Religion and American Politics

Classic and Contemporary Perspectives

EDITED BY

Amy E. Black
Wheaton College

Douglas L. Koopman
Calvin College

Larycia A. Hawkins
Wheaton College

Longman

Boston   Columbus   Indianapolis   New York   San Francisco   Upper Saddle River
Amsterdam   Cape Town   Dubai   London   Madrid   Milan   Munich   Paris   Montreal   Toronto
Delhi   Mexico City   São Paulo   Sydney   Hong Kong   Seoul   Singapore   Taipei   Tokyo

To
John C. Green, James L. Guth, Lyman A. "Bud" Kellstedt,
and Corwin E. Smidt, otherwise known as the "Gang of Four,"
with appreciation for their pioneering work and valued
contributions to the academic study of religion and politics.

Editor-in-Chief: Eric Stano
Senior Marketing Manager: Lindsey Prudhomme
Supplements Editor: Donna Garnier
Media Producer: Regina Vertiz
Production Coordinator: Scarlett Lindsay
Project Coordination, Text Design, and Electronic Page Makeup: Norine Strang,
    S4Carlisle Publishing Services
Senior Cover Design Manager: Nancy Danahy
Cover Photo: © Purestock/Getty Images
Senior Manufacturing Buyer: Dennis J. Para
Printer and Binder: Courier Corporation/Stoughton
Cover Printer: Courier Corporation/Stoughton

Library of Congress Cataloging-in-Publication Data
Religion and American politics: classic and contemporary perspectives /
    edited by Amy E. Black, Douglas L. Koopman, Larycia A. Hawkins.
        p. cm.
    ISBN-13: 978-0-13-603814-6 (pbk.)
    ISBN-10: 0-13-603814-X (pbk.)
    1.   Religion and politics—United States—Sources. 2.   United States—
Religion—Sources.   I. Black, Amy E.   II. Koopman, Douglas L.
III. Hawkins, Larycia A.
    BL2525.R449 2011
    322'.10973—dc22   2010019923

Longman
is an imprint of

www.pearsonhighered.com

1 2 3 4 5 6 7 8 9 10 — CRS — 13 12 11 10

ISBN-13: 978-0-136-03814-6
ISBN-10: 0-136-03814-X

CONTENTS

CHAPTER 4 The American Religious Landscape   104

CHAPTER 5 **Religion and Social Movements**   149

Introduction   149

Research Pieces

Primary Sources

CHAPTER 9 Religion and the Supreme Court 311

Introduction 311

Integrative Essay

Research Pieces

Primary Documents

Free Exercise Cases

Establishment Cases

PART FOUR *Religion in American Public Policy*

PREFACE

From the earliest moments in colonial history to the present day, religion has intersected with and helped shape American political culture and institutions. Scholarly interest in this connection has waxed and waned over time, but, as this book will demonstrate, the religious imprint on American politics has been strong and persistent throughout the history of the United States.

The events of September 11, 2001, starkly reminded Americans of the power of religion in international affairs and reinvigorated popular and academic interest in the intersection of religion and politics. Candidates from both major parties regularly now employ religious language and imagery in political campaigns despite a more vocal "secularist" minority. Religion infuses public discourse and issues, even as flurries of new religion cases are making their way to a Supreme Court positioned to write yet another chapter in the history of church and state jurisprudence. Books on religion and politics top bestseller lists, and broadcast and print media outlets are increasing their coverage of religion and public life.

Introduction

It is into this renewed and invigorated discussion of religion and politics that we enter. As professors and researchers interested in the connection between religion and public life, we often teach courses in religion and politics. Although we wanted to introduce our students to a wide range of voices and perspectives on the subject, we found few resources available and eventually decided to collect documents and readings ourselves. This volume is a result of that process.

In our experience, students are best challenged by reading multiple authors who vary in viewpoint, background, subject matter, and style, but we also find that they benefit from synthetic works that integrate recurring themes and ideas from the latest research. With this in mind, we designed this book as a hybrid of two common textbook formats: the edited volume of essays and the collected reader. The result is a comprehensive text that incorporates both original content from leading scholars and excerpts from classic and contemporary writings that will help students explore connections between religion and political culture, movements, institutions, and actors.

A large part of the story of religion in the United States has been that of the dominant role of Christianity and its various sects, sometimes at the expense of other religions. In recent decades, however, the range of religious voices in the public square has expanded greatly at the same time that those eschewing formal religious ties have gained in numbers and influence. The readings collected in this volume chart this progression, including reflections on and voices from the array of religious perspectives that shape the American political landscape.

Features

Each chapter opens with an introduction that describes the selections and places them in a larger theoretical context. The first selection in most of the chapters is an integrative essay, commissioned specifically for this book, that gives the reader an overview of important themes and discussions in the academic literature. In every chapter, we divide the collected readings into two sections. The first, "Research Pieces," presents excerpts from books and articles that explore key themes and controversies. The final section of each chapter, "Primary Documents," assembles primary source material related to the chapter's theme.

Together, the collection of readings offers a broad and diverse overview of central debates about religion's influence on American political history, political life, governing institutions, and public policy.

Outline of the Book

The book is divided into four parts. Part I, "Religion in the United States: Historical Legacies," traces the religious imprint on early American history in chronological order. Chapter 1 considers some of the formative religious influences in colonial America, including excerpts from the writings of influential religious thinkers and political theorists, and examples from some of the earliest written constitutions. Chapter 2, "Forging a New Nation," contains selections from key documents from the first century of the new nation, including discussions of the religious views underlying the Constitution and Bill of Rights and observations by Frenchman Alexis de Tocqueville about the role of religion in the established but still young American nation of the 1820s.

Part II, "Religion and American Political Life," examines various ways that religious values and ideas have shaped the civic culture and affected political participation. Chapter 3 includes several pieces that define, analyze, and critique civil religion in the United States and others that evaluate how religion contributes to civil society, civic responsibility, and public discourse. Chapter 4, "The American Religious Landscape," begins with a discussion of how researchers classify religious groups in the United States. The selections in this chapter describe current religious trends and consider some of the ways that race, ethnicity, and religion intersect in American politics. Chapter 5 examines the connection between religion and social movements with selections related to the abolition, prohibition, and civil rights movements. Chapter 6 focuses on the role of religious-based interest groups, especially in the last few decades. The excerpts include accounts of religious lobbying in Washington, the rise and decline of the Christian Right, and the broadening of the religious political agenda in recent years.

Part III examines intersections between religion and governing institutions, devoting one chapter to each of the three branches of American government. Chapter 7 considers the American presidency, discussing the religious background of presidents and offering examples of the use of religious rhetoric in presidential speeches. Chapter 8 turns to the legislative branch, considering ways in which religion affects congressional decision making. Excerpts include first-hand accounts from members of Congress describing their views on the relationship between religion and politics. Chapter 9 examines religion and the Supreme Court, tracing the shift from an assumed Protestant establishment to a brief attempt at a self-consciously secular state, and now beyond. The chapter includes excerpts from a few landmark Supreme Court cases that highlight developments in the constitutional interpretation of the Free Exercise and Establishment clauses.

The fourth and final part of the book, "Religion in American Public Policy," discusses both domestic and foreign policy. Chapter 10 examines the role of religious beliefs and activism in domestic politics and includes a case study of different religious approaches to environmental policy. Chapter 11 considers various perspectives on the role of religion in foreign affairs and contrasts classic and contemporary teachings from the just war and pacifist traditions. The book concludes with a short essay reflecting on the future of religion in American politics.

Acknowledgments

As with any project of this scope, this book reflects hard work and diligent assistance from many people. We are most in debt to the eight fine scholars who contributed the original essays that add great strength to this collection. They wrote strong and coherent essays that offer many new and important insights, they met their deadlines, and they accepted our editing with grace and good humor. We could not ask for a better or more competent set of collaborators.

We greatly appreciate research assistance from Erin Alderman, Brittany Belt, Jonathan Flugstad, Jonathan Hirte, Bob Hozian, Shannon Mickelson, and Kaitlin Sorenson, each of whom helped at various stages of the project. As always, Janet Miller provided assistance in extraordinary ways.

This book would not be possible without the generous support of colleagues and friends at Calvin and Wheaton Colleges and the stimulating and supportive environments we find there. We also acknowledge the generous support of the G.W. Aldeen Fund and Wheaton College Faculty Development Grants.

We would like to thank those who reviewed this text in its various stages of development. They include: Laurie M. Bagby, Kansas State University; Walton Brown-Foster, Central Connecticut State University; Kevin R. den Dulk, Grand Valley State University; Scott Fitzgerald, The University of North Carolina at Charlotte; Jane Rainey, Eastern Kentucky University; and those who reviewed anonymously.

We also want to thank the everyone at Pearson—Dickson Musslewhite at Prentice Hall for his enthusiasm for the book and help getting us started, and Eric Stano, Elizabeth Alimena, Scarlett Lindsay, and the rest of the Longman team who helped bring the project to completion. Norine Strang, Christian Holdener and their colleagues at S4Carlisle Publishing Services oversaw the production process with efficiency and skill. We are especially grateful to Beth Keister for her tireless work securing all of the permissions.

Amy Black would like to thank her co-editors for their commitment to the project and their tolerance of the flurry of e-mails to keep us all on task. This book is truly a team effort, and I am pleased that we assembled such a great team. I am especially grateful for the support and love from my family—Dan, your constant support and care for me makes the balancing act much more bearable, and Anna, your sweet spirit and joy in life have brightened even the most stressful days.

Douglas Koopman would like, too, to thank his co-editors at Wheaton for their commitment and perseverance in the project. But special thanks go to my wife Gayle for her constant faithfulness and support, and my sons Kai and Cotter for their understanding, good humor, and sometimes teasing in a project that seemed to take too long and far too often distracted from important fatherly duties.

Larycia Hawkins thanks her co-editors for their mentorship and willingness to include a junior colleague on such an important project. As always, I am indebted to my family for their love, understanding, and support of my "working vacations" to Oklahoma during the tenure of this project. A very special thanks to Elijah for being a source of joy and inspiration.

As much as we appreciate the dedication of so many people who helped made this book possible, we take responsibility for any errors that remain.

Amy E. Black
Douglas L. Koopman
Larycia L. Hawkins

About the Authors

Dr. Amy E. Black is Associate Professor and Chair of the Department of Politics and International Relations at Wheaton College, Illinois. She is the author of *Beyond Left and Right* (Baker Books, 2008), *From Inspiration to Legislation: How an Idea Becomes a Law* (Prentice Hall, 2007), and, with Douglas Koopman and David Ryden, *Of Little Faith: The Politics of George W. Bush's Faith-Based Initiatives* (Georgetown University Press, 2004), as well as book chapters and journal articles on political communication, presidential initiatives, women in politics, and religious political engagement. In 2000–2001, Dr. Black served as an American Political Science Association Congressional Fellow.

Dr. Douglas L. Koopman is Professor of Political Science at Calvin College in Grand Rapids, Michigan. Koopman has been the program director of Calvin's Paul B. Henry Institute for the Study of Christianity and Politics, interim director of its Center for Social Research, the college's William Spoelhof Teacher-Scholar-in-Residence, and, at Hope College in Holland, Michigan, the founding director of Hope's Center for Faithful Leadership. He is the author of *Hostile Takeover: The House Republican Party, 1980–1995* (Rowman and Littlefield, 1996). He is also co-author of three books: with Amy E. Black and David Ryden, *Of Little Faith: The Politics of George W. Bush's Faith-Based Initiatives* (Georgetown University Press, 2004), and with Corwin Smidt et al., *Pews, Prayers, and Participation: Religion and Civic Responsibility in America* (Georgetown, 2008) and *The Disappearing God Gap? Religion in the 2008 Presidential Election* (Oxford 2009), as well as other articles on the U.S. Congress, political parties, social policy and law, and religious faith in politics. From 1980 to 1995, Koopman worked in the U.S. House of Representatives and U.S. Senate in personal, committee, and leadership staff roles.

Dr. Larycia A. Hawkins is Assistant Professor of Politics and International Relations at Wheaton College, Illinois. She is the author of "Religion, Race, and Rhetoric: The Black Church, Interest Groups, and Charitable Choice" in *Religion, Politics, and the American Experience* (Lexington Books, 2006) and "A Live Wire? The Politics of Electricity Deregulation in Oklahoma" (*Oklahoma Policy Studies Review*, 2002). Dr. Hawkins served as a fellow of the Governing in a Global Era program at the University of Virginia's Miller Center of Public Affairs and as a Civitas Fellow at the Center for Public Justice.

CHAPTER 1

OUR MAINSTREAM RELIGIOUS HERITAGE: COLONIAL ERA TO THE AMERICAN REVOLUTION

Introduction

Integrative Essay
1.1   John Witte, Jr., *A Four-Cornered Canopy*

Research Pieces
1.2   David L. Holmes, *The Faiths of the Founding Fathers* (2006)
1.3   Andrew R. Murphy, *The Uneasy Relationship between Social Contract Theory and Religious Toleration* (1997)

Primary Sources
1.4   John Calvin, *Institutes of the Christian Religion: Book IV: C. 20, "Of Civil Government"* (1559)
1.5   William Brewster, *The Mayflower Compact* (1620)
1.6   John Winthrop, *A Model of Christian Charity* (1630)
1.7   *The Massachusetts Body of Liberties* (1641)
1.8   Roger Williams, *The Bloudy Tenent of Persecution* (July 15, 1644)
1.9   *The Cambridge Platform* (1648)
1.10 William Penn, *The Great Case of Liberty of Conscience* (1670)
1.11 John Locke, *A Letter Concerning Toleration* (1689)

Introduction

The sources gathered in this chapter illustrate some of the earliest views in Europe and the North American continent concerning the proper relationship between religious faith and political institutions. The selections illustrate some of the strongest influences on the emerging cultural and constitutional views of the elite within colonial America. On the American continent, significant theoretical advances emerged that departed from the dominant arrangements "across the pond," where a European Catholicism or an English Anglicanism were all too willing to use state power to enforce theological views and behavioral norms. In general, the primary sources and research pieces present evidence that American political thought on religion emerged from the experiences of groups seeking

1

relief from the type of dominant religious faith that at times used the "sword" of civil government to enforce its ways. Nonetheless, as the sources in this chapter indicate, the alternative vision that emerged on American soil differs significantly from the interpretation of "church–state separation" familiar to many today.

The chapter begins with John Witte's integrative essay, which describes four views of religious liberty. Two, congregational Puritans and Free Church Evangelicals, were strong advocates of different theological understandings of religious liberty and sought a state in which a fairly narrow band of religious traditions would be strongly encouraged. Two others, Enlightenment thinkers and Civic Republicans, sought to create a vibrant liberal republic. In their view, the coexistence of a variety of active religious faiths, all or nearly all of them Protestant Christian, would do much to advance the character needed for a well-functioning liberal polity.

In the first of the two research pieces, David Holmes provides an overview of the American religious landscape at the dawn of the Revolution. The discussion reveals the wide array of church–state arrangements in the colonies, from the religious tolerance and diversity of Pennsylvania and Rhode Island to the more restrictive governments of the nine colonies with established churches. Andrew Murphy's selection highlights the strong tensions between two political priorities of the American founding: religious toleration and the social contract (the idea that citizens relinquish some of their liberties in exchange for the order provided by the government). He points out that many of the founders saw the social contract as a covenant between not only a group of individuals, but between the people and God, leaving little room for the private religion of social contract theory.

The primary sources provide examples of some of the philosophical, political, and religious influences on early American thinking about the relationship between religion and the state. Calvin's "Of Civil Government" is from the *Institutes of the Christian Religion*, a massive theological treatise that is a pillar of Reformation thinking. Of particular relevance is Calvin's articulation of the proper ends of government and its officials. He attempts to separate the two "swords" of church and state and to establish on more secular grounds the duties of state officials. Ultimately, Calvin argues paradoxically for both religious dissent and public order, saying that dissent from the religious establishment in no way implies irresponsibility or disorder.

This sentiment is expressed concisely in the earliest documents of the American colonies, including "The Mayflower Compact" reproduced here. Winthrop's *Model of Christian Charity*, the more austere and detailed *Body of Liberties*, and the 1648 *Cambridge Platform* are all illustrations of the clear sense of religious mission of the colonists, and the expectation that the state would enforce the moral, if not the theological, components of these religiously inspired codes of conduct. Roger Williams's "The Bloudy Tenent of Persecution" illustrates the extent to which the boundary line between general morality and explicit theological beliefs and behavior would later be disputed. William Penn's "The Great Case of Liberty of Conscience" presages the First Amendment's Free Exercise clause, averring that individual conscience should be the cornerstone of religious freedom. The chapter ends with Locke's "A Letter Concerning Toleration," which epitomizes the idea that religious uniformity, like that propounded by the Puritans, would lead only to civil unrest. Religious toleration needed to be predicated on a social contract that divided civil interests from religious ones. For Locke, government could not coerce the soul to salvation and the church could not appoint the sovereign.

Together, these pieces present ample evidence that from an early point in colonial history, some of the new American colonists sought a relatively high degree of religious toleration, while others sought a more narrow range of religious expression. The working out of this tension would ultimately influence the shape of religious liberty in the Bill of Rights.

Integrative Essay

1.1

John Witte, Jr.

A Four-Cornered Canopy

The civic catechisms and canticles of our day still celebrate Thomas Jefferson's experiment in religious liberty. To end a millennium of repressive religious establishments, we are taught, Jefferson sought liberty in the twin formulas of privatizing religion and secularizing politics. Religion must be "a concern purely between our God and our consciences," he wrote in his famous 1802 Letter to the Danbury Baptist Association. Politics must be conducted with "a wall of separation between church and state." "Public Religion" is a threat to private religion, and must thus be discouraged. "Political ministry" is a menace to political integrity and must thus be outlawed.

These Jeffersonian maxims remain for many today the cardinal axioms of a unique American logic of religious freedom to which every patriotic individual and institution should yield. Every public school student learns the virtues of keeping his Bible at home and her prayers in the closet. Every church knows the tax law advantages of high cultural conformity and low political temperature. Every politician understands the calculus of courting religious favors without subvening religious causes. Religious privatization is the bargain we must strike to attain religious freedom for all. A wall of separation is the barrier we must build to contain religious bigotry for good.

"A page of history is worth a volume of logic," Justice Oliver Wendell Holmes, Jr. once said. And careful historical work in the past two decades has begun to call a good deal of this popular Jeffersonian logic into question. Not only are Jefferson's views on the non-establishment and free exercise of religion considerably more ambiguous than was once imagined, but the fuller account now available of the genesis and exodus of the American experiment in religious liberty suggests that Jefferson's views were hardly conventional in his own day—or in the century to follow. Indeed, the Jeffersonian model of strict separation of church and state came to constitutional prominence only in the 1940s, and then largely at the behest of the United States Supreme Court. During much of the time before that, the American experiment was devoted not so much to privatizing religion and to secularizing politics, as to protecting the private and public freedoms of all peaceable religions.

Two theological views on religious liberty were formative: those of congregational Puritans and those of Free Church Evangelicals. Two political views were equally influential: those of liberal Enlightenment thinkers and those of Civic Republicans. Exponents of these four views often found common cause and used common language, yet each group offered its own distinct political teachings on religious liberty and church-state relations. Together, these groups held up the four corners of a wide canopy of opinion about religious liberty at the time of the American founding. Following the accent of the readings, I focus on the Puritan and Evangelical views respectively.

Puritan Views

The Puritans of the New England states were heirs of the theology of religious liberty taught by European Calvinists—John Calvin, Theodore Beza, John Milton, and many others. They refined this European legacy through the efforts of William Brewster, John Winthrop, John Cotton and others in the seventeenth century. They liberalized some of this legacy through the writings of John Wise, Elisha Williams, and John Adams in the eighteenth century. They propagated their views throughout colonial America through their relentless preaching and publications, which stimulated various Presbyterians, Huguenots, Dutch Reformed, and other Calvinists in the middle and southern colonies. But it was in colonial New England, especially, that the Puritans had occasion to cast their Calvinist theological principles into constitutional practice.

The Puritans who wrote on religious liberty were concerned especially with the nature of the church, of the state, and of the relationship between them. They conceived of the church and the state as two separate covenantal associations, two seats of Godly authority in the community. Each institution, they believed, was vested with a distinct polity and calling. The church was to be governed by pastoral, pedagogical, and diaconal authorities who were called to preach the word, administer the sacraments, teach the young, and care for the poor and the needy. The state was to be governed by executive, legislative, and judicial authorities who were called to enforce law, punish crime, cultivate virtue, and protect peace and order.

In the New England communities where their views prevailed, the Puritans adopted a variety of rules designed to foster this basic separation of the offices and operations of church and state. Church officials were formally prohibited from holding political office, serving on juries, interfering in governmental affairs, endorsing political candidates, or censuring the official conduct of a statesman. Political officials, in turn, were prohibited from holding ministerial office, interfering in internal ecclesiastical government, performing clerical functions, or censuring the official conduct of a minister. To permit any such officiousness on the part of church or state officials, Massachusetts Bay Governor John Winthrop averred, "would confound those Jurisdictions, which Christ hath made distinct."

Although church and state were not to be confounded, they were still to be "close and compact," Winthrop continued. For, to the Puritans, these two institutions were inextricably linked in nature and in function. Each was an instrument of Godly authority. Each did its part to establish and maintain the community. As Puritan leader Urian Oakes put it, "I look upon this as a little model of the gloriou[s] kingdom of Christ on earth. Christ reigns among us in the commonwealth as well as in the church, and hath his glorious interest involved and wrapped up in the good of both societies respectively." The Puritans, therefore, countenanced both the coordination and the cooperation of church and state.

State officials provided various forms of material and moral aid to churches and their officials. Public properties were donated to church groups for meetinghouses, parsonages, day schools, and orphanages. Tax collectors collected tithes and special assessments to support the ministers and ministry of the congregational church. Tax exemptions and immunities were accorded to the religious, educational, and charitable organizations that they operated. Special subsidies and military protections were provided for missionaries and religious outposts. Special criminal laws prohibited interference with religious properties and services. Sabbath day laws prohibited all forms of unnecessary labor and uncouth leisure on Sundays and holy days and required faithful attendance at worship services.

Church officials, in turn, provided various forms of material and moral aid to the state. Church meetinghouses and chapels were used not only to conduct religious services but also to host town assemblies, political rallies, and public auctions, to house the community school and library, to maintain census rolls and birth, marriage, and death certificates. Parsonages were used not only to house the minister and his family but also to harbor orphans, widows, the sick, the aged, and victims of abuse and disaster. Church officials preached obedience to the authorities and imposed spiritual discipline on parishioners found guilty of crime. They encouraged their parishioners to be active in political affairs and each year offered "election day sermons" on Christian political principles. They offered learned expositions on the requirements of Godly law and occasionally offered advice to legislatures and courts, particularly on heated questions of public morality and law.

In the seventeenth century, the New England leadership left little room for individual religious experimentation. Despite their adherence to a basic separation of the offices of church and state, the New England authorities established a common Calvinist congregationalism for the community. They wrote these establishment views into their founding covenants or compacts—the Mayflower Compact of 1620 and its hundreds of colonial progeny. Separatism for them did not connote disestablishment of one religion or the toleration of other religions. Already in the 1630s, dissidents from the established faith, such as Anne Hutchinson and Roger Williams, were summarily dismissed from the colony. Immigration restrictions in Massachusetts Bay throughout the seventeenth century left little room to Catholics, Jews, or "Enthusiasts"—especially Quakers. Indeed, special laws in the late 1650s banned the Quakers and their teachings. Those Quakers who had newly arrived or newly converted were banished. Those who failed to leave were subject to flogging and the confiscation of their properties. The four Quakers who returned after banishment were hung in the Boston Common in 1659 and 1660.

Although Quakers remained unwelcome until the American Revolution, Baptists, Episcopalians, and other Protestant groups came to be tolerated in the New England colonies—partly on account of the Toleration Act passed by the English Parliament in 1689, which required all the colonies to be open to Protestant nonconformists. But the growing presence of these diverse denominations slowly shifted the Puritan understanding of liberty of conscience. Classic Calvinism taught that each person has the liberty to enter into a personal covenant relationship with God. Seventeenth-century Puritans had treated this covenant as something of a "divine adhesion contract." God set the covenantal terms for salvation in the Bible; a person had the freedom only to accept or reject them. Confronted by the realities of religious pluralism, eighteenth-century Puritan writers began to view this covenantal relationship between God and persons in more open and voluntarist terms. The covenant was made more accessible to parties of various Christian faiths, and its terms were made more open to personal deliberation and innovation. Elisha Williams put the matter thus in his famous 1744 tract on *The Essential Rights and Liberties of Protestants*:

> Every man has an equal right to follow the dictates of his own conscience in the affairs of religion. Every one is under an indispensable obligation to search the Scriptures for himself . . . and to make the best use of it he can for his own information in the will of God, the nature and duties of Christianity. And as every Christian is so bound; so he has the unalienable right to judge of the sense and meaning of it, and to follow his judgment wherever it leads him; even an equal right with any rulers be they civil or ecclesiastical.

Such formulations became increasingly common among New England Puritan writers in the later eighteenth century. It was only a short next step from this formulation to the more generic and generous religious liberty guarantee of the 1780 Massachusetts Constitution, drafted principally by John Adams:

> It is the right as well as the duty of all in society, publicly, and at stated seasons, to worship the Supreme Being, the great Creator and Preserver of the universe. And no subject shall be hurt, molested, or restrained, in his person, liberty, or estate, for worshipping God in the manner and season most agreeable to the dictates of his own conscience, or for his religious profession of sentiments; provided he doth not disturb the public peace or obstruct others in their religious worship.

It was also a natural next step to find political, if not theological, virtue in the religious pluralism of the community. Adams put this well in a later exchange with Jefferson. "Checks and balances, Jefferson," in the political as well as the religious sphere, Adams wrote, "are our only Security, for the progress of Mind, as well as the Security of Body. Every Species of Christians would persecute Deists, as either Sect would persecute another, if it had unchecked and unbalanced Power. Nay, the Deists would persecute Christians, and Atheists would persecute Deists, with as unrelenting Cruelty, as any Christians would persecute them or one another. Know thyself, Human nature!"

It was knowledge of human nature that also led the eighteenth-century Puritans to develop a system of checks and balances within the church and the state. While the offices of church and state were divinely ordained, the Puritans argued, their officials were human beings who were inherently sinful. Left to their own devices, church and state officials would invariably convert their offices into instruments of self-gain. Such official arbitrariness and abuse would inevitably lead to both popular insurrection and divine sanction. The Puritans thus advocated and adopted a variety of constitutional safeguards against autocracy and abuse within both church and state. They wrote these safeguards into their founding community covenants, like the Mayflower Compact, as well as into the separate church covenants and state covenants that each local community swore before God to uphold.

First, the Puritans argued, church and state officials must have as "godly" a character as possible, notwithstanding their inherent sinfulness. Officials were to be models of spirituality and morality for the community. Political officers were to be professing members of a locally preferred if not established church and to swear oaths of allegiance to God and the Bible. Second, both church and state officials must occupy their offices only for limited tenures. Life tenures were too dangerous, for they afforded the official the opportunity slowly to convert his office into an instrument of self-gain and self-aggrandizement. It was safer to limit the official's tenure and require periodic election and rotation of officers. Third, the Puritans advocated the development of self-limiting "republican" forms of government for both the church and the state. Rather than consolidate all forms of authority in one person or one office, they insisted on separate forms or branches of authority, each checking the sinful excesses of the other. Church authority was divided among the pastors, elders, and deacons of the consistory, state authority among executive, legislative, and judicial branches, each with a measure of responsibility and control over the other. Fourth, the Puritans adopted what they called a federalist structure of government for both the church and the state. The church was divided into semi-autonomous congregations, but each loosely conjoined and democratically represented in a broader synod or presbytery. The state was divided into semi-autonomous town governments but conjoined in a broader colonial and (later) state government. Fifth, the Puritans advocated the development of legal codes and clear statutes in the state, and clear confessions and canons in the church, so that officials were limited in their discretion. Sixth, the Puritans advocated regular popular meetings for officials to give account of themselves, and for their subjects to have occasion for discussion of important issues. In the church, this took the form of congregational meetings, in the state, the form of town meetings and popular referenda. Seventh, the Puritans advocated regularly-held democratic elections of both church and state officials. Each of these constitutional safeguards, as applied to the state, eventually found their way into the new state constitutions of New England, forged between 1776 and 1819.

Evangelical Views

The Evangelicals of colonial America had their roots in the sixteenth-century Anabaptist or Free Church movements in Europe that gave rise to the Amish, Hutterites, Mennonites, Swiss and German Brethren, and various Pietist groups. Colonial American Evangelical teachings on religious liberty and church-state relations drew powerful inspiration from the seventeenth-century "lively experiment" of Roger Williams' Rhode Island whose founding charter of 1636 granted "full liberty in religious concernm[en]ts." It also gained momentum from the "holy experiment" of religious liberty and church-state separation engineered by William Penn and his Quaker followers in Pennsylvania in 1681.

Evangelicalism did not emerge as a strong political force in America, however, until after the Great Awakening of 1720–1780 expanded its membership and message exponentially. Numerous and diverse spokesmen for the Evangelical cause rose up in the course of the later eighteenth century all along the Atlantic seaboard—Isaac Backus, John Leland, John Wesley, Charles Wesley, George Whitfield, and a host of other preachers and pamphleteers. Numerous denominational labels began to be attached to their followers—Baptists, Anabaptists, Moravians, Methodists, Wesleyans, among many others. Such labels sometimes signaled real differences in theological emphasis among these early groups, which later would harden into sharp denominational divisions. Despite these theological differences, early American Evangelicals were largely united in their insistence on liberty of conscience, disestablishment of religion, and separation of church and state. Although, outside of Rhode Island, the Evangelicals had fewer opportunities than the Puritans to institutionalize their views in the colonial era, their relentless preaching and pamphleteering had a formidable political influence on the new state and federal constitutional provisions on religious liberty drafted in the 1770s and 1780s.

Like the Puritans, the Evangelicals advanced a theological theory of religious liberty. They likewise advocated the institutional separation of church and state—the construction of "a wall of separation between the garden of the Church and the wilderness of the world," as Roger Williams put it famously in 1643. Most Evangelicals, however, went beyond the Puritans—and battled with them in the New England states—both in their definition of the rights of religious individuals and groups and in their insistence on a fuller separation of the institutions of church and state. The Evangelicals sought to protect the liberty of conscience of every individual and the freedom of association of every religious group. Their preferred method for achieving these ends was to prohibit all legal establishments of religion and, indeed, all admixtures of religion and politics. John Leland, the fiery Baptist preacher, put it thus in a proposed amendment to the Massachusetts Constitution:

> To prevent the evils that have heretofore been occasioned in the world by religious establishments, and to keep up the proper distinction between religion and politics, no religious test shall ever be requested as a qualification of any officer, in any department of this government; neither shall the legislature, under this constitution, ever establish any religion by law, give any one sect a preference to another, or force any man in the commonwealth to part with his property for the support of religious worship, or the maintenance of ministers of the gospel.

Later, Leland put the matter even more bluntly: "The notion of a Christian commonwealth should be exploded forever."

Religious voluntarism lay at the heart of the Evangelical view. "[N]othing can be true religion but a voluntary obedience unto [God's] revealed will," declared Isaac Backus, the leading Baptist light of the eighteenth century. God called the adult individual to make a conscientious choice to accept the faith. State coercion or control of this choice—either directly through persecution and repression or indirectly through withholding civil rights and benefits from those who made this choice—was an offense both to the individual and to God. A plurality of religions should coexist in the community. It was for God, not the state, to cultivate and decide which of these multiple religions should flourish and which should fade in the garden of religion. "Religious liberty is a divine right," declared preacher Israel Evans, "immediately derived from the Supreme Being, without the intervention of any created authority. . . . [T]he all-wise Creator invested [no] order of men with the right of judging for their fellow-creatures in the great concerns of religion."

Autonomy of religious governance also lay at the heart of this Evangelical view. Every religious body, Evangelicals argued, should be free from state control of their assembly and worship, state regulations of their property and polity, state incorporation of their society and clergy, state interference in their discipline and government, state collection of religious tithes and taxes. "I am as sensible of the importance of religion and of the utility of it to human society" as the Puritans are, Backus wrote. "And I concur with [them] that the fear and reverence of God and the terrors of eternity are the most powerful restraints upon the minds of men. But I am so far from thinking with [them] that these restraints would be broken down if equal religious liberty was established." Look at the long history of Christian establishment, where such forms of state intrusion on religious groups are countenanced. It has led not to pure religion. Instead, "tyranny, simony, and robbery came to be introduced and to be practiced under the Christian name." Look at communities with no religious establishments; there religion, state, and society all flourish without fail. Look at the principles of the American revolution; "all America [was] up in arms" against taxation without representation. But just as certainly as we Americans were not represented in the British Parliament, so we religious dissenters are not represented among the established civil authorities. Yet we are still subject to their religious taxes and regulations. Look at the principles of the Bible:

> God has expressly armed the magistrate with the sword to punish such as work ill to their neighbors, and his faithfulness in that work and our obedience to such authority, is enforced [by the Bible]. But it is evident that the sword is excluded from the kingdom of the Redeemer. . . . [I]t is impossible to blend church and state without violating our Lord's commands to both together. His command to the church is, Put away from among yourselves that wicked person. His command to the state is, Let both grow together until the harvest. But it has appeared for these thousand years that pure Gospel discipline in the church is very little if at all known in state establishments of religion and that instead of letting conformists thereto, and dissenters therefrom, grow together or enjoy equal worldly privileges, the sword has been employed to root up, and to prepare war against all such as put not into the mouths of the established teachers who are the means of upholding such rulers as pervert all equity.

Some Evangelicals extended the principle of church autonomy and disestablishment to argue against tax exemptions, civil immunities, property donations, and other forms of state support for all churches. Such Evangelicals feared state benevolence toward religion and religious bodies almost as much as they feared state repression. Those religious bodies that received state benefits would invariably become beholden to the state and distracted from their divine mandates. "[I]f civil Rulers go so far out of their Sphere as to take the Care and Management of religious affairs upon them," reads a 1776 Baptist Declaration, "Yea . . . Farwel to 'the free exercise of Religion.'"

The chief concern of eighteenth century Evangelicals was theological, not political. Having suffered as religious minorities for more than a century in colonial America and more than two centuries in Europe, Evangelicals sought a constitutional means to free all religion from the fetters of the law, to relieve all churches from the restrictions of the state. In so doing, most Evangelicals of the founding era—save Isaac Backus, building on his seventeenth-century hero Roger Williams—developed only the rudiments of a political theory. Most Evangelicals were content with a state that created a climate conducive to the cultivation of a plurality of religions and that accommodated all religious believers and religious bodies without conditions or controls. They pressed relentlessly to ensure that this right was inscribed in the new state and federal constitutions of the 1770s and 1780s. But once guaranteed, they retreated from political activism until returning to public life with alacrity in the 1830s forward.

Religious Foundations of American Constitutionalism

Some readers will be surprised at what they have just read. We have grown accustomed in the past half century to hearing that the First Amendment religion clauses and other constitutional provisions were based principally on secular principles born of the Western Enlightenment. We have also grown accustomed to thinking that religion has properly always been a private affair and that state officials must always remain neutral in treating competing claims of the good and the just. Whatever the merits of such a view today, it was not the principal view of the eighteenth-century American founders or their colonial predecessors. A wide variety of religious and political views helped to form America's original understandings of law and order, church and state, authority and liberty. Secular Enlightenment liberalism was certainly one such eighteenth-century view. But it was a decidedly minority view, when compared to the variety of Puritan, Evangelical, Anglican, Civic Republican, and other voices that dominated the law and politics and constitutional conventions of the day.[1]

Research Pieces

1.2

David L. Holmes

THE FAITHS OF THE FOUNDING FATHERS (2006)

"On my arrival in the United States," the famous French traveler Alexis de Tocqueville observed in the early nineteenth century, "the religious aspect of the country was the first thing that struck my attention" (Tocqueville 1992, 308). If in 1770—six years before the thirteen colonies became the United States—a different group of foreign visitors had traveled the narrow roads of the colonies, they would have agreed with de Tocqueville's later observance. The travelers would have further noted that the Americans of 1770 were either overwhelmingly Protestant or unchurched. . . . As of 1770, some one thousand Jews probably lived in the colonies. In 1790, the first federal census counted 1,243 Jews in a total American population of almost three million. By the end of the century, the new republic had synagogues in Charleston, New York, Newport, Savannah, Philadelphia, and Richmond.

In these and other port cities, the travelers would also have found scattered Roman Catholics. Most of the Roman Catholics lacked churches and priests, but some had "Mass stations"—homes or buildings where itinerant priests said Mass regularly or occasionally. The travelers would have found most of the approximately thirty-thousand Roman Catholics and virtually all of their churches located in the colonies of Maryland and Pennsylvania . . .

The Sects

In 1770, the visitors would also have seen or heard about a certain number of what in religious history are often called "sects"—groups that remained within the wide spectrum of Christian belief but that broke off into what they considered pure communities of ethics and doctrine based upon their interpretations of Scripture. . . .

. . . Persecuted in Europe, many of these groups immigrated to America during the colonial period. Following the Revolution and the subsequent separation of church and state, the United States became a fermenting vat of such Christian sects. . . .

But the principal "sect" the travelers would have encountered would have been the Quakers, or the Religious Society of Friends. Plain in appearance, believing in an Inner Light that was the presence of Christ within each person, asserting the fundamental equality of all men and women, and opposing not only trained clergy and formal worship but also military service and the swearing of oaths, the Quakers were widely dispersed. Ranking as perhaps the fifth largest of the colonial churches, they existed in substantial numbers in Rhode Island, New York, New Jersey, Maryland, Virginia, North Carolina, and especially in Pennsylvania, a colony founded under Quaker auspices.

Tolerant Pennsylvania

Pennsylvania, in fact, would have been the colony in which the travelers would have encountered the richest mosaic of sects. Because the English Quaker William Penn had founded the colony as a "Holy Experiment" where Quakers and other persecuted religious sects could live and worship freely, Pennsylvania had attracted many small religious groups by 1770. The visitors would have discovered that most of the groups had come from Germany, that all believed that they had restored practices of apostolic Christianity that mainstream Christianity had wrongly abandoned, and that virtually all were pacifistic. . . .

In colonial Pennsylvania, the visitors would also have encountered the Mennonites, the principal heirs of the radical Anabaptist (or "Rebaptizer") wing of the Reformation. The program of the Mennonites to reproduce biblical Christianity caused them not only to deviate markedly from the norms of contemporary Christian orthodoxy of the day but also to suffer persecution. Rather than baptize infants, the Mennonites baptized only converted, believing adults. Rather than regard baptism as a sacrament that washed away original sin, they viewed it as a symbolic act that ratified an inner change that had already occurred in the individual. Instead of viewing Christianity as a religion into which people were born, they taught that churches should be "gathered" out of the world and composed of believing, converted adults who had voluntarily chosen to follow Jesus Christ.

Unlike Eastern Orthodoxy, Roman Catholicism, and such mainline Protestant movements as Lutheranism, Calvinism, and Anglicanism, the Mennonites and all Anabaptists advocated the separation of church and state. Teaching that the true Christian withdrew from the fallen world and rejected its values and amusements, they opposed wearing fashionable clothes, holding public office, using the courts, swearing oaths, and serving in the military. . . . Executed in Europe by Protestant and Roman Catholic countries alike for their teachings, the Mennonites lived and worshiped openly in tolerant Pennsylvania.

In their attempt to return to first-century Christianity, all of these interpretations of Christianity differed markedly from those advocated by the mainstream of
Christianity. . . .

The Mainline Churches

In 1770, sects were only footnotes to the story of religion in America. In that year
the story focused on what were called "established churches" or "state churches."
A concept transplanted to the American colonies from Europe, an established or state
church is the official religious organization of a country or colony. The government supports it financially, legislates for it, and protects it against competition. Russia, Greece,
Scandinavia, Germany, Italy, France, Spain, the Netherlands, England, Scotland, and
other European countries all had state churches at one time. Citizens were born into
membership in churches just as they were born into citizenship in countries. From the
fourth century on, state churches represented the norm in European Christianity. Some
European countries, such as England, still have them. Of the thirteen colonies that came
to form the United States, nine had established churches during the colonial period.

Religion in New England

As the travelers worked their way down the colonies from north to south, they would
have found one tolerant religiously diverse colony in New England—Rhode Island.
Founded by Roger Williams, an exile from Puritan Massachusetts who opposed governmental coercion in religious matters, the "livelie experiment" of Rhode Island had
no established church. It guaranteed freedom of belief to all but outspoken atheists
and—for some decades—to Roman Catholics. In the words of a critic from adjacent
Massachusetts, the colony contained "Antinomians, Anabaptists, Antisabbatarians,
Arminians, Socinians, Quakers, Ranters—everything in the world but Roman Catholics
and real Christians" (Gaustad 1990, 70).

In this diverse colony, the Baptists (English Calvinists whose reading of the New
Testament caused them to reject infant baptism and to baptize only believing adults),
Quakers, Anglicans, and Congregationalists had the most members. Before he left the
ministry and became a "Seeker" after a true Christianity that he never found, Williams
had briefly been a Baptist.

By "real Christians," the Puritan critic of course meant his own Congregationalist Church, which was the established church not only in Massachusetts but also in
Connecticut and New Hampshire. The largest of four branches of Calvinist
Christianity the visitors would have observed in the colonies, Congregationalism
arguably emphasized the intellect to a greater extent than any other church in colonial
America. In the same way that other groups received their names from certain acts
(for example, the Quakers or Baptists) or modes of church governance (for example,
the Presbyterians or Episcopalians), the Congregational churches took their name
from the belief that early Christian congregations ran their own affairs and were
subject to no higher supervision than Christ.

Congregationalism originated in the movement of English Calvinists called "puritans"—a name acquired because of the efforts of its adherents to "purify" the Church of England from certain doctrines and liturgical practices that remained from its Roman Catholic past and were held to be untrue to the New Testament and to early Christian practice. The Puritan movement—both in the British Isles and in the American colonies—included the Presbyterians, the Baptists, and some Anglicans who decided to remain within England's established church.

In the backcountry of New England and especially in the colonies below it, the travelers would have encountered a third form of Calvinism—Presbyterianism (the name that Calvinism adopted in Scotland). In the area of Boston and especially in the colonies from New York to South Carolina, they would have learned of the Reformed (the name that Calvinism took on the European continent).

Except in two areas, these four groups shared the common heritage of Calvinism and displayed only minor homegrown dissimilarities in terminology and worship. Their principal differences lay in the areas of governance and baptismal practice. In matters of church government (or polity), the Congregationalists and Baptists followed a democratic form. The Presbyterians and Reformed, however (like John Calvin himself), saw the republican form with an ascending hierarchy of synods and assemblies as true to the New Testament and to early Christianity. In matters of baptism, the Baptists believed that early Christians baptized only converted adults, whereas the Congregationalists, Presbyterians, and Reformed believed that the baptism of infants was true to apostolic practice. . . .

Church historians have estimated that over 80 percent of American Christians in the colonial period—from Anglicans on the right-center of the Christian spectrum to Quakers on the left—were significantly influenced by John Calvin's teachings. Only the Roman Catholics, some of the Lutherans, and some of the "sects" remained distinctly free from Calvinist influence. Even the Quakers—on the surface a very un-Calvinistic body—were in reality the "puritans of the Puritans" and emerged in England from the left wing of the Puritan movement. . . .

As the visitors would have observed in New England, Puritans believed in the union of church and state. This teaching emerged from the Calvinist concern that every aspect of life should acknowledge God's sovereignty. In addition, it stemmed from the belief of Calvinists that God worked with humanity, as God had with the Israelites, through solemn agreements, or covenants. Only through the union of church and state, Puritans believed, could humans produce a Christian society conformed to scriptural teaching. Thus the Puritan colonies in New England were strict and intolerant on matters of doctrine and behavior, for their goal was to produce a sober, righteous, and godly Christian society. Although continually challenged by adversaries, the Puritan establishments were strong enough to survive into the early nineteenth century, longer than any other American state churches. . . .

Religion in the Middle Colonies

In their travels through New England, the foreign visitors would have seen Anglican churches, for the Church of England began to grow significantly in Connecticut, Massachusetts, and Rhode Island during the eighteenth century. Although the Puritans had previously packed off to England or to more congenial colonies any residents who openly followed Anglican usages, they were obligated (as English citizens) to tolerate Anglicanism after the passage in 1689 of the English Toleration Act. . . .

Always a minority faith in a colony whose diversity of nationality and religion rivaled that of Pennsylvania, Anglicanism nevertheless attracted many of the most influential families in New York. . . .

Religion in the Southern Colonies

In the border colony of Maryland, the foreign travelers would have encountered a colony with an unusual history. . . .

In 1770 the foreign travelers would have found that the Roman Catholics composed approximately 10 percent of the colony's population. . . .

George Calvert established Maryland not only as a place where fellow Roman Catholics could worship freely but also as a business venture. As an English citizen he was obligated to include Anglicans in the venture. He received his charter from an Anglican king (Charles I) and kept it at the pleasure of an Anglican parliament. "One can scarcely speak of tolerating in English territory," two church historians write, "a church whose 'supreme governor' was the English monarch" (Hudson and Corrigan 1992, 30). The colony's charter, in fact, presupposed that the Church of England would be Maryland's established church. Although they held the proprietorship, Roman Catholics were dominant in the colony only for a short period. Anglicans were in the majority even on the two ships that carried the first colonists. In the middle of the seventeenth century, Puritans gained substantial control, and the percentage of Roman Catholics steadily decreased as the colony grew. . . .

. . . "[T]he "Act Concerning Religion" of 1649 was passed by a legislature composed of a Protestant majority. It was an act not of religious freedom but of religious toleration— hence its alternate name, the "Maryland Toleration Act." *Religious freedom* means that citizens are free to worship in any way or not at all—and that the state protects that freedom. *Religious toleration* means that the state allows a group to exist and to worship, but retains the right to withdraw or limit that permission at any time. From 1654 to 1661 and from 1692 to the end of the Revolutionary period, Maryland, in fact, nullified its Toleration Act.

Granting religious rights only to Trinitarian Christians, Maryland's act provided for the execution or forfeiture of all lands of any resident who blasphemed or denied the doctrines of the Trinity and the divinity of Christ. It imposed fines, whipping, or imprisonment for any resident who spoke disparagingly of the Virgin Mary, the apostles, or Evangelists. Yet the act strictly enforced tolerance (as long as the act was in force) by punishing any person who dared to offend a Maryland subject by calling him or her, in a judgmental manner, a host of offensive religious terms, including "heritick, Scismatick, Idolator, puritan, Independent, Prespiterian, popish priest, Jesuite, Jesuited papist, Lutheran, Calvenist, Anabaptist, Brownist, Antinomian, Barrowist, Roundhead, Separatist, or any other name or term in a reproachfull manner relating to matter of Religion" (Maryland Toleration Act of 1649). The punishment was ten shillings or public whipping and imprisonment until such time as the aggrieved party was satisfied with the repentance of the offender. Any person who was "willfully to wrong disturbe trouble or molest any person . . . professing to believe in Jesus Christ" was also strictly punished (Maryland Toleration Act of 1649). Non-Christians were not protected at all.

Despite its limitations and shortcomings, the act represented a major advance for the time. In addition, it reflected a policy that the Calverts had followed from the colony's beginning. As the colonists boarded ships for the voyage to America, George Calvert's instructions included a caveat not to abuse each other about religion. When the colonists arrived in Maryland, Protestants and Roman Catholics initially shared a chapel in St Mary's City, the colony's first capital (Papenfuse 1999).

Thus the Maryland Toleration Act was a pioneering piece of legislation. It came decades before England's own Toleration Act or William Penn's Holy Experiment. Religious toleration generally arose from the Enlightenment, and Maryland's policy of toleration antedates the Enlightenment. But it was an act of limited religious toleration only, and for most of Maryland's colonial history it was not in force. Genuine religious freedom did not come to the United States until the late 1780s. And when it did come, it emerged from the religion of the founding fathers. . . .

1.3

Andrew R. Murphy

THE UNEASY RELATIONSHIP BETWEEN SOCIAL CONTRACT THEORY AND RELIGIOUS TOLERATION (1997)

Since the seventeenth century, the theory of the social contract has emerged as an axiom of liberal democratic political legitimacy. . . . Religious liberty, as a substantive commitment, also plays a central role in the liberal creed. The two often appear side by side: "We the people" evokes a contractarian claim in the preamble to the United States Constitution, while the principle of disestablishment, the American route to religious freedom, follows soon after in the First Amendment.

This essay has a twofold aim: first, to examine these ideas, both of which figured prominently in early modern political thought and are crucial to liberal democratic political forms and constitutional government; and second, to suggest that despite their common association in the Anglo-American tradition, they have little to do with each other and may be fundamentally at odds. . . .

I shall illustrate several contract theories and the religious politics they espouse, arguing that the historical or empirical relationship between liberalism and toleration is far more complex than scholars often assume.

The phenomenon under consideration here is *religious toleration*, a political or legal term denoting an absence of punitive sanctions for the practice of one's religion. W. F. Adeney notes that toleration proposes "a refraining from prohibition and persecution . . . . a voluntary inaction, a politic leniency [on the part of government]" (1925, 360), while Maurice Cranston calls it "a policy of patient forbearance in the presence of something which is disliked or disapproved of" (1967, 143).[2] Justifications for toleration may include utilitarianism, principles of neutrality, or respect for persons and commitments to Kantian autonomy (Horton and Nicholson 1992; Mendus and Edwards 1987; Mendus 1988). Nicholson (1985) argues persuasively that toleration must involve a positive commitment to some degree of pluralism; however, I leave aside *motivations* in this essay, essentially because such questions are difficult to settle even for individuals and become even murkier when we consider regimes.

In its most minimal form, toleration is strictly a "negative" freedom, fitting in well with classical liberalism and other traditions which stress liberty as the absence of constraint.[3] It is, at the least, a decision not to interfere with certain types of dissent. At the same time, we should not underestimate the demands that "negative" freedoms can put on regimes. Toleration may involve permitting unpopular forms of religious expression and protecting individual rights to engage in such activities. This is not *purely* negative, if by negative we mean only the *absence* of something: regimes must guarantee that tolerated groups can gather without violence or harassment. Seen this way, toleration lies at the heart of early modern political thought, providing a benchmark or minimal condition of negative freedom from which any discussion of fuller liberty must begin.[4]

Toleration and the free exercise of religion are important for contemporary reasons as well. . . .

"Liberty to that. . . . which is good, just, and honest": Puritans and toleration in Massachusetts[5]

Contractarianism of a distinctly theological sort found fertile soil in the Puritan mind through its connection with the covenantal ideal. The Puritan commonwealth, like the church, was based on voluntary consent, an "incarnation of their collective will. . . ." (Miller 1939, 418). Puritan leaders agreed that although civil government was instituted by God and necessitated by original sin (thus of divine origin), political authority arose from the consent of those governed. John Cotton referred to "the people, in whom fundamentally all power lies. . . ." (Morgan 1965, 175). Roger Williams agreed that "civil government is an ordinance of God" and that "the sovereign, original, and foundation of civil power lies in the people (1963, 249).[6] In his "Model of Christian Charity," John Winthrop noted that "for the work we have in hand it is by a mutual consent through a special overruling providence," describing the company as "knit together by this bond of love"(Winthrop 1630). Later Winthrop made his position even more explicit: "No common weal can be founded but by free consent"(1931, 422). Such views made their way into formal legal codes: "the Massachusetts Body of Liberties asserts that the body politic has ratified these [liberties] with our solemn consent"(Morgan 1965, 179).

In the thought of Roger Williams, and the controversy that his views brought about, we begin to see the varying religious implications of Puritan contractarianism. Limitation of government was Williams's inference: he linked popular sovereignty, contractarian politics, and the restriction of governmental power over church affairs. For Williams, such limitation was a means of preserving churches' purity, since political power would inevitably corrupt ("Christianity fell asleep in Constantine's bosom" [1963, 184]). Churches and states are formed voluntarily, and with divine sanction, but are charged with different missions. Posing a sharp dichotomy between spiritual and political power, he argued that coercion was proper in civil affairs, whereas religious issues could be settled only by persuasion.

The church was "like unto a corporation, society, or company of East India or Turkey merchants" (1963, 73); only when the health of the whole state was threatened by the activities of one of these "companies" was the magistrate justified in intervening in their affairs. Thus, Williams maintained that all states "[are] essentially civil, and therefore not judges, governors, or defenders of the spiritual or Christian state and worship" (1963, 3).

But Roger Williams did not represent the prevailing view of Puritan magistrates with regard to the religious implications of covenantal theories. Whereas Williams distinguished between church and state, emphasizing their different natures and functions, Winthrop cited as the "end" of the compact "to improve our lives to do more service to the Lord and increase the body of Christ whereof we are members" (Winthrop 1931, 293). The Puritans were not only covenanting with one another, but with God, under a widely shared interpretation of God's requirements. The religious nature of the covenant made possible both a code of conduct for individuals and a broad range of powers for magistrates in deciding what constituted civil or political issues.[7] Cotton saw a plan of government in Biblical texts and viewed the civil covenant as effecting what had not been possible in England.

> I am very apt to believe . . . . that the word . . . . of God [contains] a short . . . . platform, not only of theology, but also of other sacred sciences. . . . It is very suitable to God's all-sufficient wisdom, and to the fullness and perfection of the Holy Scriptures, not only to prescribe perfect rules for the right ordering of a private man's soul . . . . but also for the right ordering of a man's family, yea, of the commonwealth too, so far as both of them are subordinate to spiritual ends, and yet avoid both the churches' usurpation upon civil jurisdictions . . . . and the commonwealth's invasion upon ecclesiastical administrations (Morgan 1965, 165).

For Massachusetts Puritans, migration fused organic and contractual ideas into a communal bond incorporating both religious and political aims. The formation of a new society provided opportunities not present in existing states, possibilities for greater fidelity to Biblical guidelines. Although both church and state were based on consent, the laws of God applied to them equally. In the body politic, "every one (in his own admission) gives an implicit consent to whatever the major part shall establish, *not being against religion or the weal public . . .*" (*Liberty and the Weal Public Reconciled* 1637, 76, emphasis added). The future of New England would reflect on the colonists' performance: if they failed to walk in the Lord's ways, disaster would surely befall them, but if they remained faithful, "men shall say of succeeding plantations: the Lord make it like New England" (Winthrop 1931, 295). New England was to be the place where Biblical principles were explored and implemented, as a reflection and outgrowth of Puritan covenants.[8]

Covenant theory and contractarianism, for Puritans, described the willing acceptance of God's rule by an earthly community (c.f. Hobbes 1839, ch. 35, on Israel). During the Antinomian crisis, Winthrop reasoned that "if we here be a corporation established by free consent . . . . then no man hath right to come into us . . . . without our consent" (1931, 423). His distinction between civil and natural liberty cemented the argument against toleration, since fallen human nature merely invited depravity. In the covenant, humans *renounced* natural liberty and accepted the rule of God, and divinely informed consent trumped individual (often erroneous) conscience. Cotton also evoked "positive" liberty. One who erred on fundamental points of religion endangered his own soul and the well-being of the community, "sinning against his own conscience": thus could Cotton assert that this interpretation of "liberty of conscience sets the conscience at liberty" (1646, 8; 1972, 3). Edward Johnson urged opposition to "such as would have all sorts of sinful opinions upheld by the civil government . . . . that our Lord Christ might reign over us, both in churches and commonwealth" (1910, 140–5). Many saw in toleration a risk to their own salvation: for Nathaniel Ward, "God doth no where in his word tolerate Christian states, to give toleration to such adversaries of his Truth, if they have in their hands to suppress them" (1969, 6). Miller and Johnson describe Puritan government as "brought into being by the act of the people; but the people do not create just any sort of government, but the one kind of government which has been established by God"(1938, 189–90). The Antinomian and Williams banishments clarified the limits of acceptable public belief.[9]

Winthrop and Cotton reconciled popular sovereignty with New England political forms by an analogy of delegation: in Winthrop's words, in choosing magistrates individuals "take [men] from among [themselves] . . . . that we shall govern you and judge your cases by the rule of God's laws and our own, according to our best skill" (Miller and Johnson 1938, 206). On several occasions, Cotton approvingly quoted Bodin, pointing out that governors, not people, rule. God ruled over all, of course: the restriction of the franchise to church members followed directly from this view. The saints, as the elect, were best able to discern scriptural truths and make wise decisions for the polity. Puritan thought contains no republican ideals, no states of nature in which individuals create politics to safeguard temporal interests while theological duties remain in a distinctly separate sphere. Puritans saw the religious responsibilities of individuals, churches, and societies as immediate and overriding.

Primary Sources

1.4

John Calvin

INSTITUTES OF THE CHRISTIAN RELIGION: BOOK IV, C. 20, "OF CIVIL GOVERNMENT" (1559)

Chapter 20
Of Civil Government

1. Having shown above that there is a twofold government in man, and having fully considered the one which, placed in the soul or inward man, relates to eternal life, we are here called to say something of the other, which pertains only to civil institutions and the external regulation of manners. For although this subject seems from its nature to be unconnected with the spiritual doctrine of faith, which I have undertaken to treat, it will appear, as we proceed, that I have properly connected them, nay, that I am under the necessity Of doing so, especially while, on the one hand, frantic and barbarous men are furiously endeavouring to overturn the order established by God, and, on the other, the

flatterers of princes, extolling their power without measure, hesitate not to oppose it to the government of God. Unless we meet both extremes, the purity of the faith will perish. . . .

15. The moral law, then, (to begin with it), being contained under two heads, the one of which simply enjoins us to worship God with pure faith and piety, the other to embrace men with sincere affection, is the true and eternal rule of righteousness prescribed to the men of all nations and of all times, who would frame their life agreeably to the will of God. For his eternal and immutable will is, that we are all to worship him, and mutually love one another. The ceremonial law of the Jews was a tutelage by which the Lord was pleased to exercise, as it were, the childhood of that people, until the fulness of the time should come when he was fully to manifest his wisdom to the world, and exhibit the reality of those things which were then adumbrated by figures, (Gal. 3: 24; 4: 4). The judicial law, given them as a kind of polity, delivered certain forms of equity and justice, by which they might live together innocently and quietly. And as that exercise in ceremonies properly pertained to the doctrine of piety, inasmuch as it kept the Jewish Church in the worship and religion of God, yet was still distinguishable from piety itself, so the judicial form, though it looked only to the best method of preserving that charity which is enjoined by the eternal law of God, was still something distinct from the precept of love itself. Therefore, as ceremonies might be abrogated without at all interfering with piety, so also, when these judicial arrangements are removed, the duties and precepts of charity can still remain perpetual. But if it is true that each nation has been left at liberty to enact the laws which it judges to be beneficial, still these are always to be tested by the rule of charity, so that while they vary in form, they must proceed on the same principle. Those barbarous and savage laws, for instance, which conferred honour on thieves, allowed the promiscuous intercourse of the sexes, and other things even fouler and more absurd, I do not think entitled to be considered as laws, since they are not only altogether abhorrent to justice, but to humanity and civilised life. . . .

17. It now remains to see, as was proposed in the last place, what use the common society of Christians derive from laws, judicial proceedings, and magistrates. With this is connected another question, viz., What deference ought private individuals to pay to magistrates, and how far ought obedience to proceed? To very many it seems that among Christians the office of magistrate is superfluous, because they cannot piously implore his aid, inasmuch as they are forbidden to take revenge, cite before a judge, or go to law. But when Paul, on the contrary, clearly declares that he is the minister of God to us for good, (Rom. 13: 4), we thereby understand that he was so ordained of God, that, being defended by his hand and aid against the dishonesty and injustice of wicked men, we may live quiet and secure. But if he would have been appointed over us in vain, unless we were to use his aid, it is plain that it cannot be wrong to appeal to it and implore it. Here, indeed, I have to do with two classes of men. For there are very many who boil with such a rage for litigation, that they never can be quiet with themselves unless they are fighting with others. Law-suits they prosecute with the bitterness of deadly hatred, and with an insane eagerness to hurt and revenge, and they persist in them with implacable obstinacy, even to the ruin of their adversary. Meanwhile, that they may be thought to do nothing but what is legal, they use this pretext of judicial proceedings as a defence of their perverse conduct. But if it is lawful for brother to litigate with brother, it does not follow that it is lawful to hate him, and obstinately pursue him with a furious desire to do him harm. . . .

22. The first duty of subjects towards their rulers, is to entertain the most honourable views of their office, recognising it as a delegated jurisdiction from God, and on

that account receiving and reverencing them as the ministers and ambassadors of God. For you will find some who show themselves very obedient to magistrates, and would be unwilling that there should be no magistrates to obey, because they know this is expedient for the public good, and yet the opinion which those persons have of magistrates is that they are a kind of necessary evils. But Peter requires something more of us when he says, "Honour the king," (1 Pet. 2: 17); and Solomon, when he says, "My son, fear thou the Lord and the king," (Prov. 24: 21). For, under the term honour, the former includes a sincere and candid esteem, and the latter, by joining the king with God, shows that he is invested with a kind of sacred veneration and dignity. We have also the remarkable injunction of Paul, "Be subject not only for wrath, but also for conscience sake," (Rom. 13: 5). By this he means, that subjects, in submitting to princes and governors, are not to be influenced merely by fear, (just as those submit to an armed enemy who see vengeance ready to be executed if they resist), but because the obedience which they yield is rendered to God himself, inasmuch as their power is from God. I speak not of the men as if the mask of dignity could cloak folly, or cowardice, or cruelty, or wicked and flagitious manners, and thus acquire for vice the praise of virtue; but I say that the station itself is deserving of honour and reverence, and that those who rule should, in respect of their office, be held by us in esteem and veneration.

23. From this, a second consequence is, that we must with ready minds prove our obedience to them, whether in complying with edicts, or in paying tribute, or in undertaking public offices and burdens which relate to the common defence, or in executing any other orders. "Let every soul", says Paul, "be subject unto the higher powers." "Whosoever, therefore, resisteth the power, resisteth the ordinance of God" (Rom. 13: 1, 2). Writing to Titus, he says, "Put them in mind to be subject to principalities and powers, to obey magistrates, to be ready to every good work" (Tit. 3: 1). Peter also says, "Submit yourselves to every human creature," (or rather, as I understand it, "ordinance of man,") "for the Lord's sake: whether it be to the king, as supreme; or unto governors, as unto them that are sent by him for the punishment of evil-doers, and for the praise of them that do well" (1 Pet. 2: 13). Moreover, to testify that they do not feign subjection, but are sincerely and cordially subject, Paul adds, that they are to commend the safety and prosperity of those under whom they live to God. "I exhort, therefore," says he, "that, first of all, supplications, prayers, intercessions, and giving of thanks, be made for all men; for kings, and for all that are in authority: that we may lead a quiet and peaceable life in all godliness and honesty" (1 Tim. 2: 1, 2). Let no man here deceive himself, since we cannot resist the magistrate without resisting God. For, although an unarmed magistrate may seem to be despised with impunity, yet God is armed, and will signally avenge this contempt. Under this obedience, I comprehend the restraint which private men ought to impose on themselves in public, not interfering with public business, or rashly encroaching on the province of the magistrate, or attempting any thing at all of a public nature. If it is proper that any thing in a public ordinance should be corrected, let them not act tumultuously, or put their hands to a work where they ought to feel that their hands are tied, but let them leave it to the cognisance of the magistrate, whose hand alone here is free. My meaning is, let them not dare to do it without being ordered. For when the command of the magistrate is given, they too are invested with public authority. For as, according to the common saying, the eyes and ears of the prince are his counsellors, so one may not improperly say that those who, by his command, have the charge of managing affairs, are his hands. . . .

25. But it we have respect to the word of God, it will lead us farther, and make us subject not only to the authority of those princes who honestly and faithfully perform their duty toward us, but all princes, by whatever means they have so become, although there is nothing they less perform than the duty of princes. For though the Lord declares that ruler to maintain our safety is the highest gift of his beneficence, and prescribes to rulers themselves their proper sphere, he at the same time declares, that of whatever description they may be, they derive their power from none but him. Those, indeed, who rule for the public good, are true examples and specimens of big beneficence, while those who domineer unjustly and tyrannically are raised up by him to punish the people for their iniquity. Still all alike possess that sacred majesty with which he has invested lawful power. I will not proceed further without subjoining some distinct passages to this effect. We need not labour to prove that an impious king is a mark of the Lord's anger, since I presume no one will deny it, and that this is not less true of a king than of a robber who plunders your goods, an adulterer who defiles your bed, and an assassin who aims at your life, since all such calamities are classed by Scripture among the curses of God. But let us insist at greater length in proving what does not so easily fall in with the views of men, that even an individual of the worst character, one most unworthy of all honour, if invested with public authority, receives that illustrious divine power which the Lord has by his word devolved on the ministers of his justice and judgement, and that, accordingly, in so far as public obedience is concerned, he is to be held in the same honour and reverence as the best of kings. . .

32. But in that obedience which we hold to be due to the commands of rulers, we must always make the exception, nay, must be particularly careful that it is not incompatible with obedience to Him to whose will the wishes of all kings should be subject, to whose decrees their commands must yield, to whose majesty their sceptres must bow. And, indeed, how preposterous were it, in pleasing men, to incur the offence of Him for whose sake you obey men! The Lord, therefore, is King of kings. When he opens his sacred mouth, he alone is to be heard, instead of all and above all. We are subject to the men who rule over us, but subject only in the Lord. If they command any thing against Him, let us not pay the least regard to it, nor be moved by all the dignity which they possess as magistrates—a dignity to which, no injury is done when it is subordinated to the special and truly supreme power of God.

1.5

William Brewster

THE MAYFLOWER COMPACT (1620)

Agreement Between the Settlers at New Plymouth

IN THE NAME OF GOD, AMEN. We, whose names are underwritten, the Loyal Subjects of our dread Sovereign Lord King *James*, by the Grace of God, of *Great Britain*, *France*, and *Ireland*, King, *Defender of the Faith*, &c. Having undertaken for the Glory of God, and Advancement of the Christian Faith, and the Honour of our King and Country, a Voyage to plant the first Colony in the northern Parts of *Virginia*; Do by these Presents, solemnly and mutually, in the Presence of God and one another, covenant and combine ourselves together into a civil Body Politick, for our better Ordering and Preservation, and Furtherance of the Ends aforesaid: And by Virtue hereof do enact, constitute, and frame, such just and equal Laws, Ordinances, Acts, Constitutions, and Officers, from time to time, as shall be thought most meet and convenient for the general Good of the Colony; unto which we promise all due Submission and Obedience. IN WITNESS whereof we have hereunto subscribed our names at *Cape-Cod* the eleventh of November, in the Reign of our Sovereign Lord King *James*, of *England, France,* and *Ireland*, the eighteenth, and of *Scotland* the fifty-fourth, *Anno Domini*; 1620.

1.6

John Winthrop

A Model of Christian Charity (1630)

First . . . . We are a company professing ourselves fellow members of Christ, in which respect only, though we were absent from each other many miles, and had our employments as far distant, yet we ought to account ourselves knit together by this bond of love and live in the exercise of it. . . .

Secondly for the work we have in hand. It is by a mutual consent, through a special overvaluing providence and a more than an ordinary approbation of the churches of Christ, to seek out a place of cohabitation and consortship under a due form of government both civil and ecclesiastical. In such cases as this, the care of the public must oversway all private respects, by which, not only conscience, but mere civil policy, doth bind us. For it is a true rule that particular estates cannot subsist in the ruin of the public.

Thirdly, the end is to improve our lives to do more service to the Lord; the comfort and increase of the body of Christ, whereof we are members, that ourselves and posterity may be the better preserved from the common corruptions of this evil world, to serve the Lord and work out our salvation under the power and purity of his holy ordinances.

Fourthly, for the means whereby this must be effected. They are twofold, a conformity with the work and end we aim at. These we see are extraordinary, therefore we must not content ourselves with usual ordinary means. Whatsoever we did, or ought to have done, when we lived in England, the same must we do, and more also, where we go. That which the most in their churches maintain as truth in profession only, we must bring into familiar and constant practice; as in this duty of love, we must love brotherly without dissimulation, we must love one another with a pure heart fervently. We must bear one another's burdens. We must not look only on our own things, but also on the things of our brethren.

Neither must we think that the Lord will bear with such failings at our hands as he doth from those among whom we have lived; and that for these three reasons:

First, in regard of the more near bond of marriage between Him and us, wherein He hath taken us to be His, after a most strict and peculiar manner, which will make Him the more jealous of our love and obedience. So He tells the people of Israel, you only have I known of all the families of the earth, therefore will I punish you for your transgressions.

Secondly, because the Lord will be sanctified in them that come near Him. We know that there were many that corrupted the service of the Lord; some setting up altars before his own; others offering both strange fire and strange sacrifices also; yet there came no fire from heaven, or other sudden judgment upon them, as did upon Nadab and Abihu,[10] whom yet we may think did not sin presumptuously.

Thirdly, when God gives a special commission He looks to have it strictly observed in every article; When He gave Saul a commission to destroy Amaleck, He indented with him upon certain articles, and because he failed in one of the least, and that upon a fair pretense, it lost him the kingdom,[11] which should have been his reward, if he had observed his commission.

Thus stands the cause between God and us. We are entered into covenant with Him for this work. We have taken out a commission. The Lord hath given us leave to draw our own articles. We have professed to enterprise these and those accounts, upon these and those ends. We have hereupon besought Him of favor and blessing. Now if the Lord shall please to hear us, and bring us in peace to the place we desire, then hath He ratified this covenant and sealed our commission, and will expect a strict performance of the articles contained in it; but if we shall neglect the observation of these articles which are the ends we have propounded, and, dissembling with our God, shall fall to embrace this present world and prosecute our carnal intentions, seeking great things for ourselves and our posterity, the Lord will surely break out in wrath against us, and be revenged of such a people, and make us know the price of the breach of such a covenant.

Now the only way to avoid this shipwreck, and to provide for our posterity, is to follow the counsel of Micah, to do justly, to love mercy, to walk humbly with our God. For this end, we must be knit together, in this work, as one man. We must entertain each other in brotherly affection. We must be willing to abridge ourselves of our superfluities, for the supply of others' necessities. We must uphold a familiar commerce together in all meekness, gentleness, patience and liberality. We must delight in each other; make others' conditions our own; rejoice together, mourn together, labor and suffer together, always having before our eyes our commission and community in the work, as members of the same body. So shall we keep the unity of the spirit in the bond of peace. The Lord will be our God, and delight to dwell among us, as His own people, and will command a blessing upon us in all our ways, so that we shall see much more of His wisdom, power, goodness and truth, than formerly we have been acquainted with. We shall find that the God of Israel is among us, when ten of us shall be able to resist a thousand of our enemies; when He shall make us a praise and glory that men shall say of succeeding plantations, "may the Lord make it like that of New England." For we must consider that we shall be as a city upon a hill. The eyes of all people are upon us. So that if we shall deal falsely with our God in this work we have undertaken, and so cause Him to withdraw His present help from us, we shall be made a story and a by-word through the world. We shall open the mouths of enemies to speak evil of the ways of God, and all professors for God's sake. We shall shame the faces of many of God's worthy servants, and cause their prayers to be turned into curses upon us till we be consumed out of the good land whither we are going.

And to shut this discourse with that exhortation of Moses, that faithful servant of the Lord, in his last farewell to Israel, Deut. 30. "Beloved, there is now set before us life and death, good and evil," in that we are commanded this day to love the Lord our God, and to love one another, to walk in his ways and to keep his

Commandments and his ordinance and his laws, and the articles of our Covenant with Him, that we may live and be multiplied, and that the Lord our God may bless us in the land whither we go to possess it. But if our hearts shall turn away, so that we will not obey, but shall be seduced, and worship other Gods, our pleasure and profits, and serve them; it is propounded unto us this day, we shall surely perish out of the good land whither we pass over this vast sea to possess it.

> Therefore let us choose life,
> that we and our seed may live,
> by obeying His voice and cleaving to Him,
> for He is our life and our prosperity

1.7

THE MASSACHUSETTS BODY OF LIBERTIES (1641)

The Liberties of the Massachusets Collonie in New England, 1641

The free fruition of such liberties Immunities and priveledges as humanitie, Civilitie, and Christianitie call for as due to every man in his place and proportion without impeachment and Infringement hath ever bene and ever will be the tranquillitie and Stabilitie of Churches and Commonwealths. And the deniall or deprivall thereof, the disturbance if not the ruine of both.

We hould it therefore our dutie and safetie whilst we are about the further establishing of this Government to collect and expresse all such freedomes as for present we foresee may concerne us, and our posteritie after us, And to ratify them with our sollemne consent.

Wee doe therefore this day religiously and unanimously decree and confirme these following Rites, liberties and priveledges concerneing our Churches, and Civill State to be respectively impartiallie and inviolably enjoyed and observed throughout our Jurisdiction for ever.

1. No mans life shall be taken away, no mans honour or good name shall be stayned, no mans person shall be arested, restrayned, banished, dismembred, nor any wayes punished, no man shall be deprived of his wife or children, no mans goods or estaite shall be taken away from him, nor any way indammaged under colour of law or Countenance of Authoritie, unlesse it be by vertue or equitie of some expresse law of the Country waranting the same, established by a generall Court and sufficiently published, or in case of the defect of a law in any parteculer case by the word of God. And in Capitall cases, or in cases concerning dismembring or banishment according to that word to be judged by the Generall Court.

2. Every person within this Jurisdiction, whether Inhabitant or forreiner shall enjoy the same justice and law, that is generall for the plantation, which we constitute and execute one towards another without partialitie or delay. . .

Liberties more peculiarlie concerning the free men

58. Civill Authoritie hath power and libertie to see the Peace, ordinances and Rules of Christ observed in every church according to his word. so it be done in a Civill and not in an Ecclesiastical way.

59. Civill Authoritie hath power and libertie to deale with any Church member in a way of Civill Justice, notwithstanding any Church relation, office or interest.

60. No church censure shall degrade or depose any man from any Civill dignitie, office, or Authoritie he shall have in the Commonwealth . . .

.

.

.

.

94. *Capitall Laws.*

1. (Deut. 13. 6, 10. Deut. 17. 2, 6. Ex. 22.20)

If any man after legall conviction shall have or worship any other god, but the lord god, he shall be put to death.

2. (Ex. 22. 18. Lev. 20. 27. Dut. 18. 10.)

If any man or woeman be a witch, (that is hath or consulteth with a familiar spirit,) They shall be put to death.

3. (Lev. 24. 15, 16.)

If any person shall Blaspheme the name of god, the father, Sonne or Holie Ghost, with direct, expresse, presumptuous or high handed blasphemie, or shall curse god in the like manner, he shall be put to death.

4. (Ex. 21. 12. Numb. 35. 13, 14, 30, 31.)

If any person committ any wilfull murther, which is manslaughter, committed upon premeditated malice, hatred, or Crueltie, not in a mans necessarie and just defence, nor by meere casualtie against his will, he shall be put to death.

5. (Numb. 25, 20, 21. Lev. 24. 17.)

If any person slayeth an other suddaienly in his anger or Crueltie of passion, he shall be put to death.

6. (Ex. 21. 14.)

If any person shall slay an other through guile, either by poysoning or other such divelish practice, he shall be put to death.

7. (Lev. 20. 15, 16.)

If any man or woeman shall lye with any beaste or bruite creature by Carnall Copulation, They shall surely be put to death. And the beast shall be slaine, and buried and not eaten.

8. (Lev. 20. 13.)

If any man lyeth with mankinde as he lyeth with a woeman, both of them have committed abhomination, they both shall surely be put to death.

9. (Lev. 20. 19. and 18, 20. Dut. 22. 23, 24.)

If any person committeth Adultery with a maried or espoused wife, the Adulterer and Adulteresse shall surely be put to death.

10. (Ex. 21. 16.)

If any man stealeth a man or mankinde, he shall surely be put to death.

11. (Deut. 19. 16, 18, 19.)

If any man rise up by false witnes, wittingly and of purpose to take away any mans life, he shall be put to death.

12. If any man shall conspire and attempt any invasion, insurrection, or publique rebellion against our commonwealth, or shall indeavour to surprize any Towne or Townes, fort or forts therein, or shall treacherously and perfediouslie attempt the alteration and subversion of our frame of politie or Government fundamentallie, he shall be put to death . . .

95. A Declaration of the Liberties the Lord Jesus hath given to the Churches

1. All the people of god within this Jurisdiction who are not in a church way, and be orthodox in Judgement, and not scandalous in life, shall have full libertie to gather themselves into a Church Estaite. Provided they doe it in a Christian way, with due observation of the rules of Christ revealed in his word.

2. Every Church hath full libertie to exercise all the ordinances of god, according to the rules of scripture.

3. Every Church hath free libertie of Election and ordination of all their officers from time to time, provided they be able, pious and orthodox.

4. Every Church hath free libertie of Admission, Recommendation, Dismission, and Expulsion, or deposall of their officers, and members, upon due cause, with free exercise of the Discipline and Censures of Christ according to the rules of his word.

5. No Injunctions are to be put upon any Church, Church officers or member in point of Doctrine, worship or Discipline, whether for substance or cercumstance besides the Institutions of the lord.

6. Every Church of Christ hath freedome to celebrate dayes of fasting and prayer, and of thanksgiveing according to the word of god.

7. The Elders of Churches have free libertie to meete monthly, Quarterly, or otherwise, in convenient numbers and places, for conferences, and consultations about Christian and Church questions and occasions.

8. All Churches have libertie to deale with any of their members in a church way that are in the hand of Justice. So it be not to retard or hinder the course thereof.

9. Every Church hath libertie to deale with any magestrate, Deputie of Court or other officer what soe ever that is a member in a church way in case of apparent and just offence given in their places, so it be done with due observance and respect.

10. Wee allowe private meetings for edification in religion amongst Christians of all sortes of people. So it be without just offence for number, time, place, and other cercumstances.

96. Howsoever these above specified rites, freedomes Immunities, Authorites and priveledges, both Civill and Ecclesiastical are expressed onely under the name and title of Liberties, and not in the exact forme of Laws or Statutes, yet we do with one consent fullie Authorise, and earnestly intreate all that are and shall be in Authoritie to consider them as laws, and not to faile to inflict condigne and proportionable punishments upon every man impartiallie, that shall infringe or violate any of them.

97. Wee likewise give full power and libertie to any person that shall at any time be denyed or deprived of any of them, to commence and prosecute their suite, Complaint or action against any man that shall so doe in any Court that hath proper Cognizance or judicature thereof.

1.8

Roger Williams

THE BLOUDY TENENT OF PERSECUTION
(JULY 15, 1644)

First, the proper means whereby the civil power may and should attain its end are only political, and principally these five.

> First, the erecting and establishing what form of civil government may seem in wisdom most meet, according to general rules of the world, and state of the people.
> Secondly, the making, publishing, and establishing of wholesome civil laws, not only such as concern civil justice, but also the free passage of true religion; for outward civil peace ariseth and is maintained from them both, from the latter as well as from the former.
>> Civil peace cannot stand entire, where religion is corrupted (2 Chron. 15. 3. 5. 6; and Judges 8). And yet such laws, though conversant about religion, may still be counted civil laws, as, on the contrary, an oath doth still remain religious though conversant about civil matters.
> Thirdly, election and appointment of civil officers to see execution to those laws.
> Fourthly, civil punishments and rewards of transgressors and observers of these laws.
> Fifthly, taking up arms against the enemies of civil peace.

Secondly, the means whereby the church may and should attain her ends are only ecclesiastical, which are chiefly five.

> First, setting up that form of church government only of which Christ hath given them a pattern in his Word.
> Secondly, acknowledging and admitting of no lawgiver in the church but Christ and the publishing of His laws.
> Thirdly, electing and ordaining of such officers only, as Christ hath appointed in his Word.
> Fourthly, to receive into their fellowship them that are approved and inflicting spiritual censures against them that offend.
> Fifthly, prayer and patience in suffering any evil from them that be without, who disturb their peace.

So that magistrates, as magistrates, have no power of setting up the form of church government, electing church officers, punishing with church censures, but to see that the church does her duty herein. And on the other side, the churches as churches, have no power (though as members of the commonweal they may have power) of erecting or altering forms of civil government, electing of civil officers, inflicting civil punishments (no not on persons excommunicate) as by deposing magistrates from their civil authority, or withdrawing the hearts of the people against them, to their laws, no more than to discharge wives, or children, or servants, from due obedience to their husbands, parents, or masters; or by taking up arms against their magistrates, though he persecute them for conscience: for though members of churches who are public officers also of the civil state may suppress by force the violence of usurpers, as [J]ehoiada did Athaliah,[12] yet this they do not as members of the church but as officers of the civil state.

. . . .The God of Peace, the God of Truth will shortly seal this truth, and confirm this witness, and make it evident to the whole world, that the doctrine of persecution for cause of conscience, is most evidently and lamentably contrary to the doctrine of Christ Jesus the Prince of Peace.

Amen.

1.9

The Cambridge Platform (1648)

Chapter XVII
Of The Civil Magistrate's Power In Matters Ecclesiastical

1. It is lawful, profitable and necessary for Christians to gather themselves together into church estate, and therein to exercise all the ordinances of Christ, according unto the Word, although the consent of the magistrate could not be had thereunto; because the apostles and Christians in their time did frequently thus practice, when the magistrates, being all of them Jewish or pagan, and most persecuting enemies, would give no countenance or consent to such matters.

2. Church government stands in no opposition to civil government of commonwealths, nor any intrenches upon the authority of civil magistrates in their jurisdictions; nor any whit weakens their hands in governing, but rather strengthens them, and furthers the people in yielding more hearty and conscionable obedience unto them, whatsoever some ill affected persons to the ways of Christ have suggested, to alienate the affections of kings and princes from the ordinances of Christ; as if the kingdom of Christ in his church could not rise and stand, without the falling and weakening of their government, which is also of Christ; whereas the contrary is most true, that they may both stand together and flourish, the one being helpful unto the other, in their distinct and due administrations.

3. The power and authority of magistrates is not for the restraining of churches or any other good works, but for helping in and furthering thereof; and therefore the consent and countenance of magistrates, when it may be had, is not to be slighted, or lightly esteemed; but, on the, contrary, it is part of that honor due to Christian magistrates to desire and crave their consent and approbation therein; which being obtained, the churches may then proceed in their way with much more encouragement and comfort.

4. It is not in the power of magistrates to compel their subjects to become church members, and to partake of the Lord's Table; for the priests are reproved that brought unworthy ones into the sanctuary; then it was unlawful for the priests, so it is as unlawful to be done by civil magistrates; those whom the church is to cast out, if they were in, the magistrate ought not to thrust them into the church, nor to hold them therein.

5. As it is unlawful for church officers to meddle with the sword of the magistrate, so it is unlawful for the magistrate to meddle with the work proper to church officers.

The acts of Moses and David, who were not only princes but prophets, were extraordinary, therefore not inimitable. Against such usurpation the Lord witnessed by smiting Uzziah with leprosy for presuming to offer incense.

6. It is the duty of the magistrate to take care of matters of religion, and to improve his civil authority for the observing of the duties commanded in the first, as well as for observing of the duties commanded in the second table. They are called gods. The end of the magistrate's office is not only the quiet and peaceable life of the subject in matters of righteousness and honesty, but also in matters of godliness; yea, of all godliness. Moses, Joshua, David, Solomon, Asa, Jehoshaphat, Hezekiah, Josiah, are much commended by the Holy Ghost, for the putting forth their authority in matters of religion; on the contrary, such kings as have been failing this way, are frequently taxed and reproved of the Lord. And not only the kings of Judah, but also Job, Nehemiah, the king of Nineveh, Darius, Artaxerxes, Nebuchadnezzar, whom none looked at as types of Christ, (though were it so there were no place for any just objection) are commended in the book of God for exercising their authority this way.

7. The objects of the power of the magistrate are not things merely inward, and so not subject to his cognizance and view; as unbelief, hardness of heart, erroneous opinions not vented, but only such things as are acted by the outward man; neither is their power to be exercised in commanding such acts of the outward man, and punishing the neglect thereof, as are but mere inventions and devices of men, but about such acts as are commanded, and forbidden in the Word; yea, such as the Word does clearly determine, though not always clearly to the judgment of the magistrate or others, yet clearly in itself. In these he of right ought to put forth his authority, though oft times actually he does it not.

8. Idolatry, blasphemy, heresy, venting corrupt and pernicious opinions, that destroy the foundation, open contempt of the Word preached, profanation of the Lord's Day, disturbing the peaceable administration and exercise of the worship and holy things of God, and the like, are to be restrained and punished by civil authority.

9. If any church, one or more, shall grow schismatical, rending itself from the communion of other churches, or shall walk incorrigibly and obstinately in any corrupt way of their own, contrary to the rule of the Word; in such case, the magistrate is to put forth his coercive power, as the matter shall require. The tribes on this side Jordan intended to make war against the other tribes for building the altar of witness, whom they suspected to have turned away therein from following of the Lord.

1.10

William Penn

THE GREAT CASE OF LIBERTY OF CONSCIENCE (1670)

By Liberty of Conscience, we understand not only a mere Liberty of the Mind, in believing or disbelieving this or that principle or doctrine; but 'the exercise of ourselves in a visible way of worship, upon our believing it to be indispensably required at' our hands, that if we neglect it for fear or favor of any mortal man, we sin, and incur 'divine wrath.' Yet we would be so understood to extend and justify the lawfulness of our so meeting to worship God, as not to contrive, or abet any contrivance destructive of the government and laws of the land, tending to matters of an external nature, directly or indirectly; but so far only as it may refer to religious matters, and a life to come, and consequently wholly independent of the secular affairs of this, wherein we are supposed to transgress.

Secondly, By imposition, restraint, and persecution, we do not only mean the strict requiring of us to believe this to be true, or that to be false; and upon refusal, to incur the penalties enacted in such cases; but by those terms we mean thus much, 'any coercive let or hindrance to us, from meeting together to perform those religious exercises which are according to our faith and persuasion.'

The Question Stated

For proof of the aforesaid terms thus given, we singly state the question thus; Whether imposition, restraint, and persecution, upon persons for exercising such a liberty of conscience as is before expressed, and so circumstantiated, be not to impeach the honour of God, the meekness of the Christian religion, the authority of Scripture, the privilege of nature, the principles of common reason, the well-being of government, and apprehensions of the greatest personages of former and latter ages?

First, Then we say, that Imposition, Restraint, and Persecution, for matters relating to conscience, directly invade the divine prerogative, and divest the Almighty of a due, proper to none besides himself. And this we prove by these five particulars:

First, if we do allow the honour of our creation due to God only, and that no other besides himself has endowed us with those excellent gifts of Understanding, Reason, Judgment, and Faith, and consequently that he only is the object, as well as the author, both of our Faith, Worship, and Service; then whosoever shall interpose their authority to enact faith and worship in a way that seems not to us congruous with what he has discovered to us to be faith and worship (whose alone property it is to do it) or to restrain us from what we are persuaded is our indispensible duty, they evidently usurp this authority, and invade his incommunicable right of government over conscience: 'For the Inspiration of the Almighty gives understanding: And Faith is the gift of God,' says the divine writ.

Secondly, Such magisterial determinations carry an evident claim to that Infallibility, which Protestants have been hitherto so jealous of owning, that, to avoid the Papists, they have denied it to all but God himself.

Either they have forsook their old plea; or if not, we desire to know when, and where, they were invested with that divine excellency; and whether Imposition, Restraint, and Persecution, Were ever deemed by God the fruits of his Spirit. However, that itself was not sufficient; for unless it appear as well to us that they have it, as to them who have it, we cannot believe it upon any convincing evidence, but by Tradition only; an anti-protestant way of believing.

Thirdly, It enthrones Man as king over conscience, the alone just claim and privilege of his Creator; whose thoughts are not as mens thoughts, but has reserved to himself that empire from all the Caesars on earth: For if men, in reference to souls and bodies, things appertaining to this and the other world, shall be subject to their fellow-creatures, what follows, but that Caesar (however he got it) has all, God's share, and his own too? And being Lord of both, both are Caesar's, and not God's.

Fourthly, It defeats God's work of Grace, and the invisible operation of his eternal Spirit, (which can alone beget faith, and is only to be obeyed, in and about religion and worship) and attributes mens conformity to outward force and corporal punishments. A faith subject to as many revolutions as the powers that enact it.

Fifthly and lastly, Such persons assume the judgment of the great tribunal unto themselves; for to whomsoever men are imposedly or restrictively subject and accountable in matters of faith, worship and conscience; in them alone must the power of judgment reside: But it is equally true that God shall judge all by Jesus Christ; and that no man is so accountable to his fellow-creatures, as to be imposed upon, restrained, or persecuted for any matter of conscience whatever.

Thus, and in any more particulars, are men accustomed to intrench upon Divine Property, to gratify particular interests in the world; and (at best) through a misguided apprehension to imagine 'they do God good service,' that where they cannot give faith, they will use force; which kind of sacrifice is nothing less unreasonable than the other is abominable: God will not give his honour to another; and to him only, that searches the heart and tries the reins, it is our duty to ascribe the gifts of Understanding and Faith, without which none can please God.

1.11

John Locke

A LETTER CONCERNING TOLERATION (1689)

Honoured Sir,

Since you are pleased to inquire what are my thoughts about the mutual toleration of Christians in their different professions of religion, I must needs answer you freely that I esteem that toleration to be the chief characteristic mark of the true Church. For whatsoever some people boast of the antiquity of places and names, or of the pomp of their outward worship; others, of the reformation of their discipline; all, of the orthodoxy of their faith—for everyone is orthodox to himself—these things, and all others of this nature, are much rather marks of men striving for power and empire over one another than of the Church of Christ. Let anyone have never so true a claim to all these things, yet if he be destitute of charity, meekness, and good-will in general towards all mankind, even to those that are not Christians, he is certainly yet short of being a true Christian himself. "The kings of the Gentiles exercise leadership over them," said our Saviour to his disciples, "but ye shall not be so." The business of true religion is quite another thing. It is not instituted in order to the erecting of an external pomp, nor to the obtaining of ecclesiastical dominion, nor to the exercising of compulsive force, but to the regulating of men's lives, according to the rules of virtue and piety. . . .

I esteem it above all things necessary to distinguish exactly the business of civil government from that of religion and to settle the just bounds that lie between the one and the other. If this be not done, there can be no end put to the controversies that will be always arising between those that have, or at least pretend to have, on the one side, a concernment for the interest of men's souls, and, on the other side, a care of the commonwealth.

The commonwealth seems to me to be a society of men constituted only for the procuring, preserving, and advancing their own civil interests.

Civil interests I call life, liberty, health, and indolency of body; and the possession of outward things, such as money, lands, houses, furniture, and the like.

It is the duty of the civil magistrate, by the impartial execution of equal laws, to secure unto all the people in general and to every one of his subjects in particular the just possession of these things belonging to this life. If anyone presume to violate the laws of public justice and equity, established for the preservation of those things, his presumption is to be checked by the fear of punishment, consisting of the deprivation or diminution of those civil interests, or goods, which otherwise he might and ought to enjoy. But seeing no man does willingly suffer himself to be punished by the deprivation of any part of his goods, and much less of his liberty or life, therefore, is the magistrate armed with the force and strength of all his subjects, in order to the punishment of those that violate any other man's rights.

Now that the whole jurisdiction of the magistrate reaches only to these civil concernments, and that all civil power, right and dominion, is bounded and confined to the only care of promoting these things; and that it neither can nor ought in any manner to be extended to the salvation of souls, these following considerations seem unto me abundantly to demonstrate.

First, because the care of souls is not committed to the civil magistrate, any more than to other men. It is not committed unto him, I say, by God; because it appears not that God has ever given any such authority to one man over another as to compel anyone to his religion. Nor can any such power be vested in the magistrate by the consent of the people, because no man can so far abandon the care of his own salvation as blindly to leave to the choice of any other, whether prince or subject, to prescribe to him what faith or worship he shall embrace. For no man can, if he would, conform his faith to the dictates of another. All the life and power of true religion consist in the inward and full persuasion of the mind; and faith is not faith without believing. Whatever profession we make, to whatever outward worship we conform, if we are not fully satisfied in our own mind that the one is true and the other well pleasing unto God, such profession and such practice, far from being any furtherance, are indeed great obstacles to our salvation. For in this manner, instead of expiating other sins by the exercise of religion, I say, in offering thus unto God Almighty such a worship as we esteem to be displeasing unto Him, we add unto the number of our other sins those also of hypocrisy and contempt of His Divine Majesty.

In the second place, the care of souls cannot belong to the civil magistrate, because his power consists only in outward force; but true and saving religion consists in the inward persuasion of the mind, without which nothing can be acceptable to God. And such is the nature of the understanding, that it cannot be compelled to the belief of anything by outward force. Confiscation of estate, imprisonment, torments, nothing of that nature can have any such efficacy as to make men change the inward judgement that they have framed of things. . . .

In the third place, the care of the salvation of men's souls cannot belong to the magistrate; because, though the rigour of laws and the force of penalties were capable to convince and change men's minds, yet would not that help at all to the salvation of their souls. For there being but one truth, one way to heaven, what hope is there that more men would be led into it if they had no rule but the religion of the court and were put under the necessity to quit the light of their own reason, and oppose the dictates of their own consciences, and blindly to resign themselves up to the will of their governors and to the religion which either ignorance, ambition, or superstition had chanced to establish in the countries where they were born? In the variety and contradiction of opinions in religion, wherein the princes of the world are as much divided as in their secular interests, the narrow way would be much straitened; one country alone would be in the right, and all the rest of the world put under an obligation of following their princes in the ways that lead to destruction; and that which heightens the absurdity, and very ill suits the notion of a Deity, men would owe their eternal happiness or misery to the places of their nativity.

These considerations, to omit many others that might have been urged to the same purpose, seem unto me sufficient to conclude that all the power of civil government relates only to men's civil interests, is confined to the care of the things of this world, and hath nothing to do with the world to come.

The end of a religious society (as has already been said) is the public worship of God and, by means thereof, the acquisition of eternal life. All discipline ought, therefore, to tend to that end, and all ecclesiastical laws to be thereunto confined. Nothing ought nor can be transacted in this society relating to the possession of civil and worldly goods. No force is here to be made use of upon any occasion whatsoever. For force belongs wholly to the civil magistrate, and the possession of all outward goods is subject to his jurisdiction.

But, it may be asked, by what means then shall ecclesiastical laws be established, if they must be thus destitute of all compulsive power? I answer: They must be established by means suitable to the nature of such things, whereof the external profession and observation—if not proceeding from a thorough conviction and approbation of the mind—is altogether useless and unprofitable. The arms by which the members of this society are to be kept within their duty are exhortations, admonitions, and advices. If by these means the offenders will not be reclaimed, and the erroneous convinced, there remains nothing further to be done but that such stubborn and obstinate persons, who give no ground to hope for their reformation, should be cast out and separated from the society. This is the last and utmost force of ecclesiastical authority. No other punishment can thereby be inflicted than that, the relation ceasing between the body and the member which is cut off. The person so condemned ceases to be a part of that church.

These things being thus determined, let us inquire, in the next place: How far the duty of toleration extends, and what is required from everyone by it?

There are two sorts of contests amongst men, the one managed by law, the other by force; and these are of that nature that where the one ends, the other always begins. But it is not my business to inquire into the power of the magistrate in the different constitutions of nations. I only know what usually happens where controversies arise without a judge to determine them. You will say, then, the magistrate being the stronger will have his will and carry his point. Without doubt; but the question is not here concerning the doubtfulness of the event, but the rule of right.

But to come to particulars. I say, first, no opinions contrary to human society, or to those moral rules which are necessary to the preservation of civil society, are to be tolerated by the magistrate. But of these, indeed, examples in any Church are rare. For no sect can easily arrive to such a degree of madness as that it should think fit to teach, for doctrines of religion, such things as manifestly undermine the foundations of society and are, therefore, condemned by the judgement of all mankind; because their own interest, peace, reputation, everything would be thereby endangered.

Another more secret evil, but more dangerous to the commonwealth, is when men arrogate to themselves, and to those of their own sect, some peculiar prerogative covered over with a specious show of deceitful words, but in effect opposite to the civil right of the community. For example: we cannot find any sect that teaches, expressly and openly, that men are not obliged to keep their promise; that princes may be dethroned by those that differ from them in religion; or that the dominion of all things belongs only to themselves. For these things, proposed thus nakedly and plainly, would soon draw on them the eye and hand of the magistrate and awaken all the care of the commonwealth to a watchfulness against the spreading of so dangerous an evil. But, nevertheless, we find those that say the same things in other words. What else do they mean who teach that faith is not to be kept with heretics? Their meaning, forsooth, is that the privilege of breaking faith belongs unto themselves; for they declare all that are not of their communion to be heretics, or at least may declare them so whensoever they think fit. What can be the meaning of their asserting that kings excommunicated forfeit their crowns and kingdoms? It is evident that they thereby arrogate unto themselves the power of deposing kings, because they challenge the power of excommunication, as the peculiar right of their hierarchy. That dominion is founded in grace is also an assertion by which those that maintain it do plainly lay claim to the possession of all things. For they are not so wanting to themselves as not to believe, or at least as not to profess themselves to be the truly pious and faithful. These, therefore, and the like, who attribute unto the faithful, religious, and orthodox, that is, in plain terms, unto themselves, any peculiar privilege or power above other mortals, in civil concernments; or who upon pretence of religion do challenge any manner of authority over such as are not associated with them in their ecclesiastical communion, I say these have no right to be tolerated by the magistrate; as neither those that will not own and teach the duty of tolerating all men in matters of mere religion. For what do all these and the like doctrines signify, but that they may and are ready upon any occasion to seize the Government and possess themselves of the estates and fortunes of their fellow subjects; and that they only ask leave to be tolerated by the magistrate so long until they find themselves strong enough to effect it?

Again: That Church can have no right to be tolerated by the magistrate which is constituted upon such a bottom that all those who enter into it do thereby ipso facto deliver themselves up to the protection and service of another prince. For by this means the magistrate would give way to the settling of a foreign jurisdiction in his own country and suffer his own people to be listed, as it were, for soldiers against his own Government. Nor does the frivolous and fallacious distinction between the Court and the Church afford any remedy to this inconvenience; especially when both the one and the other are equally subject to the absolute authority of the same person, who has not only power to persuade the members of his Church to whatsoever he lists, either as purely religious, or in order thereunto, but can also enjoin it them on pain of eternal fire. It is ridiculous for any one to profess himself to be a Mahometan only in his religion, but in everything else a faithful subject to a Christian magistrate, whilst at the same time he acknowledges himself bound to yield blind obedience to the Mufti of Constantinople, who himself is entirely obedient to the Ottoman Emperor and frames the feigned oracles of that religion according to his pleasure. But this Mahometan living amongst Christians would yet more apparently renounce their government if he acknowledged the same person to be head of his Church who is the supreme magistrate in the state.

Lastly, those are not at all to be tolerated who deny the being of a God. Promises, covenants, and oaths, which are the bonds of human society, can have no hold upon an atheist. The taking away of God, though but even in thought, dissolves all; besides also, those that by their atheism undermine and destroy all religion, can have no pretence of religion whereupon to challenge the privilege of a toleration. As for other practical opinions, though not absolutely free from all error, if they do not tend to establish domination over others, or civil impunity to the Church in which they are taught, there can be no reason why they should not be tolerated.

The sum of all we drive at is that every man may enjoy the same rights that are granted to others. Is it permitted to worship God in the Roman manner? Let it be permitted to do it in the Geneva form also. Is it permitted to speak Latin in the market-place? Let those that have a mind to it be permitted to do it also in the Church. Is it lawful for any man in his own house to kneel, stand, sit, or use any other posture; and to clothe himself in white or black, in short or in long garments? Let it not be made unlawful to eat bread, drink wine, or wash with water in the church. In a word, whatsoever things are left free by law in the common occasions of life, let them remain free unto every Church in divine worship. Let no man's life, or body, or house, or estate, suffer any manner of prejudice upon these accounts. Can you allow of the Presbyterian discipline? Why should not the Episcopal also have what they like? Ecclesiastical authority, whether it be administered by the hands of a single person or many, is everywhere the same; and neither has any jurisdiction in things civil, nor any manner of power of compulsion, nor anything at all to do with riches and revenues. . . .

God Almighty grant, I beseech Him, that the gospel of peace may at length be preached, and that civil magistrates, growing more careful to conform their own consciences to the law of God and less solicitous about the binding of other men's consciences by human laws, may, like fathers of their country, direct all their counsels and endeavours to promote universally the civil welfare of all their children, except only of such as are arrogant, ungovernable, and injurious to their brethren; and that all ecclesiastical men, who boast themselves to be the successors of the Apostles, walking peaceably and modestly in the Apostles' steps, without intermeddling with State Affairs, may apply themselves wholly to promote the salvation of souls.

Farewell.

Notes

1. For sources quoted herein and further analysis, see John Witte, Jr., *Religion and the American Constitutional Experiment,* 2d ed. (Boulder: Westview Press, 2005), ch. 1–3; id. *God's Joust, God's Justice: Law and Religion in the Western Tradition* (Grand Rapids: Wm. B. Eerdmans, 2006), ch. 5–8; id., *The Reformation of Rights: Law, Religion, and Human Rights in Early Modern Calvinism* (Cambridge: Cambridge University Press, 2007).

2. See also Horton (1991), which describes toleration as the "deliberate choice not to prohibit, hinder, or interfere with conduct of which one disapproves, where one has the requisite power and knowledge" (521). This definition is repeated almost verbatim in Horton and Nicholson (1992, 2); and Horton (1993, 3).

3. See King 1976, 13ff. The classic formulation of negative and positive liberty, despite (perhaps *because of*) its polemical edge, remains Berlin 1969a.

4. When considering other social or political debates, removal of criminal penalties constitutes a similar minimum. Although such a minimum may eventually prove inadequate to secure freedom, basic toleration does set a standard from which further theorizing and action can proceed. See Galeotti 1993 on religious and cultural pluralism; Gardner 1992 on toleration and multicultural education; Horton and Mendus 1985 on racial and sexual toleration; and Jackson 1992 on campus intolerance.

5. The quotation is from John Winthrop's "Speech to the General Court," in Miller and Johnson 1938, 207.

6. The *Bloudy Tenent* was published in 1647 and, strictly speaking, belongs to a different era; however, I wish to emphasize the Puritan consensus that obtained on popular sovereignty. I admit that viewing Williams and Massachusetts Puritans solely in light of toleration obscures broad areas of agreement; see Calamandrei 1952.

7. Massachusetts Bay, however, was *not* a theocracy. The spheres were considered distinct, though civil governors were charged with the preservation of religion. See Cotton 1641, ch. 1; and *Book of Laws and Liberties*, which notes that church and state "each do help and strengthen each other" (1975, 1).

8. It is easy, however, to overstate the degree to which Puritans saw Massachusetts as an example for the world. In many ways Winthrop's ambitious language is not borne out by the larger historical record. See Bozeman 1986.

9. "The response of the Bay Colony to first the Quakers and later the Baptists was shaped by its previous experience in dealing with . . . . Anne Hutchison [and] Roger Williams" (Pestana 1991, 2).

10. Nadab and Abihu were priests, two sons of Aaron. They are known for dying after they offered 'strange fire' to God: i.e., did not follow prescribed rules in offering sacrifices to God (Leviticus 10: 1–5).

11. The Hebrew Bible in places ascribes Saul's loss of his kingdom to his failure to completely wipe out the Amalekite people (I Samuel 15:2–3, I Samuel 18).

12. The Hebrew scriptures describe Athaliah as an unfaithful usurper of the throne of Judah. Josiah was a faithful prophet of Yahweh who participated in her ouster (II Kings 11:4–20).

CHAPTER 2

FORGING A NEW NATION

Introduction

Integrative Essay

Introduction

As Chapter 1 illustrates, one of the prevailing questions about religion and public life during the colonial era was how to promote religious toleration amidst varied local religious expressions. During the fledgling years of the new republic, religion remained a focal point for the foundations of both American society and republican government. A central question facing the framers of the Constitution was how to allow varieties of religion and morality to flourish locally in ways that strengthened the newly formed union of states. The proposed solution was to guarantee constitutionally both "free exercise" and "no establishment" of religion at the national level (creating a supportive but "free" market for all faiths in the country as a whole), while letting the various states continue their current varied church-state arrangements, provided each state generally maintained a measure of official religious toleration. There was little disagreement in the early years of the republic, as George Washington wrote in his farewell address of 1796, that "[o]f all the dispositions and habits, which lead to political prosperity, Religion and Morality are indispensable supports." Yet, disagreement remained about how religion should relate to government.

Daniel Dreisbach's integrative essay describes the evolution of the debate about established state churches and the simultaneous genesis of the religion clauses that resulted from the deliberation at the Constitutional Convention. The compromise led to the emergence of a "free market" for religious expression, where all brands of religion that followed minimal standards of civic loyalty and peaceful coexistence with other faiths were welcome to participate in the marketplace of religious ideas. And it was clear that the Founders intended these competing religions to compete in this marketplace with reason and persuasion, not brute force or appeals to ecclesiastical powers or eternal punishments.

The selections in this chapter illustrate these points. The original documents, arranged mostly in chronological order, illustrate directly the development of these ideas within the minds of key founders—Adams, Madison, Jefferson, and Washington. Adams argues for the official separation of ecclesial and government offices and duties as an aid to both. With colorful and sometimes painfully graphic rhetoric, he notes his distaste for what he saw as the abuses of Catholic and Anglican church leaders, his preference for faith traditions that prefer reasonable, logical, arguments, and a more general respect for the life of the mind and the cultivation of higher thought. Madison makes a similar argument for reason-based religious conviction as he petitions the Virginia state government in protest of a bill that would use state money to pay the religious teachers of various Christian traditions, including but not exclusively the Anglicans. The Virginia Assembly heeded Madison's warning, tabling the bill and instead passing Virginia's Statute on Religious Liberty, which bears the marks of Jefferson's hand. The next two selections are official statements from President George Washington. The first proclaims a religious day of Thanksgiving, and the second, his farewell address upon leaving office, reflects the view that a deep and sincere religious faith, whatever the particulars of its theology, promotes, among other virtues, the morality and humility necessary for a peaceable and prosperous nation. Although the theological and political views of each of these founders differ in many details, these and other writings suggest that each considered how to encourage religion among the citizenry as well as the civic benefits that religion provides without providing official religious support from the national government.

In the founding era, the nation as a whole was in effect an open marketplace among religions with no formal establishment of any particular faith or sect. At the same time, the federal structure of the United States permitted a variety of different church-state relationships at the state level. Many states retained officially or semi-officially established churches, and in certain localities the "establishment" was quite strong. This mix, for the most part, allowed various religious sects to flourish peaceably, creating a distinctive culture that captured the attention of Tocqueville on his visit to the new nation. The final selection in this chapter, an excerpt from Tocqueville's 1833 observations of the role of religion in the new nation, aptly describes the American religious experiment: "In America religion is perhaps less powerful than it has been at certain periods and among certain nations; but its influence is more lasting. It restricts itself to its own resources, but of these none can deprive it; its circle is limited, but it pervades it and holds it under undisputed control."

Integrative Essay

2.1

Daniel L. Dreisbach

RELIGION AND THE CIVIL STATE
IN THE AMERICAN FOUNDING

Since the first permanent English settlements in the New World, religion has been integral to the identity and mission of the American people and their political projects.[1] The First Charter of Virginia in 1606 commended the colonists' "humble and well intended desires" to further, "by the providence of Almighty God," a noble work "in propagating [the] Christian religion to such people, as yet live in darkness and miserable ignorance of the true knowledge and worship of God." The signatories to the Mayflower Compact in 1620 undertook their voyage "for the Glory of God, and Advancement of the Christian Faith, and the Honour of our King and Country." An invocation of divine blessing and acknowledgment of a sacred mission to spread the Gospel were recurring themes in the colonial charters and other expressions of the colonists' political pursuits.

The New England Puritans, especially, believed they were called by God, in the words of Matthew 5:14, to build a "city set upon a Hill." These pious settlers committed themselves to establishing Bible commonwealths and remaking the world in conformity with God's laws, as they understood them. The Bible was often the explicit basis of early colonial charters and codes. This was true not only in New England but also in Virginia. The "Articles, Lawes, and Orders, Divine, Politique, and Martiall for the Colony in Virginea," written in 1610 and enlarged in 1611, was designed to restore discipline in the colony. Like the legal codes subsequently framed in Puritan commonwealths to the north, it bore the unmistakable influence of the Ten Commandments. It prohibited "impiously or maliciously" speaking "against the holy and blessed Trinities," blaspheming God's holy name, deriding or defying God's holy word, Sabbath breaking, murdering, bearing false witness, and committing adultery or other sexual sins.

The Bible similarly informed early colonial charters and codes in New England. For example, the "Fundamental Orders of Connecticut" (1639), arguably the first written constitution in North America, declared that a governor and his council "shall have power to administer justice according to the Lawes here established, and for want thereof according to the rule of the word of God." The "Massachusetts Body of Liberties" (1641)—sometimes described as the first bill of rights in North America—stated that "No custome or prescription shall ever prevaile amongst us in any morall cause, our meaneing is maintaine anything that can be proved to bee morallie sinfull by the word of god." These charters and code often gave specific biblical authority for provisions in them.

Most of the colonies eventually established churches, following a model they had known in Europe. Congregationalism enjoyed legal favor in New England, and the Church of England was established in the southern colonies. Religious dissenters were afforded a measure of toleration in most colonies, although they were often burdened in the exercise of their religion and denied certain civic prerogatives.

As European settlements grew in number and size throughout the colonies, the diversity of religious sects also increased. The extraordinary religious diversity in the colonies was a potential source of rivalry and conflict among denominations competing for adherents and public recognition (and, sometimes, the legal and financial favor of the civil state). Some minority sects, unfortunately, suffered persecution in their adopted homeland. The dramatic sectarian clashes capture the most attention; however, the story of religions in America is most remarkable for the amity and general respect among the diverse sects that were planted and flourished side by side in the American soil.

The religious diversity in the colonies required Americans to develop policies of, initially, religious toleration and, eventually, religious liberty. In communities where the governors and the governed are *all* of one faith, there is little demand for a policy of religious liberty. But where both civil authorities and ordinary citizens come from many denominations and where multiple sects compete for followers and public favor, peaceful coexistence requires a workable policy of toleration. Early in the colonial experience, Americans began to wrestle with these contentious issues, culminating in the bold policies of religious liberty enshrined in the Virginia Declaration of Rights (1776), Virginia Statute for Establishing Religious Freedom (1786), and First Amendment to the United States Constitution (1791).

By the time the national Constitution was crafted in the late 1780s, a declining number of Americans supported an exclusive ecclesiastical establishment in their respective states, and few advocated for a national establishment. The religious diversity in the new nation meant that the establishment of a national church was practically untenable. No denomination was sufficiently dominant to claim the legal favor of the federal regime, and there was little likelihood that a political consensus would emerge as to which sect or combination of sects should constitute a "Church of the United States." Nonetheless, many influential citizens, despite some Enlightenment influences, continued to believe religion's place (and role) in the polity must be prominent and public.

Few Americans of the seventeenth and eighteenth centuries, even among those who supported disestablishment, doubted the value and utility of a vibrant religious, specifically Christian, culture. There was a consensus that religion fosters the civic virtues and social discipline that give citizens the capacity to govern themselves. Tyrants use the whip and rod to compel social order, but this is unacceptable for a free, self-governing people. Religion, alternatively, provides an internal moral compass that prompts citizens to behave in a responsible, orderly manner. Religion was, thus, viewed as vital to self-government. For this reason, Americans frequently discussed how best to nurture popular religion and extend its influence in society.

By the mid-eighteenth century, two distinct, conflicting schools of thought had emerged regarding how best to promote a vibrant religious culture. Benjamin Rush, a respected signer of the Declaration of Independence, said "[t]here are but two ways of preserving visible religion in any country. The first is by establishments. The second is by the competition of different religious societies."

The first way, which was the practice in Europe and most of the colonies, was to maintain a legally established church. A dominant view in the early colonial period was that, because religion was indispensable to social order and political happiness, the civil state must officially and legally maintain a particular church or denomination, which citizens had a duty to support. Establishmentarians feared that a failure to establish a church with the civil state's sustaining aid would impair religion's vital influence in society.

In the second half of the eighteenth century, an unlikely coalition of religious dissenters and moderate Enlightenment rationalists advanced a second way to nurture a vibrant religious culture. They advocated terminating legal privileges for a favored church and adopting a policy of disestablishment in which all sects would be placed on an equal footing before the law. Each sect or church should be free to compete in an open marketplace of ideas where, as Thomas Jefferson confidently predicted, "truth is great and will prevail if left to herself." They contended that matters of one's belief (or disbelief) and support of a particular minister or religious society should be left to the voluntary choice of citizens; and civil rights and prerogatives should not be conditioned on a citizen's religious beliefs.

These opponents of state churches argued that disestablishment and competition among religious sects, in the words of James Madison, resulted "in the greater purity & industry of the pastors & in the greater devotion of their flocks." Disestablishment required sects to compete to survive. Churches and their clergy had to be exemplary and industrious, demonstrating to the world the purity and efficacy of their faith. Churches were forced to rely on the voluntary support of adherents rather than on the benevolence of the civil state. There was a growing belief that state churches tended to become complacent, corrupt, and intolerant.[2] Disestablishment, by contrast, facilitated a vibrant religious culture in which the best and purest religion would dominate. The combination of competition among sects, disestablishment, and religious liberty created an environment in which religions could flourish and beneficently influence public culture. This, they contended, was good for the church, good for society, and good for the civil state.

By the time of independence, eight or nine states retained an established church in some form. The Anglican Church was preferred by law throughout the south, and the Congregationalists enjoyed official favor in much of New England. A few states, like Pennsylvania and Rhode Island, steadfastly rejected Old World models of an ecclesiastical establishment and, in so doing, created new models for religious toleration and disestablished polities. These new models would eventually prevail in America.

After the separation from England, the former colonies began to revise their laws to bring them into conformity with republican principles. They gave particular attention to the model of ecclesiastical establishment inherited from England. Nowhere was this process more dramatic and, in the end, influential than in Virginia. The Virginia Convention that assembled in Williamsburg in 1776 instructed its delegates at the Continental Congress to press for independence. This bold initiative raised difficult questions about the nature of civil authority in the Commonwealth. Believing, perhaps, that they had reverted to a state of nature, the delegates thought it necessary to frame a new social compact, beginning with a declaration of man's natural rights, followed by a new plan of civil government. The assembly appointed a committee to prepare a state declaration of rights and constitution. George Mason and the young delegate from Orange County, James Madison, Jr., were among those appointed to the committee.

Mason framed initial drafts of both a declaration of rights and constitution. Although Madison was interested in all aspects of the Declaration, only the last article providing for religious toleration moved him to take action. In the first significant public act of a long and distinguished political career, Madison objected to Mason's use of the word "toleration" because it dangerously implied that religious exercise was a mere privilege that could be granted or revoked at the pleasure of the civil state and was not assumed to be a natural, unalienable right. Religious *toleration* differs from religious *liberty*. The former often assumes an established church and regards religious exercise as a revocable grant of the civil state rather than a natural right. Madison thought the right of religious exercise was a fundamental right, possessed equally by all citizens, located beyond the reach of civil magistrates and subject only to the dictates of a free conscience.

Accordingly, Madison proposed replacing Mason's statement, "all Men shou'd enjoy the fullest Toleration in the Exercise of Religion, according to the Dictates of Conscience," with the clause, "all men are equally entitled to the full and free exercise of [religion] accord[in]g to the dictates of Conscience." Mason's draft reflected the most enlightened, liberal policies of the age and went further than any previous declaration in force in Virginia, but it did not go far enough to satisfy Madison. Key to Madison's revision was the word "equally," which meant that the unlearned Baptists of central Virginia had religious rights equal to those of the aristocratic Anglicans of the Tidewater. Article XVI of the Virginia Declaration of Rights, adopted on June 12, 1776, declared:

> That religion, or the duty which we owe to our CREATOR, and the manner of discharging it, can be directed only by reason and conviction, not by force or violence; and therefore all men are equally entitled to the free exercise of religion, according to the dictates of conscience; and that it is the mutual duty of all to practise Christian forbearance, love, and charity, towards each other.

Instituting religious liberty in the place of toleration is one of America's great contributions to, and innovations of, political society.

The Massachusetts Constitution of 1780 similarly considered the prudential place of and public role for religion. The church-state model reflected in this document differed from that adopted in Virginia. It acknowledged "the duty of all men in society, publicly, and at stated seasons, to worship the SUPREME BEING." It also affirmed the citizen's right to worship "GOD in the manner and season most agreeable to the dictates of his own conscience," without being "hurt, molested, or restrained," so long as one does "not disturb the public peace, or obstruct others in their religious worship." It further stated: "As the happiness of a people, and the good order and preservation of civil government, essentially depend upon piety, religion, and morality; and as these cannot be generally diffused through a community but by the institution of the public worship of GOD, and of public instructions in piety, religion, and morality." Therefore, the Constitution authorized the legislature to mandate political bodies or religious societies to provide for religious worship and instruction, require attendance at public worship, and compel a tithe for the support of public worship and ministers. Proponents believed this arrangement appropriately balanced the establishment of one public religion with the maintenance of a protected space for various private religions in which they could worship and enjoy the support of adherents. Every polity, they thought, must maintain by law some expression of public religion responsible for disseminating throughout the community the values and civic virtues that promote social order and give citizens the capacity for self-government. A stable civil state and political prosperity could not long endure if it remained neutral or indifferent toward religion.

Against this backdrop of state constitutions, national leaders turned their attention to creating a plan of government conducive to the safety and happiness of the former colonies and the American people. The national constitution framed in Philadelphia in mid-1787, together with the First Amendment to it, defined a place and role for religion in public life. The constitutional bases for this distinctively American approach to church-state relations are Article VI, clause 3 and the First Amendment. The first declares that "no religious Test shall ever be required as a Qualification to any Office or public Trust under the United States," and the second provides that "Congress shall make no law respecting an establishment of religion, or prohibiting the free exercise thereof." The former is binding only on federal officeholders. It did not invalidate religious tests that existed under state laws. Similarly, the latter provision did not initially alter church-state arrangements and practices at the state and local levels.

The Article VI religious test ban in the original, unamended Constitution followed language instructing all national and state officeholders to take an oath or affirmation to support the Constitution. Charles Pinckney of South Carolina, who thought the national legislature should "pass no Law on the subject of Religion" (Farrand 1911, 3:599), was the chief proponent of a test ban. He purportedly told delegates at the Constitutional Convention in May 1787 that "the prevention of Religious Tests, as qualifications to Offices of Trust or Emolument . . . [, is] a provision the world will expect from you, in the establishment of a System founded on Republican Principles, and in an age so liberal and enlightened as the present" (Farrand 1911, 3:122). Three months later, Pinckney raised the subject again, this time proposing that "No religious test or qualification shall ever be annexed to any oath of office under the authority of the United States" (Farrand 1911, 2:335, 342). At the end of August, during debate on qualifications for federal office and employment, Pinckney urged the Convention to adopt the religious test ban. Following a brief debate, the delegates approved Pinckney's amendment and forwarded it to the Committee on Style, which shaped the final language incorporated into Article VI (Farrand 1911, 461, 468).

The provision generated energetic debate in the state ratifying conventions. A recurring theme emphasized the role of morality, fostered by the Christian religion, in promoting the civic virtues and social order essential to a system of self-government. The ban on religious tests, critics said, suggested inattentiveness to the vital task of selecting rulers committed to protecting and nurturing religion and morality. Once it is conceded that not all religions are conducive to good civil government and political order, then there are plausible grounds for excluding adherents of some religions from public office. Accordingly, in the words of Luther Martin of Maryland, "it would be *at least decent* to hold out some distinction between the professors of Christianity and downright infidelity or paganism." Proponents of a federal test ban framed the debate in terms of religious liberty. Oliver Ellsworth of Connecticut defended the ban, arguing that "the sole purpose and effect of it is to exclude persecution and to secure to you the important right of religious liberty." "[A] good and peaceable citizen," he continued, should receive "no penalties or incapacities on account of his religious sentiments."

The inclusion of religious tests in the laws of many states of the era indicates some measure of support for them. Moreover, religious tests coexisted with free exercise and nonestablishment provisions in some state constitutions. The founding generation apparently did not consider these concepts necessarily incompatible. Interestingly, some delegates at the Constitutional Convention who endorsed the federal ban had previously participated in crafting religious tests for their respective state laws. Can these positions be reconciled? The Constitution of 1787, as a matter of federalism, denied the national government all jurisdiction over religion, including the authority to administer religious tests. There was a consensus that religion was a matter best left to individual citizens and to their respective state governments. Many in the founding generation, it would seem, supported a federal test ban because they valued religious tests required under state laws, and they did not want the federal regime to mandate a test that would displace existing state test oaths and religious establishments (Dreisbach 1996).

A number of states conditioned their support for the proposed Constitution on the adoption of amendments—including an amendment protecting religious liberty. Early in the first Congress under the Constitution, Representative James Madison proposed the following amendment: "The civil rights of none shall be abridged on account of religious belief or worship, nor shall any national religion be established, nor shall the full and equal rights of conscience be in any manner, or on any pretext, infringed." The House gave this proposal little attention before debating the topic on August 15, 1789. Five days later, the House revisited the measure, eventually adopting this language: "Congress shall make no law establishing religion, or to prevent the free exercise thereof, or to infringe the rights of conscience." The measure was then forwarded to the Senate which, after consideration of several proposals, approved this text: "Congress shall make no law establishing articles of faith or a mode of worship, or prohibiting the free exercise of religion" (*Journal of the First Session of the Senate* 1820, 77). The House declined to accept the Senate version; thus, the matter was sent to a conference committee that drafted the final language adopted by the House on September 24, and by the Senate the following day. This text was ratified by the states and added to the Constitution in December 1791.

Although diverse interpretations can be drawn from this text and its legislative history, there is broad agreement for several modest conclusions. First, the framers proscribed the creation of a national church like the established church in England. Congress was prohibited from conferring legal preferences or special favors on one church that are denied to others. The nonestablishment provision was not meant to silence religion or require civil government to hold all religions in utter indifference. Second, the amendment affirmed that states, not the national government, had jurisdiction in matters concerning religion. Moreover, Congress was not only prohibited from establishing a national church but also denied authority to interfere with existing state religious establishments. (This purpose was turned on its head by the incorporation of the First Amendment into the Fourteenth Amendment.)[3] Third, the amendment protected citizens from actions by the federal regime inhibiting the free exercise of religion. The free exercise guarantee, at the very least, prevented Congress from compelling or prohibiting religious worship. It affirmed a right to worship God, or not, according to the dictates of conscience, free from coercion, interference, discrimination, or punishment by the national government.

While the legislative history reveals much about the First Amendment's original understanding and purposes, many questions about its application remain unanswered. For example, what role, if any, does the Constitution permit religion to play in the formulation of public policy; or to what extent is the federal government authorized to assist or encourage religion generally; or does the free exercise provision relieve a believer of an obligation to comply with a valid, facially neutral law of general applicability on the ground that the law inhibits the adherent's religious exercise? These questions plague modern church-state relations.

Ratification of the First Amendment changed little, at least initially, in church-state policies and practices in the new nation. It merely made explicit that which was already implicit in the constitutional arrangement—that is, authority in matters pertaining to religion was denied to the national government and retained by the individual, religious societies, and the respective states. At least half of the states in 1791, the year the First Amendment was ratified, retained some form of religious establishment, and a handful of states—including Connecticut, New Hampshire, and Massachusetts—continued to maintain established churches well into the nineteenth century. These church-state arrangements were untouched by the First Amendment, which explicitly restricted the federal government only. Moreover, the new national legislature continued to appoint and pay for legislative chaplains, as had been the practice in the Continental Congress. Presidents George Washington and John Adams followed the tradition set by state chief executives and the Continental Congress in setting aside days in the public calendar for prayer and thanksgiving. These and other arguably religious practices continued under the First Amendment with relatively little controversy.

The election of 1800 provided an early test for religion's place in national politics. Opponents of candidate Thomas Jefferson contended that his heterodoxy raised doubts about his fitness for high office. In an influential pamphlet published in 1800, the Presbyterian minister John Mitchell Mason declaimed that it would be "a crime never to be forgiven" for the American people to confer the office of chief magistrate "upon an open enemy to their religion, their Redeemer, and their hope, [and it] would be mischief to themselves and sin against God." Mason alleged that Jefferson's "favorite wish [is] to see a government administered without any religious principle among either rulers or ruled." He repudiated the notion gaining currency among Jeffersonians that *"Religion has nothing to do with politics"* (Mason 1800, 6, 20, 25).

Jefferson's supporters denied that their candidate was an atheist or an infidel and, in response, advanced a separationist policy that would eventually exert much influence on American politics. "Religion and government are equally necessary," intoned Tunis Wortman, "but their interests should be kept separate and distinct. No legitimate connection can ever subsist between them. Upon no plan, no system, can they become united, without endangering the purity and usefulness of both—The church will corrupt the state, and the state pollute the church" (Timoleon 1800, 7).

The incumbent, John Adams, similarly contended with political smears on account of religion. When President Adams recommended a national "day of solemn humiliation, fasting, and prayer," adversaries depicted him as a tool of establishmentarians intent on legally uniting the Presbyterian church with the new federal government (Adams 1854, 9:172-4). This allegation alarmed religious dissenters, such as the Baptists, who feared persecution by a legally established church. Disclaiming any involvement in such a scheme, Adams reported that he "was represented as . . . at the head of this political and ecclesiastical project" (Schutz and Adair 1966, 224). He thought the allegation, which drove dissenters into Jefferson's camp, cost him the election.

Once elected, President Jefferson provoked controversy by refusing to issue religious proclamations, departing from the precedent of his presidential predecessors. To his detractors, this was proof that he was an infidel, if not an atheist. On New Year's Day, 1802, the president penned a missive to a Baptist Association in Danbury, Connecticut. The New England Baptists, who had supported Jefferson in the election, were a beleaguered religious and political minority in a region where a Congregationalist-Federalist alliance dominated public life. In his letter, the president endorsed the persecuted Baptists' aspirations for religious liberty. Affirming his belief that "religion is a matter which lies solely between Man & his God" and is not among the legitimate concerns of civil government, Jefferson famously asserted that the First Amendment had built "a wall of separation between Church & State" (Dreisbach 2002, 48). According to his own account, Jefferson wanted this letter, with its figurative barrier, to explain why he, as president, had refrained from issuing executive proclamations setting aside days for public prayer and thanksgiving. Because the national government could exercise only those powers expressly granted to it by the Constitution and because no power to issue religious proclamations had been so granted, Jefferson maintained that the national government could not issue such proclamations. Insofar as Jefferson's wall was a metaphor for the First Amendment, it imposed restrictions on the national government only. As a matter of federalism, his wall had less to do with the separation between church and state than with the separation between state governments and the national government on matters pertaining to religion, such as religious proclamations. Regardless of Jefferson's understanding of the metaphor, courts and commentators have embraced the "wall of separation" as a "proof-text" for a strict separationist construction of the First Amendment and the organizing theme of church-state jurisprudence.

From the founding era to the present day, Americans have debated the prudential and constitutional relationships between church and state and between religion and politics. Few controversies today involving religion and public life raise wholly novel issues; indeed, many contemporary conflicts are variations on disputes that have engaged prior generations of Americans. Much church-state debate turns on the interpretation of the First Amendment provisions respecting the nonestablishment and free exercise of religion. Moreover, the U.S. Supreme Court has counseled that this amendment should be construed "in the light of its history and the evils it was designed forever to suppress" (*Everson v. Board of Education* 1947). Accordingly, reflection on the relations between religion and American public life in the last four centuries casts light not only on the past but also on the future of relations between the civil polity and religion.

Primary Sources

2.2

John Adams

A DISSERTATION ON THE CANON AND FEUDAL LAW (1765)

Since the promulgation of Christianity, the two greatest systems of tyranny that have sprung from this original, are the canon and the feudal law. The desire of dominion, that great principle by which we have attempted to account for so much good and so much evil, is, when properly restrained, a very useful and noble movement in the human mind. But when such restraints are taken off, it becomes an encroaching, grasping, restless, and ungovernable power. Numberless have been the systems of iniquity contrived by the great for the gratification of this passion in themselves; but in none of them were they ever more successful than in the invention and establishment of the canon and the feudal law. . . .

But another event still more calamitous to human liberty, was a wicked confederacy between the two systems of tyranny above described. It seems to have been even stipulated between them, that the temporal grandees should contribute every thing in their power to maintain the ascendancy of the priesthood, and that the spiritual grandees in their turn, should employ their ascendancy over the consciences of the people, in impressing on their minds a blind, implicit obedience to civil magistracy.

Thus, as long as this confederacy lasted, and the people were held in ignorance, liberty, and with her, knowledge and virtue too, seem to have deserted the earth, and one age of darkness succeeded another, till God in his benign providence raised up the champions who began and conducted the Reformation. From the time of the Reformation to the first settlement of America, knowledge gradually spread in Europe, but especially in England; and in proportion as that increased and spread among the people, ecclesiastical and civil tyranny, which I use as synonymous expressions for the canon and feudal laws, seem to have lost their strength and weight. The people grew more and more sensible of the wrong that was done them by these systems, more and more impatient under it, and determined at all hazards to rid themselves of it; till at last, under the execrable race of the Stuarts, the struggle between the people and the confederacy aforesaid of temporal and spiritual tyranny, became formidable, violent, and bloody.

It was this great struggle that peopled America. It was not religion alone, as is commonly supposed; but it was a love of universal liberty, and a hatred, a dread, a horror, of the infernal confederacy before described, that projected, conducted, and accomplished the settlement of America.

It was a resolution formed by a sensible people—I mean the Puritans—almost in despair. They had become intelligent in general, and many of them learned. For this fact, I have the testimony of Archbishop King himself, who observed of that people, that they were more intelligent and better read than even the members of the church, whom he censures warmly for that reason. This people had been so vexed and tortured by the powers of those days, for no other crime than their knowledge and their freedom of inquiry and examination, and they had so much reason to despair of deliverance from those miseries on that side the ocean, that they at last resolved to fly to the wilderness for refuge from the temporal and spiritual principalities and powers, and plagues and scourges of their native country.

After their arrival here, they began their settlement, and formed their plan, both of ecclesiastical and civil government, in direct opposition to the canon and the feudal systems. The leading men among them, both of the clergy and the laity, were men of sense and learning. To many of them the historians, orators, poets, and philosophers of Greece and Rome were quite familiar; and some of them have left libraries that are still in being, consisting chiefly of volumes in which the wisdom of the most enlightened ages and nations is deposited,—written, however, in languages which their great-grandsons, though educated in European universities, can scarcely read.

Thus accomplished were many of the first planters in these colonies. It may be thought polite and fashionable by many modern fine gentlemen, perhaps, to deride the characters of these persons, as enthusiastical, superstitious, and republican. But such ridicule is founded in nothing but foppery and affectation, and is grossly injurious and false. Religious to some degree of enthusiasm it may be admitted they were; but this can be no peculiar derogation from their character; because it was at that time almost the universal character not only of England, but of Christendom. Had this, however, been otherwise, their enthusiasm, considering the principles on which it was founded and the ends to which it was directed, far from being a reproach to them, was greatly to their honor; for I believe it will be found universally true, that no great enterprise for the honor or happiness of mankind was ever achieved without a large mixture of that noble infirmity. Whatever imperfections may be justly ascribed to them, which, however, are as few as any mortals have discovered, their judgment in framing their policy was founded in wise, humane, and benevolent principles. It was founded in revelation and in reason too. It was consistent with the principles of the best and greatest and wisest legislators of antiquity. Tyranny in every form, shape, and appearance was their disdain and abhorrence; no fear of punishment, nor even of death itself in exquisite tortures, had been sufficient to conquer that steady, manly, pertinacious spirit with which they had opposed the tyrants of those days in church and state. They were very far from being enemies to monarchy; and they knew as well as any men, the just regard and honor that is due to the character of a dispenser of the mysteries of the gospel of grace. But they saw clearly, that popular powers must be placed as a guard, a control, a balance, to the powers of the monarch and the priest, in every government, or else it would soon become the man of sin, the whore of Babylon, the mystery of iniquity, a great and detestable system of fraud, violence, and usurpation. Their greatest concern seems to have been to establish a government of the church more consistent with the Scriptures, and a government of the state more agreeable to the dignity of human nature, than any they had seen in Europe, and to transmit such a government down to their posterity, with the means of securing and preserving it forever. To render the popular power in their new government as great and wise as their principles of theory, that is, as human nature and the Christian religion require it should be, they endeavored to remove from it as many of the feudal inequalities and dependencies as could be spared, consistently with the preservation of a mild limited monarchy. And in this they discovered the depth of their wisdom and the warmth of their friendship to human nature. But the first place is due to religion. They saw clearly, that of all the nonsense and delusion which had ever passed through the mind of man, none had ever been more extravagant than the notions of absolutions, indelible characters, uninterrupted successions, and the rest of those fantastical ideas, derived from the canon law, which had thrown such a glare of mystery, sanctity, reverence, and right reverend eminence and holiness, around the idea of a priest, as no mortal could deserve, and as always must, from the constitution of human nature, be dangerous in society. For this reason, they demolished the whole system of diocesan episcopacy; and, deriding, as all reasonable and impartial men must do, the ridiculous fancies of sanctified effluvia from Episcopal fingers, they established sacerdotal ordination on the foundation of the Bible and common sense. This conduct at once imposed an obligation on the whole body of the clergy to industry, virtue, piety, and learning, and rendered that whole body infinitely more independent on the civil powers, in all respects, than they could be where they were formed into a scale of subordination, from a pope down to priests and friars and confessors,—necessarily and essentially a sordid, stupid, and wretched herd,—or than they could be in any other country, where an archbishop held the place of a universal bishop, and the vicars and curates that of the ignorant, dependent, miserable rabble aforesaid,—and infinitely more sensible and learned than they could be in either. . . .

They were convinced, by their knowledge of human nature, derived from history and their own experience, that nothing could preserve their posterity from the encroachments of the two systems of tyranny, in opposition to which, as has been observed already, they erected their government in church and state, but knowledge diffused generally through the whole body of the people. Their civil and religious principles, therefore, conspired to prompt them to use every measure and take every precaution in their power to propagate and perpetuate knowledge. For this purpose they laid very early the foundations of colleges, and invested them with ample privileges and emoluments; and it is remarkable that they have left among their posterity so universal an affection and veneration for those seminaries, and for liberal education, that the meanest of the people contribute cheerfully to the support and maintenance of them every year, and that nothing is more generally popular than projections for the honor, reputation, and advantage of those seats of learning. But the wisdom and benevolence of our fathers rested not here. They made an early provision by law, that every town consisting of so many families, should be always furnished with a grammar school. They made it a crime for such a town to be destitute of a grammar schoolmaster for a few months, and subjected it to a heavy penalty. So that the education of all ranks of people was made the care and expense of the public, in a manner that I believe has been unknown to any other people ancient or modern.

The consequences of these establishments we see and feel every day. A native of America who cannot read and write is as rare an appearance as a Jacobite or a Roman Catholic, that is, as rare as a comet or an earthquake. It has been observed, that we are all of us lawyers, divines, politicians, and philosophers. And I have good authorities to say, that all candid foreigners who have passed through this country, and conversed freely with all sorts of people here, will allow, that they have never seen so much knowledge and civility among the common people in any part of the world. It is true, there has been among us a party for some years, consisting chiefly not of the descendants of the first settlers of this country, but of high churchmen and high statesmen imported since, who affect to censure this provision for the education of our youth as a needless expense, and an imposition upon the rich in favor of the poor, and as an institution productive of idleness and vain speculation among the people, whose time and attention, it is said, ought to be devoted to labor, and not to public affairs, or to examination into the conduct of their superiors. And certain officers of the crown, and certain other missionaries of ignorance, foppery, servility, and slavery, have been most inclined to countenance and increase the same party. Be it remembered, however, that liberty must at all hazards be supported. We have a right to it, derived from our Maker. But if we had not, our fathers have earned and bought it for us, at the expense of their ease, their estates, their pleasure, and their blood. And liberty cannot be preserved without a general knowledge among the people, who have a right, from the frame of their nature, to knowledge, as their great Creator, who does nothing in vain, has given them understandings, and a desire to know; but besides this, they have a right, an indisputable, unalienable, indefeasible, divine right to that most dreaded and envied kind of knowledge, I mean, of the characters and conduct of their rulers. Rulers are no more than attorneys, agents, and trustees for the people; and if the cause, the interest and trust, is insidiously betrayed, or wantonly trifled away, the people have a right to revoke the authority that they themselves have deputed, and to constitute abler and better agents, attorneys, and trustees. And the preservation of the means of knowledge among the lowest ranks, is of more importance to the public than all the property of all the rich men in the country. It is even of more consequence to the rich themselves, and to their posterity. . . .

2.3

James Madison

Memorial and Remonstrance against Religious Assessments (1784)

To the Honorable the General Assembly of the Commonwealth of Virginia—A Memorial and Remonstrance

We the subscribers, citizens of the said Commonwealth, having taken into serious consideration, a Bill printed by order of the last Session of General Assembly, entitled "A Bill establishing a provision for Teachers of the Christian Religion," and conceiving that the same if finally armed with the sanctions of a law, will be a dangerous abuse of power, are bound as faithful members of a free State to remonstrate against it, and to declare the reasons by which we are determined. We remonstrate against the said Bill,

1. Because we hold it for a fundamental and undeniable truth, "that Religion or the duty which we owe to our Creator and the manner of discharging it, can be directed only by reason and conviction, not by force or violence." [Virginia Declaration of Rights, art. 16] The Religion then of every man must be left to the conviction and conscience of every man; and it is the right of every man to exercise it as these may dictate. This right is in its nature an unalienable right. It is unalienable, because the opinions of men, depending only on the evidence contemplated by their own minds cannot follow the dictates of other men: It is unalienable also, because what is here a right towards men, is a duty towards the Creator. It is the duty of every man to render to the Creator such homage and such only as he believes to be acceptable to him. This duty is precedent, both in order of time and in degree of obligation, to the claims of Civil Society . . . We maintain therefore that in matters of Religion, no man's right is abridged by the institution of Civil Society and that Religion is wholly exempt from its cognizance. True it is, that no other rule exists, by which any question which may divide a Society, can be ultimately determined, but the will of the majority; but it is also true that the majority may trespass on the rights of the minority.

2. Because if Religion be exempt from the authority of the Society at large, still less can it be subject to that of the Legislative Body. The latter are but the creatures and vicegerents of the former. Their jurisdiction is both derivative and limited: it is limited with regard to the co-ordinate departments, more necessarily is it limited with regard to the constituents. The preservation of a free Government requires not merely, that the metes and bounds which separate each department of power be invariably maintained; but more especially that neither of them be suffered to overleap the great Barrier which defends the rights of the people. The Rulers who are guilty of such an encroachment, exceed the commission from which they derive their authority, and are Tyrants. The People who submit to it are governed by laws made neither by themselves nor by an authority derived from them, and are slaves.

3. Because it is proper to take alarm at the first experiment on our liberties. We hold this prudent jealousy to be the first duty of Citizens, and one of the noblest characteristics of the late Revolution. The free men of America did not wait till usurped power had strengthened itself by exercise, and entangled the question in precedents. They saw all the consequences in the principle, and they avoided the consequences by denying the principle. We revere this lesson too much soon to forget it. Who does not see that the same authority which can establish Christianity, in exclusion of all other Religions, may establish with the same ease any particular sect of Christians, in exclusion of all other Sects? . . .

4. Because the Bill violates that equality which ought to be the basis of every law, and which is more indispensible, in proportion as the validity or expediency of any law is more liable to be impeached. If "all men are by nature equally free and independent," [Virginia Declaration of Rights, art. 1] all men are to be considered as entering into Society on equal conditions; as relinquishing no more, and therefore retaining no less, one than another, of their natural rights. Above all are they to be considered as retaining an "*equal* title to the free exercise of Religion according to the dictates of Conscience" [Virginia Declaration of Rights, art. 16]. Whilst we assert for ourselves a freedom to embrace, to profess and to observe the Religion which we believe to be of divine origin, we cannot deny an equal freedom to those whose minds have not yet yielded to the evidence which has convinced us. If this freedom be abused, it is an offence against God, not against man: To God, therefore, not to man, must an account of it be rendered. . . .

5. Because the Bill implies either that the Civil Magistrate is a competent Judge of Religious Truth; or that he may employ Religion as an engine of Civil policy. The first is an arrogant pretension falsified by the contradictory opinions of Rulers in all ages, and throughout the world: the second an unhallowed perversion of the means of salvation.

6. Because the establishment proposed by the Bill is not requisite for the support of the Christian Religion. To say that it is, is a contradiction to the Christian Religion itself, for every page of it disavows a dependence on the powers of this world: it is a contradiction to fact; for it is known that this Religion both existed and flourished, not only without the support of human laws, but in spite of every opposition from them, and not only during the period of miraculous aid, but long after it had been left to its own evidence and the ordinary care of Providence. Nay, it is a contradiction in terms; for a Religion not invented by human

policy, must have pre-existed and been supported, before it was established by human policy. . . .

7. Because experience witnesseth that ecclesiastical establishments, instead of maintaining the purity and efficacy of Religion, have had a contrary operation. During almost fifteen centuries has the legal establishment of Christianity been on trial. What have been its fruits? More or less in all places, pride and indolence in the Clergy, ignorance and servility in the laity, in both, superstition, bigotry and persecution. Enquire of the Teachers of Christianity for the ages in which it appeared in its greatest lustre; those of every sect, point to the ages prior to its incorporation with Civil policy. Propose a restoration of this primitive State in which its Teachers depended on the voluntary rewards of their flocks, many of them predict its downfall. On which Side ought their testimony to have greatest weight, when for or when against their interest?

8. Because the establishment in question is not necessary for the support of Civil Government. If it be urged as necessary for the support of Civil Government only as it is a means of supporting Religion, and it be not necessary for the latter purpose, it cannot be necessary for the former. If Religion be not within the cognizance of Civil Government how can its legal establishment be necessary to Civil Government? What influence in fact have ecclesiastical establishments had on Civil Society? In some instances they have been seen to erect a spiritual tyranny on the ruins of the Civil authority; in many instances they have been seen upholding the thrones of political tyranny: in no instance have they been seen the guardians of the liberties of the people . . . A just Government instituted to secure & perpetuate it needs them not. Such a Government will be best supported by protecting every Citizen in the enjoyment of his Religion with the same equal hand which protects his person and his property; by neither invading the equal rights of any Sect, nor suffering any Sect to invade those of another.

9. Because the proposed establishment is a departure from that generous policy, which, offering an Asylum to the persecuted and oppressed of every Nation and Religion, promised a lustre to our country, and an accession to the number of its citizens. What a melancholy mark is the Bill of sudden degeneracy? Instead of holding forth an Asylum to the persecuted, it is itself a signal of persecution. It degrades from the equal rank of Citizens all those whose opinions in Religion do not bend to those of the Legislative authority. . . .

10. Because it will have a like tendency to banish our Citizens. The allurements presented by other situations are every day thinning their number. To superadd a fresh motive to emigration by revoking the liberty which they now enjoy, would be the same species of folly which has dishonoured and depopulated flourishing kingdoms.

11. Because it will destroy that moderation and harmony which the forbearance of our laws to intermeddle with Religion has produced among its several sects. Torrents of blood have been spilt in the old world, by vain attempts of the secular arm, to extinguish Religious discord, by proscribing all difference in Religious opinion. Time has at length revealed the true remedy. Every relaxation of narrow and rigorous policy, wherever it has been tried, has been found to assuage the disease. The American Theatre has exhibited proofs that equal

and compleat liberty, if it does not wholly eradicate it, sufficiently destroys its malignant influence on the health and prosperity of the State. . . . The very appearance of the Bill has transformed "that Christian forbearance, love and charity" [Virginia Declaration of Rights, art. 16], which of late mutually prevailed, into animosities and jealousies, which may not soon be appeased. What mischiefs may not be dreaded, should this enemy to the public quiet be armed with the force of a law?

12. Because the policy of the Bill is adverse to the diffusion of the light of Christianity. The first wish of those who enjoy this precious gift ought to be that it may be imparted to the whole race of mankind. Compare the number of those who have as yet received it with the number still remaining under the dominion of false Religions; and how small is the former! Does the policy of the Bill tend to lessen the disproportion? No; it at once discourages those who are strangers to the light of revelation from coming into the Region of it; and countenances by example the nations who continue in darkness, in shutting out those who might convey it to them. Instead of Levelling as far as possible, every obstacle to the victorious progress of Truth, the Bill with an ignoble and unchristian timidity would circumscribe it with a wall of defence against the encroachments of error.

13. Because attempts to enforce by legal sanctions, acts obnoxious to so great a proportion of Citizens, tend to enervate the laws in general, and to slacken the bands of Society. If it be difficult to execute any law which is not generally deemed necessary or salutary, what must be the case, where it is deemed invalid and dangerous? And what may be the effect of so striking an example of impotency in the Government, on its general authority?

14. Because a measure of such singular magnitude and delicacy ought not to be imposed, without the clearest evidence that it is called for by a majority of citizens, and no satisfactory method is yet proposed by which the voice of the majority in this case may be determined, or its influence secured. . . .

15. Because finally, "the equal right of every citizen to the free exercise of his Religion according to the dictates of conscience" is held by the same tenure with all our other rights. . . . Either we must say, that they may controul the freedom of the press, may abolish the Trial by Jury, may swallow up the Executive and Judiciary Powers of the State; nay that they may despoil us of our very right of suffrage, and erect themselves into an independent and hereditary Assembly or, we must say, that they have no authority to enact into law the Bill under consideration. We the Subscribers say, that the General Assembly of this Commonwealth have no such authority: And that no effort may be omitted on our part against so dangerous an usurpation, we oppose to it, this remonstrance; earnestly praying, as we are in duty bound, that the Supreme Lawgiver of the Universe, by illuminating those to whom it is addressed, may on the one hand, turn their Councils from every act which would affront his holy prerogative, or violate the trust committed to them: and on the other, guide them into every measure which may be worthy of his blessing, may redound to their own praise, and may establish more firmly the liberties, the prosperity and the happiness of the Commonwealth.

2.4

Thomas Jefferson

VIRGINIA STATUTE OF RELIGIOUS LIBERTY (1786)

Whereas Almighty God hath created the mind free; that all attempts to influence it by temporal punishments or burthens, or by civil incapacitations, tend only to beget habits of hypocrisy and meanness, and are a departure from the plan of the Holy author of our religion, who being Lord both of body and mind, yet chose not to propagate it by coercions on either, as it was in his Almighty power to do; that the impious presumption of legislators and rulers, civil as well as ecclesiastical, who being themselves but fallible and uninspired men, have assumed dominion over the faith of others, setting up their own opinions and modes of thinking as the only true and infallible, and as such endeavouring to impose them on others, hath established and maintained false religions over the greatest part of the world, and through all time; that to compel a man to furnish contributions of money for the propagation of opinions which he disbelieves, is sinful and tyrannical; that even the forcing him to support this or that teacher of his own religious persuasion, is depriving him of the comfortable liberty of giving his contributions to the particular pastor, whose morals he would make his pattern, and whose powers he feels most persuasive to righteousness, and is withdrawing from the ministry those temporary rewards, which proceeding from an approbation of their personal conduct, are an additional incitement to earnest and unremitting labours for the instruction of mankind; that our civil rights have no dependence on our religious opinions, any more than our opinions in physics or geometry; that therefore the proscribing any citizen as unworthy the public confidence by laying upon him an incapacity of being called to offices of trust and emolument, unless he profess or renounce this or that religious opinion, is depriving him injuriously of those privileges and advantages to which in common with his fellow-citizens he has a natural right; that it tends only to corrupt the principles of that religion it is meant to encourage, by bribing with a monopoly of worldly honours and emoluments, those who will externally profess and conform to it; that though indeed these are criminal who do not withstand such temptation, yet neither are those innocent who lay the bait in their way; that to suffer the civil magistrate to intrude his powers into the field of opinion, and to restrain the profession or propagation of principles on supposition of their ill tendency, is a dangerous fallacy, which at once destroys all religious liberty, because he being of course judge of that tendency will make his opinions the rule of judgment, and approve or condemn the sentiments of others only as they shall square with or differ from his own; that it is time enough for the rightful purposes of civil government, for its officers to interfere when principles break out into overt acts against peace and good order; and finally, that truth is great and will prevail if left to herself, that she is the proper and sufficient antagonist to error, and has nothing to fear from the conflict, unless by human interposition disarmed of her natural weapons, free argument and debate, errors ceasing to be dangerous when it is permitted freely to contradict them:

Be it enacted by the General Assembly, That no man shall be compelled to frequent or support any religious worship, place, or ministry whatsoever, nor shall be enforced, restrained, molested, or burthened in his body or goods, nor shall otherwise suffer on account of his religious opinions or belief; but that all men shall be free to profess, and by argument to maintain, their opinion in matters of religion, and that the same shall in no wise diminish enlarge, or affect their civil capacities.

And though we well know that this assembly elected by the people for the ordinary purposes of legislation only, have no power to restrain the acts of succeeding assemblies, constituted with powers equal to our own, and that therefore to declare this act to be irrevocable would be of no effect in law; yet we are free to declare, and do declare, that the rights hereby asserted are of the natural rights of mankind, and that if any act shall be hereafter passed to repeal the present, or to narrow its operation, such act shall be an infringement of natural right.

2.5

Library of Congress

HOUSE AND SENATE DEBATES (EXCERPTS) (1789)

On June 8, 1789, James Madison introduced into the House of Representatives what were to emerge as the religion clauses of the First Amendment. What follows are all the references to these clauses in the debate on the Bill of Rights on the floor of both Houses of the First Congress.

The Debate in the House

Monday, June 8, 1789

[James Madison speaking]: Fourthly. That in article 1st, section 9, between clauses 3 and 4, be inserted these clauses to wit: The civil rights of none shall be abridged on account of religious belief or worship, nor shall any national religion be established, nor shall the full and equal rights of conscience be in any manner, or on any pretext infringed. . . .

Fifthly. That in article 1st, section 10, between clauses 1 and 2 be inserted this clause to wit: No state shall violate the equal rights of conscience, or freedom of the press, or trial by jury in criminal cases. (pp. 451–452)

Saturday, August 15, 1789

The House again went into a Committee of the Whole on the proposed amendments to the Constitution. Mr. Boudinot in the chair.

The fourth proposition being under consideration, as follows: Article 1. Section 9. Between paragraphs two and three insert "no religion shall be established by law, nor shall the equal rights of conscience be infringed."

Mr. SYLVESTER had some doubts of the propriety of the mode of expression used in this paragraph. He apprehended that it was liable to a construction different from what had been made by the committee. He feared it might be thought to abolish religion altogether.

MR. VINING suggested the propriety to transposing the two members of the sentence.

MR. GERRY said it would read better if it was, that no religious doctrine shall be established by law.

MR. SHERMAN thought the amendment altogether unnecessary, inasmuch as Congress had no authority whatever delegated to them by the Constitution to make religious establishments; he would, therefore, move to have it struck out.

MR. CARROLL—As the rights of conscience are, in their nature, of peculiar delicacy, and will little bear the gentlest touch of governmental hand; and as many sects have concurred in opinion that they are not well secured under the present constitution, he said he was much in favor of adopting the words. He thought it would tend more towards conciliating the minds of the people to the government than almost any other opinion he heard proposed. He would not contend with gentlemen about the phraseology, his object was to secure the substance in such a manner as to satisfy the wishes of the honest part of the community.

MR. MADISON said, he apprehended the meaning of the words to be, that Congress should not establish a religion, and enforced the legal observation of it by law, nor compel men to worship God in any manner contrary to their conscience. Whether the words are necessary or not, he did not mean to say, but they had been required by some of the State Conventions, who seemed to entertain an opinion that under the clause of the constitution, which gave power to Congress to make all laws necessary and proper to carry into execution the constitution, and the laws made under it, enabled them to make laws of such a nature as might infringe the rights of conscience, and establish a national religion; to prevent these effects he presumed the amendment was intended, and he thought it as well expressed as the nature of the language would admit.

MR. HUNTINGTON said that he feared, with the gentleman first up on this subject, that the words might be taken in such latitude as to be extremely hurtful to the cause of religion. He understood the amendment to mean what had been expressed by the gentleman from Virginia; but others might find it convenient to put another construction on it. The ministers of their congregations to the Eastward were maintained by contributions of those who belong to their society; the expense of building meeting-houses was contributed in the same manner. These things were regulated by bylaws. If an action was brought before a Federal Court on any of these cases, the person who had neglected to perform his engagements could not be compelled to do it; for a support of ministers, or buildings of places of worship might be construed into a religious establishment.

By the charter of Rhode Island, no religion could be established by law; he could give a history of the effects of such a regulation; indeed the people were now enjoying the blessed fruits of it. He hoped, therefore, the amendment would be made in such a way as to secure the rights of conscience, and the free exercise of religion, but not to patronize those who professed no religion at all.

MR. MADISON thought, if the word national was inserted before religion, it would satisfy the minds of honorable gentlemen. He believed that the people feared one sect might obtain a pre-eminence, or two combined together, and establish a religion, to which they would compel others to conform. He thought if the word national was introduced, it would point the amendment directly to the object it was intended to prevent.

MR. LIVERMORE was not satisfied with the amendment; but he did not wish them to dwell long on the subject. He thought it would be better if it was altered, and made to read in this manner, that Congress shall make no laws touching religion, or infringing the rights of conscience.

MR. GERRY did not like the term national, proposed by the gentleman from Virginia, and he hoped it would not be adopted by the House. It brought to his mind some observations that had taken place in the Conventions at the time they were considering the present constitution. It had been insisted upon by those who were called anti-federalists, that this form of Government consolidated the Union; the honorable gentleman's motion shows that he considers it in the same light. Those who were called anti-federalists at that time complained that they had injustice done them by the title, because they were in favor of a Federal Government, and the others were in favor of a national one; the federalists were for ratifying the constitution as it stood, and the others not until amendments were made. Their names then ought not to have been distinguished by federalists and antifederalists, but rats and antirats.

MR. MADISON withdrew his motion but observed that the words "no national religion shall be established by law," did not imply that the Government was a national one; the question was then taken on Mr. Livermore's motion, and passed in the affirmative, thirty-one for, and twenty against it. (pp. 757–759)

Monday, August 17, 1789

The committee then proceeded to the fifth proposition:

Article I. section 10. between the first and second paragraph, insert "no State shall infringe the equal rights of conscience, nor the freedom of speech or of the press, nor of the right of trial by jury in criminal cases."

MR. TUCKER—This is offered, I presume, as an amendment to the constitution of the United States, but it goes only to the alteration of constitutions of particular States. It will be much better, I apprehend, to leave the State Governments to themselves, and not to interfere with them more than we already do; and that is thought by many to be rather too much. I therefore move, sir, to strike out these words.

MR. MADISON conceives this to be the most valuable amendment in the whole list. If there were any reason to restrain the Government of the United States from infringing upon these essential rights, it was equally necessary that they should be secured against the State Governments. He thought that if they provided against the one, it was as necessary to provide against the other, and was satisfied that it would be equally grateful to the people.

MR. LIVERMORE had no great objection to the sentiment, but he thought it not well expressed. He wished to make it an affirmative proposition; "the equal rights of conscience, the freedom of speech or of the press, and the right of trial by jury in criminal cases, shall not be infringed by any State."

This transposition being agreed to, and MR. TUCKER'S motion being rejected, the clause was adopted. (pp. 783–784)

Thursday, August 20, 1789

On motion of MR. AMES, the fourth amendment was altered so as to read "Congress shall make no law establishing religion, or to prevent the free exercise thereof, or to infringe the rights of conscience." This being adopted. . . ." (p. 796)

The Debate in the Senate

All that is recorded of the debate over the religion clauses in the Senate of the First Congress is a list of motions and votes in the Senate Journal. Constitutional scholar Derek Davis summarizes the record as follows:

[The] amendment as submitted to the Senate . . . reflected a stylistic change that gave it the following reading: "Congress shall make no law establishing religion, or prohibiting the free exercise thereof, nor shall the rights of conscience be infringed." No record was left of the proceedings that brought about this stylistic change.

The Senate began deliberations on the House amendment on 3 September and continued through 9 September. The Ames amendment must have provoked controversy in the Senate, since several alternative versions were suggested in its place. In considering the House's draft, a Senate motion was first made to strike out "religion or prohibiting the free exercise thereof," and to insert, "one religious sect or society in preference to others." The motion was rejected, and then passed. Thus, the first new Senate version read, "Congress shall make no law establishing one religious sect or society in preference to others, nor shall the rights of conscience be infringed."

After further debate, the Senate rejected two alternative wordings. First, they rejected language providing, "Congress shall not make any law, infringing the rights of conscience, or establishing any Religious Sect or Society." Second, they rejected the language providing, "Congress shall make no law establishing any particular denomination of religion in preference to another, or prohibiting free exercise thereof, nor shall the rights of conscience be infringed."

Later the same day, 3 September, the Senate adopted a draft that treated religion more generically. "Congress shall make no law establishing religion, or prohibiting the free exercise thereof." Six days later, the Senate again changed its mind and adopted as its final form of the amendment, "Congress shall make no law establishing articles of faith or a mode of worship, or prohibiting the free exercise of religion."

The Senate version of the Amendment was sent to the House, which rejected it.

A House-Senate joint conference (Madison, Sherman, Vining representing the House, Ellsworth, Carroll, Paterson representing the Senate) was then created to resolve the disagreement over the religion amendment. A compromise amendment was eventually agreed upon as reported under the date of September 24, 1789. (Davis 1991, 60)

The Conference Committee

September 24, 1789

The House proceeded to consider the report of a committee of conference, on the subject matter of the amendments depending between the two houses to the several articles of amendment to the Constitution of the United States, as proposed by this House; whereupon, it was resolved, that they recede from their disagreement to all the amendments; provided that the two articles, which, by the amendments of the Senate, are now proposed to be inserted as the third and eighth articles shall be amended to read as follows: Article three, Congress shall make no law respecting an establishment of religion or prohibiting the free exercise thereof, or abridging the freedom of speech, or of the press, or the right of the people peaceably to assemble, and to petition the government for a redress of grievances.

On the motion, it was resolved, that the President of the United States be requested to transmit to the Executives of the several States which have ratified the constitution, copies of the amendments proposed by Congress, to be added thereto and like copies to the Executives of Rhode Island and North Carolina.

2.6

President George Washington

THANKSGIVING PROCLAMATION (1789)

Whereas it is the duty of all nations to acknowledge the providence of Almighty God, to obey His will, to be grateful for His benefits, and humbly to implore His protection and favor; and Whereas both Houses of Congress have, by their joint committee, requested me to *"recommend to the people of the United States a day of public thanksgiving and prayer, to be observed by acknowledging with grateful hearts the many and signal favors of Almighty God, especially by affording them an opportunity peaceably to establish a form of government for their safety and happiness:"*

Now, therefore, I do recommend and assign Thursday, the 26th day of November next, to be devoted by the people of these States to the service of that great and glorious Being who is the beneficent author of all the good that was, that is, or that will be; that we may then all unite in rendering unto Him our sincere and humble thanks for His kind care and protection of the people of this country previous to their becoming a nation; for the signal and manifold mercies and the favorable interpositions of His providence in the course and conclusion of the late war; for the great degree of tranquility, union, and plenty which we have since enjoyed; for the peaceable and rational manner in which we have been enable to establish constitutions of government for our safety and happiness, and particularly the national one now lately instituted for the civil and religious liberty with which we are blessed, and the means we have of acquiring and diffusing useful knowledge; and, in general, for all the great and various favors which He has been pleased to confer upon us.

And also that we may then unite in most humbly offering our prayers and supplications to the great Lord and Ruler of Nations and beseech Him to pardon our national and other transgressions; to enable us all, whether in public or private stations, to perform our several and relative duties properly and punctually; to render our National Government a blessing to all the people by constantly being a Government of wise, just, and constitutional laws, discreetly and faithfully executed and obeyed; to protect and guide all sovereigns and nations (especially such as have shown kindness to us), and to bless them with good governments, peace, and concord; to promote the knowledge and practice of true religion and virtue, and the increase of science among them and us; and, generally to grant unto all mankind such a degree of temporal prosperity as He alone knows to be best.

Given under my hand, at the city of New York, the 3d day of October, A.D. 1789.

2.7

President George Washington

FAREWELL ADDRESS (1796)

. . . Of all the dispositions and habits, which lead to political prosperity, Religion and Morality are indispensable supports. In vain would that man claim the tribute of Patriotism, who should labor to subvert these great pillars of human happiness, these firmest props of the duties of Men and Citizens. The mere Politician, equally with the pious man, ought to respect and to cherish them. A volume could not trace all their connections with private and public felicity. Let it simply be asked, Where is the security for property, for reputation, for life, if the sense of religious obligation desert the oaths, which are the instruments of investigation in Courts of Justice? And let us with caution indulge the supposition, that morality can be maintained without religion. Whatever may be conceded to the influence of refined education on minds of peculiar structure, reason and experience both forbid us to expect, that national morality can prevail in exclusion of religious principle.

It is substantially true, that virtue or morality is a necessary spring of popular government. The rule, indeed, extends with more or less force to every species of free government. Who, that is a sincere friend to it, can look with indifference upon attempts to shake the foundation of the fabric? . . .

Observe good faith and justice towards all Nations; cultivate peace and harmony with all. Religion and Morality enjoin this conduct; and can it be, that good policy does not equally enjoin it? It will be worthy of a free, enlightened, and, at no distant period, a great Nation, to give to mankind the magnanimous and too novel example of a people always guided by an exalted justice and benevolence. Who can doubt, that, in the course of time and things, the fruits of such a plan would richly repay any temporary advantages, which might be lost by a steady adherence to it? Can it be, that Providence has not connected the permanent felicity of a Nation with its Virtue? The experiment, at least, is recommended by every sentiment which ennobles human nature. Alas! is it rendered impossible by its vices? . . .

2.8

Nehemiah Dodge, Ephraim Robbins, and Stephen S. Nelson

ADDRESS OF THE DANBURY BAPTISTS ASSOCIATION
(OCTOBER 7, 1801)

The address of the Danbury Baptists Association in the state of Connecticut, assembled October 7, 1801. To Thomas Jefferson, Esq., President of the United States of America.

Sir,

Among the many million in America and Europe who rejoice in your election to office; we embrace the first opportunity which we have enjoyed in our collective capacity, since your inauguration, to express our great satisfaction, in your appointment to the chief magistracy in the United States: And though our mode of expression may be less courtly and pompous than what many others clothe their addresses with, we beg you, sir, to believe that none are more sincere.

Our sentiments are uniformly on the side of religious liberty—that religion is at all times and places a matter between God and individuals—that no man ought to suffer in name, person, or effects on account of his religious opinions—that the legitimate power of civil government extends no further than to punish the man who works ill to his neighbors; But, sir, our constitution of government is not specific. Our ancient charter together with the law made coincident therewith, were adopted as the basis of our government, at the time of our revolution; and such had been our laws and usages, and such still are; that religion is considered as the first object of legislation; and therefore what religious privileges we enjoy (as a minor part of the state) we enjoy as favors granted, and not as inalienable rights; and these favors we receive at the expense of such degrading acknowledgements as are inconsistent with the rights of freemen. It is not to be wondered at therefore; if those who seek after power and gain under the pretense of government and religion should reproach their fellow men—should reproach their order magistrate, as a enemy of religion, law, and good order, because he will not, dare not, assume the prerogatives of Jehovah and make laws to govern the kingdom of Christ.

Sir, we are sensible that the president of the United States is not the national legislator, and also sensible that the national government cannot destroy the laws of each state; but our hopes are strong that the sentiments of our beloved president, which have had such genial effect already, like the radiant beams of the sun, will shine and prevail through all these states and all the world, till hierarchy and tyranny be destroyed from the earth. Sir, when we reflect on your past services, and see a glow of philanthropy and good will shining forth in a course of more than thirty years we have reason to believe that America's God has raised you up to fill the chair of state out of that goodwill which he bears to the millions which you preside over. May God strengthen you for your arduous task which providence and the voice of the people have called you to sustain and support you enjoy administration against all the predetermined opposition of those who wish to raise to wealth and importance on the poverty and subjection of the people.

And may the Lord preserve you safe from every evil and bring you at last to his heavenly kingdom through Jesus Christ our Glorious Mediator.

Signed in behalf of the association,
Nehemiah Dodge, Ephraim Robbins, Stephen S. Nelson

2.9

President Thomas Jefferson

LETTER TO THE DANBURY BAPTISTS ASSOCIATION
(JANUARY 1, 1802)

To messers. Nehemiah Dodge, Ephraim Robbins, & Stephen S. Nelson, a committee of the Danbury Baptist association in the state of Connecticut.

Gentlemen,

The affectionate sentiments of esteem and approbation which you are so good as to express towards me, on behalf of the Danbury Baptist association, give me the highest satisfaction. My duties dictate a faithful and zealous pursuit of the interests of my constituents, & in proportion as they are persuaded of my fidelity to those duties, the discharge of them becomes more and more pleasing.

Believing with you that religion is a matter which lies solely between Man & his God, that he owes account to none other for his faith or his worship, that the legitimate powers of government reach actions only, & not opinions, I contemplate with sovereign reverence that act of the whole American people which declared that their legislature should "make no law respecting an establishment of religion, or prohibiting the free exercise thereof," thus building a wall of separation between Church & State. Adhering to this expression of the supreme will of the nation in behalf of the rights of conscience, I shall see with sincere satisfaction the progress of those sentiments which tend to restore to man all his natural rights, convinced he has no natural right in opposition to his social duties.

I reciprocate your kind prayers for the protection & blessing of the common father and creator of man, and tender you for yourselves & your religious association, assurances of my high respect & esteem.

(signed) Thomas Jefferson, Jan. 1, 1802.

2.10

Alexis de Tocqueville

DEMOCRACY IN AMERICA (1833)
Indirect Influence of Religious Opinions upon Political Society in the United States

The sects that exist in the United States are innumerable. They all differ in respect to the worship which is due to the Creator; but they all agree in respect to the duties which are due from man to man. Each sect adores the Deity in its own peculiar manner, but all sects preach the same moral law in the name of God. If it be of the highest importance to man, as an individual, that his religion should be true, it is not so to society. Society has no future life to hope for or to fear; and provided the citizens profess a religion, the peculiar tenets of that religion are of little importance to its interests. Moreover, all the sects of the United States are comprised within the great unity of Christianity, and Christian morality is everywhere the same.

It may fairly be believed that a certain number of Americans pursue a peculiar form of worship from habit more than from conviction. In the United States the sovereign authority is religious, and consequently hypocrisy must be common; but there is no country in the world where the Christian religion retains a greater influence over the souls of men than in America; and there can be no greater proof of its utility and of its conformity to human nature than that its influence is powerfully felt over the most enlightened and free nation of the earth.

I have remarked that the American clergy in general, without even excepting those who do not admit religious liberty, are all in favor of civil freedom; but they do not support any particular political system. They keep aloof from parties and from public affairs. In the United States religion exercises but little influence upon the laws and upon the details of public opinion; but it directs the customs of the community, and, by regulating domestic life, it regulates the state.

I do not question that the great austerity of manners that is observable in the United States arises, in the first instance, from religious faith. Religion is often unable to restrain man from the numberless temptations which chance offers; nor can it check that passion for gain which everything contributes to arouse; but its influence over the mind of woman is supreme, and women are the protectors of morals. There is certainly no country in the world where the tie of marriage is more respected than in America or where conjugal happiness is more highly or worthily appreciated, In Europe almost all the disturbances of society arise from the irregularities of domestic life. To despise the natural bonds and legitimate pleasures of home is to contract a taste for excesses, a restlessness of heart, and fluctuating desires. Agitated by the tumultuous passions that frequently disturb his dwelling, the European is galled by the obedience which the legislative powers of the state exact. But when the American retires from the turmoil of public life to the bosom of his family, he finds in it the image of order and of peace. There his pleasures are simple and natural, his joys are innocent and calm; and as he finds that an orderly life is the surest path to happiness, he accustoms himself easily to moderate his opinions as well as his tastes. While the European endeavors to forget his domestic troubles by agitating society, the American derives from his own home that love of order which he afterwards carries with him into public affairs.

In the United States the influence of religion is not confined to the manners, but it extends to the intelligence of the people. Among the Anglo-Americans some profess the doctrines of Christianity from a sincere belief in them, and others do the same because they fear to be suspected of unbelief. Christianity, therefore, reigns without obstacle, by universal consent; the consequence is, as I have before observed, that every principle of the moral world is fixed and determinate, although the political world is abandoned to the debates and the experiments of men. Thus the human mind is never left to wander over a boundless field; and whatever may be its pretensions, it is checked from time to time by barriers that it cannot surmount. Before it can innovate, certain primary principles are laid down, and the boldest conceptions are subjected to certain forms which retard and stop their completion.

The imagination of the Americans, even in its greatest flights, is circumspect and undecided; its impulses are checked and its works unfinished. These habits of restraint recur in political society and are singularly favorable both to the tranquility of the people and to the durability of the institutions they have established. Nature and circumstances have made the inhabitants of the United States bold, as is sufficiently attested by the enterprising spirit with which they seek for fortune. If the mind of the Americans were free from all hindrances, they would shortly become the most daring innovators and the most persistent disputants in the world. But the revolutionists of America are obliged to profess an ostensible respect for Christian morality and equity, which does not permit them to violate wantonly the laws that oppose their designs; nor would they find it easy to surmount the scruples of their partisans even if they were able to get over their own. Hitherto no one in the United States has dared to advance the maxim that everything is permissible for the interests of society, an impious adage which seems to have been invented in an age of freedom to shelter all future tyrants. Thus, while the law permits the Americans to do what they please, religion prevents them from conceiving, and forbids them to commit, what is rash or unjust.

Religion in America takes no direct part in the government of society, but it must be regarded as the first of their political institutions; for if it does not impart a taste for freedom, it facilitates the use of it. Indeed, it is in this same point of view that the inhabitants of the United States themselves look upon religious belief. I do not know whether all Americans have a sincere faith in their religion—for who can search the human heart?—but I am certain that they hold it to be indispensable to the maintenance of republican institutions. This opinion is not peculiar to a class of citizens or to a party, but it belongs to the whole nation and to every rank of society.

In the United States, if a politician attacks a sect, this may not prevent the partisans of that very sect from supporting him; but if he attacks all the sects together, everyone abandons him, and he remains alone.

Principal Causes which Render Religion Powerful in America

The philosophers of the eighteenth century explained in a very simple manner the gradual decay of religious faith. Religious zeal, said they, must necessarily fail the more generally liberty is established and knowledge diffused. Unfortunately, the facts by no means accord with their theory. There are certain populations in Europe whose unbelief is only equaled by their ignorance and debasement; while in America, one of the freest and most enlightened nations in the world, the people fulfill with fervor all the outward duties of religion.

On my arrival in the United States the religious aspect of the country was the first thing that struck my attention; and the longer I stayed there, the more I perceived the great political consequences resulting from this new state of things. In France I had almost always seen the spirit of religion and the spirit of freedom marching in opposite directions. But in America I found they were intimately united and that they reigned in common over the same country. My desire to discover the causes of this phenomenon increased from day to day. In order to satisfy it I questioned the members of all the different sects; I sought especially the society of the clergy, who are the depositaries of the different creeds and are especially interested in their duration. As a member of the Roman Catholic Church, I was more particularly brought into contact with several of its priests, with whom I became intimately acquainted. To each of these men I expressed my astonishment and explained my doubts. I found that they differed upon matters of detail alone, and that they all attributed the peaceful dominion of religion in their country mainly to the separation of church and state. I do not hesitate to affirm that during my stay in America I did not meet a single individual, of the clergy or the laity, who was not of the same opinion on this point. . . .

In proportion as a nation assumes a democratic condition of society and as communities display democratic propensities, it becomes more and more dangerous to connect religion with political institutions; for the time is coming when authority will be bandied from hand to hand, when political theories will succeed one another, and when men, laws, and constitutions will disappear or be modified from day to day, and this not for a season only, but unceasingly. Agitation and mutability are inherent in the nature of democratic republics, just as stagnation and sleepiness are the law of absolute monarchies.

If the Americans, who change the head of the government once in four years, who elect new legislators every two years, and renew the state officers every twelve months; if the Americans, who have given up the political world to the attempts of innovators, had not placed religion beyond their reach, where could it take firm hold in the ebb and flow of human opinions? Where would be that respect which belongs to it, amid the struggles of faction? And what would become of its immortality, in the midst of universal decay? The American clergy were the first to perceive this truth and to act in conformity with it. They saw that they must renounce their religious influence if they were to strive for political power, and they chose to give up the support of the state rather than to share its vicissitudes.

In America religion is perhaps less powerful than it has been at certain periods and among certain nations; but its influence is more lasting. It restricts itself to its own resources, but of these none can deprive it; its circle is limited, but it pervades it and holds it under undisputed control.

Notes

1. Portions of this chapter are adapted from the introduction and notes in *The Sacred Rights of Conscience: Selected Readings on Religious Liberty and Church-State Relations in the American Founding*, ed. Daniel L. Dreisbach and Mark David Hall (Indianapolis, Ind.: Liberty Fund, 2009) [hereinafter *Sacred Rights of Conscience*].

2. See Madison, A Memorial and Remonstrance against Religious Assessments (1785), in *Sacred Rights of Conscience*, 311-312 ("What have been its fruits [fruits of ecclesiastical establishments]? More or less in all places, pride and indolence in the Clergy, ignorance and servility in the laity, in both, superstition, bigotry and persecution.").

3. The U.S. Supreme Court incorporated the First Amendment religion provisions into the "liberties" protected by the Fourteenth Amendment's due process of law clause in the mid-twentieth century, thereby making them applicable to state and local authorities. This constitutional development prohibited state laws and practices "respecting an establishment of religion" or prohibiting religious exercise. The free exercise and nonestablishment of religion provisions were incorporated into the Fourteenth Amendment in *Cantwell v. Connecticut*, 310 U.S. 296, 303 (1940) and *Everson v. Board of Education*, 330 U.S. 1, 15 (1947), respectively.

CHAPTER 3

RELIGION AND AMERICAN CIVIC LIFE

Introduction

Research Pieces

3.1   Robert N. Bellah, *Civil Religion in America* (1967)
3.2   Grace Y. Kao and Jerome E. Copulsky, *The Pledge of Allegiance and the Meanings and Limits of Civil Religion* (2007)
3.3   Michael F. Bailey and Kristin Lindholm, *Tocqueville and the Rhetoric of Civil Religion in the Presidential Inaugural Addresses* (2003)
3.4   Robert D. Putnam, *Bowling Alone: The Collapse and Revival of American Community* (2000)

Primary Sources

3.5   Jean-Jacques Rousseau, *The Social Contract, Book IV, Chapter VIII: Civil Religion* (1762)
3.6   Alexis de Tocqueville, *Democracy in America* (1833), Chapters 2 and 5
3.7   President Abraham Lincoln, *Second Inaugural Address* (March 4, 1865)
3.8   General Dwight D. Eisenhower, *D-Day Message* (June 6, 1944)
3.9   President Franklin Delano Roosevelt, *D-Day Prayer* (June 6, 1944)
3.10 President John F. Kennedy, *Inaugural Address* (January 20, 1961)
3.11 President Bill Clinton, *Oklahoma City Speech* (April 23, 1995)
3.12 President George W. Bush, *Remarks at the National Day of Prayer and Remembrance* (September 14, 2001)

Introduction

Since colonial governor John Winthrop first described the New World as a "city on a hill" in the seventeenth century, scholars have noted the centrality of religion in American public life and considered its philosophical and practical consequences. Generally, the discussions of its philosophical uses analyze religion in the terms of civil religion—beliefs, symbols, and rituals connected to a specific nation that tend to encourage patriotism and place that nation in the larger context of eternal truths and values. Much of this chapter focuses on this major use of religion in American public life. But religion also has more practical utility to a nation. Its organizations are central to American civil society, a phenomenon noted by as early an observer as Tocqueville and chronicled by recent scholars such as Robert Putnam. Religious groups and people help government in two ways: first by encouraging civic skills in individuals who practice similar skills in religious bodies, and, second, by creating voluntary associations that perform many of the functions that other nations would assign to government. Together, religion can make citizens more loyal to, as well as less demanding of, government.

Robert Bellah's "Civil Religion in America," written over forty years ago, remains the cornerstone of scholarly thought on civil religion. He offers the classic definition of civil religion: "a collection of beliefs, symbols, and ritual with respect to sacred things and institutionalized into a collectivity" that exists alongside organized religion. This definition lays the groundwork for the discussion that follows.

Grace Kao and Jerome Copulsky turn our attention to the rhetoric of civil religion. They distinguish between the goals of preservationists who view civil religion as essential for cultural coherence and advocates of a more expansive and pluralist rhetoric. They also examine the "posture that civil religion takes toward the state," comparing priestly and prophetic modes of discourse.

In the next selection, Michael Bailey and Kristin Lindholm analyze one of the ceremonial staples of American political life: the presidential inaugural address. The authors examine how civil religion has changed from the early days of the nation to the present: from God's blessing to God's sanction, from a calling to live faithfully under a higher power to assuming the role of being "the cutting edge of history, the light that illuminates the path for others to follow," from success contingent upon obedience to exemption from the restraints of others, from looking to God to looking to humanity for national salvation. They caution against the dangers of self-justification and question the difference between idealism and utopianism.

More practically, religion can be a major source of social cohesion for ordinary Americans, providing both important identity and practical purpose to their lives. In *Bowling Alone*, Robert Putnam finds religion to be the "central fount of American community life and health." How does religion bind people together, and how might that be useful in civic life?

We then turn to a series of primary sources, both old and new.

Long before Bellah popularized the term, Jean-Jacques Rousseau described civil religion in his *The Social Contract*. Rousseau advocates the deliberate formation of a distinct civil religion that can coexist with any multitude of mutually tolerant religions. His arguments are interesting to consider alongside contemporary discussions of the role and place of religious ideals in the public square.

From this piece predating America's establishment we turn to one of the first outsiders to chronicle the American political philosophy, French historian Alexis de Tocqueville. Tocqueville found central, common beliefs necessary for social unity. Human action has its roots in man's idea of deity, Tocqueville argues; thus, the religious sphere is essential for political unity and should be overseen by the government. This idea raises interesting questions about the role of government and public opinion in the formulation of religious beliefs, and contrasts sharply with contemporary understandings of the role of religion in formulating political beliefs.

From these scholars of political thought we move to evidence of civil religion at work in America, with a series of speeches by American political figures spanning the last 150 years. From Abraham Lincoln to George W. Bush, we witness substantiation for the claims made by these scholars.

President Lincoln's Second Inaugural Address makes an interesting statement regarding the use of God for political ends: "Both [sides] read the same Bible and pray to the same God, and each invokes His aid against the other." With the knowledge that supporters of vastly differing perspectives find theological support for their actions, how might this change our view of civil religion and its uses in our political society?

Eight decades later, General Eisenhower and President Roosevelt both delivered public prayers on D-Day. Each spoke in sanctified terms of his undertaking: the "Great Crusade," accompanied by the world's "hopes and prayers" (Eisenhower); the "mighty endeavor . . . to set free a suffering humanity" (Roosevelt). This is priestly civil religion at its best. Does such rhetoric, sincere or not, belong on the national scene?

President Kennedy takes a step further down this path. In his inaugural address, he attributes near-divine power to the American people themselves, saying that "the energy, the faith, the devotion which we bring to this endeavor will light our country and all who serve it—and the glow from that fire can truly light the world," hearkening back to Winthrop's city on a hill.

The final two entries, by President Clinton and President Bush, demonstrate the role of civil religion and the national impulse to appeal to patriotism in the face of tragedy. The Oklahoma City bombing and the 9/11 attacks were dark moments in national history; in both situations the president sought to comfort and unite Americans in civic faith by appropriating scriptural terminology—the rhetoric of sin, God's divine purposes, the forces of evil, and the overcoming of evil with good.

Civil religion raises many questions: When, where, and in what forms are references to civil religion appropriate? Does such rhetoric provide, in the words of Kao and Copulsky, a "sacred legitimation of the social order"? Does it have inherent dangers, such as fostering undue pride and false utopianism, as Bailey and Lindholm warn? Is religion the source of communal bonding that Putnam discusses?

Each of these selections illuminates different aspects of religion in political life—whether by showcasing civil religion, pondering the potential for national self-critique, or examining the practical implications of a connection between religion and the nation. Collectively, they demonstrate that the state and religion have a pervasive influence in providing and maintaining order in American society.

Research Pieces

3.1

Robert N. Bellah

CIVIL RELIGION IN AMERICA (1967)

While some have argued that Christianity is the national faith, and others that church and synagogue celebrate only the generalized religion of "the American Way of Life," few have realized that there actually exists alongside of and rather clearly differentiated from the churches an elaborate and well-institutionalized civil religion in America. This article argues not only that there is such a thing, but also that this religion—or perhaps better, this religious dimension—has its own seriousness and integrity and requires the same care in understanding that any other religion does. . . .[1]

The Idea of a Civil Religion

The phrase civil religion is, of course, Rousseau's. . . . While the phrase civil religion was not used, to the best of my knowledge, by the founding fathers, and I am certainly not arguing for the particular influence of Rousseau, it is clear that similar ideas, as part of the cultural climate of the late eighteenth century, were to be found among the Americans. For example, Franklin writes in his autobiography:

> I never was without some religious principles. I never doubted, for instance, the existence of the Deity; that he made the world and govern'd it by his Providence; that the most acceptable service of God was the doing of good to men; that our souls are immortal; and that all crime will be punished, and virtue rewarded either here or hereafter. These I esteemed the essentials of every religion; and, being to be found in all the religions we had in our country, I respected them all, tho' with different degrees of respect, as I found them more or less mix'd with other articles, which, without any tendency to inspire, promote or confirm morality, serv'd principally to divide us, and make us unfriendly to one another.

It is easy to dispose of this sort of position as essentially utilitarian in relation to religion. In Washington's Farewell Address (though the words may be Hamilton's) the utilitarian aspect is quite explicit:

> Of all the dispositions and habits which lead to political prosperity, Religion and Morality are indispensable supports. In vain would that man claim the tribute of Patriotism, who should labour to subvert these great Pillars of human happiness, these firmest props of the duties of men and citizens. . . .

Kennedy's inaugural pointed to the religious aspect of the Declaration of Independence, and it might be well to look at that document a bit more closely. There are four references to God. The first speaks of the "Laws of Nature and of Nature's God" which entitle any people to be independent. The second is the famous statement that all men "are endowed by their Creator with certain inalienable Rights." Here Jefferson is locating the fundamental legitimacy of the new nation in a conception of "higher law" that is itself based on both classical natural law and biblical religion. The third is an appeal to "the Supreme Judge of the world for the rectitude of our intentions," and the last indicates "a firm reliance on the protection of divine Providence." In these last two references, a biblical God of history who stands in judgment over the world is indicated.

The intimate relation of these religious notions with the self-conception of the new republic is indicated by the frequency of their appearance in early official documents. For example, we find in Washington's first inaugural address of April 30, 1789:

> . . . No people can be bound to acknowledge and adore the Invisible Hand which conducts the affairs of man more than those of the United States. Every step by which we have advanced to the character of an independent nation seems to have been distinguished by some token of providential agency. . . .
>
> The propitious smiles of Heaven can never be expected on a nation that disregards the eternal rules of order and right which Heaven itself has ordained. . . . The preservation of the sacred fire of liberty and the destiny of the republican model of government are justly considered, perhaps, as deeply, as finally, staked on the experiment entrusted to the hands of the American people.

The words and acts of the founding fathers, especially the first few presidents, shaped the form and tone of the civil religion as it has been maintained ever since. Though much is selectively derived from Christianity, this religion is clearly not itself Christianity. For one thing, neither Washington nor Adams nor Jefferson mentions Christ in his inaugural address; nor do any of the subsequent presidents, although not one of them fails to mention God.[2] The God of the civil religion is not only rather "Unitarian"; he is also on the austere side, much more related to order, law, and right than to salvation and love. Even though he is somewhat deist in cast, he is by no means simply a watchmaker God. He is actively interested and involved in history, with a special concern for America. Here the analogy has much less to do with natural law than with ancient Israel; the equation of America with Israel in the idea of the "American Israel" is not infrequent.[3] What was implicit in the words of Washington already quoted becomes explicit in Jefferson's second inaugural when he said, "I shall need, too, the favor of that Being in whose hands we are, who led our fathers, as Israel of old, from their native land and planted them in a country flowing with all the necessaries and comforts of life." Europe is Egypt; America, the promised land. God has led his people to establish a new sort of social order that shall be a light unto all the nations.[4]

This theme, too, has been a continuous one in the civil religion. . . . We find it again in President Johnson's inaugural address:

> They came here—the exile and the stranger, brave but frightened—to find a place where a man could be his own man. They made a covenant with this land. Conceived in justice, written in liberty, bound in union, it was meant one day to inspire the hopes of all mankind; and it binds us still. If we keep its terms, we shall flourish.

What we have, then, from the earliest years of the republic is a collection of beliefs, symbols, and rituals with respect to sacred things and institutionalized in a collectivity. This religion—there seems no other word for it—while not antithetical to and indeed sharing much in common with Christianity, was neither sectarian nor in any specific sense Christian. At a time when the society was overwhelmingly Christian, it seems unlikely that this lack of Christian reference was meant to spare the feelings of the tiny non-Christian minority. Rather, the civil religion expressed what those who set the precedents felt was appropriate under the circumstances. It reflected their private as well as public views. Nor was the civil religion simply "religion in general." While generality was undoubtedly seen as a virtue by some, as in the quotation from Franklin above, the civil religion was specific enough when it came to the topic of America. Precisely because of this specificity, the civil religion was saved from empty formalism and served as a genuine vehicle of national religious self-understanding.

But the civil religion was not, in the minds of Franklin, Washington, Jefferson, or other leaders, with the exception of a few radicals like Tom Paine, ever felt to be a substitute for Christianity. There was an implicit but quite clear division of function between the civil religion and Christianity. Under the doctrine of religious liberty, an exceptionally wide sphere of personal piety and voluntary social action was left to the churches. But the churches were neither to control the state nor to be controlled by it. The national magistrate, whatever his private religious views, operates under the rubrics of the civil religion as long as he is in his official capacity. . . .

Civil War and Civil Religion

Until the Civil War, the American civil religion focused above all on the event of the Revolution, which was seen as the final act of the Exodus from the old lands across the waters. The Declaration of Independence and the Constitution were the sacred scriptures and Washington the divinely appointed Moses who led his people out of the hands of tyranny. The Civil War, which Sidney Mead calls "the center of American history" (1963, 12), was the second great event that involved the national self-understanding so deeply as to require expression in the civil religion. . . .

The Civil War raised the deepest questions of national meaning. The man who not only formulated but in his own person embodied its meaning for Americans was Abraham Lincoln. For him the issue was not in the first instance slavery but "whether that nation, or any nation so conceived, and so dedicated, can long endure."

. . . The phrases of Jefferson constantly echo in Lincoln's speeches. His task was, first of all, to save the Union—not for America alone but for the meaning of America to the whole world so unforgettably etched in the last phrase of the Gettysburg Address.

. . . With the Civil War, a new theme of death, sacrifice, and rebirth enters the civil religion. It is symbolized in the life and death of Lincoln. Nowhere is it stated more vividly than in the Gettysburg Address, itself part of the Lincolnian "New Testament" among the civil scriptures. Robert Lowell . . . goes on to say:

> The Gettysburg Address is a symbolic and sacramental act. . . . By his words, he gave the field of battle a symbolic significance that it had lacked. For us and our country, he left Jefferson's ideals of freedom and equality joined to the Christian sacrificial act of death and rebirth. I believe this is a meaning that goes beyond sect or religion and beyond peace and war, and is now part of our lives as a challenge, obstacle and hope. (Nevins 1964, 88–9)

Lowell is certainly right in pointing out the Christian quality of the symbolism here, but he is also right in quickly disavowing any sectarian implication. . . . The Gettysburg symbolism (". . . those who here gave their lives, that that nation might live") is Christian without having anything to do with the Christian church.

. . . The new symbolism soon found both physical and ritualistic expression. The great number of the war dead required the establishment of a number of national cemeteries. Of these, the Gettysburg National Cemetery, which Lincoln's famous address served to dedicate, has been overshadowed only by the Arlington National Cemetery. Begun somewhat vindictively on the Lee estate across the river from Washington, partly with the end that the Lee family could never reclaim it (Decker and McSween 1892, 60–7), it has subsequently become the most hallowed monument of the civil religion. Not only was a section set aside for the Confederate dead, but it has received the dead of each succeeding American war.

Memorial Day, which grew out of the Civil War, gave ritual expression to the themes we have been discussing. As Lloyd Warner has so brilliantly analyzed it, the Memorial Day observance, especially in the towns and smaller cities of America, is a major event for the whole community involving a rededication to the martyred dead, to the spirit of sacrifice, and to the American vision.[5] Just as Thanksgiving Day, which incidentally was securely institutionalized as an annual national holiday only under the presidency of Lincoln, serves to integrate the family into the civil religion, so Memorial

Day has acted to integrate the local community into the national cult. Together with the less overtly religious Fourth of July and the more minor celebrations of Veterans Day and the birthdays of Washington and Lincoln, these two holidays provide an annual ritual calendar for the civil religion. . . .

The Civil Religion Today

. . . As usual in religious polemic, [religious critics] take as criteria the best in their own religious tradition and as typical the worst in the tradition of the civil religion. Against these critics, I would argue that the civil religion at its best is a genuine apprehension of universal and transcendent religious reality as seen in or, one could almost say, as revealed through the experience of the American people. Like all religions, it has suffered various deformations and demonic distortions. At its best, it has neither been so general that it has lacked incisive relevance to the American scene nor so particular that it has placed American society above universal human values. I am not at all convinced that the leaders of the churches have consistently represented a higher level of religious insight than the spokesmen of the civil religion. . . .

Perhaps the real animus of the religious critics has been not so much against the civil religion in itself but against its pervasive and dominating influence within the sphere of church religion. As S. M. Lipset has recently shown, American religion at least since the early nineteenth century has been predominantly activist, moralistic, and social rather than contemplative, theological, or innerly spiritual (1963). Tocqueville spoke of American church religion as "a political institution which powerfully contributes to the maintenance of a democratic republic among the Americans" (1954, 310) by supplying a strong moral consensus amidst continuous political change. . . .

The churches opposed neither the Revolution nor the establishment of democratic institutions. Even when some of them opposed the full institutionalization of religious liberty, they accepted the final outcome with good grace and without nostalgia for an *ancien régime*.

The American civil religion was never anticlerical or militantly secular. On the contrary, it borrowed selectively from the religious tradition in such a way that the average American saw no conflict between the two. In this way, the civil religion was able to build up without any bitter struggle with the church powerful symbols of national solidarity and to mobilize deep levels of personal motivation for the attainment of national goals. . . .

The civil religion has not always been invoked in favor of worthy causes. . . . With respect to America's role in the world, the dangers of distortion are greater and the built-in safeguards of the tradition weaker. The theme of the American Israel was used, almost from the beginning, as a justification for the shameful treatment of the Indians so characteristic of our history. It can be overtly or implicitly linked to the idea of manifest destiny which has been used to legitimate several adventures in imperialism since the early nineteenth century.

. . . Behind the civil religion at every point lie biblical archetypes: Exodus, Chosen People, Promised Land, New Jerusalem, Sacrificial Death and Rebirth. But it is also genuinely American and genuinely new. It has its own prophets and its own martyrs, its own sacred events and sacred places, its own solemn rituals and symbols. It is concerned that America be a society as perfectly in accord with the will of God as men can make it, and a light to all the nations.

It has often been used and is being used today as a cloak for petty interests and ugly passions. It is in need—as is any living faith—of continual reformation, of being measured by universal standards. But it is not evident that it is incapable of growth and new insight.

It does not make any decision for us. It does not remove us from moral ambiguity, from being, in Lincoln's fine phrase, an "almost chosen people." But it is a heritage of moral and religious experience from which we still have much to learn as we formulate the decisions that lie ahead.

3.2

Grace Y. Kao and Jerome E. Copulsky

THE PLEDGE OF ALLEGIANCE AND THE MEANINGS AND LIMITS OF CIVIL RELIGION (2007)

This section details four ways that civil religion in general, and the Pledge of Allegiance in particular, participates in the kind of "sacred legitimation of the social order". . . . Our analysis of civil religion is based on two distinctions—the first regarding its *content* (i.e. the scope of the religious sources that can be incorporated in this civil religion), and the second, its *character* (i.e. its posture toward the state). The first distinction itself turns on the question of inclusion or exclusion: some commentators want civil religion to operate in a conservative or culturally "preservationist" fashion, while others encourage a more "pluralist" model, whereby rituals are attentive to and reflective of the increasing religious diversity of the nation. The other distinction, between priestly and prophetic modes, is especially *apropos* when rituals of civil religion involve religious language. On one reading of the Pledge of Allegiance, the phrase "one Nation under God" works as a "priestly" convention in buttressing the claims and bolstering the legitimacy of the state (i.e. "under God" means "God is on our side"). On a different reading, the phrase "one Nation under God" serves a "prophetic" agenda, so that it is God and not the state that commands American citizens' ultimate loyalty. The Pledge of Allegiance can be interpreted from all of these vantage points. By describing these possibilities and assessing the merits of each, we raise questions about the meaning, purpose, and desirability of both the Pledge of Allegiance and American civil religion.

Civil Religion and the Preservationist Impulse

Under a "preservationist" understanding of civil religion, the continued use of traditional expressions, tropes, and rituals of civil religion is necessary to maintain cultural coherence, a sense of national identity, and the stability of our central institutions. Most preservationists view America as a "Christian" (or increasingly, a "Judeo-Christian") nation and accordingly find it appropriate for our symbolic systems to reflect and reinforce that identity.[6] To illustrate, Harvard Professor Samuel Huntington interprets the entire Pledge of Allegiance controversy as "sharply pos[ing] the issue whether America is a secular or religious nation" (Huntington 2004, 81–3). Since he concludes that America *is* a "predominantly Christian nation with a secular government," whose "Anglo-Protestant" political ideals stand at the heart of our "common culture," he submits that Michael Newdow rightly feels like an "outsider" because of his atheism, just as "non-Christians may legitimately see themselves as strangers" (Huntington 2004, 82–4). While Huntington concedes that "atheists and nonbelievers" have the right to refuse to recite the Pledge or participate in any other "religiously tainted practice of which they disapprove," he still insists that all who stand outside of the cultural mainstream must accept its hegemony or face permanent alienation (Huntington 2004, 82, 106). If Huntington's diagnosis is to be accepted, rituals of civil religion such as the Pledge of Allegiance serve to articulate and reinforce a coherent national identity as well as provide a means for outsiders to become members of the political community. (Recall the fact that the Pledge of Allegiance is collectively recited by newly-minted American citizens at naturalization ceremonies.) Should these rituals be removed from public life, cultural fragmentation and disintegration of our collective identity loom as menacing possibilities. . . .

Nevertheless, the very heritage that such preservationists are striving to protect is itself a selective retrieval of certain events, symbols, memories, and interpretations—one that distorts or suppresses any evidence that does not conform to their desired image. In fact, conceptions of a "Christian" founding (or a "secular" founding, for that matter) do not take into account the maddeningly complex history of church-state relations in America. But preservationists are not just waxing nostalgic for a "golden age" of unified national identity. They are also willing to use such a vision to exclude or marginalize whomever is currently regarded as the religious or cultural Other—Quakers and other dissident Protestant sects or denominations in colonial times; Mormons in the nineteenth century; Jews and Catholics until the second half of the twentieth century; and atheists and members of many other religious traditions still now.[7]

Civil Religion and the Pluralist Impulse

While preservationists would ignore dissent from minority voices for the sake of a uniform national identity, others are calling for *civil religion,* and not these non-conformists, to change. Those who accordingly espouse a "pluralist" or a "multiculturalist" vision of civil religion encourage the expansion of the forms of civil religion even beyond this now familiar "Judeo-Christian" gloss. According to Martha Nussbaum, for example, a "reasonable 'civil religion'" for America today would include "a celebration of the diversity of traditions and comprehensive doctrines that are contained within a nation, as a source of its strength and richness" (Nussbaum 2005; cf. Rouner 1999; cf. Feldman 2005). . . .

If the preservationist desires cultural and religious differences to be reduced in the American "melting pot," pluralists advocate a patchwork quilt, by which such public displays and official recognition of a plurality of religious traditions are the means by which new and historically marginalized groups make their presence known in America civic life. As might have been expected, however, the ceremonial recognition of other religions and the expansion of civil religious expressions to include them have met with resistance and occasional hostility. . . . President Bush experienced some backlash by his evangelical Christian base for going beyond the "Judeo-Christian" script when publicly stating his belief at a press conference that Christians and Muslims pray to the "same God" (Pruden 2003). . . . The Family Research Council regarded the first-ever Congressional invocation by a Hindu priest in 2000 as " one more indication that our nation is drifting from its Judeo-Christian roots."[8] Even the Lutheran Church-Missouri Synod (LCMS) pastor who participated in an ecumenical "Prayer for America" service at Yankee stadium on September 23, 2001 faced suspension and formal charges of unionism (i.e. worshipping with non-LCMS Christians), syncretism, and idolatry by his co-religionists not so much for the *content* of his prayer, but for sharing it alongside of other Christian, Jewish, Muslim, and Hindu, and Sikh clerics (Neuchterlein 2002). One could enumerate many other examples of backlash.

It is therefore an open question whether religions outside of the dominant "Judeo-Christian" paradigm will find genuine acceptance as *bona-fide* American religions anytime soon. . . .

Priestly and Prophetic Civil Religion

In this section we deal with the posture that civil religion takes toward the state. According to Martin E. Marty, the "priestly mode" is "celebrative, affirmative, [and] culture-building" (Marty 1974, 145).[9] Interpreted in this light, civil religion serves to aid in the legitimation of the state, its institutions, and its policies, by infusing its rituals with religious rhetoric and deploying theological symbols and warrants in support of the regnant political order. In the words of Samuel Huntington: "Civil religion enables Americans to bring together their secular politics and their religious society, *to marry God and country, so as to give religious sanctity to their patriotism* and thus to *merge what could be conflicting loyalties into loyalty to a religiously endowed country*" (Huntington 2004, 103, emphasis added). In the specific case of the Pledge of Allegiance, then, the phrase "under God" could be understood to mean that "God is on our side."

In contrast to offering *priestly* endorsement, civil religion can be understood to be operating in a *prophetic* manner. As Bellah argued:

> What I meant by civil religion in America . . . was a long tradition in American public life, of which Lincoln is the absolute central exemplar, of *calling the nation to account as responsible to an authority higher than the nation, of insisting that the nation is not absolute, and making that part of our public life.* (Bellah 1986, emphasis added)

On this construal civil religion neither automatically celebrates, nor uncritically accepts, whatever the nation does, but actually makes possible quite radical political self-criticism. Thus, if *priestly* civil religion tries to give divine or transcendent sanction to "who we are," the *prophetic* type instead stresses "who we need to be" in the light of some higher, transcendent ideal.[10] For example, in his famous "I Have a Dream" speech, Dr. Martin Luther King, Jr. employed *prophetic* civil religion to champion civil rights by appealing to the still-unsatisfied promises of the Declaration of Independence and Constitution. . . .

It can be argued that *priestly* civil religion has been more popular than *prophetic* varieties. For example, in contrast to the reverent humility, sense of sin, and theological ambiguity displayed in Lincoln's Second Inaugural, most Presidential uses of civil religious rhetoric in times of war are premised on the *priestly* conviction that God *is* on America's side.[11] From another angle, the popularity of Lee Greenwood's song "God Bless the U.S.A."—in heavy rotation during Gulf War 1 (1991) and again in the aftermath of the terrorist attacks of September 11, 2001—reveals how many Americans appeal to God (or else use God-talk) in times of national crisis or tragedy. . . . Perhaps it can be concluded that Americans are fonder of the *priestly* idea of God *blessing* America than they are of *prophetic* civil religious jeremiads. Moreover, the state's interest in civil religion would seem naturally to tend toward the *priestly* mode and away from the *prophetic*.

Those who advocate a *priestly* civil religion would most likely affirm the current text of the Pledge of Allegiance. However, some *prophetic* civil religionists, concerned that rituals such as the Pledge are primarily designed to inculcate love of country rather than commitment to a set of ideals for which the country is supposed to stand, might object to its frequent use in public schools and other *fora*. While this latter group might endorse the ostensibly *religious* rationale behind the 1954 introduction of the phrase "under God" in the Pledge (i.e. to signify that the nation is under an authority higher than the state), they might be appalled by some recent strategies that defended its constitutionality by draining the phrase "one Nation under God" of any genuine religious content.

. . . It may well be the case that the state's interest in promoting civil religion in patriotic rituals will nearly always be *priestly* and not *prophetic,* since the state will want to foster patriotism and obedience—not a critical attitude toward its institutions and policies. Moreover, the American public has largely rejected appeals to *prophetic* civil religion when used to explain or justify national misfortune. Indeed, some may question the need of a *prophetic* civil religion at all, insofar as it provides the vehicle of self-criticism. For, if self-criticism with reference to an ideal is what is most desired in *prophetic* civil religion, it is important to ask whether state-sponsored civil religion is the most effective way of achieving this goal. . . . There may be times when recognition of human error, evil, or incompetence is more constructive than appeals to divine providence or divine wrath. Indeed, it is safe to say that such a *prophetic* mode of thinking about politics would continue to emanate from individuals, churches, and other religious institutions themselves (in the form of what Martin F. Marty and others have called "public religion").

This final point about the role of "public religion" for self-criticism is important, since some religious leaders criticize the very *idea and usage of civil religion itself* whether "priestly" or "prophetic," given the danger that either poses to the health and vitality of their own religious traditions. Christian ethicists such as Stanley Hauerwas and John Howard Yoder have long sought to counsel Christians in America away from both their "Constantinian" tendencies and their misguided primary allegiance to the state as opposed to the church of which Christ is the head. After all, the grand tradition of biblically-infused civil religion in America has regarded America as the "New Israel," placing America itself in a covenantal relationship with God. As we see, then, civil religion and its attendant rituals have the potential not only to offend the non-theist, but also raise difficulties for the faithful theist, as well.

Conclusion

It is clear that American civil religion, whether in its preservationist, priestly, or prophetic cast, will be objectionable to one group or another. There will never be a functional civil religion that will please all Americans. Insofar as such rituals strive to promote unity, they do so at the risk of estranging some citizens from full participation in the polity. Religious groups who have conscientiously refused to salute or pledge allegiance to the flag (e.g. Jehovah's Witnesses, Mennonites, the Elijah Voice Society, members of the Church of God) have been legally prosecuted—and in some cases, violently assaulted (Gunn 2005, 589–90; Ellis 2005).[12] By linking assent to a theological claim with an affirmation of civic loyalty, the current text of the Pledge sorts out who can and cannot be true patriots, and thereby divides, rather than unites, all Americans.

3.3

Michael F. Bailey and Kristin Lindholm

TOCQUEVILLE AND THE RHETORIC OF CIVIL RELIGION IN THE PRESIDENTIAL INAUGURAL ADDRESSES (2003)

On March 31, 1789, Robert Livingston administered the Presidential Oath of Office to the unanimously selected first President of the United States, George Washington. Washington, who scrupulously attended to how his actions could be copied by future generations, judged it fitting to elevate the occasion with the trappings of grandeur and solemnity. Going well beyond the requirements marked out by the Constitution, Washington used the moment in an extraordinarily imaginative and compelling way: he symbolically took the nation to church. Every four years since, newly elected Presidents have faithfully reenacted Washington's priestly role of consecrating the country, its principles, and its people. Even today, the inaugural addresses follow the fundamental outlines of Washington's example. Blending celebration and sobriety, greatness and humility, past accomplishments and future hope, the inaugural ceremony aims to unite a sprawling and diverse people by articulating their common political principles. More importantly for our purposes, however, by invoking God's blessing on a vision of what America can be, the addresses move beyond the political into the poetical and the divine.

   . . . It is our thesis, however, that a new expression of the divine—one more abstract and self-justificatory than the themes traditionally employed—was introduced into the inaugural addresses a few decades following the Civil War, took on new force around the time of Woodrow Wilson, and has become the dominant theme of the addresses in recent decades. This new element of divinity is nothing less than an idealized version of American democracy itself. While not fully supplanting the old civil religion, the new civil religion has largely eclipsed it. . . .

Inaugural Addresses: The Old Model

Key rhetorical elements relating to civil religion in the early inaugural addresses are: (1) modesty, (2) American exceptionalism, and (3) an emphasis on the operations of the Constitution.

Modesty

Perhaps the most striking feature of the early inaugural addresses is their modesty. . . .

These four elements of modesty—(1) belief in the experimental nature of the American project, (2) belief that success is predicated on virtuous citizens who follow the moral laws, (3) humble supplication before God, and (4) expressions of the personal inadequacies of the president—are liberally peppered throughout the addresses before the Civil War. Robert Bellah tells us that the posture of supplication and modesty reflects the American belief that "the ultimate sovereignty has been attributed to God." These elements of modesty in the early inaugural addresses are indicative of belief in a sovereign God who can be petitioned for assistance as well as the need for citizens and leaders to engage in moral behavior in order to insure that the successful American experiment remained successful. In light of the overwhelming responsibilities of the presidency, the men who were elected to the position acknowledged their own weakness before the nation. Hence, Jefferson speaks of "the weakness of my powers," Madison acknowledges his "own inadequacy," and Monroe refers to his "own deficiency" (Jefferson 1801; Madison 1809; Monroe 1817).[13]

American Exceptionalism

Side-by-side and in apparent tension with these examples of modesty, one finds the theme of American exceptionalism, the idea that citizens of the United States are a chosen people. . . .[14] As understood in the early days of the nation, American exceptionalism does not stem from an inherent superiority of Americans but from the providential work of God or, at the least, Nature's God. While especially blessed, Americans and their government have no special divine sanction. William Henry Harrison expressed this idea in his 1841 inaugural address: "We admit of no government by divine right, believing that so far as power is concerned the Beneficent Creator has made no distinction amongst men; that all are upon an equality, and that the only legitimate right to govern is an express grant of power from the governed" (Harrison 1841).

Early American exceptionalism is therefore less the belief that the United States will solve the world's problems than it is an obligation to live faithfully under God. The theme of American exceptionalism runs squarely against the American universalism—the belief that America transcends time and geography—so frequently encountered in more recent addresses. There is little sense in the early addresses that success is guaranteed; it must be earned. Therefore when Jefferson calls the United States "the world's best hope," he does so because he believes success is rooted in the virtuous citizen who "at the call of the law, would fly to the standard of the law, and would meet the invasions of the public order as his own personal concern" (Jefferson 1801). . . .

Civic Education

References to the divine and America's exceptionalism often came in the first and last sections of the addresses, serving as rhetorically ornate bookends to the core of the addresses. . . . Whereas modern addresses often soar with the possibilities of a limitless future, the civil religion of the older addresses, already sober, is further tamed by the civic education which makes up the heart of the early addresses. The purpose of this civic education is a reminder and explanation of the constitutional principles of the American system. Far from waxing eloquent on utopian dreams, the civic education of the inaugural addresses was rhetorically pedestrian, attempting to make constitutional sense of the pressing issues of the day.

. . . Such rehearsals of constitutional duty and power are more than articulations of the obvious. . . . They serve the important didactic point of emphasizing how political form—constitutional structure and processes—matters deeply to legitimate political authority and success. . . .[15]

The emphasis on form in the civic education section of the inaugural addresses does not merely complement the civil religion; it tames it. Emphasizing form reminds citizens that satisfying even the highest and most noble constitutional aspirations does not justify the use of any and all means. As importantly, it guards against the easy slide into national hubris that is possible when one believes that God has especially blessed one's nation.

Inaugural Addresses: The New Model

At first glance it may seem that the civil religion of the United States as expressed in inaugural addresses has changed little over time. This is understandable, especially when one views just the explicit mentions of God. References to the divine, such as God, Almighty and Heaven, are fairly consistent in number throughout the addresses.

Grafted onto this older civil religion, however, is a new and less articulate but surprisingly powerful sense of the divine. This new civil religion does not replace the traditional civil religion, which remains at the bookends of the addresses, but it does largely eclipse the middle civic education section. While the civic education purpose is not altogether dead, its articulation has become increasingly vague, increasingly poetic, and decreasingly wedded to the Constitution. . . . The new civil religion of idealized America does not ground us but instead unleashes us from the limits traditionally thought to bind all persons and societies.

. . . In contrast to the older addresses, the more recent addresses may be characterized by (1) immodesty, (2) American universalism, and (3) a paean to America's future. In sum we see a civil religion—predictable from Tocqueville's analysis of democracy— that is more abstract and self-justificatory than traditional civil religion.

Immodesty

. . . In contrast to the modesty of the first addresses, the more recent inaugural addresses attempt to outdo one another with their visions of grandeur. . . .

Nowhere do we find the axiomatic faith in America—and the belief that what America needs most is faith in itself—as we do in Ronald Reagan. To be American, for Reagan, is to be curiously exempt from the contingencies that face other peoples.

> The crisis we are facing today . . . does require, however, our best effort, and our willingness to believe in ourselves and to believe in our capacity to perform great deeds; to believe that together, with God's help, we can and will resolve the problems which now confront us. And, after all, why shouldn't we believe that? We are Americans. (Reagan 1981)

Another subtle sign of relative immodesty is discernible even in how modern presidents ask for God's help. The word "supplication," which was common in the first addresses, is last used in Andrew Jackson's address. Though presidents still ask for God's blessing, confidence has shifted to humanity as well. This is articulated most clearly in Nixon's closing words, where he proclaims that the nation is "sustained by our confidence in the will of God and the *promise of man*" (Nixon 1969).

No need for personal humility is expressed in the modern addresses. The call of inadequacy that studded the early addresses drops dramatically after Lincoln, who himself did not acknowledge any personal weakness. Typical of the modern presidents is Taft's comment that "anyone who has taken the oath I have just taken must feel a heavy weight of responsibility" (Taft 1909). Responsibility, true, but not inadequacy. More to the spirit is Grant's claim that "The responsibilities of the position I feel, but accept them without fear" (Grant 1869).

Just how much confidence presidents feel—or feel obligated to convey—becomes obvious in the promises presidents have made in the addresses of this past century. The first time a president uttered a promise or pledge that began with "We will. . . ." did not occur until McKinley's second address in 1900. Since McKinley's promise, there have been sixty-three other "We will" promises. Of these, 49 were uttered since Nixon's first address. The content of the promises is unlimited in scope.

Among the promises made by presidents since FDR are:

> We will bend [the new world] to the hopes of man (Johnson 1965).
> We will be as strong as we need to be for as long as we need to be (Nixon 1969).
> We will be ever vigilant and never vulnerable, and we will fight our wars against poverty, ignorance, and injustice (Carter 1977).
> We will again be the exemplar of freedom and a beacon of hope for those who do not now have freedom (Reagan 1981).
> We will not rest until every American enjoys the fullness of freedom, dignity, and opportunity as our birthright (Reagan 1985).
> We will not succumb to the dark impulses that lurk in the far regions of the soul everywhere. We shall overcome them (Clinton 1997).

In light of such grandiose promises, ranging from complete lack of vulnerability to victory over evil in the soul, the recent inaugural addresses reflect rhetorical vision of a nation without realistic political or even spiritual limits.

American Universalism

In tension with American exceptionalism—its sense of difference—is American universalism, the belief that America is less a particular culture and political system than a model for all humanity to follow. . . . This belief is not new, as we witness in Lincoln's Gettysburg Address; "Now we are engaged in a great civil war, testing whether that nation, or any nation so conceived and so dedicated, can long endure." Still, it becomes more pronounced roughly after Woodrow Wilson's second address, in which the position is articulated elegantly: "We shall be the more American if we but remain true to the principles in which we have been bred. They are not the principles of a province or of a single continent. We have known and boasted all along that they were the principles of a liberated mankind" (Wilson 1917). . . .

Paean to America

Roosevelt's paean to America is unusually elaborate but by no means unusual in content or tone. And it is in rhetoric such as Roosevelt's that we find the most significant shift in the civil religion of the United States. God is still invoked, but America's real faith is faith in America: not in the government, not in the Constitution, not, strictly speaking, in the people (though this comes closer), but in America as Idea. The American way *is* God's way. With the new civil religion, the inaugural addresses transcend politics and offer a glimpse of perfection.

The term "America" and its variants "American" and "Americans" were hardly used at all in the nation's founding and through the early presidential inaugural addresses. Though very early ardent nationalists such as Washington and Adams attempted to create a nation in words, most of the presidents reflected the more common view that the United States was a Union, not a nation. Whereas "nation" implies unity of culture and singular purpose of mind, "Union" implies a formal and constitutional agreement between independent states. Above all, Union is political and therefore more circumscribed than the concept of nation.

Consistent with Tocqueville's contention that democracies prefer the general to the specific, as the United States has democratized over time, the word "nation" has gradually replaced "Union."

. . . To be an "American," however, is something that has become vitally important over time. . . . Following Tocqueville, we speculate that in championing America, presidents use the poetic and priestly moment of the inaugural to celebrate the infinite potentialities of humanity. The new America is virtually without limits, taking on the qualities of a god. Thus we see time and again the invocation of the American spirit and the American dream. America is no longer even a place with geographical boundaries. It is spirit.

Consider the power and ambiguity of the word "American" in the inaugural addresses since Wilson. America is the secular proxy for the Kingdom of God. . . . To be American is to be at peace with the world. To be healthy. To be wealthy. To know no sense of limit. To be American is to feel the strength of humanity.

> For this is what America is all about. It is the uncrossed desert and the unclimbed ridge. It is the star that is not reached and the harvest sleeping in the unplowed ground. Is our world gone? We say 'Farewell.' Is a new world coming? We welcome it—and we will bend it to the hopes of man. (Johnson 1965)

. . . Our recent inaugural poetry tells us that America is that land where the finite merges with the infinite. It is the lot of Americans to push back or shatter the limits that shackle humanity. It is the lot of Americans to use their freedom and technological prowess to conquer nature and, with the conquering of nature, to allow humanity—not a sovereign God—to govern its destiny.

Evaluation: The Dreamy World of America

. . . We suggest that the presidential inaugural addresses have become more immodest in their claims, less rooted in moral responsibilities, less focused on the particulars of the Constitution, and more focused on America as the light of the world. . . .

One cannot be but charmed by the beauty and allure of a spiritualized America. It is not coincidental that the phrase "American Dream" is repeated frequently in the recent addresses. The American poetic ideal is indeed dreamy, capturing as it does a curious marriage of aspiration and unreality. In our more wakeful moments, however, we should ask ourselves whether we ought to embrace the new, self-transcendent civil religion. Earlier we claimed that the rhetoric accompanying the shift to a more democratized nation is troubling. While it is proper to champion the real gains of justice that characterize American history, we hold that the new civil religion poses dangers to a good polity.[16] By making America a proxy for the Kingdom of God, the concept of "American" crowds out other identities. We believe that identities such as family member, church member, employee, and other relationships have as much validity within their own spheres as does citizen. Indeed, the word "citizen" is far more circumscribed than "American" because it is rooted in particularities—to this geographical unit, this Constitution, this set of obligations and freedoms. Such particularities constantly instruct us of the contingent and partial nature of our identities as well as the concrete obligations we have to others. Political and cultural identities are of course important ways of understanding oneself, but making "American" the primary identity encourages an undifferentiated view of life that discourages diversity of thought, social pluralism, and the recognition of the specific responsibilities related to various roles.

. . . Precisely because the modern addresses champion Americanism so unwaveringly, they simultaneously encourage an odd mixture of utopianism and cynicism. . . . The fantasy presented simply cannot be fulfilled. The promise of democracy is the vague promise of *more,* and one can always have more than one has. As a result, we democrats work admirably to improve our lot but seldom rest content with what we are given.[17] The spirit of democracy, the spirit of more, the spirit of entitlement, works its way into our thinking, leaving us restless in our prosperity.

Such cynicism may also be fed by the impossible visions that are regularly placed before the people of the United States. Making promises that cannot be met, such as invulnerability, leaves presidents in the position of reinforcing the populace's distrust of public rhetoric and even, ironically, our democratic institutions. Audiences know that the United States is imperfect in areas such as crime, education, and racial relations, so holding the country up as the world's model or even savior can reinforce responses of anger, despair, and, most commonly, political apathy.

To close, we feel obligated to call for a new rhetoric of moral realism as well as a realistic (idealistic but not utopian) understanding of the limits of political life. The mark of the best epideictic speeches is to make the audience consider itself in new ways. Inaugural addresses, therefore, are occasions not simply to cater to the dispositions of the audience but to challenge citizens precisely along those moral dimensions where they are weakest. Caring for our political association should not be grounded in a hope of earthly perfection, for such hope will always disappoint. What is needed is not an expectation of future satisfaction but of present political obligations rooted in a mature understanding of the promises and limitations of the political realm. . . .

3.4

Robert D. Putnam

BOWLING ALONE: THE COLLAPSE AND REVIVAL OF AMERICAN COMMUNITY (2000)

In recent years social scientists have framed concerns about the changing character of American society in terms of the concept of "social capital." By analogy with notions of physical capital and human capital—tools and training that enhance individual productivity—the core idea of social capital theory is that social networks have value. . . .

Whereas physical capital refers to physical objects and human capital refers to properties of individuals, social capital refers to connections among individuals—social networks and the norms of reciprocity and trustworthiness that arise from them. In that sense social capital is closely related to what some have called "civic virtue." The difference is that "social capital" calls attention to the fact that civic virtue is most powerful when embedded in a dense network of reciprocal social relations. A society of many virtuous but isolated individuals is not necessarily rich in social capital. . . .

Therefore, it is important to ask how the positive consequences of social capital— mutual support, cooperation, trust, institutional effectiveness—can be maximized and the negative manifestations—sectarianism, ethnocentrism, corruption—minimized. Toward this end, scholars have begun to distinguish many different forms of social capital.

Of all the dimensions along which forms of social capital vary, perhaps the most important is the distinction between *bridging* (or inclusive) and *bonding* (or exclusive).[18] Some forms of social capital are, by choice or necessity, inward looking and tend to rein- force exclusive identities and homogeneous groups. Examples of bonding social capital include ethnic fraternal organizations, church-based women's reading groups, and fash- ionable country clubs. Other networks are outward looking and encompass people across diverse social cleavages. Examples of bridging social capital include the civil rights move- ment, many youth service groups, and ecumenical religious organizations.

Bonding social capital is good for undergirding specific reciprocity and mobilizing sol- idarity. Dense networks in ethnic enclaves, for example, provide crucial social and psy- chological support for less fortunate members of the community, while furnishing start-up financing, markets, and reliable labor for local entrepreneurs. Bridging networks, by con- trast, are better for linkage to external assets and for information diffusion. . . . Bonding so- cial capital is, as Xavier de Souza Briggs puts it, good for "getting by"; but bridging social capital is crucial for "getting ahead" (Granovetter 1973, 1360–80; Briggs 1998, 1–13). . . .

Churches and other religious organizations have a unique importance in American civil society. America is one of the most religiously observant countries in the contemporary world. With the exception of "a few agrarian states such as Ireland and Poland," observes one scholar, "the United States has been the most God-believing and religion-adhering,

---

For a more recent assessment of religion and social capital in America, see Robert D. Putnam and David E. Campbell, American Grace: How Religion Divides and Unites Us (Simon & Schuster, 2010).

fundamentalist, and religiously traditional country in Christendom," as well as "the most religiously fecund country" where "more new religions have been born. . . than in any other society'"(Lipset 1991, 187). American churches[19] over the centuries have been incredibly robust social institutions. Tocqueville himself commented at length on Americans' religiosity. Religious historian Phillip Hammond observes that "ever since the nation's founding, a higher and higher proportion of Americans have affiliated with a church or synagogue— right through the 1950s" (Hammond 1992, xiv). Although most often we think of the colonists as a deeply religious people, one systematic study of the history of religious observance in America estimates that the rate of formal religious adherence *grew* steadily from 17 percent in 1776 to 62 percent in 1980 (Finke and Stark 1992, 16). . . .

Faith communities in which people worship together are arguably the single most important repository of social capital in America. "The church is people," says Reverend Craig McMullen, the activist co-pastor of the Dorchester Temple Baptist Church in Boston. "It's not a building; it's not an institution, even. It is relationships between one person and the next"(Terry 1994, 22). As a rough rule of thumb, our evidence shows, nearly half of all associational memberships in America are church related, half of all personal philanthropy is religious in character, and half of all volunteering occurs in a religious context. So how involved we are in religion today matters a lot for America's social capital. . . .

Churches provide an important incubator for civic skills, civic norms, community interests, and civic recruitment. Religiously active men and women learn to give speeches, run meetings, manage disagreements, and bear administrative responsibility. They also befriend others who are in turn likely to recruit them into other forms of community activity. In part for these reasons, churchgoers are substantially more likely to be involved in secular organizations, to vote and participate politically in other ways, and to have deeper informal social connections (Verba, Schlozman, and Brady 1995, 282–3, 317–33, 377–84, 518–21; Macaluso and Wanat 1979, 158–169; Strate et al. 1989, 443–464; Peterson 1992, 123–139; Harris 1994, 42–68; Wald, Kellstedt, and Leege 1993, 130; Rosenstone and Hansen 1993).

Regular worshipers and people who say that religion is very important to them are much more likely than other people to visit friends, to entertain at home, to attend club meetings, and to belong to sports groups; professional and academic societies; school service groups; youth groups; service clubs; hobby or garden clubs; literary, art, discussion, and study groups; school fraternities and sororities; farm organizations; political clubs; nationality groups; and other miscellaneous groups.[20] In one survey of twenty-two different types of voluntary associations, from hobby groups to professional associations to veterans groups to self-help groups to sports clubs to service clubs, it was membership in religious groups that was most closely associated with other forms of civic involvement like voting, jury service, community projects, talking with neighbors, and giving to charity.[21]

Religiosity rivals education as a powerful correlate of most forms of civic engagement.[22] In fact religiously involved people seem simply to know more people. One intriguing survey that asked people to enumerate all individuals with whom they had had a face-to-face conversation in the course of the day found that religious attendance was the most powerful predictor of the number of one's daily personal encounters.[23] Regular church attendees reported talking with 40 percent more people in the course of the day. These studies cannot show conclusively that churchgoing itself "produces" social connectivity—probably the causal arrow between the two points in both directions—but it is clear that religious people are unusually active social capitalists.

Religious involvement is an especially strong predictor of volunteering and philanthropy. About 75–80 percent of church members give to charity, as compared with 55–60 percent of nonmembers, and 50–60 percent of church members volunteer, while only 30–35 percent of nonmembers do. In part, of course, this is because churches themselves do things that require funds and volunteers, but religious adherents are also more likely to contribute time and money to activities beyond their own congregation. Even excluding contributions to religious causes, active involvement in religious organizations is among the strongest predictors of both philanthropy and volunteering (Hodgkinson and Weitzman 1996, 5, 14, 121–31; Hodgkinson, Weitzman, and Kirsch 1990, 93–114; Rimor and Tobin 1990, 134–64; for partially contradictory evidence, see Wilson and Janoski 1995, 137–52).

In part, the tie between religion and altruism embodies the power of religious values, As Kenneth Wald, a close student of religion, observes, "Religious ideals are potentially powerful sources of commitment and motivation," so that "human beings will make enormous sacrifices if they believe themselves to be driven by a divine force"(Wald 1987, 29–30; see also Strate et al. 1989, 452). But the social ties embodied in religious communities are at least as important as religious beliefs per se in accounting for volunteerism and philanthropy[24] (Cnaan, Kasternakis, and Wineburg 1993; Jackson et al. 1995; Wilson and Musick 1997). Connectedness, not merely faith, is responsible for the beneficence of church people. Once again, the evidence does not prove beyond all doubt that churchgoing itself produces generosity, but religious involvement is certainly associated with greater attention to the needs of our brothers and sisters.

Churches have been and continue to be important institutional providers of social services. American religious communities spend roughly $15–$20 billion annually on social services. Nationwide in 1998 nearly 60 percent of all congregations (and an even higher proportion of larger congregations) reported contributing to social service, community development, or neighborhood organizing projects. Congregations representing 33 percent of all churchgoers support food programs for the hungry, and congregations representing 18 percent of all churchgoers support housing programs like Habitat for Humanity....

Faith-based organizations are particularly central to social capital and civic engagement in the African American community. The church is the oldest and most resilient social institution in black America, not least because it was traditionally the only black-controlled institution of a historically oppressed people. African Americans in all social strata are more religiously observant than other Americans. The black religious tradition distinctively encourages mixing religion and community affairs and invigorates civic activism. Both during and after the civil rights struggle, church involvement among blacks has been strongly associated with civic engagement, in part because the church provides a unique opportunity for blacks to exercise civic skills[25] (Harris 1999, esp. 59, 63–4; Lincoln and Mamiya 1990; Pattillo-McCoy 1998). C. Eric Lincoln, the sociologist of religion, says:

> Beyond its purely religious function, as critical as that function has been, the Black church in its historical role as lyceum, conservatory forum, social service center, political academy, and financial institution, has been and is for Black America the mother of our culture, the champion of our Freedom, and hallmark of our civilization. (1989)

In sum, religious involvement is a crucial dimension of civic engagement. Thus trends in civic engagement are closely tied to changing patterns of religious involvement....

Recently some skeptical sociologists have begun to question whether Americans really are as religiously observant as surveys suggest. Careful comparisons of survey responses with actual counts of parishioners in the pews suggests that many of us "misremember" whether we actually did make it to services last week. Estimates of overreporting of church attendance range as high as 50 percent[26] (Chaves and Cavendish 1994; Hadaway, Marler, and Chaves 1993) . . . In short, participation in organized worship services is probably lower today than it was twenty-five years ago and is surely lower than it was forty years ago.

Americans' involvement in the social life of the church beyond worship itself—in Sunday schools, Bible study groups, "church socials," and the like—appears to have fallen at least as fast as church membership and attendance at worship services. . . .

In sum, over the last three to four decades Americans have become about 10 percent less likely to claim church membership, while our actual attendance and involvement in religious activities has fallen by roughly 25 to 50 percent. Virtually all the postwar boom in religious participation—and perhaps more—has been erased. This broad historical pattern in religious participation—up from the first third of the century to the 1960s and then down from the 1960s to the 1990s—is very much the same pattern that we noted earlier for secular community-based organizations, as well as for political participation.

What is more, in all three cases, the more demanding the form of involvement—actual attendance as compared to formal membership, for example—the greater the decline. In effect, the classic institutions of American civic life, both religious and secular, have been "hollowed out." Seen from without, the institutional edifice appears virtually intact—little decline in professions of faith, formal membership down just a bit, and so on. When examined more closely, however, it seems clear that decay has consumed the load-bearing beams of our civic infrastructure.

The decline in religious participation, like many of the changes in political and community involvement, is attributable largely to generational differences.[27] Any given cohort of Americans seems not to have reduced religious observance over the years, but more recent generations are less observant than their parents. The slow but inexorable replacement of one generation by the next has gradually but inevitably lowered our national involvement in religious activities. . . .

I have generalized about trends in American religious participation in the aggregate over the last three decades, but in at least two important respects that is an oversimplification. First, not everyone in American society has been affected equally by the trends I have described so far. While one group of Americans has tended to withdraw from active involvement in faith-based communities, another group is as fully involved as ever. While the fraction of the population that is entirely disconnected from organized religion has increased, the fraction that is intensely involved has been relatively stable. In other words, religious dropouts have come at the expense of those whose religious involvement was modest but conventional. The result is that the country is becoming ever more clearly divided into two groups—the devoutly observant and the entirely unchurched. . . .[28] Although this polarization should not be exaggerated, it may also have a regional dimension, since there is some evidence that religious disengagement has been most marked in the North (especially the Northeast) and most limited in the southern Bible Belt.[29]

Second, the pace and direction of change has varied markedly among different denominations. Protestant and Jewish congregations have lost market share in terms of membership, while Catholics and other religions have gained. . . .

Let us summarize what we have learned about the religious entry in America's social capital ledger. First, religion is today, as it has traditionally been, a central fount of American community life and health. Faith-based organizations serve civic life both directly, by providing social support to their members and social services to the wider community, and indirectly, by nurturing civic skills, inculcating moral values, encouraging altruism, and fostering civic recruitment among church people.

Second, the broad oscillations in religious participation during the twentieth century mirror trends in secular civic life—flowering during the first six decades of the century and especially in the two decades after World War II, but then fading over the last three or four decades. As in secular life, the more intense the form of involvement, the greater the recent decline, even though a minority of the population continues to find demanding denominations especially appealing. Moreover, as in politics and society generally, this disengagement appears tied to generational succession. For the most part younger generations ("younger" here includes the boomers) are less involved both in religious and in secular social activities than were their predecessors at the same age.

Finally, American religious life over this period has also reenacted the historically familiar drama by which more dynamic and demanding forms of faith have surged to supplant more mundane forms. At least so far, however, the community-building efforts of the new denominations have been directed inward rather than outward, thus limiting their otherwise salutary effects on America's stock of social capital. In short, as the twenty-first century opens, Americans are going to church less often than we did three or four decades ago, and the churches we go to are less engaged with the wider community. Trends in religious life reinforce rather than counterbalance the ominous plunge in social connectedness in the secular community.

Primary Sources

3.5

Jean-Jacques Rousseau

THE SOCIAL CONTRACT, BOOK IV, CHAPTER VIII: CIVIL RELIGION (1762)

. . . Religion, considered in relation to society, which is either general or particular, may also be divided into two kinds: the religion of man, and that of the citizen. The first, which has neither temples, nor altars, nor rites, and is confined to the purely internal cult of the supreme God and the eternal obligations of morality, is the religion of the Gospel pure and simple, the true theism, what may be called natural divine right or law. The other, which is codified in a single country, gives it its gods, its own tutelary patrons; it has its dogmas, its rites, and its external cult prescribed by law; outside the single nation that follows it, all the world is in its sight infidel, foreign and barbarous; the duties and rights of man extend for it only as far as its own altars. Of this kind were all the religions of early peoples, which we may define as civil or positive divine right or law.

The second is good in that it unites the divine cult with love of the laws, and, making country the object of the citizens' adoration, teaches them that service done to the State is service done to its tutelary god. It is a form of theocracy, in which there can be no pontiff save the prince, and no priests save the magistrates. To die for one's country then becomes martyrdom; violation of its laws, impiety; and to subject one who is guilty to public execration is to condemn him to the anger of the gods: Sacer estod.

On the other hand, it is bad in that, being founded on lies and error, it deceives men, makes them credulous and superstitious, and drowns the true cult of the Divinity in empty ceremonial. It is bad, again, when it becomes tyrannous and exclusive, and makes a people bloodthirsty and intolerant, so that it breathes fire and slaughter, and regards as a sacred act the killing of every one who does not believe in its gods. The result is to place such a people in a natural state of war with all others, so that its security is deeply endangered.

There remains therefore the religion of man or Christianity—not the Christianity of today, but that of the Gospel, which is entirely different. By means of this holy, sublime, and real religion all men, being children of one God, recognise one another as brothers, and the society that unites them is not dissolved even at death.

But this religion, having no particular relation to the body politic, leaves the laws in possession of the force they have in themselves without making any addition to it; and thus one of the great bonds that unite society considered in severally fails to operate. Nay, more, so far from binding the hearts of the citizens to the State, it has the effect of taking them away from all earthly things. I know of nothing more contrary to the social spirit.

We are told that a people of true Christians would form the most perfect society imaginable. I see in this supposition only one great difficulty: that a society of true Christians would not be a society of men. . . .

Now, it matters very much to the community that each citizen should have a religion. That will make him love his duty; but the dogmas of that religion concern the State and its members only so far as they have reference to morality and to the duties which he who professes them is bound to do to others. Each man may have, over and above, what opinions he pleases, without it being the Sovereign's business to take cognisance of them; for, as the Sovereign has no authority in the other world, whatever the lot of its subjects may be in the life to come, that is not its business, provided they are good citizens in this life.

There is therefore a purely civil profession of faith of which the Sovereign should fix the articles, not exactly as religious dogmas, but as social sentiments without which a man cannot be a good citizen or a faithful subject. While it can compel no one to believe them, it can banish from the State whoever does not believe them—it can banish him, not for impiety, but as an anti-social being, incapable of truly loving the laws and justice, and of sacrificing, at need, his life to his duty. If any one, after publicly recognising these dogmas, behaves as if he does not believe them, let him be punished by death: he has committed the worst of all crimes, that of lying before the law.

The dogmas of civil religion ought to be few, simple, and exactly worded, without explanation or commentary. The existence of a mighty, intelligent and beneficent Divinity, possessed of foresight and providence, the life to come, the happiness of the just, the punishment of the wicked, the sanctity of the social contract and the laws: these are its positive dogmas. Its negative dogmas I confine to one, intolerance, which is a part of the cults we have rejected.

Now that there is and can be no longer an exclusive national religion, tolerance should be given to all religions that tolerate others, so long as their dogmas contain nothing contrary to the duties of citizenship. But whoever dares to say: Outside the Church is no salvation, ought to be driven from the State, unless the State is the Church, and the prince the pontiff. Such a dogma is good only in a theocratic government; in any other, it is fatal.

3.6

Alexis de Tocqueville

DEMOCRACY IN AMERICA (1833), CHAPTERS 2 AND 5

Of the Principal Source of Belief Among Democratic Nations

But obviously without such common belief no society can prosper; say, rather, no society can exist; for without ideas held in common there is no common action, and without common action there may still be men, but there is no social body. In order that society should exist and, a fortiori, that a society should prosper, it is necessary that the minds of all the citizens should be rallied and held together by certain predominant ideas; and this cannot be the case unless each of them sometimes draws his opinions from the common source and consents to accept certain matters of belief already formed.

A principle of authority must then always occur, under all circumstances, in some part or other of the moral and intellectual world. Its place is variable, but a place it necessarily has. The independence of individual minds may be greater or it may be less; it cannot be unbounded. Thus the question is, not to know whether any intellectual authority exists in an age of democracy, but simply where it resides and by what standard it is to be measured. . . .

In the United States the majority undertakes to supply a multitude of ready-made opinions for the use of individuals, who are thus relieved from the necessity of forming opinions of their own. Everybody there adopts great numbers of theories, on philosophy, morals, and politics, without inquiry, upon public trust; and if we examine it very closely, it will be perceived that religion itself holds sway there much less as a doctrine of revelation than as a commonly received opinion. . . .

How Religion in the United States Avails Itself of Democratic Tendencies

I have shown in a preceding chapter that men cannot do without dogmatic belief, and even that it is much to be desired that such belief should exist among them. I now add that, of all the kinds of dogmatic belief, the most desirable appears to me to be dogmatic belief in matters of religion; and this is a clear inference, even from no higher consideration than the interests of this world.

There is hardly any human action, however particular it may be, that does not originate in some very general idea men have conceived of the Deity, of his relation to mankind, of the nature of their own souls, and of their duties to their fellow creatures. Nor can anything prevent these ideas from being the common spring from which all the rest emanates.

Men are therefore immeasurably interested in acquiring fixed ideas of God, of the soul, and of their general duties to their Creator and their fellow men; for doubt on these first principles would abandon all their actions to chance and would condemn them in some way to disorder and impotence.

This, then, is the subject on which it is most important for each of us to have fixed ideas; and unhappily it is also the subject on which it is most difficult for each of us, left to himself, to settle his opinions by the sole force of his reason. . . .

The greatest advantage of religion is to inspire diametrically contrary principles. There is no religion that does not place the object of man's desires above and beyond the treasures of earth and that does not naturally raise his soul to regions far above those of the senses. Nor is there any which does not impose on man some duties towards his kind and thus draw him at times from the contemplation of himself. This is found in the most false and dangerous religions. . . .

I have neither the right nor the intention of examining the supernatural means that God employs to infuse religious belief into the heart of man. I am at this moment considering religions in a purely human point of view; my object is to inquire by what means they may most easily retain their sway in the democratic ages upon which we are entering.

It has been shown that at times of general culture and equality the human mind consents only with reluctance to adopt dogmatic opinions and feels their necessity acutely only in spiritual matters. This proves, in the first place, that at such times religions ought more cautiously than at any other to confine themselves within their own precincts. . . .

In continuation of this same inquiry I find that for religions to maintain their authority, humanly speaking, in democratic ages, not only must they confine themselves strictly within the circle of spiritual matters, but their power also will depend very much on the nature of the belief they inculcate, on the external forms they assume, and on the obligations they impose.

The preceding observation, that equality leads men to very general and very vast ideas, is principally to be understood in respect to religion. Men who are similar and equal in the world readily conceive the idea of the one God, governing every man by the same laws and granting to every man future happiness on the same conditions. The idea of the unity of mankind constantly leads them back to the idea of the unity of the Creator; while on the contrary in a state of society where men are broken up into very unequal ranks, they are apt to devise as many deities as there are nations, castes, classes, or families, and to trace a thousand private roads to heaven. . . .

In speaking of philosophical method among the Americans I have shown that nothing is more repugnant to the human mind in an age of equality than the idea of subjection to forms. Men living at such times are impatient of figures; to their eyes, symbols appear to be puerile artifices used to conceal or to set off truths that should more naturally be bared to the light of day; they are unmoved by ceremonial observances and are disposed to attach only a secondary importance to the details of public worship.

Those who have to regulate the external forms of religion in a democratic age should pay a close attention to these natural propensities of the human mind in order not to run counter to them unnecessarily.

I firmly believe in the necessity of forms, which fix the human mind in the contemplation of abstract truths and aid it in embracing them warmly and holding them with firmness. Nor do I suppose that it is possible to maintain a religion without external observances; but, on the other hand, I am persuaded that in the ages upon which we are entering it would be peculiarly dangerous to multiply them beyond measure, and that they ought rather to be limited to as much as is absolutely necessary to perpetuate the doctrine itself, which is the substance of religion, of which the ritual is only the form.[30] A religion which became more insistent in details, more inflexible, and more burdened with small observances during the time that men became more equal would soon find itself limited to a band of fanatic zealots in the midst of a skeptical multitude.

I anticipate the objection that, as all religions have general and eternal truths for their object, they cannot thus shape themselves to the shifting inclinations of every age without forfeiting their claim to certainty in the eyes of mankind. To this I reply again that the principal opinions which constitute a creed, and which theologians call articles of faith, must be very carefully distinguished from the accessories connected with them. Religions are obliged to hold fast to the former, whatever be the peculiar spirit of the age; but they should take good care not to bind themselves in the same manner to the latter at a time when everything is in transition and when the mind, accustomed to the moving pageant of human affairs, reluctantly allows itself to be fixed on any point. The permanence of external and secondary things seems to me to have a chance of enduring only when civil society is itself static; under any other circumstances I am inclined to regard it as dangerous. . . .

This brings me to a final consideration, which comprises, as it were, all the others. The more the conditions of men are equalized and assimilated to each other, the more important is it for religion, while it carefully abstains from the daily turmoil of secular affairs, not needlessly to run counter to the ideas that generally prevail or to the permanent interests that exist in the mass of the people. For as public opinion grows to be more and more the first and most irresistible of existing powers, the religious principle has no external support strong enough to enable it long to resist its attacks. This is not less true of a democratic people ruled by a despot than of a republic. In ages of equality kings may often command obedience, but the majority always commands belief; to the majority, therefore, deference is to be paid in whatever is not contrary to the faith.

I showed in the first Part of this work how the American clergy stand aloof from secular affairs. This is the most obvious but not the only example of their self-restraint. In America religion is a distinct sphere, in which the priest is sovereign, but out of which he takes care never to go. Within its limits he is master of the mind; beyond them he leaves men to themselves and surrenders them to the independence and instability that belong to their nature and their age. I have seen no country in which Christianity is clothed with fewer forms, figures, and observances than in the United States, or where it presents more distinct, simple, and general notions to the mind. Although the Christians of America are divided into a multitude of sects, they all look upon their religion in the same light. . . .

Another remark is applicable to the clergy of every communion. The American ministers of the Gospel do not attempt to draw or to fix all the thoughts of man upon the life to come; they are willing to surrender a portion of his heart to the cares of the present, seeming to consider the goods of this world as important, though secondary, objects. If they take no part themselves in productive labor, they are at least interested in its progress and they applaud its results, and while they never cease to point to the other world as the great object of the hopes and fears of the believer, they do not forbid him honestly to court prosperity in this. Far from attempting to show that these things are distinct and contrary to one another, they study rather to find out on what point they are most nearly and closely connected.

All the American clergy know and respect the intellectual supremacy exercised by the majority; they never sustain any but necessary conflicts with it. They take no share in the altercations of parties, but they readily adopt the general opinions of their country and their age, and they allow themselves to be borne away without opposition in the current of feeling and opinion by which everything around them is carried along. They endeavor to amend their contemporaries, but they do not quit fellowship with them. Public opinion is therefore never hostile to them; it rather supports and protects them, and their belief owes its authority at the same time to the strength which is its own and to that which it borrows from the opinions of the majority.

Thus it is that by respecting all democratic tendencies not absolutely contrary to herself and by making use of several of them for her own purposes, religion sustains a successful struggle with that spirit of individual independence which is her most dangerous opponent.

3.7

President Abraham Lincoln

SECOND INAUGURAL ADDRESS
(MARCH 4, 1865)

Fellow-countrymen:

At this second appearing to take the oath of the presidential office there is less occasion for an extended address than there was at the first. Then a statement somewhat in detail of a course to be pursued seemed fitting and proper. Now, at the expiration of four years, during which public declarations have been constantly called forth on every point and phase of the great contest which still absorbs the attention and engrosses the energies of the nation, little that is new could be presented. The progress of our arms, upon which all else chiefly depends, is as well known to the public as to myself, and it is, I trust, reasonably satisfactory and encouraging to all. With high hope for the future, no prediction in regard to it is ventured.

On the occasion corresponding to this four years ago all thoughts were anxiously directed to an impending civil war. All dreaded it, all sought to avert it. While the inaugural address was being delivered from this place, devoted altogether to saving the Union without war, insurgent agents were in the city seeking to destroy it without war—seeking to dissolve the Union and divide effects by negotiation. Both parties deprecated war, but one of them would make war rather than let the nation survive, and the other would accept war rather than let it perish, and the war came.

One eighth of the whole population was colored slaves, not distributed generally over the Union, but localized in the southern part of it. These slaves constituted a peculiar and powerful interest. All knew that this interest was somehow the cause of the war. To strengthen, perpetuate, and extend this interest was the object for which the insurgents would rend the Union even by war, while the Government claimed no right to do more than to restrict the territorial enlargement of it. Neither party expected for the war the magnitude or the duration which it has already attained. Neither anticipated that the cause of the conflict might cease with or even before the conflict itself should cease. Each looked for an easier triumph, and a result less fundamental and astounding. Both read the same Bible and pray to the same God, and each invokes His aid against the other. It may seem strange that any men should dare to ask a just God's assistance in wringing their bread from the sweat of other men's faces, but let us judge not, that we be not judged. The prayers of both could not be answered. That of neither has been answered fully. The Almighty has His own purposes. "Woe unto the world because of offenses; for it must needs be that offenses come, but woe to that man by whom the offense cometh." If we shall suppose that American slavery is one of those offenses which, in the providence of God, must needs come, but which, having continued through His appointed time, He now wills to remove, and that He gives to both North and South this terrible war as the woe due to those by whom the offense came, shall we discern therein any departure from those divine attributes which the believers in a living God always ascribe to Him? Fondly do we hope, fervently do we pray, that this mighty scourge of war may speedily pass away. Yet, if God wills that it continue until all the wealth piled by the bondsman's two hundred and fifty years of unrequited toil shall be sunk, and until every drop of blood drawn with the lash shall be paid by another drawn with the sword, as was said three thousand years ago, so still it must be said, "The judgments of the Lord are true and righteous altogether."

With malice toward none, with charity for all, with firmness in the right as God gives us to see the right, let us strive on to finish the work we are in, to bind up the nation's wounds, to care for him who shall have borne the battle and for his widow and his orphan, to do all which may achieve and cherish a just and lasting peace among ourselves and with all nations.

3.8

General Dwight D. Eisenhower

D-DAY MESSAGE
(JUNE 6, 1944)

Soldiers, Sailors and Airmen of the Allied Expeditionary Forces:

You are about to embark upon the Great Crusade, toward which we have striven these many months. The eyes of the world are upon you. The hopes and prayers of liberty-loving people everywhere march with you. In company with our brave Allies and brothers-in-arms on other Fronts you will bring about the destruction of the German war machine, the elimination of Nazi tyranny over oppressed peoples of Europe, and security for ourselves in a free world.

Your task will not be an easy one. Your enemy is well trained, well equipped and battle-hardened. He will fight savagely.

But this is the year 1944. Much has happened since the Nazi triumphs of 1940–41. The United Nations have inflicted upon the Germans great defeats, in open battle, man-to-man.

Our air offensive has seriously reduced their strength in the air and their capacity to wage war on the ground. Our Home Fronts have given us an overwhelming superiority in weapons and munitions of war, and placed at our disposal great reserves of trained fighting men. The tide has turned. The free men of the world are marching together to victory.

I have full confidence in your courage, devotion to duty, and skill in battle. We will accept nothing less than full victory.

Good Luck! And let us all beseech the blessing of Almighty God upon this great and noble undertaking.

3.9

President Franklin Delano Roosevelt

D-DAY PRAYER
(JUNE 6, 1944)

My Fellow Americans:

Last night, when I spoke with you about the fall of Rome, I knew at that moment that troops of the United States and our Allies were crossing the Channel in another and greater operation. It has come to pass with success thus far.

And so, in this poignant hour, I ask you to join with me in prayer:

Almighty God: Our sons, pride of our nation, this day have set upon a mighty endeavor, a struggle to preserve our Republic, our religion, and our civilization, and to set free a suffering humanity.

Lead them straight and true; give strength to their arms, stoutness to their hearts, steadfastness in their faith.

They will need Thy blessings. Their road will be long and hard. For the enemy is strong. He may hurl back our forces. Success may not come with rushing speed, but we shall return again and again; and we know that by Thy grace, and by the righteousness of our cause, our sons will triumph.

They will be sore tried, by night and by day, without rest—until the victory is won. The darkness will be rent by noise and flame. Men's souls will be shaken with the violences of war.

For these men are lately drawn from the ways of peace. They fight not for the lust of conquest. They fight to end conquest. They fight to liberate. They fight to let justice arise, and tolerance and goodwill among all Thy people. They yearn but for the end of battle, for their return to the haven of home.

Some will never return. Embrace these, Father, and receive them, Thy heroic servants, into Thy kingdom.

And for us at home—fathers, mothers, children, wives, sisters, and brothers of brave men overseas, whose thoughts and prayers are ever with them—help us, Almighty God, to rededicate ourselves in renewed faith in Thee in this hour of great sacrifice.

Many people have urged that I call the nation into a single day of special prayer. But because the road is long and the desire is great, I ask that our people devote themselves in a continuance of prayer. As we rise to each new day, and again when each day is spent, let words of prayer be on our lips, invoking Thy help to our efforts.

Give us strength, too—strength in our daily tasks, to redouble the contributions we make in the physical and the material support of our armed forces.

And let our hearts be stout, to wait out the long travail, to bear sorrows that may come, to impart our courage unto our sons wheresoever they may be.

And, O Lord, gives us faith. Give us faith in Thee; faith in our sons; faith in each other; faith in our united crusade. Let not the keenness of our spirit ever be dulled. Let not the impacts of temporary events, of temporal matters of but fleeting moment—let not these deter us in our unconquerable purpose.

With Thy blessing, we shall prevail over the unholy forces of our enemy. Help us to conquer the apostles of greed and racial arrogances. Lead us to the saving of our country, and with our sister nations into a world unity that will spell a sure peace—a peace invulnerable to the schemings of unworthy men. And a peace that will let all of men live in freedom, reaping the just rewards of their honest toil.

Thy will be done, Almighty God.

Amen.

3.10

President John F. Kennedy

INAUGURAL ADDRESS
(JANUARY 20, 1961)

Vice President Johnson, Mr. Speaker, Mr. Chief Justice, President Eisenhower, Vice President Nixon, President Truman, reverend clergy, fellow citizens:

We observe today not a victory of party but a celebration of freedom—symbolizing an end as well as a beginning—signifying renewal as well as change. For I have sworn before you and Almighty God the same solemn oath our forebears prescribed nearly a century and three-quarters ago.

The world is very different now. For man holds in his mortal hands the power to abolish all forms of human poverty and all forms of human life. And yet the same revolutionary beliefs for which our forebears fought are still at issue around the globe—the belief that the rights of man come not from the generosity of the state but from the hand of God.

We dare not forget today that we are the heirs of that first revolution. Let the word go forth from this time and place, to friend and foe alike, that the torch has been passed to a new generation of Americans—born in this century, tempered by war, disciplined by a hard and bitter peace, proud of our ancient heritage—and unwilling to witness or permit the slow undoing of those human rights to which this nation has always been committed, and to which we are committed today at home and around the world.

Let every nation know, whether it wishes us well or ill, that we shall pay any price, bear any burden, meet any hardship, support any friend, oppose any foe to assure the survival and the success of liberty. This much we pledge—and more.

To those old allies whose cultural and spiritual origins we share, we pledge the loyalty of faithful friends. United, there is little we cannot do in a host of cooperative ventures. Divided, there is little we can do—for we dare not meet a powerful challenge at odds and split asunder.

To those new states whom we welcome to the ranks of the free, we pledge our word that one form of colonial control shall not have passed away merely to be replaced by a far more iron tyranny. We shall not always expect to find them supporting our view. But we shall always hope to find them strongly supporting their own freedom—and to remember that, in the past, those who foolishly sought power by riding the back of the tiger ended up inside.

To those people in the huts and villages of half the globe struggling to break the bonds of mass misery, we pledge our best efforts to help them help themselves, for whatever period is required—not because the Communists may be doing it, not because we seek their votes, but because it is right. If a free society cannot help the many who are poor, it cannot save the few who are rich.

To our sister republics south of our border, we offer a special pledge—to convert our good words into good deeds—in a new alliance for progress—to assist free men and free governments in casting off the chains of poverty. But this peaceful revolution of hope cannot become the prey of hostile powers. Let all our neighbors know that we shall join with them to oppose aggression or subversion anywhere in the Americas. And let every other power know that this hemisphere intends to remain the master of its own house.

To that world assembly of sovereign states, the United Nations, our last best hope in an age where the instruments of war have far outpaced the instruments of peace, we renew our pledge of support—to prevent it from becoming merely a forum for invective—to strengthen its shield of the new and the weak—and to enlarge the area in which its writ may run.

Finally, to those nations who would make themselves our adversary, we offer not a pledge but a request: that both sides begin anew the quest for peace, before the dark powers of destruction unleashed by science engulf all humanity in planned or accidental self-destruction.

We dare not tempt them with weakness. For only when our arms are sufficient beyond doubt can we be certain beyond doubt that they will never be employed. But neither can two great and powerful groups of nations take comfort from our present course—both sides overburdened by the cost of modern weapons, both rightly alarmed by the steady spread of the deadly atom, yet both racing to alter that uncertain balance of terror that stays the hand of mankind's final war. So let us begin anew—remembering on both sides that civility is not a sign of weakness, and sincerity is always subject to proof. Let us never negotiate out of fear. But let us never fear to negotiate.

Let both sides explore what problems unite us instead of belaboring those problems which divide us.

Let both sides, for the first time, formulate serious and precise proposals for the inspection and control of arms—and bring the absolute power to destroy other nations under the absolute control of all nations.

Let both sides seek to invoke the wonders of science instead of its terror. Together let us explore the stars, conquer the deserts, eradicate disease, tap the ocean depths and encourage the arts and commerce.

Let both sides unite to heed in all corners of the earth the command of Isaiah—to "undo the heavy burdens . . . [and] let the oppressed go free."

And if a beach-head of co-operation may push back the jungle of suspicion, let both sides join in creating a new endeavor; not a new balance of power, but a new world of law, where the strong are just and the weak secure and the peace preserved. All this will not be finished in the first 100 days. Nor will it be finished in the first 1,000 days, not in the life of this Administration, nor even perhaps in our lifetime on this planet. But let us begin.

In your hands, my fellow citizens, more than mine, will rest the final success or failure of our course. Since this country was founded, each generation of Americans has been summoned to give testimony to its national loyalty. The graves of young Americans who answered the call to service surround the globe.

Now the trumpet summons us again—not as a call to bear arms, though arms we need—not as a call to battle, though embattled we are—but a call to bear the burden of a long twilight struggle year in and year out, "rejoicing in hope, patient in tribulation"—a struggle against the common enemies of man: tyranny, poverty, disease and war itself.

Can we forge against these enemies a grand and global alliance, north and south, east and west, that can assure a more fruitful life for all mankind? Will you join in that historic effort?

In the long history of the world, only a few generations have been granted the role of defending freedom in its hour of maximum danger. I do not shrink from this responsibility—I welcome it. I do not believe that any of us would exchange places with any other people or any other generation. The energy, the faith, the devotion which we bring to this endeavor will light our country and all who serve it—and the glow from that fire can truly light the world.

And so, my fellow Americans: ask not what your country can do for you—ask what you can do for your country.

My fellow citizens of the world: ask not what America will do for you, but what together we can do for the freedom of man.

Finally, whether you are citizens of America or citizens of the world, ask of us here the same high standards of strength and sacrifice which we ask of you. With a good conscience our only sure reward, with history the final judge of our deeds, let us go forth to lead the land we love, asking His blessing and His help, but knowing that here on earth God's work must truly be our own.

3.11

President Bill Clinton

OKLAHOMA CITY SPEECH
(APRIL 23, 1995)

Thank you very much. Governor Keating and Mrs. Keating, Reverend Graham, to the families of those who have been lost and wounded, to the people of Oklahoma City, who have endured so much, and the people of this wonderful state, to all of you who are here as our fellow Americans.

I am honored to be here today to represent the American people. But I have to tell you that Hillary and I also come as parents, as husband and wife, as people who were your neighbors for some of the best years of our lives.

Today our nation joins with you in grief. We mourn with you. We share your hope against hope that some may still survive. We thank all those who have worked so heroically to save lives and to solve this crime—those here in Oklahoma and those who are all across this great land, and many who left their own lives to come here to work hand in hand with you.

We pledge to do all we can to help you heal the injured, to rebuild this city, and to bring to justice those who did this evil.

This terrible sin took the lives of our American family, innocent children in that building, only because their parents were trying to be good parents as well as good workers; citizens in the building going about their daily business; and many there who served the rest of us—who worked to help the elderly and the disabled, who worked to support our farmers and our veterans, who worked to enforce our laws and to protect us. Let us say clearly, they served us well, and we are grateful.

But for so many of you they were also neighbors and friends. You saw them at church or the PTA meetings, at the civic clubs, at the ball park. You know them in ways that all the rest of America could not. And to all the members of the families here present who have suffered loss, though we share your grief, your pain is unimaginable, and we know that. We cannot undo it. That is God's work.

Our words seem small beside the loss you have endured. But I found a few I wanted to share today. I've received a lot of letters in these last terrible days. One stood out because it came from a young widow and a mother of three whose own husband was murdered with over 200 other Americans when Pan Am 103 was shot down. Here is what that woman said I should say to you today:

> The anger you feel is valid, but you must not allow yourselves to be consumed by it. The hurt you feel must not be allowed to turn into hate, but instead into the search for justice. The loss you feel must not paralyze your own lives. Instead, you must try to pay tribute to your loved ones by continuing to do all the things they left undone, thus ensuring they did not die in vain.

Wise words from one who also knows.

You have lost too much, but you have not lost everything. And you have certainly not lost America, for we will stand with you for as many tomorrows as it takes.

If ever we needed evidence of that, I could only recall the words of Governor and Mrs. Keating. If anybody thinks that Americans are mostly mean and selfish, they ought to come to Oklahoma. If anybody thinks Americans have lost the capacity for love and caring and courage, they ought to come to Oklahoma.

To all my fellow Americans beyond this hall, I say, one thing we owe those who have sacrificed is the duty to purge ourselves of the dark forces which gave rise to this evil. They are forces that threaten our common peace, our freedom, our way of life.

Let us teach our children that the God of comfort is also the God of righteousness. Those who trouble their own house will inherit the wind. Justice will prevail.

Let us let our own children know that we will stand against the forces of fear. When there is talk of hatred, let us stand up and talk against it. When there is talk of violence, let us stand up and talk against it. In the face of death, let us honor life. As St. Paul admonished us, let us not be overcome by evil, but overcome evil with good.

Yesterday Hillary and I had the privilege of speaking with some children of other federal employees—children like those who were lost here. And one little girl said something we will never forget. She said, we should all plant a tree in memory of the children. So this morning before we got on the plane to come here, at the White House, we planted a tree in honor of the children of Oklahoma.

It was a dogwood with its wonderful spring flower and its deep, enduring roots. It embodies the lesson of the Psalms—that the life of a good person is like a tree whose leaf does not wither.

My fellow Americans, a tree takes a long time to grow, and wounds take a long time to heal. But we must begin. Those who are lost now belong to God. Some day we will be with them. But until that happens, their legacy must be our lives.

Thank you all, and God bless you.

3.12

President George W. Bush

REMARKS AT THE NATIONAL DAY OF PRAYER AND REMEMBRANCE
(SEPTEMBER 14, 2001)

We are here in the middle hour of our grief. So many have suffered so great a loss, and today we express our nation's sorrow. We come before God to pray for the missing and the dead, and for those who loved them. On Tuesday, our country was attacked with deliberate and massive cruelty. We have seen the images of fire and ashes and bent steel.

Now come the names, the list of casualties we are only beginning to read:

They are the names of men and women who began their day at a desk or in an airport, busy with life.

They are the names of people who faced death and in their last moments called home to say, be brave and I love you.

They are the names of passengers who defied their murderers and prevented the murder of others on the ground.

They are the names of men and women who wore the uniform of the United States and died at their posts.

They are the names of rescuers—the ones whom death found running up the stairs and into the fires to help others.

We will read all these names. We will linger over them and learn their stories, and many Americans will weep.

To the children and parents and spouses and families and friends of the lost, we offer the deepest sympathy of the nation. And I assure you, you are not alone. Just three days removed from these events, Americans do not yet have the distance of history, but our responsibility to history is already clear: to answer these attacks and rid the world of evil.

War has been waged against us by stealth and deceit and murder. This nation is peaceful, but fierce when stirred to anger. This conflict was begun on the timing and terms of others; it will end in a way and at an hour of our choosing. Our purpose as a nation is firm, yet our wounds as a people are recent and unhealed and lead us to pray. In many of our prayers this week, there's a searching and an honesty. At St. Patrick's Cathedral in New York, on Tuesday, a woman said, "I pray to God to give us a sign that He's still here."

Others have prayed for the same, searching hospital to hospital, carrying pictures of those still missing. God's signs are not always the ones we look for. We learn in tragedy that His purposes are not always our own, yet the prayers of private suffering, whether in our homes or in this great cathedral, are known and heard and understood. There are prayers that help us last through the day or endure the night. There are prayers of friends and strangers that give us strength for the journey, and there are prayers that yield our will to a Will greater than our own.

This world He created is of moral design. Grief and tragedy and hatred are only for a time. Goodness, remembrance and love have no end, and the Lord of life holds all who die and all who mourn.

It is said that adversity introduces us to ourselves. This is true of a nation as well. In this trial, we have been reminded and the world has seen that our fellow Americans are generous and kind, resourceful and brave.

We see our national character in rescuers working past exhaustion, in long lines of blood donors, in thousands of citizens who have asked to work and serve in any way possible.

And we have seen our national character in eloquent acts of sacrifice:

Inside the World Trade Center, one man who could have saved himself stayed until the end and at the side of his quadriplegic friend.
A beloved priest died giving the last rites to a firefighter.
Two office workers, finding a disabled stranger, carried her down 68 floors to safety.
A group of men drove through the night from Dallas to Washington to bring skin grafts for burned victims.

In these acts and many others, Americans showed a deep commitment to one another and an abiding love for our country.

Today, we feel what Franklin Roosevelt called, "the warm courage of national unity." This is a unity of every faith and every background. It has joined together political parties and both houses of Congress. It is evident in services of prayer and candlelight vigils and American flags, which are displayed in pride and waved in defiance. Our unity is a kinship of grief and a steadfast resolve to prevail against our enemies. And this unity against terror is now extending across the world.

America is a nation full of good fortune, with so much to be grateful for, but we are not spared from suffering. In every generation, the world has produced enemies of human freedom. They have attacked America because we are freedom's home and defender, and the commitment of our Fathers is now the calling of our time.

On this national day of prayer and remembrance, we ask Almighty God to watch over our nation and grant us patience and resolve in all that is to come. We pray that He will comfort and console those who now walk in sorrow. We thank Him for each life we now must mourn, and the promise of a life to come.

As we've been assured, neither death nor life nor angels nor principalities, nor powers nor things present nor things to come nor height nor depth can separate us from God's love. May He bless the souls of the departed. May He comfort our own. And may He always guide our country.

God bless America.

Notes

1. Why something so obvious should have escaped serious analytical attention is in itself an interesting problem. Part of the reason is probably the controversial nature of the subject. From the earliest years of the nineteenth century, conservative religious and political groups have argued that Christianity is, in fact, the national religion. Some of them have from time to time and as recently as the 1950s proposed constitutional amendments that would explicitly recognize the sovereignty of Christ. In defending the doctrine of separation of church and state, opponents of such groups have denied that the national polity has, intrinsically, anything to do with religion at all. The moderates on this issue have insisted that the American state has taken a permissive and indeed supportive attitude toward religious groups (tax exemption, etc.), thus favoring religion but still missing the positive institutionalization with which I am concerned. But part of the reason this issue has been left in obscurity is certainly due to the peculiarly Western concept of religion as denoting a single type of collectivity of which an individual can be a member of one and only one at a time. The Durkheimian notion that every group has a religious dimension, which would be seen as obvious in southern or eastern Asia, is foreign to us. This obscures the recognition of such dimensions in our society.

2. God is mentioned or referred to in all inaugural addresses but Washington's second, which is a very brief (two paragraphs) and perfunctory acknowledgment. It is not without interest that the actual word God does not appear until Monroe's second inaugural, March 5, 1821. In his first inaugural, Washington refers to God as "that Almighty Being who rules the universe," "Great Author of every public and private good," "Invisible Hand," and "benign Parent of the Human Race." John Adams refers to God as "Providence," "Being who is supreme over all," "Patron of Order," "Fountain of Justice," and "Protector in all ages of the world of virtuous liberty." Jefferson speaks of "that Infinite Power which rules the destinies of the universe," and "that Being in whose hands we are." Madison speaks of "that Almighty Being whose power regulates the destiny of nations," and "Heaven." Monroe uses "Providence" and "the Almighty" in his first inaugural and finally "Almighty God" in his second. See *Inaugural Addresses of the Presidents of the United States from George Washington 1789 to Harry S. Truman 1949*, 82nd Congress, 2nd Session, House Document No. 540, 1952.

3. For example, Abiel Abbot, pastor of the First Church in Haverhill, Massachusetts, delivered a Thanksgiving sermon in 1799, *Traits of Resemblance in the People of the United States of America to Ancient Israel*, in which he said, "It has been often remarked that the people of the United States come nearer to a parallel with Ancient Israel, than any other nation upon the globe. Hence 'Our American Israel' is a term frequently used; and common consent allows it apt and proper" (Kohn 1961, 665).

4. That the Mosaic analogy was present in the minds of leaders at the very moment of the birth of the republic is indicated in the designs proposed by Franklin and Jefferson for a seal of the United States of America. Together with Adams, they formed a committee of three delegated by the Continental Congress on July 4, 1776, to draw up the new device. "Franklin proposed as the device Moses lifting up his wand and dividing the Red Sea while Pharaoh

was overwhelmed by its waters, with the motto 'Rebellion to tyrants is obedience to God.' Jefferson proposed the children of Israel in the wilderness 'led by a cloud by day and a pillar of fire at night' (Stokes 1950, 467–8).

5. How extensive the activity associated with Memorial Day can be is indicated by Warner: "The sacred symbolic behavior of Memorial Day, in which scores of the town's organizations are involved, is ordinarily divided into four periods. During the year separate rituals are held by many of the associations for their dead, and many of these activities are connected with later Memorial Day events. In the second phase, preparations are made during the last three or four weeks for the ceremony itself, and some of the associations perform public rituals. The third phase consists of scores of rituals held in all the cemeteries, churches, and halls of the associations. These rituals consist of speeches and highly ritualized behavior. They last for two days and are climaxed by the fourth and last phase, in which all the separate celebrants gather in the center of the business district on the afternoon of Memorial Day. The separate organizations, with their members in uniform or with fitting insignia, march through the town, visit the shrines and monuments of the hero dead, and, finally, enter the cemetery. Here dozens of ceremonies are held, most of them highly symbolic and formalized." During these various ceremonies Lincoln is continually referred to and the Gettysburg Address recited many times (Warner 1962, 8–9).

6. It is important to distinguish this *normative* preservationist approach from the more *historical* one discussed earlier and as championed by the likes of Chief Justice Rehnquist, Justice O'Connor, the petitions of *Elk Grove v. Newdow* (*Elk Grove v. Newdow* 2004), and the Executive Branch of the federal government, as represented by Solicitor General Ted Olsen's *Reply Brief for the United States as Respondent Supporting Petitioners*.

7. See Hamburger 2002 for the argument that the development of the doctrine of "the separation of church and state" was motivated by nativist, anti-Catholic prejudice in the mid-nineteenth century. See Laycock 2003 for a trenchant critique of Hamburger's claims.

8. Perhaps owing to media criticism, they later issued a clarification affirming the truth of Christianity, but conceding that "it is not our position that America's Constitution forbids representatives of religions other than Christianity from praying before Congress"(Koff 2000). We thank Professor Diana Eck for originally bringing to our attention these cases of resistance to the Hindu priest and the Dalai Lama.

9. Aside from distinguishing between *priestly* and *prophetic* modes of civil religion, Marty makes a further distinction between "the Nation under God" and "the Nation as Self-Transcendent." This latter form is when God language is absent entirely and thus the Nation itself becomes the sacred and transcendent entity (1974).

10. That is, that the nation is accountable to God, or to some ideal (e.g. "democracy"). See Marty 1974 for more on this point.

11. See White (2002) for more on the immediate negative reaction to what many now consider to have been Lincoln's greatest speech. While Lincoln is generally considered to be America's civil theologian *par excellence*, his thought raises certain difficulties. For example, the idea of America as a "new nation" proclaimed in the Gettysburg Address is based on a founding myth of voluntary migration, and the myth's overall effect-whether intended or not-has been to obscure the record of slaves and Native Americans, who were either exploited or subjected to genocidal extermination for the nation's advancement (Angrosino 2002, 249).

12. Admittedly, *legal* persecution for such conscientiousness all but abated after the *West Virginia v. Barnette* (1943) decision. Yet harassment for those who elect not to participate in Pledge of Allegiance ceremonies still continues even today.

13. Of the presidents before the Civil War, only John Adams, James Buchanan, and Abraham Lincoln offer no explicit confession of inadequacy in their addresses.

14. We acknowledge that this is a narrow construction of American exceptionalism. The many permutations of American exceptionalism have been much discussed elsewhere and need not be discussed here.

15. Emphasis on form, Tocqueville tells us, is a legacy of aristocracy (1954, 275).

16. We focus here on the implications for political society. As Christians, we believe that the rhetoric in the recent expressions of civil religion is false theology.

17. Even vacations in a democracy, Tocqueville observed, leave us exhausted (Tocqueville 1954, v.2, bk. 2, ch. 13).

18. So far as I can tell, credit for coining these labels belongs to Ross Gittell and Avis Vidal (1998, 8).

19. For simplicity's sake I use the term *church* here to refer to all religious institutions of whatever faith, including mosques, temples, and synagogues.

20. Author's analysis of General Social Survey and DDB Needham Life Style data, controlling for education, income, full-time employment, gender, marital and parental status, urban/rural residence, age, and race. This strong correlation between religiosity and associationism was reported in the 1950s (Hausknecht 1962, 54; Lazerwitz 1962).

21. Author's analysis of 1996 National Election Study.

22. In the DDB Needham Life Style surveys, attendance at church and agreement that "religion is important in my life" are more powerful predictors of club attendance, volunteering, visiting with friends, and entertaining at home than is education. On virtually all measures of civic engagement in the Roper Social and Political Trends surveys, the difference between those who attended church last week and those who did not is as large as the difference between high school and college graduates.

23. Author's analysis of a Scripps-Howard/Ohio University national survey of interpersonal communication, June 1997.

24. In the DDB Needham Life Style surveys, church attendance is a much more powerful predictor of volunteering than is agreement that "religion is important to my life."

25. The greater religiosity of African Americans is confirmed by the General Social Survey, National Election Study, Roper Social and Political Trends surveys, and DDB Needham Life Style archives, as well as Verba, Schlozman, and Brady, *Voice and Equality*.

26. See also "Symposium: Surveys of U.S. Church Attendance." According to the 1996 General Social Survey, only 2 percent of people who did not attend church "last week" report that they attended some other type of religious event or meeting. Thus the standard question does not "miss" a significant number of people who attend, say, prayer meetings *instead of* church services.

27. Author's analysis of the GSS, Roper, NES, NIMH, and DDB Needham Life Style data, as well as the time diary data. (The Gallup data are not available for secondary analysis by outside scholars.) The statistical methodology underlying this conclusion is described in Firebaugh 1989 (see also Davis 1992, 301).

28. The coefficient of variation for annualized measures of church attendance rose from 0.9 (1974–75) to 1.1 (1998–99) in both the General Social Survey and the DDB Needham Life Style archives and from 7.5 (1975) to 17.3 (1995) in the Americans' Use of Time archive (Glenn 1987, 309).

29. Between 1980 and 1990 the five states that experienced the greatest *increase* in adherence to a Christian church were Mississippi, Alabama, Louisiana, South Carolina, and Georgia, while the five states that experienced the greatest *decrease* were Vermont, New Hampshire, Maine, Oregon, and Massachusetts. See *Statistical Abstract of the United States: 1996*, table 89 (see also Hammond 1992, 165). On the other hand, this regional polarization in religiosity does *not* appear in the General Social Survey, Roper Social and Political Trends, or DDB Needham Life Style data.

30. In all religions there are some ceremonies that are inherent in the substance of the faith itself, and in these nothing should on any account be changed. This is especially the case with Roman Catholicism, in which the doctrine and the form are frequently so closely united as to form but one point of belief.

CHAPTER 4

THE AMERICAN RELIGIOUS LANDSCAPE

Introduction

Integrative Essay

Introduction

Previous chapters chronicled many of the ways religion has influenced the development of American government and civic life. This chapter charts the American religious landscape—examining changing patterns of religious belief and practice and then looking at how religion operates "on the ground" in the United States, particularly as it relates to politics.

The chapter begins with Corwin Smidt's integrative essay. Noting that religion has an important effect on how Americans interact with politics, Smidt argues that social scientists and those who use their analyses (which is nearly all of us) must conceptualize and operationalize religion well. He introduces and critiques several ways that researchers try to identify and measure religious beliefs, belonging, and behavior.

Originally published in 1955 and revised in 1960, Will Herberg's classic *Protestant—Catholic—Jew* described the role of religious affiliation in American society, noting that almost all Americans saw themselves as part of one of three religious communities—Protestants, Catholics, or Jews. He argued that the three religions were interpreted in uniquely American ways, creating widespread religious agreement and fostering unity.

In the decades since Herberg's work appeared, many researchers have offered a different view, describing an increasingly diverse American religious landscape. Mark Silk's examination of religion by region describes the strong regional variety of religious practice across the nation. Sundberg's article immediately follows. He notes the recent decline among mainline Protestant (mostly white) churches and the rise of evangelical churches, arguing that political views and ideology, more than the theological differences of denominations, increasingly define the contours of the religious landscape.

The next selection, an excerpt from Mark Chaves's pioneering work, examines religion by focusing on worshipping communities instead of individual believers. He compares Roman Catholic, black Protestant, white moderate and liberal Protestant, white conservative and evangelical Protestant, and Jewish congregations, examining the variety of politically related behaviors prevalent within each.

Kellstedt and his colleagues examine individual-level survey data to measure the influence of religion on American presidential elections since the New Deal era. In particular, they examine changing patterns of party allegiance and voting behavior among five major faith traditions: evangelical Protestants, mainline Protestants, black Protestants, white Catholics, and seculars.

The next two articles, by Harris and Kelly and Morgan Kelly, respectively, examine religion and politics through the lens of race and ethnicity. Together, they add nuance and understanding to generalizations about how two major ethnic groups with deep religious ties—African Americans and Latinos—may be redistributing their party affiliations. Fredrick C. Harris's *Something Within* demonstrates how black political elites and activists utilize black religious symbols to frame political issues and to mobilize African Americans in politics.

Amaney Jamal's work utilizes survey data to explore how mosque attendance and involvement by Muslims affects political participation. Her findings indicate that mosque involvement serves as an important conduit of both civicness and political activity, with differences in levels and types of participation for black Muslims and immigrant Muslims. These results affirm that mosques, like many churches and synagogues, can be crucial incubators of civic skills.

Given the nature of its subject matter, this chapter includes only research pieces; the primary unit of analysis is the American people themselves and how the variety of their religious beliefs, belongings, and behaviors interact with politics. Surveys that try to map this interaction are conducted regularly and provide an ongoing source of new and intriguing data. Likely the most comprehensive Internet source for access to religion surveys is the American Religious Data Archive, found at www.thearda.com. Other Internet sources of useful data and analysis include the Pew Forum on Religion and Public Life (www.pewforum.org) and the American Religious Identification Survey (www.americanreligionsurvey-aris.org).

Integrative Essay

4.1

Corwin Smidt

MAKING SENSE OF THE AMERICAN RELIGIOUS LANDSCAPE

Though the First Amendment to the U.S. Constitution prohibits the establishment of a state church, the American people are and have always been religious.[1] The establishment and free exercise clauses of the First Amendment together create a religious free-market system, fostering a multiplicity of religious bodies that appeal to different theological understandings, worship styles and liturgical preferences. No American church receives support from taxes, so each must attract members and financial contributions in order to survive. Churches must be responsive to the theological and liturgical preferences of their congregations, as dissatisfied members are free to move elsewhere or start their own tradition.

This religious contribution has contributed to high levels of religiosity in the United States. National surveys consistently reveal that nearly three of five Americans claim to be *members* of religious houses of worship and even more claim some sort of religious affiliation (a less stringent form of relationship than formal membership), with approximately two of five Americans reporting weekly church attendance. Today there are more than 1500 different faith groups in the United States.[2] This multiplicity of different religious bodies has prompted the labeling of America as "the denominational society" (Greeley 1972).

Religious pluralism and pervasiveness would have little political relevance if religion functioned merely as a relatively arbitrary preference or "taste" (e.g., if it represented nothing more than whether one prefers television comedies or soap operas). In the United States, however, people's religious characteristics shape the way they think and act politically.[3] For many Americans, religion serves as the primary foundation for the basic beliefs they express, the values they hold, and the identities they articulate. Religion thus shapes their patterns of social interaction, the people with whom they discuss politics, and the kinds of information sources they use when making electoral decisions. In turn, religion affects views on what qualities are desirable in presidential candidates, what issues are important, and the appropriateness of religious discussion in presidential campaigns. Thus, if one wishes to understand American electoral politics, one also needs to understand American religion.

Classifying Religious Adherents

Because religion influences political behavior, researchers want to explore this relationship. However, religion is multifaceted in nature (encompassing beliefs, belonging, and behavior), and it is not clear just what specific facet of religion primarily shapes political attitudes and behavior. To complicate matters further, surveys can only include a limited number of questions, often with a limited number of responses. Thus researchers must carefully weigh which religion questions to ask respondents.

In examining the relationship between religion and political variables, scholars have historically focused primarily on the belonging facet of religion. But, the plethora of religious bodies with which Americans choose to associate defies easy categorization. In more recent years, however, scholars have also begun to assess religion as a cognitive phenomenon. This essay seeks to help the reader better comprehend religion as a variable in scholarly analyses by describing these two different substantive approaches (i.e., religion as a social and religion as a cognitive phenomenon) along with some of the different analytical frameworks associated with each approach that have been used to study religion and its link to American politics.

Religion as Belonging

In linking religion to politics, social scientists have generally treated religion as a social, rather than a cognitive, phenomenon. As a social phenomenon, religion is expressed in terms of belonging—through affiliation with a local church, a specific denomination, or a religious tradition, assuming that individuals within a particular affiliation share similar experiences or perspectives. Through internal patterns of association and inter-action, as well as particular religious teachings about the way religion is linked to politics, members of each group acquire similar political attitudes and behaviors, which also can be distinguished from other groups. Accordingly, as some have argued: "Belonging can matter in politics by providing a forum in which religion can be linked to political issues, parties, candidates and activities" (Kohut et al. 2000, 13). In this sense, however, religious groups are not distinctive—they simply function like other social groups.

Conventionally, social scientists have examined religious affiliation in terms of *denominational affiliation*. But given the multiplicity of denominations in the United States, survey researchers must sift through the scores, if not hundreds, of specific affiliations reported and classify them into a manageable number of categories. Obviously, researchers can use different schema to classify these highly varied responses, and the choices they make will affect the results.

Protestant, Catholic, and Jew

Most early surveys, for example, categorized respondents by broad faith traditions, asking them whether they were "Protestant, Catholic, Jewish, something else, or noth-ing in particular." This formulation may have reflected pollsters' frustration with the complexity of American religion—or perhaps acceptance of Will Herberg's (1955) argu-ments about the relevant faith groupings in America. Even if one ignores the growing pluralism of faith traditions, the great diversity of Protestantism itself argues against us-ing such broad categories. As Stark and Glock (1968, 55) noted years ago, "When we speak of 'Protestants,' as we often do in the social sciences, we (simply) spin statistical fiction. . . .," because as a category it "includes many separately constituted groups and the only possible ground for treating them collectively would be if they shared in a common vision. [But] this is clearly not the case. . . ."

Religious Families

Other scholars have used *religious families* (e.g., Baptists, Methodists, Presbyterians, Lutherans) as the unit of analysis. While an improvement on the previous classification—and perhaps useful for some theoretical purposes—the utilization of religious families has weaknesses, given the major theological, cultural, social and racial differences that separate specific denominations within the same family. Indeed, significant theological and political differences often exist between historic denominational "kin": for example, members of the Presbyterian Church in America tend to be more theologically traditionalist and politically conservative and Republican than adherents to the Presbyterian Church, U.S.A, as do members from the Free Methodist Church in comparison with members of the United Methodist Church. The "denominational families" classification scheme can obscure rather than illuminate such important political differences between different denominations within the same religious family.

Religious Tradition

Still other researchers prefer to classify adherents by *religious tradition*, a category that includes religious denominations and congregations which exhibit similar beliefs and behaviors and are interrelated in some historical and organizational fashion (Kellstedt and Green 1993; Kellstedt et al. 1996). Such traditions, for example, evangelical Protestant and mainline Protestant, exhibit several defining characteristics (Smidt 2007). First, they have a legacy rooted in specific historical events, and they develop and change slowly. Traditions "place limits on what any given individual or groups of individuals can do within the tradition and still remain within it," and, as a result, religious traditions "shape and construct individuals and cultures" and "are not merely constructed by them" (Queen 2002, 91). In addition, members of a religious tradition exhibit a characteristic way of interpreting the world, based on common beliefs and practices, though not all members necessarily hold these particular beliefs or exhibit these behaviors. Conscious identification with a tradition is not necessary for inclusion; many Southern Baptists, for example, would not identify themselves as "evangelical," although they share religious beliefs and practices with members of denominations more comfortable with the label. As Geoffrey Layman (2001, 60) has observed, religious traditions constitute "a useful and increasingly popular conceptualization of religious belonging." The concept has proven to be to be a powerful predictor of political attitudes and behavior (see, e.g. Kellstedt and Green 1993; Kellstedt et al., 1997; Kohut et al. 2000; Layman 2001; Green 2007).

For scholars using this classification method, the question remains as to which specific denominations and faiths are to be aggregated into what particular religious traditions. Within America's overwhelmingly Christian population, for example, one can differentiate among evangelical, mainline, and black Protestant traditions, the Roman Catholic tradition, and the Eastern Orthodox tradition.[4] And, with growing religious pluralism, surveys will reveal Americans of non-Christian traditions (Judaism, Islam,

Buddhism, Hinduism), although usually in numbers too small for extensive statistical analysis within one survey itself. Finally, the unaffiliated population (Hout and Fischer 2002), can be regarded as a tradition in its own right, although it includes several "types," such as unaffiliated believers (unattached to a church or denomination but exhibiting at least modest levels of religiosity), the non-religious unaffiliated, and finally, the "anti-religious"—agnostics and atheists. Each unaffiliated group includes variation in political attitudes and behavior, in much the same ways as different affiliated groups (Green 2007; Kellstedt 2008).

Religion as a Cognitive Phenomenon

While most analysts have examined religion in terms of a social phenomenon, other scholars have examined religion more in terms of a cognitive phenomenon. Here the undergirding assumption is that individuals act more on the basis of their cognitive processes as individual actors than on the basis of their group memberships and associated social interactions.

Religious Movements

It may seem somewhat confusing to start the discussion of religion as a cognitive phenomenon by referring to religious movements, as one might initially view religious movements as social phenomena. Movements seek change, and religious movements often cross denominational boundaries and occasionally even transcend religious traditions. The charismatic movement, for example, is found within both Protestantism and Catholicism. Religious movements in the late 19th and early 20th century shaped the modern evangelical and mainline Protestant traditions (e.g., the Holiness movement, the Fundamentalist movement, the Social Gospel movement), and contemporary movements have helped to restructure American religion along theological lines.

However, movements do not have formal memberships per se. Movements are made up of many different organizations, and no single organization can encapsulate a movement. Moreover, many who see themselves as part of a movement are not formal members of any particular movement organization that serves to comprise that larger movement. Consequently, when analysts study "affiliation" with a movement, they generally do so in terms of identification with that movement (a psychological phenomenon). Moreover, the referent of the movement label is much more amorphous than a denominational label (for example, "charismatic" is less concrete than "Southern Baptist" or "Bethel United Methodist Church"). As a result, it is best to view religious movement identification as primarily a cognitive or psychological phenomenon and religious affiliation more as a sociological one, as affiliation has a much more objective foundation and social basis undergirding the concept.[5]

Attempts to categorize "evangelical" Protestants highlight the difficulties of classifying respondents religiously. Many associated with denominations in the evangelical religious tradition may not identify as evangelicals. As a result, some scholars use the label "conservative Protestant" instead (Woodberry and Smith 1998; Greeley and Hout 2006), though this strategy is perhaps even more problematic.[6] But, this discrepancy between a scholar's classification and a respondent's recognition or acceptance of such a designation is not unique to religion (e.g., a scholar might well to choose to classify someone as a political conservative based on his or her political beliefs even if such a respondent would not, if asked, identify as a political conservative).

Nevertheless, rather than asking respondents for their denominational affiliation and then classifying respondents affiliated with particular denominations as being part of the evangelical Protestant tradition, other researchers have simply asked respondents if they consider themselves "born-again or evangelical Christians." But this too is highly problematic. If someone answers affirmatively, it is unclear whether the response is in reference to "born again" or to "evangelical." Moreover, conceptually, "born again" could connote an experience, an identification, or both. The *experience* can be of two types: an identifiable point in time when an individual had a religious conversion experience, or a gradual experience in which the individual is unable to point to a specific time for the transformation. But, "born again" could also connote an *identification* with a movement or group of people, "the born-again crowd." Such ambiguities make this a poor measure for capturing evangelical respondents. And, while many (though far from all) evangelical Protestants claim to be born again (or identify as an evangelical), so do some members of other faith traditions (regardless of whether the born-again variable is assessed in terms of an experience or an identity).[7]

Religious Beliefs

A final method of classification is attempting to group respondents according to religious beliefs. Beliefs are central to any understanding of religion. As Stark and Glock (1968, 16) put it, "theology, or religious belief, is at the heart of the faith." Such emphasis assumes that human behavior is governed by cognitive processes and that individuals relate to the world in an atomistic rather than organic fashion. Thus, religion embodies the "fundamental beliefs, ideas, ethical codes, and symbols associated with a religious tradition, including what others call a theology or belief system" (Wald and Calhoun-Brown 2007, 26). These beliefs have social consequences, as "people act politically, economically, and socially in keeping with their ultimate beliefs," in that "their values, mores, and actions . . . are an outgrowth of the god or gods they hold at the center of their being" (Swierenga 1990, 154). As a result, religious beliefs should serve either as a constraint on, or a generator of, political beliefs, attitudes, and behavior.

Because beliefs are viewed as the driving force linking religion to political attitudes and behavior, their effects are understood to be more "immediate" and direct, the product of internal psychology (Wald and Smidt 1993, 32). But, if beliefs are the driving force in the linkage between religion and politics, then which beliefs are central? For example, for a respondent to be categorized as "evangelical" by the Barna Research Group he or she must claim to be born-again, state that his or her faith is very important, and adhere to seven additional beliefs.[8] The resulting categorization creates a rather arbitrary group that lacks much historical or conceptual meaning, as anyone (including Roman Catholics, Eastern Orthodox or Latter-day Saints) who meets such criteria is placed in the "evangelical" subgroup. However, in everyday practice, social (including religious) groups are defined mostly by affiliation, *not* by uniformity of belief. Not all Democrats or Republicans hold identical beliefs; nor do all Catholics or Mormons. As a result, Barna's "evangelicals" are unlikely to recognize each other as fellow believers belonging to the same religious group or exhibit any social cohesion or relative similarity in political attitudes and behavior.

Implications

The choice of one's definitional approach affects one's resultant findings. For example, the estimated proportion of evangelical Protestants within American society varies considerably by the approach adopted. Roughly speaking, evangelical Protestants constitute about a quarter of the population when measured in terms of affiliation, about one-seventh when defined in terms of identification, and less than one-tenth of the population when specified in terms of Barna's list of beliefs. Similarly, the political characteristics of those falling within the evangelical Protestant category will vary greatly by the approach adopted. Because many more African Americans fall into Barna's evangelical category than in other ways of classifying evangelicals,[9] his reported proportion of evangelicals voting Democratic in an election is far higher than when evangelicals are defined in terms of self-identification or religious affiliation.

Religion and Political Behavior

With this multiplicity of facets related to religion, the next question is: which of these best explains political behavior? For example, do religious beliefs cause people to act different politically? Or do patterns of religious belonging or affiliation? Perhaps religious behavior and level of religious commitment capture the primary effects of religion on political variables. Alternatively, might different facets of religion have distinct effects on partisan affiliations and voting decisions, and each in some way contribute to such differences?

Historically, the primary facet of religion that affected political behavior was religious affiliation. Different religious groups aligned themselves with one of the major political parties. Ethnocultural historians (e.g., Jensen 1971; Formisano 1983; Swierenga 1990) have documented this relationship during different party systems, and social scientists (e.g., Lazarsfeld et al. 1944; Berelson et al. 1954; Campbell et al. 1960) have long employed this approach to assessing religion within American politics. This relationship between religious affiliation and political preferences prevailed from the early years of the Republic through into the 1980s, as religiously one's denominational affiliation largely served as the basis of one's partisan affiliation. The different lifestyles, worldviews, and reference groups associated with people of different religious faiths helped shape their differential preferences for the two major parties and their respective platforms and candidates.

Over time, the extent to which members of a particular religious group may choose to align themselves with a specific political party has waxed and waned. During the New Deal era, Roman Catholics were highly aligned with the Democratic Party, while today their votes are much more evenly divided between the two major parties (Prendergast 1999). Nevertheless, while the specific nature of the relationship may change (e.g., while Southern Baptists may have been largely Democratic in the 1930s but largely Republicans now), the general phenomenon of religious groups aligning themselves with political parties has long been an important factor in American politics that has served to shape and color each political order. But, across these different time periods, highly religious people were found on both sides of the political divide, and both partisan sides were described largely in terms of different group affiliations.

An Emerging New Order?

Recent evidence suggests that yet another religious variable is gaining political salience, pointing to a possible new religious order in American politics, termed a "religious restructuring" by some scholars and a "theological" reordering by other scholars. Over the past five decades, religious *beliefs* and *commitment* have come to rival, and perhaps may eventually replace, religious affiliation in shaping the way in which religion relates to politics (Green 2007; Smidt et al. 2010). Religious traditionalists from a variety of affiliations align against secularists and modernists, creating the "God gap" in American politics. The God gap refers to the tendency for the more religiously observant to vote Republican and the tendency for the less religiously observant to vote Democratic. Membership in a particular religious tradition is less relevant than the strength of religious belief and commitment. Those who hold traditional religious beliefs, regardless of faith or tradition, align on one side of the political divide, while modernists are on the other.

This religious divide attracted significant attention after the 2004 election. Exit polls revealed that the largest portion of voters cited "moral values" as the most important issue of the campaign and that high percentages of those who did so voted for Bush. The mobilization of conservative Christians, particularly in states with gay marriage initiatives on the ballot, was discussed with some frequency. But, the election cleavage was perhaps best captured by the relationship between attendance at worship services and vote choice in 2004. As voters became more observant religiously, they became less likely to vote for Democrats. Following that election, a series of polls revealed that only a small minority of Americans thought the Democratic Party was "friendly to religion." These findings reflected a shift in the nature of the link between religion and political behavior.

However, recent elections also suggest that religious affiliation may still shape the electoral order more strongly than religious belief. Both the Democratic Party and Democratic presidential candidates sought to contest the perception that the Republican Party was the party of religious people while the Democratic Party was the party of secularists. And, during the 2008 presidential campaign, Barack Obama employed religious rhetoric as well as a religious strategy in seeking to win the nomination of his party and the general election in the fall.

But did the election of Obama substantially change the "God gap" in American politics? Given the margin of victory, one might anticipate that it did. Moreover, the election seemingly was fought largely over economic, rather than social, issues which might further lead one to anticipate some substantial decline in religious cleavages in voting. But, in the end, the basic patterns in religious voting found in the 2004 election continued to hold true in the 2008 election. Both religious affiliation and religious beliefs were relatively equivalent in their ability to account for presidential vote decisions in 2008 (Smidt et al. 2010). Thus, despite Obama's convincing victory, the results of the election revealed little evidence of any fundamental shift in the structure of faith-based voting.

Nevertheless, though it remains unclear whether religious beliefs and commitment will surpass religious affiliation as the primary religious determinant of political behavior, religion will continue to shape American politics. Because Americans are a fairly religious people (particularly compared to other western democracies), if a party or candidate appears to be "anti-religious" in their stance or policy positions it is likely to have politically disadvantageous consequences. But, the consequences of this religious divide in American politics move far beyond immediate electoral results. When one party is perceived as the religious party and the other as the non-religious party, it magnifies the political stakes for many of those who take their religious faith seriously. Elections become almost a "holy battle" pitting good against evil, as the election appears to be a matter of ultimate, rather than relative, concern. Political debate becomes much more heated, relationships with those affiliated with the opposite party become much less civil, and political abuses are likely to occur as the "ends begin to justify the means."

Thus, as in the past, religion will continue to shape American politics in the future. Despite the considerable difficulties in classifying religious adherents, social scientists must continue research that helps explain the particular ways in which religion shapes politics in the United States.

Research Pieces

4.2

Will Herberg

PROTESTANT—CATHOLIC—JEW (1960)

It is the thesis of the present work that both the religiousness and the secularism of the American people derive from very much the same sources, and that both become more intelligible when seen against the background of certain deep-going sociological processes that have transformed the face of American life in the course of the past generation. The distinctive character of American religiosity, so perplexing at first sight in its contradictions and discrepancies, becomes somewhat more intelligible when so interpreted, and the entire religious situation is viewed in its essential relation to the inner development of American society. American religion and American society would seem to be so closely interrelated as to make it virtually impossible to understand either without reference to the other. . . .

Of the immigrant who came to this country it was expected that, sooner or later, either in his own person or through his children, he would give up virtually everything he had brought with him from the "old country"—his language, his nationality, his manner of life—and would adopt the ways of his new home. Within broad limits, however, his becoming an American did not involve his abandoning the old religion in favor of some native American substitute. Quite the contrary, not only was he expected to retain his old religion, as he was not expected to retain his old language or nationality, but such was the shape of America that it was largely in and through his religion that he, or rather his children and grandchildren, found an identifiable place in American life.

. . . In short, while America knows no national or cultural minorities except as temporary, transitional phenomena, it does know a free variety and plurality of religions; and it is as members of a religious group that the great mass of Americans identify themselves to establish their social location once they have really sloughed off their immigrant foreignness.

For all its wide variety of regional, ethnic, and other differences, America today may be conceived, as it is indeed conceived by most Americans, as one great community divided into three big sub-communities religiously defined, all equally American in their identification with the "American Way of Life." For the third generation [of immigrants], which somehow wishes to "remember" of its background what the second generation was so anxious to "forget" and which is so concerned with finding its place in the larger community but not at the expense of its Americanness, this tripartite structure of American society into religious communities is most welcome and intelligible. And no wonder, since it has been the work largely of this third generation.

Just as sociologically we may describe the emerging social structure of America as one great community divided into three big sub-communities religiously defined, all equally American, so from another angle we might describe Protestantism, Catholicism, and Judaism in America as three great branches or divisions of "American religion." The assumption underlying the view shared by most Americans, at least at moments when they think in "nonsectarian" terms, is not so much that the three religious communities possess an underlying theological unity, which of course they do, but rather that they are three diverse representations of the same "spiritual values," the "spiritual values" American democracy is presumed to stand for (the fatherhood of God and brotherhood of man, the dignity of the individual human being, etc.). That is, at bottom, why no one is expected to change his religion as he becomes American;[10] since each of the religions is equally and authentically American, the American is expected to express his religious affirmation in that form which has come to him with his family and ethnic heritage. Particular denominational affiliations and loyalties within each of the communities (only Protestantism and Judaism come into question here, since Catholicism has no inner denominational lines) are not necessarily denied, or even depreciated, but they are held to be distinctly secondary. With some important exceptions, it is becoming more and more true that the American, when he thinks of religion, thinks of it primarily in terms of the three categories we have designated as religious communities.

All this has far-reaching consequences for the place of religion in the totality of American life. With the religious community as the primary context of self-identification and social location, and with Protestantism, Catholicism, and Judaism as three culturally diverse representations of the same "spiritual values," it becomes virtually mandatory for the American to place himself in one or another of these groups. It is not external pressure but inner necessity that compels him. For being a Protestant, a Catholic, or a Jew is understood as the specific way, and increasingly perhaps the only way, of being an American and locating oneself in American society. . . .

4.3

Mark Silk

RELIGION AND REGION IN AMERICAN PUBLIC LIFE (2005)

Introduction

In 1987, I moved from Milton, Massachusetts, to Decatur, Georgia, to take a job at the *Atlanta Journal Constitution*. The first day I went to work, the woman who lived across the street corralled my wife at the mailbox and asked what church we all belonged to. With visions of a cross burning on the front lawn, my wife allowed as how, actually, we were Jewish and did not belong to any church. Within half an hour Mrs. Jones was at the door, a list of Atlanta-area synagogues in her hand.

Back in Milton, a housewife would no more have opened a first conversation with a new neighbor by inquiring into her religious identity than she would have opened the day by running naked down the block. And during the time I spent as a journalist in Atlanta, I never had reason to doubt my original impression that religion occupied a different place in the civic culture of the South than it did in New England. As for the rest of the country, who knew? But when, after a decade, I returned to New England to start up an academic Center for the Study of Religion in Public Life, I determined to find out. The result, a decade further down the road, is the Religion by Region project, a series of volumes on religion in the public life of each of eight regions of the country.[11] The experience of editing these volumes has been educational in many ways, not the least in convincing me that to the extent that region still matters in American life—and I am convinced that it matters a lot—it is because of religion.

Even though all Americans practice and act on their religions under the regime of the First Amendment, the religions they practice, and the way and extent to which they practice them, differ substantially from region to region. These religious differences are, not coincidentally, connected to the public cultures of different parts of the country; they shape and are shaped by them. And the politics and public policies that emerge from the regions, via the politicians sent to statehouses and to Washington, likewise reflect the regional religious realities. . . .

The Religious Demography

Our regions are pretty predictable except for what we have called the Southern Crossroads, which is more or less what American historians know as the Old Southwest: Louisiana, Texas, Arkansas, Oklahoma, and Missouri. Otherwise, it is New England, the Middle Atlantic, the (rest of the) South, the Midwest (including the Plains), the Mountain West, the Pacific Northwest (which includes Alaska), and the Pacific (where Nevada and Hawaii are, not to put too fine a point on it, tacked on to California).[12] The broad features of the religious demography of these regions will come as no surprise, but the actual numbers may be a bit startling. Thus, relying on an enhanced version of the 2000 Glenmary survey of religious institutions,[13] Catholics make up over 40 percent of the population in New England (and nearly 70 percent of all religious adherents there), but constitute just 8 percent of the population of the South, and significantly less if you leave out Florida. By contrast, white Baptists make up 19 percent of the population of the South, as compared to just 1.6 percent in New England. In the Midwest, mainline Protestants constitute a higher proportion of the population than in any other region, slightly outnumbering white evangelicals. Among white Protestants, there are three times as many mainliners as evangelicals in New England, and more than twice as many in the Middle Atlantic; but everywhere else white evangelicals outnumber mainliners by substantial margins. Otherwise, you do not need me to tell you that there are a lot of Mormons in Utah (and southern Idaho), and a lot of Lutherans in the upper Midwest.

Less well known are the regional variations among the religiously unaffiliated. Nearly two out of every three people in the Pacific Northwest are unaffiliated or unaccounted for, as compared to one out of three in the Middle Atlantic and the Southern Crossroads. In both the Mountain West and the Pacific regions, the number is just short of one in two. The West—especially when you take out the Church of Jesus Christ of Latter-Day Saints—is far and away the least "churched" part of the country, and here it is important to recognize the gap between those claimed by religious institutions—membership—and how individuals identify themselves. In the Pacific Northwest, 63 percent of the people are unaffiliated or uncounted, according to the religious institutions, but only 31 percent of the people say they have no religion if you ask them directly.[14] In most parts of the country this two-to-one ratio holds: twice as many people claim a religious identity as are claimed by a religious organization. The one exception is the South, where the ratio is three to one. Specifically, the proportion of unaffiliated in the South is about the national average of 40 percent, but the number of nonidentifiers is in the low teens. . . .

Public and Private

Because of its rather peculiar religious history, New England is a place where religion is not much spoken of in civic affairs. By peculiar, I refer to the fact that the region was established as a religious exercise, and was populated for its first 200 years almost exclusively by the same ethno-religious group. And then, beginning in the middle of the 19th century, it was simply overwhelmed by Irish Catholics. After a considerable time, and a lot of ugliness, a *modus vivendi* was worked out—one in which the Catholics created their own institutions, separate and distinct from the institutions of Yankeedom. And folks learned not to press religious cases in public. So when a Howard Dean or a John Kerry (to say nothing of a Michael Dukakis) make it clear by word and deed that they are not very comfortable talking about religion in public because they are from New England, that is not because they are really saying they do not give a hoot about religion; it is because they are from New England. . . . [Given] that New England is, increasingly, heartland Democratic country, the Democratic Party's "problem" about speaking the language of faith needs to be understood as, in part, a problem of region.

The Secular Frontier

Reluctant as New Englanders are to speak about religion in public, they come in above average—indeed, ahead of the South—on the religious membership scale. America's secular frontier is, as it has always been, the Pacific Northwest—which is why we subtitled our volume on that region "The None Zone." But the denizens of the None Zone do not lack for a regional civil religion. It is called environmentalism, and it hearkens to the gospel of biodiversity. . . .

. . . To be sure, not everyone in Oregon sees things this way. Specifically, the Pacific Northwest is home to a sizable and growing minority of evangelical Protestants who regard themselves, correctly, as the counterculture in the region. And given the culture's prevailing ethos, it should not be surprising that it is only in the Pacific Northwest that a majority of evangelicals say they are against environmentalism.[15]

Varieties of Pluralism

Let me turn now to the issue of pluralism. The two most religiously diverse regions of the country are the Pacific—California, Nevada, and Hawaii—and the Middle Atlantic. But the style of pluralism—or, it might be more accurate to say, the way religion is "read" culturally—is very different. In the Pacific region (which is to say, California above all), we are in a world of fluid identities, where the dominant ethos emphasizes the individual shaping his or her own spiritual existence. As in the rest of the West (outside of Utah), religion is institutionally weak. A mix-and-match spiritual style comes naturally. . . .

By contrast, the Middle Atlantic is a place where religion carries a strong dimension of ascribed identity. It is where you come from, who you are. That this has ever been so in this region is well known to students of American religious history, and indeed we have subtitled our Middle Atlantic volume, "The Fount of Diversity.". . .

The claim I want to make is that the Middle Atlantic approach to religious pluralism got turned into a kind of ideology during and after World War II, and bade fair for a while to become *the* American way when it comes to religion. Here the key text was Will Herberg's classic *Protestant Catholic Jew*. Only in the Middle Atlantic—and really, only in New York City—could you have made a persuasive case that the religious scene really was shared on something like equal terms among Protestants, Catholics, and Jews. Equally, I would argue, only in the Middle Atlantic could you have made a persuasive case that ethnicity was turning into such a "triple melting pot"—because only in the Middle Atlantic was religion so closely identified with ethnicity.

The fact that Herberg's book actually came to define the postwar way of looking at religion in America is a remarkable testimony to the willingness of the rest of the country to buy into Middle Atlantic cultural hegemony. . . . The point I would stress here, however, is that the postwar religious regime of different tribes operating more or less in common cause now seems under assault from a different kind of regime—and not the "fluid identity" regime of California either. Rather it is a new style of religious pluralism that defines the world, Manichaean style, into "people of faith" and people of no faith. This is a hard-edged and world changing style linked to a specific moral agenda and associated with a different part of the country.

On the New Evangelical Politics

That part of the country is the Southern Crossroads, whose volume carries the subtitle "Showdown States." That religion in the Crossroads is a contact sport has something to do with the frontier character of the place, the idea that once you jumped the Mississippi all hell broke loose, and often in the form of wars and feuds. In religion, a Baptist controversialist named J. R. Graves raised hell all throughout the region, and succeeded in establishing a powerful theology of Christian republicanism in the Baptist churches. To make a long story short, this is a region where Baptists, more than their co-religionists in other parts of the country, were prepared early on to forego their scruples about separation of church and state. Beyond that, it is critical to recognize the importance of the Holiness-Pentecostal tradition, which is stronger in the Crossroads than anywhere else in the country. . . .

Again to shorten a long story, understanding religious politics in America today requires that we distinguish the Baptist strain of American evangelicalism from the Methodist one, which has given us the Holiness and Pentecostal movements. The former, Landmarkism perhaps aside, has been wary of the corruptions of the world, inclined to remove itself from the world and tend its own vine and fig tree against the return of the Lord. The latter, by contrast, contains within it a powerful willingness to take on the world and change it according to its own lights. . . .

. . . [I]t is in the Pentecostal world that old postmillennial Methodism has most powerfully and unambivalently revived and spread itself out into the wider evangelical world. . . .

On the national scene, we are now experiencing the emergence of a bifurcated model of religion versus secular that in some ways is a throwback to the early Cold War period, but without the external referent (Godless Communism). The style of discourse has various sources—including the neoconservative—but it very much partakes of the angry, confrontational style of the Crossroads, and of the Crossroad tradition of Christian republicanism. . . .

Conclusion

So that is something of what awareness of regional religious traditions and culture can contribute to an understanding of American public life today. None of this is to say that there are no national issues, or times when particular interests or concerns animate the American electorate across the board geographically. But there is a tendency, once a national election is over, for even sophisticated observers to turn from focusing on the contest for electoral votes in one state or another to a uniform explanation of what happened—as if we were, after all, one nation whose choice of president could be explained by a single overriding concern. . . .

[R]egion matters in American culture because (as I noted at the beginning) religion varies from one part of the country to another. It time for more social science research to recognize this, and proceed accordingly.

4.4

Walter Sundberg

RELIGIOUS TRENDS IN TWENTIETH-CENTURY AMERICA (2000)

Over the last half of the twentieth century, three important developments have shaped American religious life. The first is the double-sided trend of the decline of mainline churches and the growth of evangelical churches. The second is the divisive effect of political activism on the communal life of denominations. The third is the reduction of the role of religion in public life through the enforcement of the Supreme Court's legal doctrine of separation of church and state.

I. The Decline of Mainline Churches and the Growth of Evangelical Churches

"Mainline" originally referred to a commuter train route running from downtown Philadelphia to the wealthy suburbs, home of that city's high society. The term has become a sociological metaphor used to identify Protestant denominations that are largely white, affluent, and open to the secular influences of modern culture—in short, the Protestant "establishment." Eight denominations are commonly cited as belonging to the mainline: American Baptist Churches in the USA, Christian Church (Disciples of Christ), Episcopal Church, Evangelical Lutheran Church in America, Presbyterian Church (USA), Reformed Church in America, United Church of Christ, and the United Methodist Church. Except for John F. Kennedy, Jimmy Carter, and Bill Clinton, all United States Presidents who declared themselves Christian came from mainline denominations. Nearly fifty percent of all Supreme Court justices have been either Episcopalians or Presbyterians. In the House and the Senate, Episcopalians, Presbyterians, and Methodists regularly make up a plurality of the membership (Reeves 1996, 1–2).

Despite their impressive role in society, mainline denominations have suffered loss of members since 1965. The figures for the period from 1965 to 1994 are:

American Baptist Churches in the USA—3.3%
Christian Church (Disciples of Christ)—51.1%
Episcopal Church—27.0%

Evangelical Lutheran Church in America—8.5%
Presbyterian Church (USA)—13.1%
Reformed Church in America—19.8%
United Church of Christ—27.5%
United Methodist Church—22.4%

Some of these numbers are quite dramatic, others less so.[16] But it must be remembered that during this same period, the population of the United States grew by nearly thirty percent. Proportionate to population, membership decline in all these churches is alarming. Mainline denominations are steadily becoming marginalized in American religious life.

Mainline theologians and church officials rationalize membership loss by ascribing it to the effects of modern secularization. They assert that the decline of the church is inevitable because we live in a "post-Christian" era in which fewer people are attracted to organized religion. The trouble with this mainline scenario is that it does not fit the facts of religious life in America. While mainline denominations are in decline, a significant number of evangelical denominations have experienced impressive rates of growth. I define evangelical denominations as those churches that teach that the normal beginning of genuine Christian life is spiritual transformation and that combine this teaching with a conservative stance on theological, moral, and political issues. The chief examples of evangelical denominations that have enjoyed membership growth in the period from 1965 to 1994 are:

Assemblies of God +306%
Church of God (Cleveland, TN) +252%
Church of God in Christ +1,232%
Church of the Nazarene +74%
Southern Baptist Convention +45%

This growth is not an isolated phenomenon in American religious life. The Southern Baptist Convention is the largest Protestant church in America. Pentecostalist denominations like the Assemblies of God represent the fastest growing Christian movement in the history of the church. The impact of evangelical denominations is global. Worldwide, Pentecostalism has gone from 8.5 million adherents in 1958 to over 400 million today (Miller 1997, 5). In Asia, Africa, and Latin America, this movement represents nothing less than the future of Protestantism. . . .

II. The Divisive Effect of Political Activism

The second religious trend that bears examination is the divisive effect of political activism on the communal life of the church. At first glance, it would appear that there is nothing particularly distinctive in this trend. Political matters have always divided the church. In the nineteenth century, the abolitionist and secessionist movements split Baptists, Methodists, Presbyterians, Lutherans, and a host of other churches between north and south. These splits were not healed until the twentieth century. The political fights over temperance, labor unions, socialism, and America's participation in foreign wars—all have had their impact on the organizational life and spiritual health of denominations. These conflicts have not only been common; they have been necessary. There are political issues that the church must engage, even if such engagement is costly. The fight over slavery that led to the Civil War is a prime example. While the "prophetic" mantle may never have sat comfortably upon the shoulders of the institutional church, the church has nevertheless needed prophets to call it to repentance and change. From the time of H. Richard Niebuhr's *The Social Sources of Denominationalism* (1929), we have known that organized church bodies reflect more of class structure and economic status than confessional commitment in the values they hold and the political choices they make. This is wrong. The prophet brings the church back to confession.

While political conflict in the church may be common and necessary, something is going on today, especially in mainline denominations, which is, in my opinion, unprecedented. It is what I would call *the institutionalization of the prophetic office.* Since the civil rights movement of the 1960s, ecclesiastical leaders have sought not only to appeal to the consciences of individual members, but also to make denominational organizations the official agents of political and social change. They have asked members to vote on specific resolutions of action in synod meetings and conventions, set up government lobbying offices, and even attempted to enforce conformity to particular policies by pastors and congregations.

For a denomination to become involved in direct action may be effective when there is widespread support in the constituency for such action. Historic African-American churches in America and numerous Jewish organizations have a history of being effective because they have such uniform support. The Roman Catholic Church, with its immense numbers and hierarchical organization, can muster the support of literally millions of people on political matters it deems important. Even mainline denominations have had their day in the sun. In the civil rights movement, especially in the period between the famous march on Washington in August 1963 and the passing of the Voting Rights Act by Congress in 1965, mainline denominations enjoyed a significant level of unity, especially among the clergy. One survey of clergy taken in California in 1968 showed that nearly 25% had participated in civil rights demonstrations and marches (Wuthnow 1988, 146).

Over the last thirty years, mainline denominational leaders have attempted to duplicate their political success in the civil rights movement. Under the rationale of prophetic witness, they have tried to extend the paradigm of direct political action to a succession of issues: Vietnam, black power, feminism, abortion, Marxist revolution in Latin America, and homosexuality. The results have been mixed, sometimes disastrous, because the constituency in mainline churches is divided. In 1984, George Gallup did a national study that attempted to chart the differences between religious liberals and conservatives. The study allowed people to define themselves: "Are you liberal or conservative?" "43 percent of those surveyed identified themselves as religious liberals (19 percent as very liberal); 41 percent identified themselves as religious conservatives (18 percent as very conservative); and only 16 percent found it impossible to identify with one or the other of these labels" (Wuthnow 1988, 133). This is a split right down the middle. It has led to ferocious battles within denominations that threaten to undermine their effectiveness as organizations and, perhaps, their future viability.

Robert Wuthnow, professor of sociology at Princeton University, sees these battles as leading to "the restructuring of American religion." Christians are dividing politically rather than doctrinally. Thus, for example, liberal Lutherans, Presbyterians, and Episcopalians find more agreement with each other than they do with conservatives of their own confessions. Conversely, conservative Lutherans, Presbyterians, and Episcopalians make common cause against liberals in their respective churches. James Davison Hunter, professor of sociology at the University of Virginia, echoes Wuthnow when he speaks of a "cultural realignment" among American religious groups over political issues. This realignment takes the form of "pragmatic alliances . . . across faith traditions" of Protestants, Catholics, and Jews (Hunter 1991, 47). On the one side are the "orthodox" of faith traditions, who hold to an unchanging, objective standard of divine truth. On the other side are the "progressives" of these same traditions, who wish to adapt historic notions of divine truth to changing social circumstances.

Will this divisive trend lead to denominational breakup? Will churches such as the ELCA or the Presbyterian Church (USA) find the strain of political conflict so difficult that they will begin splitting up into smaller organizational units as they did in the nineteenth century because of the Civil War and other issues? A lot depends on whether or not the institutionalization of the prophetic office will continue to hold sway. When ecclesiastical leaders believe that they are doing God's will by using denominational funds to support a specific political stance, it is very difficult to get them to change course or consider another point of view. Even if such a stance adversely affects the communal life of the denomination, these leaders often dig in and will not compromise.

I do not deny the need for the prophet to speak in the church from time to time. I also acknowledge that denominations and religious organizations can be effective politically if they have the support of their constituencies. African- American churches are, as I have already stated, a prime example of such effectiveness. But when a church does not have the clear support of its members, it cannot be effective in the political realm. Who cares what the "Lutheran Church" says on a given policy if it cannot deliver the votes in support of that policy? Besides, a lot depends on the issues at stake. Who is to say, with regard to controversial matters such as feminism, abortion, homosexuality, and political "liberation," what the "prophetic" stance of the church should be? There are many issues over which Christians may legitimately disagree. The problem is that ecclesiastical leaders tend to forget this. Some are tempted to demonize their opposition and demand conformity at all costs. When religion tries to control political thought and action in this way, it can be a very dangerous thing.

4.5

Mark Chaves

CONGREGATIONS IN AMERICA (2004)

The emergence and continuing presence of the Christian right in American politics has generated a great deal of social scientific research about the relationship between religion and political activity in the United States.[17] Much of this research has used surveys of individuals to document substantial differences among religious groups in voting likelihood, voting choice, political attitudes, and overall levels of civic skills.[18] The primary conclusion emerging from this literature is that religion-based political differences among individuals are not reducible to other characteristics—race, social class, education, gender, and so on—known to generate political variation.

The vast majority of empirical research on religion and politics, however, examines individuals' political attitudes and activities abstracted from the institutional and organizational contexts in which much religion-based political activity occurs. Occasionally, research based on surveys of individuals provides glimpses into congregations' activities, as when Sidney Verba and his colleagues (Verba, Schlozman, and Brady 1995, 373) reported that, over a five-year period, 34 percent of members or regular attenders of congregations were asked by someone in authority in their congregation either to vote or to take some other form of political action, or when Andrew Kohut and colleagues (2000, 108) reported that 27 percent of monthly religious service attenders were exposed in their congregations to information on political candidates or parties. More commonly, however, previous research does not permit even indirect answers to two basic questions: To what extent do congregations engage in political activities? And in what ways do religious traditions structure congregation-based political efforts?[19]

The NCS [National Congregations Study] provides leverage on both of these questions via data on nine types of congregational political activity: (1) whether people at worship services have been told within the past twelve months of opportunities for political activity, including petitioning campaigns, lobbying, or demonstrating; (2) whether voter guides have ever been distributed to people through the congregation; (3) if voter guides have been distributed, whether they were produced by Christian right organizations;[20] whether the congregation had a group, meeting, class, or event within the past twelve months, to (4) organize or participate in a demonstration or march either in support of or opposition to some public issue or policy; (5) discuss politics; (6) get people registered to vote, or (7) organize or participate in efforts to lobby elected officials of any sort; and whether, within the past twelve months; (8) a candidate for political office or (9) an elected government official was a visiting speaker at the congregation, either at a worship service or at another event.

How Many Congregations Engage in Political Activities?

Table 4.1 shows that religious service attenders are most frequently exposed to three kinds of political activities in congregations: being told at worship services about opportunities for political participation (such as petition campaigns, lobbying, or demonstrating), receiving voter guides, and being mobilized to participate in a demonstration or march in support of or opposition to some public policy. Thirty-seven percent of religious service attenders are in congregations where opportunities for political activity were mentioned at worship services, while roughly a quarter of congregations, taken as units without respect to size, mentioned such opportunities at worship services. Approximately one fourth of religious service attenders are in congregations that distributed voter guides, and one fifth of religious service attenders are in congregations in which a group participated in a demonstration or a march. No more than 13 percent of religious service attenders are in congregations engaging in any of the remaining political activities.

Table 4.1 Congregations' Political Activities

Activity	Percent of attenders in congregations that:	Percent of congregations that:
Told people at worship services about opportunities for political activities (within the past 12 months)	37	26
Have ever distributed voter guides	27	17
Of those distributing voter guides, have distributed Christian right voter guides	39	47
Have ever distributed Christian right voter guides	7	5
Have had a group, meeting, class, or event within the past 12 months to:		
organize or participate in a demonstration or march in support of or opposition to some public issue or policy	21	9
get people registered to vote	12	9
discuss politics	13	7
organize or participate in efforts to lobby elected officials of any sort	12	4
Have had an elected government official as a visiting speaker in the past 12 months	12	6
Have had someone running for office as a visiting speaker within the past 12 months	6	4
Participated in at least one of these political activities	60	42

Are these numbers large or small? On the one hand, the level of congregation-based political activity seems low. Fifty-eight percent of congregations, containing 40 percent of religious service attenders, engage in *none* of these political activities. Scholarly and media attention to politically active congregations and congregation-based political mobilizing notwithstanding, the majority of religious congregations do not engage in political participation. Furthermore, only three of these activities are engaged in by more than 20 percent of all congregations, and only four of them are experienced by more than 20 percent of religious service attenders. As we saw with social services, the vast majority of congregations are not engaged in political activity in any extensive way. On the other hand, a majority of religious service attenders (60 percent) are in congregations that engaged in at least one of these political activities, and a sizable minority of congregations (42 percent) report political activity of some sort.

It is instructive to compare congregational involvement in politics with the involvement of other organizations whose primary purpose is *not* political action. No direct comparisons are possible with existing data, but three indirect comparisons are suggestive. A mid-1990s survey of nonprofit organizations in Minneapolis-St. Paul found that approximately one quarter of organizations reported lobbying efforts in the previous two years (Chaves, Stephens, and Galaskiewicz 2004). Only 4 percent of congregations, by contrast, report direct lobbying activity: A 2000 national survey of nonprofits large enough to file a tax return with the Internal Revenue Service ($25,000 in annual income) found that 10 percent "lobby" and 20 percent "advocate with" government officials at least *twice a month* (Berry 2003, 190). Only 7 percent of congregations below that income threshold had lobbied within the past year. Ten percent is not significantly more than 7 percent, but note the difference in intensity. It seems unlikely that many of the congregations reporting some lobbying pursued that activity twice a month on an ongoing basis.

Another national survey of nonprofit organizations found that 16 percent spent money on some sort of advocacy activity (Salamon 1995). As I just noted, 42 percent of congregations reported political activity of some sort in 1998, but most of these activities do not involve spending money, and it seems very likely that the proportion of congregations spending money on advocacy or political activity is much smaller than 16 percent. These comparisons are tentative, but they suggest that congregations engage in less of at least some types of political activity—especially direct lobbying of government officials—than other nonprofit organizations whose primary purpose is something other than politics.[21] At the same time, I should note that the very largest congregations report lobbying at a rate that approaches that of nonprofits in general. Approximately 20 percent of the largest congregations (those with more than four hundred people) reported lobbying in the past year.

Rather than comparing the extent to which congregations enter the political sphere *as congregations* with the extent to which other nonpolitical organizations enter the political sphere *as organizations,* we might instead compare the extent to which congregations and other organizations offer opportunities for political action to individuals. Verba and colleagues (Verba, Schlozman, and Brady 1995, 373) asked a sample of individuals whether they were asked to be politically active by someone in their congregation, by someone at work, or by someone from other nonpolitical organizations to which they belonged or contributed. Thirty-four percent of people affiliated with congregations said they had been asked in religious settings to be politically active,[22] compared with 19 percent of workers who were asked in the workplace and 9 percent of those associated with other nonpolitical organizations who were asked to be politically active by someone in such an organization. From the perspective of offering opportunities to individuals rather than acting as organizations in the political sphere, congregations seem to be *more* politically active than nonreligious organizations whose primary purpose is something other than politics.

Adding this comparison to the mix suggests a provocative, if tentative, conclusion. On the one hand, congregations' level of political involvement is, in absolute terms, rather low, and congregations *qua congregations* are less likely to engage in certain kinds of political activity than nonprofit organizations whose primary purpose is not politics. On the other hand, however, even at their relatively low levels of activity, congregations still might be providing more opportunities for *individual* political action than other organizations whose primary purpose is nonpolitical. Despite the thorny normative and legal issues associated with congregation-based political action in the United States, congregations engage in a fair amount of such activity. Whether we consider the level of that activity to be substantial or minimal depends somewhat on whether we focus on congregations as unified organizations or as sites at which opportunities for political action are offered to individuals. Overall, it is difficult to reach a stronger conclusion about the magnitude of congregations' political activity than the one reached by Verba and colleagues (Verba, Schlozman, and Brady 1995, 146, 373): such activity is "neither the norm nor exceptional" in congregational settings; it is "not frequent, but neither is it rare."

Religious and Race Differences in Political Activities

Table 4.2 continues this chapter's exploration of religious differences in congregations' civic activities. Unlike with other kinds of civic activities, race differences cut across denomination-based political differences in systematic and important ways, so Table 4.2 presents rates of congregational participation across five religious traditions: Roman Catholic, black Protestant, white moderate and liberal Protestant, white conservative and evangelical Protestant, and Jewish. Here . . . Protestant congregations whose

Table 4.2 Religious Tradition Differences in Congregations' Political Activities

| Activity | Percent of attenders within each tradition who attend congregations with specified political activities | | | | |
	Moderate and liberal white Protestants (n = 305)	Conservative and evangelical white Protestants (n = 439)	Black Protestants (n = 143)	Roman Catholics (n = 299)	Jews (n = 20)
Told people at worship services about opportunities for political activity (within the past 12 months)	34	28	47	45	60
Have ever distributed voter guides	20	32	28	26	25
Of those distributing voter guides, percent distributing Christian right voter guides	33	70	8	14	17
Have had a group to organize a demonstration or march	11	14	15	42	10
Have had a group to discuss politics	18	5	17	13	45
Have had a group to get people registered to vote	5	7	35	16	20
Have had a group to lobby elected officials	9	5	10	23	20
Have had an elected government official as a visiting speaker	14	9	25	8	37
Have had someone running for office as a visiting speaker	5	2	27	3	35
Participated in at least one of these political activities	57	52	71	68	90

Notes: Chi-squares associated with each row of this table are significant at least at the .01 level.

Given the small number of synagogues in the NCS sample, percentages in the "Jews" column should be interpreted cautiously. The *95%* confidence intervals around percentages in this column range from ±10 percentage points (for percentages near 0 or 100) to ±22 percentage points (for percentages near *50).* The *95%* confidence interval around percentages in the "Black Protestants" column is never more than ±8 percentage points; in the other columns it is never more than ±6 points.

regular participants are at least 80 percent African American are included in the black Protestant category whatever their denominational affiliation.

The main message in this table is that religious traditions line up differently on political activity than they do on other kinds of civic engagement. Looking at the bottom line of Table 4.2, we find that approximately 70 percent of both Catholics and black Protestants are in congregations that have engaged in at least one of these political activities compared with approximately 55 percent of white Protestants. And even with the small number of synagogues in this sample, we still may conclude with a great deal of confidence that at least 70 percent of synagogues have engaged in at least one of these types of political activity. With other types of civic activities, Jews lined up on the high end with liberal Protestants; on political activities, Jews still line up on the high end, but now with Catholics and black Protestants.

Beyond this quantitative difference, however, there are qualitative differences among these groups in the nature of their political activity.[23] Although Jewish synagogues seem to be on the high end of participation for each of these activities, Christian churches seem to specialize in particular modes of political participation, and this specialization is strongly structured by race and religious tradition. As before it would be tedious to narrate all the numbers in this table. Instead, I will describe the distinctive patterns of political activity evident within the four Christian traditions represented in Table 4.2.[24]

White Conservative and Evangelical Protestants

White conservative Protestant congregations may, overall, be less likely than Catholic or black Protestant congregations to engage in any political activity, but at the same time they specialize in distributing voter guides, especially voter guides produced by Christian right organizations. Indeed, this is the only political activity in which white conservative Protestant congregations are significantly more likely than others to engage. Thirty-two percent of conservative Protestant religious service attenders are exposed to voter guides in their congregations. Nearly that many Catholic and black Protestant attenders are exposed to voter guides, but the white conservative distinctiveness is especially evident when we consider the source of the voter guides: 70 percent of conservative Protestants in congregations distributing some sort of voter guide are in congregations that distributed voter guides produced by Christian right organizations, compared to only 33 percent of moderate and liberal white Protestants, 14 percent of Roman Catholics, and 8 percent of black Protestants.

The fact that conservative Protestant congregations distribute voter guides but do not engage much in other forms of congregational political activity is not surprising when viewed in light of the political strategies pursued by national Christian right political organizations. Many observers have pointed out that, at least since the late 1980s, conservative Protestant political organizations have embraced electoral politics, even to the point of recruiting candidates and providing campaign support for them (see for example Green, Rozell, and Wilcox 2000; Wilcox 1996). Distributing voter guides within religious congregations is an important part of this strategy; one that these results show to have been at least somewhat successful, if (as we saw in Table 4.1) reaching more than 5 percent of church attenders in the country can be considered success. At the same time, despite overt appeals on behalf of many Christian right leaders in recent years to broaden support for their political organizations among Catholics and

African Americans, black Protestant and Roman Catholic congregations remain very substantially less likely than conservative Protestant congregations to distribute voter guides produced by Christian right political organizations.

The conservative Protestant use of voter guides has, of course, received substantial attention from both scholars and journalists. This attention notwithstanding, conservative Protestants do not have a monopoly on congregation-based political activity in the United States. On the contrary; as noted earlier, Catholic and predominantly African American congregations are significantly more likely than white conservative (and liberal) Protestants to engage in some form of political activity. Extensive scholarly and media attention to the religious right obscures this fact and hides the important differences in political style typical of congregations in different religious traditions. Congregations within other major religions traditions are not less political than conservative Protestant congregations. Rather, they engage in politics in different ways.

Black Protestants

Reflecting the enduring political activism of black Protestantism at least since the civil rights era, black Protestant congregations are particularly likely to have voter registration drives and to invite political candidates and elected officials to congregations to give speeches. Thirty-five percent of those who attend African American churches are in congregations with voter registration efforts, 27 percent are in congregations that had a political candidate as a visiting speaker, and 25 percent are in congregations that had an elected official as a visiting speaker. All three of these numbers are substantially and significantly higher than the comparable percentages for congregations within other religious traditions. Overall, these results comport well with recent research finding that black Protestant congregations routinely hear speeches from political candidates, organize voter mobilization chives, and expose congregants to various political messages and solicitations (Harris 1999, chap. 6; Pattillo-McCoy 1998, 778–881; Verba, Schlozman, and Brady 1995, 383–4). African American congregations have embraced electoral politics more than white congregations, and even explicitly partisan involvement in elections seems more common and more accepted among African American churches than among white churches.

Roman Catholics

In recent years Roman Catholics have not been prominent in research on religion and politics in the United States Table 4.2 shows, however, that Roman Catholic congregations are behind only Jewish synagogues and black Protestant congregations in the likelihood of engaging in some form of politics, and they also have a distinctive way of engaging in politics. Perhaps the most surprising result in this table is that Roman Catholic congregations are substantially more likely than other congregations to attempt overtly to influence public life by lobbying elected officials and by organizing groups to demonstrate or march for or against some public issue or policy. Forty-two percent of Catholics are in congregations that have participated in a demonstration or march in the past year, three times the rate within any other tradition. Twenty-three percent have lobbied an elected official, more than twice the rate within any other Christian group. Catholics also are substantially more likely than white Protestants, though not more likely than black Protestants, to hear about opportunities for political involvement at worship services. NCS data do not contain information about the purposes for which congregations are demonstrating or lobbying. Other research, however, suggests that much of this Catholic organizing may be related to abortion (Byrnes and Segers 1992; McCarthy 1987; Byrnes 1991, chap. 9). Catholic churches also may be more open than other congregations to mobilizing efforts by community organizers in the Saul Alinsky tradition (Warren 2001; Wood 2002). Whatever the purpose of this activity, the important point here is that Catholics are *more* likely than white Protestants to be in politically active congregations, and, like congregations in other traditions, they engage in politics in distinctive ways. Specifically, Catholic congregations are more likely than others to engage in the direct action and pressure group politics of demonstrating, marching, and lobbying.

White Liberal and Moderate Protestants

Unlike for other sorts of civic activity, liberal and moderate white Protestant congregations do not stand out from others on *any* form of political involvement, but the overall pattern of results still suggests a distinctively "mainline" way of engaging in politics. These congregations are significantly more likely than white conservative Protestant congregations, but not more likely than blacks or Catholics, to have a group that discusses politics and to have someone running for office visit their congregations to give a talk. Although the high level of clerical activism that some claim characterized liberal Protestantism in the 1960s and early 1970s is not evident here, there is a sense in which these results indicate a certain political continuity in the liberal Protestant religious tradition. Robert Wuthnow and John Evans (2002) have argued that mainline Protestants do not, in general, favor their religious institutions and leaders taking a more active and visible role in public policy issues and politics. Rather, they prefer to influence public life as individuals by working behind the scenes. Thus, while moderate and liberal white Protestant congregations are relatively active when it comes to organizing political discussion groups or offering their people opportunities for political action, they are not particularly likely, relative to congregations in other traditions, to organize for the purpose of directly influencing political or electoral processes.

As is the case with other kinds of civic activities examined in this chapter, the religious traditions represented in Table 4.2, defined in terms of denominational affiliations and race, do not capture all the religious variation in congregational political activity. In particular, congregations described by informants as theologically conservative are more likely to distribute Christian right voter guides than theologically moderate and liberal congregations, whatever their race or religious denomination. This is not surprising, since many attenders in these congregations would have ideological commitments similar to those of the conservative Christian political organizations producing these guides, but it is worth noting yet again that, as Wuthnow (1988) reminded us forcefully, there is a liberal-conservative divide in American religion that crosscuts denominations.

Taken as a whole, Table 4.2 shows that congregations tend to specialize in particular forms of political action, specialization that is structured by race and religious tradition. Conservative white Protestants tend to engage in politics by distributing voter guides, especially Christian right voter guides. Black Protestants tend to register voters and open their doors to candidates and elected officials. Catholics tend to lobby elected officials and organize demonstrations and marches. Mainline Protestants tend to organize discussion groups.[25] Although none of these political activities are completely monopolized by a single religious tradition, clear modalities are present. I do not know whether the source of these affinities between religious tradition and political style lies in the nature of the issues of primary concern to different religious groups, in organizational differences among religious groups, in the preferred political strategies pursued by national leaders within different traditions, in long-term religious differences of political style and strategic repertoire, in variations across religious traditions in clergy-lay relations, in differences among religious groups in proximity to political establishments, or somewhere else. Whatever the source of these differences, it seems clear that race and religions tradition channel congregations' political activity into distinctive and recognizable paths. . . .

4.6

*Lyman Kellstedt, John Green, Corwin Smidt,
and James Guth*

FAITH TRANSFORMED: RELIGION AND AMERICAN POLITICS FROM FDR TO GEORGE W. BUSH (2007)

American Religious Groups and the Presidential Vote from FDR to George W. Bush

In most presidential elections since 1936, over 90 percent of the ballots have been by four religious communities (evangelical, mainline, and black Protestants plus white Roman Catholics) and the religiously unaffiliated, here called the "seculars." As a result, it is useful to focus on the voting behavior of these five groups. Table 4.3 presents the Republican percentage of the two-party presidential vote cast by the five groups from 1936 to 2004. The last column summarizes the GOP's net gain or loss in each group over that period. The data in this table come from a variety of sources: Gallup surveys from the late 1930s and early 1940s, the National Election Study (NES) surveys from 1948 to 2004, and the National Surveys of Religion and Politics, conducted by the authors from 1992 to 2004.[26]

Evangelical Protestants

Evangelical Protestants began the period strongly backing the candidacies of Franklin Roosevelt and Harry Truman, but by the end voted overwhelmingly Republican. Evangelicals cast 36 percent of their votes for Republican Alf Landon in 1936, but 78 percent for George W. Bush in 2004. Until 1984 evangelicals were less Republican in presidential voting than were mainline Protestants (except for 1972), but

Table 4.3 Republican Percentage of Two-Party Vote for President
by Religious Tradition, 1936–2004

Religious tradition	1936	1940	1944	1948	1952	1956	1960	1964	1968	1972	1976	1980	1984	1988	1992	1996	2000	2004	Gain/ Loss
Evangelical Protestant	36	46	48	38	63	60	60	38	69	84	51	65	74	69	69	67	74	78	+42
Mainline Protestant	48	58	60	55	72	71	70	46	72	75	64	70	72	64	57	55	60	50	+2
Black Protestant	35	38	32	6#	20	36	32	0	4	16	7	7	11	8	10	11	4	17	−18
White Catholic	18	28	33	25	49	55	17	22	40	64	44	58	55	51	46	46	50	53	+35
Secular	28	41	39	37	56	53	45	32	46	53	44	59	57	50	34	43	36	28	0
Nationwide	36	45	48	41	58	60	51	33	54	64	49	56	58	53	47	47	50	51	+15

since 1984 evangelicals have become the strongest supporters of GOP candidates, moving 42 percentage points in Republican direction between 1936 and 2004. Despite party identification that favored the Democrats as late as the 1980s, evangelicals have voted for GOP presidential aspirants at higher rates than the nation as a whole since the 1950s and especially since the 1960s.

Scholars and pundits alike have noted the recent trend that links high church attendance with Republican voting—the so-called attendance gap. Clearly, church attendance among evangelicals has had an impact on their voting behavior. Since the 1960s, those who attend church at least once a week have supported Republican candidates at higher rates than those attending less frequently. This high attendance certainly facilitates political mobilization: those who attend church most frequently are the easiest to find and activate. . . .

Indeed, evangelicals have become the religious centerpiece of the Republican party. And the movement toward the GOP has been dominated by regular church attenders, southerners, and younger evangelicals. Support for the GOP is likely to continue for the foreseeable future, as the issue positions of evangelicals line up with those of the Republican party—not only on the "social" or "moral" issues, but also on foreign policy and domestic economic issues (Guth et al. 2005; Guth, et al. 2006). . . .

Mainline Protestants

Historically, mainline Protestants have been the religious bulwark of the Republican party. As Table 4.3 shows, mainline support for GOP candidates was consistently 10 points or more above the national average from 1936 to 1992, falling just below that line in 1996, before rising again in 2000. In 2004, however, the mainline vote for Bush fell to 50 percent, the first time in the history of survey research that it dropped below the nationwide percentage. If one ignores 1936, a banner year for the Democrats, mainline voting for GOP candidates declined 8 percentage points from 1940 to 2004.

As a result, mainline Protestants no longer serve as the cornerstone of the GOP religious coalition. One is tempted to speculate that liberalism among denominational leaders and local clergy has played a part in moving mainline laity from their classic identification with the Republican party (Guth et al. 1997). Thus, in sum, the mainline Protestant domination of the GOP is a thing of the past, with declining numbers and less support for Republican candidates reducing their contribution to the GOP electoral coalition. . . .

Black Protestants

Black Protestants' affinity with the GOP ("the party of Lincoln") went back to the Civil War and the end of slavery, but these ties began to erode during the New Deal as the Democratic party came to be identified with assistance to the poor. Table 4.3 shows black Protestants still giving 38 percent of their vote to Willkie in 1940, but by the 1964 National Election Studies survey, not a single black reported voting for Goldwater, and black Protestants have voted overwhelmingly Democratic ever since, largely abandoning the party of Lincoln. Given this monolithic unity, church attendance, region, and age have not influenced black Protestants as they have white Protestant groups.

White Catholics

According to all of the best historical studies, white Catholics voted for the Democrats throughout the nineteenth century (Kleppner 1979). Table 4.3 shows that this tendency persisted until the 1970s, except for a brief flirtation with the candidacy of Dwight Eisenhower in the 1950s. The highpoints of Catholic support for Democrats came in the elections of John Kennedy in 1960 and Lyndon Johnson in 1964. By the 1970s and 1980s, however, Catholic votes were up for grabs. Republicans won on some occasions, while Democrats were victorious in others, with the Catholic vote closely mirroring the national percentages. Since 1992, the white Catholic vote has matched the national vote almost identically.

What accounts for this dramatic change over the past seventy years, a transformation unmatched except by evangelical Protestants? Has church attendance made a difference? Until the 1990s, Catholics who attended mass regularly were more likely to vote Democratic than were those who attended less consistently. This tendency changed in the 1990s, perhaps reflecting the persistent anti-abortion messages from the pulpit that may have moved observant Catholics toward the "pro-life" party, the GOP. . . .

. . . Today, all of the large white religious traditions (evangelical and mainline Protestant and Roman Catholic) exhibit the same pattern: regular church attendance, youth, and southern residence are associated with Republican voting.

Some argue that Catholics' movement toward the GOP results from the rise of this historically working-class group aligned with the Democrats toward the upper middle class and its traditional Republican ties. An alternative explanation focuses on a split between traditionalist Catholics, comfortable with the social conservatism of the Republicans and modernist Catholics, who prefer Democratic liberalism. . . .

The Secular Population

Secular citizens (those with no religious affiliation) are a more significant force in electoral politics today than in the past due to their growing numbers. Unfortunately, the role of this constituency tends to be ignored. Table 4.3 reveals that the religiously unaffiliated began the period voting Democratic, supported Eisenhower in 1952 and 1956, Kennedy in 1960, McGovern in 1972, and Reagan and Bush in the 1980s. As social issues became more prominent in the 1990s, secular voters have cast more ballots for Democratic candidates, especially in 2000 and 2004. As long as gay rights, abortion, and church-state issues are prominent, this tend is likely to continue.

Other Religious Groups

The voting behavior of other religious groups has been less important to election outcomes given their smaller size and, in some cases, their low turnout. However, despite their small national population, Jews area significant constituency in New York, California, southern Florida, and a few other locations. In addition, they maximize their impact by high turnout and have voted for Democrats in every presidential election since 1936, usually by wide margins.[27] Mormons, on other hand, are growing in number and are increasingly dispersed across the country from their base in Utah. They vote as strongly for Republicans as Jews do for Democrats. . . .

Latinos were almost absent from surveys conducted before 1970. Now the largest ethnic minority, their votes are being courted by both parties, despite historic low turnout. Few observers, however, have noticed the Catholic-Protestant differences in voting behavior found among Latinos. Latino Catholic support for Democratic candidates is consistently higher than that of Latino Protestants. The latter are theologically conservative and disproportionately Pentecostal or charismatic in their religious orientation, inclining them toward the Republican party. When the GOP takes positions on immigration that displease Latinos, both Protestants and Catholics will vote Democratic; this was the case in 1996. But when immigration is not a key issue and the so-called moral issues are central, one can expect Latino Protestants to vote Republican, as they did in 2004.[28]

Other religious groups are smaller and even less relevant to electoral outcomes. Black Catholics, for example, have never accounted for as much as 1 percent of the electorate. The evidence suggests that they are as reliably Democratic as are black Protestants. There is much speculation about the growth of other religious groups in American society, in particular Muslims (Eck 2001). Survey data, however, do not show large numbers of Muslims or, for that matter, Buddhists or Hindus.[29] These low figures may be due to high survey refusal rates for these groups or, more probably, simply reflect the fact that the numbers are really not that large. When combined into an "other religions" category, they make up over 2 percent of the sample populations since 1990, a slight increase over their numbers in previous decades. In surveys over time, these "other religions" tend to vote Democratic—the historic home of religious minorities.

In sum, data on presidential voting show dramatic changes: evangelical Protestants and white Roman Catholics have realigned, both moving in the direction of the

Republican party. Meanwhile, black Protestants and the religiously unaffiliated have gravitated toward the Democrats, the former in the 1960s and the latter since the mid-1990s. Finally, mainline Protestants have lost their key position as a Republican constituency and by 2004 were a swing group in the electorate. . . .

4.7

Fredrick C. Harris

SOMETHING WITHIN: RELIGION IN AFRICAN-AMERICAN POLITICAL ACTIVISM (1999)

The Scope of African-American Activism

In contrast to most studies on religion and black political activism, this study considers both religion and political action as multidimensional factors. Black political activism embraces what Aldon Morris, Shirley J. Hatchett, and Ronald E. Brown describe as the "orderly and disorderly" sides of the political process (1989). By "orderly and disorderly" they mean that blacks have been socialized into employing political tactics that lie both within and outside of mainstream political processes. In other words, boycotting, picketing, and joining protest marches are just as legitimate as a tool of political expression as voting, campaigning for candidates, or contacting an elected official about a problem. . . .

Black political activism—like all forms of political activities—also differs in the level of commitment actors devote to political action. Voting, for instance, takes relatively less effort than boycotting a store or organizing a neighborhood association. Taking part in a protest during the civil rights movement, for instance, required a greater level of personal commitment and risk than campaigning for a candidate in a northern city. Thus, religion's effects on black activism should vary not only because of religion's multidimensionality, but also because of the nature and context of political action. . . .

Macro and Micro Foundations of Religious Resources

The religious leadership breakfast for senatorial candidate Carol Moseley Braun was more than a routine campaign event. Later, after the breakfast, I listened again and again to the recording of Braun's visit to her own church the Sunday before the election, and I doubted that a survey of churchgoers or ministers could have fully captured the dynamics of either of those events. On the surface, the leadership breakfast could be interpreted as just another way for Braun to target ministers—as she might any other group of powerful people— as potential supporters of her congressional campaign. Yet my observations suggest that there was more going on here than a politician's self-interested pursuit of elites; indeed, they shed light on something far more complex— religion's effects on collective action and black political mobilization. . . .

. . . Scholars of the evolving micromobilization perspective (Mueller 1992), who argue that political actors draw on resources than organizations and institutions, have inspired this adaptation. "Micro" level resources, which are nonmaterial and thus less tangible—some examples are group solidarity, the symbolic articulation of political goals, and feelings of confidence in one's ability to affect political matters—play a crucial role in political mobilization.

Activities during the leadership breakfast and Braun's visits at worship services illustrate some of the ways that micro resources help actors to negotiate and formulate political goals. Members of a cultural group construct collective identities, formulate grievances, and articulate possibilities of political success through their own cultural milieu. When mobilized, these identities, grievances, and estimates of potential success interact with macro resources—funding, meeting space, and networks—that are lodged in the organizations and institutions of politicized groups (Mueller 1992, 10–11). Thus when one minister urged participants at the breakfast to commit their "prayers, time, and energy" to Braun's campaign, he identified both micro and macro foundations of political mobilization as mutually supportive sources for cooperative action.

Macro Resources

Macro resources for political mobilization are readily recognized by students of social movements and political participation. Locating them, because they are often tangible, is easier than uncovering micro resources, which are subtle and often unrecognized as sources of collective action even by the actors themselves. The ministerial breakfast easily revealed how a church could furnish political actors with organizational and institutional resources. The indigenous leadership, communication networks, easy availability of mass memberships, and social interaction of political actors at the breakfast were there for all to see. . . .

Religion, Domination, and Black Oppositional Culture

. . . Many of the cultural resources through which blacks shape oppositional worldviews evolve from their religions (Cone 1972; Raboteau 1978; Thurman 1981; Genovese 1974; Cone 1969, 1986). The use of religious language and icons in the political discourse of the former Democratic candidate, the Reverend Jesse Jackson, served as a valuable cultural resource for the mobilization of black voters during his 1984 and 1988 candidacies (Henry 1990; Barker 1988; Washington 1985; Wills 1990). Similarly, Martin Luther King and other civil rights movement activists used religious language and art to articulate views and motivate participants (Raines 1977; Branch 1988; Walker 1979; Washington 1986).

As Cheryl Townsend Gilkes observes, indigenously expressed forms of African-American Christianity like sermons and testimony "speak directly to the structures of oppression which cause black suffering"(1980, 36). This collective perspective on racial domination appears in other cultural forms of the African-American religious experience as well, particularly in music. As Wyatt T. Walker theorizes, African-American religious music operates in at least two ways. It creates an oppositional space for political reflection by "locat[ing] the people's strength of heritage, their roots, where they are and where they want to go." It also "mobilizes and strengthens the resolve for struggle," functioning as an agent of oppositional consciousness by serving as a "primary reservoir of . . . Black people's historical context" and performing as an "important factor in the process of social change"(1979, 181).

Thus African-American religious symbols, carved from the experience of white domination, promote a collective perspective of opposition in American society, which in turn fosters psychological resources for political participation such as group consciousness and feelings of political efficacy. Culture operates as a resource for mobilization by serving as a means for interpreting and legitimizing political goals.

Culture and the Construction of Collective Action Frames

Why or how political actors construct meaning for individual and collective action is often overlooked in the literature on political mobilization. With analysis I hope to illustrate that mass response to mobilization is more complex than the psychologically and organizationally centered models of activism convey. When mobilized, individuals do not detach themselves from their cultural milieu. Rather, actors make sense of political goals by developing indigenously constructed meanings drawn from shared worldviews, language, religion, experience and history.

The construction of meaning for political goals occurs in the context of what some scholars of social movements have called collective action frames, a term that refers to the way actors create "purposely constructed guides to action"(Tarrow 1992). Specifically, collective action frames "organize experience and guide action" and are a "necessary condition for movement participation, whatever its nature or intensity"(Snow et al. 1986). As Sidney Tarrow points out, action frames operate within the culture of politicized groups, providing "leaders with a reservoir of symbols with which to construct a cognitive frame for collective action"(1992, 177).

. . . [C]ulture and political goals work in tandem to influence the construction of action frames. Culture influences the goals or "preferences" of groups that emerge from "points of concern"(Laitin 1988). Group preferences evolve from the interaction of material interests with cultural ties that bind individuals into groups. Culture as well as material interests make certain preferences "obvious and important" to the members of a collectivity and thus endogenous to collective action. Without such stated goals or preferences, there can be no targeted action.

Culture also supplies material for the production of action frames. During the process of mobilization, stated objectives alone might not be sufficient for gaining an understanding of a targeted action. Instead, potential activists must, in order to reduce uncertainty about their articulated goals, make sense of these goals. Political entrepreneurs must clarify goals to potential actors by conveying them through familiar language and images. . . .

Thus, by such "linking" or "framing" of action through culture, goals are readily communicated to targeted groups, according legitimacy and certainty to action, and in turn, mobilizing. Conferring legitimacy to political action is, as Murray Edelman argues, crucial because, through symbols, actors are able to construct diverse meanings for political events that "[shape] support for causes and that [legitimize] value allocations" to actors (1985, 195). Movements that lack an existing, easily grasped, and mutually important cultural framework through which to communicate meaning will find group-based mobilization a far greater challenge.

Uncertainty, Sacred Symbols, and Action Frames

Sacred symbols, like secular ones, may be used to clarify and legitimize political goals. Culture traffics in symbols that give meaning to reality and experience. Culture is performed through ritual, a means of inventing and sustaining symbols. For those with whom sacred symbols resonate, such symbols might be more persuasive vehicles for political meaning than their secular equivalents. Sacred symbols have, as Geertz points out, a "peculiar power" that comes from "their presumed ability to identity fact with value at the most fundamental level, to give what is otherwise merely actual, a comprehensive normative import"(1973, 127).

By reducing the abstract to the familiar, sacred symbols and rituals provide meaning to articulated goals, reducing uncertainty about political action and conferring upon it a sacredly-ordained legitimacy. . . .

If people are inherently "symbolizing, conceptualizing, meaning-seeking animal(s)" (Geertz 1973, 140), rituals and symbols should act as culturally based resources for mobilization by constructing frames of action through religious meaning. Sacred symbols do not work in isolation from secular ones; in many situations they complement one another, working together to strengthen frames of action. . . .

Manipulators and Mobilizers: Strategic Uses of Rituals and Symbols

In the post–civil rights era, religious culture continues to assist black mobilization. Its current use among black political elites reveals that it is often pressed into use to serve both group and individual political interests. Political entrepreneurs strategically employ religious rituals and symbols to enhance their own legitimacy and mobilize voters behind their candidacies. The use of symbols and rituals is often subtle, as in the case of one political entrepreneur who politicized the religious ritual of "testifying" as a means of bestowing legitimacy to his election to public office. Traditionally, by testifying or "bearing witness," the converted publicly affirm their faith through expressions of appreciation and acknowledgement of God's guidance and protection. . . .

Ritual and Symbols in a Religious Culture of Opposition

. . . As I have emphasized throughout this analysis, activists use cultural material to construct frames of action, which inspire confidence in their goals by conveying information in familiar images and language. Simply put, culture figures considerably in the process of mobilization. In the case of African-American politics, sacred symbols and rituals provide the material from which to construct an action frame, giving sacredly ordained legitimacy to political goals. Given the perceived infallibility of the sacred, the impact of religious culture on mass activism could be far greater than that of secular culture.

4.8

Nathan J. Kelly and Jana Morgan Kelly

RELIGION AND LATINO PARTISANSHIP IN THE UNITED STATES (2005)

. . . The Latino population of the U.S. has grown dramatically in the past few decades, surpassing blacks as the largest minority group in the 2002 Current Population Survey. Electorally, Latinos comprised a larger proportion of voters in 2000 than in any previous election. Existing studies have focused on the low levels of participation and citizenship among Latinos, but the political importance of Latinos is increasing (Arvizu and Garcia 1996; Calvo and Rosenstone 1989; Diaz 1996; Garcia 1997; Hero and Campbell 1996; Hritzuk and Park 2000; Jones-Correa and Leal 2001; Verba et al. 1993). Since 1994, in fact, Latino participation in elections has increased at almost the same rate as their growth in the population. Given the sheer number of Latinos as well as evidence of rising naturalization and political participation levels, more attention to Latino political behavior is appropriate in order to appreciate the nature and magnitude of their current and future influence on U.S. politics. . . .

. . . Our analysis seeks to understand the interplay between religion and ethnicity in politics and to assess the determinants of partisanship in an important minority. . . .

Latino Religious Affiliation in the U.S.

Some might be inclined to dismiss the above discussion based on the assumption that there is little if any religious variation in the Latino population. After all, it is a common belief that the overwhelming majority of Latinos are Catholic. Without religious variation there would be little effect of religion on partisanship or other political attitudes and behavior. . . .

. . . [T]he stereotype that the Latino population is overwhelmingly and immutably Catholic is inaccurate and misleading. While scholars of American religion have become aware of declining attachment to Catholicism among Latinos (Greeley 1994), political scientists have paid little attention to this phenomenon. Previous studies suggest that approximately three-quarters of Latinos were affiliated with the Catholic Church during the 1980s, declining from over 80% in earlier decades (Greeley 1994; Hunt 1998). Table 4.4 indicates a further decline in Latino affiliation with the Catholic Church, with 44 percent of Latinos identifying as non-Catholics during the 1990s. While non-Catholic Latinos are mostly evangelical Protestants, our data indicate that an appreciable

Table 4.4 Religious Variation among Latinos

			a. Ethnicity			
Religious tradition	All Latinos	Mexicans	Cubans	Puerto Ricans	Other Latinos	Non-Latinos
Evangelical	23%	22%	27%	27%	23%	28%
Mainline Protestant	7%	7%	3%	4%	7%	19%
Roman Catholic	56%	59%	63%	58%	53%	26%
Other	4%	4%	7%	3%	5%	10%
Secular	9%	9%	0%	9%	12%	17%
N	951	428	30	109	384	

	b. Time in U.S.		
Religious tradition	Born and raised abroad	Raised abroad and in U.S.	Born and raised in U.S.
Evangelical	19%	23%	26%
Mainline Protestant	4%	7%	8%
Roman Catholic	61%	55%	54%
Other	5%	5%	4%
Secular	11%	10%	8%
N	241	312	398

percentage are either mainline Protestant or have no religious affiliation. Clearly, religion is not a constant factor among Latinos. . . .

Latinos, Religion and Partisanship in the United States

. . . Contrary to conventional wisdom, Latinos are diverse religiously. More Latinos than ever are not Catholic and the non-Catholic category exhibits considerable religious and political variation. The data show that an appreciable percentage of Latinos are evangelical or mainline Protestants, or have no religious affiliation. More important, these religious differences matter politically. Latinos affiliated with denominations of various religious traditions diverge in their partisan affiliations. These variations are not only present in bivariate analyses, but also persist as significant predictors when controlling for a variety of other characteristics. More specifically, we have found that affiliation with evangelical and, especially, mainline Protestant denominations increases identification with the Republican party. On the other hand, those who affiliate with no church or denomination are likely stronger Democrats than even Roman Catholics when demographic and political controls are applied.

While we do not have time-series data with which we can explicitly test dynamic hypotheses, our results also provide some leverage on the prospects for future partisan alignments among Latinos. In sum, we see two important patterns among Latinos that are central to the future of American politics. The first relates to the size of the Latino population—it has been growing and will continue to do so for many years to come. Furthermore, the geographical distribution of Latinos serves to emphasize their political importance. While Latinos are not as geographically concentrated as they once were, the largest Latino populations exist in some of the most electorally important states such as Texas, Florida, California, New York, and Illinois. Traditionally, the increasing proportion of Latinos, a disadvantaged immigrant group, has been seen as a foundation for Democratic Party success. While Latinos have been disengaged from politics in the past, the current partisan alignment among this ethnic group certainly favors Democrats as the Latino population grows and becomes more politically active. There is a second pattern, however, that might serve to moderate this Democratic advantage. Namely, there has been and will likely continue to be a decline in Catholicism among Latinos in the U.S. This religious change could serve to diminish Latino identification with the Democratic party if increasing numbers of Latinos move to evangelical and mainline Protestant churches.

4.9

Amaney Jamal

THE POLITICAL PARTICIPATION AND ENGAGEMENT OF MUSLIM AMERICANS: MOSQUE INVOLVEMENT AND GROUP CONSCIOUSNESS (2005)

. . . (M)ost studies treat religious institutions as sites for the acquisition of individual civic skills and similar vehicles that channel member concerns. Some studies have looked at the mechanisms by which ethnic religious institutions incorporate minority groups in the political process. Beyond basic associational dynamics, little is known about how minority membership in religious institutions structures political engagement.

The new studies that have begun to look at the role of religious institutions in ethnic minority communities have returned mixed results. Although some studies find that ethnic religious associations enhance mobilization, there is little consensus as to the specific processes or mechanisms that link members of ethnic religious institutions to political activity. Some studies argue that ethnic associations serve as direct mobilizers, whereas others highlight the acquisition of skills in these religious sites and their effects on political mobilization (Jones-Correa and Leal 2001; Lien et al. 2001; Verba, Schlozman, and Brady 1995). Whether ethnic religious institutions promote psychological effects, similar to group consciousness, is an issue of debate in the literature on ethnic patterns of political participation. . . .

Mosques and Political Participation

Building on this existing scholarship, my study examines the role that American mosques play in trajectories of political mobilization. In the literature of religion and politics, American mosques have received practically no attention.[30] We know very little about the political roles of mosques in the United States. Even less clear are the roles that mosques actually play in the mobilization of Muslim Americans. Are mosques linked to greater levels of political involvement for Muslim Americans? Are they conduits channeling engaged citizen concerns? Do processes of civic education and enhancement of civic skills (which thereby increase levels of civic involvement) accompany mosque participation? And do mosques foster levels of group consciousness that are useful for political activity in a manner similar to that of the politicized Black churches that Calhoun-Brown (1996) studies?

This article proceeds as follows: First, I present evidence illustrating that mosque participation is in fact associated with higher levels of various dimensions of political activity among all the Muslims in the sample. Once these data are disaggregated along ethnic lines, however, mosque participation seems significant only for Arab Muslim patterns of political activity and not significant for African American or South Asian Muslim political participation. Second, I ask whether an increase in civic skills and group consciousness accompanies mosque participation among these groups. The answer to this question will offer important insights as to whether (a) Arab Muslim political participation is related to direct mobilization and an increase in civic skills and group consciousness and (b) whether mosque participation among South Asian and African American Muslims is generating higher levels of civic skills and group consciousness.

Finally, I show that although mosque participation is associated with higher levels of civic involvement for both Arab and South Asian Muslims, this does not appear to be the case for African American Muslims. Furthermore, mosque participation is directly linked to higher levels of group consciousness among Arab and African American Muslims but not for South Asians. The differences that emerge among various Muslim ethnic populations, I argue, are a direct result of each group's ethnic experience in the United States. Arab Americans have had a stronger tradition of political participation in the United States. They have a long history of political activity aimed at both improving their own standing in the United States and influencing U.S. foreign policy in the Middle East. South Asian Muslims have played an active role in religious and civic life, yet until more recently, their spiritual and ethnic activities have not spilled over into the political sphere. African American Muslims, most of whom converted to Islam, remain more distant from the political sphere altogether. Their levels of mosque participation are associated with neither increases in levels of political activity nor civic involvement. Similar to Black churches, a notable effect of mosque participation is a higher awareness of the discrimination that affects other Muslims in the United States. Unlike Black churchgoers, however, the mosque does not necessarily serve as a vehicle of political incorporation among this subpopulation. . . .

Muslim Americans and Mosque Participation

Estimated at between 5 and 7 million, the Muslim American population is one of the fastest growing religious minorities in the country.[31] Today, American mosques number close to 1,200, a 62% increase since the 1980s. Within a 4-year period, New York City itself witnessed a two-fold increase in the number of mosques (Dodds 2002).[32] More than 20% of U.S. mosques have Islamic schools associated with them, and mosque attendance has increased 75% in the past 5 years, with approximately 1,625 Muslims linked to each mosque (Bagby, Perl, and Froehle 2001). The Muslim American community comprises both first-generation immigrants, primarily from the Middle East and South East Asia, as well as second-, third-, and fourth-generation Americans.[33] U.S. mosques gather Muslims from all sects and generations, creating expansive spaces for community and worship. Approximately 90% of contemporary U.S. mosques assemble members with mixed ethnic backgrounds. However, it is fair to say that specific ethnic groups—primarily African Americans, Arab Americans, and South Asians—dominate most mosques.

Newly emergent mosques serve as key sites for political activity and mobilization.[34] National Muslim advocacy groups, such as the Council for American Islamic Relations (CAIR), carry out voter registration drives, encourage mosque members to vote, and appeal to a wider constituency through mosque outreach campaigns.[35] The coalition-building efforts of these Muslim organizations across mosques and Arab American groups were so effective that the unified Muslim bloc vote in 2000 is thought to have been significant in many states.[36] By and large, Muslim Americans threw their support behind George W. Bush. This was a departure from their previous two-to-one support for Bill Clinton in 1996. Muslim Americans see the American political system as a place where they can actively express their opinions and concerns. In a poll administered by the Muslims and Public Sphere project at Georgetown University, 93% of Muslims reported that Muslims should participate in the U.S. political system, and 77% reported that they were involved with organizations to help the poor, the sick and homeless, or the elderly.[37] More than two thirds reported involvement with a school or youth program, and more than half (51%) stated that they have either petitioned or written the media or a politician on a given issue.[38] Patterns of civic engagement among mosque participants illustrate that this group of Muslims is actively engaged in American civic life through their local mosques.

New mosques across the United States have, in recent years, become more visibly Islamic; increasingly, architectural structures are adorned with domes and crescents . . . With the growing influence of mosques in American civic and political life, it is imperative to understand the degree to which mosques encourage political engagement and the causal mechanisms that link Muslim mosque-goers to more political activity.

Test and Hypothesis

Clearly, mosques are becoming potential sites for political activity. It is not clear, however; whether mosques are linked to broader forms of political activity across Muslim subgroups. Is this political participation the result of direct mobilization efforts? And do mosques bolster civic participation and shore up psychological benefits arising from growing forms of group consciousness? To better understand the role of the mosque in Muslim political life, I examine the importance of mosque participation on patterns of nonvoting political activity. . . .

In this study, political activity is a dependent variable based on four questions. The first question asks the following: Have you ever called or written the media or a politician on a given issue, or have you signed a petition? The second question is as follows: Have you ever attended a rally in support of a politician or cause? The third question in the survey asks the following: Have you ever given a contribution or volunteered your time or services to a political candidate? Finally, the fourth question is as follows: Would you consider yourself to be an active member of a political party? Among Muslims in the sample, 38.85% reported that they had not participated in any of these political activities, 28.66% had participated in one, 14.65% had participated in two acts, 12.42% had participated in three, and 5.41% had participated in all four acts. Political activity is coded here as a 5-point Likert-type scale variable. . . .

Controlling for key demographic variables, levels of mosque participation are directly associated with higher levels of political activity, as illustrated in Table 4.5.[39] Other demographic variables include education, marital status, and birth nationality. Those more highly educated, single, and born in the United States are more likely to be politically active. As expected by numerous studies on minority political activity, education also structures the political participation of Muslim Americans. Once the data is disaggregated along ethnic lines, however, the relationship between mosque participation and political activity becomes more complex (see Table 4.6). Although mosque participation relates to greater political activity for Arab Muslims, this relationship does not hold for South Asian or African American Muslims.[40] Among Arabs, those with higher education, who are single as opposed to married, who are women, and who are older are more likely to be politically active. As in socioeconomic status predictions, education remains significant for Arab political activity. Those who are single, older, and female might have more time on their hands to actively engage the political process.

For African Americans, the only significant variable is age; those who are older tend to be more politically involved. Mosque involvement and other demographic variables are also not pertinent for South Asian Muslim patterns of political activity. The only factor that is connected to their activity is whether respondents are U.S. born. Those born in the United States are more likely to be politically involved. Foreign-born South Asian

Table 4.5 Mosque Participation and Political Activity

	Political activity	
Independent variable	B	SE
Mosque involvement	0.141**	.065
Education	0.176***	.068
Foreign born	−0.825***	.154
Gender	0.014	.145
Age	0.008	.006
Marital status	−0.285*	.160
Constant	1.57***	.534
N	296	
Adjusted R^2	.153	

*$p < .10$. **$p < .05$. ***$p < .001$.

Note: Coefficients are unstandardized ordinary least squares regression values.

Table 4.6 Mosque Participation and Political Activity among Muslim Groups

| | Political activity | | | | | |
| | Arab Muslims | | African-American Muslims | | Asian Muslims | |
Independent variable	B	SE	B	SE	B	SE
Mosque involvement	0.435**	0.137	0.096	0.200	−0.101	0.099
Education	0.234*	0.128	0.187	0.235	0.071	0.100
Foreign born	−0.275	0.310	−0.772	0.998	−0.629*	0.371
Gender	0.624*	0.297	0.108	0.417	−0.268	0.256
Age	0.024**	0.010	0.037*	0.018	−0.015	0.009
Marital status	−0.612**	0.275	−0.267	0.414	−0.068	0.291
Constant	−1.33	1.12	0.586	1.81	2.99***	1.01
N	67		46		123	
Adjusted R^2	.190		.027		.033	

$*p < .10. **p < .05. ***p < .001.$

Note: Please note that each equation was run on the individual indicators of political activity and that significance levels and effects remained consistent across equations. Coefficients are unstandardized ordinary least squares regression values.

Muslims are less likely to be active. Poor language skills and lack of political knowledge are plausible explanations for this finding.

That the mosque is associated with political activity for Arabs and not South Asians and African Americans is telling. One would expect that if the mosque were a vehicle of political mobilization, it would consistently be tied to political activity among all mosque affiliates; however, the evidence thus far suggests that this is not the case. Although more systematic data are needed to explain why mosque participation is salient for Arab Muslim political activity and not for South Asian or African American political behavior, there are other dimensions of civic engagement that can be further examined in the data. For instance, are mosques associated with higher levels of civic involvement among these subpopulations? For Arabs, this association between mosque participation and higher levels of civic participation would mean that mosque participation is linked to both civic skills and political activity. For African American and South Asian Muslims, this would suggest that higher levels of mosque involvement can generate some form of civic capital but not necessarily be linked to political participation. Furthermore, what relationship does mosque participation have on experiences with discrimination and perceptions of intolerance and disrespect by mainstream society (measures of unfair treatment important for group consciousness)? Are mosque members more likely to be victims of discrimination and perceive mainstream society as biased against Muslims? Understanding the role of mosques and whether they attract hostility from mainstream society could further enhance our understanding as to whether mosques generate levels of group consciousness that may be useful for political involvement. . . .

Conclusion

Mosque participants are therefore situated in a unique and multi- functional locale that serves their inspirational, communal, and social needs. For Arab Muslims, mosques are directly linked to political activity, civic participation, and group consciousness. For African and Arab Americans, the mosque serves as a collectivizing forum that highlights Muslim common struggles in mainstream American society. Such common-fate attitudes and attachments unite these Muslim Americans. For South Asian Muslims, mosque participation enhances their civic participation but neither their levels of political engagement nor their levels of group consciousness.

Notes

1. When religious beliefs and practices are compared across industrialized nations, the distinctive quality of American religious life becomes particularly evident. Americans are much more likely to report weekly church attendance than those who reside in other Western cultural contexts, and they are more than twice to nearly five times more likely than residents in these other countries to pray daily. The same holds true in terms of religious beliefs, as they are far more likely than those of other Western industrialized nations to report that they believe in life after death and that they believe in miracles. Given these patterns, it is probably no surprise that Americans are also the most likely to label themselves as very religious as well. See, for example, Table 3.1 in Corwin E. Smidt, Kevin denDulk, James Penning, Stephen Monsma, and Douglas Koopman, *Pews, Prayers, and Participation: Religion and Civic Responsibility in America*. Washington, D.C.: Georgetown University Press, 2008.

2. To get an idea of just how many denominations there are, see the listing of a national directory for Christian denominations at http://christianity.about.com/od/denominations/a/denominations.htm. Accessed August 9, 2008.

3. I am not claiming that religion is the only factor shaping political preferences. While other factors may operate, religion should not be ignored. One cannot fully understand American political attitudes and behavior without understanding the religious characteristics of the American people surveyed.

4. Adding in ethno-religious factors, one should also consider Latino Protestants and Latino Catholics as distinct traditions, or at least subtraditions. In addition, there are "nontraditional

conservative" religious groups (Latter-day Saints, Jehovah's Witnesses) and other "nontraditional liberal" religious groups (Unitarians and "New Age" groups).

5. At times, both affiliation and movement identification are conceptualized as religious identities (Alwin et al. 2006), and certainly it is possible that some claims of affiliation may reflect little more than identification. Nevertheless, most respondents who claim an affiliation also report some level of worship attendance. Hence, it is better to conceptualize affiliation as reflecting primarily a sociological phenomenon, similar to gender or race, rather than as a psychological phenomenon (though obviously there are also psychological facets related to classifying oneself in terms of these types of variables as well).

6. Woodberry and Smith argue that the term "evangelical" is confusing—and it is. The problem emerges because evangelicalism is both an ongoing religious tradition with historical roots and organizational ties and a religious movement whose origins can be traced to the creation of the National Association of Evangelicals in 1942. However, the label "conservative Protestant" is probably more problematic. Not only is it unclear whether "conservative" is a theological or a political designation (the two are often conflated), but the term is ahistorical, suggesting that current "conservative" characteristics associated with the tradition are immutable and not the reflection of some particular historical era. Further, the "conservative Protestant" label can easily encompass groups such as Latter-day Saints and Jehovah's Witnesses which, though "conservative" in some

senses, fall outside the evangelical Protestant tradition on almost every social, theological, and organizational indicator.

7. For example, the Exploring Religious America Survey (PBS/U.S. News & World Report 2002) asked Christians in two separate questions whether they would describe themselves as evangelicals and as born-again. Among those who labeled themselves born-again, less than half (38 percent) also described themselves as "evangelical Christians," while more than one in four (27 percent) self-identified evangelical Christians refused to describe themselves as born-again.

8. For Barna, "born again Christians" are those who said they have made a personal commitment to Jesus Christ that is still important in their life today, and who also indicated they believe that when they die they will go to Heaven because they had confessed their sins and had accepted Jesus Christ as their savior. Respondents are not asked to describe themselves as "born again." Evangelicals then must meet this born-again criterion, plus seven other conditions. These include: (1) saying their faith is very important in their life today; (2) believing they have a personal responsibility to share their religious beliefs about Christ with non-Christians; (3) believing that Satan exists; (4) believing that eternal salvation is possible only through grace, not works; (5) believing that Jesus Christ lived a sinless life on earth; (6) asserting that the Bible is accurate in all that it teaches; and (7) describing God as the all-knowing, all-powerful, perfect deity who created the universe and still rules it today. See The Barna Update, "Presidential Race Tightens as Faith Voters Rethink Their Preferences." www.barna.org/FlexPage.aspx?Page=Barna UpdateNarrow&BarnaUpdateID=314 Accessed: August 12, 2008.

9. Because most uses of the religious tradition variable contains a category that captures the historic African-American denominations and places respondents who are affiliated with them in a black Protestant tradition, the evangelical Protestant category captures far fewer African Americans than what is obtained through an approach which classifies evangelicals simply on the basis of the religious beliefs that one holds.

10. This does not mean that *every* religion is so regarded. All religions, of course, are entitled to, and receive, equal freedom and protection under the Constitution, but not all are felt to be really American and therefore to be retained with Americanization. The Buddhism of Chinese and Japanese immigrants, for example, is definitely felt to be something foreign in a way that Lutheranism, or even Catholicism, never was; the Americanization of the Chinese or Japanese immigrant is usually felt by the immigrant himself, as well as by the surrounding American community, to involve dropping the non-American faith and becoming a Catholic or a Protestant, usually the latter.

11. The volumes, published by AltaMira Press are: *Religion and Public Life in the Pacific Northwest: The None Zone* (Patricia O'Connell Killen and Mark Silk, eds.), *Religion and Public Life in the Mountain West: Sacred Landscapes in Transition* (Jan Shipps and Mark Silk, eds.), *Religion and Public Life in the Midwest: Heartland as Common Denominator* (Philip Barlow and Mark Silk, eds.), *Religion and Public Life in New England: Steady Habits Changing Slowly* (Andrew Walsh and Mark Silk, eds.), *Religion and Public Life in the Southern Crossroads: Showdown States* (William Lindsey and Mark Silk, eds.), *Religion and Public Life in the South: In the Evangelical Mode* (Charles Reagan Wilson and Mark Silk, eds.), *Religion and Public Life in the Middle Atlantic: The Fount of Diversity* (Randall Balmer and Mark Silk, eds.). A final summary volume, written by Mark Silk and Andrew Walsh, will be titled, *One Nation, Divisible: Religion and Region in America Today*.

12. For the record, the states are apportioned among regions as follows: New England (ME, NH, VT, MA, CT, RI); Middle Atlantic (NY, NJ, PA, DE, MD, DC); South (WV, VA, KY, TN, NC, SC, GA, FL, AL, MS); Midwest (OH, MI, IN, IL, WI, MN, IA, NE, KS, ND, SD); Southern Crossroads (LA, TX, AR, OK, MO); Mountain West (MT, WY, CO, ID, UT, NM, AR); Pacific (NV, CA, HI); and Pacific Northwest (OR, WA, AK).

13. The enhancement was conducted by demographers at the Polis Center in Indianapolis. The most important addition involved supplying estimates for the traditionally African-American denominations, none of which submitted membership figures to Glenmary.

14. For data on religious self-identification we relied on the 2001 American Religious Identification Survey, conducted at the City University of New York by Barry Kosmin, Ariela Keysar, and Egon Meyer.

15. The survey data on which this is based was compiled by John Green of the University of Akron from the quadrennial surveys on religion and public issues funded by the Pew Charitable Trusts.

16. Membership figures for mainline and evangelical churches (below) are taken from *Christianity Today,* 11 August 1997, 11.

17. This section draws on Beyerlein and Chaves (2003). See that article for a more comprehensive bibliography on religion and politics and for additional detail regarding the analyses and results described in this chapter.

18. This literature is too vast to cite in its entirety. For representative examples, see Green et al. (1996); Harris (1999); Jelen (1992); Kohut et al. (2000); Leege and Kellstedt (1993); Manza and Brooks (1997); Olson and Carroll (1992); Olson (2000); Peterson (1992); Regenerus, Sikkink and Smith (1999); Verba, Schlozman, and Brady (1995); Wald, Owen, and Hill (1988); and Wilcox (1996).

19. Rather than being based on nationally representative samples of congregations, research focusing on religious institutions and political activity has been based on case studies of religiously based political organizations (for example, Wilcox 1996); case studies of particular congregations (for example, Balmer 1993: chap. 8; Wood 1994; Park 1998); surveys of individuals within a relatively small number of congregations (for example, Wald, Owen, and Hill 1988; Jelen 1992); or congregations, clergy, or activists associated with a particular political or social movement (for example, Smith 1996; McAdam 1982; Morris 1984; Hart 2001).

20. Voter guide production and distribution is not unique to Christian right groups. The League of Women Voters, for example, distributes voter guides, as does Interfaith Alliance, an association of liberal and moderate Christians. When a congregational informant said that voter guides had been distributed, he or she also was asked who wrote or produced the guides. Responses to this open-ended question allowed NCS coders to determine whether the guides were produced by an organization associated with the religious right.

21. Another comparison point is offered by the Form 990 that some charities are required to file with the IRS. In 1998, only 1.4 percent of "public charities"—organizations with 501(c)(3) IRS status—reported lobbying expenditures on their Form 990. Looking at subtypes of these organizations, we find that 4.6 percent of environmental and animal-related organizations lobbied, as did 2.8 percent of health organizations, 1.1 percent of human service organizations, 0.8 percent of arts and cultural organizations, and 0.7 percent of mutual benefit associations (Boris and Krehely 2002). These numbers are much smaller than the survey-based numbers concerning nonprofits' political activity reported in the main text, probably because lobbying activity and expenditures are underreported to the IRS.

22. Note that this number is close, as it should be, to the comparable percentage from the NCS: 37 percent of individuals are in congregations in which people are told at worship services about opportunities for political activity.

23. Guth et al. (1997) have made a similar point concerning the political activities of white Protestant clergy.

24. The religious tradition differences evident in Table 4.2 are sustained when other important variables are controlled. Readers will not be substantively misled by focusing on the simple percentages in Table 4.2. See Beyerlein and Chaves (2003) for details on multivariate analyses.

25. Given the small number of synagogues in the sample, I refrain from attempting to characterize synagogue-based political activity beyond observing that synagogues seem at least as likely to be politically active as congregations within any Christian tradition.

26. The Gallup surveys done in the 1930s and 1940s often lacked denominational specificity and rarely included questions about partisan identification and church attendance. We were able to use two surveys from 1939, two more from 1940, and one each from 1944 and 1945. The National Election Studies (NES) lacked denominational specificity until 1960. Fortunately, NES conducted a panel study from 1956 to 1960, allowing the use of 1960 denominational data for 1956. The 1956 survey asked questions about partisanship and vote choice in 1948 and 1952, as well as 1956, allowing the time series to go back to 1948. The surveys at the University of Akron were conducted by the authors beginning in 1992 and in each presidential year since. The 1992 survey allows us to reconstruct 1988 presidential choices as it asked how respondents voted in that election.

27. The Akron surveys show a small segment of Orthodox Jews tending to vote Republican in contrast to other Jews.

28. Protestant-Catholic differences among Latinos are important as are differences based on place or country of origin. Mexican Americans dwarf the small numbers of Puerto Ricans, Cuban Americans, and other Latinos in the NES surveys, making Latino subgroup analysis problematic. The Protestant-Catholic differences are even more impressive when one considers the fact that Cuban Americans are predominantly Republican and less likely to be Protestant than the larger Mexican-American population.

29. However, in data from a massive survey of over 50,000 respondents conducted in 2001 (Kosmin and Lachman 2001), the Muslim population had almost doubled since 1990, while the Buddhist and Hindu populations increased even more. Nonetheless, each of these groups was estimated to be less than 1 percent of the population in 2001. Still, these numbers are larger than the proportions of completed interviews from these groups in the surveys used for this study.

30. There are a few studies that have looked at mosques in America (Abraham 2000; Bagby 2004; Bagby, Perl, and Froehle 2001; Jamal in press).

31. There is much controversy over the exact number of the Muslim American population. The figure used in this article is the one that Muslim American groups use. These groups put their numbers at 5 to 7 million. Some argue that Muslim American groups bolster their numbers for electoral reasons. Because the census does not ask questions on religious identity, it is difficult to obtain a reliable estimate.

32. In 1980, the five boroughs contained only 8 or 9 mosques, a number that expanded, according to Marc Ferris, to about 37 in 1991. By 1994, there were more than 70 mosques; the number of mosques in New York City had doubled in 3 years (Dodds 2002).

33. The African American community makes up 30% of the Muslim American population in the United States.

34. Although the mosque has not been historically organized congregationally like churches, it nevertheless relies on rather permanent memberships.

35. Qualitative data collected by the author and participant observation substantiate this finding.

36. Analysts of Arab and Muslim political mobilization in the United States have suggested that the Arab vote and the Muslim vote have historically cancelled one another. Election 2000 witnessed a more unified stance between the two groups.

   The American Muslim Political Coordinating Council Political Action Committee included several national Muslim organizations, including CAIR, the former American Muslim Council, American Muslim Alliance, and Muslim Public Affairs Council. The American Muslim Political Coordinating Council endorsed President Bush (*American Muslim Pac endorses George W. Bush for President* 2004; Houston 2001). Furthermore, a recent representative survey of the Detroit Arab American Community (DAAS) conducted by Wayne Baker, Ronald Stockton, Sally Howell, Amaney Jamal, Ann Chih Lin, Andrew Shryock, and Mark Tessler (DAAS) revealed that 74% of Arab Muslims voted for Bush in the Detroit metro area. The American Muslim Alliance reported that 72% of the Muslim American community voted for Bush in 2000 as well.

37. There is growing concern among the Muslim community, especially post-September 11, that American Muslims do not participate in U.S. politics because of the secular nature of the United States. The Muslim Fiqh Council issued an extensive fatwa (Islamic legal edict) on the issue of participation in U.S. politics, basically stating that political participation in the United States was not only allowed but in fact a duty (*Fatwa Bank: Muslim participation in the political science in the U.S.* 2004; *American Muslim Poll: November/December 2001* 2004).

38. Please note that the Muslims in American Public Square survey is representative of Muslim communities that are in close proximity to established mosques. Although these findings may be representative of mosqued Muslim communities, it is difficult to assess their applicability to nonmosqued Muslim communities. Nonmosqued Muslim communities constitute anywhere between 65% and 70% of the total Muslim American population.

39. The question on mosque involvement is as follows: Excluding Salah (prayer) and Jumah prayer (Friday prayers), how involved are you in the activities at the mosque? Very involved, somewhat involved, somewhat not involved, or not involved at all?

40. The category *Asian Muslim* includes Afghanis, Pakistanis, Bangladeshis and Indians.

CHAPTER 5

RELIGION AND SOCIAL MOVEMENTS

Introduction

Religious actors, institutions, and language have been at the center of all major social reform efforts in the United States. Social movements promoting the abolition of slavery, women's rights, black freedom, temperance, and other causes found religion a ready tool for combating injustice. The historical record does not affirm a naked public square devoid of religious content and actors, but rather indicates that religious actors and motivations have proved instrumental to enlarging and extending liberties and freedoms ostensibly granted under the Constitution of the United States.

The research pieces in this chapter all focus on the origins and the maintenance of social movements. In the first excerpt, Christian Smith seeks to fill a gap in the academic literature, presenting a compelling argument that religion has been central to many social movements and thus merits researchers' attention. Smith describes many of the religious tools and tactics that promote social activism and discusses characteristics of religious leaders and their flocks that render them a natural fit for the sacrificial work required of social movement activism.

The next two pieces examine religious aspects of the civil rights movement. Aldon Morris's research focuses on the emergence of this movement. Morris provides a multifaceted theory that combines insights from political, economic, and sociological accounts of civil rights success. The focal point for the emergence of the civil rights movement, Morris contends, should be the local level, where activists, institutions, and resources combined to sustain "nonbureaucratic formal organizations" that were crucial to national-level civil rights successes.

The next selection from David Chappell complements the previous pieces by illuminating the importance of prophetic themes and language utilized by movement actors such as Martin Luther King Jr. In the Hebrew Scriptures, prophets are mouthpieces of God who rail against social injustice and call for governments and individuals to pursue justice for the oppressed. For example, Moses told Pharaoh to "let my people go," lest ruin fall upon Egypt. According to Chappell, such prophetic framing by civil rights activists was integral to the eventual success of the civil rights movement.

The primary sources included here showcase a range of actors who invoke religion to achieve their political goals. Decades before Abraham Lincoln called slavery the "Original Sin of the Republic," the "Declaration of Sentiments of the American Anti-Slavery Convention" called the United States to repent of the sin of slavery. Designed to mirror and expand upon the Declaration of Independence, the manifesto more directly appeals to God's law as the foundation for the anti-slavery position. Interestingly, the tactics that abolition leader William Lloyd Garrison and his comrades propose for promoting "this great, benevolent and holy cause" include enlisting the church as a means of exerting grassroots pressure for the eradication of slavery.

The next selection, excerpts from Angelina Grimké's *Appeal to Christian Women of the South*, is an impassioned religious argument against slavery. Angelina and her sister Sarah, daughters of a Southern slaveholder and judge, were among the first women in the United States to speak publicly against slavery. Addressing her Christian sisters, Grimké responds to religious arguments used in favor of the practice, referencing biblical passages to refute each one and to construct a counterargument that slavery is sin. She appeals to her readers' duty as women as she implores them to join the abolitionist cause.

In her fiery speech delivered before a women's rights convention in Akron, Ohio, former slave and traveling evangelist Sojourner Truth asserts that women of both the North and the South were united in their quest for equality. She recounts how she, like other slave women, bore physical burdens equal to men, asking rhetorically, "And ain't I a woman?" Her short but powerful speech refutes the claim of female weakness and the claim of male superiority because Christ was male; as she responds, Christ himself came from God and a woman.

The next selection, Frances Willard's "Home Protection I," illustrates the multifaceted goals of the Women's Christian Temperance Union. Willard admits the vulnerability of women to men consumed by alcohol, but asserts that the collective power of Protestant and Catholic women was central not only in the movement to ban the sale of alcohol, but also to abolition and suffrage. In her words, "God has indicated Woman, who is the born conservator of home, to be the Nemesis of Home's arch enemy, King Alcohol."

The last three primary sources peer into the religious dynamics of the civil rights movement. The "Statement by Alabama Clergymen" and Martin Luther King Jr.'s response,

"Letter from a Birmingham Jail," highlight the tension between religionists over the rationale for and the tactics of social movements. The final selection from civil rights leader Malcolm X offers an interesting critique as he condemns Martin Luther King Jr.'s invocation of religion in the quest for black freedom.

Research Pieces

5.1

Christian Smith

DISRUPTIVE RELIGION: THE FORCE OF FAITH IN SOCIAL MOVEMENT ACTIVISM (1996)

This book is about the disruptive, defiant, unruly face of religion. It is particularly concerned with religion's capacity to mobilize, promote, and abet social movements—organized efforts of challenger groups to promote or resist social change through disruptive means. . . .

Namely, on the one hand, it is clear that religion has often played, and today still plays, an absolutely central role in a number of important social and political movements. Indeed, in a host of cases, religion has served as the primary source of many of the necessary ingredients of social movement emergence and success. Yet, on the other hand, religion's important contribution to social movements remains conspicuously under-explored—arguably virtually ignored—in the academic literature on social movements. Students of disruptive politics have simply paid very little sustained, focused attention to the often-present religious dynamics in their field of study. And students of religion have done an inadequate job of building bridges from their field of study to that of social movements. Of course, scholars in both areas rarely deny the important role religion often plays in social-movement activism. But neither do they give that role the studied attention it deserves.[1] So, there remains a gaping void where there should stand a rich, illuminating body of publications. . . .

The Disruptive Potential of Sacred Transcendence

Religious believers and organizations possess a variety of assets—which we will examine below—that are useful for the promotion of social-movement activism. These include organizational resources, shared identity, normative motivational systems, public legitimacy, and so on. But many other social institutions and organizations also possess these assets, yet rarely employ them for disruptive political activism. What makes religion different in some cases? What is distinctive about religion that, under the right conditions, disposes it to disruptive collective activism? To answer that question, we need to step back and examine more closely what, sociologically speaking, religion is.

From a sociological perspective, religion is a system of beliefs and practices oriented toward the sacred or supernatural, through which the life experiences of groups of people are given meaning and direction.[2]. . .

Religion, viewed sociologically, is a particular kind of cultural meaning-system, oriented toward the sacred or supernatural. Religion affords groups of people meaning and direction by providing sets of beliefs and practices grounded not in the ordinary, mundane world, but in the divine, the transcendent, the eternal, the holy, the spiritual. . . .

Religion's investing life with meaning through sacred transcendence gives it an initially and primarily conservative thrust. By helping to explain and give meaning to the world and life as it is experienced, religion helps to justify and sustain the world and life just as it *is* experienced. By endowing life as it *is* with significance and purpose, religion provides a legitimation for the world as it is.

But that is not the complete story. For religion's very sacred transcendence—with its conservative inclinations—also contains within itself the seeds of radical social criticism and disruption. Religion provides life, the world, and history with meaning, through a sacred reality that transcends those mundane realities. But in doing so, religion establishes a perceived objective reality above and beyond temporal life, the world, and history, that then occupies an independent and privileged position to act—through those who believe the religion—back upon the mundane world. That which is sacred and transcends temporal, earthly reality also stands in the position to question, judge, and condemn temporal, earthly reality. In this way, the ultimate legitimator of the status quo can easily become its ultimate judge. This dual potential lies precisely in the ultimacy and distance that characterizes sacred transcendence itself. . . .

Neither Monocausal Idealism, Nor Materialist Reductionism

It would be misguided to think that disruptive social movements in which religion has figured prominently are exclusively religious conflicts, disconnected from matters of material production and distribution, politics, and social status. Few disruptive social conflicts are simply battles over religious belief and practices alone. Religion itself is a socially constituted reality that always exists in a social context that shapes and is shaped by religion. For this reason, in explaining social movements, it is simply impossible to separate the religious factors of belief and practice from more mundane matters of wealth, power, and prestige. All of these elements of social existence interact dynamically and mutually, and can have combined and reinforcing effects in generating disruptive social conflict. . . .

When it comes to social movements, even ones where religion plays a prominent role, religion is rarely, if ever, the exclusive bone of contention.

Having said that, however, we must also acknowledge that it would be equally misguided to think that these kinds of social movements are not "actually" about religion, but are "really" only about the more mundane—read substantive and important—matters of acquiring wealth, power, and status. To argue that religion serves as a mere epiphenomenal cloak for essentially material or political interests is simplistic and erroneous. That kind of reductionistic analysis serves merely to obscure the actual complexity of social-movement dynamics that very much need to be better understood.

In fact, in the multiple cases we have cited, the stuff of religion has helped to constitute the very substance of these social movements' grievances, identities, organizations, and strategies. . . . We would be foolish, therefore, not to recognize that religious worldviews, interests, traditions, structures, and practices themselves really do matter in shaping the mobilization, struggles, and outcomes of a multitude of social movements. We turn now to examine more precisely the variety of ways in which they can do just that.

Religious Assets for Activism

If and when religious believers or organizations initiate or become caught up in a collective mobilization for disruptive activism, what attributes or assets do they embody or possess that can help to constitute and facilitate that action? . . .

Transcendent Motivation

All social movements confront the problem of motivating their participants to make and maintain a commitment to the collective cause, especially when the activism is costly for participants. Religion offers some important and sometimes unique solutions to this problem of motivation.

Legitimation for Protest Rooted in the Ultimate or Sacred

Perhaps the most potent motivational leverage that a social-movement can enjoy is the alignment of its cause with the ultimacy and sacredness associated with God's will, eternal truth, and the absolute moral structure of the universe. People can compromise, in the end, on wage increases and job security; they can pragmatically negotiate their best political advantage on many public-policy issues. But God's will is something apart—it is not up for grabs or negotiable. What is sacred is sacred. . . The social activism of religious "true believers," therefore, often reflects an uncompromising and tenacious certainty and commitment that sustains activism in the face of great adversity. . . .

Moral Imperatives for Love, Justice, Peace, Freedom, Equity

Social movements emerge, in part, when people come to define their situations as needlessly unjust and susceptible to change. Determining this, of course, requires possessing a set of fundamental moral standards against which the status quo can be judged. In most societies, religion has served as a major source of those kinds of moral standards.

Religion not only attempts to tell us what ultimately is—Yaweh reigns sovereignly over the universe, there is no god but Allah and Mohammed is his prophet, reality is an endless succession of birth, death, and rebirth. Religion also aspires to tell us what, therefore, *should be*, how people *must* live, how the world *ought to* operate—thou shalt not murder, love your neighbor as yourself, honor the spirits of the dead, and so on. The meaning and direction for life that religion provides is inextricably tied to the ethical systems it advocates. In religion, the *is* and *the* ought, the true and the necessary assume and reinforce each other. . . .

Powerfully Motivating Icons, Rituals, Songs, Testimonies, Oratory

All religions . . . incorporate established traditions of ritual, symbols, and narrative expression that represent the worldview, express devotion, and inspire and instruct the faithful. Often these expressive and iconic traditions are elaborate, sophisticated, emotionally powerful, and imbued with the authority of centuries, if not millennia, of historical observation.

Social movements need symbols, rituals, narratives, icons, and songs. They use these to construct their collective identities, to nurture solidarity, to express their grievances, and to draw inspiration and strength in difficult times. Religion, as a major creator and custodian of powerful symbols, rituals, icons, narratives, songs, testimonies, and oratory, is well-positioned to lend these sacred, expressive practices to the cause of political activism. . . .

Ideologies Demanding Self-discipline, Sacrifice, Altruism

A world in which individuals only act to secure divisible rewards for themselves would be one devoid of social movements. For sustainable social movements require that some, perhaps many people, take risks, set examples, and pay prices on the movement's behalf, the personal costs of which are rarely fully repaid, even if the social-movement succeeds. Where does that kind of self-sacrifice come from? It can come from many places, of course, but an important source of such a self-sacrificial orientation is religion.

Most traditional religions engender in their followers an orientation of self-restraint (Bell 1976). . . . Whether it is obeying the Torah, pursuing the Noble Eightfold Path toward nirvana, taking up one's cross and following Christ, struggling in the paths of Allah, pursuing the three Hindu paths to the emancipation of moksha, or renouncing one's own righteousness and trusting only in the unmerited grace of God, religious faithfulness requires psychic or literal self-obliteration. . . .

Faith-based self sacrifice can help to generate a critical mass of participants early on, even when the cause is idealistic, unrewarding, and unpromising. . . . In short, self-sacrifice helps to transcend the "free rider" problem. And that is no small accomplishment. . . .

Legitimation of Organizational and Strategic-Tactical Flexibility

The sacred texts of all major religions are sufficiently ambiguous that they may be interpreted in disparate directions (Hart 1992, 124). It is possible, therefore, for faith based activists to find their sacred texts—perhaps especially when important political interests are at stake—legitimations for a variety of political, organizational, and tactical approaches that may satisfy their movement's needs. . . .

Organizational Resources

Social movements require more than compelling motivations, moral judgement, symbols, self-discipline, and flexibility to generate political disruption. Movements also need a variety of organizational resources by which to mobilize and through which to channel their energy. Organized religion is well-equipped to provide, when it so desires, these key resources to social movements. . . .

Trained and Experienced Leadership Resources

All established religions—by definition collective phenomena—take on some kind of organizational form that, like social movements, necessitates the operation of active leadership. Well before any social-movement in need of resources appears, religious organizations have already established functioning systems of leadership. In many cases, the religious leaders are specialists, formally or informally educated, trained, and experienced in interpersonal communications, group dynamics, and collective-identity construction. Typically, these religious leaders also enjoy influence among their followers, linkages with their colleagues, relative autonomy and flexibility in their daily schedules, and extensive contacts in their broader communities. All of these are invaluable potential assets for a burgeoning social movement. . . .

Financial Resources

Organized religion often possesses extraordinary financial resources that it can—if it so chooses—funnel, directly and indirectly, into social-movement activism. In the United States, for example, Protestant and Catholic churches each year collect from their adherents more than $39 billion in tithes and other contributions (Statistical Abstract 1994, 72). Furthermore, multiple para-church and other religious organizations raise additional hundreds of millions of dollars annually. If and when a religious organization judges that a political-activist cause falls within the bounds of its legitimate religious mission, it often possesses significant financial resources that it can contribute to the cause. . . .

Congregated Participants and Solidarity Incentives

Organized religion is well-equipped to expand the ranks of grassroots activists by providing ready-made opportunities for network- and bloc-recruitment of new members into movements. . . . Religious organizations—which comprise in the United States, for example, the largest share of all types of non-profit, voluntary organizations—can represent a veritable "field ripe for the harvest" for movement recruiters whose issues resonate with religious actors. Viewed in reverse, religious leaders committed to mobilizing disruptive activism have at their disposal ready-made, extensive recruitment networks and organizations. . . .

Pre-existing Communication Channels

In effect, the religion's established communications infrastructures—its newsletters, bulletins, weekly announcements, telephone directories, magazines, television and radio programs, address lists, journals, synods, presbyteries, and councils—that normally transmit information related to the religion's spiritual mission, become employed or are coopted to transmit information related to political activism. The synagogue telephone-tree is used to announce a rally; the worship service bulletin includes a notice about an organization's need for volunteers and donations; the denominational newsletter publishes an article about a social injustice and organizations working to respond; the Imam announces details of a planned protest at the end of Friday prayers. . . .

"Movement Midwives"

Oftentimes, newly emerging or resurging social movements are facilitated by the help of supportive, pre-existent organizations. . . . These kinds of organizations we may call "movement midwives," in recognition of their deliberate efforts to help in the "birthing" of movements, while retaining identities distinct from the movements whose births they assist. . . .

Religious organizations can and often do act as movement midwives. In the United States, for example, the Fellowship of Reconciliation, the American Friends Service Committee, *Sojourners* magazine, Clergy and Laity Concerned, New Jewish Agenda, the National Council of Churches, the Catholic Worker, and a host of other denominations, divinity schools, and para-church organizations have, over the years, worked to help spawn a number of disruptive social movements, without themselves becoming directly identified with the movements (Zald and McCarthy 1987, 73–76). These kind of organizations can, have, and do offer invaluable start-up resources for mobilizing social movements. . . .

Privileged Legitimacy

Political Legitimacy in Public Opinion

In many societies, and under certain circumstances, public opinion accords relatively greater authority to the voice of religion than to other voices. When a bishop, rabbi, ayatollah or other religious leader or teacher denounces an injustice, lodges a complaint against the government, or calls people to support a cause, it is often taken at least somewhat more seriously than the same declaration would be if spoken by a politician, business person, or secular activists. In the United States, the American public may view the voice of religion—especially grassroots religion and religion viewed as normally nonpartisan—as politically naive, perhaps, but also generally as sincere and honorable. Therefore, when religious voices speak on behalf of social movements, they can lend a valuable extra force or earnestness to the movements' causes. . . .

The Protection of Religion as a Last "Open Space"

Sometimes, authoritarian political regimes, in efforts to crush the undermining autonomy of civil society, outlaw and repress all independent associations and voluntary organizations: labor unions, social clubs, student groups, neighborhood organizations, and so on. In many societies, however, even brutal authoritarian regimes are reluctant to ban and completely repress religious institutions. Sometimes religion is untouchable because it seems too influential to challenge; other times, authoritarian regimes consider religion—wrongly—to be "apolitical," and therefore exempt from repression. For whatever reason, in many authoritarian situations, religious organizations have become the only remaining "open spaces" in civil society.

Under these conditions, religious authorities will often feel morally obliged to allow political dissidents to operate within their religious institutions, if not to proactively champion the rights of the repressed people. . . This can be a valuable protection for repressed social movements.

5.2

Aldon Morris

The Origins of the Civil Rights Movement: Black Communities Organizing for Change (1984)

Social Movement Theory and the Indigenous Approach

The present analysis of the civil rights movement is informed by three important sociological theories of social movements and collective action: classical collective behavior theory, Weber's theory of charismatic movements, and the resource mobilization theory. Insights have been drawn from those theories when appropriate, and they have served as a point of departure for further theorizing. I shall briefly present the main points of these theories and assess them in light of my findings on the civil rights movement. I shall then present the outlines of an indigenous approach to movements of the dominated. . . .

There is, besides, a more general problem with the resource mobilization perspective when applied to the civil rights movement. The present study found that such cultural factors as religious beliefs, music, and sermons, although refocused by activists, were important to the development of the movement. Similarly, it was found that charisma had an independent effect on the mobilization and organizational dynamics of the movement. The centrality of these factors is not captured by existing formulations of resource mobilization theory, because those formulations treat these fluid qualities as a residual category rather than a central component of the theory.

This study of the civil rights movement has employed an indigenous perspective. That perspective draws heavily from resource mobilization theory, adopting its emphasis on resources, organization, and rationality. It also draws from Weber by reconceptualizing his theory of charisma. The indigenous perspective supplies additional concepts and analytical statements relevant to mass-based movements of dominated groups. As the present study is confined to a single movement, the generalizability of its findings is still to be established. It is believed, however, that a number of the findings are broad in scope and relevant to understanding other movements by dominated groups.

The indigenous perspective is concerned with movements by dominated groups. A dominated group is defined as one that is excluded from one or more of the decision-making processes that determine the quantity and quality of social, economic, and political rewards that groups receive from a society.[3] Because of this exclusion, dominated groups at different times attempt to change their situation of powerlessness by engaging in nontraditional and usually nonlegitimized struggles with power holders. The task of the indigenous perspective is to examine how dominated groups take advantage of and create the social conditions that allow them to engage in overt power struggles with dominant groups.

The indigenous approach maintains that the emergence of a sustained movement within a particular dominated community depends on whether that community possesses (1) certain basic resources, (2) social activists with strong ties to mass-based indigenous institutions, and (3) tactics and strategies that can be effectively employed against a system of domination.

The basic resources enabling a dominated group to engage in sustained protest are well-developed internal social institutions and organizations that provide the community with encompassing communication networks, organized groups, experienced leaders, and social resources, including money, labor, and charisma, that can be mobilized to attain collective goals. These indigenous resources are especially important in the early phases of a movement because it is at this time that such an effort requires stable, predictable sources of funding, organization, communications, and leadership. From this perspective, indigenous resources are far more likely to be crucial in the early phases of movements, because outside resources tend to be sporadic and highly conditional, in most cases coming in response to pressure from indigenous movements already under way.[4] The significance of outside resources, in this view, lies in the help they can give in sustaining movements. However, our evidence suggests that they are not a causal determinant, because they are triggered by the strength and force of indigenous movements. The same holds true for the larger political climate, because the force of indigenous movements affects that environment, causing outside groups to act to protect or enhance their interests.

The presence of indigenous resources within a dominated community does not ensure that a movement will emerge. Rather, movements are deliberately organized and developed by activists who seize and create opportunities for protest. Social activists, in this view, play creative roles in organizing and developing movements; they must redirect and transform indigenous resources in such a manner that they can be used to develop and sustain social protest. For example, black church congregations have historically provided the money needed to sustain the church and its diverse activities. During the movement, however, activist clergymen and other church leaders had to redefine fundraising activities in such a way that additional funds could be raised to support protest activities. In some cases this even meant redefining the role of religion by broadening its scope to include supporting those efforts aimed at changing the social order. In order for activists to mobilize indigenous resources they must have access to them. Therefore, activists who have strong ties to mass-based indigenous institutions are in an advantageous position to mobilize a community for collective protest. Mass-based institutions provide activists with groups of people who are accustomed to accomplishing goals in an organized manner and with much of the money and labor force capable of being harnessed for political goals.

The availability of resources and strategically placed activists will not crystallize into a protest movement if a dominated group has not developed tactics and strategies that can be effectively used in confrontations with a system of domination. Effective tactics and strategies are those that can be employed by masses of people to generate widespread disruption of a social order. It is the widespread disruption of a society that generates the collective power of masses used by dominated groups in their struggle to redistribute power.

When a dominated group has assembled the required resources, strategically placed activists, and effective tactics and strategies for protest purposes, it has developed a local movement center. More specifically, a movement center has been established in a dominated community when that community has developed an interrelated set of protest leaders, organizations, and followers who collectively define the common ends of the group, devise necessary tactics and strategies along with training for their implementation, and engage in protest actions designed to attain the goals of the group. A local movement center is thus a distinctive form of social organization specifically developed by members of a dominated group to produce, organize, coordinate, finance, and sustain social protest. The ability of a given community to engage in a sustained protest movement depends on that community's development of a local movement center. An important sociological task is to identify and analyze the social mechanism(s) that enable protest to spread between dominated communities, broadening the scope and influence of a movement. From the indigenous perspective, sustained social movements will spread between communities that develop local movement centers. The pace, location, and volume of protest in various communities are directly dependent on the quality and distribution of local movement centers.

The term "local movement center" refers to a dynamic form of social organization. Movement centers vary in their degree of organization, hence in their capacity to produce and sustain protest. Moreover, the distribution and quality of local movement centers vary over time. An important task of social movement theory is to explicate the conditions that produce tactical innovations within movements, and to account for the timing and forms of such innovations. From the indigenous perspective tactical innovations within movements are likely to occur and succeed when local movement centers are extensive and well developed across dominated communities. Such conditions provide the internal social organization that enables activists to spread rapidly and sustain the innovations in the context of active opposition. . . .

Formal organization is an important property of local movement centers. Existing movement literature is unclear as to whether mobilization of social protest is facilitated more by formal bureaucratic organizations or loosely organized groups. The present study suggests that an intermediate form of organization can be crucial in mobilizing and coordinating protest by large numbers of people. The key organizations of the civil rights movement usually were not highly bureaucratic or loosely organized; rather, they were nonbureaucratic formal organizations such as the Montgomery Improvement Association, the Southern Christian Leadership Conference, and the Student Nonviolent Coordinating Committee. From the indigenous perspective, nonbureaucratic but formal organizations are often the most appropriate for wide-scale social protest because they facilitate mass participation, tactical innovations, and rapid decision-making. That conclusion leads to two corollaries. One, bureaucratic protest organizations of a dominated group may prevent wide-scale disruptive protest; because they inhibit mass participation, rapid decision-making, and the development of innovative tactics. Two, attacks on bureaucratic protest organizations by ruling groups during periods of political tension can precipitate new forms of mass protest by forcing activists to develop and use nonbureaucratic formal organizations, which, as noted, are more appropriately structured for mass mobilization and wide-scale protest.

Leadership is an important property of local movement centers. Protest leaders are not by-products of movements, nor is their behavior totally determined by structural imperatives. The behavior of leaders is voluntary to the extent that they engage in organization-building, mobilizing, formulation of tactics and strategies, and articulation of a movement's purpose and goals to participants and the larger society. However, I do not take a purely voluntaristic view of movement leadership. This study suggests that if most leaders are not created by their movements, they were usually leaders in other spheres of the community before the outset of the movement. It was from preexisting leadership groups that individuals were chosen as movement leaders. Furthermore, leadership in dominated communities is often characterized by conflict and disunity prior to a movement. The central question becomes: How are movement leaders chosen in those communities where deep leadership divisions exist? The present study found that this problem was solved in various black communities by choosing preexisting leaders who were well integrated into the community but were still relative newcomers not identified with conflicting factions. Finally, our data show that charismatic leadership can be an important property of movement centers in that it facilitates the mobilizing and organizing processes of movements. However, charisma is conceptualized here as a preexisting institutional process of a dominated group. This charisma is able to operate best in movements characterized by nonbureaucratic formal organizations, where bureaucratic procedures are relaxed and the more fluid and personalized qualities of charisma are freed.

Movement halfway houses help the development of movement centers by providing valuable resources that otherwise would prove costly and time-consuming to acquire. By the same token, indigenous movements provide halfway houses with opportunities to effect social change on a wider scale than they can attain alone. This mutual need increases the likelihood that halfway houses and indigenous movements will establish cooperative relationships.

The indigenous perspective takes into account that resources and the activities of individuals and groups outside a dominated community can assist in sustaining and shaping the outcome of indigenous movements. A distinction must be made, however, between resources voluntarily supplied by individuals and groups who identify with the goals of the movement and those supplied by political actors (e.g. heads of state, courts, national guards) in response to political crises created by the movement. Resources and activities by political actors, I argue, should be conceptualized as part of the social change activity sought and politically established by the movement. Hence those resources nonvoluntarily supplied by political actors are outcomes of movements rather than assistance to them. On the other hand, when groups and individuals outside of an indigenous movement voluntarily provide that movement with resources, they facilitate the social change efforts of the dominated community. What is similar about the two kinds of outside response is that both depend on the strength of an indigenous movement and the scope of change it seeks.

Finally, well-entrenched indigenous movements can generate collective action by other groups in the larger society, because a strong indigenous movement develops visible organizational structures and tactics that can be adopted by other discontented groups. In this sense, the presence of an indigenous movement serves as a resource for other groups and provides outside activists with a training ground, enabling them to learn the intricacies of social protest.

Impact of the Civil Rights Movement

The Southern civil rights movement had a profound impact on American society. First, it significantly altered the tripartite system of domination, largely dismantling those components which severely restricted the personal freedom of blacks and disfranchised them in the formal political sense. Second, the movement altered and expanded American politics by providing other oppressed groups with organizational and tactical models, allowing them to enter directly into the political arena through the politics of protest. . . .

The impact of the civil rights movement penetrated far beyond the black community. During the civil rights movement a number of other groups in the United States, including American Indians, women, farm workers, and college students shared an experience somewhat similar to the blacks': They were excluded from one or more of the main centers of power and decision-making in American society. To be sure, the extent of the exclusion varied and had different impacts on these groups. But nevertheless they were all disadvantaged, because their interests were not routinely taken into account by the powerful. In the years immediately preceding the civil rights movement these groups attempted to change their position through traditional routes or quietly bore their hardships. The civil rights movement transformed those tame and relatively ineffective approaches.

In a loud and clear voice the civil rights movement demonstrated to those groups that organized nontraditional politics was a viable method of social change, capable of bringing about the desired results far faster than traditional methods. Moreover, the civil rights movement provided excluded groups with concrete organizational (e.g. the SCLC, SNCC, the NAACP) and tactical (e.g. sit-ins, marches, boycotts) models they could follow in their struggles against oppression. Furthermore, the civil rights movement served as a training ground for many of the activists who later organized movements within their own communities. Indeed, the modern women's movement, student movement, farm workers' movement, and others of the period were triggered by the unprecedented scale of nontraditional politics in the civil rights movement.[5] Following the civil rights movement it has become commonplace for groups traditionally excluded from power to pursue their interests through demonstrations and protest.

The impact of the civil rights movement is not confined to the United States. Its influence can be seen in the antinuclear movement in Europe. Karl-Dieter Opp, a German scholar, recently wrote that participants in the antinuclear movement often maintain that the movement should be nonviolent and should employ tactics of civil disobedience, including boycotts, "sit-ins," and "go-ins" (Opp 1982). Bernadette

Devlin-McAlishey, a leader of the Irish Catholics in Northern Ireland, maintains that "there is a strong affinity between the black civil rights movement in this country and the civil rights movement in our country" (*Michigan Daily* 1982). Thus the civil rights movement has transformed the American national political community to a considerable degree and has had an impact on international politics.

5.3

David L. Chappell

A Stone of Hope: Prophetic Religion and the Death of Jim Crow (2004)

What about those who did make civil rights move? What were their ideas of human nature? Gunnar Myrdal projected his optimism onto black America. He insisted that most Negroes resisted the influence of W E. B. Du Bois and others who had become "pessimistic." Most of them had "not lost their belief that ultimately the American Creed will come out on top." Black people had even greater faith than white people in "the magic of education" (Myrdal 1962, 799,884).[6]

It is impossible to say whether Myrdal was right about the black population in general. . . . Myrdal has been roundly criticized for ignoring black culture in his study.[7] But subsequent historians have ignored what may be the most relevant aspect of black culture: the thinking of strategists of direct action in the 1950s and early 1960s. . . .

The black strategists who left a detailed record of their views do not fit Myrdal's conception. They did not think like midcentury American liberals. Whereas Myrdal and the liberals were optimistic about human development, especially about human institutions, the intellectuals of the civil rights movement stood out for their rejection of this world and its natural tendencies. They were conspicuous for their unwillingness to let social processes work themselves out and for their lack of faith in the power of education and economic development to cure society of oppressive evils. In their thinking, they were more akin to the Hebrew Prophets, Frederick Douglass, and the Reinhold Niebuhr of 1932–44 than they were to mainstream liberals.[8]

Martin Luther King's Anthropology

Martin Luther King is probably the best place to start, though historians at first exaggerated his influence and have lately been underestimating it. King appeared liberal in some respects and obviously owed a debt to liberal theology. For example, when he applied to seminary and when he later looked back on his call to the ministry, he saw the ministry as a social mission rather than a divine inspiration.[9] But he rejected the liberal optimism of the social gospel. . . . (S)cholars have overemphasized his theological liberalism and have neglected to differentiate the relative significance of his liberal opinions from that of his illiberal ones.

King expressed a strong dislike for what he called the "fundamentalism" of his father and the church in which he grew up. In that sense, he was a liberal. But in his doctrine of man—which is far more decisive in explaining his career in civil rights-King could never embrace liberal optimism. On the subject of human nature, he was closer to orthodoxy than to liberalism. Indeed, on human nature he was close to the modern conservatism of Edmund Burke.[10] Even in his papers at Crozer Theological Seminary (1948–51), before he apparently read Niebuhr, King leaned toward prophetic pessimism about man.[11] That leaning, along with his tendency to focus his pessimism on racial and economic inequality in the United States, distinguishes him from Myrdal and Schlesinger and postwar liberals in general. . . .

In the essay on Jeremiah, King sounds out the keynotes of his later speeches and public writings.[12] First, there is the prophetic belief that the nation is in moral decline. According to King, the nation is in decline partly because the national creed—far from creating the psychic tension that would inspire reform (as Myrdal would have it)—is defective and needs itself to be reformed. Jeremiah, King tells us, "realized that the covenant made at Mount Sinai had failed to accomplish its purpose. . .".

King's attraction to Jeremiah put him on the same path as Niebuhr, who in his rejection of both liberalism and neo-orthodoxy came up with "prophetic religion" as the best name for the doctrines he emphasized. King frequently referred to "prophetic Christianity" in his later writings and speeches and cited Jeremiah, Amos, and Isaiah as examples of brave men who sacrificed their social position and standing (if not their lives) when they preached to society of its corruption and insisted on total, rather than incremental, reformation.[13] . . .

The point is not that King got these emphases solely from Niebuhr. Indeed, the rather obvious point scholars lately stress, that King learned most of his abiding commitments in the black Baptist Church in which he grew up, does not conflict with the argument here. The useful thing that King learned from that rich and diverse tradition—the things he did not reject as "fundamentalist"—were compatible with what he later learned from Niebuhr. The significance of Niebuhr is not that he invented the prophetic tradition, but rather that he codified its teachings and expressed them for his contemporaries in vivid, arresting language that King understood—indeed understood better than most liberals. King understood the Niebuhrian language and found it useful, partly because of his grounding in black southern Baptist tradition, which had within it a tradition of prophetic resistance to the corrupt tendencies of this world.[14] The historian Robert Franklin identifies King with a distinct "prophetic radicalism" in the black church, a stance that was rare but well enough established to be an obvious option to King. . . . Where King ends up is what matters. King's striving to reconcile prophetic elements from his peculiar tradition with the best of the rest of American Protestantism, and with the best of the American civic tradition, made his thought converge with Niebuhr's.

King's relationship to Niebuhr is not a question of roots—historians have an occupational susceptibility to the genetic fallacy—but a question of affinities. If we hope to appreciate King and his message to America, we need to understand his grappling with Niebuhr's thought. Surely his background in black southern Baptist traditions prepared him to grapple, but that is all it did. Recent scholarship implies, in effect, that everything King needed to know he learned in kindergarten—his spiritual kindergarten, "the" black church. But it was the mature King who communicated with a world beyond his church, who brought much of his church with him into the "mainstream," who reminded his church and the mainstream how much they had in common.[15]

An "American Dilemma" or a "Theistic Dilemma"?

King did not comment on Myrdal's American Dilemma until long after he finished school (and then only superficially).[16] But he explored something parallel to Myrdal's theme, what he called the "theistic dilemma," in considerable detail at Crozer. In an essay on "the Problem of Evil," King said that theists like himself have a "dilemma": their faith tells them that the power "behind all things is good. But on every hand the facts of life seem to contradict such a faith." As a Christian, King had to believe (as he stated in an earlier essay) in "eschatological hope." But he also had to be realistic about man's life on this earth before the Second Coming. He quoted John Stuart Mill: "Nearly all things which men are hanged or imprisoned for doing to one another are nature's every day performances. Nature kills, burns, starves, freezes, poisons." Time and again, King wrote, echoing Jeremiah and Job, history shows "the just suffering while the unjust prosper." Evil was "rampant" in the universe: "Only the superficial optimist who refuses to face the realities of life fails to see this patent fact." This argument was incompatible with any Myrdalian belief that psychic guilt would compel a nation to desist from evil practices. King insisted that the problem of evil cannot be fully solved, at least not by human beings on this earth.

King's "theistic dilemma" has a greater long-term significance. The same essay shows a connection between his rejection of optimism and his later calls upon his followers for self-sacrifice. Though King considered all "solutions" to the problem of evil to be incomplete, he thought that one of them had great merit: the view that "the purpose of evil is to reform or to test." (This was superior to the theory that evil was a punishment for man's sin, since it responded to the Job- and Jeremiah-like objection that virtuous people suffer evil and evil people often avoid suffering.) King asked . . . "Who can deny that many apparent evils turn out to be goods in disguise[?] Character often develops out of hardship. Unfortunate hereditary and environmental conditions often make great and noble souls. Suffering teaches sympathy."[17] King later encouraged his followers to go into lions' dens and to walk through valleys of the shadow of death. He told them that their sacrifices could force an unwilling system to make concessions, but even if they failed in this act of protest or in this life, "unearned suffering is redemptive." That phrase is a key to King's philosophy of life, one that owes much to the example of Jeremiah and other Hebrew Prophets. It is also King's gloss on the sacrifice of Jesus, his guide to the path of His footsteps.[18]

King's message came to a pragmatic, political point: the long-suffering people must suffer still more to deliver themselves from injustice. That is the crowning injustice of oppression: those who have already paid the price of injustice must pay further to undo it, while the perpetrators and beneficiaries of injustice get off scot-free— indeed, they will probably find a way to benefit from any decrease of injustice. But this is unavoidable. The oppressed are the only ones who will hear the burden of the struggle against their oppression because they are the only ones with an interest in doing so. To expect history to follow any other path is dangerously naive. . . .

Niebuhr becomes more prominent in King's graduate school writings at Boston University from 1951 to 1954. In his notes on Jeremiah in 1952–53, King suggests that "neo-orthodoxy" could help revive a prophetic movement. Neo-orthodox thinkers "call us back to a deeper faith in God" by rejecting, as Jeremiah did, "all forms of humanistic perfectionism." Though objecting to extreme forms of neo-orthodoxy, he finds the doctrine generally useful to "those of us who are opposed to humanism in the modern world" and who seek to make "a rational defense of theism." There is an urgency in these notes: supplanting faith in man with prophetic faith in God is "the need of the hour." This urgency related to the dangers King perceived in social inequality. Rejecting humanism entailed rejecting the rich, who glorified and found success in the City of Man. In notes on the Seventy-second Psalm, King wrote: "Christianity was born among the poor and died among the rich. Whenever Christianity has remained true to its prophetic mission, it has taken a deep interest in social justice." Whenever the church has abandoned the poor, there have been "disastrous consequences." Saving Christianity means reviving its Prophets' interest in the poor. "We must never forget that the success of communism in the world today is due to the failure of Christians to live [up] to the highest ethical ten[et]s inherent in its system."[19]. . .

King alludes to Niebuhr's belief that Christianity, even orthodoxy, is sometimes subversive: "When government pretends to be divine, the Christian serves God rather than man. The Christian must constantly maintain a 'dialectical' attitude toward government." Quoting Niebuhr, King writes, democracy "'arms the individual with political and constitutional power to resist the inordinate ambition of rulers, and to check the tendency of the community to achieve order at the price of liberty.'"

King is equally attentive to Niebuhr's insistence that the corruptions of power do not justify all actions of the powerless. "Niebuhr admits that there is risk in arming men with the power of resistance, but he sees the alternative risk as worse." Here King captures Niebuhr's somewhat negative, Churchillian defense of democracy: it is the best that limited, sinful man can do. "Niebuhr makes it clear that a perfect democracy is just as impossible to reach as either the perfect society or a perfect individual. The evils of democracy are patent.". . . .

The point is not that King read or cited Niebuhr more than, say, Brightman [a theologian]. Rather, it is that what makes King a world-historical figure is his Niebuhrian pessimism about human institutions and his Niebuhrian insistence that coercion is tragically necessary to achieve justice.

Niebuhr, or—to invoke a broader tradition behind Niebuhr—prophetic Christianity, is more of a key to what happened in King's public life than the mushy generalizations scholars make about "the" black church" or "African-American tradition." It is no more useful to say that King was shaped by the black church than to say that he breathed air or was a Georgian. What sets him *off* from the black church is what makes him significant. Much of the time, black churches really did serve as opiates of the masses—as one of King's mentors, Benjamin Mays, coauthor of the long standard work, *The Negro's Church* (1933), complained.[20] What set King off from the black church is what set him off from the liberals—what led him out of both of those Egypts.[21]

Primary Sources

5.4

William Lloyd Garrison

DECLARATION OF SENTIMENTS OF THE AMERICAN ANTI-SLAVERY CONVENTION
(DECEMBER 14, 1833)

The Convention, assembled in the City of Philadelphia to organize a National Anti-Slavery Society, promptly seize the opportunity to promulgate the following DECLARATION OF SENTIMENTS, as cherished by them in relation to the enslavement of one-sixth portion of the American people.

More than fifty-seven years have elapsed since a band of patriots convened in this place, to devise measures for the deliverance of this country from a foreign yoke. The corner-stone upon which they founded the TEMPLE OF FREEDOM was broadly this— "that all men are created equal; that they are endowed by their Creator with certain in-alienable rights; that among these are life, LIBERTY, and the pursuit of happiness." At the sound of their trumpet-call, three millions of people rose up as from the sleep of death, and rushed to the strife of blood; deeming it more glorious to die instantly as freemen, than desirable to live one hour as slaves.—They were few in number—poor in resources; but the honest conviction that TRUTH, JUSTICE, and RIGHT were on their side, made them invincible.

We have met together for the achievement of an enterprise, without which, that of our fathers is incomplete, and which, for its magnitude, solemnity, and probable results upon the destiny of the world, as far transcends theirs, as moral truth does physical force.

In purity of motive, in earnestness of zeal, in decision of purpose, in intrepidity of action, in steadfastness of faith, in sincerity of spirit, we would not be inferior to them.

Their principles led them to wage war against their oppressors, and to spill human blood like water, in order to be free. *Ours* forbid the doing of evil that good may come, and lead us to reject, and to entreat the oppressed to reject, the use of all carnal weapons for deliverance from bondage—relying solely upon those which are spiritual, and mighty through God to the pulling down of strong holds.

Their measures were physical resistance—the marshalling in arms—the hostile array—the mortal encounter. *Ours* shall be such only as the opposition of moral purity to moral corruption—the destruction of error by the potency of truth—the overthrow of prejudice by the power of love—and the abolition of slavery by the spirit of repentance.

Their grievances, great as they were, were trifling in comparison with the wrongs and sufferings of those for whom we plead. Our fathers were never slaves—never bought and sold like cattle—never shut out from the light of knowledge and religion—never subjected to the lash of brutal taskmasters.

But those, for whose emancipation we are striving,—constituting at the present time at least one-sixth part of our countrymen,—are recognised by the laws, and treated by their fellow beings, as marketable commodities—as goods and chattels—as brute beasts;—are plundered daily of the fruits of their toil without redress;—really enjoy no constitutional nor legal protection from licentious and murderous outrages upon their persons;—are ruthlessly torn asunder—the tender babe from the arms of its frantic mother—the heart-broken wife from her weeping husband—at the caprice or pleasure of irresponsible tyrants;—and, for the crime of having a dark complexion, suffer the pangs of hunger, the infliction of stripes, and the ignominy of brutal servitude. They are kept in heathenish darkness by laws expressly enacted to make their instruction a criminal offence.

These are the prominent circumstances in the condition of more than TWO MILLIONS of our people, the proof of which may be found in thousands of indisputable facts, and in the laws of the slaveholding States.

Hence we maintain—

That in view of the civil and religious privileges of this nation, the guilt of its oppression is unequalled by any other on the face of the earth;—and, therefore,

That it is bound to repent instantly, to undo the heavy burden, to break every yoke, and to let the oppressed go free.

We further maintain—

That no man has a right to enslave or imbrute his brother—to hold or acknowledge him, for one moment, as a piece of merchandise—to keep back his hire by fraud—or to brutalize his mind by denying him the means of intellectual, social and moral improvement.

The right to enjoy liberty is inalienable. To invade it, is to usurp the prerogative of Jehovah. Every man has a right to his own body—to the products of his own labor—to the protection of law—and to the common advantages of society. It is piracy to buy or steal a native African, and subject him to servitude. Surely the sin is as great to enslave an AMERICAN as an AFRICAN.

Therefore we believe and affirm—

That there is no difference, *in principle*, between the African slave trade and American slavery;

That every American citizen, who retains a human being in involuntary bondage, is, according to Scripture, (Ex. 21:16) a MAN-STEALER;

That the slaves ought instantly to be set free, and brought under the protection of law;

That if they had lived from the time of Pharaoh down to the present period, and had been entailed through successive generations, their right to be free could never have been alienated, but their claims would have constantly risen in solemnity;

That all those laws which are now in force, admitting the right of slavery, are therefore before God utterly null and void; being an audacious usurpation of the Divine prerogative, a daring infringement on the law of nature, a base overthrow of the very foundations of the social compact, a complete extinction of all the relations, endearments and obligations of mankind, and a presumptuous transgression of all the holy commandments—and that therefore they ought to be instantly abrogated.

We further believe and affirm—

That all persons of color who possess the qualifications which are demanded of others, ought to be admitted forthwith to the enjoyment of the same privileges, and the exercise of the same prerogatives, as others; and that the paths of preferment, of wealth, and of intelligence, should be opened as widely to them as to persons of a white complexion.

We maintain that no compensation should be given to the planters emancipating their slaves—

Because it would be a surrender of the great fundamental principle that man cannot hold property in man;

Because SLAVERY IS A CRIME, AND THEREFORE IT IS NOT AN ARTICLE TO BE SOLD;

Because the holders of slaves are not the just proprietors of what they claim;—freeing the slaves is not depriving them of property, but restoring it to the right owner;—it is not wronging the master, but righting the slave—restoring him to himself;

Because immediate and general emancipation would only destroy nominal, not real property: it would not amputate a limb or break a bone of the slaves, but by infusing motives into their breasts, would make them doubly valuable to the masters as free laborers; and

Because if compensation is to be given at all, it should be given to the outraged and guiltless slaves, and not to those who have plundered and abused them.

We regard, as delusive, cruel and dangerous, any scheme of expatriation which pretends to aid, either directly or indirectly, in the emancipation of the slaves, or to be a substitute for the immediate and total abolition of slavery.

We fully and unanimously recognise the sovereignty of each State, to legislate exclusively on the subject of the slavery which is tolerated within its limits. We concede that Congress, *under the present national compact*, has no right to interfere with any of the slave States, in relation to this momentous subject.

But we maintain that Congress has a right, and is solemnly bound, to suppress the domestic slave trade between the several States, and to abolish slavery in those portions of our territory which the Constitution has placed under its exclusive jurisdiction.

We also maintain that there are, at the present time, the highest obligations resting upon the people of the free States, to remove slavery by moral and political action, as prescribed in the Constitution of the United States. They are now living under a pledge of their tremendous physical force to fasten the galling fetters of tyranny upon the limbs of millions in the southern States;—they are liable to be called at any moment to suppress a general insurrection of the slaves;—they authorise the slave owner to vote for three-fifths of his slaves as property, and thus enable him to perpetuate his oppression;—they support a standing army at the south for its protection;—and they seize the slave who has escaped into their territories, and send him back to be tortured by an enraged master or a brutal driver.

This relation to slavery is criminal and full of danger; IT MUST BE BROKEN UP.

These are our views and principles—these, our designs and measures. With entire confidence in the overruling justice of God, we plant ourselves upon the Declaration of our Independence, and upon the truths of Divine Revelation, as Upon the EVERLASTING ROCK.

We shall organize Anti-Slavery Societies, if possible, in every city, town and village of our land.

We shall send forth Agents to lift up the voice of remonstrance, of warning, of entreaty and rebuke.

We shall circulate, unsparingly and extensively, anti-slavery tracts and periodicals.

We shall enlist the PULPIT and the PRESS in the cause of the suffering and the dumb.

We shall aim at a purification of the churches from all participation in the guilt of slavery.

We shall encourage the labor of freemen over that of the slaves, by giving a preference to their productions;—and

We shall spare no exertions nor means to bring the whole nation to speedy repentance.

Our trust for victory is solely in GOD. We may be personally defeated, but our principles never. TRUTH, JUSTICE, REASON, HUMANITY, must and will gloriously triumph. Already a host is coming up to the help of the Lord against the mighty, and the prospect before us is full of encouragement.

Submitting this DECLARATION to the candid examination of the people of this country, and of the friends of liberty all over the world, we hereby affix our signatures to it;—pledging ourselves that, under the guidance and by the help of Almighty God, we will do all that in us lies, consistently with this Declaration of our principles, to overthrow the most execrable system of slavery that has ever been witnessed upon earth—to deliver our land from its deadliest curse—to wipe out the foulest stain which rests upon our national escutcheon—and to secure to the colored population of the United States all the rights and privileges which belong to them as men and as Americans—come what may to our persons, our interests, or our reputations—whether we live to witness the triumph of JUSTICE, LIBERTY and HUMANITY, or perish untimely as martyrs in this great, benevolent and holy cause.

5.5

Angelina E. Grimké

APPEAL TO THE CHRISTIAN WOMEN OF THE SOUTH (1836)

Respected Friends,

It is because I feel a deep and tender interest in your present and eternal welfare that I am willing thus publicly to address you. Some of you have loved me as a relative, and some have felt bound to me in Christian sympathy, and Gospel fellowship; and even when compelled by a strong sense of duty, to break those outward bonds of union which bound us together as members of the same community, and members of the same religious denomination, you were generous enough to give me credit, for sincerity as a Christian, though you believed I had been most strangely deceived. I thanked you then for your kindness, and I ask you *now,* for the sake of former confidence, and former friendship, to read the following pages in the spirit of calm investigation and fervent prayer. It is because you have known me, that I write thus unto you.

But there are other Christian women scattered over the Southern States, a very large number of whom have never seen me, and never heard my name, and who feel *no* interest whatever in *me.* But I feel an interest in *you,* as branches of the same vine from whose root I daily draw the principle of spiritual vitality—Yes! Sisters in Christ

I feel an interest in *you*, and often has the secret prayer arisen on your behalf, Lord "open thou their eyes that they may see wondrous things out of thy Law"—It is then, because I *do feel* and *do pray* for you, that I thus address you upon a subject about which of all others, perhaps you would rather not hear any thing; but, "would to God ye could bear with me a little in my folly, and indeed bear with me, for I am jealous over you with godly jealousy." Be not afraid then to read my appeal; it is *not* written in the heat of passion or prejudice, but in that solemn calmness which is the result of conviction and duty. It is true, I am going to tell you unwelcome truths, but I mean to speak those *truths in love*, and remember Solomon says, "faithful are the *wounds* of a friend." I do not believe the time has yet come when *Christian women* "will not endure sound doctrine," even on the subject of Slavery, if it is spoken to them in tenderness and love, therefore I now address *you*.

To all of you then, known or unknown, relatives or strangers, (for you are all *one* in Christ,) I would speak. . .

"The *supporters* of the slave system," says Jonathan Dymond in his admirable work on the Principles of Morality, "will *hereafter* be regarded with the *same* public feeling, as he who was an advocate for the slave trade *now is*." It will be, and that very soon, clearly perceived and fully acknowledged by all the virtuous and the candid, that in *principle* it is as sinful to hold a human being in bondage who has been born in Carolina, as one who has been born in Africa.

All that sophistry of argument which has been employed to prove, that although it is sinful to send to Africa to procure men and women as slaves, who have never been in slavery, that still, it is not sinful to keep those in bondage who have come down by inheritance, will be utterly overthrown. We must come back to the good old doctrine of our forefathers who declared to the world, "this self evident truth that *all* men are created equal, and that they have certain *inalienab*le rights among which are life, *liberty*, and the pursuit of happiness". . . .

But after all, it may be said, our fathers were certainly mistaken, for the Bible sanctions Slavery, and that is the highest authority. Now the Bible is my ultimate appeal in all matters of faith and practice, and it is to *this test* I am anxious to bring the subject at issue between us. . . .

But I shall be told, God sanctioned Slavery, yea commanded Slavery under the Jewish Dispensation. Let us examine this subject calmly and prayerfully. I admit that a species of *servitude* was permitted to the Jews, but in studying the subject I have been struck with wonder and admiration at perceiving how carefully the servant was guarded from violence, injustice and wrong. . . .

I would just ask whether American slaves have become slaves in any of the ways in which the Hebrews became servants. Did they sell themselves into slavery and receive the purchase money into their own hands? No! Did they become insolvent, and by their own imprudence subject themselves to be sold as slaves? No! Did they steal the property of another, and were they sold to make restitution for their crimes? No! Did their present masters, as an act of kindness, redeem them from some heathen tyrant to whom *they had sold themselves* in the dark hour of adversity? No! Were they born in slavery? No! No! not according to *Jewish Law*, for the servants who were born in servitude among them, were born of parents who had *sold themselves* for six years: Ex. xxi, 4. . . . Southern slaves then have *not* become slaves in any of the six different ways in which Hebrews became servants, and I hesitate not to say that American masters *cannot* according to *Jewish law* substantiate their claim to the men, women, or children they now hold in bondage. . . .

Where, then, I would ask, is the warrant, the justification, or the palliation of American Slavery from Hebrew servitude? How many of the southern slaves would now be in bondage according to the laws of Moses; Not one. You may observe that I have carefully avoided using the term *slavery* when speaking of Jewish servitude; and simply for this reason, that *no such thing* existed among that people; the word translated servant does *not* mean *slave*, it is the same that is applied to Abraham, to Moses, to Elisha and the prophets generally.

Slavery then never existed under the Jewish Dispensation at all, and I cannot but regard it as an aspersion on the character of Him who is "glorious in Holiness" for any one to assert that "*God sanctioned, yea commanded slavery* under the old dispensation." I would fain lift my feeble voice to vindicate Jehovah's character from so foul a slander. If slaveholders are determined to hold slaves as long as they can, let them not dare to say that the God of mercy and of truth *ever* sanctioned such a system of cruelty and wrong. It is blasphemy against Him. . . .

Shall I ask you now my friends, to draw the parallel between Jewish *servitude* and American *slavery*? No! For there is *no likeness* in the two systems; I ask you rather to mark the contrast. The laws of Moses *protected servants* in their *rights as men and women*, guarded them from oppression and defended them from wrong. The Code Noir of the South *robs the slave of all his rights* as a *man*, reduces him to a chattel personal, and defends the master in the exercise of the most unnatural and unwarrantable power over his slave. They each bear the impress of the hand which formed them. The attributes of justice and mercy are shadowed out in the Hebrew code; those of injustice and cruelty, in the Code Noir of America. . . .

I have thus, I think, clearly proved to you seven propositions, viz.: First, that slavery is contrary to the declaration of our independence. Second, that it is contrary to the first charter of human rights given to Adam, and renewed to Noah. Third, that the fact of slavery having been the subject of prophecy, furnishes *no excuse whatever to* slavedealers. Fourth, that no such system existed under the patriarchal dispensation. Fifth, that *slavery never* existed under the Jewish dispensation; but so far otherwise, that every servant was placed under the *protection of law*, and care taken not only to prevent all *involuntary* servitude, but all *voluntary perpetual* bondage. Sixth, that slavery in America reduces a *man* to a *thing*, a "chattel personal," *robs him* of *all* his rights as a *human being*, fetters both his mind and body, and protects the *master* in the most unnatural and unreasonable power, whilst it *throws him out* of the protection of law. Seventh, that slavery is contrary to the example and precepts of our holy and merciful Redeemer, and of his apostles.

But perhaps you will be ready to query, why appeal to *women* on this subject? *We* do not make the laws which perpetuate slavery. *No* legislative power is vested in *us; we* can do nothing to overthrow the system, even if we wished to do so. To this I reply, I know you do not make the laws, but I also know that *you are the wives and mothers, the sisters and daughters of those who do*; and if you really suppose *you* can do nothing to overthrow slavery, you are greatly mistaken. You can do much in every way: four things I will name. 1st. You can read on this subject. 2d. You can pray over this subject.

3d. You can speak on this subject. 4th. You can *act* on this subject. I have not placed reading before praying because I regard it more important, but because, in order to pray aright, we must understand what we are praying for; it is only then we can "pray with the understanding and the spirit also.". . .

. . .But why, my dear friends, have I thus been endeavoring to lead you through the history of more than three thousand years, and to point you to that great cloud of witnesses who have gone before, "from works to rewards?" Have I been seeking to magnify the sufferings, and exalt the character of woman, that she "might have praise of men?" No! no! my object has been to arouse *you*, as the wives and mothers, the daughters and sisters, of the South, to a sense of your duty as *women*, and as Christian women, on that great subject, which has already shaken our country, from the St. Lawrence and the lakes, to the Gulf of Mexico, and from the Mississippi to the shores of the Atlantic; *and will continue mightily to shake it*, until the polluted temple of slavery fall and crumble into ruin. I would say unto each one of you, "what meanest thou, O sleeper! arise and call upon thy God, if so be that God will think upon us that we perish not". . . .

What can I say more, my friends, to induce *you* to set your hands, and heads, and hearts, to this great work of justice and mercy. Perhaps you have feared the consequences of immediate Emancipation, and been frightened by all those dreadful prophecies of rebellion, bloodshed and murder, which have been uttered. "Let no man deceive you;" they are the predictions of that same "lying spirit" which spoke through the four hundred prophets of old, to Ahab king of Israel, urging him on to destruction. *Slavery* may produce these horrible scenes if it is continued five years longer, but Emancipation *never will*. . . .

And why not try it in the Southern States, if it never has occasioned rebellion; if *not a drop of blood* has ever been shed in consequence of it, though it has been so often tried, why should we suppose it would produce such disastrous consequences now? "Be not deceived then, God is not mocked," by such false excuses for not doing justly and loving mercy. There is nothing to fear from immediate Emancipation, but *every thing* from the continuance of slavery.

Sisters in Christ, I have done. As a Southerner, I have felt it was my duty to address you. I have endeavoured to set before you the exceeding sinfulness of slavery, and to point you to the example of those noble women who have been raised up in the church to effect great revolutions, and to suffer for the truth's sake. I have appealed to your sympathies as women, to your sense of duty as *Christian women*. I have attempted to vindicate the Abolitionists, to prove the entire safety of immediate Emancipation, and to plead the cause of the poor and oppressed. I have done—I have sowed the seeds of truth, but I well know, that even if an Apollos were to follow in my steps to water them, "*God only* can give the increase." To Him then who is able to prosper the work of his servant's hand, I commend this Appeal in fervent prayer, that as he "hath *chosen the weak things of the world*, to confound the things which are mighty," so He may cause His blessing, to descend and carry conviction to the hearts of many Lydias through these speaking pages. Farewell—Count me not your "enemy because I have told you the truth," but believe me in unfeigned affection,

Your sympathizing Friend,
Angelina E. Grimké

5.6

Sojourner Truth

AIN'T I A WOMAN?
(DECEMBER 1851)

Well, children, where there is so much racket there must be something out of kilter. I think that 'twixt the negroes of the South and the women at the North, all talking about rights, the white men will be in a fix pretty soon. But what's all this here talking about?

That man over there says that women need to be helped into carriages, and lifted over ditches, and to have the best place everywhere. Nobody ever helps me into carriages, or over mud-puddles, or gives me any best place! And ain't I a woman? Look at me! Look at my arm! I have ploughed and planted, and gathered into barns, and no man could head me! And ain't I a woman? I could work as much and eat as much as a man—when I could get it—and bear the lash as well! And ain't I a woman? I have borne thirteen children, and seen most all sold off to slavery, and when I cried out with my mother's grief, none but Jesus heard me! And ain't I a woman?

Then they talk about this thing in the head; what's this they call it? [member of audience whispers, "intellect"] That's it, honey. What's that got to do with women's rights or negroes' rights? If my cup won't hold but a pint, and yours holds a quart, wouldn't you be mean not to let me have my little half measure full?

Then that little man in black there, he says women can't have as much rights as men, 'cause Christ wasn't a woman! Where did your Christ come from? Where did your Christ come from? From God and a woman! Man had nothing to do with Him.

If the first woman God ever made was strong enough to turn the world upside down all alone, these women together ought to be able to turn it back, and get it right side up again! And now they is asking to do it, the men better let them.

Obliged to you for hearing me, and now old Sojourner ain't got nothing more to say.

5.7

Frances Willard

HOME PROTECTION I (1876)

So the great question narrows down to one of two (?) methods. It is not, when we look carefully into the conditions of the problem, How shall we develop more virtue in the community to offset the tropical growth of vice by which we find ourselves environed? But rather how the tremendous force we have may best be brought to bear ... and direct their full charge at short range, upon our nimble, wily, vigilant foe?

As bearing upon a consideration of that question, I lay down this proposition: All pure and Christian sentiment concerning any line of conduct which vitally affects humanity, will, sooner or later, crystallize into law. But the keystone of law can only be firm and secure when it is held in place by the arch of that keystone, which is public sentiment.

I make another statement, not so often reiterated, but just as true, viz.: The more thoroughly you can enlist in favor of your law the natural instincts of those who have the power to make that law, and to select the officers who shall enforce it, the more securely stands the law. And still another: First, among the powerful and controlling instincts in our nature stands that of self preservation, and next after this, if it does not claim superior rank, comes that of a mother's love. You can count upon that every time; it is sure and resistless as the tides of the sea, for it is founded in the changeless nature given to her from God.

Now the stronghold of the rum power lies in the fact that it has upon its side two deeply rooted appetites, namely: in the dealer, the appetite for gain, and in the drinker, the appetite for stimulants. We have dolorously said, in times gone by, that, on the human plane, we have nothing adequate to match against this frightful pair. But let us think more carefully, and we shall find that, as in nature, God has given us an antidote to every poison, and in grace a compensation for every loss; so in human society he has prepared, against alcohol, that worst foe of the social state, an enemy under whose weapons it is to bite the dust.

Think of it! There is a class in everyone of our communities—in many of them far the most numerous class—which (I speak not vauntingly; I but name it as a fact) has not, in all the centuries of wine, beer, and brandy-drinking developed, as a class, an appetite for alcohol, but whose instincts, on the contrary, set so strongly against intoxicants that if the liquor traffic were dependent on their patronage alone, it would collapse this night as though all the nitro-glycerine of Hell Gate reef had exploded under it.

There is a class whose instinct of self-preservation must forever be opposed to a stimulant which nerves, with dangerous strength, arms already so much stronger than their own, and so maddens the brain God meant to guide those arms, that they strike down the wives men love, and the little children for whom, when sober, they would die. The wife, largely dependent for the support of herself and little ones upon the brain which strong drink paralyzes, the arm it masters, and the skill it renders futile, will, in the nature of the case, prove herself unfriendly to the actual or potential source of so much misery. . . . And now I ask you to consider earnestly the fact that none of these blessed rays of light and power from woman's heart, are as yet brought to bear upon the rum-shop at the focus of power. . . . I know, and as the knowledge has grown clearer, my heart has thrilled with gratitude and hope too deep for words, that in a republic, all these now divergent beams of light can, through that magic lens, that powerful sun-glass which we name the ballot, be made to converge upon the rum-shop in a blaze of light which shall reveal its full abominations, and a white flame of heat which, like a pitiless moxa, shall burn this cancerous excrescence from America's fair form. Yes, for there is nothing in the universe so sure, so strong, as love; and love shall do all this—the love of maid for sweetheart, wife for husband, of a sister for her brother, of a mother for her son. And I call upon you who are here today, good men and brave—you who have welcomed us to other fields in the great fight of the angel against the dragon in society—I call upon you thus to match force with force, to set over against the liquor-dealer's avarice our instinct of self-preservation; and to match the drinker's love of liquor with our love of him! When you can centre all this power in that small bit of white paper which falls

"As silently as snowflakes fall upon the sod, But executes the freeman's will as lightnings do the will of God," the rum power will be as much doomed as was the slave power when you gave the ballot to the slaves. . . .

. . . God has indicated woman, who is the born conservator of home, to be the Nemesis of home's arch enemy, King Alcohol. And further, that in a republic, this power of hers may be most effectively exercised by giving her a voice in the decision by which the rum-shop door shall be opened or closed beside her home.

This position is strongly supported by evidence. About the year 1850 petitions were extensively circulated in Cincinnati (later the fiercest battle ground of the woman's crusade), asking that the liquor traffic be put under the ban of law. Bishop Simpson—one of the noblest and most discerning minds of his century—was deeply interested in this movement. It was decided to ask for the names of women as well as those of men, and it was found that the former signed the petition more readily and in much larger numbers than the latter. Another fact was ascertained which rebuts the hackneyed assertion that women of the lower class will not be on the temperance side in this great war. For it was found—as might, indeed, have been most reasonably predicted—that the ignorant, the poor (man of them wives, mothers, and daughters of intemperate men) were among the most eager to sign the petition.

Many a Hand Was Taken from the Wash-Tub

to hold the pencil and affix the signature of women of this class, and many another, which could only make the sign of the cross, did that with tears, and a hearty "God bless you." "That was a wonderful lesson to me," said the good Bishop, and he has always believed since then that God will give our enemy into our hands by giving to us an ally still more powerful, woman with the ballot against rum-shops in our land. It has been said so often that the very frequency of reiteration has in some minds induced belief that women of the better class will never consent to declare themselves at the polls. But, tens of thousands from the most tenderly-sheltered homes have gone day after day to the saloons, and have spent hour after hour upon their sanded floors, and in their reeking air—places in which not the worst politician would dare to locate the ballot box of freeman—though they but stay a moment at the window, slip in their votes, and go their way.

Nothing worse can ever happen to women at the polls than has been endured by the hour on the part of the conservative women of the churches in this land, as they, in scores of towns, have pled with rough, half-drunken men to vote the temperance tickets they have handed them and which, with vastly more of propriety and fitness they might have dropped into the box themselves. They could have done this in a moment, and returned to their homes, instead of spending the whole day in the often futile endeavor to beg from men like these the votes which should preserve their homes from the whisky serpent's breath for one uncertain year. I spent last May in Ohio, traveling constantly, and seeking on every side to learn the views of the noble women of the Crusade. They put their opinions in words like these: "We believe God led us into this work by way of the saloons,

He Will Lead Us out by Way of the Ballot

We have never prayed more earnestly over the one than we will over the other. One was the Wilderness, the other is the Promised Land."

. . .We must not forget that for every woman who joins the Temperance Unions now springing up all through the land, there are at least, a score who sympathize but do not join. Home influence and cares prevent them, ignorance of our aims and methods, lack of consecration to Christian work—a thousand reasons, sufficient in their estimation, though not in ours, hold them away from us. And yet they have this Temperance cause warmly at heart; the logic of events has shown them that there is but one side on which a woman may safely stand in this great battle, and on that side they would indubitably range themselves in the quick, decisive battle of election day, nor would they give their voice a second time in favor of the man who had once betrayed his pledge to enforce the most stringent law for the protection of their homes. There are many noble women, too, who, though they do not think as do the Temperance Unions about the deep things of religion, and are not as yet decided in their total abstinence sentiments, nor ready for the blessed work of prayer, are nevertheless decided in their views of Woman Suffrage, and ready to vote a Temperance ticket side by side with us. And there are the drunkard's wife and daughters, who from very shame will not come with us, or who dare not, yet who could freely vote with us upon this question; for the folded ballot tells no tales.

Among other cumulative proofs in this argument from experience, let us consider, briefly, the attitude of the Catholic Church toward the Temperance Reform. It is friendly, at least. . . Catholic women would vote with Protestant women upon this issue for the protection of their homes.

Again, among the sixty thousand churches of America, with their eight million members, two-thirds are women. Thus, only one-third of this trustworthy and thoughtful class has any voice in the laws by which, between the church and the public school, the rum-shop nestles in this Christian land. Surely all this must change before the Government shall be upon His shoulders. "Who shall one day reign King of Nations as he now reigns King of Saints."

Furthermore, four-fifths of the teachers in this land are women, whose thoughtful judgment, expressed with the authority of which I speak, would greatly help forward the victory of our cause. . . .

When all these facts (and many more that might be added) are marshaled into line, how illogical it seems for good men to harangue us as they do about our "duty to educate public sentiment to the level of better law," and their exhortations to American mothers to "train their sons to vote aright. . . ."

Let us, then, each one of us, offer our earnest prayer to God, and speak our honest word to man in favor of this added weapon in woman's hands, remembering that every petition in the ear of God, and every utterance in the ears of men, swells the dimensions of that resistless tide of influence which shall yet float within our reach all that we ask or need. Dear Christian women who have crusaded in the rum-shops, I urge that you begin crusading in halls of legislation, in primary meetings, and the offices of excise commissioners. Roll in your petitions, burnish your arguments, multiply your prayers. Go to the voters in your town—procure the official list and see them one by one—and get them pledged to a local ordinance requiring the votes of men and women before a license can be issued to open rum-shop doors beside your homes; go to the Legislature with the same; remember this may be just as really Christian work as praying in saloons was in those other glorious days. Let us not limit God, whose modes of operation are so infinitely varied in nature and in grace. I believe in the correlation of spiritual forces, and that the heat which melted hearts to tenderness in the Crusade is soon to be the light which shall reveal our opportunity and duty as the Republic's daughters. . . .

Let it no longer be that (women) must sit back among the shadows, hopelessly mourning over their strong staff broken, and their beautiful rod; but when the sons they love shall go forth to life's battle, still let their mothers walk beside them, sweet and serious, and clad in the garments of power.

5.8

STATEMENT BY ALABAMA CLERGYMEN
(APRIL 12, 1963)

We the undersigned clergymen are among those who, in January, issued "An Appeal for Law and Order and Common Sense," in dealing with racial problems in Alabama. We expressed understanding that honest convictions in racial matters could properly be pursued in the courts, but urged that decisions of those courts should in the meantime be peacefully obeyed.

Since that time there had been some evidence of increased forbearance and a willingness to face facts. Responsible citizens have undertaken to work on various problems which cause racial friction and unrest. In Birmingham, recent public events have given indication that we will have opportunity for a new constructive and realistic approach to racial problems.

However, we are now confronted by a series of demonstrations by some of our Negro citizens, directed and led in part by outsiders. We recognize the natural impatience of people who feel that their hopes are slow in being realized. But we are convinced that these demonstrations are unwise and untimely.

We agree rather with certain local Negro leadership which has called for honest and open negotiation of racial issues in our area. And we believe this kind of facing of issues can best be accomplished by citizens of our own metropolitan area, white and Negro, meeting with their knowledge and experience of the local situation. All of us need to face that responsibility and find proper channels for its accomplishment.

Just as we formerly pointed out that "hatred and violence have no sanction in our religious and political traditions," we also point out that such actions as incite to hatred and violence, however technically peaceful those actions may be, have not contributed to the resolution of our local problems. We do not believe that these days of new hope are days when extreme measures are justified in Birmingham.

We commend the community as a whole, and the local news media and law enforcement officials in particular, on the calm manner in which these demonstrations have been handled. We urge the public to continue to show restraint should the demonstrations continue, and the law enforcement officials to remain calm and continue to protect our city from violence.

We further strongly urge our own Negro community to withdraw support from these demonstrations, and to unite locally in working peacefully for a better Birmingham. When rights are consistently denied, a cause should be pressed in the courts and in negotiations among local leaders, and not in the streets. We appeal to both our white and Negro citizenry to observe the principles of law and order and common sense.

Signed by:

C.C.J. Carpenter, D.D., LL.D., Bishop of Alabama

Joseph A. Durick, D.D., Auxiliary Bishop, Diocese of Mobile-Birmingham

Rabbi Milton L. Grafman, Temple Emanu-El, Birmingham, Alabama

Bishop Paul Hardin, Bishop of the Alabama-West Florida Conference of the Methodist Church

Bishop Nolan B. Harmon, Bishop of the North Alabama Conference of the Methodist Church

George M. Murray, D.D., LL.D., Bishop Coadjutor, Episcopal Diocese of Alabama

Edward V. Ramage, Moderator, Synod of the Alabama Presbyterian Church in the United States

Earl Stallings, Pastor, First Baptist Church, Birmingham, Alabama

5.9

Martin Luther King Jr.

LETTER FROM A BIRMINGHAM JAIL
(APRIL 16, 1963)

My Dear Fellow Clergymen:

While confined here in the Birmingham city jail, I came across your recent statement calling my present activities "unwise and untimely." Seldom do I pause to answer criticism of my work and ideas. . .

I think I should indicate why I am here in Birmingham, since you have been influenced by the view which argues against "outsiders coming in." I have the honor of serving as president of the Southern Christian Leadership Conference, an organization operating in every southern state, with headquarters in Atlanta, Georgia. We have some eighty five affiliated organizations across the South, and one of them is the Alabama Christian Movement for Human Rights. . . . Several months ago the affiliate here in Birmingham asked us to be on call to engage in a nonviolent direct action program if such were deemed necessary. We readily consented, and when the hour came we lived up to our promise. So I, along with several members of my staff, am here because I was invited here. I am here because I have organizational ties here.

But more basically, I am in Birmingham because injustice is here. Just as the prophets of the eighth century B.C. left their villages and carried their "thus saith the Lord" far beyond the boundaries of their home towns, and just as the Apostle Paul left his village of Tarsus and carried the gospel of Jesus Christ to the far corners of the Greco Roman world, so am I compelled to carry the gospel of freedom beyond my own home town. Like Paul, I must constantly respond to the Macedonian call for aid.

Moreover, I am cognizant of the interrelatedness of all communities and states. I cannot sit idly by in Atlanta and not be concerned about what happens in Birmingham. Injustice anywhere is a threat to justice everywhere. We are caught in an inescapable network of mutuality, tied in a single garment of destiny. Whatever affects one directly, affects all indirectly. Never again can we afford to live with the narrow, provincial "outside agitator" idea. Anyone who lives inside the United States can never be considered an outsider anywhere within its bounds. . . .

I am sure that none of you would want to rest content with the superficial kind of social analysis that deals merely with effects and does not grapple with underlying causes. It is unfortunate that demonstrations are taking place in Birmingham, but it is even more unfortunate that the city's white power structure left the Negro community with no alternative.

In any nonviolent campaign there are four basic steps: collection of the facts to determine whether injustices exist; negotiation; self purification; and direct action. We have gone through all these steps in Birmingham. There can be no gainsaying the fact that racial injustice engulfs this community. Birmingham is probably the most thoroughly segregated city in the United States. Its ugly record of brutality is widely known. Negroes have experienced grossly unjust treatment in the courts. There have been more unsolved bombings of Negro homes and churches in Birmingham than in any other city in the nation. These are the hard, brutal facts of the case. On the basis of these conditions, Negro leaders sought to negotiate with the city fathers. But the latter consistently refused to engage in good faith negotiation. . . .

You may well ask: "Why direct action? Why sit ins, marches and so forth? Isn't negotiation a better path?" You are quite right in calling for negotiation. Indeed, this is the very purpose of direct action. Nonviolent direct action seeks to create such a crisis and foster such a tension that a community which has constantly refused to negotiate is forced to confront the issue. It seeks so to dramatize the issue that it can no longer be ignored. My citing the creation of tension as part of the work of the nonviolent resister may sound rather shocking. But I must confess that I am not afraid of the word "tension." I have earnestly opposed violent tension, but there is a type of constructive, nonviolent tension which is necessary for growth. . . . (W)e see the need for nonviolent gadflies to create the kind of tension in society that will help men rise from the dark depths of prejudice and racism to the majestic heights of understanding and brotherhood. . . .

My friends, I must say to you that we have not made a single gain in civil rights without determined legal and nonviolent pressure. Lamentably, it is an historical fact that privileged groups seldom give up their privileges voluntarily. Individuals may see the moral light and voluntarily give up their unjust posture; but, as Reinhold Niebuhr has reminded us, groups tend to be more immoral than individuals.

We know through painful experience that freedom is never voluntarily given by the oppressor; it must be demanded by the oppressed. Frankly, I have yet to engage in a direct action campaign that was "well timed" in the view of those who have not suffered unduly from the disease of segregation. For years now I have heard the word "Wait!" It rings in the ear of every Negro with piercing familiarity. This "Wait" has almost always meant "Never." We must come to see, with one of our distinguished jurists, that "justice too long delayed is justice denied."

We have waited for more than 340 years for our constitutional and God given rights. The nations of Asia and Africa are moving with jetlike speed toward gaining political independence, but we still creep at horse and buggy pace toward gaining a cup of coffee at a lunch counter. Perhaps it is easy for those who have never felt the stinging darts of segregation to say, "Wait." But when you have seen vicious mobs lynch your mothers and fathers at will and drown your sisters and brothers at whim; when you have seen hate filled policemen curse, kick and even kill your black brothers and sisters; when you see the vast majority of your twenty million Negro brothers smothering in an airtight cage of poverty in the midst of an affluent society; when you suddenly find your tongue twisted and your speech stammering as you seek to explain to your six year old daughter why she can't go to the public amusement park that has just been advertised on television, and see tears welling up in her eyes when she is told that Funtown is closed to colored children, and see ominous clouds of inferiority beginning to form in her little mental sky, and see her beginning to distort her personality by developing an unconscious bitterness toward white people; when you have to concoct an answer for a five year old son who is asking: "Daddy, why do white people treat colored people so mean?"; when you take a cross country drive and find it necessary to sleep night after night in the uncomfortable corners of your automobile because no motel will accept you; when you are humiliated day in and day out by nagging signs reading "white" and " colored"; when your first name becomes "nigger," your middle name becomes "boy" (however old you are) and your last name becomes "John," and your wife and mother are never given the respected title "Mrs."; when you are harried by day and haunted by night by the fact that you are a Negro, living constantly at tiptoe stance, never quite knowing what to expect next, and are plagued with inner fears and outer resentments; when you are forever fighting a degenerating sense of "nobodiness"—then you will understand why we find it difficult to wait. There comes a time when the cup of endurance runs over, and men are no longer willing to be plunged into the abyss of despair. . . .

Since we so diligently urge people to obey the Supreme Court's decision of 1954 outlawing segregation in the public schools, at first glance it may seem rather paradoxical for us consciously to break laws. One may well ask: "How can you advocate breaking some laws and obeying others?" The answer lies in the fact that there are two types of laws: just and unjust. I would be the first to advocate obeying just laws. One has not only a legal but a moral responsibility to obey just laws. Conversely, one has a moral responsibility to disobey unjust laws. I would agree with St. Augustine that "an unjust law is no law at all."

Now, what is the difference between the two? How does one determine whether a law is just or unjust? A just law is a man made code that squares with the moral law or the law of God. An unjust law is a code that is out of harmony with the moral law. To put it in the terms of St. Thomas Aquinas: An unjust law is a human law that is not rooted in eternal law and natural law. . . . All segregation statutes are unjust because segregation distorts the soul and damages the personality. It gives the segregator a false sense of superiority and the segregated a false sense of inferiority. . . . Is not segregation an existential expression of man's tragic separation, his awful estrangement, his terrible sinfulness? Thus it is that I can urge men to obey the 1954 decision of the

Supreme Court, for it is morally right; and I can urge them to disobey segregation ordinances, for they are morally wrong. . . .

Of course, there is nothing new about this kind of civil disobedience. It was evidenced sublimely in the refusal of Shadrach, Meshach and Abednego to obey the laws of Nebuchadnezzar, on the ground that a higher moral law was at stake. It was practiced superbly by the early Christians, who were willing to face hungry lions and the excruciating pain of chopping blocks rather than submit to certain unjust laws of the Roman Empire. To a degree, academic freedom is a reality today because Socrates practiced civil disobedience. In our own nation, the Boston Tea Party represented a massive act of civil disobedience. . . .

I had also hoped that the white moderate would reject the myth concerning time in relation to the struggle for freedom. I have just received a letter from a white brother in Texas. He writes: "All Christians know that the colored people will receive equal rights eventually, but it is possible that you are in too great a religious hurry. It has taken Christianity almost two thousand years to accomplish what it has. The teachings of Christ take time to come to earth." Such an attitude stems from a tragic misconception of time, from the strangely irrational notion that there is something in the very flow of time that will inevitably cure all ills. Actually, time itself is neutral; it can be used either destructively or constructively. More and more I feel that the people of ill will have used time much more effectively than have the people of good will. We will have to repent in this generation not merely for the hateful words and actions of the bad people but for the appalling silence of the good people. Human progress never rolls in on wheels of inevitability; it comes through the tireless efforts of men willing to be co workers with God, and without this hard work, time itself becomes an ally of the forces of social stagnation. We must use time creatively, in the knowledge that the time is always ripe to do right. Now is the time to make real the promise of democracy and transform our pending national elegy into a creative psalm of brotherhood. Now is the time to lift our national policy from the quicksand of racial injustice to the solid rock of human dignity. . . .

Oppressed people cannot remain oppressed forever. The yearning for freedom eventually manifests itself, and that is what has happened to the American Negro. Something within has reminded him of his birthright of freedom, and something without has reminded him that it can be gained. . . . If one recognizes this vital urge that has engulfed the Negro community, one should readily understand why public demonstrations are taking place. . . . So I have not said to my people: "Get rid of your discontent." Rather, I have tried to say that this normal and healthy discontent can be channeled into the creative outlet of nonviolent direct action. And now this approach is being termed extremist.

But though I was initially disappointed at being categorized as an extremist, as I continued to think about the matter I gradually gained a measure of satisfaction from the label. Was not Jesus an extremist for love: "Love your enemies, bless them that curse you, do good to them that hate you, and pray for them which despitefully use you, and persecute you." Was not Amos an extremist for justice: "Let justice roll down like waters and righteousness like an ever flowing stream.". . . And Abraham Lincoln: "This nation cannot survive half slave and half free." And Thomas Jefferson: "We hold these truths to be self evident, that all men are created equal . . ." So the question is not whether we will be extremists, but what kind of extremists we will be. Will we be extremists for hate or for love? Will we be extremists for the preservation of injustice or for the extension of justice? . . . Perhaps the South, the nation and the world are in dire need of creative extremists. . . .

I have heard numerous southern religious leaders admonish their worshipers to comply with a desegregation decision because it is the law, but I have longed to hear white ministers declare: "Follow this decree because integration is morally right and because the Negro is your brother." In the midst of blatant injustices inflicted upon the Negro, I have watched white churchmen stand on the sideline and mouth pious irrelevancies and sanctimonious trivialities. In the midst of a mighty struggle to rid our nation of racial and economic injustice, I have heard many ministers say: "Those are social issues, with which the gospel has no real concern." And I have watched many churches commit themselves to a completely other worldly religion which makes a strange, un-Biblical distinction between body and soul, between the sacred and the secular.

I have traveled the length and breadth of Alabama, Mississippi and all the other southern states. . . . I have looked at the South's beautiful churches with their lofty spires pointing heavenward. I have beheld the impressive outlines of her massive religious education buildings. Over and over I have found myself asking: "What kind of people worship here? . . . Where were they when Governor Wallace gave a clarion call for defiance and hatred? Where were their voices of support when bruised and weary Negro men and women decided to rise from the dark dungeons of complacency to the bright hills of creative protest?". . .

There was a time when the church was very powerful—in the time when the early Christians rejoiced at being deemed worthy to suffer for what they believed. In those days the church was not merely a thermometer that recorded the ideas and principles of popular opinion; it was a thermostat that transformed the mores of society. Whenever the early Christians entered a town, the people in power became disturbed and immediately sought to convict the Christians for being "disturbers of the peace" and "outside agitators." But the Christians pressed on. . . . By their effort and example they brought an end to such ancient evils as infanticide and gladiatorial contests.

Things are different now. . . . So often (the contemporary church) is an archdefender of the status quo. Far from being disturbed by the presence of the church, the power structure of the average community is consoled by the church's silent—and often even vocal—sanction of things as they are. . . .

Perhaps I have once again been too optimistic. Is organized religion too inextricably bound to the status quo to save our nation and the world? Perhaps I must turn my faith to the inner spiritual church, the church within the church, as the true ekklesia and the hope of the world. But again I am thankful to God that some noble souls from the ranks of organized religion have broken loose from the paralyzing chains of conformity and joined us as active partners in the struggle for freedom. . . . Some have been dismissed from their churches, have lost the support of their bishops and fellow ministers. But they have acted in the faith that right defeated is stronger than evil triumphant. . . . They have carved a tunnel of hope through the dark mountain of disappointment.

I hope the church as a whole will meet the challenge of this decisive hour. But even if the church does not come to the aid of justice, I have no despair about the future. I have no fear about the outcome of our struggle in Birmingham, even if our motives are at present misunderstood. We will reach the goal of freedom in Birmingham and all over the nation, because the goal of America is freedom. Abused and scorned though we may be, our destiny is tied up with America's destiny. Before the pilgrims landed at Plymouth, we were here. Before the pen of Jefferson etched the majestic words of the Declaration of Independence across the pages of history, we were here. For more than two centuries our forebears labored in this country without wages; they made cotton king; they built the homes of their masters while suffering gross injustice and shameful humiliation—and yet out of a bottomless vitality they continued to thrive and develop. If the inexpressible cruelties of slavery could not stop us, the opposition we now face will surely fail. We will win our freedom because the sacred heritage of our nation and the eternal will of God are embodied in our echoing demands.

Before closing I feel impelled to mention one other point in your statement that has troubled me profoundly. You warmly commended the Birmingham police force for keeping "order" and "preventing violence." I doubt that you would have so warmly commended the police force if you were to observe their ugly and inhumane treatment of Negroes. . . . (I)f you were to observe them, as they did on two occasions, refuse to give us food because we wanted to sing our grace together. I cannot join you in your praise of the Birmingham police department.

It is true that the police have exercised a degree of discipline in handling the demonstrators. In this sense they have conducted themselves rather "nonviolently" in public. But for what purpose? To preserve the evil system of segregation. Over the past few years I have consistently preached that nonviolence demands that the means we use must be as pure as the ends we seek. I have tried to make clear that it is wrong to use immoral means to attain moral ends. But now I must affirm that it is just as wrong, or perhaps even more so, to use moral means to preserve immoral ends. . . .

I wish you had commended the Negro sit inners and demonstrators of Birmingham for their sublime courage, their willingness to suffer and their amazing discipline in the midst of great provocation. One day the South will recognize its real heroes. They will be the James Merediths, with the noble sense of purpose that enables them to face jeering and hostile mobs, and with the agonizing loneliness that characterizes the life of the pioneer. They will be old, oppressed, battered Negro women, symbolized in a seventy two year old woman in Montgomery, Alabama, who rose up with a sense of dignity and with her people decided not to ride segregated buses, and who responded with ungrammatical profundity to one who inquired about her weariness: "My feets is tired, but my soul is at rest." They will be the young high school and college students, the young ministers of the gospel and a host of their elders, courageously and nonviolently sitting in at lunch counters and willingly going to jail for conscience' sake. One day the South will know that when these disinherited children of God sat down at lunch counters, they were in reality standing up for what is best in the American dream and for the most sacred values in our Judeo Christian heritage, thereby bringing our nation back to those great wells of democracy which were dug deep by the founding fathers in their formulation of the Constitution and the Declaration of Independence. . . .

Yours for the cause of Peace and Brotherhood,
Martin Luther King Jr.

5.10

Malcolm X

THE BALLOT OR THE BULLET
(APRIL 3, 1964)

Mr. Moderator, Brother Lomax, brothers and sisters, friends and enemies: I just can't believe everyone in here is a friend and I don't want to leave anybody out. The question tonight, as I understand it, is "The Negro Revolt, and Where Do We Go from Here?" or "What Next?" In my little humble way of understanding it, it points toward either the ballot or the bullet.

Before we try and explain what is meant by the ballot or the bullet, I would like to clarify something concerning myself. I'm still a Muslim, my religion is still Islam. That's my personal belief. Just as Adam Clayton Powell is a Christian minister who heads the Abyssinian Baptist Church in New York, but at the same time takes part in the political struggles . . . and Dr. Martin Luther King is a Christian Minister down in Atlanta, Georgia, who heads another organization fighting for the civil rights of black people in this country; and Rev. Galamison, I guess you've heard of him, is another Christian minister in New York who has been deeply involved in the school boycotts to eliminate segregated education; well, I myself am a minister, not a Christian minister, but a Muslim minister; and I believe in action on all fronts by whatever means necessary.

Although I'm still a Muslim, I'm not here tonight to discuss my religion. I'm not here to try and change your religion. I'm not here to argue or discuss anything that we differ about, because it's time for us to submerge our differences and realize that it is best for us to first see that we have the same problem, a common problem—a problem that will make you catch hell whether you're a Baptist, or a Methodist, or a Muslim, or a nationalist. . . . We're all in the same boat and we all are going to catch the same hell from the same man. . . . All of us have suffered here, in this country, political oppression at the hands of the white man, economic exploitation at the hands of the white man, and social degradation at the hands of the white man. . . .

Whether we are Christians or Muslims or nationalists or agnostics or atheists, we must first learn to forget our differences. If we have differences, let us differ in the closet; when we come out in front, let us not have anything to argue about until we get finished arguing with the man. . . .

If we don't do something real soon, I think you'll have to agree that we're going to be forced either to use the ballot or the bullet. It's one or the other in 1964. It isn't that time is running out—time has run out! 1964 threatens to be the most explosive year America has ever witnessed. . . . Why? It's also a political year. It's the year when all of the white politicians will be back in the so-called Negro community jiving you and me for some votes. The year when all of the white political crooks will be right back in your and my community with their false promises, building up our hopes for a letdown, with their trickery and their treachery, with their false promises which they don't intend to keep. . . .

This government has failed the Negro. This so-called democracy has failed the Negro. And all these white liberals have definitely failed the Negro. So where do we go from here? First, we need some friends. . . . To those of us whose philosophy is black nationalism, the only way you can get involved in the civil-rights struggle is give it a new interpretation. That old interpretation excluded us. It kept us out. So, we're giving a new interpretation to the civil-rights struggle, an interpretation that will enable us to come into it, take part in it. . . .

It's true we're Muslims and our religion is Islam, but we don't mix our religion with our politics and our economics and our social and civil activities—not any more. We keep our religion in our mosque. After our religious services are over, then as Muslims we become involved in political action, economic action and social and civic action. We become involved with anybody, anywhere, any time and in any manner that's designed to eliminate the evils, the political, economic and social evils that are afflicting the people of our community.

The political philosophy of black nationalism means that the black man should control the politics and the politicians in his own community; no more. . . . The political philosophy of black nationalism is being taught in the Christian church. . . . It's being taught in Muslim meetings. It's being taught where nothing but atheists and agnostics come together. . . . We want freedom *now*, but we're not going to get it saying "We Shall Overcome." We've got to fight until we overcome. . . .

We ourselves have to lift the level of our community, the standard of our community to a higher level, make our own society beautiful so that we will be satisfied in our own social circles and won't be running around here trying to knock our way into a social circle where we're not wanted. . . .

We've got to change our own minds about each other. . . . We have to see each other as brothers and sisters. We have to come together with warmth so we can develop unity and harmony that's necessary to get this problem solved ourselves. . . .

Our gospel is black nationalism. We're not trying to threaten the existence of any organization, but we're spreading the gospel of black nationalism. Anywhere there's a church that is also preaching and practicing the gospel of black nationalism, join that church. . . . Join any organization that has a gospel that's for the uplift of the black man. . . .

A segregated district or community is a community in which people live, but outsiders control the politics and the economy of that community. They never refer to the white section as a segregated community. It's the all-Negro section that's a segregated community. Why? The white man controls his own school, his own bank, his own economy, his own politics, his own everything, his own community—but he also controls yours. . . . You've got to *control* your own. Just like the white man has control of his, you need to control yours. . . .

The black nationalists aren't going to wait. Lyndon B. Johnson is the head of the Democratic Party. If he's for civil rights, let him go into the Senate next week and declare himself. . . . Tell him, don't wait until election time. If he waits too long, brothers and sisters, he will be responsible for letting a condition develop in this country which will create a climate that will bring seeds up out of the ground with vegetation on the end of them looking like something these people never dreamed of. In 1964, it's the ballot or the bullet. Thank you.

Notes

1. Inattention to religion's role in disruptive politics in the academic literature on social movements is not due to lack of notice or suggestion by some visible scholars. Mayer Zald and John McCarthy, for example, invited research into disruptive religion with their 1982 *Review of Religious Research* article, "Theological Crucibles: Social Movements in and of Religion" Yet few scholars seem to have accepted these invitations or followed their leads; nor is the inattention in the social-movement literature due to a scarcity of works on religion, politics, protest, and revolution. This chapter's bibliography alone suggests the many relevant works available. Yet, social-movement scholars appear to have made little effort to locate and utilize these works.

2. My reliance on Berger (1967) and Geertz (1973) in the following section is clear.

3. Two key statements on resource mobilization theory—Gamson, *The Strategy of Social Protest*, pp.140–43, and Tilly, *From Mobilization to Revolution*, pp. 52–55—argue that challenging groups are those excluded from the formal political process of a society, referred to as the polity. The chief aim of challenging groups is to become a part of the polity. My definition of dominated groups differs from this position in that such groups may be excluded not only from the polity but from other spheres such as the economic and cultural. Challenging behavior by dominated groups may be aimed at destroying the society.

4. In this connection Doug McAdam, "Political Process and the Black Protestant Movement 1948–1970," Ph.D. dissertation, State University of New York at Stony Brook, 1979, pp. 240, 302–6, to date the most comprehensive analysis of the funding patterns of the civil rights movement, concludes that "outside support increases sharply *following, rather than preceding*, the initial period of widespread protest activity" and that "external support, far from triggering insurgency, is actually a product of it." Emphasis added.

5. For discussions of the relationships between the civil rights movement and (1) emergence of the modern women's movement, see Jo Freeman, "The Origins of the Women's Liberation Movement," *American Journal of Sociology*, 78 (January 1973): 792–811; (2) the rise of the modern white student movement, see Clayborne Carson, *In Struggle* (Cambridge:

Harvard University Press, 1981), pp. 175–90; (3) the emergence of the farm workers' movements, see Robert J. Thomas and William H. Friedland, "The United Farmworkers Union: From Mobilization to Mechanization?" Center for Research on Social Organization, Working Paper 269, undated, University of Michigan.

6. Two scholars have shown that the black southerners' political emphasis on education was a more complex matter than Myrdal allowed. The politics and economy of the South were so restrictive that education was, like religion, one of the few avenues left open to black southerners with selfish or unselfish ambitions. See James L. Leloudis, *Schooling the New South: Pedagogy, Self, and Society in North Carolina, 1880–1920* (Chapel Hill: University of North Carolina Press, 1996), and Adam Fairclough, " 'Being in the Field of Education and Also Being a Negro . . . Seems . . . Tragic': Black Teachers in the Jim Crow South," *Journal of American History* 87 (June 2000): 65–91.

7. See Walter A Jackson, *Gunnar Myrdal and America's Conscience: Social Engineering and Racial Liberalism , 1938–1987* (Chapel Hill: University of North Carolina Press, 1990).

8. John Lewis, describing the Nashville reading group from which many SNCC leaders came, recalled that the group studies "Reinhold Niebuhr and his philosophy of nonviolent revolution." Lewis, with Michael D'Orso, *Walking with the Wind: A Memoir of the Movement* (New York: Simon and Schuster, 1998), 85. Andrew Young, in *An Easy Burden: The Civil Rights Movement and the Transformation of America* (New York: HarperCollins, 1996), 93, recalled reading Niebuhr in 1956; Niebuhr's emphasis on negotiating from strength "struck a chord in me." Niebuhr's stress on realism, on power, resonated with what Young had learned in childhood.

9. See King's application to Crozer Theological Seminary, February 1948, *PMLK*, 1:142–49, and his "Autobiography of Religious Development," Fall 1950, *PMLK* 1:359–79. The only recorded conversion experience he had came later, during the civil rights struggle.

10. Not to imply that Ralph Luker endorses this statement about Burke, but he sees a conservatism running strongly in the social gospel in black and white churches. What Arthur M. Schlesinger Sr. saw in 1932 as an increasingly radical critique of industrial capitalism was,

Luker says, in fact a conservative awareness that industrial capitalism was the radical force in society. See Luker, *The Social Gospel in Black and White: American Racial Reform, 1885–1912* (Chapel Hill: University of North Carolina Press, 1991). August Meier makes a good case that the best description of King is "The Conservative Militant," in C. Eric Lincoln, ed., *Martin Luther King, Jr.: A Profile* (New York: Hill and Wang, 1970), 144–56.

11. Kenneth L. Smith and Ira G. Zepp, in *Search for the Beloved Community: The Thinking of Martin Luther King, Jr.* (Lanham, Md.: University Press of America, 1986), emphasizes that the Prophets were the most important part of scripture for King, with the possible exception of the Sermon on the Mount.

12. Even before the scholarly work on Jeremiah, King had spoken out in prophetic tones. The first words he ever published appeared in a letter to the editor of the *Atlanta Constitution* on August 6, 1946 (*PMLK* 1:121), when he was an undergraduate at Morehouse. The *Constitution* had expressed shock at mob violence but added the characteristic southern liberal warning that any federal law to address it would make things worse. Like Isaiah, King attacked the paper and its readers for evasion and hypocrisy. Whenever "decent treatment for the Negro is urged a certain class of people hurry to raise the scarecrow of social mingling and intermarriage. . . . And most people who kick up this kind of dust know that it is simple dust to obscure the real question of rights and opportunities." Like Isaiah, King rubbed his readers' noses in their history of sin. Almost all "race mixture in America has come, not at Negro initiative, but by the acts of those very white men who talk loudest of race purity." Though he did not warn of divine retribution, his demand for basic rights, opportunities, and courtesy might have seemed as unbearable as divine retribution to *Constitution* readers. King seems to have found his voice. Martin Luther King Sr. later recalled that he and his wife had "no intimation of [King Jr.'s] developing greatness . . . until as a teenager he wrote a letter to the editor of a local paper which received widespread and favorable comment" (*PMLK*, 1:121).

13. The most thorough articulation of this "prophetic" rejection of *both* liberalism and neo-orthodoxy is in Niebuhr's *Interpretation of Christian Ethics* (New York: Harper, 1935),

but it is evident in all of his works, even those, like *Moral Man and Immoral Society* (New York: Scribner's, 1932), that regard liberalism as more prevalent than neo-orthodoxy and therefore more in need of criticism. Even the most careless reader could not come away from *Interpretation of Christian Ethics* with any thought that Niebuhr was trying to revive orthodoxy. His brother, H. Richard Niebuhr, gave "prophetic religion" a pointedly antinomian definition in his *Kingdom of God in America* (New York: Harper, 1937), 10–11. Andrew Delbanco has echoed that recently in *Puritan Ordeal*.

14. William Robert Miller, *Martin Luther King: His Life, Martyrdom, and Meaning for a New World* (New York: Weybright and Talley, 1968), 2, provides insight into the religious beliefs and practices of King's elders, whom he called "the black puritans of Auburn Avenue." On the diversity and conflict within "the" black church, see the section on African American religion and politics in the Bibliographical Essay.

15. The discussion of theological affinities must remain limited, since King's genius lay in realms other than systematic thinking. He was not a fully developed theologian but rather devoted his scholarly energy and most of his taste for intellectual subtleties to questions of social ethics. (Even in that emphasis he resembles Reinhold Niebuhr.) The effort to reduce King to what he learned as a child seems to date from Joseph R. Washington's *Black Religion: The Negro and Christianity in the United States* (Boston: Beacon Press, 1964), which states that King was "a remarkable product of the South; barely tainted by his academic exposure in the North" (p. 3). This line has been developed by others who follow the lead of the black nationalist scholar James Cone (see n. 31, below). Importantly, King condemned black folk who passively stood on the sidelines, sometimes seeming to suggest that they were as much an obstacle to freedom as active white segregationists. See King eulogy for the four girls martyred at the 16th Street Church in Birmingham in 1963, in James Melvin Washington, ed., *A Testament of Hope: The Essential Writings of Martin Luther King, Jr.* (New York: Harper and Row, 1986), 221.

16. In April 1956 King made a veiled reference to Myrdal in "Our Struggle," written by Rustin and published under King's name in

Liberation. Under the subheading, "THE LIBERAL DILEMMA," King warned that boycotters and others might die, because "many white men in the South see themselves as a fearful minority in an ocean of black men." King did not refer to any Myrdalian conflict in the minds of these white men: "They honestly believe with one side of their minds that Negroes are depraved and disease-ridden. . . . They are convinced that racial equality is a Communist idea and that those who ask for it are subversive." Such men were in conflict with forces outside, not inside, their personalities: with unbigoted white southerners. The unbigoted did have an internal dilemma, but it did not behave as Myrdal predicted. Rather than drive southerners to improve their society, "the liberal dilemma" paralyzed them. To King, the liberal dilemma would not lead to a happy ending by itself "Our Struggle," *Liberation 1,* (April 1956): 3–6, in James Melvin Washington, *Testament of Hope,* 80. See also King, *Stride toward Freedom: The Montgomery Story* (New York: Harper, 1958), 205, and "The Time for Freedom Has Come," *New York Times Magazine,* September 29, 1963, and "The American Dream," Address at Lincoln University, June 6, 1961, both in Washington, *Testament of Hope,* 161, and 208–9, respectively; and Taylor Branch, *Parting the Waters: America in the King Years,* 1954–1963 (New York: Simon and Schuster; 1988), 490. King referred to Myrdal in passing in a February 1958 speech to the National Negro Press Association, *PMLK,* 4:363.

17. The quotations in this and the previous paragraph are from "Religion's Answer to the Problem of Evil," essay for George Davis's Philosophy of Religion course, Crozer Theological Seminary, April 27, 1951 *PMLK,* 1:416–33.This essay is also of interest for its expression of dissent from Brightman (see section on King's intellectual history in the Bibliographical Essay). The editors of his papers make clear that King closely followed the work of J. S. Whale, *The Christian Answer to the Problem of Evil* (London: Student Christian Movement Press, 1936), and H. F. Rail, *Christianity: An Inquiry into Its Nature and Truth* (New York: Scribner, 1940). They do not make clear that King wound up with a very Niebuhrian notion of order, which he seems to have cribbed from Rail. Order, King says, brings us all that is good and beautiful; but order; which brings, for example, the predictable vaporization of water

with heat, inevitably brings "tornadoes, flood and destruction in which the good suffer with the evil." This exactly parallels Niebuhr's emphasis in *Moral Man* that social order, which is better than anarchy, cannot be achieved or maintained without injustice.

18. See King's exam answers on the theology of the Bible (November 1953), which state that Jeremiah and Job "make it clear that the righteous do suffer and the wicked do prosper." Jeremiah was the first to question the Deuteronomic principle that evil in the world was simply "punishment for sin." King also argues that Isaiah's "suffering is not due to something that he has done, but is *vicarious* and *redemptive.* Through his suffering[,] knowledge of God is sp[r]ead to the unbelieving Gentiles[,] and those unbelievers seeing that this suffering servant is innocent will become conscious of their sins and repent and thereby be redeemed." *PMLK,* 2:207–8. The refrain, "unearned suffering is redemptive" appears in King's "Pilgrimage to Nonviolence," in *Stride toward Freedom,* 103. It also appears in "Suffering and Faith," *Christian Century,* April 1960, 510; in "Love, Law, and Civil Disobedience," *New South* (December 1961): 3ff.; in the "I Have a Dream" speech at the Lincoln Memorial in 1963; and in King's eulogy for the four girls martyred at the 16th Street Church in Birmingham—all reprinted in James Melvin Washington, *Testament of Hope,* 41, 47, 219, and 221–22.

19. Notecards on Jeremiah and Psalm 72 (1952–53), *PMLK,* 2:165–66.

20. Mays and Joseph Nicholson, *The Negro's Church* (New York: institute of Social and Religious Research, 1933); see also Mays, Commencement Address at Howard University, June 1945, *Journal of Negro Education* (Summer 1945): 527–34. The only way to avoid fascism in the United States was to "Christianize" the country, Mays said. But he thought it necessary first to Christianize the churches, for at present "the Church is subservient both to State and to society"; the church must stop being "priestly" and become "prophetic" (p. 528).

21. In an essay on the affinities between King and Thomas Merton, Albert Raboteau wisely argues that the course of both exceptional thinkers could not have been determined by their backgrounds. King stood apart from "the prophetic tradition within African-American religion"—just as Merton stood apart from

much of "the contemplative tradition within monasticism." To Raboteau, "it was not traditions per se, but what King and Merton took from them, or better, the ways in which King and Merton were transformed by them, that made all the difference." Irresistible as the wisdom of this observation is, however, Raboteau goes on to show Merton as much more self-conscious and decisive in separating himself from the general run of contemplative monks than King ever was in separating himself from prophets. Raboteau shows King separating himself, in fact, from just about everything *but* the company of prophets—that and God's love for the human race, which is ever looking for ways to murder His prophets. Raboteau, *A Fire in the Bones: Reflections on African-American Religious History* (Boston: Beacon Press, *1995),* 169–71.

CHAPTER 6

RELIGIOUS GROUPS IN THE POLITICAL PROCESS

Introduction

Interest groups and lobbyists are both revered and reviled for their role in the American political system. Religious interest groups are a case in point. They have helped claimants bring important cases to the courts, raising challenges to existing interpretations of the Constitution's religion clauses. Religious interest groups have also entered the political fray, lobbying for issues of concern to them, stirring up controversy with pointed voter guides that critics contend blur the lines between church and state. This chapter explores these themes and others.

We begin with Kimberly Conger's integrative essay that discusses the role of religious interest groups in general and then focuses in particular on the tactics of the Christian Right to illustrate how religious interest groups are similar to yet different from other interest groups.

The next selection, Allen Hertzke's *Representing God in Washington*, is a landmark study that illustrates how the congressional culture tames the tactics and rhetoric of religious lobbies. One of Hertzke's major insights is that while religionists typically approach politics as purists, they may also act as pragmatists who weigh when to "go for broke" and when to compromise in the name of a partial victory.

Whereas Hertzke emphasizes Congress as the center of activity for religious interest groups, Kevin den Dulk shifts the focus to the federal courts as another prime locale for the activities and efforts of religious interest groups. Den Dulk's essay traces the link between evangelical political activism and rights advocacy, explaining how evangelical interest groups have promoted their policy goals through legal challenges in the courts.

Edward Cleary's piece, "Religion at the Statehouse: The California Catholic Conference," reminds us that religion and politics pervade every layer of federalism in the United States. Cleary's focus on the California Catholic Conference demonstrates the power and presence of religious lobbies at the state level. Although driven by the imperatives of Catholic social teaching, such as the preferential option for the poor, the group uses secular language in its advocacy work. The grassroots and organizational assets of the California Catholic Conference rival those of other state-level interest groups, but its priorities rooted in faith take precedence over portraying an image of power.

The primary sources included in this chapter provide examples of two types of interest group writings: voter guides and *amicus curiae* briefs. The first two selections are voter guides designed to direct the voting behavior of co-religionists. The "2008 Christian Coalition Voter Guide" is our first example. Introduced in 1992, these guides were an important tool for rallying grassroots support for candidates who shared the goals of the Christian Right. The next selection, an excerpt from a voter guide published by the Muslim Public Affairs Council, indicates that the tactic has gained ground among a wide range of religious interest groups.

The last two primary sources highlight how religious interest groups in the United States pursue their goals through the courts. These excerpts from *amicus curiae* (or "friend of the court") briefs, legal arguments submitted on behalf of groups who have an interest in a case under appeal, respond to the Supreme Court case *Van Orden v. Perry* (2005), which challenged the constitutionality of a public display of the Ten Commandments on the grounds of the Texas Capitol. The American Center for Law and Justice brief contends that the Ten Commandments, while rooted in the Judeo-Christian tradition, constitute a cultural artifact that most Americans (termed "reasonable observers") and even the government recognize as foundational to American law and jurisprudence. The second brief, submitted by the Hindu American Association on behalf of several minority religious groups, argues that the Ten Commandments are not universally accepted and tend to exclude the concerns of minority religions in the United States. The Court ultimately decided that the Texas Capitol monument was not constitutional, in part validating the arguments of the Hindu Association. In a companion case decided at the same time, however, the Court's ruling reflected the arguments of the American Center for Law and Justice, upholding the validity of Ten Commandments displays in particular contexts.

Integrative Essay

6.1

Kimberly H. Conger

RELIGIOUS INTEREST GROUPS AND THE AMERICAN POLITICAL PROCESS

Interest groups are central to an understanding of the American political process. Pluralist theory argues that the best way to understand American politics is through the analysis of group interaction—that policies result from the competition of organized groups for access to government and influence over policy and the benefits government can provide. The pluralist insight is at least as old as the Founding. Madison in Federalist 10 observed the "zeal for different opinions concerning religion, concerning government, and many other points" and argued that "the regulation of these various and interfering interests forms the principal task of modern legislation."

Pluralist theory notes that political interests compete with each other for scarce policy resources. The vast majority of these political interests are represented by interest groups—organizations of a few or many people, elites or average citizens, who have banded together to try to convince the government to do something. Similarly, a myriad of religious interest groups help represent the ideas and opinions of religious citizens and elites across the political and theological spectrum to decision-makers in all branches and at all levels of American government. Although religious interest groups tend to form and behave in ways similar to their secular counterparts, religious groups face a different set of challenges and experience more varied levels of success. In this essay, I first define interest groups in general and describe why and how they seek influence in government and public policy. Then I look at specifically religious interest groups, discuss their wide variety, and examine how they relate to one another and to their larger religious constituencies. Finally, I more closely examine the Christian Right and its role in creating the most prominent set of religious citizen interest groups in the last generation.

Interest Groups: A Brief Introduction

An interest group is best defined as: *An organized group of individuals sharing common objectives who actively attempt to influence policymakers in all three branches of the government and at all levels.* This active attempt to influence policymakers can take a variety of forms. Probably the most prevalent activity in which interest groups are involved is lobbying decision makers: members of Congress, state legislators, and bureaucratic officials at both the federal and state level. Lobbying involves not simply trying to convince a decision-maker of one's preferred policy position (though it is certainly that), but also educating decision-makers on the more detailed aspects of the questions and policies under consideration. Members of Congress, for example, often need specialized information that they do not have the time or the staff resources to collect themselves. Many members use lobbyists who generally share their personal views (frequently representatives of interest groups) to gather information on policies outside their areas of expertise (see, e.g., Austen-Smith 1993). Decision-makers need information, and interest groups can provide that information while appropriately achieving their primary reason for existence, representing their members and supporters.

The characteristics of an interest group's members and supporters help to define two broad categories of interest groups: elite and citizen groups. Elite-level groups are made up primarily of businesses, unions or other associations that are generally formed to protect the economic interests of their members. Individual citizens cannot join these groups, and citizens' interests are rarely represented by elite groups. The vast majority of interest groups at both the federal and state level are elite groups. At the other end of the spectrum are citizen groups, those designed to represent the opinions and needs of ordinary citizens. These groups generally have to offer incentives for individuals to join. Groups like the American Association of Retired People (AARP) offer selective benefits exclusively to their members such as retail and prescription drug discounts. While people may join primarily for these benefits, the group can educate its members on policy issues and claim to speak for a large body of constituents when lobbying. Few other citizen groups have the size and stature of the AARP, but many work in similar ways to gain membership and influence government.

Some individuals join interest groups for purposive benefits, that is, they join in order to seek policy change (Olson 1965). This is frequently the impetus for joining religious interest groups. Policy-oriented citizen groups tend to live and die by member contributions and grants from philanthropic foundations. Thus, when a group's issue receives significant attention in the media and in government, it will tend to have the constituency and resources to try to influence the policy discussion, but when attention to the issue declines, they tend to fade away.

Citizen groups tend to employ indirect tactics in addition to direct lobbying in their efforts to influence government. Because effective direct lobbying is expensive and subject to criticism of "insider" corruption, many citizen groups utilize "outsider" lobbying efforts, such as e-mail or letter-writing campaigns, to advocate for change. For example, in efforts to influence policy, some interest groups that encourage their membership to write to their legislators also provide a template letter detailing their position on a policy and legislator contact information. In state government, these efforts can be even more effective than lobbying. Legislators get so little contact from their constituents that concerted efforts like these present a large response to a policy issue (Conger 2009). Some citizen groups also employ protests and rallies, along with general public education through press releases and outreach programs. In general, their greatest strength is their ability to mobilize individual political participation beyond voting, and they leverage that strength into influence with a wide-variety of decision makers.

Religious Interest Groups

Religious interest groups face the same array of strategic and tactical lobbying choices as other interest groups. But what frequently separates religious groups from their secular counterparts is that the stated motivation of religious groups originates in convictions and values that transcend the world of politics. Members of religious groups, therefore, often work for societal change both within and beyond the political arena. Many scholars believe that it is this motivation and commitment that allows religious groups to succeed even in the face of scarce resources and indifferent decision-makers (Aminzade and Perry 2001; Campbell and Yonish 2003). Other scholars argue that the skills learned in conducting the business of religious congregations—civic skills like how to run a committee meeting and contact public officials—help create individuals who are more likely to be involved in the political process (Verba, Schlozman, and Brady 1995). The variety and identity of religious groups in the United States runs the gamut from church-based denominational groups to issue-oriented citizen groups, from large, well-funded and highly organized associations to shoe-string operations with an email list, and from Evangelical to Catholic to Jewish and even Muslim and Buddhist. As the size and scope of government has increased, especially since the New Deal, the number and variety of religious groups has grown as well. To understand the role of religious groups in the broad contemporary expanse of American politics and policy making, we look first at the elite level and then turn to citizen groups.

Elite-Level Religious Interest Groups

Elite-level religious interests generally represent Christian denominations or regional and national bodies of non-Christian religious groups. They are active on both the right and the left, though many elite-level religious groups lean more to the left than the right (as we will see below, the right is more represented by citizen interest groups). Many elite interests are involved with social issues, and some are very involved with protecting religious freedom in the United States and abroad. Perhaps the most well-known of these elite-level interest groups is the National Council of Churches. Formed in 1908 as the Federal Council of Churches, it is an ecumenical group focused on building cooperation among its mainline Protestant constituent denominations. Like many other religious groups, much of the NCC's focus on public policy is an outgrowth of what was originally a purely religious function. So, the NCC and other groups like it have a distinct, though closely related, organization which focuses on public policy advocacy. The NCC's Justice and Advocacy commission has been widely active on environmental and social justice issues. They lobby and perform educational functions for both their constituents and law-makers, following the general pattern of elite-level interest groups.

Many of the denominations represented by the NCC also have their own public policy groups and advocacy offices in Washington, DC, promoting the particular witness and policy positions of the individual denomination. Often, they also have separate social services arms with a presence in Washington, DC as well. Lutheran Services of America, for example, is a joint project of the Evangelical Lutheran Church and the Lutheran Church—Missouri Synod that forms an umbrella advocacy organization for over 300 Lutheran social service organizations nationwide. While each denomination office may advocate for public policy that follows its individual interpretation of what the Bible calls Lutherans to believe, they band together on social service issues.

Similarly, the Catholic Church has many entities that advocate for a wide range of policies and programs in Washington. The US Conference of Catholic Bishops operates much like Protestant denominational organizations. Its primary goal is religious in that it is the main decision-making body for Catholics in the US. But as part of its role in interpreting religious requirements for Catholics, it takes public stands on public policy issues across a wide range of topics related to human life, family life, social justice, and global solidarity. Catholic Charities USA, on the other hand, while firmly under the guidance of the Council of Bishops, focuses its efforts on social welfare and justice policy, and advocates specifically on behalf of its myriad social service providers for resources from the Federal Government.

In both the Protestant and Catholic cases, elite-level interest groups grow out of the beliefs and non-political commitments of each religious tradition that seek to represent the denomination as a whole. This process of non-political beliefs informing and motivating political activity is also evident among non-Christian elite-level interest groups in the United States. Groups like the American Israel Public Affairs Committee, the American Jewish Congress, and the Council on American-Islamic Relations focus both on promoting public policy based on their religious values and on the practical necessities in terms of regulation and resources for the social welfare service providers they govern. For example the Council on American-Islamic relations has sought to protect the civil liberties of Muslim Americans following the September 11, 2001 terrorist attacks through litigation on behalf of Muslims incorrectly detained on suspicion of terrorism and charity groups incorrectly accused of funding foreign terrorists (e.g., Walsh 2009).

Citizen Religious Interest Groups: The Case of the Christian Right

Perhaps more visible to the average citizen are religious citizen groups. These are religiously guided and motivated groups whose membership base is comprised of individuals who primarily influence politics through grassroots activism. While there have been religious citizen groups along the entire ideological spectrum for decades, most of the popular and scholarly attention in recent decades has focused on those on the ideological right. In particular, much research has looked at the Christian Right, politically conservative and activist Evangelicals and fundamentalists who have lobbied individually and through citizen interest groups at both the national and state levels over the past thirty years. The story of the Christian Right demonstrates some of the ways in which religious lobbying and interest groups have changed over time and the ways in which they have become more sophisticated—and successful—players in the American political arena.

The Christian Right is an umbrella term for politically active social traditionalists who employ explicitly Christian arguments in advancing their goal of altering American values to an earlier and, in their view, more "Christian" era of personal and public morality. In the movement's early days, this was expressed primarily in opposition to abortion, pornography, obscenity in media, sex education in schools, and support for prayer and Bible reading in public schools. More recently, groups under this umbrella have added opposition to euthanasia, embryonic stem-cell research, and gay marriage to the agenda. Although most Christian Right organizations share these issue positions, the movement also encompasses groups who promote stay at home motherhood, homeschooling, and teaching creationism in schools. In general, movement supporters want to see their vision of a moral society enacted in this country for the common good.

The Christian Right has had significant organizational success and public notice. In its early days, most of these organizations emphasized national level policy and were heavy on leadership and light on individual membership. Never monolithic, the movement spawned a plethora of single-issue organizations focused on the right to life, opposition to the Equal Rights Amendment, and the promotion of Christian schools. Utilizing the nation-wide network of Christian radio stations, many of these organizations were able to proclaim their messages to large numbers of conservative Evangelicals.

One exception to the single-issue concentration was Jerry Falwell's Moral Majority, Inc. calling for a return to Christian morality in all venues of public life, the Moral Majority empowered Evangelical and fundamentalist leaders to action and mobilized thousands of church congregations by holding voter registration drives and educating them about issues and modes of political activity. Although Christian Right groups had been gaining influence, the Moral Majority's entrance into mainstream politics on the side of the conservative Ronald Reagan was the movement's first appearance on the radar screen of most political journalists and academics. While the Moral Majority was able to generate a considerable amount of attention, due primarily to the oversized public persona of Jerry Falwell, it had neither the size nor organizational stability to be effective for the long run. As such, other groups gained prominence in the 1980s. Concerned Women for America, the Eagle Forum, the American Family Association, and the Family Research Council (originally affiliated with James Dobson's Focus on the Family) all began in the 1970s and 1980s and focused on promoting national public policy change backed up by a large and stable grassroots strategy.

The 1980s were a time of great promise for the Christian Right and its supporters. Ronald Reagan was a conservative president who had "endorsed" conservative Evangelicals at a Christian Broadcasters Association Meeting in 1980 (Smith 2000, 62). Evangelical Christians were also appointed to executive branch positions in the Reagan White House and the federal agencies. However, very little substantive change occurred during Reagan's eight years on the national policy issues of primary concern to the religious right (Wilcox 2000). Some argued that the lack of real progress meant that Republicans were using conservative religious groups to win elections only, and paid lip-service to their issue agenda (Blumenthal 1994).

By the mid to late 1980s, the top-down mobilization efforts of many of the national organizations were beginning to bear fruit at other levels of government. Conservative political activists were able to recruit new members for state-level and national Christian Right groups, and Evangelical and Fundamentalist pastors were stepping into the broader policy influencing efforts. Many were preaching about social issues from their pulpits for the first time, and Christian Radio and print media were reinforcing the messages that individuals heard in churches on Sundays. Into the mix of heightened awareness and disappointment with a conservative administration came Pat Robertson, who decided to run against George H.W. Bush, the sitting Vice-President, for the Republican presidential nomination in 1988.

In Robertson, the Christian Right had one of its own running for president. He was a Pentecostal preacher with a large television presence, a social and economic conservative, from a politically experienced family. Robertson was not, perhaps, the best candidate to reach out to the GOP's other main factions. He ran well at the start of the Republican primaries, winning the Iowa straw poll and coming in second to Vice-President George H. W. Bush in the Michigan primary. But issues of personal and policy competence and the internal theological and philosophical divisions within the Christian Right and its constituent interest groups plagued Robertson's campaign, as his Pentecostal theology alienated many fundamentalists and conservative Evangeli-cals. While Robertson's ability to attract GOP voters faded away after the initial state contests, his ability to bring Christian Right leaders into GOP party leadership positions is longer-lasting (Moen 1992, 113).

Scratch the surface of the contemporary Christian Right and you find that much of the leadership got its start in the Robertson campaign (Conger and McGraw 2008). Many activists entered politics by volunteering for the campaign. In it, they learned a lot about politics in general, but more importantly, they learned how grassroots politics, and specifically the Republican parties at the state level, worked. Many of these activists went on to found and staff the new citizen-level Christian Right interest groups that were springing up all around the country. Their candidate may have failed to achieve the presidency, but they recognized that there were many opportunities for influence and policy impact at the state level.

In 1989, out of the remnants of his campaign organizations, Robertson founded the Christian Coalition. The local successor to the Moral Majority (which folded in the mid-1980s), the Christian Coalition embodied the notion that national politics were not fruit-ful for the Christian Right. Focusing on state and local elections and issues, the Christian Coalition established affiliated state organizations in nearly every state. This was the re-sult of a conscious effort to include primarily state-level organizations that were already in existence (Diamond 1998, 76). Utilizing the support base created and nourished by the original organizations, the Coalition became truly that, a coordinator for many state-level affiliates. With its emphasis on the practical side of politics, the organization also emphasized conservative economic issues at both the national and state level in addi-tion to the religious conservative moral agenda.

With the increasing power of the Christian Coalition, the focus of Christian Right po-litical action significantly shifted to the local sphere. Christian Right leaders, including Pat Robertson, believed that Christian Right activists and supporters would have more opportunities to influence politics at local levels. They believed that their numbers would make more difference in getting the "right" people elected at the state and local level than seeking to wield that numeric power in a centralized way in Washington, DC. Many Christian Right organization members and movement supporters began to seek positions in state and local government, particularly on local school boards and in state legislatures.

National politics gave the Christian Right a new reason for existence in the 1992 presidential elections. With a newly elected Democratic president, the Christian Right had a new enemy around which to mobilize conservative support. Bill Clinton gave much ammunition to the Christian Right in the first two years of his administration. Clinton's stances on issues such as gays in the military, abortion rights, and nationalized healthcare all served as significant rallying points for many members of the movement. This "crisis" poised members of the movement to seek power and influence in new ways. The hard campaign work by Christian Right activists and astonishing voter turnout of their rank and file supporters in the 1994 midterm congressional election is widely credited with producing the Republican landslide that gave the party majorities in the House and Senate. Voter mobilization by Christian Right groups in the states, in addition to general and widespread dissatisfaction with the Clinton administration's policies, led to record levels of voter turnout by religious conservatives of all theologi-cal persuasions. This unprecedented mobilization, in conjunction with an unusually high number of open seats in the House, made Christian Right supporters the margin of victory (estimates range from 10–15% of the voting population) in a great number of close congressional races (Rozell and Wilcox 1995, 255–256).

While much of the public attention in the 1994 elections focused on national politics, the election really marked a sea change in the movement's base from the federal to the state level. In the push to get conservative Republicans elected to Congress, not only were significant networks of mobilized individuals built, but the state-level interest groups formed in the wake of the Robertson campaign gained significant stature both in terms of supporters and resources and in terms of visibility and impact on state and local politics.

The most visible interest groups involved both in mobilizing grassroots supporters and changing both state and national public policy were becoming state-level Christian Coalition chapters. Generally headed by the most prominent Christian Right leader in the state, these state chapters focused on practical politics and on teaching people how to become involved, how to lobby, and how to run for office. While involved in social issues such as abortion and school-based sex education in nearly every state, the Christian Coalition focused on electoral politics. State level coalitions produced voter guides for offices at all levels of the political process. While technically non-partisan, these guides clearly delineated the candidate for whom the Coalition believed Christians should vote. There were accusations from many non-favored candidates that the guides misrepresented their voting and opinion records (Wilcox and Joe 1998), and over time, fewer and fewer churches allowed the coalition to openly distribute the guides for fear of losing their tax-exempt status. As the national organization faced more legal and financial troubles after the 2000 election, most state level coalitions disbanded, and some changed their names and continued to operate as individual, state-level interest groups.

The Christian Coalition's arc of success and failure ushered in another model of Christian Right interest groups created by those who observed and learned from that history. The "research foundation," a model pioneered by the national Family Research Council and mirrored by affiliated organizations in over 30 states, is now a prominent model. These groups focus much more specifically on public policy than did the Christian Coalition. Even though most of their policy recommendations are conservative and geared toward Republican decision-makers, they are officially non-partisan and work hard to keep that status. Activists in these organizations prefer to be thought of as part of the "pro-family" movement and tend to work on conservative family economic policy—mainly tax-cuts and other programs designed to allow families to live on one income—along with their traditional focus on abortion policy, sex education, and the newer and more immediate focus on opposing same-sex marriage. Contemporary activists within these groups seem to be much more practically minded than their predecessors. They are focused on the day-to-day realities of trying to get state-level policies enacted or changed; they spend quite a bit of time writing legislation for sympathetic state legislators and lobbying their friends and enemies in the statehouse and governor's mansion. In many states, these family research institutes are the primary contemporary face of the Christian Right and much of the movement's leadership prefers this model to the more nationally managed model of the past.

Although the movement continues to have very little policy success at the national level, it is clear that the Christian Right's focus on the states and its activities based on state interest groups have had an impact on state level policy and on state and national elections. State Christian Right interest groups have succeeded in banning gay marriage by constitutional Amendment or "Defense of Marriage" acts in 42 states (Sorens,

Muedini, and Ruger 2008), restricting the abortion license in 34 states (Sorens, Muedini, and Ruger 2008), and passing myriad other social behavior policies on the state level. At the national level, however, the movement's one conspicuous success was the election of George W. Bush to the White House for two terms. Certainly Evangelicals and other social conservatives contributed to the vote totals in his victories. But even if they had not, Bush's Evangelical faith and general social conservatism gave the movement a voice in Washington. Over time, many national Christian Right interest groups became disillusioned with the cost of their access to the president who required their support of the Iraq war, something far outside their traditional domestic policy issues. But rank and file Christian Right supporters deeply identified with and strongly supported President Bush in his campaigns and his policy positions, giving impetus for grassroots mobilization. Many interest group leaders capitalized on this in their battles to ban same-sex marriage at the state level in 2004.

Some believe that the same-sex marriage issue reinvigorated a movement that had lost some of it reason for being after the September 11th, 2001 terrorist attacks. That may perhaps have been true at the national level, and there is no doubt that the same-sex marriage issue energized grassroots activists all over the country. But this perspective fails to recognize the wide variety of issues on which the movement has been active at the state level for over a decade now. The division of labor among groups allows them to share an activist core and a grassroots constituency but to reach out to new supporters on the margins. In Indiana, for example, Advance America has taken the lead on protecting churches from the state's newly implemented state property tax plan. By contrast, the Indiana Family Institute has taken the lead on the state's constitutional amendment banning gay marriage, while Indiana Right to Life focuses on abortion, and Indiana American Family Association works at the local level to change zoning laws to ban adult bookstores and other outlets for pornography and obscenity. Thus, many of the Christian Right's primary policy issues are addressed in the state, but by different coteries of Christian Right interest groups, operating in different spheres. This pattern, to a greater or lesser degree, is repeated in states all over the country.

This division of labor is both a cause and an outgrowth of the movement activists' growing political sophistication. As activists dug deeper into the political process in order to be more effective at policy change, they recognized that no single group would have the ability to accomplish what an array of overlapping groups could. This fragmentation, seen as a problem by some in the larger movement, has been a strength at the state level because it creates a broader base of supporters. Individuals can be active on one issue without agreeing to support an organization on a variety of other issues with which they may disagree. This situation has also created an environment where groups focused on issues ancillary to the main body of Christian Right issues have flourished in particular political contexts.

Most prominently, and in many cases even older than the Christian Right movement, is the Pro-Life movement and its attendant organizations. The Pro-Life movement is not really part of the Christian Right because its primary constituency is socially conservative Roman Catholics. There is a significant degree of overlap between the two movements in terms of support and grassroots activism, but the Catholic Right to Life's opposition to birth control and other, more fundamental theological divisions have been a barrier to full acceptance of Right to Life organizations by the primarily Protestant Evangelical Christian Right. Conversely, the Christian Right's broader agenda that deals with many issues besides abortion is seen as taking up non-essential issues by the mainly Catholic Right to Life movement. In some states, this has translated into two pro-life interest groups, one Catholic and one Protestant. In others, it has simply meant that the Christian Right lends support to the pro-life organization when possible, but continues to pursue its own larger agenda.

The other movement that has significant but not complete overlap with Christian Right groups is the Homeschooling movement and its wide range of related interest groups spread across the country. There are groups in every state in the country that are specifically political, whose reason for existence is to protect legal homeschooling and lobby on its behalf to state decision-makers. Homeschoolers generally share the political commitments of the Christian Right, with some being even more socially and morally conservative. And certainly the Christian Right supports the rights of homeschoolers. But like the pro-life movement, while there is considerable overlap between the Christian Right and homeschoolers an organizational fusion appears unlikely.

Citizen Religious Interest Groups on the Left

The Christian Right serves as the best case study of citizen-based religious interest groups at both the national and state level. The movement has significantly changed the political landscape for the relationship between religion and politics in this country since its advent over 30 years ago. Much of the political activity by religious people on the left side of the American political spectrum has occurred in the elite level interest groups discussed earlier in this essay. There are some religious citizen groups on the left, and while some pre-date the Christian Right, most have sprung up in reaction to the movement or to its policy commitments. Drawing from the protests against the Vietnam War, Sojourners was founded in 1971 and has been a consistent critical voice opposing the Christian Right from the perspective of the Evangelical Left. Never truly gaining a following of state-based organizations, many Sojourners supporters focus their efforts in church-based activities promoting peace and social justice. Sojourners was deeply involved in advocating for religiously based social justice during the 2008 election. Most prominently, it held a presidential candidate forum for Democrats in which candidates Barack Obama, John Edwards, and Hillary Clinton were asked a wide variety of questions about their personal faith and how it impacted their policy positions. This forum and the general level of comfort with religious ideas displayed by some Democratic candidates signaled the party has begun to recognize its need for religious voters and is seeking to make religious activists and interest groups supporters on the left more comfortable with its candidates.

Faith in Public Life concentrates on helping religious people on the left impact national policy debates by serving as a clearing house for many small and more local groups. It emerged before the 2008 presidential election and while it seems to have the potential to build a movement on the left similar in scale and bread to the Christian Right, its eventual impact remains to be seen. Other national religious left groups focus on particular policy issues, primarily dealing with social justice issues like ending hunger (Bread for the World), environmental issues (Interfaith Power and Light), and peace and human rights (Pax Christi).

At the state-level, one of the more prominent religious left groups that has a presence in a number of states is the Religious Coalition for Reproductive Choice. Like other citizen and elite groups on the religious left, this organization is more strongly affiliated with congregation-based actions rather than individual state organizations; it opposes abortion restrictions and focuses on social justice for women.

As we have seen from looking at religious interest groups in general and more specifically at the history and activities of the Christian Right, religious interest groups are an important component of the larger pattern of interest group behavior and structures in the United States. Like their secular counterparts, these groups lobby decision-makers, educate their supporters, and mobilize citizens and elites to seek change in American public policy. As the interest group universe has grown, so has the number and variety of religious interest groups, who are active in all three branches of government and at all levels. This vitality in religious interest groups is not limited to Evangelical or even Christian interest groups; Muslim, Jewish, and even Buddhist groups are actively seeking to represent their faith communities in the political process. Religious interest groups have consistently played a role in the creation of public policies concerning moral values, social justice, and the provision of social welfare services. These groups will endure because of their commitment to ideals larger than politics and the fact that the consistency of their religious and political witness makes them unique in the universe of American interest groups.

Research Pieces

6.2

Allen Hertzke

REPRESENTING GOD IN WASHINGTON: THE ROLE OF RELIGIOUS LOBBIES IN THE AMERICAN POLITY (1988)

Religious Political Activism and the Congressional Milieu

Often critics of religious groups, on the Right and the Left, focus on speeches, pronouncements, and resolutions to illustrate the militancy and dangerous extremism of their adversaries. The militant rhetoric of fundamentalists and the "leftist" pronouncements of liberal Protestants provide ample ammunition for such attacks. Thus People for the American Way and other secular critics of the fundamentalists have a field day quoting the militant rhetoric of this new social movement. Jerry Falwell: "One day Jesus is going to come and strike down all the Supreme Court rulings in one fell swoop." Tim LeHaye: "250,000 secular humanists control the basic institutions of America, including broadcast media, public schools, and the Methodist Church."[1] Similarly, critics of liberal church leaders find plenty of evidence that the latter are "unpatriotic apologists for Marxism" in statements such as these: "Our nation today is the very fount of violence in many places in the Third World" (Reichley 1985, 266). . . .

. . . While these statements do tell us something about their originators, they tell us little about concrete efforts to affect national policy. Even the most "prophetic" or militant groups, when they seek to influence the Congress, adapt to its norms and priorities. The congressional milieu, I would argue, exercises a powerful influence on partisans, and "movement" rhetoric inevitably seems to give way to lobby strategies aimed at change on the margins. In this section I amplify on this theme and demonstrate the ways in which the Congress, or better, the congressional milieu, influences the religious groups.

One place where congressional influence appears is in the language of the lobby craft. For those concerned that "religious fanatics" are entering politics, the evidence should be reassuring. The norms and rules of the game appear to mold the message. For example, religious lobbyists, in general, did not feel it was wise to use overtly religious language in attempting to convince legislators of their position. As James Dunn of the Baptist Joint Committee put it,

> When we interpret for our *constituency* we use biblical themes and Christian principles; but when we move across the street and start rendering to Caesar what is Caesar's, we explain in terms of social utility and not our theological rootage. We enter the political marketplace of ideas. We don't talk about sin, but about the greatest good for the greatest number—not that we don't see sin. (interview with author) . . .

The Bread for the World lobby director echoed this theme: "We don't say vote for this because you're Christian. It's because we are Christians that we are concerned. It's in the outreach to the church that we use religious language" (interview with author). Ed Snyder of the Friends Committee on National Legislation observed, "We don't use words that would set off people. We use words that have universal appeal. We don't tend to use religious language, yet we do speak of 'reconciliation'" (interview with author). While this theme was echoed by a number of lobbyists, the clearest indication of a strategic avoidance of religious language came, ironically, from the fundamentalists. Said Jones of the Moral Majority,

> We are not a religious organization, and we have some nonreligious people who support us because of our stand for a strong national defense. We don't try to use scripture or words of Christ to convince people. If we started to use scripture we would bleed ourselves to death. We want to influence government. (interview with author)

While the Concerned Women for America distinguishes itself from the Moral Majority by self-consciously identifying itself as a Christian organization, its lobbyists, too, avoid religious themes:

> We are motivated by religious values, but don't use the Bible to persuade. We guide our truth around their mental roadblocks. We speak to congressmen in terms that give respect to their goals and attitudes. On the ERA, for example, we make a constitutional case, argue facts. If a congressman says "I'm for the ERA, I think equal pay for equal work is good"; we say "but the constitutional amendment cannot govern private action." We don't quote Ephesians 5 and 6 ("Wives, be subject to your husbands . . ."). (interview with author)

Curiously, some of the mainline Protestant lobbies have not developed such clear strategic guidelines. The lobby director for the United Methodists, for example, mused that perhaps they needed to employ more clearly religious language:

> It would strengthen our position if we used the language in resolutions (which is religiously oriented). Most people on the Hill are church-related. And Reagan is being influenced by people who talk God language to him in a way we are not. I don't want to be viewed as a politician. I don't want the church to be viewed as a lobbyist. The church has a broader calling. (interview with author)

While all religious lobbies adapt themselves to the congressional milieu to a greater or lesser extent, one of the most dramatic findings to emerge from the analysis of interview data was the extent to which the fundamentalist groups have adopted pragmatic strategies aimed at lobby success, a finding that contrasts sharply with the militant and uncompromising image of them that often emerges from the pages of the elite press. In part this pragmatism is due to their dependence on key legislators to sponsor their proposals. As challengers of the status quo, fundamentalist leaders are particularly dependent on sympathetic legislators. As Gary Jarmin of Christian Voice summarized it: "In lobbying you always need a chief sponsor, and you need to adjust your priorities to theirs. You need that lead, the point man for legislation, someone who will go to the mat on it, or we don't introduce" (interview with author). In contrast, many of the liberal Protestant lobbyists have spent the Reagan years attempting to block legislation rather than initiate it (with the possible exception of Bread for the World). Another reason for this new tactical pragmatism is the fundamentalists' dependence upon constituent support, both financial and political. As the Moral Majority lobbyist described it, that organization had to start showing some success to maintain contributions from members: "In 1981 the Moral Majority went through a difficult period. We didn't have victories, and we needed victories for our membership" (interview with author). The leaders learned that pragmatic, incrementalist strategies were the means to ensure some victories, however partial. Jones, indeed, was unabashed about admitting the implications of such a shift; "Incremental approaches take us out of the business of being radical. We are not for radical change; we're for incremental change" (interview with author). This sentiment is echoed by the lobbyist for Concerned Women for America, "I have difficulty on purist approach on abortion or tuition tax credits. We have to eat the elephant a bit at a time. We have to accept partial victories. And we have some tension with membership on these problems" (interview with author). The last statement indicates that fundamentalists, too, suffer from tension over the difference between winning and witnessing to religious absolutes. Jones echoed Ferris: "Our pragmatic stance has produced tension. Prolife groups wrote Falwell calling him a murderer, because he said there should be exceptions on abortion in cases where life of the mother is in danger and in cases of rape and incest" (interview with author). In spite of tension with some members, fundamentalist leaders think that strategic adaptation is essential to effective representation of their constituents. Fundamentalists want to win, to have an impact, and they appear willing to compromise to succeed. As one congressional aide put it, they seem more motivated because, "They don't have what they want" (interview with author).

In the 1960s Saul Alinsky taught radical community organizers that "The price of a successful attack is a constructive alternative" (Alinsky 1972, 130). Fundamentalist leaders now seem to be applying that rule to their work. On abortion, for example, the lobby work is linked to other efforts:

> In a way the prolife movement closed their eyes to the real needs of unwed mothers. Since 1973 it has been seen as too negative. So the Moral Majority has moved into the issue by providing an alternative to abortion with our Save-a-Baby clinics. We work with teens, either to learn how to be a mother or to put up for adoption. We allowed the prochoice people to frame the issue so they would be perceived as caring. Framing the issue is the key to success. (interview with author) . . .

. . . Jones mentioned several cases in which it was deemed strategic for the organization to offer an alternative to a measure they were opposing. One example was the Genocide Treaty:

> A good idea, but practical implications were bad. Helms wanted to oppose outright. But we didn't want to compromise our pro-Jew stance. So we 1) reiterated our support for Israel, our pro-Jew stance, 2) said there was a need for a genocide treaty, but not this one, and 3) offered to present an alternative, which we are currently drafting. (interview with author)

This last example illustrates another way in which fundamentalist leaders show strategic inclinations. They have forged, or are attempting to forge, alliances with a number of "strange bedfellows." The most obvious, of course, is the pro-Israel stand, which has nudged Jewish leaders to rethink their hostile responses to the New Religious Right. Hyman Bookbinder of the American Jewish Committee noted a shift in his own thinking: "Things are not so simple, we are not saying that everything Falwell favors we reject. We are for discipline and traditional values, and maybe pornography and abortions went too far" (interview with author). Intriguingly, while Bookbinder noted that there was some tension between Jewish groups and liberal Protestants over Israel, he acknowledged the support from the fundamentalists: "We don't like Falwell's reasons for supporting Israel, but will accept support wherever we can" (interview with author). Fundamentalist lobbyists seem willing to forge coalitions wherever they can, with Catholics on abortion, with Jews on Israel, even with the National Council of Churches on IRS legislation. The approach is strategic. In contrast, the leader of the Methodist lobby seemed to be moving that organization in a different direction with respect to coalitional work; "We are now re-evaluating these coalitions, looking at stronger criteria for coalition involvement, specifically affirmative action criteria" (interview with author). There is some evidence, consequently, that the assessment of one senatorial aide may be partially correct: "The conservatives will transform faster than the liberals. They [the fundamentalists] like it out of the cloister, are more open to moderation than the NCC crowd" (interview with author).

Summary

Washington religious leaders, whether they wish to characterize what they do as lobbying or not, do engage in diverse strategies aimed at influencing congressional decision-making. Moreover, they are increasingly attempting to bring "pressure" on members of

Congress through the mobilization of constituents, which, given the potentially broad base of churches, has important implications for the American polity. . . . While this is especially true of the fundamentalists, it is also a growing strategy of the "mainline" Protestant leaders, who are striving to develop lists of "hot names"—denominational members who share their activist vision of Gospel imperatives. Further, the congressional milieu fosters a tactical pragmatism on the part of religious groups, some of which maintain radical long-term goals but must engage the process in incremental steps. Particularly for those groups who wish to win and not just "witness," the norms and rules of the game dictate a molding of political messages into acceptable—meaning consensus producing—forms. Moreover, a growing reliance on grassroots mobilization seems to heighten leaders' interest in tactical pragmatism. Whether they lobby for Moral Majority and Concerned Women for America on the Right, or NETWORK, Bread for the World, and the United Church of Christ on the Left, leaders who rely on constituent mobilization for power acknowledged that they strive for tangible legislative successes to keep their networks alive. Since, as one scholar observed, "success = compromise" (Berry 1984, 121), this organizational imperative moves groups toward an accommodation with the system they are attempting to influence. Religious lobbyists, in short, do influence public policy, but are themselves influenced by their participation in the national public square.

6.3

Kevin R. den Dulk

IN LEGAL CULTURE, BUT NOT OF IT: THE ROLE OF CAUSE LAWYERS IN EVANGELICAL LEGAL MOBILIZATION (2006)

In the 1960s, most observers would not have predicted that Jerry Falwell, the fundamentalist preacher, was destined to lead a political movement. Even Falwell was dubious about the prospect. "I would find it impossible" he declared in a 1965 sermon, "to stop preaching the pure saving gospel of Jesus Christ, and begin doing anything else—including participating in civil-rights reforms" (FitzGerald 1981, 63). But by 1979 Falwell had established a political presence as a leader in the Moral Majority, and in that role he helped to spearhead the creation of the Moral Majority Legal Defense Foundation, a short-lived attempt in 1981 to pursue the parent organization's goals in court. . . . [T]he Moral Majority Legal Defense Foundation would defend believers from abridgements of their freedoms and help reclaim a Judeo-Christian heritage that had been lost in thirty years of "secularist" interpretations of the Constitution. What he had once declared impossible had now become quite real: Falwell was participating in the politics of rights. . . .

. . . Although studies of rights mobilization suggest that lawyers working with or within the civil rights movement tended to privilege litigation at its outset, evangelical activism, like other more recent movements, took the opposite trajectory. Although a mass-based moralist campaign preceded and in fact fostered evangelicalism's eventual development of legal expertise and litigation strategies, evangelical leaders and grassroots activists in the movement initially used the manifold tactics of public protest. Nevertheless, the movement itself was always intimately linked to the politics of rights. Indeed, the moral grievances that generated the evangelical political resurgence quickly became wedded to specific rights-claims in the late 1970s and early 1980s—the *right* to life or the *right* to practice one's faith, among others—to such an extent that the distinction between moral/religious grievances and legal rights was blurred. . . .

I examine two key elements of the rights mobilization of cause lawyers in the evangelical movement. First, I argue that these lawyers were remarkably adaptive and appropriating; they were not wholly oppositional to or uncompromising about rights . . . Second, I suggest the key mechanism for this appropriation was the influence of certain intellectuals within the evangelical movement itself. . . .

Evangelicals and Conservative Rights Mobilization: Some Theoretical Preliminaries

Religious and other socially conservative groups have been heavily involved in litigation over abortion, pornography, and education at least since the late 1970s (Ivers 1998; Brown 2002; den Dulk 2001), and groups associated with economic conservatism have argued their cause in courts since the turn of the century (Epstein 1985; Hatcher 2005). Sociolegal research has often assumed that these forms of conservative advocacy, religious or otherwise, are by definition a reactionary and inherently antiegalitarian phenomenon. . . .

Yet the story of evangelical rights mobilization is more complex than a straightforward account of reactionary conservatism. Evangelical rights mobilization *was* a response to certain progressive rights-claims, but it did not so much reflect an opposition between egalitarian and antiegalitarianism as it revealed a conflict over different understandings of equality itself. Put another way, evangelicals accepted the basic terms of political debate, but reframed their arguments to reflect an alternative understanding of rights and equality. . . .

. . . Like other cause lawyers (Sarat and Scheingold 1998; Scheingold and Sarat 2004), evangelical lawyers found ideological and tangible support not only within the legal profession but also in their broader community, and they were particularly influenced by evangelical intellectuals who directly targeted lawyers for rights-based activism. . . . Moreover, while Posner (2001) and others suggest that increasing specialization of knowledge has diminished the importance of conventional public intellectuals, I would suggest that specialization has *heightened* the influence of evangelical intellectuals within the tradition, who have provided religious context for the bewildering array of technological advancements, new ideas, and moral controversies endemic in modern life. Intellectuals in the evangelical tradition have been particularly adept in explaining and evaluating such concepts as "rights," "equality," "freedom," and "rule of law" through the eyes of religious worldview. Indeed, evangelical intellectuals have developed relatively coherent notions of "legality," as Ewick and Silbey (1998) understand the term, which have shaped evangelical cause lawyers' motivations and tactics.

Evangelicals and the Religious Vocation of Law

It is somewhat surprising, however, that evangelicals have paid so much attention to legal ideas and activism. As noted earlier, evangelical belief about public life is peculiarly ambivalent, a simultaneous attraction to and repulsion from political and social engagement. George Marsden (1991, 110), a leading historian of evangelicalism, calls this structure of belief a "tension between . . . revivalism and polemics," an inclination to shift focus between spiritual regeneration of the individual and of society as a whole. Modern "evangelicalism" (from the Greek for "gospel") is a legacy of episodic revivalist fervor in Britain and the United States during the eighteenth and nineteenth centuries. In the present day, it is best characterized neither by a specific institutional manifestation (compared to the Catholic Church, evangelicalism is highly decentralized and schismatic) nor a set of demographic characteristics (e.g., the average evangelical today shares roughly the same socioeconomic status as the average American). Instead, evangelicalism's primary unifying feature is a passionate commitment to a set of ideas, particularly the tenets of traditionalist Protestant Christianity: the overwhelming sin of the individual, eternal salvation through Christ's death and resurrection, the final authority and historicity of the biblical text, and personal spiritual transformation (e.g., the once-in-a-lifetime "born again" experience). . . .

Evangelicals avoided courts as a place for cultural contestation well into the 1970s. Despite three decades of separationist efforts in church-state law led by the American Jewish Congress, American Jewish Committee, and Americans United (Sorauf 1976; Ivers 1995), as well as a burgeoning and increasingly organized push by NOW, NARAL, and the ACLU to secure abortion rights through litigation, evangelical legal advocates were virtually nonexistent. Not only was there no serious effort to sponsor cases, threaten litigation, or file *amicus* briefs to influence abortion or education litigation at the federal appellate level; there was also no evangelical movement or organization in existence at the time that could engage in the politics of rights in any venue. Extrajudicially, some individuals pushed a rights agenda through proposals for legislation or constitutional amendments, especially in the area of school prayer. But these proposals were so rare and their support so weak and diffuse that they can hardly be taken as an indicator of the legal mobilization of evangelicals as a group. . . .

It was not until intellectuals and other elites within the broader world of evangelicalism became convinced that "secular forces" must be confronted in terms of a theology of activist politics that evangelical cause lawyers emerged and rights-advocacy groups began to form in the mid-1970s. To foster this mobilization, elites had to do more than merely publicize grievances and opportunities for redress (McCann 1994); they had to provide a religious justification for why progressive rights-mobilization was a threat at all and why their fellow evangelicals ought to mobilize to combat it. As evangelical leaders began to nudge their fellow religionists out of apolitical isolation, a small group of evangelical attorneys began to see cause lawyering as a distinctively religious vocation. Although they served clients, their underlying commitment was to advance a set of "transcendent" values (see Sarat and Scheingold 1998). . . .

Meanwhile, other evangelical opinion leaders and activists were raising the specter of abortion and issuing even more explicit calls for Christian cultural (and particularly legal) engagement. In 1975, several prominent evangelicals, concerned that abortion had become a "Catholic issue," formed the Christian Action Council "to remind non-Roman Catholic Christians that virtually all Christians from the beginning have been against permissive abortion and for the protection of human life" (Anonymous 1976). Francis Schaeffer, an American pastor and writer who operated L'Abri Fellowship in Switzerland as a ministry to young evangelical academics and intellectuals, provided another bridge between ideas and action. He authored widely read books, such as *How Shall We Then Live?* (1976) and *Whatever Happened to the Human Race?* (1979), both accompanied by popular film series. These works, as well as Schaeffer's *Christian Manifesto* in 1981, argued that the *Roe* decision was a culmination of the steady movement of American constitutionalism away from its traditional bedrock in biblical principles. . . Schaeffer reminded his audience repeatedly of the biblical theme that government received its ultimate authority from God and no one else. To reinforce his point, he was particularly fond of invoking the seventeenth-century Scottish theologian Samuel Rutherford, whose declaration of the rule of law (*lex rex*, or "the law is king") against the arbitrary "divine right of kings" provided a framework for Schaeffer's overall critique. For Schaeffer, the courts, not the rule of law, had become king (1981)—a perspective whose resonance has only deepened among evangelicals since Schaeffer's time.

Schaeffer's influence extended to a number of fronts in the burgeoning pro-life movement and beyond . . . Schaeffer would hearken back to another legacy of the civil rights movement, namely, the use of courts. He struck directly at the heart of evangelical apathy in the legal arena, chiding the attorneys in his audience for ignoring the dramatic change in recent decades:

> Where were the Christian lawyers during the crucial shift from forty years ago to just a few years ago? Surely the Christian lawyers should have seen the change taking place and stood on the wall and blown the trumpets loud and clear. A non-lawyer like myself has a right to feel somewhat let down because the Christian lawyers did not blow the trumpets clearly between, let us say, 1940 and 1970. (1981, 47)

Coupled with the exhortations of other evangelical elites, Schaeffer's explicit challenges to attorneys represented an important evangelical experience: the *calling* to law. For evangelicals, to respond to a call is to spiritualize vocation, that is, to begin to discern a divine plan for one's life and, especially in the legal realm, to respond with obedience to a religious obligation that is bound up with a political cause. . . .

The role of religious leaders and activists is built into the process of discerning the call to a legal vocation. Some evangelical attorneys, like John Whitehead, founder of one of the first evangelical firms in 1982, fell under the direct tutelage of pastors and religious intellectuals. Indeed, his choice for the firm's name—the Rutherford Institute—was an obvious paean to Schaeffer's influence.[2] Many others sought guidance from "spiritually mature" colleagues in the legal profession. The Christian Legal Society institutionalized this kind of religious mentorship and helped channel the call of some of its members into church-state law through its own public interest firm, the Center for Law and Religious Freedom (CLRF), founded in 1975. Many interviewees traced their first experiences with answering a call to CLS.[3] . . .

Evangelical intellectuals and opinion leaders also passed on their concern with the *legitimacy* of ideas to the new class of evangelical attorneys. Scholarship through law reviews and law-related books served as an outlet to help validate evangelical ideas in the secular legal community by showing the consistency between legal norms and values and evangelical ideas. It was a vehicle for taking part in the debate over progressive rights-claims, while attempting to redefine the terms of that debate (Schlozman and Tierney 1986, 362–64). . . .

By the early 1980s, then, the CLRF, Rutherford, and several other movement law firms had been created to answer the call to cause lawyering. Many more were on the way, including most notably the American Center for Law and Justice (founded in 1990) and Alliance Defense Fund (1994). Movement elites were directly involved in establishing this second wave of rights-advocacy groups. Pat Robertson founded the ACLJ, drawing from the resources of his media (Christian Broadcasting Network), electioneering and mass mobilization (the Christian Coalition), and academic (Regent University) interests. A group of many other prominent evangelicals, including James Dobson of Focus on the Family and the late Bill Bright of Campus Crusade for Christ, founded the Alliance Defense Fund.

The callings pursued by these various groups took many different forms. Many advocates mobilized law for defensive purposes by protecting the autonomy of churches and religious schools; others used advocacy to transform the culture as a whole by focusing on abortion, same sex relations, and other matters of morality policy. . . .

Rights Mobilization and Equality in Education

In the late 1970s and 1980s, evangelical attorneys began an effort to carve out cultural space in public educational institutions, where evangelism was particularly widespread. To national parachurch organizations like InterVarsity Christian Fellowship or Campus Crusade for Christ, not to mention myriad local fellowships, Bible studies, and campus churches, access to public facilities or other campus resources is a tool to help them evangelize secular universities. From the beginning, such groups as the Rutherford Institute, the CLRF, and later the ACLJ and ADF were at the forefront of battles over "equal access"—the principle that religious and nonreligious individuals and groups alike ought to have the same opportunities to public goods. In fact, the CLRF pioneered the principle: it helped take the seminal equal access case, *Widmar v. Vincent* (1981), to the Supreme Court; it led the intriguing coalition of evangelical and civil liberties groups that pushed through the Equal Access Act in 1984 (Hertzke 1988: ch. 6), applying the equal access principle to public high schools across the country; and it provided leadership in *Widmar* 's progeny in federal and state courts, including *Board of Education v. Mergens* (1990), *Lamb's Chapel v. Center Moriches Union Free School District* (1993), and *Rosenberg v. University of Virginia* (1995).

But what motivates the Center's involvement in this body of case law? The CLRF's *amicus* brief in *Widmar* provides a hint. Declaring its concern over "the core values of religious liberty," CLRF describes the "nature of the religious command and obligation" that motivated the Christian students who were denied access to facilities at a public university. In particular, the CLRF invoked biblical mandates, including the Great Commission,[4] to suggest that evangelism was a central part of the students' expression of faith. Because the Court had upheld the right of other religious groups to evangelize in certain public fora, CLRF reasoned that the students in this case should have the same protection. Basic legal equality demanded it.

Of course, CLRF presented this argument to a judicial audience, but linking student evangelism to religious exercise was not simply a legal strategy. The CLRF advocates for equal access because its attorneys believe that evangelism is part of their calling. One of the earliest directors of CLRF characterized the issue this way:

> Our mission [was] to prepare and preserve the ground [for evangelism] through law. The window *is* law. . . . I once asked [several prominent evangelists], "What are you doing to keep the window open?" And they said, "We're praying, Sam." And I said, "Not enough. If my wife had a brain tumor and I said all we are doing is praying because my God is a mighty God and he can save and heal and he can take care of that tumor, you would say to us, 'We admire your faith, but go to the doctor.'" So when it comes to religious liberty this idea of just praying without going to a lawyer is inadequate, superficial, and unbiblical. (interview with author)

The reference to the Bible here points to a religious idea underlying equal access lawyering. Without exception, CLRF respondents claimed that their approach to equal access is a direct result of institutionalizing the biblical command to "do unto others as you would have them do unto you" (interview with author). In fact, without prompting, a recent director of CLRF said in an interview that a consistent application of the Golden Rule is "the single most important thing in my strategic decision-making" (interview with author). The comment, reiterated in nearly every other interview with CLRF staff, illustrates a convergence between the normative imperatives of evangelicals and their mobilization of law. A biblical mandate affected both whether and how CLRF would get involved in the issue of equal access.

One might question how deep this commitment to *equal* access runs. Although CLRF's motive for advocating equal access was to open the public square to other Christians, the group has been careful to tolerate other uses of the principle. By focusing on equal access, the CLRF itself attempts to "witness" through the legal process by not claiming any special constitutional protections. Using an evangelical moral calculus, this may appear a costly strategy: advocates open the door to beliefs and practices that are anathema. For example, several gay and lesbian organizations that seek to establish chapters in high schools around the country have used the equal access doctrine. But CLRF, rather than working out legal distinctions to exclude these groups, has not opposed the principle's wider application. One attorney described CLRF's willingness to support equal access for all groups as an opportunity for evangelism because it presents Christians as sincere, consistent with principle, and fair (interview with author). The evangelistic priority served as a strategic bar to exclusionary legal tactics. . . .

Conclusion

These experiences of cause lawyers for the evangelical movement may appear unique. Few religious traditions have mobilized—or counter mobilized—law in quite the same way. . . .

6.4

Edward L. Cleary

RELIGION AT THE STATEHOUSE: THE CALIFORNIA CATHOLIC CONFERENCE (2003)

While a great surge in interest in politics and religion in the United States occurred at the national level over the last ten years, extensive activity has gone on largely unnoticed at the state level (see Yamanc 1998).[5] Systematic studies of politics and religion at the state level are virtually unknown except for a few attempts to analyze hot issues, such as abortion (Byrnes and Segers 1992; Segers and Byrnes, 1995).

Among religious organizations active at this level, probably few match the Roman Catholic Church in terms of the resources it allocates to political activism. It is at the state level that the church centers its largest lobbying efforts. It is also here that policy decisions most strongly affect the allocation of government resources, monetary and symbolic, often through religious organizations. In brief, as the power of state government has expanded over the past generation, so too have state interest groups increased in number and diversity (Thomas and Hrebenar 1999).

The California Catholic Conference, with a staff of ten, represents the largest religious lobby in the state. Much is at stake to warrant this commitment of resources. Catholic Charities, part of the conference's lobbying efforts, alone receives about $1 billion per year. The conference addresses a wide range of issues from opposing the death penalty and protecting the homeless to having Cesar Chavez Day proclaimed a yearly state event.

A public theology that has been developing gradually in the United States in the last thirty years drives the efforts of the California Catholic Conference, as it does a number of other state conferences. While formulated largely in the United States, this theology derives from 110 years of worldwide Catholic social teaching. This public theology resembles contemporary Latin American social theology. In concert with the Catholic Church's "option for the poor," Catholic public theology in the U.S. attempts to defend the weak and the vulnerable. . . .

Mandate for Conference

. . . The CCC presents itself as "the official voice of the Catholic community in California's public policy arena." Dissenting Catholics have not raised a systematic challenge to this claim. Thus the question of who speaks for the church—an age-old one—is here presented as a settled issue. . . .

Recent research suggests that the California Conference reflects contemporary Catholic values. The single most commonly held value in Catholic identity is helping the poor with 97 percent of Catholics stating that helping the needy is an important element in their identity (Davidson 1997, 167; Froehle and Gautier 2000, 27–28). Further, in contrast to other groups, Catholics show an unusually high level of readiness to have the government assist the poor (Froehle and Gautier 2000, 34–35). . . .

. . . In the larger sphere of religion and politics, lobbying is only one of many instruments that church leaders worldwide employ. Lobbying contrasts to the alternatives that typically include writing and publishing joint pastoral letters, appeals from parish pulpits, promoting large scale demonstrations, and inspiring or even empowering thousands of lay leaders to become political activists. . . .

. . . In California, the choice of lobbying as the major instrument of public policy advocacy has been singularly effective. The bishops seldom use joint pastoral letters on public policy. They have not fostered mass demonstrations as a favored instrument nor have they relied on base Christian communities as allies. . . . The strength of the conference derives, in part, from its claim to represent Catholic institutions. The Catholic Church forms the largest bloc in the state in important sectors; for example, it is the largest private provider of healthcare, social services, and education in the state. Twelve diocesan Catholic Charities agencies annually serve more than one million persons. These clients come from diverse ethnicities, social classes, and religious backgrounds. Fifty Catholic hospitals serve five million patients a year. Catholic universities and other schools educate almost 300,000 students. The language of advocacy used by the California Conference to define its mission employs universal, not sectarian, description. The conference professes to promote preferential care for human life, the weak and vulnerable, the rights of workers, food and income security for "our low-income neighbors," and the environment. None of these issues, as such, are specifically "Catholic." The church in itself—that is, in its parishes and human resources—is also formidable. Its 1,067 parishes in twelve dioceses cover every corner of the state. The New Historical Atlas of Religion in America shows Catholics' pervasive presence. In all but one California county, the Catholic Church is the largest denomination. In the single exception, Trinity County, the church is the second largest denomination (fragmentation of the other churches, not overall percentage, help to explain this dominance). Nor is the presence new. The state began with large numbers of Catholics and Catholic institutions already present in the territory. In 1890, the Catholic Church was the largest religious presence in three-quarters of the counties. Since then Los Angeles and counties to the north and east have become predominately Catholic (Gaustad and Barlow 2000, 319–321).

Politicians can quickly grasp the universal reach of such an institution. Its 3,737 priests and twenty-nine bishops offer upper and middle- management strength to say nothing of the thousands of women religious and lay persons employed by church institutions and presumably loyal to church interests. . . .

Priority Issues and Policy Positions

The conference looks over the proposals and sets its priorities. Some bills, for instance, regarding highway construction hold little interest. But the conference selects many others as relating directly or indirectly to the church's public policy agenda. Conference members select what they call "first tier" priorities among the bills. . . .

. . . The California Catholic Conference acts as an activist on behalf of marginalized groups as well as representing its own interests. As legislation is proposed, lobbyists from the conference swing into action. Besides talking with legislators and their staffs, conference members begin preparing one-page background papers (in English and Spanish) for others to join in their lobbying efforts. Each paper describes the substance of the issue, how it arose, church teaching (as on social justice) that relates to the issue, and many "talking points." The latter briefly describe facts, such as California classifying one-quarter of its children as "poor," or previous tax cuts doing little to support working families. Conference lobbyists appear similar in their activities to secular lobbyists, but they also differ in fundamental ways. They do not attend the fundraising events that form a large part of the "schmoozing efforts" of most lobbyists. They make no money offers and avoid the appearance of bestowing favors upon senators or assembly persons. . . .

. . . [T]he conference reinforces its efforts by Catholic Lobby Day. This is held at a crucial time in April, not long after spring recess and just as legislative policy committees are about to hear and report bills introduced into their houses. Catholics from all over the state are encouraged to participate in the day-long event. Thus, the conference sees itself as open, participatory, and having a mission of educating the larger church on political issues presumed to be important to a citizen with Catholic social justice values.

The conference and especially Executive Director Edward E. Dolejsi, have extended their efforts widely beyond its Sacramento office . . . He brings interested parties up to date on current legislation that affects them or their clients. He lectures on the obligations of Catholic citizenship and the role of the conference. . . .

. . . Dolejsi came to California after being executive director of the Washington state Catholic Conference for ten years. Dolejsi has enjoyed a fairly long career as a Catholic lobbyist as have directors in other states. Among directors and associates, one can note the trend toward professionalization. Thirteen directors hold law degrees; other directors or staff often possess advanced degrees or have acquired special expertise in health or social services. Their expertise serves them well in understanding the complexities of law and legislation surrounding the issues that have formed the core of interests that define the California Conference. Recurring issues include education, family relations, immigration, and migrant farm workers. The conference has a special interest in public schooling. Conference lobbyists have expressed concern about the poor performance of public schools, especially those enrolling economically disadvantaged students. They have also championed tax breaks for teachers who find living on their salaries in California increasingly difficult. Concerns about the welfare of families often coincide with school issues. Recently, the conference has stressed support for parental rights as part of the larger discussion of the conduct of education. Some issues are intractable, having been on the policy table without resolution for decades. One such issue involves the rights of immigrants. . . .

. . . The Catholic Church in California has been intimately involved with the struggle for immigrant rights. The California Catholic Conference, coming into play only in the last twenty years, joined the struggle in its later manifestations. While most media attention has gone to illegal immigrants, many immigrants to California are there legally but often find legal handicaps in their living conditions. The conference has sought to protect, at a minimum, rights that are fundamental to their economic and social well-being, attempting to preserve a balance and recognizing various rights in conflict. The conference has solidly supported attempts of legal immigrants without their social security numbers to obtain drivers licenses.

California is one of the world's largest consumers of migrant labor for agribusiness. The California Conference has taken special interest in supporting supervision of farm worker recruiters and the requirement that they have surety bonds. It continues to press for consistent improvement in sometimes inhumane housing arrangements.

The conference's efforts continue a longstanding church accompaniment of Cesar Chavez and the farm worker movement. This support was bitterly opposed by ranch and agribusiness owners. This conflict, too long to detail here, is part of the larger history of the church and organized labor. A recent achievement in the farm worker struggle occurred when a statue of Chavez was erected in Sacramento and a special day was proclaimed in his honor as an annual state event.

Chavez is seen as much more than a labor organizer. He and Dorothy Day have become modern icons for the type of spirituality that the conference would like to see embraced by California's Catholics (Bokenkotter 1998). It is an engaged spirituality, especially inclined toward supporting and most of all empowering the weaker and more vulnerable persons and groups in the state. As Dolejsi says of the conference and the poor, "The poor are the natural soil of the Church in California. We are, at bottom, attempting to be prophetic in their behalf."

This study of the confluence of church and politics within California affords only a partial but important view of church and state. Understanding religion and politics would be enhanced considerably by comparative research on other Catholic conferences or on the larger view of state religious lobbying. Distinctive political cultures and secular political trends within states provide one framework for comparing religious group as lobbyists. Demographic trends provide another way to explore differences in governmental structures, policy, and politics. In contrast to the wide and almost exclusive burst of recent studies about national politics and religion, state politics and religion offers a wide field for the future studies.

Primary Sources

6.5

Christian Coalition of America

2008 CHRISTIAN COALITION VOTER GUIDE (2008)

Voter guides provide the electorate with tools for making decisions about political candidates and policy issues. On their face, voter guides are not controversial. It is not a violation of IRS regulations to disseminate voter guides, but some claim that voter guides proffered by religious groups leave the faithful little question concerning for whom to vote. You be the judge.

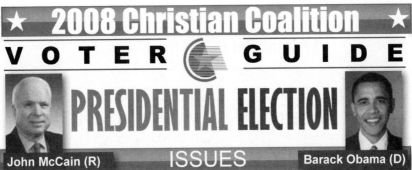

2008 Christian Coalition ★
VOTER (GUIDE
PRESIDENTIAL ELECTION

John McCain (R)	ISSUES	Barack Obama (D)
Supports	Education vouchers that allow parents to choose public or private school for their children	Opposes
Opposes	Sex education for children in kindergarten through 12th grade	Supports
Opposes	Increase in federal income tax rates	Supports
Supports	Appointing judges that will adhere to a strict interpretation of the Constitution	Opposes
Opposes	Further restrictions on the right to keep and bear arms	Supports
Opposes	Public funding of abortions, (such as govt. health benefits and Planned Parenthood)	Supports
Supports	Parental notification for abortions by minors	Opposes
Supports	Legislation mandating health care for infants surviving abortions	Opposes
Opposes	Granting sexual preference a protected minority status under existing civil rights laws	Supports
Opposes	Allowing adoption of children by homosexuals	Supports
Supports	Enforcing the 1993 law banning homosexuals in the military	Opposes
Supports	Prohibiting public funding for art that is pornographic or anti-religious	Opposes
Supports	Tax credits for purchasing private health insurance	Opposes
Supports	Allowing federal funding for faith-based charitable organizations	Opposes
Supports	Tax credits for investment in renewable sources of energy, (such as wind, solar & biomass)	Supports
Supports	Legislation to enact a "cap & trade" system to reduce carbon dioxide emissions	Supports

www.johnmccain.com   www.barackobama.com

★ Vote on November 4 ★

6.6

Muslim Public Affairs Council

ACTIVATE 08 VOTER GUIDE: 2008 ELECTION: A LOOK AT THE CANDIDATES AND THE ISSUES

Voting from an Islamic Perspective

The future of our country will be decided as Americans cast their votes this November for the next president of the United States. In looking to the coming months, the Muslim American community must remain steadfast in our commitment to political and civic participation in accordance to the guiding principles of our religion.

As Muslims, we believe that the message of Islam is sent as guidance to humankind for the betterment of life everywhere (Quran 34:28, 21:107). In American society, the most effective way for Muslim Americans to share their values, the values of Islam, is through participation in its democracy. American civil society is a dynamic institution shaped by the participation of its members. As Muslims, the Quran encourages us to engage with any project that seeks to do good (5:2). In America this project is society, which can be improved by our participation within it.

Prophet Muhammed (peace be upon him) himself participated in an alliance held by the chiefs of the tribes to ensure justice in society (Treaty of Fudul), saying "If I am invited to be part of such a treaty, I will join." It is a duty upon us, then, to follow in the footsteps of the Prophet and participate in society in order to create better policies for our nation.

According to the Quran and the Prophet Muhammad (pbuh), the only way to make the values of Islam beneficial and relevant is to have a voice within pluralistic democratic society, and to stand for our Islamic beliefs as well as the principle of justice. We must concern ourselves with each candidate's plan for economic reform, accessible health care, foreign policy, alternative energy, as well as the various other substantive issues that affect not only the Muslim American community, but all Americans. We cannot not sit idly by and let others make the decisions that affect all of us.

As Muslims, we must strive to model our lives on the teachings of the Quran and the life of the Prophet, which advocate for active participation, not isolation in society. We, as Muslim Americans, believe that making our voice heard is a duty upon us, and in a democracy that voice becomes audible primarily by voting. Voting is not just allowed by Islam, it is mandated by it.

What You Need to Know about Muslim American Voters

Like other immigrant communities, Muslims immigrated to the United States to pursue educational and economic opportunities, or to seek refuge from conflict or persecution. Muslims began arriving in large numbers in the 1960s, establishing themselves in cities and towns across America. They integrated themselves into the local community and maintained their faith and cultural traditions in such institutions as the mosque and Muslim community centers.

Despite having lived in the United States for at least three generations and having been successful participants in the American dream, little was known about Muslim Americans and their values, experiences, and attitudes on various issues until recently. While the U.S. Census Bureau is legally forbidden from inquiring about an individual's religious affiliation, several other independent surveys have been able to estimate the number of Muslims in America. The Pew Research Center approximates that there are 1.5 million adult Muslim Americans, while the oft-cited 6–7 million is based on a 2001 survey conducted by researchers from Hartford Institute for Religious Research.

It is often thought that most Muslims are Arabs, but actual numbers indicate that the largest ethnic majority of American Muslims are in fact African American, constituting 35% of the native-born Muslim American population. South Asians comprise 18%, while Arabs make up 24% of Muslims in America.

According to a February 2006 Gallup poll of Muslim Americans, most individuals are in support of the idea that religion and democracy are compatible, an attitude that results from religion playing an important part in their life. With regard to governance, 65% of Muslim Americans believe that religious leaders should not have a direct role in the policy-making process, and 28% believe that the role of those leaders should be limited to advising government officials who hold this responsibility. Therefore, it is a misconception that for Muslims, religion is not compatible with democracy. Instead, Muslim Americans value democratic principles to the same extent that they do their religious beliefs.

In general, Muslims feel more integrated into American society, which has resulted in an increasing trend of political and civic participation at the mosque and university level.

6.7

Van Orden v. Perry

Brief of *Amicus Curiae* American Center for Law and Justice in Support of Respondents (2005)

Summary of Argument

... By including a monument containing a non-sectarian version of the Decalogue among numerous other historical monuments and displays on the grounds of its State Capitol, Texas does not violate the Establishment Clause. This Court should affirm the judgment of the court below.

Argument the History and Ubiquity of Governmental and Other Recognition of the Decalogue's Secular Role Ensures That Public Displays of the Ten Commandments Convey a Message which Is Predominantly Secular

As the court below succinctly put it: "History matters here." 351 F. 3d at 181. Indeed, this Court has held that the "history and ubiquity" of a practice is one of the elements of the endorsement test. . . .

. . . This case cannot be properly evaluated without an understanding of the "history and ubiquity" of the Decalogue as both a source and symbol of law in American culture. In fact, an understanding of the Commandments' role in the development of Western law, and a survey of judicial, executive, legislative and other secular references to and depictions of the Ten Commandments demonstrates that symbolic use of the Decalogue—such as that exemplified by Texas' display of the Eagles' monument—is at least as ubiquitous and as much a part of "our Nation's cultural landscape," *Newdow*, 124 S. Ct. at 2322, as other traditional practices expressly or implicitly approved by this Court. . . .

A. The Foundational Role of the Decalogue in the Development of Anglo-American Law

The portion of the Hebrew Scriptures called the Ten Commandments, or the Decalogue, is an integral part of the legal heritage of Western civilization. To require its removal from the walls of American courthouses and other public settings because it refers to the God of Israel as a source of fundamental legal obligations would be similar to requiring the removal of the Declaration of Independence because it refers to "Nature's God" and to "the Creator" and to "divine providence" as the source of the equality of all persons and of the universal rights of life, liberty and the pursuit of happiness. Indeed, if one were to eliminate religious references from our legal history, one would reduce the timeframe of that history to very recent generations.

The founders of the American Republic, in carrying over to it many features of the English law inherited from the colonial period, were highly conscious of the historical sources of that law, including its source in Biblical law and morals.

The founding fathers were entirely familiar with, and strongly influenced by, the great treatise of William Blackstone entitled *Commentaries on the Laws of England*, published in 1765, in which he wrote that there are two main sources of human law, namely, a law of nature, which "God has enabled human reason to discover," and a divine law, "whose doctrines are to be found only in holy scripture." "Upon these two foundations," Blackstone wrote, "depend all human laws; that is to say, no human laws should be suffered to contradict these"[6] (Blackstone 1765; Altschuler 1996; Boorstin 1958). . . .

. . . Under the influence of Calvinism in the later 17th and early 18th centuries an even stronger emphasis was placed on Mosaic law, including the Decalogue, and on the Biblical sources of English law.

Although Calvinism remained especially strong in the American colonies, it eventually had to compete with other forms of Protestantism and also with Deism. All these belief-systems shared, however, a strong belief both in the religious foundation of moral values and in the moral foundations of legal principles. . . .

. . . It is hardly an establishment of religion officially to recognize that the Ten Commandments were understood by our ancestors to be the source of the division of law into branches of constitutional law, criminal law, family law, property law, contract law, and tort law.

Not only the authors of the United States Constitution but also their successors who are authorized to interpret it have preserved the historical dimension of American law. The continuity of its development over generations and centuries, which is reflected in the doctrine of precedent as well as in legal scholarship, is symbolized in the display of the Ten Commandments, which for centuries has been considered to be a historical source of universal legal obligations.

B. Evidence of Judicial Recognition of Decalogue's Foundational Role

1. The U.S. Supreme Court On at least seven occasions, members of this Court have noted the foundational role of the Ten Commandments in the development of our legal system.[7] . . .

2. The State Supreme Courts There are well over a hundred references to the Ten Commandments in the reported decisions of the state supreme courts. . . .

Without listing or citing the scores of references to the Decalogue in the decisions of the lower federal and state courts, the foregoing sampling must suffice to demonstrate the point; namely, the judicial branch of our government has historically, unhesitatingly made the connection between the Ten Commandments and our legal system—the same connection made by the reasonable observer when viewing the monuments displayed at the Texas State Capitol.

C. Recognition by the Executive Branch

Presidential recognition of the Ten Commandments' role in our legal system and culture has not been wanting. Besides frequent references to the general concept of civic order being based on divine law[8] several U.S. Presidents have made specific reference to the foundational role of the Decalogue; for example. . . .

. . . To Woodrow Wilson is attributed the following:

If we had the eyes to see the subtle elements of thought which constitute the gross substance of our present habit, both as regards the sphere of private life and as regards the action of the State, we would easily discover how very much we "owe to the Jews for the Ten Commandments and other contributions to Western Law" (*Equity Inv., v. Paris,* 1981). . . .

D. Legislative Recognition

Because, as Justice Frankfurter observed, "innumerable civil regulations . . . reinforce commands of the decalogue" (*McGowan v. Maryland* 1961), it should come as no surprise to find that, historically, the foundational role of the Commandments has found expression in legislation. It is no exaggeration to say that the Ten Commandments, *literally,* have been part of our legal system for over a millennium. . . .

. . . The ubiquity of the Ten Commandments in our history also manifests itself in the legal codes of the thirteen original colonies. It may fairly be said that all of the colonies incorporated the Decalogue—in whole or in part—in their legal codes (See Lutz 1998). After independence, the Commandments continued to exert an obvious and strong influence on legislation, even legislation drafted by ardently anti-Establishment lawmakers such as Jefferson and Madison. . . .

Aside from the broad and undeniable influence of the Mosaic law on our legal system in general (Kirk 1991, 11–49; Novak 2001), it is clear that specific provisions of the Ten Commandments continue to directly influence and, indeed, be incorporated into our legal codes as even a cursory look at our criminal codes will attest. . . .

. . . The Sabbath observance Commandment was deemed to have broad secular application by the Court itself in *McGowan v. Maryland,* 366 U.S. 420 (1961). The Commandment against "using the Lord's name in vain" is applied in daily secular life, especially in law and politics, where witnesses and government officials still swear to tell the truth or uphold the law "so help me God" (*ACLU of Ohio Found., Inc. v. Ashbrook* 2004). . . .

E. Recognition by Depiction on Public Property

More than once, members of this Court have pointed to the depiction of Moses and the Ten Commandments in the Court's own courtroom to illustrate acceptable accommodation by government of a religious practice or display (*Lynch v. Donnelly* 1984, 677; *County of Allegheny v. American Civil Liberties Union* 1989, 652–53). . . .

Courthouses and other public buildings across the nation abound with depictions of Moses and the Ten Commandments. . . .

The ubiquity of the Ten Commandments as a universally recognizable symbol of Law is thus seen in the incorporation of the Decalogue into the artwork and architecture of our public buildings where our laws are made, interpreted, and executed. In a far more literal sense than the legislative prayer at issue in *Marsh,* the Ten Commandments have become "part of the fabric of our society" (*Marsh v. Chambers* 1983, 792).

F. Recognition in Secular and Popular Culture

It is also significant to note the way in which the Ten Commandments have become part of secular and popular culture and discourse. This not only distinguishes their use as a symbol from more quintessentially religious symbols such as crucifixes and crèches, but also underscores the fact that, for a reasonable observer, no message of religious disapproval or disenfranchisement automatically follows from a governmental display of the Decalogue.

The cultural ubiquity of the Decalogue is perhaps best illustrated by the frequency with which the phrase "Ten Commandments of . . ." is used in our culture—not connected with religion at all—to convey a set of important, authoritative rules or guidelines for a variety of activities. A survey of periodicals, articles and books from such diverse, secular disciplines as medicine, sociology, business and agriculture shows literally hundreds of titles using the phrase "Ten Commandments of . . ." in purely secular settings. . . .

It seems unlikely that a "reasonable observer," who embodies "a community ideal of social judgment, as well as rational judgment" (*Capitol Hill Review and Advisory Board v. Pinette* 1995), would perceive a message of approval or disapproval of his or her religious choices when, after overindulging on Thanksgiving, he or she picks up a copy of "The Ten Commandments of buying TV fitness gadgets." App. C. . . .

The point, of course, is that references to the Decalogue in completely secular contexts are so ubiquitous in American society that the reasonable observer does not automatically think "religion" every time he or she sees a depiction of or comes across the words "The Ten Commandments." On the contrary, the ubiquity in our culture of such references makes it highly probable that a reasonable observer viewing a display like that at the Texas State Capitol in the secular historical context in which it appears would have no difficulty ascertaining the predominantly secular message to be conveyed.

Conclusion

The widespread and longstanding recognition by government and secular society of the Decalogue's foundational role is firmly embedded in American culture and, like the traditions and practices catalogued by this court in *Marsh* and *Lynch*, is "part of the fabric of our society." . . .

6.8

Van Orden v. Perry

BRIEF FOR THE HINDU AMERICAN FOUNDATION AND OTHERS, REPRESENTING THE INTERESTS OF HINDUS, BUDDHISTS, AND JAINS, AS *AMICI CURIAE* IN SUPPORT OF REVERSAL (2005)

. . . The *Amici Curiae* represented herein submit this brief to offer the perspective of adherents to several non-Judeo-Christian faiths and to explain why, from that perspective, the Ten Commandments Monument on the grounds of the Texas Capitol has the effect of expressing an inherent government preference for Judeo-Christian religions over non-Judeo-Christian religions.

Amici include non-profit organizations and worship communities in Hindu,[9] Jain,[10] Buddhist[11] and other non-Judeo-Christian traditions[12] (collectively, the "Non-Judeo-Christian Religions"). Collectively, they reflect the religious sentiments of millions of Americans, including some of the fastest growing religious groups in the United States. . . .

. . . Each *Amicus* is well situated to assist the Court in understanding the viewpoint of non-Judeo-Christians. Each represents people whose theologies differ in profound respects from one or more of the Commandments and with the concept of "law" as divine injunction that the Decalogue reflects. Because their religious traditions are not Judeo-Christian, *Amici* provide a unique perspective—albeit one shared by millions of Americans—on the effect of the Ten Commandments monument on non-Judeo-Christians, and why it should be found to violate the Establishment Clause under this Court's First Amendment jurisprudence.

Summary of the Argument

The maintenance of the Ten Commandments Monument on the grounds of the Texas State Capitol violates the Establishment Clause because the Monument is inherently religious, serves no historic purpose, and does not lose its religious character through juxtaposition with secular images. It depicts the Ten Commandments, a cornerstone of Judeo-Christian theology, in the traditional shape of the "Biblical Stones." Non-Judeo-Christians, including *Amici,* who do not adhere to the religious views that the Ten Commandments either state or symbolize cannot fail to perceive the placement of such a monument on the grounds of the Texas Capitol as an endorsement of Judeo-Christian beliefs over their own. The maintenance of the Monument therefore has the primary effect of advancing the Judeo-Christian beliefs to which a majority of Texans subscribe.

In reaching a contrary conclusion, the lower courts committed two principal errors. First, they concluded that the Ten Commandments Monument was "non-sectarian" simply because it favored no Judeo-Christian sect or denomination over any other. The courts below completely ignored the effect of the Ten Commandments Monument on non-Judeo-Christians, whose beliefs regarding the nature of God and the relationship between man and God differ greatly from those enshrined in the Monument and for whom the Monument is clearly and unavoidably "sectarian." By ignoring the effect of the Monument on non-Judeo-Christians, they disregarded the requirements of this Court's Establishment Clause jurisprudence.

Second, the lower courts relied heavily on the forty years the Monument stood without challenge on the grounds of the Texas Capitol. The Establishment Clause is a bedrock constitutional limitation on the power of government and a violation of that limitation should not be countenanced simply because no one has complained for over forty years. Many of this Court's Establishment Clause decisions struck down state-sponsored religious practices—mandatory school prayer, for example—that had been observed far longer than forty years. Moreover, the inference drawn by the lower courts that the absence of complaint evidences the inoffensiveness of the Monument overlooks the historically tiny population of non-Judeo-Christians in Texas—a population that has reached significant numbers only in recent years. With the recent increase of religious diversity, in both Texas and the nation as a whole, comes a host of Establishment Clause issues that would never before have come to the fore. The Fifth Circuit's reliance on the historical absence of challenge during a period of much greater religious homogeneity effectively allowed majoritarianism to trump Establishment Clause requirements.

Amici respectfully submit that the lower courts reached the wrong conclusion here in part because they failed to properly consider the effect of the Ten Commandments Monument on those who do not adhere to Judeo-Christian religions. *Amici* urge this Court to rectify that mistake. . . .

Background on the Non-Judeo-Christian Religions and How Their Theologies Conflict with the Religious Precepts Set Forth on the Ten Commandments Monument[13]

. . . Followers of the Non-Judeo-Christian Religions did not begin to arrive in this country in appreciable numbers until about 1975. They came to the United States, like many generations of immigrants before them, seeking religious and political liberty and better lives for themselves and theft families. Recognizing their religious minority status, they nevertheless expected to find a nation in which the Constitution guaranteed that Government would not favor one religion over another. In the eyes of the Non-Judeo-Christian Religions, the Ten Commandments Monument is inconsistent with this Constitutional guarantee.

1. *Hinduism.* . . . Several core aspects of Hindu theology directly conflict with the precepts set forth on the Ten Commandments Monument, and with the religious anthropology that the Decalogue symbolizes, with the result that a Hindu viewing the Ten Commandments Monument would perceive the state as preferring or endorsing Judeo-Christian beliefs at variance with his or her own.

Hinduism propounds a theology of panentheistic monotheism, recognizing that God can be called many names and may take many forms, and that the means or ways to salvation are many.[14] Hindu theology does not place proscriptions on how to pray, and each person may choose which form of God to pray to on his or her own path to self-realization. Moreover, Hindus do not conceive of God as a specific, single entity separate from other living things, in stark contrast to the portrayal of the God who delivered the Ten Commandments in *Exodus*. Rather, for Hindus, God is omnipresent *(anantam)* and within all living things (Chinmayananda n.d., 230). Thus, Hindus cannot reconcile their non-dualistic teachings with the very First Commandment, which mandates the exclusion of all divine manifestations other than the Judeo-Christian God. For the same reason, the teachings of Hinduism cannot be squared with the reference to "the Lord thy God" in the Fourth Commandment.

Nor can Hindus accept the First Commandment's prohibition against "graven images." The use of *murtis* (sacred representations of God in any of God's various forms) is central to the practice of the religion for virtually all Hindus.[15] These consecrated images represent the presence of God and help devotees offer their devotion to God (Wakin 2004).[16]

Additionally, Hindu theology does not proscribe the time or manner of prayer to God (Chinmayananda n.d., 449, 7:21).[17] Hinduism teaches that God, the one Supreme Being, is omnipotent *(sarva-shaktitva)* and need not rest. For example, Hindu philosophy holds that God created the universe with a single inhalation (Krishnananda 1975, 251, 2:4:10; Chinmayananda n.d., 527–30, 9:7–9).[18] Hindus feel no compulsion to refrain from work or other activities on any particular holy day of the week. The concept of six days of creation and a seventh day for rest, the Sabbath, is absent from Hindu theology. The Third Commandment's directive on the Texas Monument to "[r]emember the Sabbath Day, to keep it holy" is alien to Hinduism. . . .

Argument

As demonstrated above, there are fundamental differences between the precepts set forth on the Ten Commandments Monument and Hindu, Buddhist and Jain teachings regarding the very essence of religion, i.e., the existence and/or nature of God and the relationship between human beings and God. To *Amici* and their co-religionists, the Ten Commandments Monument is not a list of universal ethical truisms or mere "ceremonial deism;" it is not a history lesson; it cannot be dismissed as a *de minimis* affront to the Non-Judeo-Christian Religions. Instead, it expresses concepts that conflict with the most basic beliefs of these religions. . . .

I. The Primary Effect of the Ten Commandments Monument on Members of the Non-Judeo-Christian Religions Is to Confirm That Texas Endorses the Particular Majority Religious View Reflected in the Monument

The Establishment Clause undergirds our increasingly pluralistic society. Waves of immigrants—Christians of all denominations, Jews, Muslims, Hindus, Buddhists, Jains, Sikhs, Zoroastrians and others—have come to this country with the expectation that they will find the freedom to worship in their own way without becoming a political outsider as a consequence of doing so.

The Establishment Clause is phrased as an absolute: "Congress shall make no law respecting an establishment of religion. . . ." It admits no exceptions for majority sentiment, historical inertia or administrative expedience. It contains no sunset provision, limitations period or grandfather clause.

The Fifth Circuit's ruling was in error. The Ten Commandments Monument violates the Establishment Clause under the facts of this case, i.e., placement in the Texas Capitol of a central symbol of Judeo-Christian beliefs, a religious symbol that by its nature, history and content reflects fundamental differences with *Amici's* non-Judeo-Christian theology. The Fifth Circuit declared the text on the Ten Commandments Monument to be "non-sectarian" (*Van Orden v. Perry 2003*)[19] as the text did not favor one set of Judeo-Christian beliefs over another. But the text and the Monument plainly favor Judeo-Christian beliefs over other religious beliefs. For practitioners of non-Judeo-Christian faiths, the Ten Commandments Monument is manifestly sectarian. Its presence on the grounds of the Texas Capitol is perceived by reasonable non-Judeo-Christian observers as an inherently religious symbol that cannot be divorced from its overtly Judeo-Christian nature and history. The Fifth Circuit's ruling was error and should be reversed. . . .

B. The Effect of the Ten Commandments Monument on Followers of the Non-Judeo-Christian Religions Is to Signal an Endorsement of Particular Religious Views
The effect of placing a six-foot monument of a central Judeo-Christian religious text at the seat of state government is to underscore the government's endorsement of the particular views espoused by that text. This Court has permitted explicitly religious conduct or speech in governmental settings or at public events only when the context makes clear that the government is not endorsing the beliefs espoused in the speech . . .

The inference of government endorsement is particularly strong here because the Ten Commandments undoubtedly reflect the religious views of the majority of Texans. An adherent of a non-Judeo-Christian faith in Texas for any length of time cannot help but be aware of his or her status as part of a religious minority. Texas is part of the "Bible Belt." For the State of Texas to place on its Capitol grounds a monument to one of the central symbols of the religious majority, and have it be the only outdoor monument with explicitly religious symbols, is in itself powerfully suggestive of official endorsement (*Van Orden v. Perry* 2003, 175–176).[20]

It is important to emphasize that *Amici* do not take issue with the specific ethical teachings of the Ten Commandments. *Amici* share with all people of good faith the belief that human beings should not kill each other, should not steal from each other, and should honor their parents. The Ten Commandments Monument is not presented, however, as a mere set of universally shared ethical or legal norms. . . . The Monument's message cannot be divorced by a reasonable viewer from its biblical origins and its religious symbolism and connotations. . . .

The Ten Commandments are an important religious symbol, a symbol that conveys a religious message very different from the religious views of the followers of the Non-Judeo-Christian Religions. The effect of non-Judeo-Christians having to confront this religious symbol in the seat of government should have been part of the Fifth Circuit's reasonable observer analysis. Failure to consider these issues is reversible error and consideration of these issues compels a finding that the Monument violates the Establishment Clause. . . .

II. The Ten Commandments Monument Violated the Establishment Clause Forty Years Ago and Continues to Do So Today

The Fifth Circuit's conclusions were based in significant part on the finding that the Ten Commandments Monument has stood on the grounds of the Texas Capitol for forty years without recorded complaint. This must mean, the Court reasoned, that reasonable observers do not view it as an endorsement of religious belief. This reasoning is fatally flawed.

Surely it cannot be the law of the land that those who would violate the Constitution need only do so in a way that their actions go unchallenged for an extended period of time. Such a rule would ensure that the most egregious constitutional violations could go unremedied. Moreover, such a rule ignores the specific historical reasons why the Ten Commandments Monument has not previously been challenged, at least by those represented by *Amici*.

Establishment Clause jurisprudence should not enshrine the historical views of the unchallenged majority, but should reflect the increasing and increasingly important religious diversity of the United States. . . .

B. The History of *Amici* in Texas (and the United States) Explains Why Followers of the Non-Judeo-Christian Religions Had Not Previously Openly Complained about the Ten Commandments Monument
The lower courts reasoned that if anyone had religious objections to the Ten Commandments Monument, someone would have raised them long before the instant action had been brought. This reasoning is flawed, however, because very few adherents of non-Judeo-Christian faiths were present in 1961 or for many years thereafter to voice any complaint. Texas cannot use its own historical lack of religious diversity to justify its continued sponsorship of the undeniably sectarian Ten Commandments Monument. The Fifth Circuit's reliance on the historical absence of debate elevates majoritarianism over Establishment Clause jurisprudence.

Until recently, the *Amici* were too small a minority in Texas to be expected to voice their objections to the Ten Commandments Monument. Hindus, Buddhists and Jains primarily immigrated to the United States from Asian countries after 1965 (Melton 2003, 197–198) . Immigration from Asia was stunted during and after World War I because of a significant anti-Asian prejudice (Melton 2003, 197–198). This bias led to the enactment of the Asian Exclusion Act of 1917 (see Melton 2003, 198),[21] which severely limited Asian immigration for a half century under a strict quota system. With the passage of the Immigration and Nationality Act of 1965, limitations on immigration to the United States were relaxed, and quotas from Asian countries were raised to the same level as European countries (see Melton 2003, 198). Nevertheless, it was some years before those immigrants could become citizens, further inhibiting their political voice. Accordingly, Hindu, Buddhist and Jain immigrants could not have been expected to openly challenge the Ten Commandments Monument in 1961.[22]

In recent years the number of Asian immigrants has been steadily rising and, not surprisingly, so has the number of followers of the *Amici's* religions. For example, according to the 2003 U.S. Census, the number of Hindus, Buddhists, and Jains in the United States approximately tripled from 648,000 in 1990 to 1,933,000 in 2001 (United States Census Bureau; The Pluralism Project at Harvard University).[23] This trend is similar in Texas. For example, the first Hindu *mandir* in the nation was built in the late 1970s (Tweed and Prothero 1999, 289). Today there are forty in Texas alone (The Pluralism Project at Harvard University n.d.). There are also currently over 100 Buddhist temples and five Jain temples in Texas (The Pluralism Project at Harvard University n.d.).

Finally, the Fifth Circuit's ruling is inconsistent with the history and purpose of the Establishment Clause. It was not lost on the Framers that the United States was created in large part by the emigrations of religious dissidents. The drafters of the Bill of Rights devised the Establishment Clause as a means of protecting the religious views of those who dissent or disagree by ensuring that state power would never throw its weight behind any religion or religion in general. As the population of the United States grows ever more religiously diverse, the original purpose of the Establishment Clause becomes evermore critical. The Ten Commandments Monument is sectarian and violates the Establishment Clause today, just as it did forty years ago. That it took forty years for religious pluralism to give rise to an impetus to challenge Texas' actions is no defense. This is especially true with regard to followers of the Non-Judeo-Christian Religions represented *by Amici.*

Conclusion

The Ten Commandments Monument is a large granite monument in the traditional shape of the Biblical Stones engraved with a message from the Judeo-Christian God and sitting on the path to the seat of political power in a predominantly Christian state. The lower courts erred by failing to consider the effect of this Monument on non-Judeo-Christians, such as the followers of the religions represented by *Amici.* As set forth above, the Ten Commandments Monument sends the message to such non-Judeo-Christians that the State of Texas endorses Judeo-Christian religions and that Judeo-Christians are insiders while all others are outsiders. *Amici* urge this Court to consider such effects and conclude that the Ten Commandments Monument violates the Establishment Clause of the First Amendment.

Notes

1. Both quotes were taken from People for the American Way literature.
2. In addition to Schaeffer, Whitehead sought out the late Rousas John Rushdooney, a Christian "reconstructionist" who believed that the Old Testament law is still in universal effect. Whitehead never wholly subscribed to reconstructionism, but Rushdooney did provide "intellectual focus" and a network of other evangelical elites when Whitehead was beginning his career (Whitehead 1999).
3. Interviews with McFarland; Ericsson; Bradley Jacobs, HSDLA (formerly CLRF); and Gregory Baylor, CLRF.

4. In the New Testament passage of Matthew 28: 18–20, Christ is recorded as leaving his disciples with these words: "All authority in heaven and on earth has been given to me. Therefore go and make disciples of all nations, baptizing them in the name of the Father, and of the Son, and of the Holy Spirit, and teaching them to obey everything I have commanded you. And surely I am with you always, to the very end of the age" (NIV).

5. Yamanc's 1998 dissertation is an exception. . . . He investigated the role of religious advocacy organizations at the Wisconsin state legislature.

6. The founding generation learned its law from Blackstone's *Commentaries on the Laws of England*. . . . As historian Daniel Boorstin puts it, "In the history of American institutions, no other book—except the Bible—has played so great a role. . ."

7. The late Chief Justice Warren attributed such a role to the Bible in general: "I believe the entire Bill of Rights came into being because of the knowledge our forefathers had of the Bible and their belief in it. . .," quoted in TIME, Feb. 15, 1954.

8. For example:
   ". . . the propitious smiles of Heaven can never be expected on a nation that disregards the eternal rules of order and right which Heaven itself has ordained. . ." (Washington 1789).

   "enlightened by a benign religion, professed, indeed, and practiced in various forms, yet all of them inculcating honesty, truth, temperance, gratitude, and the love of man; acknowledging and adoring an overruling Providence. . ." (Jefferson 1801).

   "If we shall suppose that American slavery is one of those offenses which, in the providence of God, must needs come, but which, having continued through His appointed time, He now wills to remove. . . shall we discern therein any departure from those divine attributes which the believers in a living God always ascribe to Him?" (Lincoln 1865).

   "And yet the same revolutionary beliefs for which our forbears fought are still at issue around the globe – the belief that the rights of man come not from the generosity of the state, but from the hand of God" (Kennedy 1961).

9. The following *Amici* are devoted to Hinduism: The Hindu American Foundation; Arsha Vidya Pitham; Arya Samaj of Michigan; The Hindu International Council Against Defamation; Hindu University of America, Inc.; Navya Shastra; and Saiva Siddhartha Church.

10. *Amicus,* The Federation of Jain Associations in North America, is devoted to Jainism.

11. *Amicus,* Dr. Robert A.F. Thurman, is a world-renowned Buddhist scholar and Professor of Indo-Tibetan Studies at Columbia University.

12. *Amicus,* The Interfaith Freedom Foundation, represents Muslims, Sikhs, Hindus, Buddhists, Jews and other religious minorities.

13. A complete description of Hinduism, Buddhism and Jainism, and the many schools of thought of each of these religions that have emerged over their long histories, is beyond the scope of this brief.

14. This concept is known in Sanskrit as *samadarshinah,* or "equal vision" (Chinmayananda n.d., 313–14, 5:18). ("Sages look with an equal eye upon a BRAHMANA endowed with learning and humility, on a cow, on an elephant, and even a dog and an outcaste." Commentary stating in part, "Everywhere [God] realizes the presence of the same Truth, whatever be the container."); *see also id.* at 230, 5:2 ("[I]n whatever way men approach Me, even so do I reward them; My path do men tread in all ways . . . .").

15. For example, Sri Pramukh Swami Maharaj of the Bochasanwasi Shri Ashar Purushottam Sanstha propounded prayers involving *murtis* as one of the defining aspects of Hinduism.

16. This is not to say that Hindus worship *murtis.* The idea that Hindus "worship idols" is a very common misconception. Hindus do not believe that the *murti* or home is actually the Divine Being itself. Hindus fully understand that the Divine itself is much greater than the physical image. The misconception that Hindus worship idols has been perpetuated for over 500 years, and continues to date. For example, in 2004, Orthodox Jewish Rabbis in New York and Israel forbade the use of Indian hair in wigs because of the misconception that Hindus worship idols.

17. ("Whatsoever form any devotee desires to worship with faith – that [same] faith of his I make [firm and] unflinching." Commentary stating in part, ". . . the Common Truth that holds together the multiple universe of names and forms." "It is very well-known that, all men do not worship at the same altar.").

18. (Commentary stating in part, "[i]t is the eternally composed and already existent Vedas that are manifested like a man's breath—without any thought or effort on [H]is part"); explaining that creation is a continuous and

cyclical process, which takes no effort on the part of God).

19. (describing the Monument as having "a large panel display[ing] a nonsectarian version of the text of the Commandments") [hereinafter "5th Cir. Opinion"].

20. The following additional factors bolster the endorsement effect of the Ten Commandments Monument on the Non-Judeo-Christian Religions: (1) the Monument is on the State Capitol grounds; (2) the Monument is owned and maintained by the state; (3) the Texas Capitol grounds are not a public forum; (4) there is no disclaimer of the explicitly religious message on the Monument; (5) the Monument is in the traditional shape and form of the Biblical Stones and contains numerous Judeo-Christian symbols such as the Chi Rho, Stars of David, the All-Seeing Eye in an equilateral triangle and ancient Hebrew text in tablets; (6) none of the other sixteen monuments on the grounds of the Texas Capitol are religious and many, if not all, reflect government endorsed speech; and (7) as the District Court recognized, the context of the Monument does not suggest that it is part of a display regarding the history of lawmaking. In short, the context of the Monument does nothing to dispel its overwhelmingly religious impact, particularly when viewed by those outside of the Judeo-Christian context. In terms of context, the Ten Commandments Monument is similar to the stand-alone crèche this Court struck down in *Allegheny*, not the contextualized and secularized Christmas display that passed constitutional muster in *Lynch*.

21. Immigration Act of 1917, ch. 29, 39 Stat. 874 (1917) (repealed 1952). The 1952 Act, although repealing the 1917 Asian Exclusion Act, retained the same restrictive quotas found in the 1917 Act. Immigration & Nationality Act of 1952, ch. 477, 66 Stat. 163 (1952) (amended 1965, 79 Stat. 911).

22. The few non-Judeo-Christians who may have been present in Texas in 1961 may not have felt emboldened to challenge to Monument. Congress had not yet passed The Civil Rights Act of 1964 and the country would not see the first strong enforcement of civil rights laws for several years. The lower courts wrongly assumed that asserting an objection to the Monument in 1961 would have taken no more courage than it would today.

23. At Table 79 (finding that between 1990 and 2001, respectively, the number of Hindus grew from 227,000 to 766,000 and the number of Buddhists grew from 401,000 to 1,082,000); (the number of Jains grew from 20,000 to 75,000).

CHAPTER 7

RELIGION AND
THE PRESIDENCY

Introduction

Despite the many and varied influences of religion on American politics, few explorations of the presidency give serious attention to how religion affects the office. Upon reflection, this is an unusual fact. Americans have always been and remain a religious people, with a high level of religious practice and widespread adherence to traditional religious beliefs even in the modern era. In that context, it would be surprising if the only public official elected nationwide by those same Americans was *not* religious.

Presidents from recent decades have been more, rather than less, openly religious. Contrary to the assumption that modernity would bring increasing secularization, it may be that the changing expectations of the nation and presidency in the post–World War II era amplified the religious dimensions of the office. The constant efforts at outreach and coalition building common in political campaigning are now standard and institutionalized in the presidency. The 24/7 news cycle and the feeling of intimacy of nonstop electronic, particularly visual, coverage of the presidency emphasize the personal aspects of the one holding the presidential office. Americans come to expect a "full" and "real" picture of their elected leader, and religious faith and practice is logically an important aspect of the president's biographical sketch. As the size of the institutional presidency expands, and as the media intrudes further into the presidential office and person, the focus on a president's religion might well be expected to grow.

In their essay commissioned for this volume, Mark Rozell and Harold Bass describe many points of connection between religion and the presidency, noting that "neglecting or misunderstanding the religion factor contributes to an incomplete understanding of presidents and the presidency." They identify several areas where religion influences executive behavior and policy, providing an overview of religion's role in presidential elections, interest group politics, staffing, and policy agendas.

The first of the two research pieces is an excerpt from the concluding chapter of Gary Scott Smith's recent landmark study of religion and eleven American presidents. Smith demonstrates the extent to which all presidents act on religious convictions of some sort, considers the role of presidents in shaping national discussions of church–state issues, comments on how presidents employ civil religion and understandings of divine providence, and discusses how citizens often use religious morality to evaluate presidential character.

Next, Charles Dunn identifies ten "theological dimensions of presidential leadership," demonstrating how a theological framework can enrich our understanding of the American presidency and the many individuals who have held that office. He then offers a classification scheme that charts the ideology and theology of presidents through Ronald Reagan.

The primary source selections that follow reveal some of the ways in which American presidents themselves speak of and about religion. Presidents symbolize the nation, and often employ religious language to encourage joint and noble efforts. Most of the excerpts reflect that trait. The first selection offers insight into Abraham Lincoln's private anguish over the Civil War. Found by his secretary after Lincoln's assassination, the note was apparently written after the Confederate victory at Manassas.

The next selection includes excerpts from John F. Kennedy's speech to Protestant ministers in the midst of the 1960 presidential campaign. Kennedy attempts to allay fears that a Catholic president would be unduly influenced by the church and its leadership, describing his views on separation of church and state and proclaiming: "I do not speak for my church on public matters; and the church does not speak for me."

Jimmy Carter represents a sharp contrast to Kennedy's campaign; Carter's open discussion of the importance of his personal faith in the 1976 campaign was a marked change from his predecessors. His emphasis on religion and values appealed to many voters longing for a leader with honesty and integrity after the divisiveness of the Watergate scandal. Carter's inaugural address, reprinted in its entirety here, is replete with religious rhetoric and themes.

Four years later, Ronald Reagan reached out to voters with a different tone and manner. Drenched in the rhetoric of civil religion, Reagan's speech at the Republican National Convention in Denver calls out to America's religious history; speaks of compacts, covenants, and manifest destiny; and offers the promise "to recapture our destiny, to take it into our own hands."

The next speech, George W. Bush's First Inaugural Address, is also reprinted in its entirety. In the 2000 campaign, Bush often spoke of his personal faith and the importance of his religious conversion. When asked in a primary debate to name the political philosopher with whom he most identified, Bush famously replied, "Christ, because he changed my heart." While criticized by many commentators, his reply seemed to cement the impression in voters' minds of the centrality of the Christian faith in his life and probably helped his nomination efforts, especially among the evangelical wing of the Republican Party. In this first speech as president, Bush interweaves biblical references and lines from famous hymns with nods to America's growing religious diversity, such as his groundbreaking reference to mosques.

We end the chapter with an excerpt of President Barack Obama's June 4, 2009, address in Cairo, Egypt. The speech illustrates a sophisticated interpretation of the operation of faith in public life even as it connects major religious traditions to very practical issues of international affairs.

As the selections in this chapter make clear, religion has influenced the president as well as the presidency, the individual and the office. To neglect either is to have an incomplete view of American politics and religion.

Integrative Essay

7.1

Mark J. Rozell and Harold F. Bass

RELIGION AND THE U.S. PRESIDENCY

Despite a significant and vastly growing literature on the intersection of religion and politics in the U.S., the role of religion in the presidency remains a neglected subject. Most such works focus on the religious beliefs and practices of certain chief executives widely known to have been men of deep faith. In the modern era, presidents who professed their faith openly and attracted political support by so doing—Jimmy Carter and George W. Bush especially—have received the bulk of the analysis. The importance of faith to many other presidents of deep religious convictions but more muted public display has attracted less interest. Often, studies of presidencies have either ignored religion or inaccurately characterized these leaders as non-religious men who merely used rhetorical appeals to faith for politically calculated reasons. Gary Scott Smith (2007; 2005), one of the few scholars doing serious in-depth analysis of the role of religion to the presidency, states: "Even though thousands of volumes have been written about America's presidents, we do not know much about the precise nature of their faith or how it affected their performance and policies" (Smith 2005, 6).

Neglecting or misunderstanding the religion factor contributes to an incomplete understanding of presidents and the presidency. Serious works are available on religion and the American founding period and on the religious beliefs and practices of the nation's founders and early presidents, Abraham Lincoln, and certain modern presidents such as Jimmy Carter, Ronald Reagan, and George W. Bush. Recent years have also seen the proliferation of highly polemical popular works on the importance of faith to certain presidents. During the George W. Bush era in particular there was a near explosion of books and essays on the president's religiosity; some lavishing praises on him as a man of genuine faith commitment and others characterizing him as a captive of the conservative evangelical-led religious right movement. Both such agenda-driven accounts and the bulk of scholarly work on the presidency have tended to ignore the importance of the faith convictions of the less religiously demonstrative presidents as well as the role of faith in shaping presidential selection, forming the basis for some interest groups in presidential elections, informing the organization of the executive office, and influencing policy agendas in the executive branch.

Incomplete Analysis of Presidents' Religion

Part of the widespread discomfort with writing about religion and the presidency is the belief that the U.S. constitutional system supports what Thomas Jefferson called a "wall of separation between church and state." Large bodies of scholarship and judicial opinions have taken Jefferson's famous phrase to advocate the strict separationist view. However, religion scholar Thomas J. Buckley, S.J. (2007) and constitutional law scholar Daniel Dreisbach (2002) have shown that this statement from Jefferson's 1802 letter to the Danbury Baptist Association has often been taken out of context as a call for absolute separation. Their close examinations of Jefferson's presidential addresses, private correspondences, and the public papers of his administration reveal that the third president contributed significantly to the development of American civil religion, perhaps more so than any of his contemporaries. Jefferson even directed government funds to support the work of Christian missionary groups to "civilize" and to convert Native American Indians (Buckley 2007, 41).

Incomplete analysis of Thomas Jefferson's presidency is just one example of the tendency among scholars to overlook the role of faith in the presidency by examining only public religious behavior (i.e. religious rhetoric in speeches or regular church attendance) when assessing religious commitment. Scholars have erroneously placed a number of presidents of the modern era in the nonreligious category. For example, many perceived a publicly concealed religiosity as a lack of serious faith commitment on Harry S Truman's part. Elizabeth Edwards Spalding (2007) argues that Truman, the second Baptist to serve in the White House, was deeply religious but uncomfortable with overt displays of faith and skeptical of those who claimed that their own religion gave them a favored relationship with God. She also traces the influence of Truman's faith on his foreign policy, particularly the Cold War, which he saw as a moral clash against atheistic communism. For example, Truman reached out to religious groups to aid the West in the Cold War. He gave a policy address at a Catholic college to showcase his desire to enlist the support of the Church in combating communism and he made efforts to establish formal relations between the U.S. and the Vatican. Truman also wrote to the president of the Baptist World Alliance: "To succeed in our quest for righteousness we must, in St. Paul's luminous phrase, put on the armor of God" (Spalding 2007, 103).

Many scholars have characterized Dwight D. Eisenhower as perhaps the least religious of any of the modern presidents because he all but abandoned his strongly religious upbringing after entering West Point and was open about his aversion to organized religion. They cite the president-elect's comment in a December 1952 address to the Freedom Foundation: "Our form of government has no sense, unless it is grounded in a deeply felt religious faith, and I don't care what it is" (Holl 2007, 120). Historian Jack Holl argues that the president's biographers have mostly gotten the story wrong, observing that, "no one emphasizes the influence of Eisenhower's deeply ingrained religious beliefs on his public life and work" (2007, 120). Four years prior to being elected president, Eisenhower said that "I am the most intensely religious man I know" (Holl 2007, 119). Eisenhower was the first president to write his own inaugural prayer, was baptized in the White House, approved "one nation, under God" being added to the Pledge of Allegiance and "In God We Trust" to the U.S. currency, and appointed a new office of special assistant for religion in his administration.

Like Eisenhower, Ronald Reagan did not attend church while president and appeared to harbor an aversion to organized religion. Reagan biographers have characterized him as generally indifferent to religion, except to the extent that he could attract the political support of religiously-motivated voters with his conservative positions on social issues. This conventional view of Reagan has held for years. However, Paul Kengor (2004) who reviewed Reagan's private papers and letters and interviewed many of the people closest to the former president finds that Reagan was a deeply religious man. According to Kengor, the neglect and misunderstanding of Reagan's religiosity "leaves an unbridgeable gap in our own understanding of Reagan and what made him tick, especially in the great calling of his political life: his Cold War crusade against the Soviet Union" (Kengor 2007, 175). Like Truman, Reagan perceived the struggle of the Cold War as not merely strategic but moral. Reagan avoided church attendance as president largely due to security concerns. He had regularly attended services prior to his presidency, and resumed after he left office. Thus Kengor argues that those who only observed what appeared to be Reagan's outward indifference to religion while in office misunderstood his true sentiments.

Interest in the relationship between religion and the presidency took off during the George W. Bush presidency due to his exceptional openness about his faith and the belief that his policy agenda was driven significantly by his religiosity. While it is true that Bush was much less constrained about expressing his religiosity publicly than many past presidents, it is an exaggeration to claim that he was unique in this regard among America's chief executives. In the modern era, for example, such presidents as Jimmy Carter and Bill Clinton have been at least as open about their faith, and perhaps even more so. One study showed that Bill Clinton invoked Christ in presidential speeches more often than Bush per number of years in office (Kengor 2004, 2; Penning 2007, 210).

Religion and Presidential Selection

One of the challenges in studying the religion-presidency intersection is that all presidents find it politically expedient at times to connect religious themes to policy goals or use religious rhetoric to sustain political support. However, it is not always clear whether presidents do so because they believe that they have to, or because it comes naturally to them. In the electoral context, presidential aspirants find it particularly advantageous to evoke religious identity and themes.

Although Article VI of the Constitution stipulates that "no religious test shall ever be required as a qualification for any office or public trust under the United States," the presidential selection process shows certain norms with regard to the religion of presidential aspirants. The most compelling is the clear expectation that the president be a person of faith. All our presidents to date have made this claim, at least nominally. A 2004 poll indicated that almost 60% of likely voters surveyed believed that it is important that the president believes in God and be deeply religious (Banks 2004).

Well into the 20th century, that faith was presumed to be Protestant Christianity. In the 1920s, Governor Al Smith of New York, a Democrat, became the first Roman Catholic to receive serious consideration for a major party's presidential nomination. After falling short in 1920 and 1924, he finally prevailed in 1928; but the campaign featured considerable anti-Catholicism, and Smith suffered a decisive general election defeat. Three decades later, Sen. John F. Kennedy's presidential prospects turned on whether his Catholicism would prove to be an insurmountable obstacle. The 1956 Bailey Memorandum, ostensibly written by the Democratic Party chair in Connecticut, but actually prepared by a Kennedy aide, asserted that the shifting mid-century electoral landscape actually gave a Catholic candidate, who could mobilize rising numbers of Catholic voters in key states, an advantage (White 1961, 240–3; Sorensen 1965, 81–3).

During the course of the 1960 nomination contest, Kennedy delivered a key speech to an assembly of Protestant ministers in Houston, Texas, in which he assured them that his faith would not compromise his exercise of the powers and duties of the office of president (White 1961, 391–393; see full text of the speech later in the chapter). This pledge to separate his private faith from his public responsibilities resonated well with mid-century American culture and society, but contrasts starkly with the current expectation that personal faith will and should inform public policy positions.

Kennedy won the nomination convincingly, and the election narrowly, amid abiding concerns among Protestants. He remains the only Roman Catholic president to date, although the Democrats have subsequently nominated Catholics for vice president (Edmund Muskie, 1968; Sargent Shriver, 1972; Geraldine Ferraro, 1984; Joseph Biden, 2008) and president (John Kerry, 2004). Following Kennedy's election in 1960, the Republican Party nominated William E. Miller, a Roman Catholic, for vice president in 1964.

No person of Jewish faith has ever received a major party presidential nomination. Sen. Barry Goldwater (AZ), the 1964 Republican nominee, was of Jewish descent on his father's side, but he identified himself as an Episcopalian. Sen. Joseph Lieberman (CT), an Orthodox Jew, received the Democratic vice presidential nomination in 2000. In this instance, the effect on public opinion and electoral behavior appeared negligible.

In 1968 and 2008 Mormons figured prominently in the Republican presidential nominating contests. Governor George Romney (MI) was a leading contender in 1968 for the nomination won by Quaker Richard Nixon. Four decades later, Romney's son, Mitt, was a strong candidate. The elder Romney's faith was commonly noted, but it did not prove especially controversial in his pursuit of the party nomination. Indeed, what garnered the most attention was the fact that his parents were Mormon missionaries serving in Mexico when he was born, raising questions because of the constitutional requirement that the president be a natural born citizen. In contrast, his son's religious identity appeared much more noteworthy and controversial in 2008, reflecting both the rising salience of religion in American politics and significant changes in the nomination process that provided venues for the expression of religious sensitivities.

Another recent development with regard to the religious backgrounds of presidential aspirants is the presence of former clergy in the nominating contests of the parties: Jesse Jackson in 1984 and 1988 for the Democrats; Pat Robertson in 1988 and Mike Huckabee in 2008 for the Republicans. The success of Robertson and Huckabee in some nomination contests is evidence of the rise of evangelical interests in the body politic in general and the Republican Party in particular.

Religion is present in the presidential nomination process not only as a characteristic of the candidates but also as a source of coalition building. Contests for the presidency have long featured the mobilization of voters based on religious affiliations. Traditionally identifying with the Democratic Party, Catholics and Jews provided stable electoral foundations for Democratic presidential nominees, while mainline Protestants did the same for the Republicans. These identifications generally paralleled socioeconomic ones, with the Republicans capturing the support of the more established elements of society and the Democrats the more marginal. Similarly, religious identities often correlated with regional and residential ones. For example, Democratic strongholds in the urban Northeast housed substantial numbers of Catholics and Jews. In turn, White Protestants in what used to be called the Solid South were once a key part of the Democratic presidential coalition.

More recent developments have modified these traditional patterns, as parties, candidates, and campaigns have sought to attract support from religiously-rooted voters based on issues and ideologies. Democrats have claimed the enthusiastic support of African-American Protestants with commitments to civil rights. Republicans have appealed to some Jewish voters by advocating a strong pro-Israel stance and have made inroads with some Catholic voters with their pro-life position on abortion. Moreover, upward class mobility has made the GOP more attractive to middle-class Catholics.

However, the most important development along these lines in recent decades has been the mobilization of evangelicals. Evangelicals were once relatively disengaged from the electoral process and their voting behavior was best explained by other factors, notably class and region. For example, the traditional inclination of Southern Baptists to vote Democratic reflected a regional norm, reinforced by their lower-middle class position in Southern society.

The 1970s saw dramatic changes in this pattern for several reasons. Economic development moved evangelicals upward within the middle class, and several issues emerged on the political agenda that enraged and engaged the evangelical community. These included controversial Supreme Court decisions proscribing public prayer in public schools and expanding abortion rights. In addition, cultural changes in the 1960s and 1970s threatened the traditional values of evangelicals.

In 1976, a self-proclaimed evangelical successfully sought the Democratic presidential nomination and went on to win the general election. Jimmy Carter brought attention to and mobilized this segment of the population. Four years later, frustrated by many of his policies, particularly on women's rights and abortion, evangelicals largely deserted Carter's reelection bid and instead supported Republican nominee Ronald Reagan. Since then, this constituency has been a vital component in the presidential coalitions assembled by Republican Party nominees.

Republicans have benefited not only from the support of evangelicals but from the emergence of a broader religiosity gap. Those who frequently attend religious services, regardless of religious affiliation, are more likely to vote Republican than those who rarely or never attend. This electoral shift has proven significant in the post–New Deal era resurgence in Republican presidential fortunes, and is particularly helpful in explaining narrow GOP victories in the presidential contests in 2000 and 2004.

Changes in the presidential nomination process including the expansion of primaries and participatory caucuses afford interest groups, some of them faith-based, new avenues for involvement in presidential selection. This has resulted in the development of channels of communication within presidential candidate organizations in both parties that systematically reach out to religious voters.

In the array of power brokers and kingmakers who attempt to influence voter preferences for presidential nominations, those who claim to speak for religious interests have become quite prominent in the Republican coalition. They have included Jerry Falwell (Moral Majority), Charles Colson (Prison Fellowship), Ralph Reed (Christian Coalition), James Dobson (Focus on the Family), Gary Bauer (American Values), and Richard Land (Southern Baptist Convention Ethics and Religious Liberty Commission).

Iowa's caucuses, since 1972 the opening salvo in the delegate selection contests for the national party conventions, have played a critical role in structuring the ensuing nomination campaigns. They have consistently featured enthusiastic participation by social conservatives motivated by religion in what is frequently a multi-candidate race, providing high visibility for religious interests. For example, in 1976 Jimmy Carter's dark horse candidacy was propelled by winning a strong 27.6% of the caucus delegates, leading the Democratic field of candidates. In 1988, Pat Robertson, head of the Christian Coalition, garnered the support of almost 25% of the Republicans, finishing in second place. In 2000, Alan Keyes and Gary Bauer, both appealing to the Christian conservatives in the electorate, got a combined 23%. Eight years later, Mike Huckabee won the GOP contest in Iowa with 34.4% of the vote due to high evangelical turnout. The placement of the Iowa caucuses, and media publicity surrounding them, virtually guarantee that the early stages of the nomination contests will focus attention on the preferences of religiously-motivated participants.

Religious Interests and the Presidency

One common way that institutional presidency scholars have confronted the topic of religion is through the pluralist lens of interest representation. This approach has figured prominently in considerations of presidential selection, staffing, and policy-making. The pluralist perspective views politics as the arena where groups organize and compete in efforts to translate their private interests into public policy through electioneering and lobbying. Students of interest groups observe that whereas the presidency is rarely the primary focus of group activity, it is a significant one nevertheless. Interactions between presidents and pressure groups are on the rise, owing to a heightened role for the president in domestic policy making and to the proliferation of interest groups. The place of religious interests in the campaign often foreshadows their subsequent contributions to presidential politics and policy-making.

In this regard, religion is treated in essentially a secular fashion. Religion is represented as a descriptive demographic category, addressed alongside such counterparts as socio-economic status, race, ethnicity, region, age, and gender in shaping political behavior. Because discussions of interest representation in electoral coalitions and presidential policy-making identify and include religious interests in the context of overlapping and competing identities, insufficient attention has been given to the distinctive character of religion as a descriptive category (see Mitchell 2007). What makes religious groups noteworthy and problematical, compared with their more numerous secular counterparts, is their transcendent character. This feature arguably heightens the intensity of commitment of religious people and diminishes their willingness to compromise with and accommodate competing interests.

Just as modern reforms of the presidential nomination process have provided religious interests with expanded opportunities for involvement in presidential selection, the establishment and expansion of the White House Office has provided new avenues and institutions for interaction between the president and religious groups. Modern presidents and their staff assistants engage in systematic outreach to religious interests to draw them into and maintain their presence within the presidential electoral coalition. In turn, religious activists make known to the White House their expectations and demands with regard to nominations, appointments, policies, and priorities.

Presidential Staffing

A successful presidential campaign presents the incumbent with the opportunity to staff the administration, and key campaign aides typically follow the president into office. Religious interests operate in reciprocal fashion. After successfully supporting a favored candidate for the presidential nomination and general election, leaders of religious interest groups seek to influence public policies. They do so by seeking the appointment of acceptable candidates for presidential nominations and government offices, and by promoting their policy agendas.

Party leaders often look to the president for input before the election of the national party chair. In the New Deal era, a period dominated by Democratic presidents Franklin D. Roosevelt and Harry S Truman, the Democratic Party chair was always a Roman Catholic. After a post-convention interlude in 1960, the Democrats resumed this pattern under Presidents Kennedy and Johnson until 1969. This afforded symbolic representation to a key electoral constituency. Early on, it also provided substantial patronage opportunities, though these receded considerably over the decades.

More important, the creation of the Executive Office of the President in 1939, the cornerstone of which is the White House Office, has given presidents a location to house key assistants, many drawn from the campaign organization. Close at hand, they oversee the president's pursuit of political and policy objectives. Reflecting bureaucratic patterns, the White House Office has experienced dramatic growth in size, accompanied by division of labor and specialization.

In this organizational setting, attention to representation and cultivation of interest groups has been a presidential priority, and religious interests have been included from the outset (see Pika 1987–1988). Early on, President Harry S Truman identified a specific aide,

David Niles, as his liaison with minorities, notably Catholics and Jews. His successors followed suit. President Dwight Eisenhower enlisted Frederick Fox, a Congregationalist minister, as a presidential assistant to deal with volunteer groups in general and religious ones in particular. One of President Lyndon Johnson's top aides, Bill Moyers, had been a Southern Baptist seminarian a decade earlier.

Presidents Richard Nixon and Gerald Ford institutionalized this previously informal commitment to group representation. In 1974, Ford established the Office of Public Liaison (OPL), formalizing outreach to groups from the White House Office. Henceforth, organized interests, including religious ones, have benefited from its presence, enjoying varying degrees of access and attention.

Over the past three decades, the number and visibility of religious liaisons on White House staffs has heightened considerably. In 1979 President Jimmy Carter, alienated from the evangelical community that had rallied to his 1976 presidential candidacy, brought Robert Maddox, a Southern Baptist pastor from his home state of Georgia, into the White House. Nominally a speechwriter, Maddox's real assignment was to communicate with and assuage the restive evangelicals, working with their leaders, as the re-election campaign neared. Ronald Reagan assigned Morton Blackwell, a campaign aide who had dealt with evangelicals, to the Office of Public Liaison in a parallel capacity. In his second term, he deployed Gary Bauer, who was closely tied to the evangelical community, as a domestic policy adviser. Vice President George H.W. Bush enlisted Doug Wead, an ordained Assemblies of God minister, to assist his 1988 presidential campaign in garnering evangelical support. After the election he brought Wead into the White House as a special assistant to continue these outreach efforts.

Bill Clinton continued this now-familiar pattern of designating a White House aide as liaison with the religious community, locating Flo McAtee in this capacity within the Office of Public Liaison. The George W. Bush White House featured particularly high-level opportunities for evangelical leaders to make their concerns known, including weekly conference calls with the Office of Public Liaison. Another OPL staffer provided outreach to the Jewish community. Further, the office of political affairs, under the supervision of Karl Rove, deputy chief of staff, proved especially attentive to evangelical needs and interests. In addition, Michael Gerson, Bush's chief speechwriter and policy adviser, brought a strong evangelical background and orientation to his assignment.

The Bush White House merits mention on another institutional front. On assuming office in 2001, the president fulfilled a campaign pledge and established by executive order the White House Office of Faith-Based and Community Initiatives. This office is charged with expanding the role of faith-based bodies in the delivery of social services through the provision of federal grants.

Any discussion of modern presidents and their religious advisors has to make mention of the extraordinarily enduring role that Billy Graham has played in the post-World War II era. This prominent evangelist has enjoyed access and provided counsel to every president since Harry Truman. Beset by personal scandal, Clinton also brought Graham and other prominent pastors to the White House to provide him with spiritual counsel.

These appointments and offices demonstrate the growing propensities of modern presidents to place on their White House staffs assistants who can communicate with religious constituencies in the electoral environment. From the president's perspective, these interactions are linked to re-election efforts. They also pertain to policy initiatives.

Presidential Policy Agendas and Religion

Nineteenth-century presidents rarely advanced ambitious policy agendas, typically deferring to Congress. With some conspicuous exceptions, particularly emancipation, religion did not feature prominently in presidential policy-making until the beginning of the 20th century. The Progressive Era coincided with and contributed to an expansion of presidential power, and the reform agenda of the period was infused with social justice concerns advanced by Protestants and Catholics alike. For Protestants, it was the social gospel articulated by Walter Rauschenbusch in *Christianity and the Social Crisis* (1907). For Catholics, Leo XIII's papal encyclical *Rerum Novarum* (1891) heightened sensitivities to the plight of the working class in industrializing society and led to calls for responsive public policies. Early 20th century presidents Theodore Roosevelt and Woodrow Wilson associated themselves with these causes in their Square Deal and New Freedom agendas. Franklin Roosevelt did so with the New Deal, and Lyndon Johnson's Great Society, with its commitment to civil rights and the expansion of the welfare state, reflected these emphases as well. Bill Clinton's New Covenant was an effort to advance these themes at century's end.

The literature on interest groups makes clear that their efforts to influence the public policy agenda involved mobilization and counter-mobilization. Successes by one group encouraged emulation by others. In part as a reaction to perceived excesses of Johnson's Great Society as well as discontent with modern cultural norms, the Christian Right emerged around 1980 as a major force in American politics. A pro-life stance on abortion became the forefront of the Christian Right policy agenda. Freedom of religious expression, against claims that it fosters religious establishment, has been another priority. President Reagan and his Republican successors have rhetorically embraced this agenda and it has figured prominently in their judicial nominations, though never advancing far in the legislative process.

On the foreign policy front, presidential policy leadership is less constrained. In the post-World War II era, religious interests and convictions have undergirded several presidential policies. U.S. presidents framed the Cold War as a struggle against "godless" communism on behalf of religious believers. Consistent U.S. foreign policy support for Israel is rooted in the Judeo-Christian heritage of the West. President Carter's commitment to human rights as a foundation for his foreign policy was an expression of his deeply-held religious beliefs. Similarly, George W. Bush often connected his religious beliefs with his "freedom agenda."

Thus, religious interests clearly occupy a seat at the table of presidential politics and policy. In recent decades, this position has been enhanced by profound organizational changes in presidential politics and policy-making that broaden the avenues for influencing outcomes. Presidential campaign-based channels of communication carry over into the administrations, wherein presidential outreach efforts and reciprocal interest group lobbying explicitly represent religious interests. In concert, they have opened new avenues of access and interaction.

Research Pieces

7.2

Gary Scott Smith

FAITH AND THE PRESIDENCY: FROM GEORGE WASHINGTON TO GEORGE W. BUSH (2006)

This examination of the lives of eleven presidents [Washington, Jefferson, Lincoln, Theodore Roosevelt, Wilson, Franklin Roosevelt, Eisenhower, Kennedy, Carter, Reagan, and George W. Bush] demonstrates that their faith has been vitally important to a substantial number of the occupants of the Oval Office. . . .[1]

Despite their differences, all eleven presidents emphasized the nation's religious heritage, trumpeted the value of religion, called for spiritual renewal, and underscored the relationship between religious faith and morality. . . . From George Washington to George W. Bush, they argued that God rules the universe, that the dictates of reason and revelation reinforce one another and supply a basis for both individual morality and public policy, and that religious faith best sustains the nation's constitutional democracy and provides the strongest safeguard and support for republican virtue and liberty (Levenick and Novak 2005). They all accepted Washington's exhortation in his general order of July 2, 1776: "Let us therefore rely upon the goodness of the Cause, and the aid of the supreme Being, in whose hands Victory is, to animate and encourage us to great and noble Actions". . . .[2] All eleven used religious motifs to define and defend the nation's goals and purposes. Most of them argued that faith in God was essential to sustaining America's traditional values, strengthening its resolve, and solving its problems. Both Roosevelts, Wilson, Eisenhower, Kennedy, Reagan, and Bush emphasized patriotic piety, conventional morality, and the evils of autocracy, fascism, communism, or terrorism (Fairbanks 1982, 336–7, 342) . . . view[ing] the United States as carrying out a godly mission by striving to defeat these wicked forces and create a more righteous international order. . . .

Many of these presidents had deeply held religious beliefs, but they expressed their faith in different ways. Except for Wilson, Carter, and Bush, they were intensely private about their religious convictions.[3] These three presidents and Lincoln were the most personally devout. Of these eleven chief executives, only Jefferson and Wilson extensively studied Christian theology. Although all of them highly regarded and read the Bible, Jefferson, Lincoln, Wilson, Carter, and Bush read it most faithfully and knew it the best. Only Franklin Roosevelt and Reagan did not attend church regularly while president. . . . They all declared that they needed God's counsel to carry out their momentous responsibilities. Their faith helped these presidents (Kennedy to a much lesser extent) gain perspective, establish priorities, be confident about their decisions, endure trials, and accept defeats (Abshire 2003). These presidents also regularly employed religious rhetoric in their speeches to comfort the grieving; challenge citizens to promote justice, righteousness, and compassion; appeal to commonly held spiritual values; win support for their campaigns or policies; and invoke God's blessing on America and thank him for his guidance (e.g. Barnes 2003; Mattingly 2005).

These presidents have been both lauded and lambasted for their faith. Although many have praised their personal piety and the influence of their religious convictions on various actions and policies, others have complained that some chief executives have mistakenly (and dangerously) claimed to know God's will on vital issues or that their faith influenced them to adopt policies that have harmed the nation. . . . As the scholarly community and the culture became more secular and skeptical, substantial concerns were raised about the religiosity of some twentieth-century presidents. "A lot of people are worried about Presidents' taking their cues from on high," journalist Hugh Sidey wrote in 1984. "Woodrow Wilson's fervor sank his marvelous ideas about peace. Jimmy Carter's conviction that he had a special relationship with God and could get answers through prayer instead of the National Security Council may have been the biggest cause of his ineptitude. Reagan is at his worst when he is thumping his Bible and counting God among his Cabinet." Many accuse Bush of believing that God directs his policy making. Critics also complain that presidents have often used the Bible selectively and inappropriately to advance their own political interests, ignored many of its central teachings, and frequently quoted it out of context. Instead of using the Bible to scrutinize and criticize American actions, detractors protest, they have generally employed it to justify them. They wanted "God on their side" to help them legitimate their ideas and give them "moral satisfaction" and used "only enough of the Bible or their Christian convictions [to] accomplish their political objectives" (Thomas and Dobson 1999). Moreover, critics allege, they have portrayed God as sanctifying and expediting America's agenda.

Presidential Convictions

. . . Some maintain that presidents should confine their religious convictions to their private lives and prevent them from intruding on their work. Voicing this concern, Abraham Foxman, national director of the Anti-Defamation League, argues that when Bush prays "as a private person practicing his own faith, God bless, but when it becomes part of the official function of the president," it is "inappropriate." Others counter that committed Christians, Jews, and Muslims, like other citizens, should be able to support or oppose political policies based on their personal perspective of what is morally right, prudent, feasible, and good for society. . . . Is it "really so preposterous," others add, for a "person who represents the will of the public . . . to discuss his personal convictions?" Is it inappropriate for a country where 90 percent of the citizens believe in God to "elect a leader who shares this fundamental belief?" (Williams 2005).

Like other Americans, presidents should be able to express and act on their religious convictions. They bring to their public service the totality of who they are as people, which is shaped in part by their faith. Although none of them tried to "impose" his personal religious views on the citizenry, the subjects of this study believed that their ideological commitments should direct their actions and policies. Several factors make it difficult for presidents and other elected officials to bring Christian values to bear directly on political life: the pressures of political life, their desire for public approval, the complex, demanding nature of diplomacy, and the necessity of appealing to and satisfying conflicting interest groups (Colson 1987, 176). Nevertheless, the influence of their faith is evident in many ways, including Washington's quest to guarantee religious liberty, Jefferson's to ensure peace, Lincoln's to end slavery, Theodore Roosevelt's to settle the 1902 coal strike, Wilson's to devise the Treaty of Versailles, Franklin Roosevelt's to remedy the ills of the Great Depression, Eisenhower's to reduce armaments, Kennedy's to procure black Civil Rights, Carter's to promote human rights around the globe, Reagan's to combat communism, and Bush's to encourage faith-based initiatives.

The Separation of Church and State

. . . Presidents, because of their duties, visibility, and influence have played an important role in this debate over the intent of the First Amendment. Through their personal religious practices, rhetoric, and policies, they have a significant impact on American attitudes about church–state relations (Hutcheson 1988, 236). All the presidents in this study supported Madison and Jefferson's basic position on the first issue: The government cannot directly fund religious worship or proselytizing. They sometimes inflamed the debate over the second issue ["of sponsoring or endorsing public acts of worship or public displays of religious devotion" (Monsma 2002, 261–3)] by leading the nation in prayer or including scriptural passages in issuing proclamations or giving addresses. Many of the presidents in this study, most significantly Washington and Jefferson, strongly promoted religious liberty. Carter, Reagan, and Bush criticized communist nations for restricting the religious freedom of their citizens. Only Lincoln dealt with this issue at length at home, as he wrestled with how to maintain citizens' religious liberty while thwarting disloyalty to the Union and efforts to undermine its purposes. Numerous chief executives, especially since Franklin Roosevelt, have been deeply involved in disputes involving [whether the government may fund faith-based services].

Identifying three possible responses to these church–state issues helps clarify these debates. The first, the strict separation position, advocates very limited aid to "educational and social programs of faith-based groups" and strong safeguards to protect the free exercise rights of religious citizens. Its proponents believe that religion is important, but because it is private and personal, government should neither aid nor impede it. The second approach—formal neutrality—contends that the "government should not use religion as a category either to confer special benefits or to withhold benefits generally available." The government must not single out religious groups for distinctive benefits or liabilities. Some fear that this position will weaken free exercise provisions. Labeled both "positive neutrality" and "substantive neutrality," the third stance calls for examining not only whether a law or governmental action "is neutral in a technical legal sense" but also "whether its effects are neutral."

. . . These eleven presidents provided governmental support for religion in numerous ways. All of them except Jefferson proclaimed days of public prayer and thanksgiving to God, deeming them constitutionally permissible and beneficial (Jefferson 1808). They officially recognized Christian, Jewish, and, more recently, Muslim holidays. Many of them prayed in the White House with religious groups. Eisenhower and all his successors spoke at the national prayer breakfasts in Washington that began in the 1950s. These eleven presidents typically endorsed such practices as chaplains in the military and Congress, the inclusion of the phrase "under God" in the Pledge of

Allegiance, prayers by chaplains at inaugurals, prayer in the public schools, and government funding of private religious schools. . . .

While strongly promoting scriptural values of righteousness, peace, justice, and compassion, all eleven presidents respected the separation of church and state. Although they celebrated the nation's Judeo-Christian heritage and emphasized the importance of religion to the well-being of the nation, they did not use the power of their office to push any distinctively sectarian beliefs, practices, or aims or to give special privileges to their own denominations. They all asserted that religious faith helped promote virtue, civility, and social order and wanted the federal government and religious groups to work together to elevate the nation's morality and remedy its social ills.

All of these presidents insisted that the government could supply "friendly aid" to religious groups as long as it did not favor some over others. Although Jefferson, Kennedy, and Carter, because of philosophical commitments and political pressures, adopted the strict separationist position of no government aid most fully, they still promoted religion through various means. Their life experiences, ideological convictions, and religious supporters, as well as the prevailing political climate, prompted other presidents, most notably Wilson, Franklin Roosevelt, Eisenhower, Reagan, and Bush, to prefer the positive neutrality position. To them, the nation's traditional religious values provided a bulwark for combating evil opponents—German autocrats, Nazis, communists, and terrorists—and for rallying the support of the American people. Some of these eleven presidents led the nation in prayer (Roosevelt on D-Day and Eisenhower at his first inaugural), and many of them repeatedly exhorted Americans to pray about domestic and foreign issues. Most of them gave more government support to religion than members of Americans United for the Separation of Church and State argue is permitted by the Constitution or prudent, and Kennedy and Carter maintained a more rigid separation than scores of scholars and religious leaders think is constitutionally required.[4]

Civil Religion

From Washington to Bush, "presidents have symbolized, and in some cases defined, the civil religion or public faith that has held this diverse society together" (Monsma 2002, 232). . . . Presidents have usually employed broad religious language and eschewed specific Christian or Protestant terms. They have typically referred to God by generic titles and avoided mentioning Jesus or Christian doctrines. . . . They have used civil religion to sanctify the political order, reinforce cherished ideals, appeal to principles shared by the country's many religious communities, and assure citizens that God uses the United States to accomplish his purposes (especially to defeat evil and spread democracy) and endorses its policies. Often linking piety with patriotism and love of God with love of country, the subjects of this study stated or intimated that God's hand was evident in the creation and preservation of the United States. . . .

Scholars distinguish between priestly civil religion, which offers God's comfort and solace to people in the midst of tragedy and affliction, and prophetic civil religion, which uses biblical themes to challenge citizens' attitudes and actions. All eleven presidents functioned more as priests than as prophets. They asserted that God had chosen and blessed the United States, provided spiritual inspiration, and consoled their countrymen after tragedies (Marty 1974, 144–7; Linder 1996). However, they all sometimes used the rhetoric of civil religion to exhort citizens to reevaluate the nation's goals and actions and to accentuate and seek to implement its best values. When employing the prophetic role, presidents challenged Americans to evaluate "the country's actions in relation" to God's will and standards, condemned the "idolatry of religious nationalism," and urged them to repent of their "corporate political sins" (Linder and Pierard 1991). . . .

Deeply desiring to hold the nation's disparate elements together, the presidents examined in this study often employed the rhetoric and symbols of civil religion in their efforts to promote unity or provide comfort in times of national trial and tragedy. In the absence of a national church or sanctioned religious credo, and given Americans' substantial religious diversity, their use of this form of discourse is quite understandable. Despite its strong Judeo Christian heritage, the United States has no official religion. Therefore, when speaking to or for the American people, presidents have tended, no matter what their own personal faith, to use broad, generalized language. More than many critics admit, these presidents employed civil religious rhetoric to criticize the nation's shortcomings and failure to incarnate or implement transcendent standards. Unfortunately, however, they too often used this vocabulary to justify U.S. policies, actions, and principles and to exaggerate its righteousness.

America as God's Chosen Nation

The idea that America is a chosen nation has had a powerful impact on its history. From the Puritan attempt to build a city upon a hill, to Thomas Paine's vision of America as an "asylum for Mankind," to current arguments that the United States is a refuge for the world's politically oppressed, this concept has inspired millions. . . .

By their words and actions, presidents have done much to promote this idea. Although none of the subjects of this study claimed that America was the new Israel, all of them asserted that God selected the United States to perform a special mission: to spread democracy, liberty, and biblical morality to the world. They argued that its seemingly miraculous birth; rapid spread across the continent; remarkable increase in population, industry, affluence, and might; successful assimilation of millions of people of diverse ethnic and religious backgrounds; modeling of republican government; and pivotal role in deciding the outcome of international wars all testified to God's choice, use, and blessing of America. Its success and support encouraged people in countries around the globe to throw off the shackles of despotism and embrace democracy. As Eisenhower put it, "The American experiment has, for generations, fired the passion and the courage of millions elsewhere seeking freedom, equality, [and] opportunity" (Eisenhower 1961). While assigning America an exalted role and responsibility, none of these eleven presidents contended that God approved of all of its actions. They insisted that God wanted to use the United States to benefit the world and exhorted citizens to obey biblical standards. Undoubtedly speaking for all of them, Franklin Roosevelt declared in his final State of the Union Address: "We pray that we may be worthy of the unlimited opportunities God has given us" (Roosevelt 1945). . . .

Lincoln was much less willing than the other presidents examined in this study—most notably Washington, Wilson, both Roosevelts, Reagan, and Bush—to say that God supported his side. He was also much more ambivalent than the rest of them about whether God had selected the United States to accomplish his purposes, calling it God's "almost chosen nation." While repeatedly asserting, as they did, that God directed history, Lincoln rejected the belief that God is on our side that inspired the campaigns and foreign policies of numerous other occupants of the Oval Office (Miller 2002). This was much easier to do because he fought against his former countrymen with whom he shared many commonalities and with whom he sought reconciliation, not a foreign power whose people differed in race, culture, and creed and who thwarted America's interests or sought world domination. Yet to his credit, Lincoln persistently refused what must have been a strong temptation to identify his side with God's righteousness and justice.

Given their conviction that America is a chosen nation, not surprisingly, almost all of them believed that God selected them to be president and saw themselves as his instrument. In the words of Woodrow Wilson, "God ordained that I should be the next President of the United States," and no mortal "could have prevented that." Although most of them did not state this claim so boldly, they were inspired by their belief that God had "called" them. This conviction prompted them to pray for God's guidance in leading the nation and to seek to discern his will. Although some of them have been accused of believing that God specifically revealed his will to them, none of them made this claim. Lincoln was the most explicit in declaring that "the Almighty has his own purposes" that people often did not comprehend, but all the subjects of this study strove to discover God's plans for the United States. Although many of them spoke of feeling more confident about important decisions after praying, none of them asserted that God directly told him to take a particular course of action (Marty 2003; Dowd [, Mark] 2004; Dowd [, Maureen] 2004; Suskind 2004). . . .

Presidential Character

Throughout the nation's history, most Americans have expected their presidents to have sterling character. Although some complain that focusing on the personal morality of statesmen diverts attention from the more important matters of political philosophy and programs, the issue of character has played a significant role in selecting and evaluating presidents. . . .

. . . As Richard Hutcheson argues, for many Americans, character is closely connected to "religiously grounded morality." Most of the presidents examined in this study have been men of exemplary character, but they have not led flawless lives. Critics accuse all eleven of lying to advance their agendas, safeguard their reputations, or supposedly promote the national interest. They claim that Washington, Jefferson, Wilson, Franklin Roosevelt, Eisenhower, and Kennedy had sexual relations outside marriage, violating biblical moral standards and their commitments to their wives.[5]

Good character, Reeves maintains, is an essential ingredient in "the complex mix of qualities that make an outstanding president and a model leader for a democratic people" (Reeves 1991, 419). Many of the chief executives who are considered great were men of exceptional character. Many Americans agree that "office and the country [are] better served by having Presidents who exemplify the best qualities of integrity, honesty, morality, and strength of character." Nevertheless, scholars generally rate several men widely considered to have had the most integrity (including John Quincy Adams,

Hoover, and Carter) as among the least effective presidents. Their admirable character helped them endure extensive criticism as they dealt with ideological divisions, social unrest, and economic difficulties and urged Americans to eschew selfishness and pursue the common good (Chambers 1998). On the other hand, some who were less upright (including Franklin Roosevelt and Kennedy) were very successful presidents (Phelps 2001; Pfiffner 2000). In the final analysis, their exemplary character, often sustained by their faith, helped numerous presidents, including Washington, Lincoln, Theodore Roosevelt, Eisenhower, and Reagan, lead effectively.

A Final Assessment

Billy Graham exaggerates when he argues that every president has left the office "with a very deep religious faith," but the tremendous responsibilities and pressures and the trials and tribulations of the presidency have inspired many of these eleven chief executives to develop a stronger faith (Alley 1972, 120). Crises often drive people to a deeper appreciation of their religious heritage and a closer relationship with God. Many of these presidents testified that the burdens of the office prompted them to seek God's guidance and assistance more than ever before. As we have seen, their faith was important to many presidents and helped inform the way they viewed the world, fulfilled their responsibilities, made decisions, and chose and implemented policies. Although George W. Bush is more outspoken about his faith than most of his predecessors, religious convictions have helped shape and guide the attitudes and actions of many occupants of the Oval Office. Arthur Schlesinger Jr.'s complaint that a "tide of religiosity" is "engulfing a once secular republic" as a result of Bush's presidency displays a misunderstanding of both the presidency and American history (Jacoby 2004, back cover).

. . . While recognizing that the world's many religions and ideologies and countries' clashing interests made it very difficult to base international relations on biblical principles, these presidents nonetheless often tried to do so. At times, they demonized their enemies or cloaked America's self-serving goals in moral rhetoric, but they frequently pursued policies they believed were based on biblical norms and would benefit other nations. Some claim it is morally obligatory to assess the ethical implications of political, military, and strategic factors and to seek to do God's will on earth (Lally 1958, 314). "Great presidents not only encourage the public to strive for the noblest ideals and the highest principles," Reeves maintains, "but pursue the goals in practice" (Reeves 1997, 418). The presidents examined in this study tried to achieve many of humanity's most admirable ideals through their domestic and foreign policies. . . .

Many of the contestants in this animated debate pay insufficient attention to American history . . . I have aimed to steer a course between those who depict the founders and many presidents as devout, conventional Christians and those who portray them as deists, skeptics, and secularly minded men. Faith—although not always orthodox, Christian faith—had a powerful influence on the thoughts and actions of many presidents. Their understanding of the separation of church and state did not lead these chief executives to confine their religious convictions to their private lives. Instead, their faith affected their work in important ways. . . .

7.3

Charles W. Dunn

THE THEOLOGICAL DIMENSIONS OF PRESIDENTIAL LEADERSHIP: A CLASSIFICATION MODEL (1984)

Importance of Presidential Theology

. . . The importance of a theological understanding of presidential leadership may be established in several ways. First, the presidency quite often is referred to in theological terms, such as "faith in the presidency," "trust in presidential leadership," "a sacred office," "confidence in presidential leadership," or "saving the presidency."

Second, leading presidential analysts, observers, and presidents themselves have used theological analogies, metaphors, and similes to describe the presidency. Theodore Roosevelt referred to the office as a "bully pulpit" while Franklin Roosevelt said it is "preeminently a place of moral leadership. . . ."

Campaigns for the presidency offer a third reason for understanding the theological dimensions of presidential leadership. The 1976 and 1980 presidential campaigns present excellent verbal as well as visual examples of theological symbol manipulation by presidential candidates. In 1976, candidate Jimmy Carter said he was "born again," a not-so-subtle code word from John 3 designed to woo the substantial segment of the American electorate that claims to be "born again." And the Sunday immediately prior to election day, President Ford, an Episcopalian, was prominently pictured shaking hands with the Southern Baptist Convention's best known conservative preacher, W. A. Criswell, while entering the front door of the First Baptist Church, Dallas, Texas. In 1980 candidate Ronald Reagan appeared before a theologically conservative meeting hosted by the Religious Roundtable in Texas where he proclaimed his faith in the Genesis account of creation and expressed support for prayer in the public schools.

Still a fourth reason for expanding our understanding concerns the use of theological rhetoric in support of public policy aims, Lincoln's Gettysburg Address, his Second Inaugural and his earlier "house divided" speech are replete with numerous theological themes. But perhaps more than any other president, William McKinley's policy toward the Philippines reveals the significant relationship between theology and public policy.

> The truth is I didn't want the Philippines, and when they came to give us a gift from the gods I did not know what to do with them I sought counsel. . . . I walked the floor of the White House night after night until midnight, and I am not ashamed to tell you gentlemen, that I went down on my knees and prayed to Almighty God for light and guidance more than one night. And late one night it came to me this way—I don't know how it was but it came . . . there was nothing left for us to do but to take them all, and to educate the Filipinos, and uplift and civilize and Christianize them, and by God's grace do the very best we could by them as our fellowmen for whom Christ died.
> (Novak 1974, 154) . . .

Fifth, a substantial body of scholarship, particularly among sociologists, theologians, and historians, documents a civil religion replete with its own terminology generally considered inoffensive to a broad theological spectrum. . . .

While William McKinley's Philippine statement may be considered outside the accepted boundary lines of the civil religion, both conservative and liberal presidents on the whole have drawn liberally from biblical and theological terminology to establish the credibility of their political aspirations and policy objectives. Many of the most famous of all political slogans have biblical and theological overtones, such as "the white man's burden" and "manifest destiny," that helped presidents and others inspire the populace. . . .

Sixth, in at least some instances, religious or theological advice has been sought and given to presidents, including Reinhold Niebuhr to Franklin Roosevelt, Billy Graham to several presidents, such as Kennedy, Johnson, and Nixon and Jerry Falwell to Ronald Reagan. Sometimes their advice has been received both substantively and symbolically as when Presidents Kennedy, Johnson, and Nixon publicly announced and had pictures taken of their public policy discussions with Billy Graham.

Seventh, presidents cannot ignore, except at their own potential political peril, political movements with a theological base, such as the abolitionist movement prior to the Civil War that existed principally because of theological forces and the Nuclear Freeze and Moral Majority movements of today. The abolitionist movement with its uncompromising theologically based opposition to slavery kept "the feet of presidents to the fire" in the prosecution of their cause. . . .

Church joining, if not faithful attendance, is an eighth reason for understanding the impact of theology and religion on presidents. Perhaps the best example of this occurred in 1952 when the Democratic candidate Adlai Stevenson, a Unitarian, became a Presbyterian, and a nonchurchmember, General Eisenhower, also became a Presbyterian. As shown in Table 7.1 presidents tend to be members of or to attend the safe or mainline denominational churches, such as Methodist, Presbyterian, Episcopalian, and Baptist. President Nixon took the unusual course of holding Sunday morning worship services in the White House with leading clergy from several denominations presiding.

The moderating influence of the safe or mainline churches on presidential behavior suggests a ninth reason. Or it could be said that politics itself tends to moderate the theological and religious convictions of presidents. . . .

The essential point is that like their political ideology, the theology of most Americans tends to be in the middle, i.e., neither hot nor cold. Thus, the middle of the electorate, we may reasonably argue, pressures presidents to conform to them.

Finally the national party platforms, particularly in recent years, present a contrast between conservative and liberal theological convictions perhaps best shown in the 1980 platforms wherein they differed sharply on such issues as school prayer, abortion, ERA (equal rights amendment for women) and others. That presidents feel the theological pressure from these platforms maybe shown with respect to Jimmy Carter; who though personally opposed to abortion for theological reasons, would not take a stand against the mainstream of his party on this issue. Also, in 1980 George Bush had to agree to support the Republican Platform that contained several theologically based planks which he opposed.

Not only do these ten reasons offer sufficient justification for examining the relationships between presidential behavior and theological convictions, but they also begin to unveil differences between and among presidents. . . .

Table 7.1 Church Preferences of Presidents: Attendance and/or Membership

1.	George Washington	Episcopalian
2.	John Adams	Unitarian
3.	Thomas Jefferson	Unitarian*
4.	James Madison	Episcopalian
5.	James Monroe	Episcopalian
6.	John Quincy Adams	Unitarian
7.	Andrew Jackson	Presbyterian
8.	Martin Van Buren	Dutch Reformed
9.	William H. Harrison	Episcopalian
10.	John Tyler	Episcopalian
11.	James K. Polk	Methodist
12.	Zachary Taylor	Episcopalian
13.	Millard Fillmore	Unitarian
14.	Franklin Pierce	Episcopalian
15.	James Buchanan	Presbyterian
16.	Abraham Lincoln	Presbyterian*
17.	Andrew Johnson	Methodist
18.	Ulysses S. Grant	Methodist
19.	Rutherford B. Hayes	Methodist
20.	James A. Garfield	Disciples of Christ
21.	Chester A. Arthur	Episcopalian
22.	Grover Cleveland	Presbyterian
23.	Benjamin Harrison	Presbyterian
24.	Grover Cleveland	Presbyterian
25.	William McKinley	Methodist
26.	Theodore Roosevelt	Dutch Reformed
27.	William H. Taft	Unitarian
28.	Woodrow Wilson	Presbyterian
29.	Warren G. Harding	Baptist
30.	Calvin Coolidge	Congregationalist
31.	Herbert C. Hoover	Friend (Quaker)
32.	Franklin D. Roosevelt	Episcopalian
33.	Harry S Truman	Baptist
34.	Dwight D. Eisenhower	Presbyterian
35.	John F. Kennedy	Roman Catholic
36.	Lyndon B. Johnson	Disciples of Christ
37.	Richard M. Nixon	Friend (Quaker)
38.	Gerald R. Ford	Episcopalian
39.	Jimmy Carter	Baptist
40.	Ronald Reagan	Presbyterian
41.	George H. W. Bush	Episcopalian
42.	Bill Clinton	Baptist
43.	George W. Bush	Methodist
44.	Barack Obama	United Church of Christ

*Church preference; never joined any church.

Source: Compiled by C. W. Dunn (editors' update: George H. W. Bush to present).

Presidential Ideology and Theology

Through . . . studying the principal biographical and autobiographical sources on all American presidents from Washington through Reagan, Figures 7.1–7.4 classify the presidents on an ideological continuum from conservative to liberal and on a theological continuum from conservative to liberal. . . .

Still another problem is in classifying the early presidents, especially those of the Unitarian persuasion which is today uniformly considered theologically liberal, since, during the early period of American history, Unitarian thought tended to be much more conservative than it is today. Thus, by today's standards, Unitarian presidents like the two Adams would generally fit the conservative side of the theological comparison more than the liberal.

While any classification system presents loopholes and difficulties in making precise classifications, they can be very helpful if one recognizes their limitations and does not try to press them to do more than what they were intended to do, namely to provide guidance in understanding presidential behavior. Among the conclusions that may be drawn from Figures 7.1–7.4 are these:

First, the ideological and theological components tend to reinforce one another. Liberal presidents ideologically also tend to be liberal presidents theologically while conservative presidents ideologically tend to be theologically conservative.

Second, one cannot always determine which came first, the "chicken or the egg," that is, whether a president is liberal primarily because of ideology or theology. Superficially, the safe conclusion would be that theology tends to reinforce ideology more than the other way around, but then we do not have sufficient evidence to conclude that

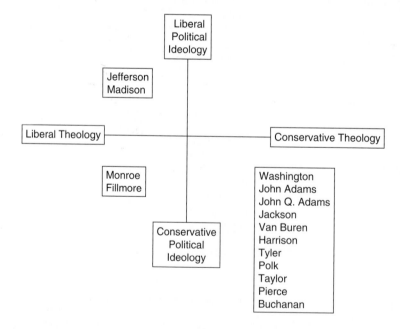

Figure 7.1 The Ideological and Theological Tendencies of Presidents: Washington–Buchanan

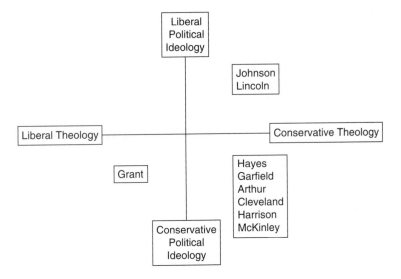

Figure 7.2 The Ideological and Theological Tendencies of Presidents: Lincoln–McKinley

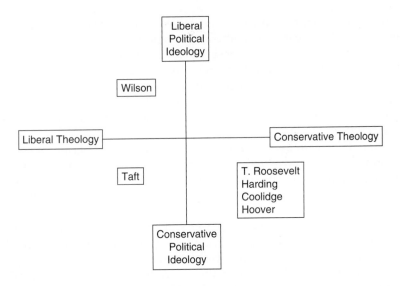

Figure 7.3 The Ideological and Theological Tendencies of Presidents: T. Roosevelt–Hoover

firmly. One principal support for this conclusion is that presidents generally speak more about their ideology than their theology.

Third, some presidents appear never to give serious thought to their theological convictions. In such instances theology would definitely tend to reinforce more than to direct their ideological positions.

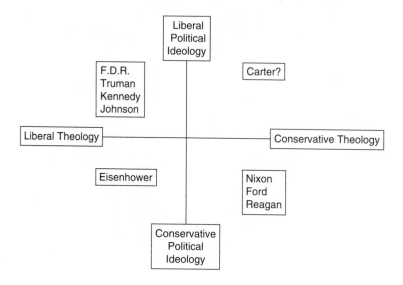

Figure 7.4 The Ideological and Theological Tendencies of Presidents: F.D.R.–Reagan

Fourth, what cannot be shown are the degrees of conservatism and liberalism. To wit, Walter Mondale is clearly more liberal ideologically and theologically than Jimmy Carter, and Ronald Reagan is more conservative than Richard Nixon.

Fifth, those in the conservative-conservative quadrant are more likely to be Republicans and those in the liberal-liberal quadrant are more likely to be Democrats. This adds further evidence to the conclusion that theological liberals are more comfortable in the Democratic Party and theological conservatives are more at ease in the Republican Party.

Sixth, since Lyndon Johnson all presidents have either symbolically or substantively (or both) professed to be conservative theologically. . . . Another way to look at it is that from Nixon through Reagan, presidents have tended to go beyond the trappings of inoffensive civil religion to show the nation more clearly and dramatically their personal theological and religious convictions.

Seventh, the difficulty in placing Jimmy Carter also helps to reveal why he had difficulty governing. He made much use of theologically conservative symbols in capturing the Democratic nomination for president in 1976 and also in winning the office, ironically the Democratic Party with a theologically liberal base in its platform and majority in Congress somewhat put President Carter in a vise between two irreconcilable points of view. He, a person of at least symbolically conservative theological convictions, had difficulty leading a party of definite liberal theological and ideological convictions.

Eighth, while presidents in the conservative-conservative quadrant dominated the first three eras of presidents, those in the liberal-liberal quadrant dominate the fourth era. This pattern conforms to the historical theological pattern as conservative theology dominated most of American history until the latest era. Now after a period of liberal theological domination, there has been a conservative theological resurgence that at least to some extent is reflected among the presidents as our most recent presidents have made greater efforts to appear more conservative theologically, evidently in response to a latent arousal of grassroots theological conservatism.

Generals or Footsoldiers

The evidence tends to suggest that presidents are not generals on the theological battlefield. In a democratic sense as elected officials, they generally respond more to public pressures on theological issues than they lead the public. Then too as individuals they tend not to have strong theological convictions. The political experience, if not the presidency itself, evidently has the effect of moderating strongly held theological convictions among presidents. In an effort not to be offensive, presidents usually identify with mainline churches and use inoffensive language often called the language of the "civil religion" that attracts, but does not alienate, a cross section of the religious among the electorate.

Presidents are not immune, however, to theological pressures for a variety of reasons. For example, theologically based political movements, such as liberally oriented ones on the Vietnam War and the nuclear freeze issues and conservative ones on issues like ERA and abortion, force presidents to respond. Party platforms with theologically based planks may also substantially influence presidential leadership.

In theological warfare over public policy then, presidents are important figures on the battlefield, but in rank they are probably somewhere between generals and footsoldiers.

Primary Sources

7.4

President Abraham Lincoln

MEDITATION ON THE DIVINE WILL
(SEPTEMBER 1862)

The will of God prevails. In great contests each party claims to act in accordance with the will of God. Both may be, and one must be, wrong. God cannot be for and against the same thing at the same time. In the present civil war it is quite possible that God's purpose is something different from the purpose of either party—and yet the human instrumentalities, working just as they do, are of the best adaptation to effect His purpose. I am almost ready to say that this is probably true—that God wills this contest, and wills that it shall not end yet. By his mere great power, on the minds of the now contestants, He could have either saved or destroyed the Union without a human contest. Yet the contest began. And, having begun He could give the final victory to either side any day. Yet the contest proceeds.

7.5

President John F. Kennedy

ADDRESS TO THE GREATER HOUSTON MINISTERIAL ASSOCIATION
(SEPTEMBER 12, 1960)

Reverend Meza, Reverend Reck, I'm grateful for your generous invitation to state my views.

While the so-called religious issue is necessarily and properly the chief topic here tonight, I want to emphasize from the outset that I believe that we have far more critical issues in the 1960 campaign; the spread of Communist influence, until it now festers only 90 miles from the coast of Florida—the humiliating treatment of our President and Vice President by those who no longer respect our power—the hungry children I saw in West Virginia, the old people who cannot pay their doctors bills, the families forced to give up their farms—an America with too many slums, with too few schools, and too late to the moon and outer space. These are the real issues which should decide this campaign. And they are not religious issues—for war and hunger and ignorance and despair know no religious barrier.

But because I am a Catholic, and no Catholic has ever been elected President, the real issues in this campaign have been obscured—perhaps deliberately, in some quarters less responsible than this. So it is apparently necessary for me to state once again—not what kind of church I believe in, for that should be important only to me—but what kind of America I believe in.

I believe in an America where the separation of church and state is absolute; where no Catholic prelate would tell the President—should he be Catholic—how to act, and no Protestant minister would tell his parishioners for whom to vote; where no church or church school is granted any public funds or political preference, and where no man is denied public office merely because his religion differs from the President who might appoint him, or the people who might elect him.

I believe in an America that is officially neither Catholic, Protestant nor Jewish; where no public official either requests or accept instructions on public policy from the Pope, the National Council of Churches or any other ecclesiastical source; where no religious body seeks to impose its will directly or indirectly upon the general populace or the public acts of its officials, and where religious liberty is so indivisible that an act against one church is treated as an act against all.

For while this year it may be a Catholic against whom the finger of suspicion is pointed, in other years it has been—and may someday be again—a Jew, or a Quaker, or a Unitarian, or a Baptist. It was Virginia's harassment of Baptist preachers, for example, that led to Jefferson's statute of religious freedom. Today, I may be the victim, but tomorrow it may be you—until the whole fabric of our harmonious society is ripped apart at a time of great national peril.

Finally, I believe in an America where religious intolerance will someday end, where all men and all churches are treated as equals, where every man has the same right to attend or not to attend the church of his choice, where there is no Catholic vote, no anti-Catholic vote, no bloc voting of any kind, and where Catholics, Protestants, and Jews, at both the lay and the pastoral levels, will refrain from those attitudes of disdain and division which have so often marred their works in the past, and promote instead the American ideal of brotherhood.

That is the kind of America in which I believe. And it represents the kind of Presidency in which I believe, a great office that must be neither humbled by making it the instrument of any religious group nor tarnished by arbitrarily withholding it—its occupancy from the members of any one religious group. I believe in a President whose views on religion are his own private affair, neither imposed upon him by the nation, nor imposed by the nation upon him as a condition to holding that office.

I would not look with favor upon a President working to subvert the first amendment's guarantees of religious liberty; nor would our system of checks and balances permit him to do so. And neither do I look with favor upon those who would work to subvert Article VI of the Constitution by requiring a religious test, even by indirection. For if they disagree with that safeguard, they should be openly working to repeal it.

I want a Chief Executive whose public acts are responsible to all and obligated to none, who can attend any ceremony, service, or dinner his office may appropriately require of him to fulfill; and whose fulfillment of his Presidential office is not limited or conditioned by any religious oath, ritual, or obligation.

This is the kind of America I believe in—and this is the kind of America I fought for in the South Pacific, and the kind my brother died for in Europe. No one suggested then that we might have a divided loyalty, that we did not believe in liberty, or that we belonged to a disloyal group that threatened—I quote—"the freedoms for which our forefathers died."

And in fact this is the kind of America for which our forefathers did die when they fled here to escape religious test oaths that denied office to members of less favored churches—when they fought for the Constitution, the Bill of Rights, the Virginia Statute of Religious Freedom—and when they fought at the shrine I visited today, the Alamo. For side by side with Bowie and Crockett died Fuentes, and McCafferty, and Bailey, and Badillo, and Carey—but no one knows whether they were Catholics or not. For there was no religious test there.

I ask you tonight to follow in that tradition—to judge me on the basis of 14 years in the Congress, on my declared stands against an Ambassador to the Vatican, against unconstitutional aid to parochial schools, and against any boycott of the public schools—which I attended myself. And instead of doing this, do not judge me on the basis of these pamphlets and publications we all have seen that carefully select quotations out of context from the statements of Catholic church leaders, usually in other countries, frequently in other centuries, and rarely relevant to any situation here. And always omitting, of course, the statement of the American Bishops in 1948 which strongly endorsed Church–State separation, and which more nearly reflects the views of almost every American Catholic.

I do not consider these other quotations binding upon my public acts. Why should you?

But let me say, with respect to other countries, that I am wholly opposed to the State being used by any religious group, Catholic or Protestant, to compel, prohibit, or prosecute the free exercise of any other religion. And that goes for any persecution, at any time, by anyone, in any country. And I hope that you and I condemn with equal fervor those nations which deny their Presidency to Protestants, and those which deny it to Catholics. And rather than cite the misdeeds of those who differ, I would also cite the record of the Catholic Church in such nations as France and Ireland, and the independence of such statesmen as De Gaulle and Adenauer.

But let me stress again that these are my views.

For contrary to common newspaper usage, I am not the Catholic candidate for President.

I am the Democratic Party's candidate for President who happens also to be a Catholic.

I do not speak for my church on public matters; and the church does not speak for me. Whatever issue may come before me as President, if I should be elected, on birth control, divorce, censorship, gambling or any other subject, I will make my decision in accordance with these views—in accordance with what my conscience tells me to be in the national interest, and without regard to outside religious pressure or dictates. And no power or threat of punishment could cause me to decide otherwise.

But if the time should ever come—and I do not concede any conflict to be remotely possible—when my office would require me to either violate my conscience or violate the national interest, then I would resign the office; and I hope any conscientious public servant would do likewise.

But I do not intend to apologize for these views to my critics of either Catholic or Protestant faith; nor do I intend to disavow either my views or my church in order to win this election.

If I should lose on the real issues, I shall return to my seat in the Senate, satisfied that I'd tried my best and was fairly judged.

But if this election is decided on the basis that 40 million Americans lost their chance of being President on the day they were baptized, then it is the whole nation that will be the loser, in the eyes of Catholics and non-Catholics around the world, in the eyes of history, and in the eyes of our own people.

But if, on the other hand, I should win this election, then I shall devote every effort of mind and spirit to fulfilling the oath of the Presidency—practically identical, I might add, with the oath I have taken for 14 years in the Congress. For without reservation, I can, "solemnly swear that I will faithfully execute the office of President of the United States, and will to the best of my ability preserve, protect, and defend the Constitution—so help me God."

7.6

President Jimmy Carter

INAUGURAL ADDRESS
(JANUARY 20, 1977)

For myself and for our Nation, I want to thank my predecessor for all he has done to heal our land.

In this outward and physical ceremony we attest once again to the inner and spiritual strength of our Nation. As my high school teacher, Miss Julia Coleman, used to say: "We must adjust to changing times and still hold to unchanging principles."

Here before me is the Bible used in the inauguration of our first President, in 1789, and I have just taken the oath of office on the Bible my mother gave me a few years ago, opened to a timeless admonition from the ancient prophet Micah: "He hath showed thee, O man, what is good; and what doth the Lord require of thee, but to do justly, and to love mercy, and to walk humbly with thy God" (Micah 6:8).

This inauguration ceremony marks a new beginning, a new dedication within our Government, and a new spirit among us all. A President may sense and proclaim that new spirit, but only a people can provide it.

Two centuries ago our Nation's birth was a milestone in the long quest for freedom, but the bold and brilliant dream which excited the founders of this Nation still awaits its consummation. I have no new dream to set forth today, but rather urge a fresh faith in the old dream.

Ours was the first society openly to define itself in terms of both spirituality and of human liberty. It is that unique self-definition which has given us an exceptional appeal, but it also imposes on us a special obligation, to take on those moral duties which, when assumed, seem invariably to be in our own best interests.

You have given me a great responsibility—to stay close to you, to be worthy of you, and to exemplify what you are. Let us create together a new national spirit of unity and trust. Your strength can compensate for my weakness, and your wisdom can help to minimize my mistakes.

Let us learn together and laugh together and work together and pray together, confident that in the end we will triumph together in the right.

The American dream endures. We must once again have full faith in our country and in one another. I believe America can be better. We can be even stronger than before.

Let our recent mistakes bring a resurgent commitment to the basic principles of our Nation, for we know that if we despise our own government we have no future. We recall in special times when we have stood briefly, but magnificently, united. In those times no prize was beyond our grasp.

But we cannot dwell upon remembered glory. We cannot afford to drift. We reject the prospect of failure or mediocrity or an inferior quality of life for any person. Our Government must at the same time be both competent and compassionate.

We have already found a high degree of personal liberty, and we are now struggling to enhance equality of opportunity. Our commitment to human rights must be absolute, our laws fair, our natural beauty preserved; the powerful must not persecute the weak, and human dignity must be enhanced.

We have learned that "more" is not necessarily "better," that even our great Nation has its recognized limits, and that we can neither answer all questions nor solve all problems. We cannot afford to do everything, nor can we afford to lack boldness as we meet the future. So, together, in a spirit of individual sacrifice for the common good, we must simply do our best.

Our Nation can be strong abroad only if it is strong at home. And we know that the best way to enhance freedom in other lands is to demonstrate here that our democratic system is worthy of emulation.

To be true to ourselves, we must be true to others. We will not behave in foreign places so as to violate our rules and standards here at home, for we know that the trust which our Nation earns is essential to our strength.

The world itself is now dominated by a new spirit. Peoples more numerous and more politically aware are craving and now demanding their place in the sun—not just for the benefit of their own physical condition, but for basic human rights.

The passion for freedom is on the rise. Tapping this new spirit, there can be no nobler nor more ambitious task for America to undertake on this day of a new beginning than to help shape a just and peaceful world that is truly humane.

We are a strong nation, and we will maintain strength so sufficient that it need not be proven in combat—a quiet strength based not merely on the size of an arsenal, but on the nobility of ideas.

We will be ever vigilant and never vulnerable, and we will fight our wars against poverty, ignorance, and injustice—for those are the enemies against which our forces can be honorably marshaled.

We are a purely idealistic Nation, but let no one confuse our idealism with weakness.

Because we are free we can never be indifferent to the fate of freedom elsewhere. Our moral sense dictates a clearcut preference for these societies which share with us an abiding respect for individual human rights. We do not seek to intimidate, but it is clear that a world which others can dominate with impunity would be inhospitable to decency and a threat to the well-being of all people.

The world is still engaged in a massive armaments race designed to ensure continuing equivalent strength among potential adversaries. We pledge perseverance and wisdom in our efforts to limit the world's armaments to those necessary for each nation's own domestic safety. And we will move this year a step toward ultimate goal— the elimination of all nuclear weapons from this Earth. We urge all other people to join us, for success can mean life instead of death.

Within us, the people of the United States, there is evident a serious and purposeful rekindling of confidence. And I join in the hope that when my time as your President has ended, people might say this about our Nation:

> that we had remembered the words of Micah and renewed our search for humility, mercy, and justice;
>
> that we had torn down the barriers that separated those of different race and region and religion, and where there had been mistrust, built unity, with a respect for diversity;
>
> that we had found productive work for those able to perform it;
>
> that we had strengthened the American family, which is the basis of our society;
>
> that we had ensured respect for the law, and equal treatment under the law, for the weak and the powerful, for the rich and the poor;
>
> and that we had enabled our people to be proud of their own Government once again.

I would hope that the nations of the world might say that we had built a lasting peace, built not on weapons of war but on international policies which reflect our own most precious values.

These are not just my goals, and they will not be my accomplishments, but the affirmation of our Nation's continuing moral strength and our belief in an undiminished, ever-expanding American dream.

7.7

Ronald Reagan

NOMINATION ACCEPTANCE ADDRESS
(JULY 17, 1980)

. . . Mr. Chairman, Mr. Vice-President-to-be, this convention, my fellow citizens of this great nation:

With a deep awareness of the responsibility conferred by your trust, I accept your nomination for the Presidency of the United States. I do so with deep gratitude. And I think also I might interject on behalf of all of us our thanks to Detroit and the people of Michigan and to this city for the warm hospitality we've enjoyed. And I thank you for your wholehearted response to my recommendation in regard to George Bush as the candidate for Vice President.

I'm very proud of our party tonight. This convention has shown to all America a party united, with positive programs for solving the nation's problems, a party ready to build a new consensus with all those across the land who share a community of values embodied in these words: family, work, neighborhood, peace and freedom. . . .

More than anything else, I want my candidacy to unify our country, to renew the American spirit and sense of purpose. I want to carry our message to every American, regardless of party affiliation, who is a member of this community of shared values.

Never before in our history have Americans been called upon to face three grave threats to our very existence, any one of which could destroy us. We face a disintegrating economy, a weakened defense and an energy policy based on the sharing of scarcity. . . .

We need a rebirth of the American tradition of leadership at every level of government and in private life as well. The United States of America is unique in world history because it has a genius for leaders—many leaders—on many levels. . . .

"Trust me" government asks that we concentrate our hopes and dreams on one man; that we trust him to do what's best for us. But my view of government places trust not in one person or one party, but in those values that transcend persons and parties. The trust is where it belongs—in the people. The responsibility to live up to that trust is where it belongs, in their elected leaders. That kind of relationship, between the people and their elected leaders, is a special kind of compact.

Three-hundred-and-sixty years ago, in 1620, a group of families dared to cross a mighty ocean to build a future for themselves in a new world. When they arrived at Plymouth, Massachusetts, they formed what they called a "compact," an agreement among themselves to build a community and abide by its laws.

This single act—the voluntary binding together of free people to live under the law—set the pattern for what was to come.

A century and a half later, the descendants of those people pledged their lives, their fortunes, and their sacred honor to found this nation. Some forfeited their fortunes and their lives; none sacrificed honor.

Four score and seven years later, Abraham Lincoln called upon the people of all America to renew their dedication and their commitment to a government of, for and by the people. Isn't it once again time to renew our compact of freedom; to pledge to each other all that is best in our lives; all that gives meaning to them—for the sake of this, our beloved and blessed land?

Together, let us make this a new beginning. Let us make a commitment to care for the needy; to teach our children the values handed down to us by our families; to have the courage to defend those values and virtues and the willingness to sacrifice for them.

Let us pledge to restore, in our time, the American spirit of voluntary service, of cooperation, of private and community initiative; a spirit that flows like a deep and mighty river through the history of our nation.

As your nominee, I pledge to you to restore to the Federal Government the capacity to do the people's work without dominating their lives. I pledge to you a Government that will not only work well but wisely, its ability to act tempered by prudence, and its willingness to do good balanced by the knowledge that government is never more dangerous than when our desire to have it help us blinds us to its great power to harm us. . . .

. . . Now this evening marks the last step, save one, of a campaign that has taken Nancy and me from one end of this great nation to the other, over many months and thousands and thousands of miles. There are those who question the way we choose a President, who say that our process imposes difficult and exhausting burdens on those who seek the office. I have not found it so.

It is impossible to capture in words the splendor of this vast continent which God has granted as our portion of His creation. There are no words to express the extraordinary strength and character of this breed of people we call Americans. Everywhere we've met thousands of Democrats, Independents and Republicans from all economic conditions, walks of life bound together in that community of shared values of family, work, neighborhood, peace and freedom. They are concerned, yet, they're not frightened. They're disturbed, but not dismayed. They are the kind of men and women Tom Paine had in mind when he wrote, during the darkest days of the American Revolution, "We have it in our power to begin the world over again."

Nearly 150 years after Tom Paine wrote those words, an American President told the generation of the Great Depression that it had a "rendezvous with destiny." I believe that this generation of Americans today has a rendezvous with destiny. . . .

The time is now, my fellow Americans, to recapture our destiny, to take it into our own hands. And to do this it will take many of us, working together. I ask you tonight, all over this land, to volunteer your help in this cause so that we can carry our message through out the land. . . .

I have thought of something that's not a part of my speech and worried over whether I should do it. Can we doubt that only a Divine Providence placed this land, this island of freedom, here as a refuge for all those people in the world who yearn to breathe free? Jews and Christians enduring persecution behind the Iron Curtain; the boat people of Southeast Asia, Cuba, and of Haiti; the victims of drought and famine in Africa, the freedom fighters of Afghanistan, and our own countrymen held in savage captivity.

I'll confess that I've been a little afraid to suggest what I'm going to suggest. I'm more afraid not to. Can we begin our crusade joined together in a moment of silent prayer?

God bless America.

Thank you.

7.8

President George W. Bush

INAUGURAL ADDRESS
(JANUARY 20, 2001)

President Clinton, distinguished guests and my fellow citizens, the peaceful transfer of authority is rare in history, yet common in our country. With a simple oath, we affirm old traditions and make new beginnings.

As I begin, I thank President Clinton for his service to our nation.

And I thank Vice President Gore for a contest conducted with spirit and ended with grace.

I am honored and humbled to stand here, where so many of America's leaders have come before me, and so many will follow.

We have a place, all of us, in a long story—a story we continue, but whose end we will not see. It is the story of a new world that became a friend and liberator of the old, a story of a slave-holding society that became a servant of freedom, the story of a power that went into the world to protect but not possess, to defend but not to conquer.

It is the American story—a story of flawed and fallible people, united across the generations by grand and enduring ideals.

The grandest of these ideals is an unfolding American promise that everyone belongs, that everyone deserves a chance, that no insignificant person was ever born.

Americans are called to enact this promise in our lives and in our laws. And though our nation has sometimes halted, and sometimes delayed, we must follow no other course.

Through much of the last century, America's faith in freedom and democracy was a rock in a raging sea. Now it is a seed upon the wind, taking root in many nations.

Our democratic faith is more than the creed of our country, it is the inborn hope of our humanity, an ideal we carry but do not own, a trust we bear and pass along. And even after nearly 225 years, we have a long way yet to travel.

While many of our citizens prosper, others doubt the promise, even the justice, of our own country. The ambitions of some Americans are limited by failing schools and hidden prejudice and the circumstances of their birth. And sometimes our differences run so deep, it seems we share a continent, but not a country.

We do not accept this, and we will not allow it. Our unity, our union, is the serious work of leaders and citizens in every generation. And this is my solemn pledge: I will work to build a single nation of justice and opportunity.

I know this is in our reach because we are guided by a power larger than ourselves who creates us equal in His image.

And we are confident in principles that unite and lead us onward.

America has never been united by blood or birth or soil. We are bound by ideals that move us beyond our backgrounds, lift us above our interests and teach us what it means to be citizens. Every child must be taught these principles. Every citizen must uphold them. And every immigrant, by embracing these ideals, makes our country more, not less, American.

Today, we affirm a new commitment to live out our nation's promise through civility, courage, compassion and character.

America, at its best, matches a commitment to principle with a concern for civility. A civil society demands from each of us good will and respect, fair dealing and forgiveness.

Some seem to believe that our politics can afford to be petty because, in a time of peace, the stakes of our debates appear small.

But the stakes for America are never small. If our country does not lead the cause of freedom, it will not be led. If we do not turn the hearts of children toward knowledge and character, we will lose their gifts and undermine their idealism. If we permit our economy to drift and decline, the vulnerable will suffer most.

We must live up to the calling we share. Civility is not a tactic or a sentiment. It is the determined choice of trust over cynicism, of community over chaos. And this commitment, if we keep it, is a way to shared accomplishment.

America, at its best, is also courageous.

Our national courage has been clear in times of depression and war, when defending common dangers defined our common good. Now we must choose if the example of our fathers and mothers will inspire us or condemn us. We must show courage in a time of blessing by confronting problems instead of passing them on to future generations.

Together, we will reclaim America's schools, before ignorance and apathy claim more young lives.

We will reform Social Security and Medicare, sparing our children from struggles we have the power to prevent. And we will reduce taxes, to recover the momentum of our economy and reward the effort and enterprise of working Americans.

We will build our defenses beyond challenge, lest weakness invite challenge.

We will confront weapons of mass destruction, so that a new century is spared new horrors.

The enemies of liberty and our country should make no mistake: America remains engaged in the world by history and by choice, shaping a balance of power that favors freedom. We will defend our allies and our interests. We will show purpose without arrogance. We will meet aggression and bad faith with resolve and strength. And to all nations, we will speak for the values that gave our nation birth.

America, at its best, is compassionate. In the quiet of American conscience, we know that deep, persistent poverty is unworthy of our nation's promise.

And whatever our views of its cause, we can agree that children at risk are not at fault.

Abandonment and abuse are not acts of God; they are failures of love.

And the proliferation of prisons, however necessary, is no substitute for hope and order in our souls.

Where there is suffering, there is duty. Americans in need are not strangers, they are citizens, not problems, but priorities. And all of us are diminished when any are hopeless.

Government has great responsibilities for public safety and public health, for civil rights and common schools. Yet compassion is the work of a nation, not just a government.

And some needs and hurts are so deep they will only respond to a mentor's touch or a pastor's prayer. Church and charity, synagogue and mosque lend our communities their humanity, and they will have an honored place in our plans and in our laws.

Many in our country do not know the pain of poverty, but we can listen to those who do. And I can pledge our nation to a goal: When we see that wounded traveler on the road to Jericho, we will not pass to the other side.

America, at its best, is a place where personal responsibility is valued and expected.

Encouraging responsibility is not a search for scapegoats, it is a call to conscience. And though it requires sacrifice, it brings a deeper fulfillment. We find the fullness of life not only in options, but in commitments. And we find that children and community are the commitments that set us free.

Our public interest depends on private character, on civic duty and family bonds and basic fairness, on uncounted, unhonored acts of decency which give direction to our freedom.

Sometimes in life we are called to do great things. But as a saint of our times has said, every day we are called to do small things with great love. The most important tasks of a democracy are done by everyone.

I will live and lead by these principles: to advance my convictions with civility, to pursue the public interest with courage, to speak for greater justice and compassion, to call for responsibility and try to live it as well.

In all these ways, I will bring the values of our history to the care of our times.

What you do is as important as anything government does. I ask you to seek a common good beyond your comfort; to defend needed reforms against easy attacks; to serve your nation, beginning with your neighbor. I ask you to be citizens: citizens, not spectators; citizens, not subjects; responsible citizens, building communities of service and a nation of character.

Americans are generous and strong and decent, not because we believe in ourselves, but because we hold beliefs beyond ourselves. When this spirit of citizenship is missing, no government program can replace it. When this spirit is present, no wrong can stand against it.

After the Declaration of Independence was signed, Virginia statesman John Page wrote to Thomas Jefferson: "We know the race is not to the swift nor the battle to the strong. Do you not think an angel rides in the whirlwind and directs this storm?'"

Much time has passed since Jefferson arrived for his inauguration. The years and changes accumulate. But the themes of this day he would know: our nation's grand story of courage and its simple dream of dignity.

We are not this story's author, who fills time and eternity with his purpose. Yet his purpose is achieved in our duty, and our duty is fulfilled in service to one another.

Never tiring, never yielding, never finishing, we renew that purpose today, to make our country more just and generous, to affirm the dignity of our lives and every life.

This work continues. This story goes on. And an angel still rides in the whirlwind and directs this storm.

God bless you all, and God bless America.

7.9

President Barack Obama

A New Beginning
(Cairo, Egypt, June 4, 2009)

I am honored to be in the timeless city of Cairo, and to be hosted by two remarkable institutions. For over a thousand years, Al-Azhar has stood as a beacon of Islamic learning, and for over a century, Cairo University has been a source of Egypt's advancement. Together, you represent the harmony between tradition and progress. I am grateful for your hospitality, and the hospitality of the people of Egypt. I am also proud to carry with me the goodwill of the American people, and a greeting of peace from Muslim communities in my country: assalaamu alaykum.

We meet at a time of tension between the United States and Muslims around the world—tension rooted in historical forces that go beyond any current policy debate. The relationship between Islam and the West includes centuries of co-existence and co-operation, but also conflict and religious wars. More recently, tension has been fed by colonialism that denied rights and opportunities to many Muslims, and a Cold War in which Muslim-majority countries were too often treated as proxies without regard to their own aspirations. Moreover, the sweeping change brought by modernity and globalization led many Muslims to view the West as hostile to the traditions of Islam.

Violent extremists have exploited these tensions in a small but potent minority of Muslims. The attacks of September 11th, 2001 and the continued efforts of these extremists to engage in violence against civilians has led some in my country to view Islam as inevitably hostile not only to America and Western countries, but also to human rights. This has bred more fear and mistrust.

So long as our relationship is defined by our differences, we will empower those who sow hatred rather than peace, and who promote conflict rather than the cooperation that can help all of our people achieve justice and prosperity. This cycle of suspicion and discord must end.

I have come here to seek a new beginning between the United States and Muslims around the world; one based upon mutual interest and mutual respect; and one based upon the truth that America and Islam are not exclusive, and need not be in competition. Instead, they overlap, and share common principles—principles of justice and progress; tolerance and the dignity of all human beings.

I do so recognizing that change cannot happen overnight. No single speech can eradicate years of mistrust, nor can I answer in the time that I have all the complex questions that brought us to this point . . . As the Holy Koran tells us, "Be conscious of God and speak always the truth." That is what I will try to do—to speak the truth as best I can, humbled by the task before us, and firm in my belief that the interests we share as human beings are far more powerful than the forces that drive us apart.

Part of this conviction is rooted in my own experience. I am a Christian, but my father came from a Kenyan family that includes generations of Muslims. As a boy, I spent several years in Indonesia and heard the call of the azaan at the break of dawn and the fall of dusk. As a young man, I worked in Chicago communities where many found dignity and peace in their Muslim faith.

As a student of history, I also know civilization's debt to Islam. It was Islam—at places like Al-Azhar University—that carried the light of learning through so many centuries, paving the way for Europe's Renaissance and Enlightenment. It was innovation in Muslim communities that developed the order of algebra; our magnetic compass and tools of navigation; our mastery of pens and printing; our understanding of how disease spreads and how it can be healed. Islamic culture has given us majestic arches and soaring spires; timeless poetry and cherished music; elegant calligraphy and places of peaceful contemplation. And throughout history, Islam has demonstrated through words and deeds the possibilities of religious tolerance and racial equality.

I know, too, that Islam has always been a part of America's story. The first nation to recognize my country was Morocco. In signing the Treaty of Tripoli in 1796, our second President John Adams wrote, "The United States has in itself no character of enmity against the laws, religion or tranquility of Muslims." And since our founding, American Muslims have enriched the United States. They have fought in our wars, served in government, stood for civil rights, started businesses, taught at our Universities, excelled in our sports arenas, won Nobel Prizes, built our tallest building, and lit the Olympic Torch. And when the first Muslim-American was recently elected to Congress, he took the oath to defend our Constitution using the same Holy Koran that one of our Founding Fathers—Thomas Jefferson—kept in his personal library.

So I have known Islam on three continents before coming to the region where it was first revealed. That experience guides my conviction that partnership between America and Islam must be based on what Islam is, not what it isn't. And I consider it part of my responsibility as President of the United States to fight against negative stereotypes of Islam wherever they appear.

But that same principle must apply to Muslim perceptions of America. Just as Muslims do not fit a crude stereotype, America is not the crude stereotype of a self-interested empire. The United States has been one of the greatest sources of progress that the world has ever known. We were born out of revolution against an empire. We were founded upon the ideal that all are created equal, and we have shed blood and struggled for centuries to give meaning to those words—within our borders, and around the world. We are shaped by every culture, drawn from every end of the Earth, and dedicated to a simple concept: E pluribus unum: "Out of many, one."

Much has been made of the fact that an African-American with the name Barack Hussein Obama could be elected President. But my personal story is not so unique. The dream of opportunity for all people has not come true for everyone in America, but its promise exists for all who come to our shores—that includes nearly seven million American Muslims in our country today who enjoy incomes and education that are higher than average.

Moreover, freedom in America is indivisible from the freedom to practice one's religion. That is why there is a mosque in every state of our union, and over 1,200 mosques within our borders. That is why the U.S. government has gone to court to protect the right of women and girls to wear the hijab, and to punish those who would deny it.

So let there be no doubt: Islam is a part of America. And I believe that America holds within her the truth that regardless of race, religion, or station in life, all of us share common aspirations—to live in peace and security; to get an education and to work with dignity; to love our families, our communities, and our God. These things we share. This is the hope of all humanity.

Of course, recognizing our common humanity is only the beginning of our task. Words alone cannot meet the needs of our people. These needs will be met only if we act boldly in the years ahead; and if we understand that the challenges we face are shared, and our failure to meet them will hurt us all. . . .

That does not mean we should ignore sources of tension. Indeed, it suggests the opposite: we must face these tensions squarely. And so in that spirit, let me speak as clearly and plainly as I can about some specific issues that I believe we must finally confront together.

The first issue that we have to confront is violent extremism in all of its forms.

In Ankara, I made clear that America is not—and never will be—at war with Islam. We will, however, relentlessly confront violent extremists who pose a grave threat to our security. Because we reject the same thing that people of all faiths reject: the killing of innocent men, women, and children. And it is my first duty as President to protect the American people.

The situation in Afghanistan demonstrates America's goals, and our need to work together. Over seven years ago, the United States pursued al Qaeda and the Taliban with broad international support. We did not go by choice, we went because of necessity. . . . We would gladly bring every single one of our troops home if we could be confident that there were not violent extremists in Afghanistan and Pakistan determined to kill as many Americans as they possibly can. But that is not yet the case.

That's why we're partnering with a coalition of forty-six countries. And despite the costs involved, America's commitment will not weaken. Indeed, none of us should tolerate these extremists. They have killed in many countries. They have killed people of different faiths—more than any other, they have killed Muslims. Their actions are irreconcilable with the rights of human beings, the progress of nations, and with Islam. The Holy Koran teaches that whoever kills an innocent, it is as if he has killed all mankind; and whoever saves a person, it is as if he has saved all mankind. The enduring faith of over a billion people is so much bigger than the narrow hatred of a few. Islam is not part of the problem in combating violent extremism—it is an important part of promoting peace. . . .

Let me also address the issue of Iraq. Unlike Afghanistan, Iraq was a war of choice that provoked strong differences in my country and around the world. . . .

Today, America has a dual responsibility: to help Iraq forge a better future—and to leave Iraq to Iraqis. I have made it clear to the Iraqi people that we pursue no bases, and no claim on their territory or resources. Iraq's sovereignty is its own. . . .

So America will defend itself respectful of the sovereignty of nations and the rule of law. And we will do so in partnership with Muslim communities which are also threatened. The sooner the extremists are isolated and unwelcome in Muslim communities, the sooner we will all be safer.

The second major source of tension that we need to discuss is the situation between Israelis, Palestinians and the Arab world.

America's strong bonds with Israel are well known. This bond is unbreakable. It is based upon cultural and historical ties, and the recognition that the aspiration for a Jewish homeland is rooted in a tragic history that cannot be denied.

Around the world, the Jewish people were persecuted for centuries, and anti-Semitism in Europe culminated in an unprecedented Holocaust. . . . On the other hand, it is also undeniable that the Palestinian people—Muslims and Christians—have suffered in pursuit of a homeland. . . . [T]he situation for the Palestinian people is intolerable. America will not turn our backs on the legitimate Palestinian aspiration for dignity, opportunity, and a state of their own.

For decades, there has been a stalemate: two peoples with legitimate aspirations, each with a painful history that makes compromise elusive. But if we see this conflict only from one side or the other, then we will be blind to the truth: the only resolution is for the aspirations of both sides to be met through two states, where Israelis and Palestinians each live in peace and security.

That is in Israel's interest, Palestine's interest, America's interest, and the world's interest. . . . To play a role in fulfilling Palestinian aspirations, and to unify the Palestinian people, Hamas must put an end to violence, recognize past agreements, and recognize Israel's right to exist.

At the same time, Israelis must acknowledge that just as Israel's right to exist cannot be denied, neither can Palestine's. The United States does not accept the legitimacy of continued Israeli settlements. . . .

America will align our policies with those who pursue peace. . . . All of us have a responsibility to work for the day when the mothers of Israelis and Palestinians can see their children grow up without fear; when the Holy Land of three great faiths is the place of peace that God intended it to be; when Jerusalem is a secure and lasting home for Jews and Christians and Muslims, and a place for all of the children of Abraham to mingle peacefully together as in the story of Isra, when Moses, Jesus, and Mohammed (peace be upon them) joined in prayer.

The third source of tension is our shared interest in the rights and responsibilities of nations on nuclear weapons.

This issue has been a source of tension between the United States and the Islamic Republic of Iran. For many years, Iran has defined itself in part by its opposition to my country, and there is indeed a tumultuous history between us. . . .

It will be hard to overcome decades of mistrust, but we will proceed with courage, rectitude and resolve. There will be many issues to discuss between our two countries, and we are willing to move forward without preconditions on the basis of mutual respect. . . .

I understand those who protest that some countries have weapons that others do not. No single nation should pick and choose which nations hold nuclear weapons. That is why I strongly reaffirmed America's commitment to seek a world in which no nations hold nuclear weapons. . . .

The fourth issue that I will address is democracy.

I know there has been controversy about the promotion of democracy in recent years, and much of this controversy is connected to the war in Iraq. So let me be clear: no system of government can or should be imposed upon one nation by any other.

That does not lessen my commitment, however, to governments that reflect the will of the people. Each nation gives life to this principle in its own way, grounded in the traditions of its own people. America does not presume to know what is best for everyone, just as we would not presume to pick the outcome of a peaceful election. But I do have an unyielding belief that all people yearn for certain things: the ability to speak your mind and have a say in how you are governed; confidence in the rule of law and the equal administration of justice; government that is transparent and doesn't steal from the people; the freedom to live as you choose. Those are not just American ideas, they are human rights, and that is why we will support them everywhere. . . .

The fifth issue that we must address together is religious freedom.

Islam has a proud tradition of tolerance. . . . I saw it firsthand as a child in Indonesia, where devout Christians worshiped freely in an overwhelmingly Muslim country. That is the spirit we need today. People in every country should be free to choose and live their faith based upon the persuasion of the mind, heart, and soul. . . . Among some Muslims, there is a disturbing tendency to measure one's own faith by the rejection of another's. The richness of religious diversity must be upheld—whether it is for Maronites in Lebanon or the Copts in Egypt. And fault lines must be closed among Muslims as well, as the divisions between Sunni and Shia have led to tragic violence, particularly in Iraq.

Freedom of religion is central to the ability of peoples to live together. We must always examine the ways in which we protect it. . . .

The sixth issue that I want to address is women's rights. . . .

Our daughters can contribute just as much to society as our sons, and our common prosperity will be advanced by allowing all humanity—men and women—to reach their full potential. I do not believe that women must make the same choices as men in order to be equal, and I respect those women who choose to live their lives in traditional roles. But it should be their choice. That is why the United States will partner with any Muslim-majority country to support expanded literacy for girls, and to help young women pursue employment through micro-financing that helps people live their dreams.

Finally, I want to discuss economic development and opportunity.

I know that for many, the face of globalization is contradictory. The Internet and television can bring knowledge and information, but also offensive sexuality and mindless violence. Trade can bring new wealth and opportunities, but also huge disruptions and changing communities. . . .

But all of us must recognize that education and innovation will be the currency of the 21st century, and in too many Muslim communities there remains underinvestment in these areas. I am emphasizing such investments within my country. . . .

On education, we will expand exchange programs, and increase scholarships, like the one that brought my father to America, while encouraging more Americans to study in Muslim communities. . . .

On economic development, we will create a new corps of business volunteers to partner with counterparts in Muslim-majority countries. . . .

On science and technology, we will launch a new fund to support technological development in Muslim-majority countries, and to help transfer ideas to the marketplace so they can create jobs. And today I am announcing a new global effort with the Organization of the Islamic Conference to eradicate polio. And we will also expand partnerships with Muslim communities to promote child and maternal health.

All these things must be done in partnership. Americans are ready to join with citizens and governments; community organizations, religious leaders, and businesses in Muslim communities around the world to help our people pursue a better life.

The issues that I have described will not be easy to address. . . . I know there are many—Muslim and non-Muslim—who question whether we can forge this new beginning. Some are eager to stoke the flames of division, and to stand in the way of progress. Some suggest that it isn't worth the effort—that we are fated to disagree, and civilizations are doomed to clash. . . . But if we choose to be bound by the past, we will never move forward. And I want to particularly say this to young people of every faith, in every country—you, more than anyone, have the ability to remake this world. . . .

It is easier to start wars than to end them. It is easier to blame others than to look inward; to see what is different about someone than to find the things we share. But we should choose the right path, not just the easy path. There is also one rule that lies at the heart of every religion—that we do unto others as we would have them do unto us. This truth transcends nations and peoples—a belief that isn't new; that isn't black or white or brown; that isn't Christian, or Muslim or Jew. It's a belief that pulsed in the cradle of civilization, and that still beats in the heart of billions. It's a faith in other people, and it's what brought me here today.

We have the power to make the world we seek, but only if we have the courage to make a new beginning, keeping in mind what has been written.

The Holy Koran tells us, "O mankind! We have created you male and a female; and we have made you into nations and tribes so that you may know one another."

The Talmud tells us: "The whole of the Torah is for the purpose of promoting peace."

The Holy Bible tells us, "Blessed are the peacemakers, for they shall be called sons of God."

The people of the world can live together in peace. We know that is God's vision. Now, that must be our work here on Earth. Thank you. And may God's peace be upon you.

Notes

1. Numerous others shared many of the same convictions, most notably John Adams, James Madison, John Quincy Adams, Andrew Jackson, Rutherford Hayes, James Garfield, Grover Cleveland, Benjamin Harrison, William McKinley, Herbert Hoover, Harry Truman, Gerald Ford, George H. W. Bush, and Bill Clinton.

2. George Washington Papers, Library of Congress, 1741–99.

3. Carter, however, displayed much less personal piety than many other presidents whose faith was not nearly as strong. Ribuffo suggests that "because he was so pious, Carter felt little need for official declarations of piety" (Ribuffo 1989, 151).

4. Few Americans, except outspoken secularists, want a naked public square. Mainline, evangelical, and fundamentalist Protestants, Catholics, Jews, and Muslims all insist that public life should rest on basic religious values. Although Americans disagree about whether public buildings should be allowed to display the Ten Commandments, most of them concur that their principles-reverence for God, honesty, fidelity, integrity, and respect for life and property-should direct corporate as well as individual life. Two Christian intellectuals have especially promoted this argument: Richard John Neuhaus, editor of the journal *First Things* and author of *The Naked Public Square* (Grand Rapids, MI: Eerdmans, 1984), and Yale Law School professor Stephen Carter, who wrote *The Culture of Disbelief: How American Law and Politics Trivialize Religious Devotion* (New York: Basic Books, 1993) and *God's Name in Vain: The Wrongs and Rights of Religion in Politics* (New York: Basic Books, 2000). They contend that the effort to broaden the concept of the separation of church and state in order to eliminate religious perspectives, values, and symbols from public life and to inhibit the participation of

religious groups in discussions of public policy is at odds with the First Amendment as it has been understood throughout American history. In *Divided by God: America's Church-State Problem and What We Should Do About It*, New York University law professor Noah Feldman argues that the current debate over religion in the public arena is largely between two camps he labels "legal secularists" and "values evangelicals." He insists that almost all Americans want to ensure that the nation's religious division and diversity does not pull us apart. "Values evangelicals think that the solution lies in finding and embracing traditional values we can share;" "legal secularists think that we can maintain our national unity only if we treat religion as a personal, private matter." He proposes a bargain: greater tolerance for the public expression of religion "in exchange for tighter restrictions on government funding" of religious institutions and activities. He urges values evangelicals to "reconsider their position in favor of state support for religious institutions and re-embrace the American tradition of institutionally separated church and state" because "state funding actually undercuts, rather than promotes, the cohesive national identity that evangelicals" want to restore. See also Michelle Goldberg, 2005.

5. Jefferson was a bachelor during his first alleged indiscretion and a widower during his second.

CHAPTER 8

RELIGION AND CONGRESS

Introduction

Research Pieces

8.1   Peter Benson and Dorothy Williams, *Religion on Capitol Hill: Myths and Realities* (1982)

8.2   James L. Guth, *Religion and Roll Calls: Religious Influences on the U.S. House of Representatives, 1997–2002* (2007)

8.3   Elizabeth Anne Oldmixon, *Uncompromising Positions: God, Sex, and the U.S. House of Representatives* (2005)

8.4   Michelle Gabriel, *Prayer Groups Proliferate on Capitol Hill* (2003)

8.5   Representative David Price, *The Congressional Experience* (2004)

Primary Sources

8.6   Senator Joseph Lieberman, *Statement of Senator Joe Lieberman on the Nomination of John Ashcroft for Attorney General* (February 1, 2001)

8.7   Senator Rick Santorum, *The Press and People of Faith in Politics* (August 2008)

8.8   Representative Nancy Pelosi, *Nancy Pelosi Delivers Speech at National Hispanic Prayer Breakfast* (June 16, 2005)

8.9   Senator Barack Obama, *"Call to Renewal" Keynote Address* (June 28, 2006)

8.10 Senator John Danforth, *Onward, Moderate Christian Soldiers* (June 17, 2007)

Introduction

The selections in this chapter explore the relationship between religion and Congress and are rooted in the theoretical tradition of political science. Hannah Pitkin asserts that representation involves making the absent present. Thus, when running for office from their districts, many members of Congress articulate their fitness for office with appeals based on versions of "Trust me. I'm like you. Send me to Washington to protect the values you and I share." Because so many of the American people are religious, one set of public values quite plausibly reflected in Washington is religious values.

    The articles in this chapter contribute to a deeper operational understanding of Congress. Knowledge about how members of Congress operate as individuals within the institution is as important as the operational aspects of how a bill becomes a law. To the extent that national representative bodies are representative in religious ways, studying religion in Congress provides insight into the broader topic of the role of religion in America, especially its politically relevant manifestations.

While little scholarship has studied religious factors in congressional behavior, there are some useful works in the field. For many decades, congressional scholars all but ignored asking questions about the potential influence of religion on Congress and its members. One of the first books to engage such questions came not from political science, but from psychology. In *Religion on Capitol Hill* (excerpted here), Peter Benson and Dorothy Williams interviewed legislators in the 1970s. Although many political scientists scrutinized Benson and Williams's methods, the project represents an important landmark in the study of Congress because it probed the religious beliefs and behaviors of its members.

Religion is now commonly conceptualized by social scientists as including dimensions of "belief, behavior, and belonging," and the articles selected for this chapter provide a window into each of these dimensions of religion. While it makes sense to surmise that the religious activities of national legislators will likely mirror those of their constituents in many ways, certainly these elite politicians are different as well. How might that be so? On average, members of Congress are more educated than their constituents. The fact that a significant percentage of members of Congress are attorneys or businesspersons, coupled with the tasks of legislating, suggests that many possess strong critical thinking and persuasion skills. Thus, one might expect members of Congress to approach religion in a more systematic way than their typical constituents and to articulate that thinking when called upon to do so. We might also expect that members of Congress, as partisans elected in an increasingly polarized party system, are more extreme and politicized individuals than their average constituents. Perhaps politicization and polarization affect whether members of Congress employ religious language in defense of issue positions and how they do so once employed.

The first selection is an excerpt from Benson and Williams's classic, but controversial, psychological study. The researchers advance a more detailed scholarly conversation about the public and private roles of religion in Congress. Their findings suggest that substantive and reasonably well-organized religious thinking and motivation are widespread among members of Congress, even among those who do not express their religion publicly.

Two more recent pieces are representative of works that examine religious influences on legislators. James Guth's analysis of how religious factors influence voting in the House of Representatives explores the connections between district religiosity, member religiosity, and member voting behavior. Guth and his colleagues gathered data to create religious profiles of legislators that offer details beyond simple descriptions of their religious affiliation, adding measures of legislators' theological perspectives and religious involvement.

The next selection, an excerpt from Elizabeth Anne Oldmixon's *Uncompromising Positions*, offers another window into decision making in the U.S. House of Representatives. Combining analysis of roll-call voting data, characteristics of legislative districts, and information from interviews with members and key staff, Oldmixon considers how and why legislators decide how to vote on legislation related to "culture war" issues such as abortion and homosexuality.

Michelle Gabriel's news article highlights the proliferation of prayer groups in Congress, offering a glimpse of some of the ways senators and representatives from both sides of the aisle interact informally with colleagues on matters of personal faith. In particular, the story discusses how Congressional prayer groups offer unique places of religious "belonging".

The selection by North Carolina Democrat David Price, excerpted from a textbook he wrote about Congress, is an atypical description of typical and regular patterns of religious interaction with congressional issues and personalities. Not only is Representative Price a longstanding member of the U.S. House of Representatives, he is also a former political science professor who holds an advanced religious degree. On the basis of this uniquely informed reflection on his experience, Price outlines several propositions to support his views concerning how religious faith and political life and action can and do interrelate in the realm of Congress.

The Price article is also a nice transition to the set of primary sources for this chapter. Five statements on the interaction between faith and public life/public policy from prominent current or recent members of the House and Senate are included here. These members constitute a representative cross section of the political spectrum and religious traditions within the Congress. While the five statements reflect differences in tone, theology, and the policy conclusions drawn, they all affirm the theme of this chapter that many active and successful politicians do not check their religious belonging, belief, and behavior at the door when they enter public life.

The primary documents section begins with an excerpt from Connecticut Senator Joe Lieberman's speech on the Senate floor in which he described his reasons for voting against Attorney General nominee John Ashcroft. Senator Lieberman, an Orthodox Jew, made national news when he accepted Al Gore's invitation to join the 2000 Democratic ticket as the party's nominee for vice president.

The next selection is a speech by former Pennsylvania Republican representative and senator Rick Santorum, given in the midst of the 2008 presidential election campaign at a forum organized by the Oxford Centre for Religion and Public Life. In the speech, Santorum describes what he views as unfair and uninformed media treatment as an openly religious and politically conservative politician. He also criticizes the use by Barack Obama and other Democrats of religious language and themes in campaigns, questioning their depth and sincerity.

Providing a significant contrast in approach and content from Santorum's reflections, the next speech is a keynote address to the National Hispanic Prayer Breakfast from then-Democratic leader, and soon to become Speaker of the House, Nancy Pelosi. In this speech, Rep. Pelosi connects her Roman Catholic faith with her work promoting Democratic programs and policies.

In the next selection, also from a Democrat, then-Senator Barack Obama explains his faith journey from his childhood in a "not particularly religious household" to his decision as an adult to embrace Christianity and join a United Church of Christ congregation. Arguing that the Democratic Party should be more welcoming of people of faith, Obama offers suggestions to progressive and conservative leaders for approaching religion and politics.

The chapter concludes with a newspaper editorial by John Danforth, an ordained Episcopal minister and former Republican senator from Missouri who represents the moderate wing of the Republican Party. Danforth utilizes a metaphor from the hymn "Onward, Christian Soldiers" in order to challenge the notion that conservative Christian voices have hegemony in the Republican ranks.

Research Pieces

8.1

Peter Benson and Dorothy Williams

RELIGION ON CAPITOL HILL: MYTHS AND REALITIES (1982)

Religion and the Myths Disproved

What can we make of the religion-politics connection? What can we expect to be different as a result of our knowledge about it? To begin with, it rids us of some misleading notions that have led down some divisive and unproductive paths in the past.

The evidence strongly suggests that the U.S. Congress, far from being a hotbed of secular humanism, agnosticism, and atheism, is instead made up of a preponderance of people to whom religion is important, most of whom belong to a church or synagogue, and most of whom engage in both the public and the private practice of their faith.

We know that members of Congress are not less religious than the rest of the American public; if anything, in some ways of defining religiousness, they are more religious than the American public.

We know that being religiously committed does not automatically brand one as a political conservative, but that a goodly number of the committed tend to be liberal in voting pattern, and some among the committed are the most liberal of any in Congress. And when we look at a particular brand of conservatism—that represented by the New Christian Right—we still find conservatives and liberals holding many beliefs in common.

We know that it can be shown with some certainty that a member's type of religious belief is predictably connected with a member's type of voting issues.

We know that evangelical Christians in Congress are not a united voting bloc. On the contrary, the members who score highest on our evangelical measures tend to divide and cluster at opposite ends of the political liberal-political conservative continuum. On the voting measures we used, few evangelicals are politically lukewarm or moderate.

It is hard to let go of some of our favorite myths. However, the shattering of a myth now and then can do wonders for one's outlook on life. It lets new light in. Now that some of the mist has cleared, there may be assumptions to reexamine and a private collection of villains and heroes who now require new labels.

With the myths shattered the public experiences some new uncertainties in place of the assurances that the old stereotypes provided. There was a time when the public believed one could expect the evangelical candidate to be conservative. One could expect the liberal candidate to be less subject to influence by religious principles. One could expect the candidate backed by the New Christian Right to be more religious than the other candidate. The trouble with those expectations was that there was a potential for later disappointment when the candidate, once elected, turned out not to support the "right" causes.

Voting, like politics, is an inexact science. A voter can never be certain what characteristics, biases, tendencies, and convictions come along with the person for whom the ballot is cast. The choice is difficult. Candidates for a given office often sound rather alike. If one understands politics and religion about equally well, or knows the political world better than the religious world, those politically tuned perceptions are probably a good index to the voting choices that must be made.

However, if you are a person who wants to vote intelligently and whose ear is much better attuned to religious issues than to political issues, it may be possible to use that religiously astute ear as you listen to candidates. Does the message mark him or her as more of a Legalist or more of a People-Concerned type? Does the candidate sound more like a Nontraditional or a Self-Concerned? In the religious realm, does the candidate seem to want to urge the morality that he/she espouses onto all of society? Does the candidate talk more about the need for control and for adherence to the laws of God, or about encouraging the development of people's God-given potential? These are matters central to the religious identities that connect to some voting issues. If our evidence is correct, what you hear in the religious realm may turn up in related voting patterns, once the candidate is elected.

Religion—A Less Global View

Many people, in thinking about religion, tend to think in large, sometimes loosely defined categories, making some general assumptions that, if they are led to look at them carefully they would agree the evidence does not entirely support.

One of our first convictions is that religion for most is more than window-dressing, more than something tacked onto life. One clergyman described the tacked-on religion as being treated in many conversations as if it were a kind of green glop that can be splashed onto things to make them seem religious. Live as you like, but splash on a little green glop by sitting through a worship service now and then. Conduct a business meeting in which all members employ against each other their sharpest manipulative skills in an effort to get their own way, but splash on the green glop of religiosity by opening or closing the meeting with prayer. We found some evidence that some in Congress may adhere to the green-glop theory, but they are a minority. Some, too sophisticated to think of religion in that way, still think in general categories that show up in sentences that begin "Catholics tend to. . . ." or "Jews usually are. . . ." or "Religious people are . . . ." There is something dynamic about religious belief, when taken seriously, that causes it to be integrated into the person's total perception of life, into his or her motives and ways of dealing with people and decisions. This integration process produces great variety among religious people, so that, like snowflakes, no two of them are exactly alike.

Not only does religion exert power in life, but there seems to be evidence that its development is interactive—the person interacting with the religious messages he or she receives to develop a particular religious type. Obviously there is some process at work that causes members of the same denomination, hearing the same kinds of messages delivered from the religious institution, to turn out to have very different sets of belief. Individuals may be quite active participants in the development of their own religious world view and posture, finding and internalizing the religious themes and messages that best accord with who they are.

If we assume that most persons can be located in a religious type, a number of significant questions emerge. What accounts for one's location in a religious type? Why have some become Self-Concerned religionists while others are People-Concerned? Do people move, across their life span, from one type to another? Once a person is established as a Self-Concerned religionist, is no further change likely? Could there be a sequential movement from one type to another throughout life, as there is evidence for in stages of moral reasoning? And if people move, by what process does it occur? . . .

Religious Types in Later Congresses

How representative are our discoveries, and how durable? The facts and interpretations presented in this book are based on interviews with eighty members of the Ninety-sixth Congress, whose term ran from 1978 to 1980. Do our myth-shattering discoveries hold true for that entire body of 535 members? We think the eighty are a good representation of the entire Ninety-sixth Congress, as shown in chapter 2, although we do not want to overstate that claim. Having achieved contact with a sample that closely matches the entire Congress as to Senate-House membership, political party, region, religious affiliation, sex, age, education, and voting record, everything we know about research would say that our sample accurately represents the whole. . . .

Religion in the Wider World

Although much of what we have presented has meaning in the Congress, our discoveries also say some important things about religion. We think it likely that the religious themes and religious types described in this study would find their counterparts almost anywhere in the general population. We believe that this book has implications in the wider world. Although the six religious types were discovered in analysis of interviews with members of Congress, the religious scales and types afford new descriptive labels and definitions that can help us understand varieties of religious belief and expression throughout the Judeo-Christian world, and perhaps beyond. It seems likely that other populations, people in other walks of life—scientists, homemakers, clergy, academics, the general public—could easily find a home in one of the six types. The proportions of the six types might vary, but all could fairly easily be found and identified.[1]

If this generalization of the types to the population at large is possible, we then have new categories in which to diagnose and reexamine our own religious tendencies. We have occasion to evaluate the nature of the filter with which we hear and incorporate certain messages (". . . some seed fell into good soil") and fail to hear others (". . . and some seed fell on rocky ground"). We have opportunity to observe whether our religious type compels our own behavior only when patently religious matters are at issue, or whether we carry that tendency into other areas of life. If we are Legalists religiously, are we also Legalists at home and at our place of work?

A corollary discovery may be that there is considerable potential for dialogue across different religious groups. A widespread warming of relationships between individuals and small groups from different denominations has occurred over the past twenty years or so. This warming has enabled them to work meaningfully in joint historical and liturgical studies, social action projects, and a variety of other enterprises. This phenomenon is probably further evidence of the truth that religious types spread across the denominations. When representatives of Catholic, Lutheran, Presbyterian, and Jewish faiths have found themselves able to work well together, it may have been because they are of similar religious types and thus are able to work from shared assumptions, in spite of the division of churchly allegiance and divergent ritual. With that recognition they have been able to band together to work on common ground, from common assumptions.

Religious Tension—Friend or Foe?

One of the cherished hopes we may one day have to relinquish is the warmly good-hearted assumption that since a given group of people is composed entirely of a single religious tradition, it ought to be able to agree. Reason, experience, and the evidence of our research combine to discourage that hope. Religious people receive the message of their faith in such markedly different ways that people with equal religious conviction and commitment (insofar as these can be measured) often express themselves in sharply opposing kinds of behavior. . . .

One of the major messages carried in the mass of data summarized in this book is that religion affects people differently, even those who take it equally seriously, and therefore the tensions that exist in our varying points of view are not likely to go away. We have not all the same gifts—nor the same perceptions, nor the same agendas, nor the same ways of living our religion.

But that is not altogether bad news. Though tension and struggle are painful, good often comes of them. The religious establishment as well as the rest of society needs a variety of pressures to keep it on course. Some must sound the note of caution, some give the challenge to action, some point the way to change, some point to the value of stability and tradition. Part of our American belief in the value of pluralism causes us to see that the church, the Congress—indeed, all of society—is best served when all sides continue to speak their convictions. The tensions are essential to the health of the organism, provided of course that there also exist enough mutual respect, trust, and shared area of agreement so that the tension does not tear it apart.

It is here that members of the New Christian Right go astray, and with them others—individual people, whole denominations, cults—who believe that theirs is the only way. As was illustrated in chapter 8, all of the positions expressed in the religious themes can be supported with Scripture. The New Christian Right and other "only way" people find themselves on shaky grounds and lose potential friends when they declare that the only message Scripture has to deliver is the one they claim as support for their position.

Given the admission of this continuing tension, what is the value of pointing out the tension? By looking straight at those things that divide us, and acknowledging those divisions, we can sometimes move away from the scene of battle and look again at what unites us, at where the agreements and concurrences are. A visible difference is usually more manageable than an invisible and unacknowledged one. The "management" may be only a matter of avoiding the disputed territory whenever circumstances make it possible. When avoidance is impossible, we may shorten the conflict by recognizing and acknowledging the other's already known and stated position. . . .

When it comes to the question of religion, of the ways in which we understand God and ourselves and what that relationship means, when it comes to the question of our commitment to our religious beliefs and the ways in which we live them out, there is very little difference between the members of Congress and the rest of us.

We elect them from among us. Though we often view them as the enemy—the they in Washington who vote our taxes and delimit our freedoms—in the immortalized words of Pogo: "We have met the enemy, and they is us." The same varieties of pressures, longings, and dreams motivate us all. The same personal hurts and physical limitations and human suffering assail us. August as the congressional office seems to most of us, and awed as one nearly always is by the power it wields, before God the office holder and the home-town voter are much the same. What we have learned about Congress, therefore, we have probably also to some extent learned about ourselves. Perhaps as we reflect on what we see through this window on one of the hitherto unexplored comers of life, we will find some new understanding, some increased respect, some common ground for hope.

8.2

James L. Guth

RELIGION AND ROLL CALLS: RELIGIOUS INFLUENCES ON THE U.S. HOUSE OF REPRESENTATIVES, 1997–2002 (2007)

In recent years political scientists have made enormous strides in understanding the influence of religion on political attitudes and behavior, both in the mass public and among political activists.

In stark contrast, the literature on religion's influence among public officials is much more preliminary. Work on religion in Congress, especially, still suffers from the problems that frustrated political scientists in early efforts to analyze religion's electoral role, namely, difficulties in measuring religious factors. In recent years, however, scholars have developed far better measures of religious affiliation, behavior and belief when dealing with the mass public. The importance of multiple measures of religion lies in the fact that religion is multidimensional, with "belonging, believing and behaving" facets (Layman 2001).

Indeed, the two major approaches to understanding the impact of religion on American political alignments put primary emphasis on different aspects of religion. The *ethnoreligious* perspective, long dominant among political historians and some social scientists, argues that denominational affiliation or membership in religious traditions is the primary mediator of religious influence on electoral politics (see, for example, McCormick 1974; Manza and Brooks 1999). More recently, proponents of *religious restructuring* or, more popularly, "culture war" perspectives have argued that religious beliefs produce the real political divisions among Americans, as "orthodox" believers oppose "progressives"(Wuthnow 1988; Hunter 1991). As we have shown elsewhere, both perspectives are helpful in understanding the electoral influences of religion (Guth et al. 2005; Guth et al. 2006; Green et al. 2007) and the impact of religion on party elites (Layman 2001; Green and Jackson 2007). It seems only natural then, that the same framework should be used to analyze one product of the electoral process, decision-making in Congress. Such an approach is not only more likely to uncover the full effects of religion on legislative behavior, but will also allow us to connect developments in the party system with the actions of political elites.

The multiple religious measures necessary for such an approach are almost entirely absent, however, from the study of Congress. Given difficulties in acquiring information on members' beliefs and religious activities, scholars have almost invariably relied on easily available public information on "religious affiliation," by default adopting a crude ethnoreligious approach, rather than attempting to acquire measures on religious belief and practice to test the restructuring or culture wars model as well. In this essay, we demonstrate the utility of a more comprehensive approach. As part of a long-term project using interviews, participant observation and extensive web searches, we have assembled a massive amount of information on House members' religious affiliations, behavior and beliefs. This data base permits us not only to place members in their correct religious tradition, but also to assess their religious participation levels and degree of theological "traditionalism" (see Guth 2007 for more details).[2]

Our presentation proceeds as follows. After providing a brief religious profile of the House from 1997–2002, we show that legislator voting reflects the same religious patterns that we find in the mass public and among political activists, both in terms of the members' own religious traits and those of their constituents. We then consider whether the influence of religion is channeled through historical religious traditions, religious commitment, or theological orientation. We also consider whether legislative behavior stems primarily from the member's own religious traits, or is also influenced directly by the religious composition of the district.

Results

Table 8.1 reports the results of our classification efforts, locating House members in their appropriate religious traditions, assessing their religious involvement, and judging their theological perspectives. The distribution of religious affiliations reveals the continuation of some historic tendencies: white evangelical Protestants are still underrepresented in comparison with their one-quarter of the national population, claiming less than one-sixth of House members, while mainline Protestants count about twice the proportion of their one-sixth of the citizenry. Combining White Catholics and Hispanic Catholics produces a Catholic percentage

Table 8.1 Religious Traits of U.S. House Members, 1997–2002

	N=	Percent of Membership	Democratic Percent of Group	GOP Percent of Group
Member Faith Tradition				
Evangelical	92	17.3	14.1	85.9
Latter-day Saints	15	4.2	20.0	80.0
Mainline	165	31.0	36.4	63.6
White Catholic	132	24.8	52.3	47.7
All Others	32	6.0	40.6	59.4
Black Protestant	34	6.4	100.0	0.0
Hispanic Catholic	23	4.3	91.3	8.7
Jewish	32	6.0	87.5	12.5
Secular	8	1.5	100.0	0.0
Religious Activity				
None Known	167	31.3	61.7	38.3
Member Only	79	14.8	53.2	46.8
Regular Attender	119	22.3	40.3	59.7
Office/Activist	168	31.5	32.7	67.3
Theological Orientation				
Modernist	40	7.5	87.5	12.5
Undetermined	222	41.7	65.8	34.2
Centrist	138	25.9	41.3	58.7
Traditionalist	133	25.0	7.5	92.5
ALL	**533**	**100**	**46.5**	**53.5**

reasonably in line with the national population, although the former may be slightly over-represented and the latter, under-represented. Similarly, Black Protestants are somewhat under-represented and Jewish legislators more numerous than population numbers would suggest. House members also tend to be fairly active religiously and those whose theological orientation can be determined tend to be centrist or traditionalist.

The partisan location of religious groups is more interesting. As in the electorate, evangelicals in Congress are overwhelmingly Republican, as are Latter-day Saints. Mainline Protestants are still solidly in the GOP camp, while white Catholic legislators show a slight Democratic bias. Not surprisingly, Hispanic Catholic, Jewish, Black Protestant, and Secular legislators are overwhelmingly Democratic, reflecting similar patterns in the electorate. Looking at it from the other direction, the House GOP is largely a mainline (37 percent), evangelical (28 percent), and white Catholic (22 percent) body, while the Democratic caucus is more diverse with white Catholics (28 percent), mainliners (24 percent), Black Protestants (14 percent), and Jews (13 percent) all having substantial contingents. As in the mass public, Republican legislators tend to be more religiously active than Democrats and more overtly traditionalist as well.

Does voting behavior vary systematically by religious affiliation, activity, and belief? As Table 8.2 shows, the answer is clearly "yes." As the first column reveals,

Table 8.2 Religion and Ideological /Partisan Orientations, House of Representatives, 1997–2002. Mean scores.* (*N* = 533)

	DW-Nominate (Liberalism)	Social Issue Liberalism	Economic Issue Liberalism	Foreign Policy Liberalism	Party Unity Scores (Democratic)
Overall Mean=	−.0489	46.17	47.40	47.41	−7.37
Member Faith Tradition					
Evangelical	−.3771	19.43	25.27	25.21	−68.11
LDS	−.3599	25.56	28.32	27.51	−59.38
Mainline	−.1426	41.29	39.89	41.14	−28.18
White Catholic	−.0156	47.60	52.27	50.60	3.35
All Others	−.0137	51.32	48.84	49.33	−15.32
Black Protestant	.3322	75.01	73.15	70.21	74.44
Hispanic Catholic	.3425	77.32	76.48	75.05	77.58
Jewish	.5035	83.14	80.07	83.83	91.49
Secular	.5511	87.22	81.69	83.74	92.95
Eta=	.589	.638	.598	.589	.547
Theological Traditionalism					
Modernist	.3544	73.76	74.08	76.96	70.80
Not Ascertained	.1423	61.17	59.49	59.13	29.37
Centrist	−.1050	42.86	44.73	45.30	−17.75
Traditionalist	−.4313	16.36	22.04	21.24	−80.87
Eta=	.589	.664	.596	.606	.551
Religious Activity					
Unknown/None	.1059	59.02	57.17	56.82	21.56
Membership	−.0079	49.43	50.96	49.71	3.33
Active Member	−.0965	42.85	45.10	45.79	−16.60
Office Held	−.1884	34.18	37.61	38.09	−34.38
Eta=	.278	.344	.285	.265	.259
Religious Constituencies					
Pearson's r=					
Evangelical	−.402**	−.507**	−.464**	−.425**	−.292**
Latter-day Saints	−.090*	−.091*	−.128**	−.122**	−.080
Mainline	−.350**	−.377**	−.357**	−.323**	−.307**
White Catholic	.049	.061	.105*	.060	.004
Black Protestant	.334**	.293**	.286**	.318**	.275**
Hispanic Catholic	.191**	.265**	.223**	.210**	.198**
Jewish	.286**	.321**	.314**	.255**	.217**

religious traditions vary rather strongly on Poole and Rosenthal's general ideological measure (DW-Nominate), with evangelicals the most conservative, followed closely by Latter-day Saints, and at a distance by mainline Protestants. White Catholics fall very slightly to the liberal side of the mean, Hispanic Catholics and Black Protestants much more so, while Jewish and Secular members hold down the liberal end of the continuum. The *eta* statistic for difference of means suggests a fairly strong relationship.

The theological scale also has a powerful relation with all the voting scores, with modernist members the most liberal, followed by those whose theology cannot be ascertained and then by centrists, with traditionalists having the most conservative (and Republican) voting scores. The relationship is strongest on social issues, but not by very much. The religious activity scale is clearly less powerful, as shown by the *etas*, even though the patterns are consistent across the voting scores. Although the religiously inactive are the most liberal, and the most active are the most conservative, the differences between categories are much smaller than for the other religious measures. The greater conservatism of the religiously active is probably an artifact of the tendency for traditionalists to be more involved in religious institutions than their centrist and modernist counterparts are. The multivariate analyses later tend to support this conjecture.

If the personal religious traits of members are strongly associated with their legislative decisions, is the same true of constituency religious factors? A hoary theme of the congressional voting literature is the role that constituents play in legislative decisions. Of course, the problem is always to find the relevant constituency variables to use in the analysis. Here we will draw on the best available data: the religious composition of House districts, based on the 1990 Glenmary Research Center census.[3] As the bottom of Table 8.2 shows, House voting does bear a reasonable relationship to district religious composition. Evangelical membership has a distinctly conservative impact on all the voting scores; so, to a lesser extent, does mainline Protestant membership, followed by LDS numbers. White Catholic membership predicts only a modestly higher score on economic liberalism, but larger Black Protestant, Hispanic Catholic and Jewish populations are solidly associated with liberalism. Thus, the influence of constituency religion parallels that of member religious traits.

This raises the classic issue of the relative influence of personal and constituency traits on legislator behavior. Where we find, as in this case, that legislative action seems to respond to constituencies, does this suggest that districts tend to elect members who share their own traits and attitudes? Or do representatives defer to their constituency, even if their own traits and opinions differ? We cannot completely resolve this question, but Table 8.3 throws some light on it. To assess the relative impact of member and constituency religious traits we include both in regressions predicting our five voting scores. We enter dummy variables for each major ethnoreligious tradition (with "All Others" serving as the omitted reference category), the measures of member religious activity and theology, and the percentage of district residents from various religious groups.

Table 8.3 presents a fairly consistent picture. With the single exception of greater White Catholic liberalism on economic issues, member affiliation with the three largest religious traditions has no direct impact on voting, once other religious factors are in the equation. Clearly, theological orientation is by far the strongest predictor on all five measures, with traditionalism having a negative relationship with policy liberalism and Democratic party voting. Thus, for evangelicals, mainline Protestants, and white Catholics it is their location on the theological scale that influences voting. On the other

Table 8.3 Religious Variables, Ideology and Partisanship in the House of Representatives, 1997–2002 (standardized regression coefficients, OLS analysis) (N = 533)

	DW-Nominate	Social Issue Liberalism	Economic Issue Liberalism	Foreign Policy Liberalism	Party Unity Scores (Democratic)
Member Faith Tradition					
Evangelical	−.013	−.045	.004	−.008	−.008
Latter-day Saints	.030	.005	.046	.021	.021
Mainline	.034	.061	.036	.037	.037
White Catholic	.070	.035	.114**	.090	.090
All Others	—	—	—	—	—
Black Protestant	.099	.119*	.117*	.120*	.120*
Hispanic Catholic	.171**	.153**	.197**	.177**	.177**
Jewish	.161**	.162**	.172**	.150**	.150**
Secular	.156**	.143**	.137**	.147**	.147**
Belief and Practice					
Theology	−.426**	−.422**	−.406**	−.454**	−.454**
Activity	.055	.034	.063	.090*	.090*
District Religion					
Evangelical	−.099*	−.212**	−.153**	−.139*	−.139*
Latter-day Saint	−.035	−.050	−.091*	−.069	−.069
Mainline	−.093	−.107*	−.118*	−.080*	−.080*
White Catholic	.049	.032	.085	.055	.055
Black Protestant	.211**	.140**	.151*	.173**	.173**
Hispanic Catholic	−.033	.017	.003	.004	.004
Jewish	.043	.014	.013	−.014	−.014
Adjusted R squared	.501		.609		.527

hand, it is membership in several minority ethnoreligious groups that produces liberal and Democratic votes. Once again, a combined ethnoreligious and culture wars model seems to produce the best results in predicting voting behavior—this time in the U.S House of Representatives, rather than in the electorate.

Constituencies seem to influence voting primarily by electing members who share their general religious orientation, as most constituency coefficients are insignificant when member traits are in the equation. Still, Table 8.3 shows that some district religious constituencies may have an added independent impact. The proportion of evangelical Protestants in a district increases conservative and Republican voting on all five scores, while Black Protestant membership consistently has the opposite effect. That these are the most faithful Republican and Democratic religious constituencies, respectively, suggests that members—especially those from other traditions—pay them special attention.

The only other notable constituency effect is the mild conservatizing influence of main-line Protestant numbers.

A review of Tables 8.1, 8.2, and 8.3 will leave connoisseurs of the literature on religious voting in recent national elections with a strong sense of *déjà vu* (perhaps all over again). Evangelicals and Latter-day Saints have been strongly Republican in recent elections, mainline Protestants and white Catholics have been swing groups, while religious minorities and secular voters have contributed disproportionately to the Democratic coalition. Even more important, perhaps, theological traditionalists have backed the GOP, while modernists have supported the Democrats. The fact that representatives from these traditions and theological perspectives and from districts dominated by them are located in analogous political space in Congress should not be surprising. And that religious measures alone account for half or more of the variance in voting scores is impressive.

Conclusions

Our data on the House of Representatives present a *prima facie* case for the explanatory power of religious factors. Using variables that permit us to test the impact of belonging, behaving and believing on legislative voting, we find some support for both the restructuring thesis that the contemporary influence of religion derives from the theological orientations of members and for the older ethnoreligious perspective that emphasizes denominational affiliation. Theological orientation shows a consistently strong influence on the legislative voting scores examined here: traditionalists tend toward political conservatism and Republican voting across the board, while modernists are consistently liberal or Democratic. Indeed, for the three largest Christian traditions—evangelical and mainline Protestants and white Catholics—it is now this facet of religion that shapes member choices. The apparent bivariate differences between these traditions seen in Table 8.2 are accounted for by the varying numbers of factional groups within each tradition. Thus, the solid conservatism of evangelical Protestants reflects their overwhelming theological traditionalism, not some specific historic doctrinal or ethnic trait. Similarly, the "centrist" position of Catholic members reflects the more even balance among theological factions in their House contingent, not primarily "moderate" political tendencies inherent in Catholicism. On the other side, the influence of membership in the historic religious traditions—based on ethnicity, religious ethos and unique historical experience—is still seen in the tendency for Black Protestants, Jews, and Seculars to adhere to more liberal and Democratic positions.

The analysis shows that much of religion's influence is channeled indirectly through changes in the religious composition of the two legislative parties, changes which track those transforming the mass electorate (see Green et al. 2007). What some observers (D'Antonio and Tuch 2004) have seen as the declining influence of religion (as measured by affiliation) in legislative voting over recent decades is better understood as the development of more powerful theological lines of cleavage within the House and the institutionalization of these religious influences within party structures.

8.3

Elizabeth Anne Oldmixon

UNCOMPROMISING POSITIONS: GOD, SEX, AND THE U.S. HOUSE OF REPRESENTATIVES (2005)

Inspired by the Sermon on the Mount, Puritan leader John Winthrop preached to the early European settlers in North America that they should model themselves as "a city upon a hill" (Winthrop 1630). In the years that followed, this image of America as a Godly "city upon a hill" became a popular metaphor for the nation. Although the Founders ultimately designed a decidedly secular government, Winthrop's sermon demonstrates that well before the founding, the rhetoric of the nascent American community was infused with religious themes and a sense of providence. As President Reagan noted in his 1989 farewell address, Winthrop coined this phrase as a way to "describe the America he imagined" (Reagan 1989). In that America, religious values were considered an unfailingly positive force. Winthrop regarded the relationship between the new American community and their God as a "covenant" that placed shared responsibilities and shared admonitions on the group as a whole.

Although Winthrop imagined religion to be a positive, unifying social force, the reality is that in the current era religion is a source of conflict. Religion provides communities with a set of correct beliefs and practices on which to model their lives. Yet the effort to realize these shared values brings cultural groups into the public arena, often in opposition to other groups. Indeed, in the twentieth century alone, religious values inspired different visions of the good life and animated both liberal and conservative political activism in support of those visions. The Catholic Church, for example, is a longstanding participant in political discourse, engaging in anti-death penalty activism while promoting economic social justice. Black churches are enduring centers of political activism in the African American community. In the mid-twentieth century they were joined by liberal Protestant churches and Jewish groups in their effort to end the status quo of American apartheid. The political conflicts over the regulation of pornography and alcohol have been infused with religious rhetoric. At the state and local levels, discussions of science curricula in education are unmistakably marked by a subtext of religious disagreement. Even in the areas of foreign policy and immigration policy, religious values strongly influence mass and elite-level preferences. Religion may not always be a source of political conflict, but it can be—and in a pluralistic society it likely will be. When this conflict occurs, cultures compete for legitimacy in the public space, and political institutions must provide resolution.

In the current era, American political institutions are called on to manage a highly salient conflict between two longstanding cultural groups of Americans: those who embrace religious traditionalism and those who embrace progressive sexual norms. In this book I investigate the politics of that conflict as it is manifested in the U.S. House of Representatives. I trace the development of these two cultures in contemporary American politics and then move to a discussion of legislative decision-making and leadership tactics. The underlying theoretical argument is that cultural conflict produces an absolutist politics that complicates traditional legislative norms. As legislators indicate, cultural issues draw on religious values and therefore are not amenable to compromise politics. To shepherd culturally significant bills through the legislative process, congressional leaders must develop strategies to overcome that difficulty. Adopting a weak form of partisanship that builds bipartisan coalitions provides one possible strategy, but the inclination of the Republican majority has been to embrace models of strong party government. . . .

Making Moral Decisions

Because cultural conflict is the stuff of electioneering, cultural issues make their way onto the congressional agenda once the polls have closed. Legislators then find themselves in a position to make moral decisions. Tatalovich and Smith (2001) make the point that moral or cultural conflicts arise out of competing concerns for social status. One group, typically on the left, fights for equalization and recognition of their social status. Another group, typically on the right, perceives the status claims of this new group as a threat to its status and joins the battle to fight for preservationist policies. These issues, therefore, do not draw on traditional class-based economic considerations. Hence, my expectation for this analysis was that economic predictors would have minimal influence on elite decision making. Cultural theory predicts that phenomena that are representative of sociocultural values should structure decision making. In particular, Republican partisanship, ideological conservatism, and legislator identification as Roman Catholic or a religious conservative were expected to produce support for religious traditionalism.

In personal interviews, legislators and staff repeatedly indicated that certain issues are different. Certain issues tap fundamental ethical considerations—and reproductive policy, homosexuality, and (to a lesser extent) school prayer are among those issues. Interview respondents indicated that when they consider these issues, their decision making is guided by internal values rather than economic or electoral considerations. Many respondents specifically referenced the importance of religious faith in decision making. Because cultural issues are easy issues, however, there tends to be correspondence between legislator attitudes and modal district preferences—at least, that is how legislators perceive the dynamic. As a result, basing decision making on personal ethical principles lacks significant electoral risk. To varying degrees, religion, party, and ideology all inform moral decision making, as expected.

The Catholic effect is particularly significant. Both elite Catholic identification and district-level Catholicism are associated with higher levels of legislator support for religious traditionalism. The presence of religious conservative constituencies also is associated with higher levels of legislator support for religious traditionalism, although elite identification as a religious conservative is not for the most part. One might have expected the opposite result because whereas religious conservatives thematically have a singular policy focus and can concentrate their effort on traditional relationships, Catholics do not. The Catholic agenda comprises traditional moral issues, on one hand, and social justice issues on the other. Even the Catholic bishops are divided with regard to which set of issues deserves a pride place (Byrnes 1993). Thus, in theory the linkage between Catholicism and elite decision making could be muddled—but it is not. The seamless effect of Catholic identification may be attributable to the work of the Catholic hierarchy in establishing social teaching and the work of congregations in socializing members. This question warrants further investigation.

Managing Moral Decisions

Legislators and staff indicated in interviews that a significant impediment to policymaking is that cultural issues may defy the normal legislative process, which inevitably requires compromise, give and take. The ideological extremes in both congressional parties are the locus of this problem. They do not want to compromise because the normative stakes are too high. Legislators may differ in opinion on energy policy, but at least compromise in this area does not damn anyone to hell, constitute an assault on western civilization, or indicate misogyny. With culturally significant issues, the bias is slanted toward standing one's ground. As Rep. (and political scientist) David Price (D-N.C.) notes, "[T]here's bias that being ethical means standing alone, and your individual integrity takes precedence over everything else. Of course I'm not about to minimize the importance of individual integrity, but what I'm saying is that often individual integrity might direct us to the kind of role we need to play in the institution as opposed to a kind of contrarian view which suggests that we think we're the only righteous person here in Sodom on the Potomac. You know, that kind of a case needs to be made for cooperative work on a committee and in a party setting . . . I think there's an ethical burden of proof on the person who will not cooperate in doing what needs to be done to bring policies to fruition."[4]

Rep. Price's point is well made. Standing on principle may garner electoral points; it may reduce an individual legislator's internal dissonance; it may even be regarded as heroic. It probably is not a good way to govern, however, if legislators want to accomplish anything.

Obvious compromise positions are available on cultural issues that would be widely popular among the American people. Legislatively, it is difficult to produce those compromise policies because issues take on a nonnegotiable framing that is embraced by the elites and the base constituencies of both parties. This framing creates a partisan incentive within the House of Representatives to sacrifice moderated consensus for absolutist partisanship. As a result, for the most part policymaking is either incremental or nonexistent, although there are a handful of notable exceptions. Yet in the U.S. constitutional system, legislators have the responsibility to, well, legislate. This responsibility often entails resolving regional, economic, and ideological differences, thereby overcoming factious tendencies (Madison 1787). Perhaps, then, the most laudable legislators are those who sacrifice their fundamental principles in the name of consensual policy development. The alternative is legislators who stand their ground—at the expense of fulfilling their responsibilities to the public.

The strength of democratic governance in the United States is based on the ability of Congress—the national deliberative institution—to identify issues of common concern and manage them effectively (Dodd 1993). Congress has done this very well in the face of national traumas, such as war and economic depression. It has overcome wedge issues in the past. Therefore, the student of Congress has reason to be optimistic about the ability of the institution to address cultural wedge issues in the current context. Doing so will require skilled leaders who build winning coalitions across party and coalition lines, while sacrificing ideological extremists. To be clear: The onus is on the leadership of *both* congressional parties.

Over the past decade, the Republican majority in the House has embraced a style of strong party governance. Although this style left the party wobbly after the 105th Congress, House Republicans have reclaimed their lost seats and are reasonably skilled at passing partisan legislation. With a working majority and less need to accommodate the minority party, the 109th Congress might be characterized by conditional party government. Given the political context, this approach clearly makes sense. If any party since the end of the New Deal/Roosevelt Congresses could legitimately claim a mandate—and I use that term with some skepticism—it almost is certainly the current Republican Party.[5] Not only are the Republicans operating under unified government, President Bush garnered a majority of the vote in 2004 and the Republicans picked up seats in both legislative chambers When Speaker Hastert was asked about the possibility of major tax reform in Bush's second term, Hastert responded, "I think this is the only time in generations that you might have a chance to be able to do it."[6]

Hastert senses the opportunity. Republicans have the votes, so observers of politics should expect Republicans to pursue ambitious goals. The problem for House Republicans is that they still confront a more moderate Senate. So they may not win, and they may have to moderate their reform agenda. Nevertheless, their best opportunity to rack up significant legislative victories is in the 109th Congress (2005–2006). Developing a record of legislative accomplishment on cultural issues, however, probably requires a more constructive approach to party governance. Since the Republicans took over as the majority party their management of these issues has included constructive elements and produced important incremental results, but cultural issues also have been a vehicle for partisan confrontation. Thus, efforts to seriously bridge cultural cleavages to build shifting coalitions have been few. Moreover, even when the Republicans made such efforts, Democrats have not always been amenable to coordination. They appear no more willing to sacrifice their ideological extremes than Republicans.

The distribution of preferences on abortion and gay relationships—as captured by the exit poll data—suggests, however, that the public supports a middle-ground approach to cultural policy making. Developing a record of accomplishment on these issues, then, requires that Congress craft policy around that middle ground. Again, this strategy will require sacrificing the ideological extremes in both parties, which may be unrealistic. Nevertheless, policy that reflects the moderate preferences of the American people requires legislative compromise. Alternatively, both parties can continue to engage in polemics, ratcheting up the tenor of cultural conflict as an homage to their bases. That strategy will win votes in the short run, but it will produce a dearth of real legislative accomplishment in this area.

8.4

Michelle Gabriel

PRAYER GROUPS PROLIFERATE ON CAPITOL HILL (2003)

Congresswoman Denise Majette has a lot of reasons to pray.

"As a freshman member of Congress in the minority party, I need to be constantly connected to the Holy Spirit to stay strong," Majette, a Democrat from Georgia, said.

Before they debate issues that affect millions of Americans' lives, many legislators meet for informal prayer sessions and Bible studies. Organized prayer breakfasts also are held weekly for Senate and House members, which Rep. Zach Wamp, R-Tenn., called "the finest hour of the week."

Although the Constitution forbids them to tamper with religious expression and practice in their roles as elected officials, in private, congressional members feel free to bend God's ear about some of the nation's most pressing issues.

"I've met with a senator friend of mine to pray about the world and pray about other countries and each other," said Wamp. "There's a lot of prayer. It's a huge source of strength for members of Congress."

Rep. Todd Tiahrt, R-Kan., attends Bible study classes at the Capitol and hosts impromptu prayer sessions with friends. "It's sort of a time of listening and a brief closing prayer in my office," Tiahrt said. "I found prayer doesn't hurt anyone and it's often a source of strength."

Daniel Dreisbach, a professor of justice, law and society at American University in Washington, said despite the constraints of the First Amendment, church and state have been linked since the time of the Founding Fathers. In the country's earliest years, he noted, worship services were commonplace on public grounds and Congress often dabbled in religious matters. The appointment and salaries of Senate and House chaplains were among the first agenda items of the first Congress.

Today, as Congress continues to open sessions with prayer and observes a National Day of Prayer established in 1952, some groups say that religion and politics are inexorably linked.

Praying in congressional offices "shows that they're not divorcing their religious views from their public office," said Annie Laurie Gaylor, co-founder of the Freedom From Religion Foundation, a group advocating church-state separation.

But Dreisbach said prayer in Congress is allowed, provided it's voluntary. "We don't ask people to shed their religious beliefs once they step into the halls of government," he said.

Dreisbach said religious beliefs are as ingrained as political affiliation—an undeniable part of a person's beliefs. He said discussing religion or engaging in prayer are no different from rooting for a baseball team or discussing the weather, as long as they are done in private—a position Wamp shares.

"The Scripture says you're not to do it publicly or proudly but to find a place, maybe in a closet, so (prayer) is a private, personal thing," Wamp said. "People should not beat their chest about it."

Gaylor agreed that private prayer at work is permissible, but the members of Congress must be careful not to impose their views on their staff or visitors. Or, she said, they could pray elsewhere.

"There are a plethora of tax-exempt churches right around the corner from the Capitol," Gaylor said. "Why don't they pray there?"

Because there are so many prayer breakfasts, prayer meetings and private praying going on in the Capitol and nearby House and Senate office buildings, congressmen need to realize there may be a feeling of pressure to participate among congressional staff and others on Capitol Hill, said Melissa Rogers, visiting professor of religion and public policy at Wake Forest University Divinity School.

"Because Washington is a place for networking, people who do take part in these activities should make it clear to their subordinates that it's not an expectation in any way," she said.

Gaylor said that there is a "coercive" element to formal and informal prayer groups. "It's like telling staff people, 'If you want to get in good with your boss, you have to be praying,'" she said.

Congressmen and staff members should make it clear that neither promotions nor penalties are linked with prayer participation—and make sure their actions reflect their words, Rogers said.

Robert Boston, a spokesman for Americans United for the Separation of Church and State, said informal prayer groups are preferable to religious expression funded by state dollars—for instance, the House and Senate chaplains.

Sen. Chuck Grassley, R-Iowa, is part of both formal and informal prayer groups in Congress. He attends weekly Senate prayer breakfasts, and also prays in private.

"I regularly take time to pray by myself and with others to offer thanks and seek guidance," Grassley said. "As a Christian, I believe that God wants us to talk to him about anything in our life."

Wamp said he notices more people than ever praying on the Hill, especially in the wake of Sept. 11.

"We hit our knees as a country on Sept. 11, and I hope we stayed there," he said. "I believe we have. I think prayer influences a number of congresspeople's daily lives." Jennifer Smith, spokeswoman for the Center for Christian Statesmanship founded by conservative pastor D. James Kennedy of Fort Lauderdale, Fla., said prayer transcends politics.

"Capitol Hill can be a really stressful arena to work in and . . . it's important that believers know they aren't out there fighting the battle alone," she said. "The prayer that happens on Capitol Hill is a really important part of (congressmen's) days."

Tiahrt said many members of Congress, who keep hectic schedules, find structure and repose in prayer.

"(Congress) is such a different lifestyle," he said. "I pray for my family quite a bit. Family is eternal, and this job only lasts two years."

8.5

Representative David Price

The Congressional Experience (2004)

The Two Realms

The relation of the sacred and the secular has inspired theological discussion for thousands of years. The Jewish and Christian faiths are distinctive in setting up a problematic relationship, a tension, between the kingdom of God and earthly kingdoms. In some of the earliest writings in the Hebrew scriptures, the book of Samuel, a great ambivalence is expressed about the very idea of an earthly king in Israel, so that it "may be like all the nations" (1 Samuel 8:20). That ambivalence about the political realm reappears in various forms throughout the Bible.

Theologians have related the sacred and the secular, the religious and the political, in a variety of ways. This variety was best analyzed in H. Richard Niebuhr's masterful *Christ and Culture*, where a "series of typical answers" to this "perennial Christian perplexity" were elaborated (Niebuhr 1956, 2). Some theologians have seen worldly kingdoms as a vehicle for divine law. Others have seen this world as virtually abandoned by God. Most theologians, however, have tried to keep those two views in tension. God's word has been interpreted as both a call and a guide to social involvement. Yet God's word remains transcendent, always imperfectly embodied in our institutions, always standing in judgment over them. Other religious traditions have been much more single-minded, either in renouncing the world or in identifying earthly and Godly rule. Judaism and Christianity, over most of their histories, have maintained the tension and thus have witnessed recurring debates about what the relationship should be. I do not aim to contribute to that debate so much as to reflect on it and its implications for our contemporary American situation. My thoughts fall into six related propositions, the first being that religious faith powerfully and positively shapes our political advocacy and practice.

Our capacity to compartmentalize our lives is often quite remarkable. This was particularly evident as the civil rights movement challenged the southern church in the 1960s; people who were loving and generous in their personal relationships often saw no contradiction in their support of social practices and laws that denied others their humanity. But such compartmentalization is ultimately untenable. Many in my generation found guidance in the writings of Reinhold Niebuhr, whose interpretation of the relation of the religious ethic of love to politics is still helpful today. A love ethic can never be perfectly embodied in politics, he taught, but it nonetheless compels its adherents to seek justice as a proximate public expression of love. To fail to pursue justice in our common life is just as surely a betrayal of the ethic of love as it would be to reject a neighbor's need face-to-face.

William Lee Miller brought the point home in a gloss on Jesus' familiar parable of the Good Samaritan. The Samaritan came upon a man who had been robbed and wounded. He bandaged his wounds and took him to an inn for care and safekeeping, thus proving himself a true neighbor, in contrast to the priest and Levite who "passed by on the other side." What if the Samaritan had come by the same spot next day and found another man robbed and wounded? And then suppose he met wounded and victimized travelers again and again. How long would it take him to conclude that his individual acts of kindness were not enough, that the road needed to be patrolled? "Would there not be something deficient," Miller asked, "in the faith that never [sought] to prevent the attacks on travelers? What if the servant of God would give his last bread to a starving stranger in a bread line, yet never think to ask questions about the economic conditions that cause the bread line to exist?" (Miller 1958, 24).[7]

The civil rights movement led many people of faith to rediscover the Hebrew prophets and their call for justice that "rolled down like waters" (Amos 5:24). Rabbi Abraham Joshua Heschel, who worked closely with Martin Luther King, tellingly placed the call to social justice in the context of prayer, the most personal and "inward" of religious acts:

> Religion as an establishment must remain separated from the government. Yet prayer as a voice of mercy, as a cry for justice, as a plea for gentleness, must not be kept apart. Let the spirit of prayer dominate the world. Let the spirit of prayer interfere in the affairs of man. Prayer is private, a service of the heart; but let concern and compassion born of prayer dominate public life. (Heschel 1996, 261)

This explains what Heschel said upon returning from the voting rights march in Selma in 1963: "I felt my legs were praying" (Waskow 1998).

Translating religious convictions into social action is not always simple or straightforward. In the years prior to World War II, for example, Niebuhr challenged those who interpreted the love ethic to counsel nonresistance and pacifism. Such a view, he said, owed more to Enlightenment notions of human perfectibility than to a "Christian realism" that, in taking full account of human sin and the will to power, recognized "that justice [could] be achieved only by a certain degree of coercion on the one hand, and by resistance to coercion and tyranny on the other hand" (Davis and Good 1960, 148).

While such realism warns against oversimplifying the task of "achieving justice in a sinful world," it also recognizes that world for what it is and thus preserves a tension between religious ideas and their historical manifestations. Our basic American political values have readily identifiable religious roots. But our religious traditions also prompt an ongoing critique of our faltering efforts to realize liberty and justice, just as they offer a corrective to the excesses of individualism and materialism in American life.

My second proposition is that in a pluralistic democracy we must seek common ground with people of diverse traditions and those whose values do not have conventional religious roots. I remember discussions in the 1960s among people whose involvement in the civil rights movement stemmed from religious convictions as to whether persons from radically different backgrounds and traditions could work together effectively for the cause. Of course, the answer to that was yes. We bring our deepest convictions and insights to our political advocacy, but at the same time, we recognize the validity of other traditions and the common ethical ground we share. In politics, we debate the issues, not the doctrines. We debate with people whose theological and philosophical perspectives differ, and we can often find a basis for concerted action. This is the happy experience of American democracy.

My third point is that if we cannot find common ground, there may be good reason for stopping short of embodying our religious and moral precepts in civil law. In the absence of a broader supportive consensus, it is often preferable to leave the individual and communal expression of conscience free.

Theologians have long debated the question put by Thomas Aquinas: "Whether an effect of law is to make men good?" (quoted in Bigongiari 1953, 24–6).[8] Our religious traditions contain lawlike moral codes that continue to shape civil law. There are also reciprocal effects, despite protestations that "you can't legislate morality." The legal order inculcates rudimentary moral standards, and obedience to the law may habituate one to at least the external forms of goodness. But morality is prior to the law, and its imperatives are never exhausted by religious or civil codes. Nor can the legal order compel behavior that is, in the deepest sense, moral. This is partly because of inevitable flaws in human law and partly because law, in its generality, falls short of the individual's moral potential. Most fundamentally, however, it is because the instrumentalities of law and government cannot compel the good will and "clean heart" from which morality springs.

Our religiously inspired judgments as to what is moral and our political judgments as to what can and should be embodied in law are related, but they are not the same thing. Their relationship is problematic even in a homogeneous religious setting. And in a country where multiple religious and ethical traditions flourish, we should move cautiously indeed in enshrining in civil law moral precepts that lack substantial support beyond a specific religious tradition. The U.S. Constitution, former New York governor Mario Cuomo acknowledged, "guarantees my right to try to convince you to adopt my religion's tenet as public law. . . . The question for the religious public official then [becomes]. . . . Should I try?" Cuomo's suggested criterion for crossing that threshold was the presence of consensus, or the "plausibility of achieving that consensus," on the basis of convictions shared in the community at large (Price 2004, 14–5).[9]

It is thus perfectly consistent, for example, for one who is convinced that abortion is always wrong to conclude that it is not prudent to embody a prohibition of abortion in civil law. Other criteria may also apply: For example, should religiously inspired disapproval of certain behaviors, such as same-gender sexual relations, be translated into laws that violate the principles of civil liberty, nondiscrimination, and equal opportunity—or into opposition to laws that would implement these fundamental and broadly shared democratic values? The answer, I believe, is no. Such judgments are partly prudential judgments, based on the necessary ground rules of a pluralistic society. But they are also theologically grounded judgments, based on an understanding of the voluntaristic character of religious obedience and of the limits and dangers—not least, to religious liberty—of placing the authority of the state behind any group's moral agenda.

This leads to my fourth point: that religious toleration and the separation of church and state are essential protections of the freedom of religious expressing and practice. In the midst of the controversy over the use of religion in my first congressional campaign, a local minister allied with the incumbent was quoted as saying that my view represented that of a "pluralistic person in a pluralistic society." That statement is worth examining. I would readily acknowledge commitment to a pluralistic society, a society in which the expression of religious conviction is free and unimpeded. However, that does not mean that I am a "pluralistic person." In fact, the genius of a pluralistic society is its ability to combine a strength of conviction, a rootedness in tradition, with a respect for the convictions and traditions of others. And when we stand up for toleration and religious freedom, we're not suggesting that somehow our religious convictions are weak or indecisive. On the contrary, we're standing up for the strength of those convictions and defending our right to express them.

Governor Cuomo, a practicing Catholic, put it this way: "To assure our freedom, we must allow others the same freedom even if occasionally it produces conduct which we hold to be sinful . . . I protect my right to be a Catholic by preserving your right to believe as a Jew, a Protestant or a non-believer or anything else you choose" (Cuomo 1984, 4–5). That states a basic truth, I believe, about American democracy.

The first amendment to the U.S. Constitution contains two complementary protections of religious freedom: Government is not to "establish" religion, but neither is it to prohibit "the free exercise thereof." There are to be no state-sponsored religious exercises and no religious tests, formal or informal, for political participation or election to office. Those precepts protect the freedom of religious expression we all possess. At the same time, the state is not to discriminate against religion or place undue burdens on religious practice. For example, the so-called equal access statute at the federal level, ensuring that religiously oriented school organizations will not be discriminated against because of their orientation, has been upheld by the Supreme Court (*Westside Community Board of Education v. Mergens* 1990). After school hours, such clubs can use meeting rooms and school facilities on the same basis as other organizations.

Maintaining a delicate and judicious balance between the antiestablishment and free exercise principles is a continuing challenge for our country. Fortunately a serious threat in the form of the so-called Religious Freedom Amendment to the Constitution fell considerably short of the required two-thirds vote in the House of Representatives in 1998. This amendment, a project of the religious right, went considerably beyond the school prayer amendments of years past. It purported to improve on the first amendment in ways that would have broken down the barriers to state-sponsored religious exercises and government aid to sectarian institutions.[10] An impressive alliance of mainline religious organizations worked to defeat the amendment, and it was significant how many of the members opposing it spoke not only of protecting constitutional democracy, of which freedom from religious coercion is a cornerstone, but also of protecting freedom for the unimpeded expression of religious faith and conviction. What religious freedom is about, and what the proposed amendment threatened, is not only civil liberty but also religious faithfulness.

The boundary between establishment and free exercise was also at issue in the 2001–2002 debates over President Bush's faith-based initiative. Religious organizations and congregations had long utilized federal funding to build community centers in urban neighborhoods, provide housing for the elderly and disabled, shelter the homeless, deliver hot meals to elderly shut-ins, and provide other services. They normally carried out these activities through affiliated but legally distinct entities—often called 501(c)(3) organizations from the relevant section of the tax code—which prevented federal funds from being used for religious worship or proselytization and ensured nondiscriminatory practices in hiring and the choice of beneficiaries. This is what Bush sought to change. His legislative proposals and the executive order he ultimately issued weakened the barriers to the funding of sectarian activity and removed them with respect to discrimination in hiring. From the perspective of my district, where faith-based initiatives had flourished for years, this had the appearance of "fixing" a system that was not broken. In any event, it raised serious first amendment questions, which is why the initiative stalled in the Senate and the courts are still sorting out charitable choice issues.

My fifth point is that our religious traditions point up the limitations as well as the possibilities of politics and give us a realistic perspective on political power. These traditions reject cynicism and the placing of arbitrary limits on our aspirations, but they also provide a realistic view of human nature and the pervasiveness of sin and self-interest in society. We should have no illusions about the evils of which human beings, individually and collectively, are capable. Our task in politics therefore becomes not only to utilize power for the common good but also to check the inevitable abuses of power, to make the best of a sinful world. Reinhold Niebuhr's most quoted line is pertinent here: "Man's capacity for justice makes democracy possible; but man's inclination to injustice makes democracy necessary" (Davis and Good 1960, 186). No policy or program, even the most well intentioned, can escape the taint of self-interest and self-seeking. Consequently the task of democracy is not only to realize our positive aspirations but also to provide a check against inevitable miscarriages of justice and abuses of power.

The framers of the Constitution believed that no governmental power could safely go unchecked. They therefore "contriv[ed] the interior structure of the government [so] that its several constituent parts [might], by their mutual relations, be the means of keeping each other in their proper places." James Madison's reflections on these arrangements revealed a persistent streak of Calvinism among these heirs of the Enlightenment:

> It may be a reflection on human nature that such devices should be necessary to control the abuses of government. But what is government itself but the greatest of all reflections on human nature? If men were angels, no government would be necessary. If angels were to govern men, neither external nor internal controls on government would be necessary. In framing a government which is to be administered by men over men, the great difficulty lies in this: You must first enable the government to control the governed; and in the next place oblige it to control itself. A dependence on the people is, no doubt, the primary control on the government; but experience has taught mankind the necessity of auxiliary precautions (Madison 1961, 1992).

Thus do we draw on our religious traditions in recognizing the distortions and dangers to which the exercise of political power is liable and in protecting ourselves against them.

It is important to distinguish this realistic view from the more simplistic antipower ideology that persistently rears its head in American politics. Government is hardly the only realm in which power exists or can be abused; political power can be used to counter or control economic or other kinds of power. Realism requires that we not only attend to the dangers of strengthening a given organ of government but also ask what powers and interests might fill the vacuum if it is weakened. There is nothing automatically efficacious about checkmated governmental institutions; a simplistic distrust of power is sometimes a poor guide to what is required to make institutions function accountably and effectively. What the realism rooted in our religious traditions offers is, rather, an awareness of the admixture of self-interest and self-seeking in all human endeavors, of the necessity to use power deliberately as we pursue the common good, and also of the need for checks and safeguards as we recognize the vulnerability of such power to distortion and abuse.

A final and related point is this: Our religious traditions warn against absolutizing anyone's political power or program, regarding this as a form of idolatry. The very worst kind of pride is often religious pride: equating our own point of view, our own interest or ideology, with the will of God. Here too Heschel spoke with eloquence:

> We must not regard any human institution or object as being an end in itself. Man's achievements in this world are but attempts, and a temple that comes to mean more than a reminder of the living God is an abomination. (Heschel 1972, 415)

There is a story in the book of Samuel that, as far as I know, is unique in the ancient world. King David, at the height of his power and prestige, commits a grievous sin, and the lowly prophet Nathan visits him and calls him to account, pronouncing God's judgment: "Why have you despised the word of the Lord, to do what is evil in his sight?" (2 Samuel 12:9). God's word stands above even David, king of all Israel. The conviction that no person or institution stands above or is to be identified with God's will is at the very heart of our religious traditions.

The American statesman who best understood this was Abraham Lincoln. Recall the words of his second inaugural address, all the more remarkable for being uttered after almost four years of civil war:

> Both [sides] read the same Bible, and pray to the same God; and each invokes His aid against the other. It may seem strange that any men should dare to ask a just God's assistance in wringing their bread from the sweat of other men's faces; but let us judge not, that we be not judged. The prayers of both could not be answered—that of neither has been answered fully. (Stern 1940, 841)

Niebuhr once wrote that this passage "puts the relation of our moral commitments in history to our religious reservations about the partiality of our moral judgments more precisely than, I think, any statesman or theologian has put them"[11](Miller 1980, 8). Lincoln expressed the moral commitment against slavery in uncompromising terms, along with his determination to "finish the work we are in." But there followed the religious reservation, the recognition that ultimate judgment belonged to God alone, the refusal, even in this extreme instance, to presume an absolute identification between his own cause and God's will.

On another occasion, responding to a clergyman who expressed the hope that the Lord was on the side of the Union, Lincoln reportedly said, "I know that the Lord is always on the side of the right. But it is my constant anxiety and prayer that I and this nation should be on the Lord's side" (Carpenter 1867, 282). We are too quick to claim that God is on our side, to claim divine sanction for the program that we are promoting or the power that we seek, and sometimes to demonize our opponents. "As all 'God-fearing' men of all ages," Niebuhr warned, we "are never safe against the temptation of claiming God too simply as the sanctifier of whatever we most fervently desire" (Niebuhr 1952, 173). The crucial question is the one that Lincoln asked: Are we on the Lord's side? We ought never to lose that sense of God's transcendence and of the fallibility of all our human efforts, political and otherwise. This is the ultimate reason for rejecting the political pretensions and religious arrogance of those who equate their own program with God's will. Here too we look not only to the tenets of pluralism and the U.S. Constitution but to the deepest insights of our religious traditions themselves. For these traditions counsel a kind of religious humility, a sense that our own strivings are always subject to God's judgment.

The imperatives of faith will continue to require and inspire political action. The fact that others may put a religious label on policies too easily or quickly or opportunistically does not make the imperative of faith any less compelling. But there are good reasons (rooted not only in democratic experience but also in the theology of divine transcendence and human sinfulness) for refusing to identify any particular ideology or political program with the will of God and for rebuking those who presume to do so. "For my thoughts are not your thoughts, neither are your ways my ways, says the Lord" (Isaiah 55:8).

Primary Sources

8.6

Senator Joseph Lieberman

STATEMENT OF SENATOR JOE LIEBERMAN ON THE NOMINATION OF JOHN ASHCROFT FOR ATTORNEY GENERAL
(FEBRUARY 1, 2001)

I have known John Ashcroft for almost 40 years, as a college classmate, a fellow State Attorney General and a colleague in the Senate. Throughout that time, our views on important issues very often have diverged, but I have never had reason to doubt his sincerity or his integrity. It strikes me in this regard that the often-noted and sometimes derided notion that Senators judge their colleagues more leniently than outsiders misses an important point. It is not that we reflexively defer to our former colleagues. It is instead that we as human beings find it tremendously difficult to pass judgment on those we have worked with and know well. And it is because I have known Senator Ashcroft for so long that I find the conclusion I have reached—which is to oppose his nomination—so awkward and uncomfortable. But that is where my review of the record regarding this nomination and my understanding of the Senate's responsibility under the advice and consent clause lead me. . . .

. . . In short, although I believe that the Constitution casts the Senate's advice role as a limited one and counsels Senators to be cautious in withholding their consent, I nevertheless have opposed nominees where their policy positions, statements or actions made me question whether they would be able to administer the agency they had been nominated to head in a credible and appropriate manner. Regretfully, I conclude that such a determination is again warranted on this critically important nomination—because of the record of the nominee and because of the position for which he has been nominated. . . .

Before yielding the floor, I would like to comment on one more issue that has come up during the consideration of this particular nomination: Senator Ashcroft's religious beliefs and his public profession of his faith. During the time since the President nominated Senator Ashcroft, many have argued—too often privately—that Senator Ashcroft's deeply held beliefs and his religious practices somehow cast suspicion on his ability to serve as Attorney General. I emphatically reject—and am confident my colleagues will also reject—any suggestion that Senator Ashcroft's religious beliefs bear in any manner at all on the consideration of his nomination.

All across this nation, tens of millions of Americans of a multitude of faiths daily and weekly make professions of faith privately and publicly that elevate, order and give purpose to their lives and enrich the life of our society. To suggest that all of us who believe with a steadfast faith in a Supreme Being as the Universe's ultimate Sovereign have an obligation to mute one of our faith's central tenets if we wish to serve in government is not to advance the separation of Church and State, but instead to erect a barrier to public service by Americans of faith which is totally unacceptable. To consider the private religious practices of a nominee or a candidate for public office which are different from most—whether Pentecostal Christian, Orthodox Jewish, Shia Muslim or any other denomination—as a limitation on that person's capacity to hold that office is profoundly unfair and wrong.

Nowhere in the First Amendment or anywhere else in the Constitution or in the jurisprudence surrounding them is there any suggestion that of all the values systems that those in public life are permitted to draw upon to inform their views and their actions, religion stands alone as being off limits. Let us remember that the Constitution and the Bill of Rights were drafted by people of faith whose belief in the Creator was the direct source of the rights with which they endowed us and which we enjoy to this day. To suggest that one may justify his or her views on abortion, environmental protection or any other issue with reference to a system of secular values, but not by drawing upon a tradition of religious beliefs, seems to me to be at odds not only with the freedom of religion and expression enshrined in the First Amendment, but also with the daily experience of the vast majority of our fellow citizens. The First Amendment tells us that we may not impose our religion on others. It most decidedly does not say that we may not ourselves use our religion to inform our public and private statements and positions.

So it is Senator Ashcroft's record, not his religion, that we should judge today. I admire Senator Ashcroft for his private and public adherence to his faith, but for the reasons stated above, based on his record, I will vote against his confirmation.

8.7

Former U.S. Senator and Representative Rick Santorum, R-PA.

THE PRESS AND PEOPLE OF FAITH IN POLITICS
(AUGUST 2008)

Thank you. I appreciate the opportunity to be here and share some thoughts with you. And actually I very much look forward to dialog and discussion and questions you might have.

Terry (Mattingly) gives a very gracious introduction, and I think what you can gather from that introduction is that I am someone who was in public life whose faith was very much, for good or bad, where I wore it on my sleeve. I didn't deliberately do it that way. But to me, the old saying that "you can't check your faith at the door when you go into your office" really meant something to me. You were either a person whose faith was important in every aspect of your life, or faith really wasn't important to you.

And so when I got into the United States Senate, believe it or not, a very interesting story talked about many times to groups, of my own journey really accelerated when I came to the Senate. I came to the United States Senate, and I found God, which is not something I would not say is a common thing, but it's more common than you might think. That leaders in the United States, particularly folks on the Republican side of the aisle—which I always term as the party of faith—you'll find, I'm always amazed, at the number of my colleagues whose faith has deepened because of their political involvement and because of the responsibility being thrust upon them.

And so that happened to me, and as a result, I felt compelled to be much more outspoken about the role that faith played in my own public life. And as a result of that, I was labeled by the media and my opponents as a theocrat. That somehow because I dared to allow faith to influence the decisions that I made—not dictate, but certainly influence the decisions that I made—that I was somehow trying to impose a theocratic rule over the United States.

What I found overwhelmingly in the American press corps is a bunch of non-believers who don't understand faith whatsoever. I mean, the idea of TIME Magazine naming me one of the top 25 evangelicals was sort of funny, if it wasn't so pathetic that they don't understand what they're even talking about. At least (Richard John) Neuhaus, who I think would have been the only other Catholic—I think I've talked about this before. But he was first a Protestant. So you can at least—Neuhaus was a convert—so you might sort of peg him as an evangelical.

But the press in this country is overwhelmingly ignorant—completely ignorant—of faith. Most of the people in the press, I've found, have no faith themselves. And when you discuss faith, it's as if you're discussing voo-doo or some sort of bizarre theory that's sort of nice if you want to go to church on Sunday and you want to do that. But it has no application to the governing of the United States because in their mind this is a very secular country that separates church and state. They have accepted the idea that faith is illegitimate in the public square.

And the idea now that you see the Democrats trying to come and talk about faith is, to me, just a charade. I don't think it's serious at all. I think it is purely a political calculation. I think that they know that they are doing poorly among certain voters who care about that. So they are just making a sob (sic) to them saying, "Look, we understand you. We can talk your language." Not to say that there aren't some who are sincere. But I'm talking overall, the Democratic Party—with the Nancy Pelosis, the Harry Reids, the Howard Deans, the folks who are orchestrating this effort—are using probably some people, who are in fact devout believers who are Democrats, as pawns in an attempt to try to get votes or at least decrease the intensity of the vote against them in certain states where they know if they don't do that, they're gonna have a hard time winning presidential elections or other elections.

So, to me, this issue, like many others in America, is evidence of what I see as a very great divide in American politics. And it's on cultural grounds; it's on religious grounds; it's on national-security grounds. This is a country that is wrestling with its own Judeo-Christian identity. And the party of the left, which is the Democratic Party, the secular party, which is the Democratic Party, the party of Europe, which is the Democratic Party.

It was just such an affirmation of this belief to see Barack Obama in Germany. He is the party of Europe. They love him over there. Why? Because it is a very secular world. It's a very secular culture. It's a socialistic culture. It is exactly what Barack Obama wants to see America. It's exactly what Howard Dean envisions for America. If you look at everything they do, they point to the journey of Western Europe as the journey they want to replicate here in America.

This is the better society. When I hear Barack Obama talk about how flawed — deeply flawed — America is and how much change is necessary, he speaks in wonderful glowing terms without getting specific. What he really wants is a more secular, government-driven, top-down, elitist culture, which is more reflective of what we're seeing in Western Europe.

And the press is probably one step ahead of him, I would argue. I can tell you experiences I've had with members of the press corps that have come up to me quietly, almost whispering in my ear, and say, "I'm a believer. Don't tell anybody. I don't want to be outed in this country." It is that bad. And I'm sure you've had lots of folks you've talked to here in the press corps who'll tell you that's not the case, who'll tell you that the press corps here and the media here is representative of a wide swath of different viewpoints. And that faith is important to them. It's baloney. It's absolute baloney. The reporting does not reflect it.

And I can tell you that the people that I've dealt with, they have a fundamental misunderstanding and mistrust of people of faith in public life. They see them as a threat to what they see as the secular religion of America.

And so, I'm glad that you're here and that you're interested in this topic. It is a battle that many of us, and I think many across America—Terry talks about (the state of Pennsylvania being) Philadelphia, Pittsburgh and Alabama in between—that the Alabama part of Pennsylvania, and in fact, not Philadelphia, but much of Pittsburgh, which is a socially conservative town. They see what's going on. They see the attempts of the mainstream media. They see the attempts of Hollywood, and the elites in academia, trying to change this culture from the top down. And trying to do things, as I make the argument in my book,[12] to break down the Church and to break down the family and to make it more dependent on the other institutions of our society, which they control, which is the media, academia and the government.

And so that is sort of the life struggle here in America. We are, in my opinion, inching ever more closely and successfully because the people who tell the story, in the mainstream media, Hollywood and academia have a lot more power right now than mom and dad at home. And churches, if you look at the where the future of America goes, and look at what children spend their time consuming, the average American kid spends 7 plus hours a day—teenagers and younger—spend 7 plus hours a day in front of some media content. Computers. Video games. Television. Movie. CD. They're consuming media 7 plus hours a day.

They obviously, if they're in school six hours plus a day, they're consuming from the liberal academia, which is public schools through higher education. Contrast that with the average American kid spends 10 minutes talking with their mom or dad a day. And on average goes to church, most kids and most Americans still go to church, on average spent 10 minutes a day in church.

So compare the time the parents and the churches, which are the counter-cultural trends, versus what children are consuming from the mainstream media, which is all on the other side. And you can see that America is in the process of violent change.

And the media, particularly reporters, are part and parcel of that because they have been educated at those institutions, elitist institutions, and they are in the media, whether it's Hollywood or whether it's the news media, which has a very definite point of view and does not tolerate people. They are completely intolerant of people who have different points of view when it comes to faith.

If you go back 50 years, I don't think you would find that in the mainstream media. You certainly wouldn't find that in Hollywood. Hollywood was not a seedbed of radical thought in trying to transform the culture. The mainstream media was much more in touch with traditional American values.

Academia was never, for the last hundred years, never in touch with traditional American values. And the fact that the elites have gone to those institutions and have ended up in the newsroom and ended up in Hollywood and ended up in those places. They have sown the seeds that have are now being planted in the broader American culture.

So that's how I see it.

8.8

Representative Nancy Pelosi

NANCY PELOSI DELIVERS SPEECH AT NATIONAL HISPANIC PRAYER BREAKFAST
(JUNE 16, 2005)

Buenos dias. Gracias, Reverend Hector Cortez, for your kind words and warm welcome.

President Luis Cortes, it is wonderful to see you again. After I addressed this gathering two years ago, I was honored by your visit to my office to outline an initiative that you had just launched—the Hispanic Capacity Project. Congratulations on the progress this project has made in meeting the needs of the community, and truly providing, "nueva esperanza."

Congratulations also on being named one of the 25 most influential evangelicals in America by *Time* magazine. That is a strong measure of your leadership, and the influence that Nueva Esperanza has had in improving the lives of so many Hispanic families.

It is an honor to join all of you once again as House Democratic Leader. As you may know, I come from San Francisco. St. Francis of Assisi is our patron saint. It was St. Francis who said, "Preach the gospel, and sometimes use words."

Thank you for preaching the gospel through your work. After all, it is our faith that enables us to lift the work we do to a higher purpose. It is our faith that leads us to believe in the dignity and worth of every person, and to pursue the policies that affirm that value. And it is our faith that teaches us to respect the diversity of all of God's children, and to demonstrate that respect by allowing all people to live up to their God-given potential.

That is why so many of the policies we pursue should not be viewed as legislation, or regulations, or programs. They should be statements of our values.

The Bible says "Honor thy father and thy mother." Preaching the gospel in our deeds means working to guarantee the strength of Social Security, which is such a life-line for so many Hispanic seniors, survivors, and people with disabilities. Millions of Hispanic seniors depend on Social Security for more than half of their retirement income. And for the majority of elderly Hispanic women, Social Security represents their only retirement income.

We must not let Social Security's guaranteed benefit become a guaranteed gamble.

In the Book of Hebrews it is written: "Make level paths for your feet, so that the lame may not be disabled, but rather healed." Today, creating those 'level paths' means providing health care access for all.

Right now, one in three Hispanics under the age of 65 does not have access to health insurance. A child's chance to grow and learn requires good health; a family's chance to succeed depends on the physical ability to work; and all of those depend on access to health care.

Democrats believe that access to health care is a right, and not a privilege. Whether it is fighting for jobs, or increasing the minimum wage, or access to health care, or pro-tecting Social Security—all of the battles we fight are to strengthen America by allowing more people to achieve its promise.

Nowhere is this clearer than in two areas that, in combination, have truly made our country the great nation we are today: immigration and education.

In Leviticus, the Israelites are told by God: "When a newcomer lives with you in your land, do not mistreat him. The newcomer living with you must be treated as one of your native-born. Love him as yourself, for you were newcomers in Egypt."

We are all newcomers to this country. America was built by newcomers who brought their hope, optimism, and determination to build a better life for themselves and their families.

With each wave of immigrants, America has become not only more diverse, but also more open and equal; not only culturally richer, but also spiritually stronger. And it is your faith, commitment to family, and love of country that strengthen America today.

Your story is the story of America. And together, we can write the next chapter. To do that, we need a thoughtful, comprehensive immigration policy.

What we don't need is vigilantism, and that is why I support the McCain-Kennedy-Gutierrez-Kolbe bill. This initiative will truly secure our borders. It will allow families to be reunified. And it will allow millions of immigrant workers to come out of the shadowy world they are now forced to inhabit, and work openly with the respect they deserve. I hope the President will join me in supporting it.

And America truly becomes the land of opportunity for the newest Americans when we guarantee a quality education for all. I know that education is of the highest priority to the Hispanic community.

Families cannot do it alone. It requires a strong public policy commitment. You are doing your part, and more Latinos are going to college than ever before.

But as we send our young people to college, we must not send them into crushing debt. We must also enable more Latino high school students to graduate with the prospect of going on to college by reducing the high school dropout rate. And we must enable every elementary school-age child to learn and to dream in safe, modern schools where children can learn, teachers can teach, and parents can participate.

Just this week, House Democrats announced a comprehensive education agenda called "Strengthening our Schools." This initiative will mean better schools, better teachers, and a better chance to go to college for the 8 million Latino children currently in our schools. Education is truly the doorway to opportunity, and we must do more to open that door wider to all Americans.

Our Founding Fathers understood that faith was a deeply personal commitment, but they also recognized that Americans are a faith-filled people, and the personally-held faith of millions leads to great acts of conscience, charity, and community.

In 1960, when John F. Kennedy was running for President, his critics raised questions about whether his faith should disqualify him from the presidency. Then-Senator Kennedy went to a gathering of ministers in Houston, and said in his address the issue is "not what kind of church I believe in . . . but what kind of America I believe in."

The America he believed in is the one we believe in today: one in which each person can practice his or her own faith in his or her own way; one in which the hopes and dreams of every child are met with an education system that gives them the knowledge and opportunity to achieve them; one in which we make the stunning advances in health and medicine available to all who need them; one in which poverty is eradicated, and the strength of our economy grants all who are willing to work an opportunity to succeed; one in which a lifetime of work provides a retirement of dignity and independence; and one in which we recognize that our strength comes from our diversity.

This is certainly true of the Democrats in the House who I am privileged to lead.

There are more Hispanics serving in the House of Representatives today than at any time in American history. This includes Congressman Bob Menendez of New Jersey, Chairman of the Democratic Caucus, the first Latino in history elected to the Leadership in Congress.

In addition to the contributions Hispanic-Americans are making to the professional and civic life of America, we are particularly grateful to those who are serving in America's defense. Overseas, more than 200 Hispanic-American soldiers have given their lives in Iraq and Afghanistan, and hundreds more have been wounded. We mourn the loss of those who have made the supreme sacrifice. And we are deeply grateful for the courage, the patriotism, and the sacrifice of all who are serving.

Our mission is to build an America and a future worthy of their sacrifice. An America that is strong, secure, and welcoming. An America that is a place of "nueva esperanza."

That is the America we believe in. That is the America we aspire to create. And by working together and preaching the gospel—sometimes using words—that is the America we can achieve.

Thank you. God bless you. And God bless America.

8.9

Senator Barack Obama

"Call to Renewal" Keynote Address
(June 28, 2006)

Today I'd like to talk about the connection between religion and politics and perhaps offer some thoughts about how we can sort through some of the often bitter arguments that we've been seeing over the last several years. . . . [and] tackle head-on the mutual suspicion that sometimes exists between religious America and secular America.

I want to give you an example that I think illustrates this fact. As some of you know, during the 2004 U.S. Senate General Election I ran against a gentleman named Alan Keyes. Mr. Keyes is well-versed in the Jerry Falwell–Pat Robertson style of rhetoric that often labels progressives as both immoral and godless.

Indeed, Mr. Keyes announced towards the end of the campaign that "Jesus Christ would not vote for Barack Obama. Christ would not vote for Barack Obama because Barack Obama has behaved in a way that it is inconceivable for Christ to have behaved."

Jesus Christ would not vote for Barack Obama.

Now, I was urged by some of my liberal supporters not to take this statement seriously, to essentially ignore it.

But what they didn't understand. . . . was that I had to take Mr. Keyes seriously, for he claimed to speak for my religion, and my God. He claimed knowledge of certain truths.

Mr. Obama says he's a Christian, he was saying, and yet he supports a lifestyle that the Bible calls an abomination.

Mr. Obama says he's a Christian, but supports the destruction of innocent and sacred life.

And so what would my supporters have me say? Should I say that a literalist reading of the Bible was folly? Should I say that Mr. Keyes, who is a Roman Catholic, should ignore the teachings of the Pope?

Unwilling to go there, I answered with what has come to be the typically liberal response in such debates—namely, I said that we live in a pluralistic society, that I can't impose my own religious views on another, that I was running to be the U.S. Senator of Illinois and not the Minister of Illinois.

But Mr. Keyes's implicit accusation that I was not a true Christian nagged at me, and I was also aware that my answer did not adequately address the role my faith has in guiding my own values and my own beliefs.

Now, my dilemma was by no means unique. In a way, it reflected the broader debate we've been having in this country for the last thirty years over the role of religion in politics.

For some time now, there has been plenty of talk among pundits and pollsters that the political divide in this country has fallen sharply along religious lines. Indeed, the single biggest "gap" in party affiliation among white Americans today is not between men and women, or those who reside in so-called Red States and those who reside in Blue, but between those who attend church regularly and those who don't.

Conservative leaders have been all too happy to exploit this gap, consistently reminding evangelical Christians that Democrats disrespect their values and dislike their Church, while suggesting to the rest of the country that religious Americans care only about issues like abortion and gay marriage; school prayer and intelligent design.

Democrats, for the most part, have taken the bait. At best, we may try to avoid the conversation about religious values altogether, fearful of offending anyone and claiming that—regardless of our personal beliefs—constitutional principles tie our hands. At worst, there are some liberals who dismiss religion in the public square as inherently irrational or intolerant, insisting on a caricature of religious Americans that paints them as fanatical, or thinking that the very word "Christian" describes one's political opponents, not people of faith.

Now, such strategies of avoidance may work for progressives when our opponent is Alan Keyes. But over the long haul, I think we make a mistake when we fail to acknowledge the power of faith in people's lives . . . and I think it's time that we join a serious debate about how to reconcile faith with our modern, pluralistic democracy.

And if we're going to do that then we first need to understand that Americans are a religious people. 90 percent of us believe in God, 70 percent affiliate themselves with an organized religion, 38 percent call themselves committed Christians, and substantially more people in America believe in angels than they do in evolution.

This religious tendency is not simply the result of successful marketing by skilled preachers or the draw of popular mega-churches. In fact, it speaks to a hunger that's deeper than that—a hunger that goes beyond any particular issue or cause. . . .

And I speak with some experience on this matter. I was not raised in a particularly religious household, as undoubtedly many in the audience were. My father, who returned to Kenya when I was just two, was born Muslim but as an adult became an atheist. My mother, whose parents were non-practicing Baptists and Methodists, was probably one of the most spiritual and kindest people I've ever known, but grew up with a healthy skepticism of organized religion herself. As a consequence, so did I.

It wasn't until after college, when I went to Chicago to work as a community organizer for a group of Christian churches, that I confronted my own spiritual dilemma.

I was working with churches, and the Christians who I worked with recognized themselves in me. They saw that I knew their Book and that I shared their values and sang their songs. But they sensed that a part of me that remained removed, detached, that I was an observer in their midst.

And in time, I came to realize that something was missing as well—that without a vessel for my beliefs, without a commitment to a particular community of faith, at some level I would always remain apart, and alone.

And if it weren't for the particular attributes of the historically black church, I may have accepted this fate. But as the months passed in Chicago, I found myself drawn—not just to work with the church, but to be in the church.

For one thing, I believed and still believe in the power of the African-American religious tradition to spur social change, a power made real by some of the leaders here today. Because of its past, the black church understands in an intimate way the Biblical call to feed the hungry and cloth the naked and challenge powers and principalities. And in its historical struggles for freedom and the rights of man, I was able to see faith as more than just a comfort to the weary or a hedge against death, but rather as an active, palpable agent in the world. As a source of hope.

And perhaps it was out of this intimate knowledge of hardship—the grounding of faith in struggle—that the church offered me a second insight, one that I think is important to emphasize today.

Faith doesn't mean that you don't have doubts.

You need to come to church in the first place precisely because you are first of this world, not apart from it. You need to embrace Christ precisely because you have sins to wash away—because you are human and need an ally in this difficult journey.

It was because of these newfound understandings that I was finally able to walk down the aisle of Trinity United Church of Christ on 95th Street in the South Side of Chicago one day and affirm my Christian faith. It came about as a choice, and not an epiphany. I didn't fall out in church. The questions I had didn't magically disappear. But kneeling beneath that cross on the South Side, I felt that I heard God's spirit beckoning me. I submitted myself to His will, and dedicated myself to discovering His truth.

That's a path that has been shared by millions upon millions of Americans—evangelicals, Catholics, Protestants, Jews and Muslims alike; some since birth, others at certain turning points in their lives. It is not something they set apart from the rest of their beliefs and values. In fact, it is often what drives their beliefs and their values.

And that is why that, if we truly hope to speak to people where they're at—to communicate our hopes and values in a way that's relevant to their own—then as progressives, we cannot abandon the field of religious discourse.

Because when we ignore the debate about what it means to be a good Christian or Muslim or Jew; when we discuss religion only in the negative sense of where or how it should not be practiced, rather than in the positive sense of what it tells us about our obligations towards one another. . . . others will fill the vacuum, those with the most insular views of faith, or those who cynically use religion to justify partisan ends. . . .

I am not suggesting that every progressive suddenly latch on to religious terminology—that can be dangerous. Nothing is more transparent than inauthentic expressions of faith. As Jim has mentioned, some politicians come and clap—off rhythm—to the choir. We don't need that.

In fact, because I do not believe that religious people have a monopoly on morality, I would rather have someone who is grounded in morality and ethics, and who is also secular, affirm their morality and ethics and values without pretending that they're something they're not. They don't need to do that. None of us need to do that.

But what I am suggesting is this—secularists are wrong when they ask believers to leave their religion at the door before entering into the public square. Frederick Douglass, Abraham Lincoln, Williams Jennings Bryan, Dorothy Day, Martin Luther King—indeed, the majority of great reformers in American history—were not only motivated by faith, but repeatedly used religious language to argue for their cause. So to say that men and women should not inject their "personal morality" into public policy debates is a practical absurdity. Our law is by definition a codification of morality, much of it grounded in the Judeo-Christian tradition.

Moreover, if we progressives shed some of these biases, we might recognize some overlapping values that both religious and secular people share when it comes to the moral and material direction of our country. We might recognize that the call to sacrifice on behalf of the next generation, the need to think in terms of "thou" and not just "I," resonates in religious congregations all across the country. And we might realize that we have the ability to reach out to the evangelical community and engage millions of religious Americans in the larger project of American renewal. . . .

While I've already laid out some of the work that progressive leaders need to do, I want to talk a little bit about what conservative leaders need to do—some truths they need to acknowledge.

For one, they need to understand the critical role that the separation of church and state has played in preserving not only our democracy, but the robustness of our religious practice. Folks tend to forget that during our founding, it wasn't the atheists or the civil libertarians who were the most effective champions of the First Amendment. It was the persecuted minorities, it was Baptists like John Leland who didn't want the established churches to impose their views on folks who were getting happy out in the fields and teaching the scripture to slaves. It was the forbearers of the evangelicals who were the most adamant about not mingling government with religious, because they did not want state-sponsored religion hindering their ability to practice their faith as they understood it.

Moreover, given the increasing diversity of America's population, the dangers of sectarianism have never been greater. Whatever we once were, we are no longer just a Christian nation; we are also a Jewish nation, a Muslim nation, a Buddhist nation, a Hindu nation, and a nation of nonbelievers. . . .

This brings me to my second point. Democracy demands that the religiously motivated translate their concerns into universal, rather than religion-specific, values. It requires that their proposals be subject to argument, and amenable to reason. I may be opposed to abortion for religious reasons, but if I seek to pass a law banning the practice, I cannot simply point to the teachings of my church or evoke God's will. I have to explain why abortion violates some principle that is accessible to people of all faiths, including those with no faith at all.

Now this is going to be difficult for some who believe in the inerrancy of the Bible, as many evangelicals do. But in a pluralistic democracy, we have no choice. Politics depends on our ability to persuade each other of common aims based on a common reality. It involves the compromise, the art of what's possible. At some fundamental level, religion does not allow for compromise. It's the art of the impossible. If God has spoken, then followers are expected to live up to God's edicts, regardless of the consequences. To base one's life on such uncompromising commitments may be sublime, but to base our policy making on such commitments would be a dangerous thing. . . .

Finally, any reconciliation between faith and democratic pluralism requires some sense of proportion.

This goes for both sides.

Even those who claim the Bible's inerrancy make distinctions between Scriptural edicts, sensing that some passages—the Ten Commandments, say, or a belief in Christ's divinity—are central to Christian faith, while others are more culturally specific and may be modified to accommodate modern life.

The American people intuitively understand this, which is why the majority of Catholics practice birth control and some of those opposed to gay marriage nevertheless are opposed to a Constitutional amendment to ban it. Religious leadership need not accept such wisdom in counseling their flocks, but they should recognize this wisdom in their politics.

But a sense of proportion should also guide those who police the boundaries between church and state. Not every mention of God in public is a breach to the wall of separation—context matters. It is doubtful that children reciting the Pledge of Allegiance feel oppressed or brainwashed as a consequence of muttering the phrase "under God." I didn't. Having voluntary student prayer groups use school property to meet should not be a threat, any more than its use by the High School Republicans should threaten Democrats. And one can envision certain faith-based programs—targeting ex-offenders or substance abusers—that offer a uniquely powerful way of solving problems.

So we all have some work to do here. But I am hopeful that we can bridge the gaps that exist and overcome the prejudices each of us bring to this debate. And I have faith that millions of believing Americans want that to happen. No matter how religious they may or may not be, people are tired of seeing faith used as a tool of attack. They don't want faith used to belittle or to divide. They're tired of hearing folks deliver more screed than sermon. Because in the end, that's not how they think about faith in their own lives. . . .

8.10

Senator John Danforth

ONWARD, MODERATE CHRISTIAN SOLDIERS
(JUNE 17, 2007)

It would be an oversimplification to say that America's culture wars are now between people of faith and nonbelievers. People of faith are not of one mind, whether on specific issues like stem cell research and government intervention in the case of Terri Schiavo,[13] or the more general issue of how religion relates to politics. In recent years, conservative Christians have presented themselves as representing the one authentic Christian perspective on politics. With due respect for our conservative friends, equally devout Christians come to very different conclusions.

It is important for those of us who are sometimes called moderates to make the case that we, too, have strongly held Christian convictions, that we speak from the depths of our beliefs, and that our approach to politics is at least as faithful as that of those who are more conservative. Our difference concerns the extent to which government should, or even can, translate religious beliefs into the laws of the state.

People of faith have the right, and perhaps the obligation, to bring their values to bear in politics. Many conservative Christians approach politics with a certainty that they know God's truth, and that they can advance the kingdom of God through governmental action. So they have developed a political agenda that they believe advances God's kingdom, one that includes efforts to "put God back" into the public square and to pass a constitutional amendment intended to protect marriage from the perceived threat of homosexuality.

Moderate Christians are less certain about when and how our beliefs can be translated into statutory form, not because of a lack of faith in God but because of a healthy acknowledgement of the limitations of human beings. Like conservative Christians, we attend church, read the Bible and say our prayers.

But for us, the only absolute standard of behavior is the commandment to love our neighbors as ourselves. Repeatedly in the Gospels, we find that the Love Commandment takes precedence when it conflicts with laws. We struggle to follow that commandment as we face the realities of everyday living, and we do not agree that our responsibility to live as Christians can be codified by legislators.

When, on television, we see a person in a persistent vegetative state, one who will never recover, we believe that allowing the natural and merciful end to her ordeal is more loving than imposing government power to keep her hooked up to a feeding tube.

When we see an opportunity to save our neighbors' lives through stem cell research, we believe that it is our duty to pursue that research, and to oppose legislation that would impede us from doing so.

We think that efforts to haul references of God into the public square, into schools and courthouses, are far more apt to divide Americans than to advance faith.

Following a Lord who reached out in compassion to all human beings, we oppose amending the Constitution in a way that would humiliate homosexuals.

For us, living the Love Commandment may be at odds with efforts to encapsulate Christianity in a political agenda. We strongly support the separation of church and state, both because that principle is essential to holding together a diverse country, and because the policies of the state always fall short of the demands of faith. Aware that even our most passionate ventures into politics are efforts to carry the treasure of religion in the earthen vessel of government, we proceed in a spirit of humility lacking in our conservative colleagues.

In the decade since I left the Senate, American politics has been characterized by two phenomena: the increased activism of the Christian right, especially in the Republican Party, and the collapse of bipartisan collegiality. I do not think it is a stretch to suggest a relationship between the two. To assert that I am on God's side and you are not, that I know God's will and you do not, and that I will use the power of government to advance my understanding of God's kingdom is certain to produce hostility.

By contrast, moderate Christians see ourselves, literally, as moderators. Far from claiming to possess God's truth, we claim only to be imperfect seekers of the truth. We reject the notion that religion should present a series of wedge issues useful at election time for energizing a political base. We believe it is God's work to practice humility, to wear tolerance on our sleeves, to reach out to those with whom we disagree, and to overcome the meanness we see in today's politics.

For us, religion should be inclusive, and it should seek to bridge the differences that separate people. We do not exclude from worship those whose opinions differ from ours. Following a Lord who sat at the table with tax collectors and sinners, we welcome to the Lord's table all who would come. Following a Lord who cited love of God and love of neighbor as encompassing all the commandments, we reject a political agenda that displaces that love. Christians who hold these convictions ought to add their clear voice of moderation to the debate on religion in politics.

Notes

1. Editors' note: In chapter 8, Benson and Williams describe six types of religion present in the U.S. Congress: Legalistic, Self-Concerned, Integrated, People-Concerned, Nontraditional, and Nominal. These are ranked on thirteen different scales, each categorized into theological emphases, views of the institutional church, and religious themes present. The first four types hold definite similarities—members of these groups tend to speak well of the church/society relationship, acknowledge the importance of religion in their lives, attend religious services with some degree of regularity, and are able to speak somewhat knowledgeably about religion. However, while these four types share these characteristics, they are, in fact, distinct groups with separate patterns of behavior based upon these basic underlying principles. The last two groups are also distinctive, even in regard to foundational beliefs. The Nontraditionals see God as more of an uninvolved, abstract higher power, a view lending itself to contemporary accusations of secular humanism. Finally, the Nominalists are those who show little enthusiasm for religion; personal commitment is low, and maintaining a light façade of religious involvement is most likely done for the sake of expediency. (For more on this, see Benson and Williams, ch. 8, pp. 107–139.)

2. The author wishes to thank Lyman Kellstedt, Corwin Smidt and John Green for their assistance on the research project reported here.

3. Here we use data from the 1990 Glenmary Research Center's census of religious bodies (Bradley et al. 1990). The allocation of membership by congressional district was carried out by John C. Green, a member of the research team producing the current project. His estimates have been used in other studies of congressional voting (e.g. Oldmixon et al. 2005).

4. Interview with the author, July 19, 2000.

5. The Democrats of the 89th Congress, during the Johnson Administration, offer stiff competition.

6. *Fox News Sunday,* November 7, 2004.

7. See Luke 10:29–37.

8. On the "clean heart," see Psalm 51:10.

9. "As I understood my own religion," Cuomo said of his Catholicism, "it required me to accept the restraints it imposed in my own life, but it did not require that I seek to impose all of them on all New Yorkers."

10. The text of the proposed amendment was as follows: "To secure the people's right to acknowledge God according to the dictates of conscience: Neither the United States nor any State shall establish any official religion, but the people's right to pray and to recognize their religious beliefs, heritage, or traditions on public property, including schools, shall not be infringed. Neither the United States nor any State shall require any person to join in prayer or other religious activity, prescribe school prayers, discriminate against religion, or deny equal access to a benefit on account of religion" (House Joint Resolution 78, 105th Congress). My floor statement on the proposal may be found in *Congressional Record,* daily ed., June 4, 1998, pp. H4074-75; also see the statements of Reps. Vic Fazio and Bill Hefner, pp. H4093-94.

11. I am drawing here on Miller's insightful exegesis. For further exposition of the Second Inaugural as "almost a perfect model of the difficult but not impossible task of remaining loyal and responsible toward the moral treasures of a free civilization on the one hand while yet having some religious vantage point over the struggle," with an application of the model to the post-World War II conflict with communism, see Niebuhr 1952, 171–4.

12. Santorum, Rick. "It Takes A Family: Conservatism and the Common Good" ISI Books, Wilmington, Delaware, 2005.

13. Editors' note: Between 1998 and 2005, a legal battle in the Florida state courts over the removal of a feeding tube from a brain-damaged woman, Terri Schiavo, raged between Schiavo's husband, who believed his wife to be in a persistent vegetative state, and her parents, who believed Schiavo to be capable of some recovery. After the U.S. Supreme Court refused to hear appeals several times, members of Congress and President George W. Bush passed an emergency bill forcing the case into the U.S. District Courts. However, the District Court refused to overturn the order, thus upholding the decision of the Florida state courts, siding with Schiavo's husband. A final Supreme Court appeal from Schiavo's parents was refused. This case raised questions of both the right to die and of government and judicial intervention. It also became a public rallying point for various interest groups on either side of the debate.

CHAPTER 9

RELIGION AND THE SUPREME COURT

Introduction

At least since Chief Justice Marshall's 1803 declaration in *Marbury v. Madison*, that "it is emphatically the province and duty of the judicial department to say what the law is," federal judges have had the power to make law. The Supreme Court and other federal judges continue to follow Justice Marshall's charge in this most famous case—"saying" what the law is, in some cases mechanically applying clear principles to new facts, but in many other cases crafting new principles from debated propositions and reasons. Such behavior applies to all of constitutional law, including the First Amendment's religion clauses.

In the integrative essay that opens this chapter, Paul Wahlbeck examines Supreme Court judicial decision making in religion cases through three common academic approaches—as policy decisions reflecting the preferences of the justices deciding the case, as reasoned legal conclusions closely following legal precedents, and, third, as strategic decisions determined by the political context inside and outside the Court. Each approach provides partial insight into the Court's decisions on religion cases, but Wahlbeck finds that strategic issues, particularly internal ones facing individual justices seeking to shape the majority opinion, have the greatest explanatory power.

Thomas Buckley focuses on Blaine amendments, constitutional provisions in more than two-thirds of the states that demand stricter church/state separation than the federal First Amendment requires. Buckley notes the partisan and anti-Catholic roots of such amendments. On their face, Blaine amendments restrict government support of any sectarian school, service, or agency. In effect, supporters sought to buttress a pre-existing Protestant culture in schools and other public institutions and weaken potential competitors, particularly Catholic schools.

The next selection, an excerpt from Jeffrey Toobin's *The Nine*, casts light on a newly successful strategy of lowering the separationist wall and its chief contemporary proponent, Jay Sekulow, of the American Center on Law and Justice (ACLJ). Essentially, Sekulow developed the legal strategy of defending religious expression as free speech and found a receptive audience in recent Supreme Courts.

One perennial issue facing the federal courts is public display of religious symbols—crosses in military cemeteries, "In God We Trust" on our currency, and displays of religious symbols in or near state and local government buildings. An excerpt from *A People's History of the Supreme Court* by Peter Irons discusses the opinions in two "Ten Commandments" cases decided in 2005, *McCreary County v. ACLU*, which struck down a Kentucky display, and *Van Orden v. Perry*, which upheld a slightly different display in Texas.

The final research piece, a short excerpt from David O'Brien's *Storm Center*, briefly reviews the religious background of Supreme Court justices, and the accidental, intermittent, and short-lived "Catholic" and "Jewish" seats of the twentieth century. As he shows, the Supreme Court began as a firm bastion of mainline Protestant establishment but no longer follows that model.

The primary sources section includes excerpts from a few of the many landmark Supreme Court religion cases. First are three major "free exercise" cases—*Cantwell v. Connecticut* (1940), *Sherbert v. Verner* (1963), and *Employment Division v. Smith* (1990)—that illustrate the unsettled nature and fine line-drawing of many of these cases. Similarly, the chapter excerpts three major establishment cases, *Lemon v. Kurtzman* (1971), and its famous but ill-followed three-part test, *Zelman v. Simmons-Harris* (2002), which appears to break new ground in permissible public–religious cooperation, and *Locke v. Davey* (2004), a less faith-friendly ruling that illustrates the continued role of the Supreme Court in drawing the boundaries of church and state.

The history of the Supreme Court and its rulings indicates an erratic pattern of support for some aspects of faith in the public square. The founders accepted state laws that permitted established churches while firmly asserting no federal establishment of religion. And a look behind the surface of the separationist Blaine amendment reveals attempts to support one religious tradition at the expense of all others. In this context, Supreme Court decisions of the last few decades fit the longer pattern of ambivalent support of faith in the public square.

Integrative Essay

9.1

Paul Wahlbeck

JUDICIAL DECISION MAKING AND RELIGION CASES

On April 17, 1990, the Supreme Court of the United States announced its decision in *Employment Division v. Smith*. The Court considered whether the denial of unemployment benefits is constitutional when the person was fired for ingesting peyote, a hallucinogenic drug, during a Native American religious ceremony. The Court ruled that there is no constitutional violation unless the use of peyote was banned because of its religious motivation. Justice Antonin Scalia, writing for the Court, stated that the Free Exercise Clause "does not relieve an individual of the obligation to comply with a law that incidentally forbids (or requires) the performance of an act that his religious belief requires (or forbids)" (*Employment Division v. Smith* 1990). Siding with Justice Scalia against this religious exercise claim were Chief Justice William H. Rehnquist and Justices Byron R. White, John Paul Stevens, and Anthony Kennedy.

In 2005, the Supreme Court announced its decisions in two cases that challenged the display of the Ten Commandments on public grounds. One case involved a 6-foot granite monument inscribed with the Ten Commandments displayed on the Texas State Capitol grounds (*Van Orden v. Perry* 2005). The second case challenged two Kentucky counties that hung "large, gold-framed copies of an abridged text of the King James version of the Ten Commandments" in their courthouses (*McCreary County v. American Civil Liberties Union of Kentucky* 2005). The Supreme Court treated these two disputes differently, ruling that the Texas display passed constitutional muster while the Kentucky display was an unconstitutional establishment of religion. Although Justice Stephen Breyer proved to be the pivotal voter in these cases, former Chief Justice Rehnquist and Justices Scalia, Thomas, and Anthony M. Kennedy sided in favor of the religious displays.

These cases present a puzzle: why do Supreme Court justices make the decisions they do? Why do they support religious expression in some cases, but limit it in others? It is striking that two of the five justices (Chief Justice Rehnquist and Justice Scalia) who heard all three cases did not consistently uphold religious expression but rather swung from opposition to individual religious expression to support for governmental religious displays. Do the usual accounts of judicial behavior explain these divergent decisions, or are rulings on religious cases exceptional? After a brief outlining of three models of judicial decision-making, this chapter examines how well each model explains how judges reach decisions in religious cases.

Explanations of Judicial Decision Making

Recognizing that judicial decisions constitute significant policy statements that affect the choices available to private citizens, government officials, and judges, the study of judicial politics assumes that courts are political institutions and judges are political actors. The Supreme Court's written opinions, as Segal and Spaeth (2002, 357) note, represent "the core of the Court's policymaking process," articulating legal principles that guide lower courts and others. These rulings establish expectations about what behavior is appropriate behavior in a wide range of societal interactions and determine the grounds for sanctioning violations of those expectations (Knight 1992). Court rulings not only influence the behavior of private parties and organizations; they also have distributional consequences when one interest is favored over another (Knight 1992; Hurst 1956). Three theories suggest how judges reach these decisions.

The first model of judicial decision-making—the policy preference model—posits that judges' decisions on these important policy questions are influenced by their personal views of good public policy. As Oliver Wendell Holmes said, "Every important principle which is developed by litigation is in fact and at bottom the result of more or less definitely understood views of public policy" (Holmes 1881, 35). Political scientists explain political behavior using rational choice theory, which assumes that decision-makers choose alternatives that maximize the utility they derive from a choice (Elster 1986). In the context of the Supreme Court, "A major goal of all justices is to see the law reflect their preferred policy positions, and they will take actions to advance this objective" (Epstein and Knight 1998, 11). Rohde and Spaeth (1976) found evidence that justices are swayed by their positions on the issues presented in a case as well as their attitudes toward the specific litigants. In the end, this perspective leads us to hypothesize that justices will vote for the outcome that is most compatible with their individual preferences.

The second explanation of judicial decision making is the legal model, which maintains that judges are guided by the law when making decisions. Judges, according to this perspective, are constrained by the norm of following precedent (Knight and Epstein 1996). While judges' preferences influence their choices, this norm establishes the expectation that they will apply legal rules or standards, whether derived from statutes, the Constitution, prior court decisions, or other authoritative sources, to the case facts presented to them. Segal (1984) empirically tested the legal model using the Supreme Court's search and seizure decisions.[1] After identifying the legal standards governing the Court's Fourth Amendment jurisprudence, Segal used case facts to determine whether each standard was satisfied and found that the legal fact model successfully explained Supreme Court decisions.

A third explanation of judicial behavior, which builds on principles central to the legal and preference models, focuses on the strategic choices made by Supreme Court justices. Strategic decisions are those in which the utility derived from a choice is conditioned on the decision of another actor (Epstein and Knight 1998). Two principal strategic limitations on behavior have been identified in the literature—internal and external. Internal constraints are the benefits derived from a justice's decision as influenced by the choices made by that justice's colleagues (Epstein and Knight 1998; Maltzman, Spriggs, and Wahlbeck 2000). The author of a legal opinion cannot simply express his or her sincere preferences, but must accommodate the views of colleagues as well, bargaining over opinion content (Maltzman, Spriggs, and Wahlbeck 2000; Wahlbeck, Spriggs, and Maltzman 1998). External constraints are most frequently imposed by Congress. In order to write opinions that are efficacious in establishing or guiding legal policy, the Court must moderate its views to discourage Congress from passing legislation overturning its decisions (Meernik and Ignagni 1997; Spiller and Gely 1992).

While I focus on these three explanations, there are a number of additional factors that play a role in judicial decision making. Justices lack complete, perfect information about the available policy alternatives and their consequences and are influenced by interest groups who file amicus curiae briefs. Also, since the Supreme Court relies on other actors to enforce and implement its decisions, it is dependent on the discretion of lower courts and other implementers to faithfully follow its decisions.

Policy Preferences and Decision Making in Religious Cases

Of these three theories, the most commonly held is the policy preference model, which has been borne out with a wealth of evidence. This model assumes that justices make decisions that comport with their policy preferences. "Each member of the Court," argue Rohde and Spaeth (1976, 72), "has preferences concerning the policy questions faced by the Court, and when the justices make decisions they want the outcomes to approximate as nearly as possible those policy preferences." Political scientists test the proposition that justices' votes are influenced by their preferences in a number of ways: examining the interagreement among justices in separate opinions (i.e. concurrences and dissents) (Pritchett 1948), the effect of party affiliation (Tate 1981), and the change of policy preferences over time (Martin and Quinn 2002). Segal and Cover (1989) found that the pair-wise correlation between a justice's ideology and his or her subsequent voting behavior is as high as 80% for justices nominated between 1953 and 1987.

An examination of the justices' votes in religious cases from the 1953 to 2007 Supreme Court terms reveals that these decisions are explained, at least in part, by the justices' policy preferences. The decisions in *Employment Division v. Smith, Van Orden*, and *McCreary County*, although seemingly contradictory, fit a pattern: conservative justices support government regulation of private religious expression while also supporting government endorsement of religion. Put another way, there is an inverse relationship between support for the expression of religion when comparing Free Exercise claims and Establishment Clause claims.[2]

Justices' support of religion in Free Exercise and Establishment Clause cases varies, as seen in Table 9.1.[3] Former Chief Justice Rehnquist supported religious exercise claims in 20% of those cases, while seven justices supported those claimants in more than 90% of cases. The average ideology of justices who supported the position of litigants seeking free exercise of religion was liberal, including Justices William J. Brennan, Jr., Thurgood Marshall, Harry A. Blackmun, Ruth Bader Ginsburg, and David Souter.[4] These are the same justices who typically support civil liberty claimants.[5] In contrast, the justices opposing free exercise claims were moderate to conservative: Lewis F. Powell, White, Rehnquist, Kennedy, O'Connor, and Warren E. Burger.

The patterns suggest that conservative justices tend to favor mainstream religious groups (the in-group), while liberal justices lean toward minority religious expression (the out-group). In most establishment cases, like those prescribing prayer or Bible reading in schools, laws being challenged are examples of government established support for the dominant religious group in a community. In contrast, religious exercise cases

Table 9.1 Justices' Support for Religious Claims, 1953–2007 Terms

Justice (Years of Service)	Percent Support for Free Exercise Claims (Number of Cases)	Percent Support for Government in Establishment Claims (Number of Cases)
Earl Warren (1953–1969)	60.0 (5)	50.0 (6)
Hugo L. Black (1937–1971)	60.0 (5)	33.3 (9)
William O. Douglas (1939–1975)	100.0 (6)	0.0 (17)
John M. Harlan (1955–1971)	66.7 (3)	20.0 (5)
William J. Brennan, Jr. (1956–1990)	81.8 (22)	19.0 (42)
Potter Stewart (1958–1981)	91.7 (12)	54.2 (24)
Byron R. White (1962–1993)	52.4 (21)	82.9 (41)
Arthur J. Goldberg (1962–1965)	100.0 (1)	0.0 (1)
Abe Fortas (1965–1969)	100.0 (1)	0.0 (2)
Thurgood Marshall (1967–1991)	77.8 (18)	16.7 (36)
Warren E. Burger (1969–1986)	60.0 (10)	83.3 (30)
Harry A. Blackmun (1970–1994)	72.2 (18)	31.6 (38)
Lewis F. Powell (1972–1987)	54.6 (11)	58.6 (29)
William H. Rehnquist (1972–2005)	20.0 (20)	91.5 (47)
John Paul Stevens (1975–)	52.4 (21)	5.1 (39)
Sandra Day O'Connor (1981–2006)	50.0 (14)	50.0 (32)
Antonin Scalia (1986–)	50.0 (12)	95.0 (20)
Anthony M. Kennedy (1988–)	62.5 (8)	72.2 (18)
David H. Souter (1990–2009)	100.0 (4)	7.1 (14)
Clarence Thomas (1991–)	80.0 (5)	92.9 (14)
Ruth Bader Ginsburg (1993–)	66.7 (3)	0.0 (12)
Stephen G. Breyer (1994–)	100.0 (3)	36.4 (11)
John G. Roberts, Jr. (2005–)	100.0 (1)	—

Note: Justices' ideology is denoted by shading: liberal justices are marked by the darkest grey, moderates by a lighter grey, and conservatives by white. A justice's ideology is derived from Martin and Quinn (2007).
Source: Spaeth (2008), *The Original United States Supreme Court Judicial Database, 1953–2007 Terms.*

usually pit religious outsiders against the government. Table 9.2 presents the religious groups that have been involved in religious litigation from the 1953 to 2007 terms. It is rare that a religious exercise claim involved Catholics or Protestants, as litigants are generally adherents of minority religious beliefs, like Jehovah Witnesses or Native American religions. The data reveal that the average ideology of justices supporting the religious exercise claimant was significantly different than those opposing the religious adherent, but only when the litigant came from a non-Christian religious tradition. When a litigant came from a Christian tradition, conservative justices were significantly more supportive of the free exercise claim.

The Law and Decision Making in Religious Cases

The second explanation for judicial decision making is that justices are guided by certain legal principles in making decisions. Two groups of scholars applied Segal's test of

Table 9.2 Religious Affiliations in Free Exercise Cases

Religious Affiliation	Number of Cases	Percent of Free Exercise Cases
Native American Religions	5	18.5
Evangelical/Protestant	5	18.5
Jehovah Witness	3	11.1
Jewish	3	11.1
Amish	2	7.4
Seventh Day Adventist	2	7.4
Muslim	1	3.7
Santeria	1	3.7
Krishna	1	3.7
Catholic	1	3.7
Serbian Orthodox	1	3.7
Unknown	2	7.4
Total	27	99.9

Source: Spaeth (2008), *The Original United States Supreme Court Judicial Database, 1953–2007 Terms;* Decisions of the Supreme Court of the United States.

the legal model to religious cases. Joseph Ignagni examined Establishment Clause cases (1994a; 1994b) and Free Exercise cases (1993). Ignagni operationalized the legal principles governing Establishment Clause jurisprudence with seven variables, and found that three fact-based variables influenced the Court's decision in cases where government aid was supplied to religious groups: whether the aid could be described as a general welfare service, whether the aid affected all groups equally, and whether the law required surveillance or inspection of religious institutions (1994a). In another study, Ignagni studied justices' votes. After controlling for the predilections of the justices, including their preferences on these policies, he still found support for fact-based legal variables (1994b).

Kritzer and Richards (2003) took this analysis of Establishment Clause cases a step further by examining the impact of doctrinal change. They posited that there may be regimes - series of key judicial precedents - that "structure the way in which the Supreme Court justices evaluate key elements of cases in arriving at decisions in a particular legal area" (Richards and Kritzer 2002, 308). This suggests that the influence of key legal facts, including those explored by Ignagni, may change when the Court issues a decision that alters legal doctrine. They hypothesize that the Supreme Court's landmark decision in *Lemon v. Kurtzman* (1971), when the Court barred direct government funding to religious schools created a regime shift in Establishment Clause doctrine. Using the legal facts identified by Ignagni (1994a; 1994b), Kritzer and Richards (2003) found a discernable shift in the weight accorded to these legal facts following *Lemon*. These findings bolstered their expectation that the law and legal doctrine can affect judicial decision making.

Beyond doctrinal influences, another important facet of the legal model is the assumption that lawyers have the capacity to influence Supreme Court justices through their arguments. Not all attorneys are equal, and experienced lawyers enjoy an advantage over their colleagues who have not participated as frequently in litigation. Galanter (1974) argued that "repeat players" possess several advantages. First, knowledge of institutional incumbents (i.e., judges or justices) allows lawyers to tailor their argument to the preferences of the presiding judges. For example, an experienced attorney would likely target the median justice on the Court, like former Justice O'Connor or Justice Kennedy. A second advantage is experience with the give and take of oral argument and other facets of the judicial process. Arguing a case before the High Court can be daunting even to the most accomplished attorneys. As one practitioner told Kevin McGuire, "I think it's normally a lawyer who's arguing his first case who will get totally thrown by the kinds of questions that the justices ask and who won't be properly prepared for what it's all about. So the experienced advocate, while he or she cannot always guess what the questions are, can come a lot closer than somebody who's not used to it" (McGuire 1993, 188).

Researchers who tested this hypothesis using an attorney's number of appearances before the Court as a proxy for experience found that prior experience has many benefits. Experienced attorneys possess greater credibility than less practiced lawyers (Johnson, Wahlbeck, and Spriggs 2006) and are more likely to prevail (McGuire 1995). This relationship holds true in religious cases before the Supreme Court. When a litigant is represented by the more experienced practitioner, the Court supports that litigator's position nearly two-thirds of the time.[6] In most cases (including religious cases) however, the attorney who argues before the Supreme Court has never appeared at oral arguments before. Most attorneys argued only one religion case from 1971 to 1993. Thus, the evidence suggests court decisions are influenced by both legal precedent and the lawyers arguing religious cases.

Strategic Explanations of the Supreme Court's Religion Cases

While most judicial scholars explain court decisions as a product of preferences or the law, the most recent trend has focused on the strategic context in which decisions are made. This perspective posits that Supreme Court justices are not free agents who can make decisions independently, but must be cognizant of the views held by their colleagues and actors in the other branches of government. Here I focus on the internal constraints operative within the Court itself.

Justices have leverage with the author of the Court's majority opinion, as the author needs the support of other justices to speak for the Court. To move the Court's opinion closer to their ideal policy point, justices employ a wide range of tactics: expressions of hesitance about joining the opinion, memoranda that state specific reservations with an opinion, threats to withhold their vote or to join the dissent if their concerns are not met, draft opinions that concur in the opinion or judgment of the Court, and the switching of votes (Spriggs, Maltzman, and Wahlbeck 1999). These tactics can prompt the author to moderate his or her views and move the opinion closer to the preferred views of the justice (Wahlbeck, Spriggs, and Maltzman 1998).

Beyond quantitative analysis of the bargaining over Supreme Court opinions, there have been interesting studies of the Court's internal deliberation in particular cases. Schwartz (1986), for example, used the retired justices' papers to examine the opinion-writing process in the Court's decision governing busing to advance school desegregation (*Swann v. Charlotte-Mecklenburg Board of Education* 1971). The Chief Justice, Warren E. Burger, was in the minority of the justices who opposed busing. However, he chose to write the Court's opinion himself, and his "lack of votes induced [him] to agree to rewrite and ultimately to issue a *Swann* opinion that the [other justices] were willing to accept. But the final opinion still was not as forthright as it would have been had it been written by [a supporter of busing]"(Schwartz 1986, 187).

A similar storyline might emerge from a study of the Establishment Clause cases. It appears, for example, that Chief Justice Burger's colleagues restricted his expression of his sincere preferences in the opinions. The justices' papers reveal in *Lemon v. Kurtzman* (1971) that Justice Harlan objected to Burger's attempt to tie "the non-entanglement principle entirely to the Free Exercise clause," rather than viewing it as "deducible from the Establishment and Free Exercise clauses taken together" (Harlan 1971). Harlan directly asked Chief Justice Burger to omit a phrase in Burger's draft opinion that concluded that the programs in question created excessive entanglement "and thus conflict with the Free Exercise Clause." Indeed, the final, published version of the opinion broadens this conclusion to state that the government's entanglement results in a "conflict with the Religion Clauses" (*Lemon v. Kurtzman* 1971, 620). Thus, one can surmise that Burger was hindered in pursuing his sincere policy preference by his colleagues' views.

Chief justices have exceptional capacity to shape policy as the leader of the Court. Although the Chief has a single vote like the Supreme Court's associate justices, the chief enjoys some prerogatives, like opinion assignment, that afford the opportunity to set the Court's agenda. Kobylka (1989) explored the leadership of Chief Justice Warren Burger in religious Establishment Clause cases. He concluded that Chief Justice Burger came close to altering Establishment Clause doctrine, but failed when he was unable to hold the "middle" or median justice. Burger's influence over this policy domain waxed and waned. In two periods during Burger's tenure as chief (1969–1972 and 1978–1983 terms), he exercised influence on the Court, but was in dissent much of the time in two other periods (1973–1977 and 1984–1985 terms).

In the first period, Burger led the Court in reshaping doctrine to comport with his vision of good legal policy. He assigned the majority opinion to himself in five of the six Establishment Clause cases decided between 1969 and 1972, paving the way for an accommodationist policy—"[accommodating] indirect state support for religious activities" (Kobylka 1989, 550). Other justices held a separatist view, opposing government support of religion. Burger's early success was seen in *Walz v. Tax Commission* (1970) where he created a new constitutional requirement—no excessive entanglement between church and state. He added to this doctrinal development in *Lemon v. Kurtzman* (1971) where he articulated a three-part test for assessing a challenged law: the law possesses a secular legislative purpose, the primary effect is not to advance or inhibit religion, and the law does not result in excessive government entanglement with religion. Although the Court reached a separatist result in *Lemon*, striking down the state aid to teachers in nonpublic schools, Burger was able to institutionalize his accommodationist preference in the excessive entanglement prong of the *Lemon* test.

Despite these early successes, Burger was not able to fulfill his vision of remaking Establishment Clause policy. He lost three out of four battles over cases seeking to apply *Lemon* between 1973 and 1977. A coalition of three moderate justices (Stewart, Blackmun, and Powell) determined the outcome of these four cases, upholding one parochaid law, invalidating a second, and partially rejecting two other laws. Though Burger's influence was greater between 1978 and 1983 when the Court decided eight cases, striking four laws as constitutionally flawed, these cases were too narrow to advance doctrinal development (Kobylka 1989). The more significant development was Justices White's and Rehnquist's adoption of the *Lemon* test to advance accommodationist objectives. As Kobylka put it, "these decisions dulled *Lemon*'s separationist edge and brought it back with Burger's vision. Court watchers saw the 'wall of separation' to be crumbling" (1989, 558). Burger's influence over policy development was not sustained in the final two years of his tenure as Chief Justice, however, as he found himself in the minority in the most important cases (Kobylka 1989, 559).

Kobylka argued that Burger's struggle with reorienting the Establishment Clause doctrine stemmed from his personal leadership capacity, the context of the bench, and the political environment. Burger's leadership strategies were not well developed, as he initially exhibited "insensitivity in monopolizing majority and plurality opinions" (Kobylka 1989, 561). As his tenure as chief justice continued, he modified his tactics by diversifying his opinion assignments to other justices, assigning opinions to White and Rehnquist, who were the most extreme justices in his coalition. He was also limited in his ability to establish an accommodationist jurisprudence by the composition of the Court. Burger enjoyed only a slim majority with the assured hostility of Justices Brennan, Marshall, Stevens, and Blackmun. Moreover, public officials passed legislation that ran counter to the Court's previous decisions: "With governments largely ignoring decisions with which they disagreed, and with the Solicitor General actively seeking the reversal of 'objectionable' precedents, the hesitancy of the centrist justices to go along with Burger, lest the Court be seen as caving in to overtly political pressures, may have been heightened" (Kobylka 1989, 562).

Conclusion

What then explains judicial decision making in religious cases? Each theory—the policy preferences model, the legal model, and the strategic decision-making model—provides insight into the Court's decisions. Justices seek decisions that comport with their view of good legal policy, but they do not act without fetters. They are constrained by the norm of following precedent and the law and must keep the views of their colleagues in mind. There is give-and-take among the justices, who must sometimes settle for decisions that do not conform perfectly with their policy preferences. Returning to the high-profile cases introduced at the beginning, we find that the justices' decisions in *Employment Division* and the Ten Commandment display cases were shaped by policy preferences, the law, and dynamics on the bench.

It is perhaps time to acknowledge that neither legal explanations nor policy preference explanations provide a complete understanding of Supreme Court decision making. Although each explanation can provide useful insights into judicial behavior standing alone, they each leave unexplained a portion of judicial behavior. George and Epstein (1992) confronted this dilemma in their study of the Supreme Court's capital punishment decisions, finding that what they called the political model overpredicted conservative outcomes in more recent years, while the legal model overstated the Court's liberal tendencies. A better explanation, they discovered, incorporated elements of each model—what they called an integrated model.

The strategic model has the advantage of recognizing the role of both policy preferences and legal constraints (among other constraints). Justices, as rational decision makers, seek to maximize their goals, including their policy preferences, but have to do that within the bounds of formal rules and informal norms. The principal norm in the American legal system is stare decisis, that is, the expectation that judges will adhere to precedent when rendering decisions. When decisions can be explained by policy preferences and the law, as we have seen in the domain of religion cases, it is another indicator that strategic explanations are valuable tools for understanding judicial (and more broadly, political) decision making.

Research Pieces

9.2

Thomas E. Buckley

A MANDATE FOR ANTI-CATHOLICISM: THE BLAINE AMENDMENT (2004)

In recent years a better understanding of American history has gradually moved the U.S. Supreme Court away from a strict separationist perspective on church and state and toward a greater accommodation of religion. In *Agostini v. Felton* (1997) and *Mitchell v. Helms* (2000), the majority of justices expanded possibilities for government aid to church-related schools. Then in *Zelman v. Simmons-Harris* (2002), the court approved the Cleveland voucher program, which allows poor students to use public money to pay for private and parochial school tuition. Voucher cases in other states, most notably Florida, have been less successful, because state courts have determined that such programs violated state constitutional prohibitions that are stricter than the First Amendment's establishment clause. But the 19th-century history of such state provisions, commonly known as Blaine amendments, is instructive. As its recent rulings demonstrate, the Supreme Court has been reading that history.

In 1870, James Gillespie Blaine was 40 years old and a rising star in the Republican Party. After he served in the Maine Legislature, that state elected him to the U.S. House of Representatives, where he soon occupied the speaker's chair. His political trajectory and that of his party had risen together. Down Pennsylvania Avenue in the White House sat his friend, Ulysses S. Grant, whom he hoped to succeed in office. In addition to the presidency, the Republicans controlled both houses of Congress and were now completing a Southern reconstruction policy designed to gather the newly emancipated and enfranchised African-Americans into the political fold of Abraham Lincoln.

The advancement of public schools represented a key element in that program as well as an important part of the Republican drive for cultural homogeneity in post-Civil War America. The schools would lift up Southern blacks and Americanize newly arrived immigrants, especially Irish and German Catholics. Following the program laid out by

Horace Mann in the 1840's, public education would inculcate a nondenominational Protestant morality through Bible reading, hymn singing and the use of the McGuffey readers. The result would be a law-abiding, hard-working, broadly based middle-class society that embodied the values of capitalism embedded in Republican ideology.

The Catholic Church, most notably in the person of Archbishop John Baptist Purcell of Cincinnati, resisted this vision of an essentially Protestant culture. Though a religious minority in that city, Catholics formed the largest single denomination, with 23 parishes. By 1870 Purcell's Catholic school system enrolled 12,000 students in Cincinnati, in comparison with 19,000 attending public schools. The archbishop wanted his schools to share in the public school fund. The New York Legislature had recently passed a bill introduced by William Marcy Tweed, the Democratic boss of New York's Tammany Hall, to provide public funds to private schools in the city and county of New York enrolling at least 200 students. Agitation existed for similar measures in places where Catholics were numerous. The New York law was soon repealed, and Purcell failed to get a share in the funds. But, confronted by the pervasively Protestant character of the public schools-the chief irritant to Catholics-a majority of the Cincinnati school board determined that Bible reading and other religious exercises should be discontinued. After a series of court battles, the Ohio Supreme Court ultimately upheld this decision.

Protestants committed to fostering a religiously based morality in the schools were outraged by the court's action. In their view, Catholic immigrants who disagreed with this public policy should go home. By Protestant definition, Catholics owed allegiance to a foreign ruler in Rome, where the First Vatican Council had just upped the ante by proclaiming papal infallibility. Adherence to authoritarian, antidemocratic Romanism rendered Catholic claims of American loyalty dubious at best. Fallout from Cincinnati's Bible war merged with the school-funding issue in New York and spread across the nation.

Perhaps the most extreme anti-Catholic reaction was the proposal in 1870 of an amendment to the U.S. Constitution proposed by Judge Elisha Hurlbut of New York, an expert in constitutional law. It would empower Congress to ban "any foreign hierarchical power . . . founded on principles or dogmas antagonistic to republican institutions." Some read in Hurlbut's proposal the opening salvo of an anti-Catholic, nationalistic campaign akin to Otto von Bismarck's Kulturkampf, which was gathering steam in Germany. Moreover, the campaign to identify the United States as a Christian Protestant nation, which had begun during the Civil War, now revived with the efforts of Supreme Court Justice William Strong and the National Reform Association to amend the U.S. Constitution's preamble to read: "Recognizing Almighty God as the source of all authority and power in civil government, and . . . the Lord Jesus Christ as the Governor among the nations, His revealed will as the supreme law of the land, in order to constitute a Christian government," we the People, etc.

Although such proposals proved too extreme to rally widespread support in Congress, they showed the way to politicians anxious to distract voters from the financial mismanagement and gross scandals of the Grant administration. A Protestant minority, including such notable clergymen as Henry Ward Beecher, was willing to eliminate overtly Protestant religious exercises from the schools. But Beecher and his friends drew the line at public funding for Catholic schools. Where worried Protestants read signs of moral crisis and Catholic threat in the school fights, others saw political opportunity. School funding rather than school prayer became the defining issue. Constitutional amendment became the method. And political gain provided an important motivation.

A vigorous dose of anti-Catholicism always enlivened an otherwise dull speech. As the future President Rutherford B. Hayes informed Blaine in June 1875, the "school question" had rendered the state Republican convention "enthusiastic." The party had "been losing strength in Ohio for several years by emigration of Republican farmers," he explained. "In their place have come Catholic foreigners . . . We shall crowd them on the school and other state issues." Running on a blatantly anti-Catholic platform, Hayes narrowly captured the Ohio governorship that fall, despite the economic depression and the scandals enveloping the national Republican Party.

Grant seized the moment. In a speech in December 1875, the president proposed that Congress approve a constitutional amendment formally separating church and state, provide for the taxation of church property and forbid the states from allocating public funds to any schools that taught "sectarian tenets." Sectarian meant Catholic. A week later Blaine offered his amendment on the floor of the House. It included the most popular of the Grant proposals. After extending the language of the First Amendment to the states, it provided that "no money raised by taxation in any state for the support of public schools, or derived from any public fund thereof, nor any public lands devoted thereto, shall ever be under the control of any religious sect, nor shall any money so raised or lands so devoted be divided between religious sects or denominations."

As the University of Chicago law professor Philip Hamburger has demonstrated in his superb study, *Separation of Church and State* (Harvard Univ. Press, 2002), Blaine's proposal directly challenged Catholic efforts for school funding while leaving nondenominational Protestantism securely entrenched in public education. It was designed to secure the nomination for Blaine. Hayes's victory in Ohio had made him an instant "reform" Republican candidate. Blaine's friends were concerned. Apart from the school issue, Hayes had failed to excite the voters. One Republican politician urged that Blaine needed only to make "a good speech on the School question" to "cinch the nomination." But Blaine's Catholic cousin, Ellen Ewing Sherman was not so sure. She and her husband, the Civil War general William Tecumseh Sherman, wanted him in the White House, but Ellen Sherman warned that his proposals for "the State Constitutions and school laws" would hurt him "among our Irish friends and Catholics."

Blaine lost anyway. Though he entered the Republican convention in June as the front-runner, allegations that he had accepted bribes from the Union Pacific Railroad fatally damaged his chances for the nomination; and the delegates eventually chose the squeaky clean Hayes, everyone's second choice. They also recognized Hayes's single successful issue in his Ohio campaign by incorporating Blaine's amendment into their national platform. That August it almost passed Congress, winning 180 to 7 in the House of Representatives but failing to gain the necessary two-thirds majority in the Senate.

Iowa and Illinois, however, had already placed variants of the Blaine Amendment in their state constitutions, and Congress quickly mandated that all states admitted to the Union after 1876 must follow suit. Washington State, for example, incorporated the following proviso in its 1889 constitution: "All schools maintained or supported wholly or in part by the public funds shall be forever free from sectarian control or influence."

Earlier this year in *Locke v. Davey*, a 7-to-2 Supreme Court majority decided that the state of Washington could deny a scholarship to a student seeking a "devotional theology degree." But the justices avoided directly ruling on the Blaine Amendment statement in Washington's constitution. Instead they pointed out approvingly that the guidelines for the scholarship program permitted students to attend "pervasively religious" institutions and take courses in "devotional theology."

Thirty-seven states have clauses modeled after the Blaine Amendment, and cases challenging such provisions are coming up in Michigan, South Dakota and elsewhere. A 19th-century concern has become a burning issue in 21st-century church-state jurisprudence. The question the U.S. Supreme Court will face is whether such provisions placed in state constitutions a century or more ago violate the religious liberty provided by the First Amendment.

As for Blaine, he finally received the long-desired Republican presidential nomination in 1884. His defeat in that year's election has been attributed largely to a Republican charge, which he never made or endorsed, that the Democratic Party was one of "Rum, Romanism and Rebellion." That attack galvanized the Democrats. Blaine later said he could never have condemned "that ancient faith in which my mother lived and died." The son of a Catholic mother and Presbyterian father, he was raised as a Presbyterian. Among his cousins was a Jesuit priest, Thomas Sherman, son of the general. Given his relatives, Blaine may have hoped and expected, as some scholars assert, that the amendment he sponsored would not pass. Perhaps his anti-Catholicism had been "just politics" after all. Shortly after he lost the 1876 Republican nomination, Maine put Blaine in the Senate. The next month, when that body defeated his amendment by a two-vote margin, Senator Blaine was absent.

9.3

Jeffrey Toobin

THE NINE: INSIDE THE SECRET WORLD OF THE SUPREME COURT (2007)

The backlash to these rulings [*Minersville School District v. Gobitis, Virginia Board of Education v. Barnette, Engle v. Vitale*] was not long in coming. Prayer and Bible reading had been staples of American public education for generations. The court-ordered end to such religious observance in public schools was soon followed by the chaotic late 1960s. The cause-and-effect was debatable, but for many Christians there was a clear connection between the increased secularization of public life and the licentiousness and disorder that followed. In this period, Rev. Billy Graham, in an indirect way, and then Rev. Pat Robertson, in explicit terms, merged their religious messages with a conservative political agenda. In the election of 1980, Rev. Jerry Falwell mobilized what he called the Moral Majority to defeat a Democratic president and a generation of liberal senators. By the time Bill Clinton was elected president, the evangelical movement represented the core of his conservative opposition. The twin pillars of their agenda were clear—one against legalized abortion, the other for public religious expression, especially prayer in schools.

By the midnineties, after *Casey*, there was no point in pushing an antiabortion agenda on a Court that had made up its mind on the issue. But the issue of religious expression was wide open. Curiously, although the evangelical movement had amassed enormous political clout, it had not cultivated comparable leadership in the legal arena. But all social movements in America eventually find a strategist who sets their course in the courts—their Thurgood Marshall or Ruth Bader Ginsburg—and this was the moment when the evangelicals discovered theirs. Oddly enough, their savior, Jay Sekulow, turned out to be a nice Jewish boy from Brooklyn. . . .

His family tracked the migration pattern of the country as a whole—city to suburb to Sun Belt, in his case, Brooklyn to Long Island to Atlanta. . . . Sekulow settled on a college close to his home, Atlanta Baptist College.

Sekulow was drifting through the mandatory Bible classes when a friend, whom he regarded at the time as a "Jesus freak," challenged him to study the Book of Isaiah. Sekulow knew that Jews were supposed to believe that someday the Messiah would come—but that he hadn't come yet. Still, in reading the passages about the Messiah, Sekulow thought he recognized the description—it was Jesus Christ. Sekulow still considered himself a Jew, but one who believed that Jesus was the savior. In time, Sekulow learned that there were other Jews who shared his belief and they were called "Jews for Jesus." At a ceremony in February 1976, Sekulow marched to the front of a Jews for Jesus church service and announced that he had committed his life to Jesus Christ. . . .

. . . Sekulow . . . signed on as the general legal counsel for the national Jews for Jesus organization, and it turned out that the group had a case that was heading to the Supreme Court. Sekulow decided to argue it himself and wound up changing American constitutional law.

Jews for Jesus believes its members should engage in missionary work to seek out converts. Their best-known (or notorious) form of proselytizing consists of aggressive leafleting, especially in public places like airports. In response to this practice, which was frequently annoying to passengers, the governing board of Los Angeles International Airport banned all "First Amendment activities" on its grounds. On July 6, 1984, pursuant to the policy, airport police evicted Alan Howard Snyder, "a minister of the Gospel" in Jews for Jesus, for distributing religious literature. Before Sekulow became involved in the matter, his colleagues in California sued to invalidate the airport rule.

The original theory of the case was straightforward. Proselytizing was a form of religious activity among Jews for Jesus followers. A blanket ban on the practice thus interfered with their First Amendment right to the "free exercise" of their religion. That was how these cases had customarily been argued. Religious expression was always defended under the Free Exercise Clause.

But Sekulow's relative ignorance about the Constitution turned out to be his best weapon. Sure, cases involving religion were always argued under the Free Exercise Clause. But Sekulow came up with a different theory. The First Amendment, after the religion clauses, goes on to say that Congress shall make no law "abridging the freedom of speech." (In a series of cases after World War II, the Court said that the First Amendment was binding against states and localities as well as Congress.) Sekulow thought the eviction of the Jews for Jesus minister was a speech case, not a religion case. What the airport was doing was censoring free speech—and it didn't matter whether the speech concerned religion or politics, which was the more familiar basis for free speech claims. What made Sekulow's idea so appealing was that the Court had been far more generous in extending protection to controversial speech than to intrusive religious activities. Sekulow could draw on a legion of cases where the justices protected all sorts of obnoxious expression, including distributing obscenity . . . Sekulow wondered how these activities could be permitted but not the polite distribution of pamphlets.

So did the justices. At the oral argument on March 3, 1987, Sekulow later recalled in a speech, "I had walked into the courtroom thinking about Jesus and how he overturned the moneychangers' tables at the Temple. Jesus was an activist. He stood up for what he knew was right. I drew strength from his example." But in front of the justices, Sekulow didn't even mention religion. He said the case was solely about free speech. Sekulow knew he was on to something when he heard his adversary list all the supposed reasons that the airport banned the Jews for Jesus leafleters. At one point, Thurgood Marshall, who was by then ailing, crotchety, and usually silent on the bench, roused himself and growled, "Can I ask you a question? What is wrong with what these people do?"

"Nothing is wrong with what they do," the lawyer said.

"Well, how can you prohibit something that doesn't do anything wrong?"

Marshall had gone to the heart of the matter. For all the airport's rationalizations, the case was about the censorship of an unpopular group—exactly what the speech clause of the First Amendment was designed to prevent. The vote in *Board of Airport Commissioners of the City of Los Angeles v. Jews for Jesus, Inc.* was unanimous, with O'Connor writing for the Court that the ordinance violated the First Amendment.

Sekulow immediately began putting his insight to work for the broader evangelical movement. A group of students at Westside High School in Omaha wanted to start a Christian club, to read the Bible and pray together after class. The principal and local board of education turned the group down, saying that to permit a Christian student group in a public school would amount to an "establishment" of religion, in violation of the First Amendment. Sekulow took the appeal to the Supreme Court.

Again, Sekulow steered away from the religion arguments under the First Amendment. To him, the case was about the free speech rights of the students. If other youth groups could use the school facilities, why not the Christian kids? Once more, Sekulow won overwhelmingly, with O'Connor again writing the opinion and only Stevens in dissent. More importantly, O'Connor essentially gave Sekulow and his allies a road map for expanding the place of religion in public schools. In the key passage in *Board of Education of Westside Community Schools v. Mergens*, O'Connor wrote, "There is a crucial difference between government speech endorsing religion, which the Establishment Clause forbids, and private speech endorsing religion, which the Free Speech and Free Exercise Clauses protect. We think that secondary school students are mature enough and are likely to understand that a school does not endorse or support student speech that it merely permits on a nondiscriminatory basis." The Court was saying that religious activity was welcome at public schools, as long as it was students and not teachers or administrators who initiated it. Evangelical students and their parents were only too happy to accept the invitation.

Sekulow's victory in the *Mergens* case in 1990 drew Pat Robertson's attention. The son of a senator and a graduate of Yale Law School himself, Robertson had established himself a political, financial, and religious powerhouse. He had started the Christian Broadcasting Network in 1960 and soon found that he needed $7,000 per month to keep it on the air. So he ran a telethon seeking seven hundred people to give $10 apiece, and he called the program *The 700 Club*. Based in Virginia Beach, the network and its signature program launched Robertson's vast empire, which included, by the 1980s, broadcast, real estate, cable operations, and even a university, Regent, with more than a thousand students. (Later, he sold just one part of his operation to ABC for $1.9 billion.) In 1988, Robertson ran a respectable race for the Republican presidential nomination, which included besting Vice President George H. W. Bush in the Iowa caucuses, but he had never figured out a reliable way to bring his fight to the courts.

So in 1990, he asked Sekulow to join him in starting a conservative counterpart to the American Civil Liberties Union. Like the ACLU, the new entity would not limit itself to a single issue—such as abortion or school prayer—but instead represent a complete political agenda. Even the name of the new operation would announce an institutional rival to the ACLU; it was called the American Center for Law and Justice, the ACLJ. . . .

. . . [C]ases flooded the ACLJ. In many of them, the question was how much of a Christian message the evangelicals could get into the schools. Organized prayer was out; Christian student groups were in. What, then, about non-student evangelical groups using school property after hours?

That was Sekulow's first major case under Robertson's auspices. New York state law allowed community groups to use school property for "social, civic, and recreational meetings" that were "nonexclusive and open to the general public." Lamb's Chapel, a small evangelical church on Long Island, asked to use the Center Moriches school district's facilities to show a series of six films featuring lectures by James Dobson, a central figure in the national evangelical movement. . . . The school district rejected the request to show the films, because they "appear to be church related." Sekulow took the case to the Supreme Court.

There, from the start, Sekulow stuck with his trademark argument. "Mr. Chief Justice and may it please the Court," he began. "This case is about censorship of Lamb's Chapel's speech, which was entertained for the purpose of having a film series at the school facilities to show and discuss contemporary family issues. The direct targeting of religious purpose as an exclusion under the access policy of the school district is both content based and viewpoint based, and does not meet constitutional scrutiny." Like the Jews for Jesus leafleters in L.A. and the Christian students in Omaha, the Lamb's Chapel evangelicals were victims of government repression, not the advance agents of a state religion.

"So what provision of the Constitution are you relying on?" O'Connor asked.

"First Amendment, as applied to the states through the Fourteenth, freedom of speech."

"Which part of it?"

"Free speech."

Religion couldn't be privileged under the Constitution, Sekulow insisted, but it couldn't be penalized, either. "The way I understand the respondents' argument, the atheists are in, the agnostics are in, the communists are in, the religion is not in," Sekulow told the justices. "This is the type of viewpoint discrimination that this Court has not sanctioned." The result, in *Lamb's Chapel v. Center Moriches Union Free School District*, was another unanimous victory for Sekulow. . . .

By the midnineties, the issue was settled. According to the standards of Supreme Court litigation, Sekulow had emerged out of nowhere to revolutionize an important rule of law. As a result of his efforts, it was clear that if a school, airport, or other public forum was going to open up its facilities to some individuals or groups, the authorities couldn't exclude religious speakers from the list.

9.4

Peter Irons

A People's History of the Supreme Court: The Men and the Women Whose Cases and Decisions Have Shaped Our Constitution (2006)

Religion cases make up only a small fraction of the Supreme Court's docket, but they often ignite political and legal fires among partisans on both sides of the growing church–state divide in American society. Although the *Santa Fe* decision in 2000 settled the school-prayer debate, in the courts if not the southern towns in which "voluntary" prayer continued, conflicts over other religion issues brought new cases to the Court in the subsequent five years. The razor-thin presidential victory of George W. Bush in 2000 not only placed a "born-again" Christian conservative in the Oval Office, but also encouraged Religious Right legal groups to hope that Supreme Court justices had read the election returns and would be more receptive to arguments that "we are a religious people whose institutions presuppose a Supreme Being," as Justice William O. Douglas— one of the Court's great liberals—had written in 1952.

It was not the Religious Right, however, but church-and-state separationists who initiated a trio of cases that challenged invocations of a "Supreme Being" in such institutions as public schools, courthouses, and state capitals. . . .

. . . The issue in these cases, which began in two rural Kentucky counties and the Texas capital of Austin, involved public displays of the Ten Commandments. Whether or not the justices relished another round of arguments in divisive religion cases is impossible to say, but they had little choice, since federal appellate courts had issued conflicting rulings on Ten Commandments displays. Such a "circuit split" virtually guaranteed Supreme Court review, to provide a uniform legal standard for lower-court judges.

Unlike the words "under God" in the Pledge, which refer to no particular deity and could been seen—as Justice O'Connor noted in Michael Newdow's case—as a form of "ceremonial deism," the Ten Commandments come straight from the Bible and are sacred only to Jews and Christians. "I am the Lord your God," states the first, followed by the command that "You shall have no other gods before me." Jews and Christians differ on the precise wording of the Commandments, as do Catholics and Protestants, and even different Protestant denominations. None of these religious believers, however, dispute theft divine inspiration and source. Even nonbelievers agree that three of the Commandments—proscribing murder, theft, and perjury—have a legitimate place in American law, although the proscription of adultery has lost its legal sanction in most states, along with "taking the Lord's name in vain" and working on the Sabbath. Most people also agree that honoring one's parents and not coveting your neighbors' property are good moral principles.

But the disputes that brought the Kentucky and Texas cases before the Court were not over standards for legal and moral behavior, but over whether the undeniable and solely religious nature of the first five Commandments—and the inclusion of the last five in the same biblical text—proscribes their display in public places. Recent polls show that more than 70 percent of the public and almost 90 percent of evangelical Christians support such displays. Even federal judges, whose legal commandments include the Constitution's first ten amendments, have lined up on opposite sides in Ten Commandments cases, as the Supreme Court recognized when it agreed to umpire this dispute.

The cases before the Court in 2005 came from very different communities. McCreary and Pulaski counties, which adjoin each other, are close to the Tennessee border in southeastern Kentucky and are overwhelmingly rural, white, low income, and Christian, with Southern Baptists predominating. Austin, in contrast, is a booming, cosmopolitan city with more than two hundred thousand residents, the center of Texas state government, surrounded by high-tech industries and high-income suburbs, and the home of the University of Texas.

The Ten Commandments displays in these communities were also very different. In 1999, McCreary and Pulaski county officials, prodded by the Kentucky legislature, placed framed copies of the Commandments on their courthouse walls. The governing bodies of both counties passed resolutions authorizing the displays as recognitions of "our Christian heritage." One Pulaski resident, Paul Lee, a World War II veteran, saw the courthouse display and promptly called the ACLU office in Louisville. "Our forefathers saw fit to say that church is separate from the state and vice versa," he said, "and I want to keep it that way." In McCreary two residents, David Howe and Louanne Walker, also volunteered to become ACLU plaintiffs. Howe was a retired disk jockey and Walker was the cousin of Jimmie Greene, who headed McCreary's governing board and became a defendant in the case. "I was kind of shocked,' Greene said about his cousin's stand. "You know, this is a small county," Walker replied, "and I'd say most of the people are in favor of having the Ten Commandments posted in the courthouse. I'm not against the Ten Commandments. I'm just a firm believer in separation of church and state."

Confronted with the ACLU lawsuit, county officials in both McCreary and Pulaski first responded by surrounding the Ten Commandments with other documents, including excerpts from the Declaration of Independence, the Mayflower Compact, and a quote from Abraham Lincoln praising the Bible. But these all contained references to God, and a federal judge ordered the counties to remove them. At that point, a Religious Right legal group, Liberty Counsel, founded by the Reverend Jerry Falwell, offered the counties free legal representation. Liberty Counsel's legal director, Mathew Staver, urged his clients to broaden the displays with copies of the Bill of Rights, the lyrics to the "Star Spangled Banner," and the Magna Carta, and to label the displays as "Foundations of American Law." But the federal district judge again ruled against the counties, and the U.S. Court of Appeals for the Sixth Circuit upheld that decision.

The Austin display of the Ten Commandments differed both in age and in location. In 1961, the Fraternal Order of Eagles had donated a six-foot granite monument, etched with the Commandments, and with a cross and a Star of David on its base. State officials placed it in a grassy area between the Capitol and state supreme court buildings. The grounds also included seventeen other plaques and statues, commemorating events and prominent figures in Texas history, although none were dose to the Commandments monument.

The Texas display stood for more than forty years before anyone complained. The man who did was Thomas Van Orden, a former lawyer who had lost his license after falling into a crippling depression and failing to file papers for his clients. One journalist wrote that Van Orden "sleeps nightly in a tent in a wooded area; showers and washes his clothes irregularly; hangs out in a law library; and survives on food stamps and the good graces of friends who give him a few bucks from time to time." Van Orden had lost his career and family, but not his legal skills. Passing the Ten Commandments monument one day in 2002 on his way to the state law library, he decided to file a lawsuit against it in federal court, with Governor Rick Perry as the first defendant, using the library's books and computers to draft a complaint "I wrote myself to the Supreme Court," he later said. Representing himself, Van Orden lost in both the federal district and appeals courts, which held the Ten Commandments monument did not "endorse" religion. Determined to reach the Supreme Court, Van Orden—unlike Michael Newdow—decided that he needed an experienced advocate, and called Erwin Chemerinsky, a noted Duke University law professor. Chemerinsky, who had earlier advised Newdow on his briefs, had never heard of Van Orden, but agreed to argue his case. "I have nothing but the greatest admiration and respect for him," Chemerinsky said of his client. "He's extremely intelligent and articulate, and I think he did an excellent job of briefing and arguing the case" in the lower courts.

Court watchers in the media and the legal community were divided over whether the Court would uphold or strike down the Ten Commandments displays in the Kentucky and Texas cases, and the justices did not tip their hands during the oral arguments, peppering the lawyers on both sides with questions that focused on the histories of the displays. As it turned out, two separate majorities decided the two cases in June 2005, with their divergent outcomes reflecting the Court's difficulty in finding a consistent judicial standard in Establishment Clause cases. Rather than finding any "bright line" to guide their interpretation, the justices—as they had in earlier cases—looked to the "context" and "setting" of public displays of religious symbols and sentiments.

Ruling in *McCreary County v. ACLU of Kentucky*, the title for the two Kentucky cases, five justices agreed that the "purpose" behind the courthouse displays was to endorse the religious message of the Commandments. Writing for himself and Justices Ginsburg, Breyer, and Stevens, Justice Souter held that subsequent displays of more secular documents did not erase the clearly religious purpose of the first, which displayed "an unmistakably religious statement dealing with religious obligations and with morality subject to religious sanction." Souter dismissed the revised displays as a "litigating position" adopted by county officials who "were simply reaching for any way to keep a religious document on the walls of courthouses constitutionally required to embody religious neutrality."

The Court's swing votes, Justices O'Connor and Kennedy, swung in opposite directions in these cases. Justice O'Connor joined the *McCreary County* majority with a separate concurring opinion. "It is true that many Americans find the Commandments in accord with their personal beliefs," she wrote, tacitly acknowledging public support for their display. "But we do not count heads before enforcing the First Amendment." The fact that virtually all McCreary and Pulaski county residents were Christians, although O'Connor did not mention this fact, could not allow that religious majority to proclaim their beliefs on courthouse walls. The Constitutions religion clauses, she concluded, "protect adherents of all religions, as well as those who believe in no religion at all."

Although Chief Justice Rehnquist had not attended the oral arguments because of illness, he read the transcripts and joined Justices Thomas and Kennedy in Justice Scalia's dissent in the *McCreary County* case. Reflecting his view that the Establishment Clause did not protect religious minorities or nonbelievers from majoritarian sentiment,

Scalia denounced "the demonstrably false principle that the government cannot favor religion over irreligion" in public places. It was "entirely clear from our Nation's historical practices," he wrote, "that the Establishment Clause permits this disregard" of those who do not accept "monotheistic" beliefs.

The majority coalition shifted to the other side in the Texas case, *Van Orden v. Perry*, with five justices upholding the Ten Commandments monument on the Texas Capitol grounds. This case produced seven opinions among the nine justices, another reflection of judicial discord over the Establishment Clause. Chief Justice Rehnquist, joined by Scalia, Thomas, and Kennedy, wrote a brief plurality opinion that conceded the "religious significance" of the Commandments. But that did not prohibit their public display. "Simply having religious content or promoting a religious message consistent with a religious doctrine does not run afoul of the Establishment Clause," Rehnquist wrote.

The swing vote in the *Van Orden* case, it turned out, was that of Justice Breyer, who switched sides from *McCreary County* in a concurring opinion. The factor that most influenced Breyer was that the Texas monument had stood for more than forty years before Thomas Van Orden challenged its display. "Those forty years," Breyer wrote, "suggest that the public visiting the capitol grounds has considered the religious aspect of the tablets' message as part of what is a broader moral and historical message reflective of a cultural heritage." In contrast, the plaintiffs in *McCreary County* had promptly objected to the courthouse displays. This was about as fine a distinction between the cases that anyone could find, with Breyer playing the role of Solomon in proposing to split the Establishment Clause baby in half, satisfying hardly anyone on either side, both on the Court and in the American public.

Among the four dissenters, Justice Souter replied most directly to Breyer's reliance on the forty years that had passed before Van Orden challenged the Ten Commandments monument. Breyer seemed to suggest, Souter wrote, "that forty years without a challenge shows that . . . the religious expression is too tepid to provoke a serious reaction. I doubt that a slow walk to the courthouse, even one that took forty years, is much evidentiary help in applying the Establishment Clause." Justice Stevens, on his part, decried Rehnquist's "simplistic commentary on the various ways in which religion has played a role in American life," and denounced "the plurality's wholehearted validation of an official state endorsement of the message that there is one, and only one, God."

9.5

David O'Brien

STORM CENTER: THE SUPREME COURT IN AMERICAN POLITICS (2008)

Religion, race, and gender have historically been barriers to rather than bases for appointments to the Court. The overwhelming majority (92) of the 110 justices have come from established Protestant religions: fifty-five from old-line faiths—Episcopalian, Unitarian, Congregationalist, and Quaker—and thirty-seven from others, such as Baptist, Methodist,

Lutheran, and Disciples of Christ. Of the remaining eighteen, eleven were Catholics and seven were Jews.

Religion has political symbolism, but it played little role in judicial selection until the twentieth century. The "Catholic seat" and the "Jewish seat" were created accidentally, rather than by presidential efforts to give the Court religious balance. Representation, of course, is purely symbolic. Catholics and Jews do not have well-defined positions, for example, on statutory interpretation. Nor does the appointment of a Catholic or a Jew guarantee that the views of each faith will be reflected in the justices' voting.

The first Catholic, Chief Justice Taney, was appointed in 1835, but religion had little to do with Jackson's selection of his friend and adviser. Thirty years after Taney's death, the next Catholic was named. Edward White was appointed in 1894, but again religion played a minor role, though in 1910 President Taft was urged to promote him to the post of chief justice because he was "a democrat, a Catholic, and from the South."[7] From White's appointment until 1949, the Court always included one, and usually two, Catholics: Joseph McKenna served from 1898 to 1925; Pierce Butler from 1923 to 1939; and Frank Murphy from 1940 to 1949. For almost thirty years (from 1898 to 1925), there were two Catholics on the Court, even though Catholics lacked the political influence they later acquired in the New Deal coalition. Roosevelt rewarded Catholic supporters with an unprecedented number of lower federal court judgeships, but he did not do the same with his appointments to the Courts.[8] When Murphy died in 1949, Truman did not feel compelled to appoint another Catholic. None sat on the high bench until Eisenhower's appointment of Brennan in 1956. Devoted to bipartisanship, Eisenhower wanted "a very good Catholic, even a conservative Democrat," in order to "show that we mean our declaration that the Court should be nonpartisan."[9] By contrast, Reagan appointed two Catholics, Antonin Scalia and Anthony Kennedy, even though he paid no attention to his nominees' religious affiliations in his quest to infuse a sharply conservative judicial philosophy into the Court. When nominated in 1991 by President George H.W. Bush, Justice Clarence Thomas belonged to a charismatic Episcopal Church, but he was raised as a Catholic, went to parochial schools, and later attended a seminary. Following his appointment, in 1996 he again began attending a Catholic Church. Like Reagan, President George W. Bush named two Catholics: Chief Justice John G. Roberts Jr., and Justice Samuel Alito Jr.

In 1853, President Millard Fillmore offered a position to Judah Benjamin, but Benjamin wanted to stay in the Senate. Not until President Woodrow Wilson's appointment of Brandeis in 1916 did the Court acquire its first Jewish justice. Opposition was not necessarily anti-Semitic but based largely on antagonism toward Brandeis's progressive legal views and reform politics. Seven prior ABA presidents, including William Howard Taft, proclaimed that Brandeis was "not a fit person to be a member of the Supreme Court of the United States."[10] After Brandeis's appointment, an expectation of a "Jewish seat" developed. With the confirmation of Cardozo in 1932 and his subsequent replacement by Frankfurter, two Jewish justices sat on the Court until Brandeis retired in 1939. When Frankfurter stepped down in 1962, the Jewish factor mattered, and Kennedy named Arthur Goldberg, his secretary of labor.[11] Three years later, Johnson persuaded Goldberg to become ambassador to the United Nations, and his vacancy was filled by the president's friend Abe Fortas. After Fortas's resignation in 1969, no other Jew sat on the high court until 1993, when it was joined by Justice Ruth Bader Ginsburg. Less than a year later, President

Clinton named a second Jewish justice, Stephen Breyer. As a result of Reagan's, George H.W. Bush's, Clinton's and George W. Bush's appointments, the Court has five Catholic and two Jewish justices, more non-Protestants than at any other time in the Court's history.

Although politically symbolic, religious representation on the Court never amounted to a quota system. Catholics and Jews were more often selected because of personal and ideological compatibility with the president. "There is no such thing as a Jewish seat," Goldberg observed, though his religion was a factor that Johnson considered when coaxing him to leave the Court. Johnson was intent on appointing Fortas, regardless of his religion. The two had known each other since the New Deal, and in 1964 LBJ had unsuccessfully urged Fortas to become attorney general. Fortas also initially declined appointment to the Court because he wanted "a few more years of activity."[12] Johnson persisted, and in the end Fortas reluctantly agreed to enter the marble temple. In sum, although once symbolically important, religious representation is no longer deemed crucial. "In contrast to Frankfurter, Goldberg, and Fortas," as Justice Ginsburg observed, "no one regarded [her] and Breyer as filling a Jewish seat."[13]

Primary Documents
Free Exercise Cases

9.6

Cantwell v. Connecticut

---

310 U.S. 296 (1940)

Editors' note: Due to space limitations, most footnotes for the court cases have been omitted.

MR. JUSTICE ROBERTS, delivered the opinion of the Court.

Newton Cantwell and his two sons, Jesse and Russell, members of a group known as Jehovah's witnesses, and claiming to be ordained ministers, were arrested in New Haven, Connecticut, and each was charged by information in five counts, with statutory and common law offenses. After trial in the Court of Common Pleas of New Haven County, each of them was convicted on the third count, which charged a violation of §6294 of the General Statutes of Connecticut, and on the fifth count, which charged commission of the common law offense of inciting a breach of the peace. . . .

The court held that the charge was not assault or breach of the peace or threats on Cantwell's part, but invoking or inciting others to breach of the peace, and that the facts supported the conviction of that offense.

First. We hold that the statute, as construed and applied to the appellants, deprives them of their liberty without due process of law in contravention of the Fourteenth Amendment. The fundamental concept of liberty embodied in that Amendment embraces the liberties guaranteed by the First Amendment. The First Amendment declares that Congress shall make no law respecting an establishment of religion or prohibiting the free exercise thereof. The Fourteenth Amendment has rendered the legislatures of the states as incompetent as Congress to enact such laws. The constitutional inhibition of legislation on the subject of religion has a double aspect. On the one hand, it forestalls compulsion by law of the acceptance of any creed or the practice of any form of worship. Freedom of conscience and freedom to adhere to such religious organization or form of worship as the individual may choose cannot be restricted by law. On the other hand, it safeguards the free exercise of the chosen form of religion. Thus, the Amendment embraces two concepts, freedom to believe and freedom to act. The first is absolute, but, in the nature of things, the [310 U.S. 296, 304] second cannot be. Conduct remains subject to regulation for the protection of society. The freedom to act must have appropriate definition to preserve the enforcement of that protection. In every case, the power to regulate must be so exercised as not, in attaining a permissible end, unduly to infringe the protected freedom. No one would contest the proposition that a state may not, by statute, wholly deny the right to preach or to disseminate religious views. Plainly, such a previous and absolute restraint would violate the terms of the guarantee. It is equally clear that a state may, by general and non-discriminatory legislation, regulate the times, the places, and the manner of soliciting upon its streets, and of holding meetings thereon, and may in other respects safeguard the peace, good order, and comfort of the community—without unconstitutionally invading the liberties protected by the Fourteenth Amendment. The appellants are right in their insistence that the Act in question is not such a regulation. If a certificate is procured, solicitation is permitted without restraint, but, in the absence of a certificate, solicitation is altogether prohibited. . . .

Second. We hold that, in the circumstances disclosed, the conviction of Jesse Cantwell on the fifth count must be set aside. Decision as to the lawfulness of the conviction demands the weighing of two conflicting interests. The fundamental law declares the interest of the United States that the free exercise of religion be not prohibited and that freedom to communicate information and opinion be not abridged. The state of Connecticut has an obvious interest in the preservation and protection of peace and good order within her borders. We must determine whether the alleged protection of the State's interest, means to which end would, in the absence of limitation by the Federal Constitution, lie wholly within the State's discretion, has been pressed, in this instance, to a point where it has come into fatal collision with the overriding interest protected by the federal compact.

Conviction on the fifth count was not pursuant to a statute evincing a legislative judgment that street discussion of religious affairs, because of its tendency to provoke disorder, should be regulated, or a judgment that the playing of a phonograph on the streets should in the interest of comfort or privacy be limited or prevented. Violation of an Act exhibiting such a legislative judgment and narrowly drawn to prevent the supposed evil, would pose a question differing from that we must here answer. Such a declaration of the State's policy [310 U.S. 296, 308] would weigh heavily in any challenge of the law as infringing constitutional limitations. Here, however, the judgment is based on a common law concept of the most general and undefined nature. The court below has held that the petitioner's conduct constituted the commission of an offense under the state law, and we accept its decision as binding upon us to that extent.

The offense known as breach of the peace embraces a great variety of conduct destroying or menacing public order and tranquility. It includes not only violent acts, but acts and words likely to produce violence in others. No one would have the hardihood to suggest that the principle of freedom of speech sanctions incitement to riot or that religious liberty connotes the privilege to exhort others to physical attack upon those belonging to another sect. When clear and present danger of riot, disorder, interference with traffic upon the public streets, or other immediate threat to public safety, peace, or order, appears, the power of the state to prevent or punish is obvious. Equally obvious is it that a state may not unduly suppress free communication of views, religious or other, under the guise of conserving desirable conditions. Here we have a situation analogous to a conviction under a statute sweeping in a great variety of conduct under a general and indefinite characterization, and leaving to the executive and judicial branches too wide a discretion in its application.

Having these considerations in mind, we note that Jesse Cantwell, on April 26, 1938, was upon a public street, where he had a right to be and where he had a right peacefully to impart his views to others. There is no showing that his deportment was noisy, truculent, overbearing or offensive. He requested of two pedestrians permission to play to them a phonograph record. The permission was granted. It is not claimed that he [310 U.S. 296, 309] intended to insult or affront the hearers by playing the record. It is plain that he wished only to interest them in his propaganda. The sound of the phonograph is not shown to have disturbed residents of the street, to have drawn a crowd, or to have impeded traffic. Thus far he had invaded no right or interest of the public, or of the men accosted.

The record played by Cantwell embodies a general attack on all organized religious systems as instruments of Satan and injurious to man; it then singles out the Roman Catholic Church for strictures couched in terms which naturally would offend not only persons of that persuasion, but all others who respect the honestly held religious faith of their fellows. The hearers were, in fact, highly offended. One of them said he felt like hitting Cantwell, and the other that he was tempted to throw Cantwell off the street. The one who testified he felt like hitting Cantwell said, in answer to the question 'Did you do anything else or have any other reaction?' 'No, sir, because he said he would take the victrola and he went.' The other witness testified that he told Cantwell he had better get off the street before something happened to him, and that was the end of the matter, as Cantwell picked up his books and walked up the street.

Cantwell's conduct, in the view of the court below, considered apart from the effect of his communication upon his hearers, did not amount to a breach of the peace. One may, however, be guilty of the offense if he commit acts or make statements likely to provoke violence and disturbance of good order, even though no such eventuality be intended. Decisions to this effect are many, but examination discloses that, in practically all, the provocative language which was held to amount to a breach of the peace consisted of profane, indecent, or abusive remarks directed to the person of the hearer. Resort to epithets or [310 U.S. 296, 310] personal abuse is not in any proper sense communication of information or opinion safeguarded by the Constitution, and its punishment as a criminal act would raise no question under that instrument.

We find in the instant case no assault or threatening of bodily harm, no truculent bearing, no intentional discourtesy, no personal abuse. On the contrary, we find only an effort to persuade a willing listener to buy a book or to contribute money in the interest of what Cantwell, however misguided others may think him, conceived to be true religion.

In the realm of religious faith, and in that of political belief, sharp differences arise. In both fields the tenets of one man may seem the rankest error to his neighbor. To persuade others to his own point of view, the pleader, as we know, at times resorts to exaggeration, to vilification of men who have been, or are, prominent in church or state, and even to false statement. But the people of this nation have ordained in the light of history, that, in spite of the probability of excesses and abuses, these liberties are, in the long view, essential to enlightened opinion and right conduct on the part of the citizens of a democracy.

The essential characteristic of these liberties is that, under their shield, many types of life, character, opinion and belief can develop unmolested and unobstructed. Nowhere is this shield more necessary than in our own country, for a people composed of many races and of many creeds. There are limits to the exercise of these liberties. The danger in these times from the coercive activities of those who in the delusion of racial or religious conceit would incite violence and breaches of the peace in order to deprive others of their equal right to the exercise of their liberties, is emphasized by events familiar to all. These and other transgressions of those limits the States appropriately may punish. [310 U.S. 296, 311] Although the contents of the record not unnaturally aroused animosity, we think that, in the absence of a statute narrowly drawn to define and punish specific conduct as constituting a clear and present danger to a substantial interest of the State, the petitioner's communication, considered in the light of the constitutional guarantees, raised no such clear and present menace to public peace and order as to render him liable to conviction of the common law offense in question.

The judgment affirming the convictions on the third and fifth counts is reversed, and the cause is remanded for further proceedings not inconsistent with this opinion.

Reversed.

9.7

Sherbert v. Verner

---

374 U.S. 398 (1963)

MR. JUSTICE BRENNAN delivered the opinion of the Court.

Appellant, a member of the Seventh-day Adventist Church, was discharged by her South Carolina employer because she would not work on Saturday, the Sabbath Day of her faith. When she was unable to obtain other employment because from conscientious scruples she would not take Saturday work, she filed a claim for [374 U.S. 398, 400] unemployment compensation benefits under the South Carolina Unemployment Compensation Act. That law provides that, to be eligible for benefits, a claimant must be "able to work and . . . available for work"; and, further, [374 U.S. 398, 401] that a claimant is ineligible for benefits "[i]f . . . he has failed, without good cause . . . to accept available suitable work when offered him by the employment office or the employer. . . ."

II

We turn first to the question whether the disqualification for benefits imposes any burden on the free exercise of appellant's religion. We think it is clear that it does. In a sense the consequences of such a disqualification to religious principles and practices may be only an indirect result of welfare legislation within the State's general competence to enact; it is true that no criminal sanctions directly compel appellant to work a six-day week. But this is only the beginning, not the end, of our [374 U.S. 398, 404] inquiry.[14] For "[i]f the purpose or effect of a law is to impede the observance of one or all religions or is to discriminate invidiously between religions, that law is constitutionally invalid even though the burden may be characterized as being only indirect." . . .

Significantly, South Carolina expressly saves the Sunday worshipper from having to make the kind of choice which we here hold infringes the Sabbatarian's religious liberty. When, in times of "national emergency," the textile plants are authorized by the State Commissioner of Labor to operate on Sunday, "no employee shall be required to work on Sunday . . . who is conscientiously opposed to Sunday work; and if any employee should refuse to work on Sunday on account of conscientious . . . objections he or she shall not jeopardize his or her seniority by such refusal or be discriminated against in any other manner." S.C. Code, 64-4. No question of the disqualification of a Sunday worshipper for benefits is likely to arise, since we cannot suppose that an employer will discharge him in violation of this statute. The unconstitutionality of the disqualification of the Sabbatarian is thus compounded by the religious discrimination which South Carolina's general statutory scheme necessarily effects.

III

We must next consider whether some compelling state interest enforced in the eligibility provisions of the South Carolina statute justifies the substantial infringement of appellant's First Amendment right. It is basic that no showing merely of a rational relationship to some colorable state interest would suffice; in this highly sensitive constitutional area, "[o]nly the gravest abuses, endangering paramount interests, give occasion for permissible limitation," *Thomas v. Collins*, 323 U.S. 516, 323 U.S. 530. [374 U.S. 398, 407] No such abuse or danger has been advanced in the present case . . .

IV

In holding as we do, plainly we are not fostering the "establishment" of the Seventh-day Adventist religion in South Carolina, for the extension of unemployment benefits to Sabbatarians in common with Sunday worshippers reflects nothing more than the governmental obligation of neutrality in the face of religious differences, and does not represent that involvement of religious with secular institutions which it is the object of the Establishment Clause to forestall. See *School District of Abington Township v. Schempp*, ante, p. 203. Nor does the recognition of the appellant's right to unemployment benefits under the state statute serve to abridge any other person's religious liberties. Nor do we, by our decision today, declare the existence of a constitutional right to unemployment benefits on the part [374 U.S. 398, 410] of all persons whose religious convictions are the cause of their unemployment. This is not a case in which an employee's religious convictions serve to make him a non-productive member of society. See note 2 supra. Finally, nothing we say today constrains the States to adopt any particular form or scheme of unemployment compensation. Our holding today is only that South Carolina may not constitutionally apply the eligibility provisions so as to constrain a worker to abandon his religious convictions respecting the day of rest. This holding but reaffirms a principle that we announced a decade and a half ago, namely that no State may "exclude individual Catholics, Lutherans, Mohammedans, Baptists, Jews, Methodists, Non-believers, Presbyterians, or the members of any other faith, because of their faith, or lack of it, from receiving the benefits of public welfare legislation." *Everson v. Board of Education*, 330 U.S. 1, 16.

In view of the result we have reached under the First and Fourteenth Amendments' guarantee of free exercise of religion, we have no occasion to consider appellant's claim that the denial of benefits also deprived her of the equal protection of the laws in violation of the Fourteenth Amendment.

The judgment of the South Carolina Supreme Court is reversed, and the case is remanded for further proceedings not inconsistent with this opinion.

It is so ordered. . . .

MR. JUSTICE HARLAN, whom MR. JUSTICE WHITE joins, dissenting.

. . . What the Court is holding is that if the State chooses to condition unemployment compensation on the applicant's availability for work, it is constitutionally compelled to carve out an exception—and to provide benefits—for those whose unavailability is due to their religious convictions. Such a holding has particular significance in two respects. [374 U.S. 398, 421]

. . . The secular purpose of the statute before us today is even clearer than that involved in *Braunfeld*. And just as in *Braunfeld*—where exceptions to the Sunday closing laws for Sabbatarians would have been inconsistent with the purpose to achieve a uniform day of rest and would have required case-by-case inquiry into religious beliefs—so here, an exception to the rules of eligibility based on religious convictions would necessitate judicial examination of those convictions and would be at odds with the limited purpose of the statute to smooth out the economy during periods of industrial instability. Finally, the indirect financial burden of the present law is far less than that involved in *Braunfeld*. Forcing a store owner to close his business on Sunday may well have the effect of depriving him of a satisfactory livelihood if his religious convictions require him to close on Saturday as well. Here we are dealing only with temporary benefits, amounting to a fraction of regular weekly wages and running for not more than 22 weeks. . . .

Second, the implications of the present decision are far more troublesome than its apparently narrow dimensions would indicate at first glance. The meaning of today's holding, as already noted, is that the State must furnish unemployment benefits to one who is unavailable for work if the unavailability stems from the exercise of religious convictions. The State, in other words, must single out for financial assistance those whose behavior is religiously motivated, even though it denies such assistance to others whose identical behavior (in this case, inability to work on Saturdays) is not religiously motivated . . . .

9.8

Employment Division v. Smith

494 U.S. 872 (1990)

JUSTICE SCALIA delivered the opinion of the Court.

This case requires us to decide whether the Free Exercise Clause of the First Amendment permits the State of Oregon to include religiously inspired peyote use within the reach of its general criminal prohibition on use of that drug, and thus permits the State to deny unemployment benefits to persons dismissed from their jobs because of such religiously inspired use.

I

. . . Respondents Alfred Smith and Galen Black (hereinafter respondents) were fired from their jobs with a private drug rehabilitation organization because they ingested peyote for sacramental purposes at a ceremony of the Native American Church, of which both are members. When respondents applied to petitioner Employment Division (hereinafter petitioner) for unemployment compensation, they were determined to be ineligible for benefits because they had been discharged for work-related "misconduct". The Oregon Court of Appeals reversed that determination, holding that the denial of benefits violated respondents' free exercise rights under the First Amendment. [494 U.S. 872, 875]

On appeal to the Oregon Supreme Court, petitioner argued that the denial of benefits was permissible because respondents' consumption of peyote was a crime under Oregon law. . . .

Before this Court in 1987, petitioner continued to maintain that the illegality of respondents' peyote consumption was relevant to their constitutional claim. We agreed . . . .

On remand, the Oregon Supreme Court held that respondents' religiously inspired use of peyote fell within the prohibition of the Oregon statute, which "makes no exception for the sacramental use" of the drug. 307 Ore. 68, 72–73, 763 P.2d 146, 148 (1988). It then considered whether that prohibition was valid under the Free Exercise Clause, and concluded that it was not. The court therefore reaffirmed its previous ruling that the State could not deny unemployment benefits to respondents for having engaged in that practice.

We again granted certiorari. 489 U.S. 1077 (1989).

II

Respondents' claim for relief rests on our decisions in *Sherbert v. Verner, supra, Thomas v. Review Bd. of Indiana Employment Security Div., supra,* and *Hobbie v. Unemployment Appeals Comm'n of Florida,* 480 U.S. 136 (1987), in which we held that a State could not condition the availability of unemployment insurance on an individual's willingness to forgo conduct required by his religion. As we observed in *Smith I,* however, the conduct at issue in those cases was not prohibited by law. We held that distinction to be critical, for "if Oregon does prohibit the religious use of peyote, and if that prohibition is consistent with the Federal Constitution, there is no federal right to engage in that conduct in Oregon," and "the State is free to withhold unemployment compensation from respondents for engaging in work-related misconduct, despite its religious motivation." 485 U.S. at 672. Now that the Oregon Supreme Court has confirmed that Oregon does prohibit the religious use of peyote, we proceed to consider whether that prohibition is permissible under the Free Exercise Clause.

A

The Free Exercise Clause of the First Amendment, which has been made applicable to the States by incorporation into the [494 U.S. 872, 877] Fourteenth Amendment, see *Cantwell v. Connecticut*, 310 U.S. 296, 303 (1940), provides that "Congress shall make no law respecting an establishment of religion, or *prohibiting the free exercise thereof. . . .*" U.S. Const. Amdt. I (emphasis added). The free exercise of religion means, first and foremost, the right to believe and profess whatever religious doctrine one desires. Thus, the First Amendment obviously excludes all "governmental regulation of religious beliefs as such." . . .

But the "exercise of religion" often involves not only belief and profession but the performance of (or abstention from) physical acts: assembling with others for a worship service, participating in sacramental use of bread and wine, proselytizing, abstaining from certain foods or certain modes of transportation. It would be true, we think (though no case of ours has involved the point), that a state would be "prohibiting the free exercise [of religion]" if it sought to ban such acts or abstentions only when they are engaged in for religious reasons, or only because of the religious belief that they display. It would doubtless be unconstitutional, for example, to ban the casting of "statues that are to be used [494 U.S. 872, 878] for worship purposes," or to prohibit bowing down before a golden calf.

Respondents in the present case, however, seek to carry the meaning of "prohibiting the free exercise [of religion]" one large step further. They contend that their religious motivation for using peyote places them beyond the reach of a criminal law that is not specifically directed at their religious practice, and that is concededly constitutional as applied to those who use the drug for other reasons. They assert, in other words, that "prohibiting the free exercise [of religion]" includes requiring any individual to observe a generally applicable law that requires (or forbids) the performance of an act that his religious belief forbids (or requires). As a textual matter, we do not think the words must be given that meaning. . . .

We have never held that an individual's religious beliefs [494 U.S. 872, 879] excuse him from compliance with an otherwise valid law prohibiting conduct that the State is free to regulate. . . .

The only decisions in which we have held that the First Amendment bars application of a neutral, generally applicable law to religiously motivated action have involved not the Free Exercise Clause alone, but the Free Exercise Clause in conjunction with other constitutional protections. . . .

The present case does not present such a hybrid situation, but a free exercise claim unconnected with any communicative activity or parental right. Respondents urge us to hold, quite simply, that when otherwise prohibitable conduct is accompanied by religious convictions, not only the convictions but the conduct itself must be free from governmental regulation. We have never held that, and decline to do so now. There being no contention that Oregon's drug law represents an attempt to regulate religious beliefs, the communication of religious beliefs, or the raising of one's children in those beliefs, the rule to which we have adhered ever since *Reynolds* plainly controls. . . .

B

Respondents argue that even though exemption from generally applicable criminal laws need not automatically be extended to religiously motivated actors, at least the claim for a [494 U.S. 872, 883] religious exemption must be evaluated under the balancing test set forth in *Sherbert v. Verner*, 374 U.S. 398 (1963). . . .

Values that are protected against government interference through enshrinement in the Bill of Rights are not thereby banished from the political process. Just as a society that believes in the negative protection accorded to the press by the First Amendment is likely to enact laws that affirmatively foster the dissemination of the printed word, so also a society that believes in the negative protection accorded to religious belief can be expected to be solicitous of that value in its legislation as well. It is therefore not surprising that a number of States have made an exception to their drug laws for sacramental peyote use. See, e.g., Ariz. Rev. Stat. Ann. 13-3402(B)(1)-(3) (1989); Colo. Rev. Stat. 12-22-317(3) (1985); N.M. Stat. Ann. 30-31-6(D) (Supp. 1989). But to say that a non-discriminatory religious practice exemption is permitted, or even that it is desirable, is not to say that it is constitutionally required, and that the appropriate occasions for its creation can be discerned by the courts. It may fairly be said that leaving accommodation to the political process will place at a relative disadvantage those religious practices that are not widely engaged in; but that unavoidable consequence of democratic government must be preferred to a system in which each conscience is a law unto itself or in which judges weigh the social importance of all laws against the centrality of all religious beliefs.

Because respondents' ingestion of peyote was prohibited under Oregon law, and because that prohibition is constitutional, Oregon may, consistent with the Free Exercise Clause, deny respondents unemployment compensation when their dismissal results from use of the drug. The decision of the Oregon Supreme Court is accordingly reversed.

It is so ordered.

Establishment Cases

9.9

Lemon v. Kurtzman

---

403 U.S. 602 (1971)

MR. CHIEF JUSTICE BURGER delivered the opinion of the Court.

These two appeals raise questions as to Pennsylvania and Rhode Island statutes providing state aid to church-related elementary and secondary schools. Both statutes are challenged as violative of the Establishment and Free Exercise Clauses of the First Amendment and the Due Process Clause of the Fourteenth Amendment.

Pennsylvania has adopted a statutory program that provides financial support to nonpublic elementary and [403 U.S. 602, 607] secondary schools by way of reimbursement for the cost of teachers' salaries, textbooks, and instructional materials in specified secular subjects. Rhode Island has adopted a statute under which the State pays directly to teachers in nonpublic elementary schools a supplement of 15% of their annual salary. Under each statute state aid has been given to church-related educational institutions. We hold that both statutes are unconstitutional. . . .

II

. . . The language of the Religion Clauses of the First Amendment is at best opaque, particularly when compared with other portions of the Amendment. Its authors did not simply prohibit the establishment of a state church or a state religion, an area history shows they regarded as very important and fraught with great dangers. Instead they commanded that there should be "no law respecting an establishment of religion." A law may be one "respecting" the forbidden objective while falling short of its total realization. A law "respecting" the proscribed result, that is, the establishment of religion, is not always easily identifiable as one violative of the Clause. A given law might not establish a state religion, but nevertheless be one "respecting" that end in the sense of being a step that could lead to such establishment and hence offend the First Amendment.

In the absence of precisely stated constitutional prohibitions, we must draw lines with reference to the three main evils against which the Establishment Clause was intended to afford protection: "sponsorship, financial support, and active involvement of the sovereign in religious activity." *Walz v. Tax Commission,* 397 U.S. 664, 668 (1970).

Every analysis in this area must begin with consideration of the cumulative criteria developed by the Court over many years. Three such tests may be gleaned from our cases. First, the statute must have a secular legislative purpose; second, its principal or primary effect must be one that neither advances nor inhibits religion, *Board of Education v. Allen,* 392 U.S. 236, 243 (1968); [403 U.S. 602, 613] finally, the statute must not foster "an excessive government entanglement with religion." *Walz, supra,* at 674.

Inquiry into the legislative purposes of the Pennsylvania and Rhode Island statutes affords no basis for a conclusion that the legislative intent was to advance religion. On the contrary, the statutes themselves clearly state that they are intended to enhance the quality of the secular education in all schools covered by the compulsory attendance laws. There is no reason to believe the legislatures meant anything else. A State always has a legitimate concern for maintaining minimum standards in all schools it allows to operate. As in *Allen,* we find nothing here that undermines the stated legislative intent; it must therefore be accorded appropriate deference.

In Allen the Court acknowledged that secular and religious teachings were not necessarily so intertwined that secular textbooks furnished to students by the State were in fact instrumental in the teaching of religion. 392 U.S. at 248. The legislatures of Rhode Island and Pennsylvania have concluded that secular and religious education are identifiable and separable. In the abstract we have no quarrel with this conclusion.

The two legislatures, however, have also recognized that church-related elementary and secondary schools have a significant religious mission, and that a substantial portion of their activities is religiously oriented. They have therefore sought to create statutory restrictions designed to guarantee the separation between secular and religious educational functions and to ensure that State financial aid supports only the former. All these provisions are precautions taken in candid recognition that these programs approached, even if they did not intrude upon, the forbidden areas under the Religion Clauses. We need not decide whether these legislative precautions restrict the principal or primary effect of the programs to the point where they do not offend the Religion [403 U.S. 602, 614] Clauses, for we conclude that the cumulative impact of the entire relationship arising under the statutes in each State involves excessive entanglement between government and religion. . . .

V

. . . The sole question is whether state aid to these schools can be squared with the dictates of the Religion Clauses. Under our system, the choice has been made that government is to be entirely excluded from the area of religious instruction and churches excluded from the affairs of government. The Constitution decrees that religion must be a private matter for the individual, the family, and the institutions of private choice, and that while some involvement and entanglement are inevitable, lines must be drawn.

The judgment of the Rhode Island District Court in No. 569 and No. 570 is affirmed. The judgment of the Pennsylvania District Court in No. 89 is reversed, and the case is remanded for further proceedings consistent with this opinion.

9.10

Zelman v. Simmons-Harris

536 U.S. 639 (2002)

CHIEF JUSTICE REHNQUIST delivered the opinion of the Court.

The State of Ohio has established a pilot program designed to provide educational choices to families with children who reside in the Cleveland City School District. The question presented is whether this program offends the Establishment Clause of the United States Constitution. We hold that it does not.

There are more than 75,000 children enrolled in the Cleveland City School District. The majority of these children are from low-income and minority families. Few of these families enjoy the means to send their children to any school other than an inner-city public school. For more than a generation, however, Cleveland's public schools have been among the worst performing public schools in the Nation. . . .

It is against this backdrop that Ohio enacted, among other initiatives, its Pilot Project Scholarship Program, Ohio Rev. Code Ann. §§3313.974–3313.979 (Anderson

1999 and Supp. 2000) (program). The program provides financial assistance to families in any Ohio school district that is or has been "under federal court order requiring supervision and operational management of the district by the state superintendent." §3313.975(A). Cleveland is the only Ohio school district to fall within that category.

The program provides two basic kinds of assistance to parents of children in a covered district. First, the program provides tuition aid for students in kindergarten through third grade, expanding each year through eighth grade, to attend a participating public or private school of their parent's choosing. §§3313.975(B) and (C)(1). Second, the program provides tutorial aid for students who choose to remain enrolled in public school. §3313.975(A). . . .

The program has been in operation within the Cleveland City School District since the 1996–1997 school year. In the 1999–2000 school year, 56 private schools participated in the program, 46 (or 82%) of which had a religious affiliation. None of the public schools in districts adjacent to Cleveland have elected to participate. More than 3,700 students participated in the scholarship program, most of whom (96%) enrolled in religiously affiliated schools. Sixty percent of these students were from families at or below the poverty line. In the 1998–1999 school year, approximately 1,400 Cleveland public school students received tutorial aid. This number was expected to double during the 1999–2000 school year.

The program is part of a broader undertaking by the State to enhance the educational options of Cleveland's schoolchildren in response to the 1995 takeover. That undertaking includes programs governing community and magnet schools. . . .

In July 1999, respondents filed this action in United States District Court, seeking to enjoin the reenacted program on the ground that it violated the Establishment Clause of the United States Constitution. In August 1999, the District Court issued a preliminary injunction barring further implementation of the program, 54 F. Supp. 2d 725 (ND Ohio), which we stayed pending review by the Court of Appeals, 528 U.S. 983 (1999). In December 1999, the District Court granted summary judgment for respondents. 72 F. Supp. 2d 834. In December 2000, a divided panel of the Court of Appeals affirmed the judgment of the District Court, finding that the program had the "primary effect" of advancing religion in violation of the Establishment Clause. 234 F. 3d 945 (CA6). The Court of Appeals stayed its mandate pending disposition in this Court. App. to Pet. for Cert. in No. 01–1779, p. 151. We granted certiorari, 533 U.S. 976 (2001), and now reverse the Court of Appeals.

The Establishment Clause of the First Amendment, applied to the States through the Fourteenth Amendment, prevents a State from enacting laws that have the "purpose" or "effect" of advancing or inhibiting religion. *Agostini* v. *Felton*, 521 U.S. 203, 222–223 (1997) ("[W]e continue to ask whether the government acted with the purpose of advancing or inhibiting religion [and] whether the aid has the 'effect' of advancing or inhibiting religion" (citations omitted)). There is no dispute that the program challenged here was enacted for the valid secular purpose of providing educational assistance to poor children in a demonstrably failing public school system. Thus, the question presented is whether the Ohio program nonetheless has the forbidden "effect" of advancing or inhibiting religion.

To answer that question, our decisions have drawn a consistent distinction between government programs that provide aid directly to religious schools, *Mitchell* v. *Helms*, 530 U.S. 793, 810–814 (2000) (plurality opinion); *id.*, at 841–844 (*O'Connor, J.*, concurring in judgment); *Agostini, supra*, at 225–227; *Rosenberger* v. *Rector and Visitors of Univ. of Va.*, 515 U.S. 819, 842 (1995) (collecting cases), and programs of true private choice, in which government aid reaches religious schools only as a result of the genuine and independent choices of private individuals, *Mueller* v. *Allen*, 463 U.S. 388 (1983); *Witters* v. *Washington Dept. of Servs. for Blind*, 474 U.S. 481 (1986); *Zobrest* v. *Catalina Foothills School Dist.*, 509 U.S. 1 (1993). While our jurisprudence with respect to the constitutionality of direct aid programs has "changed significantly" over the past two decades, *Agostini*, *supra*, at 236, our jurisprudence with respect to true private choice programs has remained consistent and unbroken. Three times we have confronted Establishment Clause challenges to neutral government programs that provide aid directly to a broad class of individuals, who, in turn, direct the aid to religious schools or institutions of their own choosing. Three times we have rejected such challenges. . . .

Mueller, *Witters*, and *Zobrest* thus make clear that where a government aid program is neutral with respect to religion, and provides assistance directly to a broad class of citizens who, in turn, direct government aid to religious schools wholly as a result of their own genuine and independent private choice, the program is not readily subject to challenge under the Establishment Clause. A program that shares these features permits government aid to reach religious institutions only by way of the deliberate choices of numerous individual recipients. The incidental advancement of a religious mission, or the perceived endorsement of a religious message, is reasonably attributable to the individual recipient, not to the government, whose role ends with the disbursement of benefits. As a plurality of this Court recently observed:

"[I]f numerous private choices, rather than the single choice of a government, determine the distribution of aid, pursuant to neutral eligibility criteria, then a government cannot, or at least cannot easily, grant special favors that might lead to a religious establishment." *Mitchell*, 530 U.S., at 810.

See also *id.*, at 843 (O'Connor, J., concurring in judgment) ("[W]hen government aid supports a school's religious mission only because of independent decisions made by numerous individuals to guide their secular aid to that school, 'no reasonable observer is likely to draw from the facts . . . an inference that the State itself is endorsing a religious practice or belief'" (quoting *Witters*, *supra*, at 493 (O'Connor, J., concurring in part and concurring in judgment))). It is precisely for these reasons that we have never found a program of true private choice to offend the Establishment Clause.

We believe that the program challenged here is a program of true private choice, consistent with *Mueller*, *Witters*, and *Zobrest*, and thus constitutional. As was true in those cases, the Ohio program is neutral in all respects toward religion. It is part of a general and multifaceted undertaking by the State of Ohio to provide educational opportunities to the children of a failed school district. It confers educational assistance directly to a broad class of individuals defined without reference to religion, *i.e.*, any parent of a school-age child who resides in the Cleveland City School District. The program permits the participation of *all* schools within the district, religious or nonreligious. Adjacent public schools also may participate and have a financial incentive to do so. Program benefits are available to participating families on neutral terms, with no reference to religion. The only preference stated anywhere in the program is a preference for low-income families, who receive greater assistance and are given priority for admission at participating schools.

There are no "financial incentive[s]" that "ske[w]" the program toward religious schools. *Witters*, *supra*, at 487–488. Such incentives "[are] not present . . . where the aid is allocated on the basis of neutral, secular criteria that neither favor nor disfavor religion, and is made available to both religious and secular beneficiaries on a nondiscriminatory basis." *Agostini, supra,* at 231. The program here in fact creates financial *dis*incentives for religious schools, with private schools receiving only half the government assistance given to community schools and one-third the assistance given to magnet schools. Adjacent public schools, should any choose to accept program students, are also eligible to receive two to three times the state funding of a private religious school. Families too have a financial disincentive to choose a private religious school over other schools. Parents that choose to participate in the scholarship program and then to enroll their children in a private school (religious or nonreligious) must copay a portion of the school's tuition. Families that choose a community school, magnet school, or traditional public school pay nothing. Although such features of the program are not necessary to its constitutionality, they clearly dispel the claim that the program "creates . . . financial incentive[s] for parents to choose a sectarian school." *Zobrest,* 509 U.S., at 10.3 . . .

In sum, the Ohio program is entirely neutral with respect to religion. It provides benefits directly to a wide spectrum of individuals, defined only by financial need and residence in a particular school district. It permits such individuals to exercise genuine choice among options public and private, secular and religious. The program is therefore a program of true private choice. In keeping with an unbroken line of decisions rejecting challenges to similar programs, we hold that the program does not offend the Establishment Clause.

The judgment of the Court of Appeals is reversed.

It is so ordered.

9.11

Locke v. Davey

---

540 U.S. 712 (2004)

CHIEF JUSTICE REHNQUIST delivered the opinion of the Court.

The State of Washington established the Promise Scholarship Program to assist academically gifted students with postsecondary education expenses. In accordance with the State Constitution, students may not use the scholarship at an institution where they are pursuing a degree in devotional theology. We hold that such an exclusion from an otherwise inclusive aid program does not violate the Free Exercise Clause of the First Amendment.

The Washington State Legislature found that "[s]tudents who work hard . . . and successfully complete high school with high academic marks may not have the financial ability to attend college because they cannot obtain financial aid or the financial aid is insufficient." Wash. Rev. Code §28B.119.005 (Supp. 2004). In 1999, to assist these high-achieving students, the legislature created the Promise Scholarship Program, which provides a scholarship, renewable for one year, to eligible students for postsecondary education expenses. Students may spend their funds on any education-related expense, including room and board. The scholarships are funded through the State's general fund, and their amount varies each year depending on the annual appropriation, which is evenly prorated among the eligible students. Wash. Admin. Code §250-80-050(2) (2003). The scholarship was worth $1,125 for academic year 1999–2000 and $1,542 for 2000–2001.

To be eligible for the scholarship, a student must meet academic, income, and enrollment requirements. A student must graduate from a Washington public or private high school and either graduate in the top 15% of his graduating class, or attain on the first attempt a cumulative score of 1,200 or better on the Scholastic Assessment Test I or a score of 27 or better on the American College Test. §§250-80-020(12)(a)-(d). The student's family income must be less than 135% of the State's median. §250-80-020(12)(e). Finally, the student must enroll "at least half time in an eligible postsecondary institution in the state of Washington," and may not pursue a degree in theology at that institution while receiving the scholarship. §§250-80-020(12)(f)-(g); see also Wash. Rev. Code §28B.10.814 (1997) ("No aid shall be awarded to any student who is pursuing a degree in theology"). Private institutions, including those religiously affiliated, qualify as "eligible postsecondary institution[s]" if they are accredited by a nationally recognized accrediting body. See Wash. Admin. Code §250-80-020(13). A "degree in theology" is not defined in the statute, but, as both parties concede, the statute simply codifies the State's constitutional prohibition on providing funds to students to pursue degrees that are "devotional in nature or designed to induce religious faith." Brief for Petitioners 6; Brief for Respondent 8; see also Wash. Const., Art. I, §11.

A student who applies for the scholarship and meets the academic and income requirements is notified that he is eligible for the scholarship if he meets the enrollment requirements. E.g., App. 95. Once the student enrolls at an eligible institution, the institution must certify that the student is enrolled at least half time and that the student is not pursuing a degree in devotional theology. The institution, rather than the State, determines whether the student's major is devotional. Id., at 126, 131. If the student meets the enrollment requirements, the scholarship funds are sent to the institution for distribution to the student to pay for tuition or other educational expenses. See Wash. Admin. Code §250–80–060.

Respondent, Joshua Davey, was awarded a Promise Scholarship, and chose to attend Northwest College. Northwest is a private, Christian college affiliated with the Assemblies of God denomination, and is an eligible institution under the Promise Scholarship Program. Davey had "planned for many years to attend a Bible college and to prepare [himself] through that college training for a lifetime of ministry, specifically as a church pastor." App. 40. To that end, when he enrolled in Northwest College, he decided to pursue a double major in pastoral ministries and business management/administration. Id., at 43. There is no dispute that the pastoral ministries degree is devotional and therefore excluded under the Promise Scholarship Program.

At the beginning of the 1999–2000 academic year, Davey met with Northwest's director of financial aid. He learned for the first time at this meeting that he could not use his scholarship to pursue a devotional theology degree. He was informed that to receive the funds appropriated for his use, he must certify in writing that he was not pursuing such a degree at Northwest. He refused to sign the form and did not receive any scholarship funds.

Davey then brought an action under 42 U. S. C. §1983 against various state officials (hereinafter State) in the District Court for the Western District of Washington to enjoin the State from refusing to award the scholarship solely because a student is pursuing a devotional theology degree, and for damages. He argued the denial of his scholarship based on his decision to pursue a theology degree violated, *inter alia*, the Free Exercise, Establishment, and Free Speech Clauses of the First Amendment, as incorporated by the Fourteenth Amendment, and the Equal Protection Clause of the Fourteenth Amendment. After the District Court denied Davey's request for a preliminary injunction, the parties filed cross-motions for summary judgment. The District Court rejected Davey's constitutional claims and granted summary judgment in favor of the State.

A divided panel of the United States Court of Appeals for the Ninth Circuit reversed. 299 F. 3d 748 (2002). The court concluded that the State had singled out religion for unfavorable treatment and thus under our decision in *Church of Lukumi Babalu Aye, Inc.* v. *Hialeah*, 508 U.S. 520 (1993), the State's exclusion of theology majors must be narrowly tailored to achieve a compelling state interest. 299 F. 3d, at 757–758. Finding that the State's own antiestablishment concerns were not compelling, the court declared Washington's Promise Scholarship Program unconstitutional. *Id.*, at 760. We granted certiorari, 538 U.S. 1031 (2003), and now reverse.

The Religion Clauses of the First Amendment provide: "Congress shall make no law respecting an establishment of religion, or prohibiting the free exercise thereof." These two Clauses, the Establishment Clause and the Free Exercise Clause, are frequently in tension. See *Norwood* v. *Harrison*, 413 U.S. 455, 469 (1973) (citing *Tilton* v. *Richardson*, 403 U.S. 672, 677 (1971)). Yet we have long said that "there is room for play in the joints" between them. *Walz* v. *Tax Comm'n of City of New York*, 397 U.S. 664, 669 (1970). In other words, there are some state actions permitted by the Establishment Clause but not required by the Free Exercise Clause.

This case involves that "play in the joints" described above. Under our Establishment Clause precedent, the link between government funds and religious training is broken by the independent and private choice of recipients. See *Zelman* v. *Simmons-Harris*, 536 U.S. 639, 652 (2002); *Zobrest* v. *Catalina Foothills School Dist.*, 509 U.S. 1, 13–14 (1993); *Witters* v. *Washington Dept. of Servs. for Blind*, 474 U.S. 481, 487 (1986); *Mueller* v. *Allen*, 463 U.S. 388, 399–400 (1983). As such, there is no doubt that the State could, consistent with the Federal Constitution, permit Promise Scholars to pursue a degree in devotional theology, see *Witters*, *supra*, at 489, and the State does not contend otherwise. The question before us, however, is whether Washington, pursuant to its own constitution, which has been authoritatively interpreted as prohibiting even indirectly funding religious instruction that will prepare students for the ministry, see *Witters* v. *State Comm'n for the Blind*, 112 Wash. 2d 363, 369–370, 771 P. 2d 1119, 1122 (1989); cf. *Witters* v. *State Comm'n for the Blind*, 102 Wash. 2d 624, 629, 689 P. 2d 53, 56 (1984) ("It is not the role of the State to pay for the religious education of future ministers"), rev'd, 474 U.S. 481, *supra*, can deny them such funding without violating the Free Exercise Clause.

. . . [W]e believe that the entirety of the Promise Scholarship Program goes a long way toward including religion in its benefits.[15] The program permits students to attend pervasively religious schools, so long as they are accredited. As Northwest advertises, its "concept of education is distinctly Christian in the evangelical sense." App. 168. It prepares *all* of its students, "through instruction, through modeling, [and] through [its] classes, to use . . . the Bible as their guide, as the truth," no matter their chosen profession. *Id.*, at 169. And under the Promise Scholarship Program's current guidelines, students are still eligible to take devotional theology courses. Davey notes all students at Northwest are required to take at least four devotional courses, "Exploring the Bible," "Principles of Spiritual

Development," "Evangelism in the Christian Life," and "Christian Doctrine," Brief for Respondent 11, n. 5; see also App. 151, and some students may have additional religious requirements as part of their majors. Brief for Respondent 11, n. 5; see also App. 150–151.

In short, we find neither in the history or text of Article I, §11 of the Washington Constitution, nor in the operation of the Promise Scholarship Program, anything that suggests animus towards religion.[16] Given the historic and substantial state interest at issue, we therefore cannot conclude that the denial of funding for vocational religious instruction alone is inherently constitutionally suspect.

Without a presumption of unconstitutionality, Davey's claim must fail. The State's interest in not funding the pursuit of devotional degrees is substantial and the exclusion of such funding places a relatively minor burden on Promise Scholars. If any room exists between the two Religion Clauses, it must be here. We need not venture further into this difficult area in order to uphold the Promise Scholarship Program as currently operated by the State of Washington.

The judgment of the Court of Appeals is therefore

Reversed.

JUSTICE SCALIA, with whom JUSTICE THOMAS joins, dissenting.

In *Church of Lukumi Babalu Aye, Inc.* v. *Hialeah,* 508 U.S. 520 (1993), the majority opinion held that "[a] law burdening religious practice that is not neutral . . . must undergo the most rigorous of scrutiny," *id.,* at 546, and that "the minimum requirement of neutrality is that a law not discriminate on its face," *id.,* at 533. The concurrence of two Justices stated that "[w]hen a law discriminates against religion as such, . . . it automatically will fail strict scrutiny." *Id.,* at 579 (Blackmun, J., joined by *O'Connor, J.,* concurring in judgment). And the concurrence of a third Justice endorsed the "noncontroversial principle" that "formal neutrality" is a "necessary conditio[n] for free-exercise constitutionality." *Id.,* at 563 (*Souter, J.,* concurring in part and concurring in judgment). These opinions are irreconcilable with today's decision, which sustains a public benefits program that facially discriminates against religion.

I

We articulated the principle that governs this case more than 50 years ago in *Everson* v. *Board of Ed. of Ewing,* 330 U.S. 1 (1947):

"New Jersey cannot hamper its citizens in the free exercise of their own religion. Consequently, it cannot exclude individual Catholics, Lutherans, Mohammedans, Baptists, Jews, Methodists, Non-believers, Presbyterians, or the members of any other faith, because of their faith, or lack of it, from receiving the benefits of public welfare legislation." *Id.,* at 16 (emphasis deleted).

When the State makes a public benefit generally available, that benefit becomes part of the baseline against which burdens on religion are measured; and when the State withholds that benefit from some individuals solely on the basis of religion, it violates the Free Exercise Clause no less than if it had imposed a special tax.

That is precisely what the State of Washington has done here. It has created a generally available public benefit, whose receipt is conditioned only on academic performance, income, and attendance at an accredited school. It has then carved out a solitary course of study for exclusion: theology. Wash. Rev. Code §28B.119.010(8) (Supp. 2004); Wash. Admin. Code §250-80-020(12)(g) (2003). No field of study but religion is singled out for disfavor in this fashion. Davey is not asking for a special benefit to which others are not entitled. Cf. *Lyng* v. *Northwest Indian Cemetery Protective Assn.*, 485 U.S. 439, 453 (1988). He seeks only *equal* treatment—the right to direct his scholarship to his chosen course of study, a right every other Promise Scholar enjoys. . . .

The Court does not dispute that the Free Exercise Clause places some constraints on public benefits programs, but finds none here, based on a principle of "'play in the joints.'" *Ante*, at 4. I use the term "principle" loosely, for that is not so much a legal principle as a refusal to apply *any* principle when faced with competing constitutional directives. There is nothing anomalous about constitutional commands that abut. A municipality hiring public contractors may not discriminate *against* blacks or *in favor of* them; it cannot discriminate a little bit each way and then plead "play in the joints" when hauled into court. If the Religion Clauses demand neutrality, we must enforce them, in hard cases as well as easy ones. . . .

In any case, the State already has all the play in the joints it needs. There are any number of ways it could respect both its unusually sensitive concern for the conscience of its taxpayers *and* the Federal Free Exercise Clause. It could make the scholarships redeemable only at public universities (where it sets the curriculum), or only for select courses of study. Either option would replace a program that facially discriminates against religion with one that just happens not to subsidize it. The State could also simply abandon the scholarship program altogether. If that seems a dear price to pay for freedom of conscience, it is only because the State has defined that freedom so broadly that it would be offended by a program with such an incidental, indirect religious effect.

What is the nature of the State's asserted interest here? It cannot be protecting the pocketbooks of its citizens; given the tiny fraction of Promise Scholars who would pursue theology degrees, the amount of any citizen's tax bill at stake is *de minimis*. It cannot be preventing mistaken appearance of endorsement; where a State merely declines to penalize students for selecting a religious major, "[n]o reasonable observer is likely to draw . . . an inference that the State itself is endorsing a religious practice or belief." *Id.*, at 493 (*O'Connor, J.*, concurring in part and concurring in judgment). Nor can Washington's exclusion be defended as a means of assuring that the State will neither favor nor disfavor Davey in his religious calling. Davey will throughout his life contribute to the public fisc through sales taxes on personal purchases, property taxes on his home, and so on; and nothing in the Court's opinion turns on whether Davey winds up a net winner or loser in the State's tax-and-spend scheme.

No, the interest to which the Court defers is not fear of a conceivable Establishment Clause violation, budget constraints, avoidance of endorsement, or substantive neutrality—none of these. It is a pure philosophical preference: the State's opinion that it would violate taxpayers' freedom of conscience *not* to discriminate against candidates for the ministry. This sort of protection of "freedom of conscience" has no logical limit and can justify the singling out of religion for exclusion from public programs in virtually any context. The Court never says whether it deems this interest compelling (the opinion is devoid of any mention of standard of review) but, self-evidently, it is not.[17]

Notes

1. Although Segal grounded this model in legal standards, discussing at length the constitutional requirements and judicial interpretations, he included the caveat that "such a model is not necessarily inconsistent with policy preferences" (1984, 892). Segal and Spaeth argue that "facts obviously affect the decisions of the Supreme Court, but on that point the attitudinal model does not differ from the legal model. The models differ in that proponents of the legal model conjoin facts with legalistic considerations . . . , while proponents of the attitudinal model describe the justices' votes as an expression of the fact situations applied to their personal policy preferences" (2002, 319).

2. The pair-wise correlation for justices' support rates between 1953 and 2007 Terms was -0.59 (p = 0.004).

3. These data are taken from Spaeth (2008), examining orally argued decisions that resulted in a signed opinion. Religious and civil liberty cases were identified using Spaeth's issue and value coding.

4. The justices' votes were obtained from Spaeth (2008) and the justices' ideology scores were derived from Martin and Quinn (2007). The cite is correct as 2007.

5. A difference in means test reveals that the difference between the average ideology of a civil liberties supporter and the average ideology of a free exercise supporter is not statistically significant.

6. I examined the Supreme Court's decision to identify the attorney who argued a case before the Court. Then, using a search in Westlaw for that attorney's name, I determined the number of prior cases that an attorney had argued before the Supreme Court.

7. L.R. Wilfry to the President, October 31, 1910, Edward White Papers, Library of Congress, Manuscripts Division, Washington, D.C.

8. See Memorandum for the Attorney General, November 27, 1942, and Comparative List Showing Religion of Judges Appointed during the Periods of 1922–1933 and 1933–1942, Francis Biddle Papers, Box 2, Franklin D. Roosevelt Presidential Library, Hyde Park, New York.

9. Note on telephone conversation with Attorney General Brownell, September 9, 1956, Dwight David Eisenhower Diaries, Box 11, Dwight David Eisenhower Presidential Library, Abilene, Kansas.

10. Quoted in Memorandum on Confirmation of Justice Louis Brandeis, White House Central Files, Fortas/Thornberry Series, Chron. File, Lyndon Baines Johnson Presidential Library, Austin, Texas. See, generally, A.T. Mason, *Brandeis: A Free Man's Life* (New York: Viking Press, 1946).

11. Kennedy Interview, at 319, John F. Kennedy Presidential Library, Waltham, Massachusetts.

12. Letter to the President, July 19, 1965, White House Central Files-Federal Government, Box 535, Lyndon Baines Johnson Presidential Library, Austin, Texas.

13. Justice Ruth Bader Ginsburg, "From Benjamin to Breyer: Is There a Jewish Seat?" 24 *The Supreme Court Historical Quarterly* no. 3 (2003).

14. In a closely analogous context, this Court said: ". . . the fact that no direct restraint or punishment is imposed upon speech or assembly does not determine the free speech question. Under some circumstances, indirect 'discouragements' undoubtedly have the same coercive effect upon the exercise of First Amendment rights as imprisonment, fines, injunctions or taxes. A requirement that adherents of particular religious faiths or political parties wear identifying arm-bands, for example, is obviously of this nature." *American Communications Assn. v. Douds*, 339 U.S. 382, 402. Cf. *Smith v. California*, 361 U.S. 147, 153–155.

15. Washington has also been solicitous in ensuring that its constitution is not hostile towards religion, see *State ex rel. Gallwey v. Grimm*, 146 Wash. 2d 445, 470, 48 P. 3d 274, 286 (2002) ("[I]t was never the intention that our constitution should be construed in any manner indicating any hostility toward religion." (citation omitted)), and at least in some respects, its constitution provides greater protection of religious liberties than the Free Exercise Clause, see *First Covenant Church of Seattle v. Seattle*, 120 Wash. 2d 203, 223–229, 840 P. 2d 174, 186–188 (1992) (rejecting standard in *Employment Div., Dept. of Human Resources of Ore. V. Smith*, 494 U.S. 872 (1990), in favor of more protective rule); *Munns v. Martin*, 131 Wash. 2d 192, 201, 930 P. 2d 318, 322 (1997) (holding a city ordinance that imposed controls on demolition of historic structures inapplicable to the Catholic Church's plan to demolish an old

school building and build a new pastoral center because the facilities are intimately associated with the church's religious mission). We have found nothing in Washington's overall approach that indicates it "single[s] out" anyone "for special burdens on the basis of . . . religious callings" as *Justice Scalia* contends, *post,* at 6.

16. Although we have sometimes characterized the Establishment Clause as prohibiting the State from "disproving of a particular religion or religion in general," *Church of Lukumi Babalu Aye, Inc. v. Hialeah,* 508 U.S. 520, 532 (1993) (citing cases), for the reasons noted *supra,* the State has not impermissibly done so here.

17. The court argues that those pursuing theology majors are not comparable to other Promise Scholars because "training for religious professions and training for secular professions are not fungible." *Ante,* at 7. That may well be, but all it proves is that the State has a *rational basis* for treating religion differently. If that is all the Court requires, its holding is contrary not only to precedent, see *supra,* at 1, but to common sense. If religious discrimination required only a rational basis, the Free Exercise Clause would impose no constraints other than those the Constitution already imposes on all government action. The question is not whether theology majors are different, but whether the differences are substantial enough to justify a discriminatory financial penalty that the State inflicts on no other major. Plainly they are not.

Equally unpersuasive is the Court's argument that the State may discriminate against theology majors in distributing public benefits because the Establishment Clause and its state counterparts are themselves discriminatory. See *ante,* at 7–8, 9–10. The Court's premise is true at some level of abstraction—the Establishment Clause discriminates against religion by singling it out as the one thing a State may not establish. All this proves is that a State has a compelling interest in not committing *actual* Establishment Clause violations. Cf. *Widmar v. Vincent,* 454 U.S. 263, 271 (1981). We have never inferred from this principle that a State has a constitutionally sufficient interest in discriminating against religion in whatever other context it pleases, so long as it claims some connection, however attenuated, to establishment concerns.

CHAPTER 10

DOMESTIC POLICY DEBATES

Introduction

In her integrative essay that opens this chapter, Katherine Knutson explores the role of religion in the policy process. After describing some of the ways in which religion informs and shapes policy debates, Knutson provides an overview of several of the "key policy debates in which religious groups have taken part." As she notes, religious voices have been important in public policy advocacy throughout American history, often animating the discussion on opposing sides of the debate.

In the first research piece, Hugh Heclo introduces and briefly outlines three levels of interaction between religion and public policy: institutional, behavioral, and philosophical. The institutional level concerns the relationship between religious and governmental organizations, what we often call "church and state." The second level, behavioral, includes the ways in which religious affiliation affects a person's view on politics. A third level, the philosophical, considers the public philosophies that grow out of religious commitments and beliefs.

The next piece by Douglas Koopman explains the strengths and limitations of the term *morality politics* to describe symbolic values issues with obvious religious and moral dimensions. Religious organizations and groups have often been active on such issues, including abortion, homosexuality, and the role of religion in the public square. More recently, however, religious actors across the political spectrum have broadened their engagement to a range of issues.

The primary sources in this chapter offer several examples of public statements from religious leaders or organizations that seek to define or redefine the connection between a religious group and its commitments to politics and public policy. Although the publication of official statements can never ensure that the faithful will follow the pronouncements, such documents provide leadership and set an important tone by establishing the official policy for an organization or church or by encouraging participants in a religious movement to chart a new course.

The first example, the final section of a 1946 statement approved at a special meeting of the Federal Council of Churches (FCC), an affiliation of denominations primarily from the mainline Protestant tradition, was the first of several FCC resolutions to openly condemn racism and racial segregation. Describing discrimination as a "violation of the gospel of love and human brotherhood," the statement paved the way for member denominations to pass similar resolutions and to promote racial reconciliation.

The next selection, the "Chicago Declaration of Evangelical Social Concern," is reprinted in its entirety. This statement was the work of a group of evangelical leaders concerned about social justice issues who met in Chicago, Illinois, to call for an expanded evangelical policy agenda. The signatories founded the organization Evangelicals for Social Action as a result.

Written in response to the economic policies of the Reagan administration, the United States Conference of Catholic Bishops' pastoral letter "Economic Justice for All" is an example of one of the many documents that contribute to Catholic social teaching. The excerpts included here are a portion of the introduction as well as a few of the bishops' recommendations on how Catholics should work to "lift up the human and ethical dimensions of economic life."

The selection that follows is an excerpt from "An Evangelical Manifesto," a statement released by a group of evangelical pastors, academics, and leaders who speak to those inside and outside of evangelicalism, seeking "to address the confusions and corruptions that attend the term *Evangelical*" and calling fellow evangelicals to a renewed focus on essential beliefs and practices. These leaders call for political engagement that is "neither privatized nor politicized," calling for evangelical participation in the public square and a robust commitment to religious liberty.

The chapter concludes with a short case study, collecting several religious statements on environmental politics that showcase a range of perspectives from a variety of religious groups. The first selection, the International Catholic-Jewish Liaison Committee's "A Common Declaration on the Environment," resulted from a gathering in Vatican City in 1998. Formed as a result of decisions made at the Second Vatican Council, the Committee's goals include improving understanding and cooperation between Catholics and Jews.

The National Council of Churches (NCC), a broad-based, predominantly mainline Protestant coalition of more than fifty denominations in the United States, holds a General Assembly each year and adopts resolutions committing its member churches to particular courses of action. The 2006 "Resolution on Global Warming," reprinted here in its entirety, is reflective of the NCC's pronouncements that promote environmental awareness, conservation, and regulation.

The final two statements reflect the views of two groups of evangelical leaders who hold significantly different views about how to respond to global climate change. The first statement, a call to action from a group of pastors, college presidents, and organization leaders working together as the Evangelical Climate Initiative (ECI), describes climate change as a serious problem requiring a response and calls on church leaders to "teach the truths communicated here but also seek ways to implement the actions that follow from them." The selection that follows, a letter from a group of evangelical pastors and leaders called the Cornwall Alliance for the Stewardship of Creation, is a direct response to the ECI call to action. Contending that the scientific evidence concerning the extent of global warming and its predicted effects is far from conclusive, the letter concludes that "the most prudent response is not to try (almost certainly unsuccessfully and at enormous cost) to prevent or reduce whatever slight warming might really occur."

Integrative Essay

10.1

Katherine E. Knutson

RELIGION AND PUBLIC POLICY

Ask casual observers of American politics what political issues religious groups care about, and they will likely respond with "abortion" or "same-sex marriage." For the past two decades these issues have dominated news headlines, but, while important, they represent only the tip of the iceberg of the presence of religion in public policy debates.

Historically, religion plays an important role in the formation of public policy in the United States. Religious voices have been involved in every major policy debate and, perhaps surprisingly, have often represented conflicting perspectives in these debates. In this essay, I examine the contours of religion and public policy in the United States by first exploring the ways religion is used in the policy process and second, providing an overview of a few of the key policy debates in which religious groups have taken part. This discussion of religion and public policy first requires a brief examination of the process of public policy formation and the nature of religion in America.

Public Policy Formation

Policy formation is a complex process occurring at multiple venues and including a multitude of participants. Policies are debated and formed at the national level by Congress (through legislative statute or constitutional amendment proposals), the Executive Branch (through the use of Executive Orders or bureaucratic rulemaking), and the courts (through the clarification of the constitutionality of laws). Policies passed by the federal government affect the entire nation and may also have international effects if they involve aspects of foreign policy or trade. The federal structure of the American government allows policy debate and formation at the state and local levels; in state legislatures, school board meetings, town councils, governors' offices, and state courts. Policies adopted by a state or local government generally affect what happens within the jurisdiction of that government, but as with federal policy, state or local laws may affect other states or localities.

These various locales of policy formation are called "venues." People interested in changing public policies must assess both which venue is most appropriate for effecting the desired change (for example, which venue has jurisdiction over the policy in question) and which venue is most likely to be receptive to their demands. Policy debates may shift between venues when one level or branch of government decides it should act on the issue, but also in response to the activities of individuals or groups interested in the debate (Baumgartner and Jones 1994). Religious groups take advantage of the multiple venues of policymaking in their attempts to influence public policies.

Religion in America

In addition to factors related to the process of policy formation, the nature of religion and religiosity in America plays an important role in shaping the relationship between religion and public policy. America is notable for its high levels of religiosity, its Judeo-Christian tradition, and its religious diversity. As a nation founded on principles of religious liberty by people of religious faith, the country has long struggled with the balance between a protection of the "separation of church and state" and a government that is loosely based on the principle of majority rule.[1] The First Amendment to the Constitution protects the right to participate in the public sphere, yet many argue that policies reflecting particular religious values should not be codified into public law.

While the country is distinctive in its religiosity—85% of Americans say they are "sure" or "fairly certain" that God exists and 58% report that religion is "very important" to them—religious expression takes many forms (Kohut et al. 2000). Scholars identify a number of major religious traditions that are important to consider when examining the topic of religion and public policy in the U.S. These include Mainline Protestants, evangelical Protestants, Black Protestants, Catholics, and Jews (Kellstedt and Green 1993). Other important groups include historic peace denominations (Quakers, Mennonites), The Church of Jesus Christ of Latter-Day Saints (Mormons), Hispanic Protestants, Hispanic Catholics, and Muslims. Recently, scholars have noted that conservative members of some religious traditions share more in common with conservative members of other traditions than with progressive members of their own group (Hunter 1991). For example, the political beliefs of many progressive evangelical Protestants resemble those of progressive Catholics more than those of conservative evangelicals. This trend results in shifting and sometimes surprising coalitions in public policy advocacy.

The combination of these factors makes the study of religion and public policy quite complex. In this essay I focus on two questions that help structure an analysis of the impact of religion on public policy. First, how is religion used in the formation of public policy? Second, what issues are religious groups interested in and how have these priorities shifted over time? I conclude the essay with some observations about the role religion might play in the formation of public policy in upcoming years.

Religion in Policy Formation

Religious institutions, adherents, and beliefs play multiple roles in the formation of public policy, four of which merit our attention. First, religious beliefs often motivate individual policymakers or citizens to hold particular political beliefs. For example, many within the Judeo-Christian tradition point to mandates within religious texts to support public policies that help the poor or marginalized. The Bible contains literally hundreds of references to caring for the poor. As a result, some of the strongest voices for increased spending on income support programs such as food stamps and international aid to impoverished countries come from religious communities. Similarly, many individuals and elected officials cite their interpretation of biblical texts as the primary reason for their opposition to homosexual practice and same-sex marriage.

Research clearly indicates that the religious beliefs of many Americans actively shape and influence their political positions. In a study of the impact of religious beliefs on political opinions, scholars found that "religion does matter—and in some cases it matters more than any other factor"(Kohut et al. 2000, 52). This is particularly true for "social, sexual, and cultural issues," such as abortion, stem cell research, pornography, and gambling, even when controlling for the impact of other demographic variables. Religion influences Americans on both ends of the ideological spectrum, though this is manifest in different ways, with some religious citizens concerned about economics and social justice while others focus on issues of personal morality.

Elected officials and policymakers are not immune to the influence of religious beliefs, though it can be difficult to gauge the extent of this influence. One study of Members of Congress found that religious beliefs play a role in voting decisions by shaping their very approach to politics (Benson and Williams 1986). Eighty percent of the Members of Congress interviewed reported that religion had a "perceptible influence" on their votes in Congress. Other research found that this trend held true for members of state legislatures as well (Yamane and Oldmixon 2006).

Second, religion affects public policy when policymakers and advocates invoke the language and symbols of religion to discuss policies. Employment of religious rhetoric is rarely restricted to a single side of any debate. Opponents of embryonic stem cell research, for example, argue that the manipulation of an embryo is an attempt to "play God" and results in immoral destruction of life. Supporters, meanwhile, argue that banning promising lines of research when so many people are suffering from conditions that might be remedied by such research is itself immoral. Participants use these types of morality-based appeals to frame the debate as one that requires action because of the moral imperative it poses.

These types of arguments are particularly persuasive in American society because of the high levels of religiosity. In psychological terms, the use of morality-based argumentation in political debates "primes" individuals to consider their religious beliefs when making decisions on political issues (Sniderman, Brody, and Tetlock 1991). For example, Americans might not inherently see the connection between global warming and their religious beliefs, but some religious leaders have sought to reframe the issue as biblically mandated "creation care." For example, former Vice President for Governmental Affairs of the National Association of Evangelicals (NAE) Reverend Richard Cizik argued "If you are for the sanctity of life and ignore the health impact of the environment on the unborn, I think that is a limited understanding of how everything is connected in life"(Vu 2007). By connecting religious arguments to public policy debates, religious and political leaders can create situations in which the religious beliefs of an individual become salient to political decision making.

Once political leaders make decisions, they may invoke religion to provide moral legitimacy to the policies. Requesting God's blessing over a political activity—particularly military action—is commonplace. Phrases such as "God bless America" and "so help me God" are common refrains in political speeches. At the start of military action in Iraq in 2003, President George W. Bush addressed the nation to justify the war. In concluding his arguments, he drew upon the religious beliefs of Americans saying, "I know that the families of our military are praying that all those who serve will return safely and soon. Millions of Americans are praying with you for the safety of your loved ones and for the protection of the innocent"(White House Press Release 2003).

Third, religious groups use the networks developed through houses of worship and common belief systems to mobilize citizens to action on policy issues. Constitutionally protected freedoms of speech and association mean that religious adherents may legally join together to promote their political beliefs, though tax law and the non-profit status of houses of worship and some interest groups constrain some political behavior. For example, tax law prohibits non-profit institutions like churches, mosques, and synagogues from direct endorsement of political candidates. However, they are able to lobby for and against public policies, and they may establish independent political entities that can participate more broadly in the political process.

Many denominations and religious groups maintain policy offices in Washington, D.C. to coordinate their response to political developments.[2] The Methodist church was the first to do so when, in 1916, the denomination established an office to promote its position on prohibition. Three years later, the National Catholic Welfare Conference established an office to advance anti-poverty measures on behalf of American Catholics. Today Washington-area offices represent nearly all major Christian religious groups and denominations as well as other religious traditions. The Religious Action Center of Reform Judaism, for example, is active on issues ranging from bilingual education policy to gun control to policy towards Israel. Another major player is the United States Catholic Conference. The USCC drafts policy positions based on Catholic theology, which have the potential to influence the beliefs and political behavior of the nearly one quarter of Americans who identify as Catholics (Coleman 2003).

In addition to these types of efforts, a range of membership-based interest groups reflect the policy interests of religious citizens. One of the oldest groups of this type is the Women's Christian Temperance Union, founded in 1874 to mobilize support for prohibition of alcohol and, later, women's suffrage. Today, some of the largest and most visible religious interest groups are found on the conservative end of both the political and theological spectrum. The Family Research Council (FRC) is one of the largest and most powerful of these groups. Founded in 1983, the organization is at the forefront of many policy debates, especially those dealing with sexuality, human life, and religious liberty. Religious interest groups on the left tend to focus on different types of issues than their counterparts on the right. Bread for the World and Sojourners/Call to Renewal are two of the most influential of these. In October of 2008, for example, the Sojourners/Call to Renewal website focused on policy issues such as fighting poverty, immigration reform, Iran, farm worker wages, the Iraq war, and genocide in Darfur. In contrast, the FRC website highlighted abortion, same-sex marriage in California, and conscience rights (laws defending the right of health care workers not to participate in abortions or sterilizations).

Fourth, religion impacts public policy when religious institutions themselves become agents of policy implementation. Religious institutions have a long history of providing services such as education and health care with funding from the government. Many houses of worship sponsor services such as food banks, English classes, and childcare facilities. One of the largest religious-based providers of social services is Catholic Charities USA, which has been operating in the United States since 1910. One scholar found that two-thirds of the organization's budget comes from government grants (Coleman 2003, 251). In recent years, the government has made it easier for religious institutions to gain government funding for such programs without being forced to sacrifice their religious character.[3]

In summary, religion, as expressed through individual beliefs, political rhetoric, group mobilization and religious institutions, is of obvious importance in the formation of public policies. Despite the common perception of a clear separation between church and state, religion influences everyday policy debate and decision-making. It is to these debates and decisions that we now turn.

Policy Debates

While the religious dimension of debates over abortion and same-sex marriage has received much media attention in recent years, the issues in which religious groups take interest are varied and have shifted over time. Some policy debates focus on issues that affect religious belief or practice directly, while others concern policies that religious groups or individuals care about as a result of religious beliefs. The following section briefly highlights some of the major policy debates in which religious voices have played a part.[4] It is organized into broad policy areas: free exercise, sex and the body, civil rights, immigration, education, social services, and foreign policy. Each subsection includes a brief overview of a handful of the specific policy debates in which religious individuals and groups have taken interest.

Free Exercise

While the First Amendment enshrines the free exercise of religion in the U.S. Constitution, it leaves many gray areas to be addressed by a range of government venues, particularly the courts, often pitting a minority religious group against the majority. Questions of whether the U.S. could demand that the Mormon church abandon its practice of polygamy as a condition for the statehood of Utah,[5] whether Oregon could make the smoking of a hallucinogenic drug used in Native American religious ceremonies illegal,[6] or whether a Florida city could pass a law banning animal sacrifice to specifically interfere with the religious practices of Santeria[7] are just a few examples of free exercise debates. Courts ruling on free exercise cases often distinguish between the expression of religious beliefs and the actions an individual might take as a result of those beliefs, finding it constitutional to limit some of the latter.

Debates over the free exercise of religion are likely to intensify as America becomes more religiously diverse. The beliefs and practices of new, or growing, religious groups may run contrary to the dominant Judeo-Christian beliefs. In one recent case, Muslim taxi drivers in Minnesota refused to carry passengers carrying alcohol because they believed Islamic law forbids such contact. The Metropolitan Airports Commission, which oversees transportation at the airport, implemented fines for cab drivers who took such steps. Related battles are being played out across the country as Muslims press their employers for accommodation for prayer breaks and religious holidays (Bazar 2008).

Sex and the Body

Religious groups are perhaps most visible in policy debates concerning the regulation of sex and the body. Debates over contraception and, more recently, abortion frequently feature religious and moral language, and religiously motivated individuals and groups have been at the forefront of such debates. While a coalition of conservative religious groups have led the fight against legalized abortion, some religious groups support keeping abortion legal. The group Catholics for a Free Choice, for example, advocates abortion rights despite the Catholic Church's official and vehement opposition to such rights. Recent policy debates concerning abortion focus on procedures such as late term abortion (also known as partial-birth abortion), access to emergency contraception (the so-called "morning after" pills), and parental consent laws. Because the *Roe vs. Wade* decision legalizing first trimester abortions grants states significant control over policy concerning second and third trimester abortions, many groups have focused their attention on influencing abortion policy in individual states through legislation, referenda or constitutional amendments.

Policies concerning sexual orientation also receive considerable attention from religious groups. In 1991, one gay and two lesbian couples in Hawaii sued for the right to marry. In the following years, nearly every state passed a state law or constitutional amendment to outlaw same-sex marriage and prevent the state from recognizing same-sex marriage licenses issued by other states. Groups such as the Family Research Council, Traditional Values Coalition, Christian Coalition, and Concerned Women for America organized and funded the campaigns in many states. In several states, the Catholic Church, the Mormon Church, and churches affiliated with the Southern Baptist Convention were also strong participants in the debate (Stenger 2008).

More recently, several state courts, including those in Vermont, Massachusetts, Connecticut, California, and Iowa ruled in favor of couples seeking same-sex marriage rights. In response to the California decision in 2008, a coalition led primarily by religious individuals, churches, and interest groups campaigned successfully to overturn the ruling by passing Proposition 8, a state constitutional amendment defining marriage as between one man and one woman. As with other debates, though, religious voices supported both sides. Religious groups such as Dignity USA, Equal Partners in Faith, and Soulforce, along with the United Church of Christ, Metropolitan Community Churches, Quakers, and Unitarian Universalists campaigned in opposition to laws and amendments denying marriage rights to same-sex couples.

Civil Rights

Religious groups have a long history of involvement in debates over civil rights. In early debates over slavery, individuals drew on religious beliefs and texts to justify both support for and opposition to slavery. Many white Christians from the south claimed the institution was "divinely ordained," while many northern churches helped lead the antislavery movement (Noll 2008). As one scholar of religion in America argues, the Civil War "was also fundamentally a religious war fought over how to interpret the Bible and how to promote moral norms in national public life"(Noll 2008, 43). Though religious difference was not the sole cause of the Civil War, it certainly set the context for it.

Approximately 100 years later, religious motivations were again on display in the Civil Rights Movement led, in large part, by the Reverend Martin Luther King, Jr. and the Southern Christian Leadership Conference. African-American churches provided strong networks used to organize and support protests of civil rights violations (Morris 1999). Leaders within African American churches fused Christian theology with principles of nonviolence to effectively challenge institutionalized oppression. These leaders were joined in their efforts by Jews, white mainline Protestants and white Roman Catholics, though much of the momentum for joining the Civil Rights Movement came from the elites within these religious traditions (Noll 2008; Verter 2002). As with the debate over slavery, supporters of segregation used religion to justify their position, though no strong leaders emerged and these arguments failed to gain traction with a significant portion of the population (Noll 2008).

Immigration

Religious identification plays a major role in historic and contemporary debates over immigration. In the first major waves of immigration in the early 1900s, much of the hostility towards new immigrants was based on the fact that many were Catholics from countries such as Ireland and Italy, and were perceived as a threat to the dominant Protestant population. A more recent debate over immigration reform sparked massive nation-wide demonstrations in the spring of 2006. The U.S. House of Representatives debated a bill that would have made it a federal crime to assist individuals without documentation (Hondagneu-Sotelo 2007). Religious groups such as the National Conference of Catholic Bishops and the National Hispanic Association of Evangelicals were leading participants in rallies opposing this legislation. These groups drew upon religious texts emphasizing care for immigrants, such as the passage in the book of Leviticus (recognized by both Jews and Christians) that instructs, "The alien living with you must be treated as one of your native-born" (Lev. 19:34 NIV).

Throughout the tense debate in Congress, Catholic leaders along with leaders from mainline Protestant denominations, Hispanic evangelical churches, and the historic peace churches advocated policies that created more opportunities for family reunification, protected human rights, and provided a path to citizenship for undocumented immigrants already in the country. Meanwhile, many white evangelicals opposed proposals that included a path to citizenship. In public opinion polls, over 60% of white evangelicals agree that the growing number of immigrants "threatens traditional American customs and values" and "are a burden because they take our jobs, housing and health care." One particularly interesting finding in studies of public opinion is that individuals who attend church more frequently, regardless of the denomination, express more favorable views of immigrants and immigration than those who attend less often (Smith 2006).

Education

America's system of public schools has been at the center of numerous policy debates prominently featuring religious groups. Schools are controlled primarily by local school boards, though they are subject to additional standards and funding dictated by state and federal governments. One of the fiercest battles involves the teaching of scientific theories about the development of life on Earth. Following the 1859 publication of Charles Darwin's *The Origin of Species*, science textbooks for secondary students began to include the theory of evolution. Conflict between the theory of evolution and the traditional Judeo-Christian belief that humans were created by God grew as more students enrolled in secondary schools and were thus exposed to the teaching of evolution (Larson 1985). As the challenge to creationism grew, several states responded with anti-evolution legislation supported by the fundamentalist movement.[8] By 1930, the legislatures of twenty states had debated laws banning the teaching of evolution, and Tennessee, Mississippi, and Arkansas had passed such laws (George 2001). Curricula remain an issue today as school boards debate the teaching of Intelligent Design, which critics claim is a thinly veiled attempt to teach creationism under a different name, and the development of humanities classes that use religious texts, such as the Bible, to study issues of religion and faith from a scholarly perspective.

Another current education debate involves the use of school vouchers to allow students to attend the school of their choice—including religious schools—where public schools are failing. Government funding of religious schools was addressed by a string of court cases beginning in the 1960s, which generally found that public funds could not be used to pay for private religious schools.[9] However, the Supreme Court did uphold the right of states to create private school tuition tax credit laws as long as the money went to parents and not directly to schools (*Mueller v. Allen* 1983). In more recent years, the Court has shifted its position, upholding indirect government funding of religious schools (*Zelman v. Simmons-Harris* 2002). The Catholic Church along with groups such as the evangelical-dominated Home School Legal Defense Fund actively advocate for school vouchers. In contrast, religious groups that advocate strict separation of church and state, such as the Baptist Joint Committee and the American Jewish Congress, strongly oppose vouchers.

Social Services

Religious groups have been at the forefront of policy debates over welfare and anti-poverty measures, arguing for governmental assistance in advancing moral mandates to care for the poor. In 1969, Mainline Protestants, Catholics, and Jews collaborated in support of President Nixon's proposed Family Assistance Plan, which would have guaranteed a minimum income to families with children (Steensland 2002), framing it as a basic human right. In Congress, representatives such as Tony Hall (Democrat from Ohio from 1970–2003) draw on religious beliefs and cite scripture to justify their support for anti-poverty measures. In 1993, Representative Hall staged a 22-day hunger strike to call attention to world hunger (Hertzke 2006). More recently, in the summer of 2007, leaders of religious interest groups such as Bread for the World and Faith in Public Life identified reform of the Farm Bill as one of their top legislative priorities. These groups, motivated by their religious beliefs, viewed provisions of the bill that dealt with poverty and hunger as moral issues that required a response from churches and faith-based groups.

Religious groups also take an active role in the debate over federal housing policy. Groups such as Habitat for Humanity, the National Conference of Catholic Bishops, and the Religious Action Center of Reform Judaism have been leaders in the fight for affordable housing for the poor. These groups view provision of low-income housing as a fundamentally moral question and tend to situate the issue of low-income housing within the larger context of poverty and economic justice. In a press release from March 2003 the RAC argued that, "Jewish tradition teaches that poverty is a powerless condition; homelessness is a dehumanizing experience . . . Jewish history, including expulsion and ghettoization, has taught us about the pain and indignity of not having a stable home. Thus we are called on by our religious obligations and our history to provide for the poor and the homeless."

Foreign Policy

Finally, religious beliefs have shaped a great deal of American foreign policy. Religious believers have been behind many anti-war movements in U.S. history, including protests against the Vietnam and Iraq wars. In the 1970s and 1980s, mainline Protestant, Roman Catholic, and Quaker groups helped lead the opposition to U.S. support of military dictatorships in Central America (Kurtz and Fulton 2002). At the same time, religion has also been used to encourage American military involvement. Religiously-motivated individuals urged President Franklin D. Roosevelt to intercede on behalf of the persecuted Jews in World War II. Similarly, some of the strongest support for military action in Iraq and Afghanistan comes from religious adherents, particularly evangelical Protestants. Financial and military support for Israel can also be traced to the advocacy of American Jews and supporters of Israel within the evangelical tradition.

More recently, faith-based groups such as International Justice Mission and Christian Solidarity Worldwide have been major advocates for greater concern for human rights and international religious freedom in U.S. foreign policy. Religious groups support legislation to limit sex trafficking and promote international religious freedom. Faith-based groups in the United States have also highlighted human rights abuses in Darfur, China, and North Korea. Movements such as the Save Darfur Coalition and the ONE Campaign draw support from faith communities and emphasize interfaith approaches to solving world crises (Hertzke 2006).

Conclusion

While some point to the doctrine of "separation of church and state" to suggest that there is no room for religion in the public square, it is clear that religious beliefs and religiously-motivated individuals have played a major role in the development and implementation of public policy in the U.S. Furthermore, there is no evidence that their influence will diminish any time in the near future. Using the four roles of religion in shaping U.S. public policy outlined in this essay, what then can we expect to see in the years to come?

Given the high levels of religiosity and salience of religious beliefs, the influence of religion on individual decision-makers, whether they be citizens in the voting booth or elected officials voting on legislation, is unlikely to dissipate. In fact, the impact may become even stronger as religious leaders connect a wider range of political issues to religious beliefs. Recently such connections have included the global AIDS epidemic, the genocide in Sudan, the effects of globalization, and developments in biotechnology. These recent trends also suggest a growing role for voices on the religious left, even in debates involving issues such as sexuality and reproduction traditionally dominated by religious conservatives.

Elected officials will continue to draw upon religious and moral language to legitimize political decisions because such language resonates with the public. In fact, politicians are sometimes criticized when they are unable to speak the language of faith, as presidential contender Senator John McCain learned in the 2008 campaign (Carnes 2009). Religious leaders on the Right were initially hesitant to support his candidacy. Some, like influential leader Dr. James Dobson even went so far as to publically announce that he would not vote for McCain as "a matter of conscience"(Boyer 2008). After McCain's selection of Sarah Palin as a running mate, Dobson shifted his position and endorsed McCain.

We may also see shifts in the freedom of leaders to mobilize extant religious networks for political ends. Religious leaders have begun to push the boundaries of restrictions on political speech. During the 2008 presidential campaign, pastors from around the country purposely violated federal tax law by making political endorsements from the pulpit. This act of civil disobedience, sponsored by a conservative Christian group, sought to establish grounds for a legal case to overturn the restriction on political speech.

Given the religious nature of America, the strength of religious institutions and their success in providing social services, the government is likely to continue to turn to religious institutions to help implement public policies. The Supreme Court's ruling on school vouchers provided a legal foundation for the indirect transfer of government money to religious organizations. George W. Bush's establishment of a faith-based office in the White House and President Obama's continuation of it will likely encourage ongoing partnerships between religious organizations and the federal government. While debates over the rights of religious institutions to proselytize and discriminate in hiring will continue, the government would be unable to meet the needs of citizens without the help of these faith-based groups.

In short, religion plays a large and important role in the formation of public policy, and has done so throughout American history. Religious actors have participated in political debates on a variety of issues and represented a range of viewpoints, often with conflicting applications of religious precepts. While many observers are critical of the mixing of religion and politics, the continued participation of these faith-based voices in public discourse, policy advocacy, and political campaigns contributes to a vigorous American democracy.

Research Pieces

10.2

Hugh Heclo

RELIGION AND PUBLIC POLICY: AN INTRODUCTION (2001)

... The major interactions between religion and public policy seem to occur at three different levels.[10]

The first is *institutional*. Here attention focuses on the way organized structures of religion and government impinge on each other and together on society. It is a perspective that comes most naturally to Americans because it is genetically encoded, so to speak, with their nation's founding understanding of itself. The bland phrase "separation of church and state" conceals what was the most historically unique and audacious thing about America's experiment in self-government—the commitment to a free exercise of religion (Noonan 1998). It is on this institutional level, with national and then state government, that one encounters the contests over government sponsorship of religious organizations and disputed infringements on groups claiming the unfettered exercise of religious liberties. Less obviously, it is also where one finds religious and public agencies grinding against each other in the conduct of such things as educational and welfare policies.

The second area of interconnectedness between religion and public policy can be termed *behavioral*. By this, one means nothing grander than the idea that through religious attachments people are moved to act in public ways (e.g., voting, community organizing, and other political activities). It is important to notice that there is a direct, though paradoxical, link between these first and second dimensions. The hands-off distancing between religious and government institutions has meant that in America religion could be a free-forming and immensely rich resource for the nation's politics. The astute observer Alexis de Tocqueville concluded that his American informants were correct—the main reason religion held great sway over their country was the separation of church and state: "by diminishing the apparent power of religion one increased its real strength" (1966, 273). Thus since Tocqueville's visit in 1831, Americans in religious association have created and sustained movements promoting the abolition of slavery, women's rights, prison and asylum reform, child welfare and worker protection, mothers pensions, liquor regulation, racial desegregation, and civil rights legislation. People moved to action through religious affiliations have also been an important resource in more routine party politics and elections.

The third dimension of connections between religion and public policy is more difficult to put into words. But one senses, almost instinctively, that something very important is still missing if we simply give an account of organized institutions and politically relevant behaviors. Lacking a better term, we might call this third sphere *philosophical*. Here one is trying to capture the intersections of religion and policymaking that involve ideas and modes of thought bearing on the fundamental ordering of a society's public life. It is the arena people are operating in when they speak about culture wars or the nation's need for a moral vision. It is the substructure of ideas on the basis of which some people cringe and others rejoice when a presidential candidate talks about his personal relationship to Jesus Christ. Religion is not only a source of moral principles (as well as masks for hypocrisy) in public debate. It is also the ground of competing public philosophies for the nation, which can include the religious injunction to keep explicit religion out of politics.

The philosophical level is not about abstract thought experiments but ties back into the first two dimensions. Consider that aspect of public philosophy contending for separations of church and state. In keeping the new national government out of religious matters, the formal Constitution was constructed, as some have described it, as a "godless" document (Kramnick and Moore 1996).[11] This is not because religion was unimportant to the society but because it was too important. As a matter of prudent political predictions—in the behavioral dimension noted above—the Founders understood why the Constitution had best keep essentially silent on matters of religion and God. In general, the dangers of political division based on religion were fresh in historic memories of Europe's religious wars. More particularly, the fragile coalition behind the proposed Constitution would be endangered by any statements about religion and devotion to God that might compete with the abundant state and local government dealings on the subject.

Yet, in relating calculations of political behavior and institutional design, the Founders were also drawing on a deeper set of understandings already present in society. These were ideas about individual conscience identified with Protestantism, and they were refined and elevated during decades-long encounters among concrete communities of religious believers and dissenters in the American colonies. Thus behind the separating of church and state loomed an emerging cultural commitment to the free exercise of religion. This state-limiting, free exercise norm was mainly a religious achievement pursued in search of genuine religiosity. Generally speaking, its champions were not secular philosophers but religious people who were convinced that religion could never be authentic if it was directly or indirectly coerced through government (Noonan 1998).

The point, then, is that institutional, behavioral, and philosophical categories are three interrelated, not separate perspectives. . . .

The Inescapable Coupling

Whether we like it or not, the connections between religion and public policy choices are profound and unavoidable. Government policy and religious matters are not the same thing, but neither are they isolated from each other. The two are distinct but not separate.

The two domains intertwine because both claim to give authoritative answers to important questions about how people should live. Both are concerned with the pursuit of values in an obligational way. To put it another way, both religion and public policies deal in "oughts" and do so in terms of commands rather than idle suggestions or passing speculations.

Obviously, religion tells people how they should live. It can be less obvious that public policy also presents directives for living out some answers and not others. It does so because policy represents certain choices for society and those choices are backed up by the coercive power of government. Like it or not, modern government policy is invariably in the business of mandating, promoting, discouraging, or prohibiting some ways of life and not others. The point, then, is this. In a very deep, substantive way, the City of God and the City of Man are inescapably engaged in transactions with each other. . . .[12]

Nevertheless, it is also true to say that religion and policy are not the same thing. Religion points toward matters of ultimate meaning understood as humans stand in relation to the sacred and supernatural. Concerned with what is timeless, unchanging, and holy, religion is about the Absolute, or it is about nothing. By contrast, the courses of action pursued by government—its policies—are societal engagements with the here and now. Its meanings are proximate. At least in democratic (as opposed to totalitarian) government, policymaking acknowledges itself to be contingent, potentially erroneous, and changeable.

But exactly at this point we risk falling into another trap of simplistic, stereotyped thinking about our subject. Are religious people therefore to be seen as the ones who make absolutist pronouncements and the irreligious mind as the only one capable of tolerance? Is serious religion necessarily intolerant and are godless people the ones who can be counted on to engage the diverse public audience with persuasion rather than with asserting dogma? Not at all. This way of parsing the subject obscures too much of the spiritual possibilities in religion as well as the inhumane possibilities in secularism. It denies the possibility of a religious faith that, sensing the eternal and transcendent, renders relative and contingent all human institutions and claims to truth—including dogmatic religiousness as a form of idolatry (Tinder 1995). Likewise, if there can be contingent, humbling dimensions to lived religion, there can also be absolutist assumptions and dogmatically imposed faith surrounding supposedly contingent, secular policies. Religion and policy mark a continuous flashpoint in public life because the two touch precisely along that horizon where the great thing needful is to keep relative things relative and absolutes absolute.[13]

If nothing else, these introductory comments should raise warning flags: thinking about religion and public policy requires thinking in complex rather than simplistic ways. Doing so means harkening to what might be taken to be the first commandment of all religions—to "pay attention," to look past the surface of things and not assume that what meets the eye is all that is going on.

10.3

Douglas Koopman

RELIGION AND AMERICAN PUBLIC POLICY: MORALITY POLITICS AND BEYOND (2009)

The Study of Public Policy

Because there are thousands of different policies enacted by national, state, and local governments, scholars have developed several approaches to analyze them more capably. One relatively common approach is to differentiate between and among various types of public policy according to "their effect on society and the relation-ships among those involved in policy formation" (Anderson 2006, p. 11). This approach typically divides public policy into three broad categories: (1) distributive policies that involve allocation of services or benefits to particular segments of the population, (2) regulatory policies that impose restrictions or limitations on the behavior of individuals or groups, and (3) redistributive policies that involve deliber-ate efforts by the government to shift the allocation of resources and wealth from the "haves" to the "have nots."

A second approach focuses on the "stages" of policy making—formation, imple-mentation, and evaluation. Although some criticize these divisions as overly rigid (Cochran, Mayer, Carr, and Cayer 2006, p. 7) such categories are frequently used as a heuristic device to isolate and focus attention on these particular aspects of policy making.

Finally, analysts have examined public policy making in terms of specific substan-tive areas. In fact, most major texts in the field typically divide the subject matter into chapters on the policy process and chapters on major public policies. In terms of the lat-ter, the focus tends to be on broad areas of policy like health, environment, and defense.[14]

The Emergence of "Morality Policy" as a Field of Study

Although moral issues have been evident within American politics since the founding, the use of the terms *morality politics* and *morality policies* by social scientists is, in fact, quite recent. These terms rise out of earlier studies of "symbolic" and "value" politics (Gusfield 1963; Edelman 1964). When policy analysts contrast these concepts with their opposites—"material" and "substantive"—one almost detects disappointment, if not disdain, that such types of policies even emerge in American politics. . . .

But just how should one label these noneconomic policy issues in a disciplinary subfield that had focused on economic policies that could be negotiated quietly by experts, interest groups, and elected officials in incremental bargaining? Symbolic and status issues were a category of policy issues that seemed to operate under different rules—and a category of issues that, starting in the 1960s, seemed to be proliferating. As a result, scholars began writing about a "moral" category of public policy issues. . . .

However, it was Meier (1994; 1999) who popularized, if not coined, the term *morality politics*, cleverly labeling it as "the politics of sin." He argues that morality policies reflect the way in which core social values interact with the policy of the state, because they embody disputes over the values and behaviors that are endorsed or rejected by the gov-ernment (Meier 1999, p. 681). Thus, morality policy would appear to be a subtype of re-distributive policy, although with one important difference: Morality policies redistribute "values," whereas redistributive policies redistribute "economic" rewards. Nevertheless, despite these differences, both involve zero-sum games, with the policy outcomes clearly signifying the "winners" and "losers" in the process.

To understand why morality policy constitutes a distinct class of public policy, it is necessary to specify what scholars have argued are its defining characteristics (e.g. Tatalovich and Daynes 1988; Nice 1992; Meier 1994; Mooney and Lee 1995; Haider-Markel and Meier 1996). As noted earlier, morality policy involves "debate over first principles," in which at least one side portrays the issue as one of morality or sin and uses moral arguments in its policy advocacy.[15] Thus, at the center of morality policy debate is conflict over fundamental values about which no consensus exists among members of society.

Several other characteristics flow from this defining quality (Mooney 2001, pp. 7–8). The first is its perceived simplicity, involving "easy issues"(Carmines and Stimson 1980). Because the debate is about first principles, and not instrumental values, almost anyone can legitimately claim to be well informed. Second, because the morality policy debate is characterized by conflicts over first principles, the issues are usually highly salient to the general public (Mooney and Lee 1995; Haider-Markel and Meier 1996). A third characteristic flows from the second—namely, that morality politics is characterized by high levels of citizen participation (Carmines and Stimson 1980; Haider-Markel 1999). Fourth, in morality politics, compromise is difficult to achieve, unlike in other policy arenas.[16] And, finally, in cash-strapped governmental settings, such policies require little expenditure or bureaucratic time and attention in that they do not transfer economic assets.

Morality policies hold a special attraction to ambitious politicians who seek to benefit from appeals to the electorate. However, ambition is not the only reason why politicians may latch on to morality issues; many are forced to respond to public opinion out of self-preservation (Mooney 2001). Because of their salience, elected officials who wish to retain their positions will likely adopt positions on such issues that reflect constituency attitudes. Furthermore, although the typical drivers of economic regulatory policy are linked to sociological variables like income and urbanization, those that drive morality policy are either religious factors (e.g., the dominant religious traditions in a state or district) or "political" factors such as tight electoral and partisan competition (Mooney 2001). . . .[17]

Morality Policy as an Analytical Tool

Scholars of morality policy have focused on a rather narrow band of issues, primarily those "moral" issues that have dominated media coverage. The link that these studies make to religion is understandable, because religious groups and religiously backed moral claims are common in debates on such matters as abortion, gay rights, the death penalty, and gambling.

. . . [M]orality politics exhibits certain distinct characteristics. It is characterized by controversies over deeply held values that are easily grasped by the public—not disputes over "mere" economic matters. Public accessibility suggests that these issues do not need expert commentary or elite framing, both of which cloud the issues and make the choices relative. Practitioners in morality policies tend to argue their issue positions in terms of clear right and wrong, morally unambiguous, language. Morality policy outcomes involve official "signaling" of approved and disapproved behaviors, and thus those groups with identities that are connected to those particular behaviors. In morality politics, characteristics common to other policy areas—interest group resolution, "policy learning" by individuals and state officials from others, gradualism, and incrementalism—are quite uncommon. Public appeals on moral issues typically have a religious coloration. Such issues generally invite public participation and comment, and there is evidence that "direct democracy" plays more of a role in morality, than in other, policy decisions.[18]

However, few issues, if any, are purely and always moral. Outside of a very few "pure" morality policies (e.g., possibly the teaching of creationism), the morality policy model serves more as a useful analytical tool than a fully descriptive snapshot of reality. Even for morality policy scholars, different issues "fit" differently. None fit perfectly, and some "morph" into more traditional policy dynamics later on. As has been noted, even scholars working within the morality policy framework have concluded that moralization is subject to particular contexts and linkages; reality is simply more complex.

In the end, the scholarship on morality policies reveals various strengths and limitations. Its strengths include making comparisons and distinctions. Indeed, morality politics starts with Lowi's notion that "politics follows policies," and that moral *policies* lead to a new kind of moral poli*tics*. The most useful contribution is the point that moral policies in pure form do not fit the typical, and otherwise quite useful, models of public policy analysis.

Because the two major American political parties broadly agree on democratic capitalism, the cleavages and contests between them are likely to be based increasingly on noneconomic or moral issues. That these grievances are natural seems to be the case, resulting from the nature of American culture, our political structures, and the federalization of many policy issues. And, issues considered to be merely symbolic in the 1970s have developed into major bones of contention, leading to the establishment of a field of study labeled *morality policy*.

Nevertheless, some of the limitations of the morality policy framework have become more evident over time. First, some specific issues within this framework have been studied more than others. Of course, this is not an inherent problem to the approach, but it does limit our ability to assess how well the framework may be applied to a breadth of political issues. A more substantial problem is that few political matters and public policies are "purely" moral in their outline and process. Sometimes policy disputes appear to be a clash of moralities, sometimes policy proposals lose their moral qualities over extended periods of time, and sometimes that happens quickly as they get linked to other policies, soon operating in much the same way as traditional economic policies. . . .

Primary Sources

10.4

Federal Council of the Churches of Christ in America

THE CHURCH AND RACE RELATIONS
(MARCH 5–7, 1946)

What Must the Church Do?

Christians in America, more than ever before, honestly desire that quality of Christian fellowship which strengthens brethren of one racial group through the mutual helpfulness of brethren of all racial groups. Efforts directed toward such mutual helpfulness are frequently confused and ineffectual because of the segregation pattern which defeats good-will. Men of God will find themselves frustrated and defeated when they attempt to live out their Christian impulses within a racially segregated society.

The Church Must Choose

Either the Church will accept the pattern of segregation in race relations as necessary, if not desirable, and continue to work within this pattern for the amelioration of racial tensions or it will renounce the pattern of segregation as unnecessary and undesirable.

The Federal Council of the Churches of Christ in America hereby renounces the pattern of segregation in race relations as unnecessary and undesirable and a violation of the Gospel of love and human brotherhood. Having taken this action, the Federal Council requests its constituent communions to do likewise. As proof of their sincerity in this renunciation they will work for a non-segregated Church and a non-segregated society.

The Church when true to its higher destiny, has always understood that its gospel of good news has a two-fold function, namely:

To create new men with new motives
To create a new society wherein such men will find a friendly environment within which to live their Christian convictions.

The churches of America, while earnestly striving to nurture and develop individuals of racial good-will, have at the same time neglected to deal adequately with the fundamental pattern of segregation in our society which thwarts efforts of men of good-will. This must be corrected. Churches should continue to emphasize the first function; however, they must launch a comprehensive program of action in fulfillment of the second function. This is imperative now.

The Church Must Eliminate Segregation from Its Own Life

In order that the Church may remove the validity of the charge which the world makes when it says, "Physician, heal thyself," we urge our constituent communions to correct their own practice of segregation. With this end in view, it is recommended that each communion take steps to ascertain the facts concerning the practice of racial segregation within its own life and work, and formulate a plan of action inthe following areas:

Membership

Are all children of God welcomed into the membership of the communion's parish, churches or are there some who are excluded by the color with which God has endowed them? What actions are necessary to correct this practice? We urge this practice upon the churches of all racial and nationality groups.

Fellowship

Does racial segregation create a chasm which places profound limitations upon Christian fellowship within the life of a given geographical community? If so, what can be done to remove these limitations?

Worship

What is the extent of racial segregation in the services of worship provided by our communion? Are Worship opportunities available to racially mixed groups with sufficient frequency to make such worship a normal expression of our common worship to God without racial self-consciousness and embarrassment?

Service

What is the extent of racial segregation in the administrative practices provided in schools, colleges, seminaries, hospitals, camps, young people's conferences and similar church-related institutions under the control of our communion? What are the steps that should now be authorized and carried out by the responsible boards of the communion to overcome these defects?

Employment

Do the local churches, state and area judicatories, national boards and general ecclesiastical offices provide opportunities for the employment of persons at all levels drawn from racial minority groups? If so, is the proportion of such interracial employment fair? If not, what legislative actions and administrative procedures should be proposed within each communion to bring employment practices within its entire life into conformity with the Christian goal of a non-segregated society?

The Church, having chosen to renounce the segregation pattern as a violation of its Gospel of love, and having outlined steps by which the practice of segregation may be corrected within its own life, must next direct her attention to the community within which the Christian Church functions.

The Church Should Initiate the Clinical Approach as One Method of Resolving Race Tensions

In order that the community may sense the transforming power of organized religion in relieving community tensions arising from the segregation pattern locally, we urge upon churches and Church Councils the value of Race Relations Clinics to affect the daily lives of people where they live and work.

Such clinics seek to discover factually what are the actual tension points in interracial living and, in the light of such facts, what constructive steps may be taken to alleviate these tensions. The churches, through ministerial associations and councils of churches, take the initiative in enlisting the co-operation of the leaders of social, labor, business and civic agencies of the community. The fact-finding process and the diagnosis based thereon deal with such questions as discrimination in employment, housing, education, health and leisure-time activities. It further analyzes the communities' resources, including the churches, to ascertain where they integrate and serve Negroes and other minority racial groups as well as where they fail. By this means they seek to develop methods of factual analysis and through democratic agreement formulate a community-wide plan of action to change the policies and practices that have created tensions and segregation patterns.

We have outlined what we believe to be certain glaring defects in the ideals and purposes of our Protestant churches in the matter of race relations, calling special attention to the un-Christian character and unfortunate results of the segregation pattern. We are not unmindful of the heroic services done by the churches through their schools, colleges and other institutions in improving the condition of Negro and other minority groups, but we believe that these efforts will not accomplish their full results unless the Christian Church again accepts as a definite goal the practice of the early Christians in accepting all racial groups into the same religious society on the basis of equality.

10.5

Chicago Declaration of Evangelical Social Concern
(November 25, 1973)

As evangelical Christians committed to the Lord Jesus Christ and the full authority of the Word of God, we affirm that God lays total claim upon the lives of his people. We cannot, therefore, separate our lives from the situation in which God has placed us in the United States and the world.

We confess that we have not acknowledged the complete claim of God on our lives.

We acknowledge that God requires love. But we have not demonstrated the love of God to those suffering social abuses.

We acknowledge that God requires justice. But we have not proclaimed or demonstrated his justice to an unjust American society. Although the Lord calls us to defend the social and economic rights of the poor and oppressed, we have mostly remained silent. We deplore the historic involvement of the church in America with racism and the conspicuous responsibility of the evangelical community for perpetuating the personal attitudes and institutional structures that have divided the body of Christ along color lines. Further, we have failed to condemn the exploitation of racism at home and abroad by our economic system.

We affirm that God abounds in mercy and that he forgives all who repent and turn from their sins. So we call our fellow evangelical Christians to demonstrate repentance in a Christian discipleship that confronts the social and political injustice of our nation.

We must attack the materialism of our culture and the maldistribution of the nation's wealth and services. We recognize that as a nation we play a crucial role in the imbalance and injustice of international trade and development. Before God and a billion hungry neighbors, we must rethink our values regarding our present standard of living and promote a more just acquisition and distribution of the world's resources.

We acknowledge our Christian responsibilities of citizenship. Therefore, we must challenge the misplaced trust of the nation in economic and military might—a proud trust that promotes a national pathology of war and violence which victimizes our neighbors at home and abroad. We must resist the temptation to make the nation and its institutions objects of near-religious loyalty.

We acknowledge that we have encouraged men to prideful domination and women to irresponsible passivity. So we call both men and women to mutual submission and active discipleship.

We proclaim no new gospel, but the Gospel of our Lord Jesus Christ who, through the power of the Holy Spirit, frees people from sin so that they might praise God through works of righteousness.

By this declaration, we endorse no political ideology or party, but call our nation's leaders and people to that righteousness which exalts a nation.

We make this declaration in the biblical hope that Christ is coming to consummate the Kingdom and we accept his claim on our total discipleship until he comes.

10.6

United States Conference of Catholic Bishops

ECONOMIC JUSTICE FOR ALL: PASTORAL LETTER ON CATHOLIC SOCIAL TEACHING AND THE U.S. ECONOMY (1986)

Why We Write

7. In our letter, we write as pastors, not public officials. We speak as moral teachers, not economic technicians. We seek not to make some political or ideological point but to lift up the human and ethical dimensions of economic life, aspects too often neglected in public discussion. We bring to this task a dual heritage of Catholic social teaching and traditional American values.

8. As *Catholics*, we are heirs of a long tradition of thought and action on the moral dimensions of economic activity. The life and words of Jesus and the teaching of his Church call us to serve those in need and to work actively for social and economic justice. As a community of believers, we know that our faith is tested by the quality of justice among us, that we can best measure our life together by how the poor and the vulnerable are treated. This is not a new concern for us. It is as old as the Hebrew prophets, as compelling as the Sermon on the Mount, and as current as the powerful voice of Pope John Paul II defending the dignity of the human person. . . .

Principal Themes of the Pastoral Letter

12. The pastoral letter is not a blueprint for the American economy. It does not embrace any particular theory of how the economy works, nor does it attempt to resolve disputes between different schools of economic thought. Instead, our letter turns to Scripture and to the social teachings of the Church. There, we discover what our economic life must serve, what standards it must meet. Let us examine some of these basic moral principles.

13. *Every economic decision and institution must be judged in light of whether it protects or undermines the dignity of the human person. The pastoral letter begins with the human person.* We believe the person is sacred—the clearest reflection of God among us. Human dignity comes from God, not from nationality, race, sex, economic status, or any human accomplishment. We judge any economic system by what it does *for* and *to* people and by how it permits all to *participate* in it. The economy should serve people, not the other way around.

14. *Human dignity can be realized and protected only in community.* In our teaching, the human person is not only sacred but also social. How we organize our society—in economics and politics, in law and policy—directly affects human dignity and the capacity of individuals to grow in community. The obligation to "love our neighbor" has an individual dimension, but it also requires a broader social commitment to the common good. We have many partial ways to measure and debate the health of our economy: Gross National Product, per capita income, stock market prices, and so forth. The Christian vision of economic life looks beyond them all and asks, Does economic life enhance or threaten our life together as a community?

15. *All people have a right to participate in the economic life of society.* Basic justice demands that people be assured a minimum level of participation in the economy. It is wrong for a person or a group to be excluded unfairly or to be unable to participate or contribute to the economy. For example, people who are both able and willing, but cannot get a job are deprived of the participation that is so vital to human development. For, it is through employment that most individuals and families meet their material needs, exercise their talents, and have an opportunity to contribute to the larger community. Such participation has a special significance in our tradition because we believe that it is a means by which we join in carrying forward God's creative activity.

16. *All members of society have a special obligation to the poor and vulnerable.* From the Scriptures and church teaching, we learn that the justice of a society is tested by the treatment of the poor. The justice that was the sign of God's covenant with Israel was measured by how the poor and unprotected—the widow, the orphan, and the stranger—were treated. The kingdom that Jesus proclaimed in his word and ministry excludes no one. Throughout Israel's history and in early Christianity, the poor are agents of God's transforming power. "The Spirit of the Lord is upon me, therefore he has anointed me. He has sent me to bring glad tidings to the poor" (Lk. 4:18). This was Jesus' first public utterance. Jesus takes the side of those most in need. In the Last Judgment, so dramatically described in St. Matthew's Gospel, we are told that we will be judged according to how we respond to the hungry, the thirsty, the naked, the stranger. As followers of Christ, we are challenged to make a fundamental "option for the poor"—to speak for the voiceless, to defend the defenseless, to assess life styles, policies, and social institutions in terms of their impact on the poor. This "option for the poor" does not mean pitting one group against another, but rather, strengthening the whole community by assisting those who are the most vulnerable. As Christians, we are called to respond to the needs of *all* our brothers and sisters, but those with the greatest needs require the greatest response.

17. *Human rights are the minimum conditions for life in community.* In Catholic teaching, human rights include not only civil and political rights but also economic rights. As Pope John XXIII declared, "all people have a right to life, food, clothing, shelter, rest, medical care, education, and employment." This means that when people are without a chance to earn a living, and must go hungry and homeless, they are being denied basic rights.

Society must ensure that these rights are protected. In this way, we will ensure that the minimum conditions of economic justice are met for all our sisters and brothers.

18. *Society as a whole, acting through public and private institutions, has the moral responsibility to enhance human dignity and protect human rights.* In addition to the clear responsibility of private institutions, government has an essential responsibility in this area. This does not mean that government has the primary or exclusive role, but it does have a positive moral responsibility in safeguarding human rights and ensuring that the minimum conditions of human dignity are met for all. In a democracy, government is a means by which we can act together to protect what is important to us and to promote our common values.

19. *These six moral principles are not the only ones presented in the pastoral letter, but they give an overview of the moral vision that we are trying to share.* This vision of economic life cannot exist in a vacuum; it must be translated into concrete measures. Our pastoral letter spells out some specific applications of Catholic moral principles. We call for a new national commitment to full employment. We say it is a social and moral scandal that one of every seven Americans is poor, and we call for concerted efforts to eradicate poverty. The fulfillment of the basic needs of the poor is of the highest priority. We urge that all economic policies be evaluated in light of their impact on the life and stability of the family. We support measures to halt the loss of family farms and to resist the growing concentration in the ownership of agricultural resources. We specify ways in which the United States can do far more to relieve the plight of poor nations and assist in their development. We also reaffirm church teaching on the rights of workers, collective bargaining, private property, subsidiarity, and equal opportunity . . .

Chapter IV

A New American Experiment: Partnership for the Public Good

295. . . . . The founders of the nation set out to establish justice, promote the general welfare, and secure the blessings of liberty for themselves and their posterity. Those who live in this land today are the beneficiaries of this great venture. Our review of some of the most pressing problems in economic life today shows, however, that this undertaking is not yet complete. Justice for all remains an aspiration; a fair share in the general welfare is denied to many. In addition to the particular policy recommendations made above, a long-term and more fundamental response is needed. This will call for an imaginative vision of the future that can help shape economic arrangements in creative new ways. We now want to propose some elements of such a vision and several innovations in economic structures that can contribute to making this vision a reality. . . .

C. Partnership in the Development of National Policies

317. . . . . To encourage our fellow citizens to consider more carefully the appropriate balance of private and local initiative with national economic policy, we make several recommendations.

318. *First, in an advanced industrial economy like ours, all parts of society, including government, must cooperate in forming national economic policies.* Taxation, monetary policy, high levels of government spending, and many other forms of governmental regulation

are here to stay. A modern economy without governmental interventions of the sort we have alluded to is inconceivable. These interventions, however, should help, not replace, the contributions of the other economic actors and institutions and should direct them to the common good. . . .

319. *Second, the impact of national economic policies on the poor and the vulnerable is the primary criterion for judging their moral value.* Throughout this letter we have stressed the special place of the poor and the vulnerable in any ethical analysis of the U.S. economy. National economic policies that contribute to building a true commonwealth should reflect this by standing firmly for the rights of those who fall through the cracks of our economy: the poor, the unemployed, the homeless, the displaced. Being a citizen of this land means sharing in the responsibility for shaping and implementing such policies.

320. *Third, the serious distortion of national economic priorities produced by massive national spending on defense must be remedied.* Clear-sighted consideration of the role of government shows that government and the economy are already closely intertwined through military research and defense contracts. Defense-related industries make up a major part of the U.S. economy and have intimate links with both the military and civilian government; they often depart from the competitive model of free-market capitalism. Moreover, the dedication of so much of the national budget to military purposes has been disastrous for the poor and vulnerable members of our own and other nations. The nation's spending priorities need to be revised in the interests of both justice and peace (USCCB, *The Challenge of Peace*, 270–271).[19]

D. Cooperation at the International Level

322. If our country is to guide its international economic relationships by policies that serve human dignity and justice, we must expand our understanding of the moral responsibility of citizens to serve the common good to the entire planet. Cooperation is not limited to the local, regional, or national level. Economic policy can no longer be governed by national goals alone. The fact that the "social question has become worldwide" (Pope Paul VI, *On the Development of Peoples*, 3) challenges us to broaden our horizons and enhance our collaboration and sense of solidarity on the global level. The cause of democracy is closely tied to the cause of economic justice. The unfinished business of the American experiment includes the formation of new international partnerships, especially with the developing countries, based on mutual respect, cooperation and a dedication to fundamental justice. . . .

Chapter V

D. Commitment to a Kingdom of Love and Justice

363. Confronted by this economic complexity and seeking clarity for the future, we can rightly ask ourselves one single question: How does our economic system affect the lives of people — *all* people? Part of the American dream has been to make this world a better place for people to live in; at this moment of history that dream must include everyone on this globe. Since we profess to be members of a "catholic" or universal Church, we all must raise our sights to a concern for the well-being of everyone in the

world. Third World debt becomes our problem. Famine and starvation in sub-Saharan Africa become our concern. Rising military expenditures everywhere in the world become part of our fears for the future of this planet. We cannot be content if we see ecological neglect or the squandering of natural resources. In this letter we bishops have spoken often of economic interdependence; now is the moment when all of us must confront the reality of such economic bonding and its consequences and see it as a moment of grace—a *kairos*—that can unite all of us in a common community of the human family. We commit ourselves to this global vision. . . .

10.7

Evangelical Manifesto Steering Committee

AN EXECUTIVE SUMMARY OF "AN EVANGELICAL MANIFESTO: A DECLARATION OF EVANGELICAL IDENTITY AND PUBLIC COMMITMENT"
(MAY 7, 2008)

Editors' note: This is an abbreviated version of the full Evangelical Manifesto, which can be read at www.EvangelicalManifesto.com

Keenly aware of this hour of history, we as a representative group of Evangelicals in America address our fellow-believers and our fellow-citizens.[20] We have two purposes: to clarify the confusions that surround the term *Evangelical* in the United States, and to explain where we stand on issues that cause consternation over Evangelicals in public life.

The global era challenges us to learn how to live with our deepest differences—especially religious differences that are ultimate and irreducible. These are not just differences between personal worldviews but between entire ways of life co-existing in the same society.

1. Our Identity

First, we reaffirm our identity. *Evangelicals are Christians who define themselves, their faith, and their lives according to the Good News of Jesus of Nazareth.* (The Greek word for good news was *euangelion,* which translated into English as *evangel.*) This Evangelical principle is the heart of who we are as followers of Jesus. It is not unique to us. We assert it not to attack or to exclude, but to remind and to reaffirm, and so to rally and to reform.

Evangelicals are one of the great traditions in the Christian Church. We stand alongside Christians of other traditions in both the creedal core of faith and over many issues of public concern. Yet we also hold to Evangelical beliefs that are distinct—distinctions we affirm as matters of biblical truth, recovered by the Protestant Reformation and vital for a sure knowledge of God. We Evangelicals are defined theologically, and not politically, socially, or culturally.

As followers of Jesus Christ, Evangelicals stress a particular set of beliefs that we believe are true to the life and teachings of Jesus himself. Taken together, they make us who we are. We place our emphasis on. . . .

1. Jesus, fully divine and fully human, as the only full and complete revelation of God and therefore the only Savior.
2. The death of Jesus on the cross, in which he took the penalty for our sins and reconciled us to God.
3. Salvation as God's gift grasped through faith. We contribute nothing to our salvation.
4. New life in the Holy Spirit, who brings us spiritual rebirth and power to live as Jesus did, reaching out to the poor, sick, and oppressed.
5. The Bible as God's Word written, fully trustworthy as our final guide to faith and practice.
6. The future personal return of Jesus to establish the reign of God.
7. The importance of sharing these beliefs so that others may experience God's salvation and may walk in Jesus' way.

Sadly, we repeatedly fail to live up to our high calling, and all too often illustrate our own doctrine of sin. The full list of our failures is no secret to God or to many who watch us. If we would share the good news of Jesus with others, we must first be shaped by that good news ourselves.[21]

2. Our Place in Public Life

Second, we wish to reposition ourselves in public life. To be Evangelical is to be faithful to the freedom, justice, peace, and well-being that are at the heart of the good news of Jesus. Fundamentalism was world-denying and politically disengaged at its outset, but Evangelicals have made a distinguished contribution to politics—attested by causes such the abolition of slavery and woman's suffrage, and by names such as John Jay, John Witherspoon, Frances Willard, and Sojourner Truth in America and William Wilberforce and Lord Shaftesbury in England.

Today, however, enormous confusion surrounds Evangelicals in public life and we wish to clarify our stand through the following assertions:

First, we repudiate two equal and opposite errors into which many Christians have fallen. One error is to privatize faith, applying it to the personal and spiritual realm only. Such dualism falsely divorces the spiritual from the secular and causes faith to lose its *integrity.*

The other error, made by both the religious left and the religious right, is to politicize faith, using faith to express essentially political points that have lost touch with biblical truth. That way faith loses its *independence,* Christians become the "useful idiots" for one political party or another, and the Christian faith becomes an ideology. Christian beliefs become the weapons of political factions.

Called to an allegiance higher than party, ideology, economic system, and nationality, we Evangelicals see it our duty to engage with politics, but our equal duty never to be completely equated with any party, partisan ideology, or nationality. The politicization of faith is never a sign of strength but of weakness.

Second, we repudiate the two extremes that define the present culture wars in the United States. On one side, we repudiate the partisans of a *sacred public square*, those who would continue to give one religion a preferred place in public life.

In a diverse society, it will always be unjust and unworkable to privilege one religion. We are committed to religious liberty for people of all faiths. We are firmly opposed to theocracy. And we have no desire to coerce anyone or to impose beliefs and behavior on anyone. We believe in persuasion.

On the other side, we repudiate the partisans of a *naked public square*, those who would make all religious expression inviolably private and keep the public square inviolably secular. This position is even less just and workable because it excludes the overwhelming majority of citizens, who are still profoundly religious. Nothing is more illiberal than to invite people into the public square but insist that they be stripped of the faith that makes them who they are.

We are committed to a *civil public square – a vision of public life in which citizens of all faiths are free to enter and engage the public square on the basis of their faith, but within a framework of what is agreed to be just and free for other faiths as well.* Every right we assert for ourselves as Christians is a right we defend for all others.

Third, we are concerned that a generation of culture warring, reinforced by understandable reactions to religious extremism around the world, has created a powerful backlash against all religion in public life among many educated people. If this hardens into something like the European animosity toward religion in public life, the result would be disastrous for the American republic and would severely constrict liberty for people of all faiths. The striking intolerance shown by the new atheists is a warning sign.

We call on all citizens of goodwill and believers of all faiths and none to join us in working for a civil public square and the restoration of a tough-minded civility that is in the interests of all.

Fourth, we are concerned that globalization and the emerging global public square have no matching vision of how to live with our deepest differences on the global stage. In the Internet era, everyone can listen to what we say even when we are not speaking to everyone. Global communication magnifies the challenges of living with our deepest differences.

As the global public square emerges, we warn of two equal and opposite errors: *coercive secularism* and *religious extremism*.

We also repudiate the two other positions. First, those who believe their way is the only way and the way for everyone, and are therefore prepared to coerce them. This position leads inevitably to *conflict*.

Second, those who believe that different values are relative to different cultures, and who therefore refuse to allow anyone to judge anyone else or any other culture. This position sounds tolerant at first, but it leads directly to the ills of *complacency*. In a world of such evils as genocide, slavery, female oppression, and assaults on the unborn, there are rights that must be defended, evils that must be resisted, and interventions into the affairs of others that are morally justified.

Fifth, we warn of the danger of a two-tier global public square. This is a model of public life which reserves the top tier for cosmopolitan secular liberals, and the lower tier for local religious believers. Such an arrangement would be patronizing as well as severely restricting religious liberty and justice.

We promote a civil public square, and we respect for the rights of all, even those with whom we disagree. Contrary to those who believe that "error has no rights," we respect the right to be wrong. But we also insist that "the right to believe anything" does not mean that "anything anyone believes is right." Rather, respect for conscientious differences also requires respectful debate.

We do not speak for all Evangelicals. We speak only for ourselves, *yet not to ourselves*. We invite all our fellow-Christians, our fellow-citizens, and people of different faiths to take note of these declarations and to respond where appropriate.

We pledge that in a world of lies, hype, and spin, we publish this declaration in words that, under God, we make our bond. People of the Good News, we desire not just to speak the Good News but to embody and be good news to our world and to our generation.

Domestic Policy Case Study: Environmental Issues

10.8

International Catholic-Jewish Liaison Committee

A COMMON DECLARATION ON THE ENVIRONMENT
(MARCH 23–26, 1998)

Across the world people are becoming increasingly aware that certain forms of human activity are leading to environmental damage and seriously limiting the possibility of a sustainable development for all. Climate change, air and water pollution, desertification, resource depletion, and loss of biodiversity are among the consequences. While many have contributed to this damage, all must learn to live in a way which respects the integrity of the delicate balance that exists among the earth's ecosystems. Nor can we ignore the relation between the effect on the environment of population increase in certain areas and of heightened economic expectation among peoples.

Governments, commerce, industry, and agriculture must also collaborate if individuals and communities are to be able to exercise their right to live in a sound and healthy environment.

Concern for the environment has led both Catholics and Jews to reflect on the concrete implications of their belief in God, Creator of all things. In turning to their sacred scriptures, both have found the religious and moral foundations for their obligation to care for the environment. While they may differ in interpretations of some texts or in their methodological approaches, Jews and Catholics have found such broad agreement on certain fundamental values that they are able to affirm them together.

1. All of Creation Is Good and Forms a Harmonious Whole, Rich in Diversity (Genesis 1–2)

God created everything that exists, each according to its kind. "And God saw that it was good." Nothing, therefore, is insignificant; nothing should be recklessly destroyed as if devoid of purpose. Modification of species by genetic engineering must be approached with great caution. Everything is to be treated with reverence, as part of a whole willed by God to be in harmony. It was a willful act of disobedience that first broke this harmony (Genesis 3:14–19).

2. The Human Person—Male and Female—Is Part of Creation and Yet Distinguished from It, Being Made in the Image and Likeness of God. (Genesis 1:26)

The respect due to each person, endowed with a God-given dignity, allows for no exception and excludes no ones. Life is precious. We are to affirm it, to promote it, to care for and cherish it. When harm is done to the environment, the lives of both individuals and communities are profoundly affected. Any social, economic, or political activity that directly or indirectly destroys life or diminishes the possibility for people to live in dignity is counter to God's will.

3. The Human Person, Alone of All Creation, Has Been Entrusted with the Care of Creation. (Genesis 1:26–30; 2:15–20)

The human person has an immense responsibility, that of caring for all of creation. No person or group can use the resources of this earth as proprietor, but only as God's steward who destined these goods for all. Assuring that individuals and communities have access to what is necessary to sustain life in dignity is an expression of this stewardship, as is a reverent and moderate use of created goods.

4. Land and the People Depend on Each Other. (Leviticus 25; Exodus 23; Deuteronomy 15)

We all depend on the land, source of our sustenance. While human activity renders the land productive, it can also exhaust it, leaving only desolation. In the Jubilee Year, a time for God, liberty is to be proclaimed throughout the land, debts forgiven, and slaves freed. Also the land is to lie fallow so that it, too, can be restored.

A recognition of the mutual dependence between the land and the human person calls us today to have a caring, even loving, attitude towards the land and to regulate its use with justice, the root of peace.

5. Both Jews and Catholics Look to the Future, a Time of Fulfillment

Our responsibility for all that dwells in the earth and for the earth itself extends into the future. The earth is not ours to destroy (cf. Dt 20:19), but to hand on in trust to future generations. We cannot, therefore, recklessly consume its resources to satisfy needs that are artificially created and sustained by a society that tends to live only for the present. We also need to act, together whenever feasible, to assure that sound practices, guaranteed by law, are established in our countries and local communities for the future preservation of the environment.

Care for creation is also a religious act. Both Catholics and Jews use water, fire, oil, and salt as signs of God's presence among us. As part of God's creation, we offer its fruits in prayer and worship, and the Psalmist does not hesitate to summon all of creation to join in praising God (Psalms 96, 98, 148).

Respect for God's creation, of which we are a part, must become a way of life. We therefore call upon our respective religious communities and families to educate children, both by teaching and example, to fulfill the trust that God has confided to us.

The earth is the Lord's and the fullness thereof; the world and those who dwell therein (Psalms 24:1)

10.9

General Assembly of the National Council of Churches USA

RESOLUTION ON GLOBAL WARMING (2006)

RESOLUTION:

The National Council of Churches has stated:

> The rapidly expanding dimensions of (human) "dominion" over the earth and its physical resources call for new and deeper commitment to the Christian doctrine of stewardship. Natural resources, human techniques and institutions all together constitute an interlocking and interacting system of amazing complexity, precision and balance.
>
> An ecologically just society will be guided by the values of sustainability, fairness, and participation. Sustainability refers to the earth's limited capacity to provide resources and to absorb the pollution resulting from their use. Sustainability requires that biological and social systems which nurture and support life not be depleted or poisoned. Fairness refers to . . . an equitable distribution of the total benefits and costs.

Whereas the impacts of global warming, as currently predicted and understood by leading scientists and scientific bodies around the world including the National Aeronautics and Space Administration, the National Academy of Sciences, and the Intergovernmental Panel on Climate Change, will dramatically and negatively alter God's gracious gift of creation and Whereas the predicted impacts of global warming will have a disproportionate impact on those living in poverty and hunger, the elderly and infants, and those least responsible for the emissions of green house gases.

Be It Therefore Resolved That the National Council of Churches in Christ:

1. Expresses its deep concern for the pending environmental, economic, and social tragedies threatened by global warming to creation, human communities, and traditional sacred spaces
2. Urges the Federal Government to respond to global warming with greater urgency and leadership and gives support for mandatory measures that reduce the absolute amount of greenhouse gas emissions, and in particular emissions of carbon dioxide, to levels recommended by nationally and internationally recognized and respected scientific bodies.
3. Urges the Federal, State and Local Governments to support and invest in energy conservation and efficiency, sustainable and renewable, and affordable and sustainable transportation
4. Calls for business and industry to respond to global warming with increased investment in conservation and more efficient and sustainable energy technologies that are accessible, sustainable, and democratic.
5. Stands firmly with all of God's children by urging that adaptive measures and financial support be forthcoming from government and industry to aid those directly impacted by global warming and in particular those least able to relocate, reconstruct, or cope with the current and pending impacts of climate change
6. Calls on all Christians, people of faith and people of good will the world over to lead by example and seek active means whereby they may, individually and in community, quickly reduce their emissions of green house gas emissions and speak out for engagement by their elected officials on matters of global warming.

10.10

Evangelical Climate Initiative

CLIMATE CHANGE: AN EVANGELICAL CALL TO ACTION
(JANUARY 2006)

Preamble

As American evangelical Christian leaders, we recognize both our opportunity and our responsibility to offer a biblically based moral witness that can help shape public policy in the most powerful nation on earth, and therefore contribute to the well-being of the entire world.[22] Whether we will enter the public square and offer our witness there is no longer an open question. We are in that square, and we will not withdraw.

We are proud of the evangelical community's long-standing commitment to the sanctity of human life. But we also offer moral witness in many venues and on many issues. Sometimes the issues that we have taken on, such as sex trafficking, genocide in the Sudan, and the AIDS epidemic in Africa, have surprised outside observers. While individuals and organizations can be called to concentrate on certain issues, we are not a single-issue movement. We seek to be true to our calling as Christian leaders, and above all faithful to Jesus Christ our Lord. Our attention, therefore, goes to whatever issues our faith requires us to address.

Over the last several years many of us have engaged in study, reflection, and prayer related to the issue of climate change (often called "global warming"). For most of us, until recently this has not been treated as a pressing issue or major priority. Indeed, many of us have required considerable convincing before becoming persuaded that climate change is a real problem and that it ought to matter to us as Christians. But now we have seen and heard enough to offer the following moral argument related to the matter of human-induced climate change. We commend the four simple but urgent claims offered in this document to all who will listen, beginning with our brothers and sisters in the Christian community, and urge all to take the appropriate actions that follow from them.

Claim 1: Human-Induced Climate Change Is Real

Since 1995 there has been general agreement among those in the scientific community most seriously engaged with this issue that climate change is happening and is being caused mainly by human activities, especially the burning of fossil fuels. Evidence gathered since 1995 has only strengthened this conclusion.

Because all religious/moral claims about climate change are relevant only if climate change is real and is mainly human-induced, everything hinges on the scientific data. As evangelicals we have hesitated to speak on this issue until we could be more certain of the science of climate change, but the signatories now believe that the evidence demands action:

- The Intergovernmental Panel on Climate Change (IPCC), the world's most authoritative body of scientists and policy experts on the issue of global warming, has been studying this issue since the late 1980s. (From 1988–2002 the IPCC's assessment of the climate science was Chaired by Sir John Houghton, a devout evangelical Christian.) It has documented the steady rise in global temperatures over the last fifty years, projects that the average global temperature will continue to rise in the coming decades, and attributes "most of the warming" to human activities.
- The U.S. National Academy of Sciences, as well as all other G8 country scientific Academies (Great Britain, France, Germany, Japan, Canada, Italy, and Russia), has concurred with these judgments.
- In a 2004 report, and at the 2005 G8 summit, the Bush Administration has also acknowledged the reality of climate change and the likelihood that human activity is the cause of at least some of it.[23] (GRID-Arendal 2001)

In the face of the breadth and depth of this scientific and governmental concern, only a small percentage of which is noted here, we are convinced that evangelicals must engage this issue without any further lingering over the basic reality of the problem or humanity's responsibility to address it.

Claim 2: The Consequences of Climate Change Will Be Significant, and Will Hit the Poor the Hardest

The earth's natural systems are resilient but not infinitely so, and human civilizations are remarkably dependent on ecological stability and well-being. It is easy to forget this until that stability and well-being are threatened.

Even small rises in global temperatures will have such likely impacts as: sea level rise; more frequent heat waves, droughts, and extreme weather events such as torrential rains and floods; increased tropical diseases in now-temperate regions; and hurricanes that are more intense. It could lead to significant reduction in agricultural output, especially in poor countries. Low-lying regions, indeed entire islands, could find themselves under water. (This is not to mention the various negative impacts climate change could have on God's other creatures.)

Each of these impacts increases the likelihood of refugees from flooding or famine, violent conflicts, and international instability, which could lead to more security threats to our nation.

Poor nations and poor individuals have fewer resources available to cope with major challenges and threats. The consequences of global warming will therefore hit the poor the hardest, in part because those areas likely to be significantly affected first are in the poorest regions of the world. Millions of people could die in this century because of climate change, most of them our poorest global neighbors.

Claim 3: Christian Moral Convictions Demand Our Response to the Climate Change Problem

While we cannot here review the full range of relevant biblical convictions related to care of the creation, we emphasize the following points:

- Christians must care about climate change because we love God the Creator and Jesus our Lord, through whom and for whom the creation was made. This is God's world, and any damage that we do to God's world is an offense against God Himself (Gen. 1; Ps. 24; Col. 1:16).
- Christians must care about climate change because we are called to love our neighbors, to do unto others as we would have them do unto us, and to protect and care for the least of these as though each was Jesus Christ himself (Mt. 22:34–40; Mt. 7:12; Mt. 25:31–46).
- Christians, noting the fact that most of the climate change problem is human induced, are reminded that when God made humanity he commissioned us to exercise stewardship over the earth and its creatures. Climate change is the latest

evidence of our failure to exercise proper stewardship, and constitutes a critical opportunity for us to do better (Gen. 1:26–28).

Love of God, love of neighbor, and the demands of stewardship are more than enough reason for evangelical Christians to respond to the climate change problem with moral passion and concrete action.

Claim 4: The Need to Act Now Is Urgent. Governments, Businesses, Churches, and Individuals All Have a Role to Play in Addressing Climate Change—Starting Now.

The basic task for all of the world's inhabitants is to find ways now to begin to reduce the carbon dioxide emissions from the burning of fossil fuels that are the primary cause of human-induced climate change.

There are several reasons for urgency. First, deadly impacts are being experienced now. Second, the oceans only warm slowly, creating a lag in experiencing the consequences. Much of the climate change to which we are already committed will not be realized for several decades. The consequences of the pollution we create now will be visited upon our children and grandchildren. Third, as individuals and as a society we are making long-term decisions today that will determine how much carbon dioxide we will emit in the future, such as whether to purchase energy efficient vehicles and appliances that will last for 10–20 years, or whether to build more coal-burning power plants that last for 50 years rather than investing more in energy efficiency and renewable energy.

In the United States, the most important immediate step that can be taken at the federal level is to pass and implement national legislation requiring sufficient economy-wide reductions in carbon dioxide emissions through cost-effective, market-based mechanisms such as a cap-and-trade program. On June 22, 2005 the Senate passed the Domenici-Bingaman resolution affirming this approach, and a number of major energy companies now acknowledge that this method is best both for the environment and for business.

We commend the Senators who have taken this stand and encourage them to fulfill their pledge. We also applaud the steps taken by such companies as BP, Shell, General Electric, Cinergy, Duke Energy, and DuPont, all of which have moved ahead of the pace of government action through innovative measures implemented within their companies in the U.S. and around the world. In so doing they have offered timely leadership.

Numerous positive actions to prevent and mitigate climate change are being implemented across our society by state and local governments, churches, smaller businesses, and individuals. These commendable efforts focus on such matters as energy efficiency, the use of renewable energy, low CO_2 emitting technologies, and the purchase of hybrid vehicles. These efforts can easily be shown to save money, save energy, reduce global warming pollution as well as air pollution that harm human health, and eventually pay for themselves. There is much more to be done, but these pioneers are already helping to show the way forward.

Finally, while we must reduce our global warming pollution to help mitigate the impacts of climate change, as a society and as individuals we must also help the poor adapt to the significant harm that global warming will cause.

Conclusion

We the undersigned pledge to act on the basis of the claims made in this document. We will not only teach the truths communicated here but also seek ways to implement the actions that follow from them. In the name of Jesus Christ our Lord, we urge all who read this declaration to join us in this effort.

10.11

Cornwall Alliance for the Stewardship of Creation

AN OPEN LETTER TO THE SIGNERS OF "CLIMATE CHANGE: AN EVANGELICAL CALL TO ACTION" AND OTHERS CONCERNED ABOUT GLOBAL WARMING
(JUNE 11, 2007)

"They only asked us to remember the poor—the very thing I was eager to do."

—The Apostle Paul, Galatians 2:10

Widespread media reports tell of a scientific consensus that:

- the world is presently experiencing unprecedented global warming;
- the main cause of it is rising atmospheric carbon dioxide because of human use of fossil fuels for energy; and
- the consequences of continuing this pattern will include (1) rising sea levels that could inundate highly populated and often poor low-lying lands, (2) more frequent deadly heat waves, droughts, and other extreme weather events, (3) increased tropical diseases in warming temperate regions, and (4) more frequent and intense hurricanes.

Recently eighty-six evangelical pastors, college presidents, mission heads, and other leaders signed "Climate Change: An Evangelical Call to Action," under the auspices of the Evangelical Climate Initiative. The document calls on the federal government to pass national legislation requiring sufficient reductions in carbon dioxide emissions to fight global warming and argues that these are necessary to protect the poor from its harmful effects.

In light of all this, many people are puzzled by the Interfaith Stewardship Alliance's opposition to such calls. Do we not *care* about the prospect of catastrophic global warming? Do we not *care* that with rising temperatures the polar ice caps will melt, and the sea will inundate low island countries and coastal regions? Do we not *care* that the world's poor might be most hurt by these things?

Yes, we care. But we also believe, with economist Walter Williams, that "truly compassionate policy requires dispassionate analysis." That is the very motive for our opposing drastic steps to prevent global warming. In short, we have the same motive proclaimed by the Evangelical Climate Initiative in its "Call to Action."

But motive and reason are not the same thing. It matters little how well we mean, if what we do actually harms those we intend to help.

That is why we take the positions we do. In . . . "A Call to Truth, Prudence, and Protection of the Poor: An Evangelical Response to Global Warming," we present extensive evidence and argument against the extent, the significance, and perhaps the existence of the much-touted scientific consensus on catastrophic human-induced global warming.[24] Further, good science—like truth—is not about counting votes but about empirical evidence and valid arguments. Therefore we also present data, arguments, and sources favoring a different perspective:

- Foreseeable global warming will have moderate and mixed (not only harmful but also helpful), not catastrophic, consequences for humanity—including the poor—and the rest of the world's inhabitants.
- Natural causes may account for a large part, perhaps the majority, of the global warming in both the last thirty and the last one hundred fifty years, which together constitute an episode in the natural rising and falling cycles of global average temperature. Human emissions of carbon dioxide and other greenhouse gases are probably a minor and possibly an insignificant contributor to its causes.
- Reducing carbon dioxide emissions would have at most an insignificant impact on the quantity and duration of global warming and would not significantly reduce alleged harmful effects.
- Government-mandated carbon dioxide emissions reductions not only would not significantly curtail global warming or reduce its harmful effects but also would cause greater harm than good to humanity—especially the poor—while offering virtually no benefit to the rest of the world's inhabitants.
- In light of all the above, the most prudent response is not to try (almost certainly unsuccessfully and at enormous cost) to prevent or reduce whatever slight warming might really occur. It is instead to prepare to adapt by fostering means that will effectively protect humanity—especially the poor—not only from whatever harms might be anticipated from global warming but also from harms that might be fostered by other types of catastrophes, natural or manmade.

We believe the harm caused by mandated reductions in energy consumption in the quixotic quest to reduce global warming will far exceed its benefits. Reducing energy consumption will require significantly increasing the costs of energy—whether through taxation or by restricting supplies. Because energy is a vital component in producing all goods and services people need, raising its costs means raising other prices, too. For wealthy people, this might require some adjustments in consumption patterns—inconvenient and disappointing, perhaps, but not devastating. But for the world's two billion or more poor people, who can barely afford sufficient food, clothing, and shelter to sustain life, and who are without electricity and the refrigeration, cooking, light, heat, and air conditioning it can provide, it can mean the difference between life and death.

Along with all the benefits we derive from economic use of energy, another consideration—a Biblical/theological one—points in the same direction. The stewardship God gave to human beings over the earth—to cultivate and guard the garden (Genesis 2:15) and to fill, subdue, and rule the whole earth (Genesis 1:28)—strongly suggests that caring for human needs is compatible with caring for the earth. As theologian Wayne Grudem put it, "It does not seem likely to me that God would set up the world to work in such a way that human beings would eventually destroy the earth by doing such ordinary and morally good and necessary things as breathing, building a fire to cook or keep warm, burning fuel to travel, or using energy for a refrigerator to preserve food."

Whether or not global warming is largely natural, (1) human efforts to stop it are largely futile; (2) whatever efforts we undertake to stem our small contributions to it would needlessly divert resources from much more beneficial uses; and (3) adaptation strategies for whatever slight warming does occur are much more sensible than costly but futile prevention strategies. Therefore, we believe it is far wiser to promote economic growth, partly through keeping energy inexpensive, than to fight against potential global warming and thus slow economic growth. And there is a side benefit, too: wealthier societies are better able and more willing to spend to protect and improve the natural environment than poorer societies. Our policy, therefore, is better not only for humanity but also for the rest of the planet.

We recognize that reasonable people can disagree with our understanding of the science and economics. But this is indeed our understanding.

Please join us in endorsing **"A Call to Truth, Prudence, and Protection of the Poor: An Evangelical Response to Global Warming"** http://www.cornwallalliance.org/docs/Call_to_Truth.pdf). To do so, send an e-mail with your name, degree(s) (with subject, level, and granting institution), professional title, professional affiliation (for identification purposes only), mailing address, e-mail address, and (for verification) phone number to Stewards@CornwallAlliance.org. If you have questions, please e-mail the same address.

Notes

1. I say "loosely" based because many aspects of policymaking in America require a supermajority. For example, passage of a bill in the Senate requires a filibuster-proof majority of 3/5ths and passage of a constitutional amendment requires a 2/3rds vote in both chambers of Congress and ratification by 3/4ths of the states.

2. Denominational lobbies face some difficulty in that they speak for large groups of members, yet most members of the denominations are unaware of what the Washington office does or even of the office's existence since most Americans join houses of worship for spiritual rather than political reasons. The disconnection between lobbyists and members is particularly problematic for Mainline Protestant groups.

3. This was the intention behind the Faith Based Initiative advocated by President George W. Bush in 2000. One of Bush's first actions as President was to establish the Office of Faith Based and Community Initiatives to help religious institutions apply for federal grants to provide social services and to prevent discrimination against these groups in the awarding of government grants. For a more detailed history of the policy, see (Black, Koopman, and Ryden 2004).

4. This overview leaves out many areas in which religious voices have participated including debates over prohibition, the environment, physician assisted suicide, racial profiling, judicial nominations, capital punishment, nuclear disarmament, child vaccinations, tax policy, gambling, divorce law, campaign finance laws, women's rights, and drug policy, to name just a few.

5. The U.S. Supreme Court upheld laws passed by Congress that outlawed polygamy in the case *Reynolds v. United States* (1879). Before Utah could be admitted as a state, Congress required the LDS Church to change its position on polygamous marriage.

6. The U.S. Supreme Court upheld an Oregon policy that banned the use of peyote in the case *Employment Division v. Smith* (1990). The decision was especially significant because it reflected a change in the way the Court interpreted the free exercise clause of the

Constitution, making it easier for states to restrict aspects of religious practice.

7. The U.S. Supreme Court ruled against a city ordinance targeting the religious group in the case *Church of the Lukumi Babalu Aye v. City of Hialeah* (1993).

8. The movement was titled "fundamentalism" because adherents accepted a list of "fundamental" tenets of Christian faith published in a series of pamphlets in the early 1900s.

9. See, for example, *Swart v. South Burlington* (1961), *Brusca v. State of Missouri State Board of Education* (1971), *Lemon v. Kurtzman* (1971).

10. The schema is adapted from Mark Noll's introduction in Mark A. Noll, ed., *Religion and American Politics* (New York: Oxford University Press, 1990).

11. Explanations for the Constitution's godless language are examined historically by John F. Wilson, "Religion, Government, and Power in the New American Nation," in Noll, *Religion and American Politics*, 77–91; and Daniel L. Dreisbach, "In Search of a Christian Commonwealth," *Baylor Law Review* 48:4 (1996):927–1000.

12. Deeper interpretations of the historical transformation in these transactions cannot be dealt with here. A provocative account is Marcel Gauchet's *The Disenchantment of the World: A Political History of Religion* (Princeton: Princeton University Press, 1997). For a valuable counterpoint, see Charles Taylor's foreword to Gauchet's book as well as his *Sources of the Self* (Cambridge, MA: Cambridge University Press, 1989) and *A Catholic Modernity?* Marianist Award Lecture (Dayton, Ohio, 1996).

13. This is exactly the viewpoint Richard Niebuhr identified behind the Founders commitment to religious freedom. See his 1939 lecture "Limitations of Power and Religious Liberty" reproduced in Harvard Divinity School, *Religion & Values in Public Life* 3:2 (1995).

14. This rather unsettled nature of religion and public policy may be one reason why undergraduate public policy textbooks typically avoid religious matters in their content and discussion. Usually, the first half of these introductory textbooks discusses public policy in general, whereas the second half is generally divided into large topical public policy categories. Most textbooks usually start the second half with chapters on fiscal and budget policy, and then move to large social programs such as welfare, retirement, and health care. Next come chapters on the environment and energy, and typically one or two chapters on foreign and military policy end the book. A few exceptions (e.g. Peters 2006) might touch on "morality politics" in a chapter on cultural issues, in which issues as abortion, gay rights, and church-state separation might be addressed. But, generally, the undergraduate public policy student seems unlikely to encounter much discussion of the interaction between religion and public policy, an unfortunate limitation given the persistence of religious belief in the nation and the increasing presence of religious rhetoric and groups in the public square and the policy-making world.

15. Mooney (2001) argues that this characterization could fit economic policy areas if at least one side perceived the issue as involving first principles of right and wrong.

16. Although Meier is pessimistic about making and enforcing moral policies, he does suggest one possible means out of this dilemma is through the reframing of issues in ways that work with established policy-making procedures within the political branches of government. Such a reframing could entail presenting the debate as a more ambiguous clash of different, although widely held, values (e.g. abortion as a clash between the preservation of life and the privacy and freedom rights of a pregnant female). If core values clash, although policy still needs to be made, perhaps a more typical process might transpire. Another potential reframing could be to link a "sin" issue to a public good (such as linking state allowance of sponsorship of gambling to higher funding for popular functions such as education), converting moral politics into more redistributive politics.

17. In addition to Mooney, Raymond Tatalovich has been a major contributor to the study of morality policies. He and Byron Daynes published a widely used edited volume in the field (Tatalovich and Daynes 1988). Their first 1988 edition was published as Social Regulatory Policy, but by the third, 2005, edition, the title had changed to Moral Controversies in American Politics (Tatalovich and Daynes 2005). The usual issues—abortion, death penalty, gay rights, pornography—are in each. Other issues—animal rights, English as an official language, school prayer, gun control, and hate crimes—fall in and out of editions, but the core remains.

18. It is also quite likely that morality policies are debated more often, and more publicly, in America than elsewhere.

19. National Conference of Catholic Bishops, *The Challenge of Peace: God's Promise and Our Response* (Washington DC: USCC Office of Publishing and Promotion Services, 1983).

20. The terms "an Evangelical" and "Evangelicals" are proper nouns, rather than common nouns, and should be spelled with an upper case—as are the terms Roman Catholic, Orthodox, and Protestant, or Christian, Jew, and Muslim.

21. This brief expression of repentance is more fully developed in the full Evangelical Manifesto.

22. Cf. "For the Health of the Nation: An Evangelical Call to Civic Responsibility," approved by National Association of Evangelicals, October 8, 2004.

23. See also the main IPCC website, www.ipcc.ch. For the confirmation of the IPCC's findings from the U.S. National Academy of Sciences, see *Climate Change Science: An Analysis of Some Key Questions* (2001); http://books.nap .edu/html/climatechange/summary.html. For the statement by the G8 Academies (plus those of Brazil, India, and China) see Joint Science Academies Statement: Global Response to Climate Change, (June 2005): http:// nationalacademies.org/onpi/06072005.pdf. Another major international report that confirms the IPCC's conclusions comes from the Arctic Climate Impact Assessment. See their *Impacts of a Warming Climate*, Cambridge University Press, November 2004, p.2; http://amap.no/acia/. Another important statement is from the American Geophysical Union, "Human Impacts on Climate," December 2003, http://www.agu.org/sci_soc/ policy/climate_change_position.html. For the Bush Administration's perspective, see *Our Changing Planet: The U.S. Climate Change Science Program for Fiscal Years 2004 and 2005*, p.47; http://www.usgcrp.gov/usgcrp/ Library/ocp2004-5/default.htm. For the 2005 G8 statement, see http://www.number-10.gov .uk/output/Page7881.asp.

24. See Cornwall Alliance for the Stewardship of Creation, "A Call to Truth, Prudence, and Protection of the Poor: An Evangelical Response to Global Warming," June 11, 2007.

CHAPTER 11

FOREIGN POLICY DEBATES

Introduction

Research Pieces

11.1 Samuel Huntington, *The Clash of Civilizations* (1996)
11.2 Madeleine Albright, *The Mighty and the Almighty* (2006)
11.3 Walter Russell Mead, *God's Country?* (September/October 2006)

Primary Sources

11.4 St. Thomas Aquinas, *The Summa Theologica. Part II, Question 40* (Circa 1274)
11.5 *The Schleitheim Confession of Faith: Brotherly Union of a Number of Children of God Concerning Seven Articles* (February 24, 1527)
11.6 Mennonite Central Committee, *A Commitment to Christ's Way of Peace* (February 1993)
11.7 United States Conference of Catholic Bishops, *Statement on Iraq* (November 13, 2002)

Introduction

The terrorist attacks of September 11, 2001, brought into sharp relief the intersection between religion and foreign policy. Most of the world, including "experts" in government and the academy, were caught unaware. But as the readings in this chapter indicate, religion is ever present in the global realm and influences politics in many important ways.

In the excerpt from *The Clash of Civilizations*, Samuel Huntington asserts that cultural aspects of civilizations, including religion, represent their essence. Divisions along cultural lines form the basis for political struggles between the five major civilizations of the world. Religion, Huntington claims, is at the crux of potentially high-conflict clashes, especially those between Islam and the West. While some scholars and pundits viewed the September 11 attacks as confirmation of Huntington's thesis, others saw this as an overly simplistic interpretation. For example, noted historian Edward Said maintains that Huntington reduces complex and contested notions—Islam and the West—down to a few factors salient to proving his version of foreign policy. His critics notwithstanding, Huntington's theory must be a part of any informed discussion of foreign policy in the post–Cold War era.

Former Secretary of State Madeline Albright argues that the State Department ignores religion at the world's peril. In her memoir, *The Mighty and the Almighty*, she details how the realist approach to international relations overlooked cultural factors such as religion, which she now deems central to a smart foreign policy. She calls for dialogue across religious boundaries in the name of peace.

Walter Russell Mead's "God's Country" argues that evangelicals are the most influential religious group shaping contemporary American foreign policy. The result in recent years has been a focus upon human rights and continued strong support of the state of Israel. Certainly, Mead's piece challenges policy makers and academics not only to consider closely the influence of religion, but also to take note of the role of particular strands of religion in the making and conduct of foreign policy.

Although the intersection of religion and foreign policy has received short shrift in modern writings and governmental policies, the primary sources demonstrate that religious teachings and doctrine relevant to international affairs date back many centuries. For example, St. Aquinas' work, *The Summa Theologica*, is an example of early Catholic teaching that extends the Great Commandment to love God and to love one's neighbor to the battlefield—love your enemy, even in the midst of war. The Schleitheim Confession, written by Anabaptists who had been persecuted for their beliefs, details a different interpretation of the Great Commandment to love neighbor and self. Jesus Christ's peaceful example and teachings in the Sermon on the Mount motivated the Anabaptists to eschew war altogether.

The next two readings offer modern interpretations of classic Catholic and Anabaptist teachings. The United States Conference of Catholic Bishops statement at the height of tensions about how to address Saddam Hussein and alleged weapons of mass destruction in Iraq illustrates how the church continues to apply the Just War doctrine to engage questions of war and peace. The Mennonite Central Committee's statement from 1994 reaffirms its modern commitment to the principles of peace outlined in 1527 at Schleitheim.

As these sources demonstrate, foreign policy debates are not merely considerations of military power and economic interests. Religion frames disputes between states and shapes foreign policy decisions within states by government actors. As Secretary of State Albright cautioned, we ignore religion in foreign policy at our peril.

Research Pieces

11.1

Samuel Huntington

THE CLASH OF CIVILIZATIONS (1996)

Core State and Fault Line Conflicts

Civilizations are the ultimate human tribes, and the clash of civilizations is tribal conflict on a global scale. In the emerging world, states and groups from two different civilizations may form limited, ad hoc, tactical connections and coalitions to advance their interests against entities from a third civilization or for other shared purposes. Relations between groups from different civilizations however will be almost never close, usually cool, and often hostile. . . . Cold peace, cold war, trade war, quasi war, uneasy peace, troubled relations, intense rivalry, competitive coexistence, arms races: these phrases are the most probable descriptions of relations between entities from different civilizations. Trust and friendship will be rare.

Intercivilizational conflict takes two forms. At the local or micro level, *fault line conflicts* occur between neighboring states from different civilizations, between groups from different civilizations within a state, and between groups which, as in the former Soviet Union and Yugoslavia, are attempting to create new states out of the wreckage of old. Fault line conflicts are particularly prevalent between Muslims and non-Muslims. . . . At the global or macro level, *core state conflicts* occur among the major states of different civilizations. The issues in these conflicts are the classic ones of international politics, including:

1. relative influence in shaping global developments and the actions of global international organizations such as the U.N., IMF [International Monetary Fund], and World Bank;

2. relative military power, which manifests itself in controversies over nonproliferation and arms control and in arms races;

3. economic power and welfare, manifested in disputes over trade, investment, and other issues;

4. people, involving efforts by a state from one civilization to protect kinsmen in another civilization, to discriminate against people from another civilization, or to exclude from its territory people from another civilization;

5. values and culture, conflicts over which arise when a state attempts to promote or to impose its values on the people of another civilization;

6. occasionally, territory, in which core states become front line participants in fault line conflicts.

These issues are, of course, the sources of conflict between humans throughout history. When states from different civilizations are involved, however, cultural differences sharpen the conflict. In their competition with each other, core states attempt to rally their civilizational cohorts, to get support from states of third civilizations, to promote division within and defections from opposing civilizations, and to use the appropriate mix of diplomatic, political, economic, and covert actions and propaganda inducements and coercions to achieve their objectives. Core states are, however, unlikely to use military force directly against each other, except in situations such as have existed in the Middle East and the Subcontinent where they adjoin each other on a civilizational fault line. Core state wars are otherwise likely to arise under only two circumstances. First, they could develop from the escalation of fault line conflicts between local groups as kin groups, including core states, rally to the support of the local combatants. This possibility, however, creates a major incentive for the core states in the opposing civilizations to contain or to resolve the fault line conflict.

Second, core state war could result from changes in the global balance of power among civilizations. . . . [T]he history of Western civilization is one of "hegemonic wars" between rising and falling powers. . . . The missing hegemonic war in Western history is that between Great Britain and the United States, and presumably the peaceful shift from the Pax Britannica to the Pax Americana was in large part due to the close cultural kinship of the two societies. The absence of such kinship in the shifting power balance between the West and China does not make armed conflict certain but does make it more probable. The dynamism of Islam is the ongoing source of many relatively small fault line wars; the rise of China is the potential source of a big intercivilizational war of core states.

Islam and the West

Some Westerners . . . have argued that the West does not have problems with Islam but only with violent Islamist extremists. Fourteen hundred years of history demonstrate otherwise. The relations between Islam and Christianity, both Orthodox and Western, have often been stormy. Each has been the other's Other. . . . Across the centuries the fortunes of the two religions have risen and fallen in a sequence of momentous surges, pauses, and countersurges. . . .

The causes of this ongoing pattern of conflict lie not in transitory phenomena such as twelfth-century Christian passion or twentieth-century Muslim fundamentalism. They flow from the nature of the two religions and the civilizations based on them. Conflict was, on the one hand, a product of difference, particularly the Muslim concept of Islam as a way of life transcending and uniting religion and politics versus the Western Christian concept of the separate realms of God and Caesar. The conflict also stemmed, however, from their similarities. Both are monotheistic religions, which, unlike polytheistic ones, cannot easily assimilate additional deities, and which see the world in dualistic, us-and-them terms. Both are universalistic, claiming to be the one true faith to which all humans can adhere. Both are missionary religions believing that their adherents have an obligation to convert nonbelievers to that one true faith. From its origins Islam expanded by conquest and when the opportunity existed Christianity did also. The parallel concepts of "jihad" and "crusade" not only resemble each other but distinguish these two faiths from other major world religions. Islam and Christianity, along with Judaism, also have teleological views of history in contrast to the cyclical or static views prevalent in other civilizations.

The level of violent conflict between Islam and Christianity over time has been influenced by demographic growth and decline, economic developments, technological change, and intensity of religious commitment. . . .

A comparable mix of factors has increased the conflict between Islam and the West in the late twentieth century. First, Muslim population growth has generated large numbers of unemployed and disaffected young people who become recruits to Islamist causes, exert pressure on neighboring societies, and migrate to the West. Second, the Islamic Resurgence has given Muslims renewed confidence in the distinctive character and worth of their civilization and values compared to those of the West. Third, the West's simultaneous efforts to universalize its values and institutions, to maintain its military and economic superiority, and to intervene in conflicts in the Muslim world generate intense resentment among Muslims. Fourth, the collapse of communism removed a common enemy of the West and Islam and left each the perceived major threat to the other. Fifth, the increasing contact between and intermingling of Muslims and Westerners stimulate in each a new sense of their own identity and how it differs from that of the other. Interaction and intermingling also exacerbate differences over the rights of the members of one civilization in a country dominated by members of the other civilization. Within both Muslim and Christian societies, tolerance for the other declined sharply in the 1980s and 1990s.

The causes of the renewed conflict between Islam and the West thus lie in fundamental questions of power and culture. *Kto? Kovo?* Who is to rule? Who is to be ruled? The central issue of politics defined by Lenin is the root of the contest between Islam and the West. There is, however, the additional conflict, which Lenin would have considered meaningless, between two different versions of what is right and what is wrong and, as a consequence, who is right and who is wrong. So long as Islam remains Islam (which it will) and the West remains the West (which is more dubious), this fundamental conflict between two great civilizations and ways of life will continue to define their relations in the future even as it has defined them for the past fourteen centuries.

These relations are further roiled by a number of substantive issues on which their positions differ or conflict. Historically one major issue was the control of territory, but that is now relatively insignificant. . . . The effective end of Western territorial imperialism and the absence so far of renewed Muslim territorial expansion have produced a geographical segregation so that only in a few places in the Balkans do Western and Muslim communities directly border on each other. Conflicts between the West and Islam thus focus less on territory than on broader intercivilizational issues such as weapons proliferation, human rights and democracy, control of oil, migration, Islamist terrorism, and Western intervention. . . .

In the 1980s and 1990s the overall trend in Islam has been in an anti-Western direction. In part, this is the natural consequence of the Islamic Resurgence and the reaction against the perceived *"gharbzadegi"* or Westoxication of Muslim societies. . . . Muslims fear and resent Western power and the threat which this poses to their society and beliefs. They see Western culture as materialistic, corrupt, decadent, and immoral. They also see it as seductive, and hence stress all the more the need to resist its impact on their way of life. Increasingly, Muslims attack the West not for adhering to an imperfect, erroneous religion, which is nonetheless a "religion of the book," but for not adhering to any religion at all. In Muslim eyes Western secularism, irreligiosity, and hence immorality are worse evils than the Western Christianity that produced them. . . .

These images of the West as arrogant, materialistic, repressive, brutal, and decadent are held not only by fundamentalist imams but also by those whom many in the West would consider their natural allies and supporters. . . .

. . . Both popular and intellectually serious Muslim publications repeatedly describe what are alleged to be Western plots and designs to subordinate, humiliate, and undermine Islamic institutions and culture.[1]

The reaction against the West can be seen not only in the central intellectual thrust of the Islamic Resurgence but also in the shift in the attitudes toward the West of governments in Muslim countries. The immediate postcolonial governments were generally Western in their political and economic ideologies and policies and pro-Western in their foreign policies. . . . One by one, however, pro-Western governments gave way to governments less identified with the West or explicitly anti-Western in Iraq, Libya, Yemen, Syria, Iran, Sudan, Lebanon, and Afghanistan. Less dramatic changes in the same direction occurred in the orientation and alignment of other states including Tunisia, Indonesia, and Malaysia. The two staunchest Cold War Muslim military allies of the United States, Turkey and Pakistan, are under Islamist political pressure internally and their ties with the West subject to increased strain. . . .

. . . The West's close friends in the Muslim world are now either like Kuwait, Saudi Arabia, and the Gulf sheikdoms dependent on the West militarily or like Egypt and Algeria dependent on it economically. . . .

Growing Muslim anti-Westernism has been paralleled by expanding Western concern with the "Islamic threat" posed particularly by Muslim extremism. Islam is seen as a source of nuclear proliferation, terrorism, and, in Europe, unwanted migrants. These concerns are shared by both publics and leaders. . . .

Given the prevailing perceptions Muslims and Westerners have of each other plus the rise of Islamist extremism, it is hardly surprising that following the 1979 Iranian Revolution, an intercivilizational quasi war developed between Islam and the West. It is a quasi war for three reasons. First, all of Islam has not been fighting all of the West. Two fundamentalist states (Iran, Sudan), three nonfundamentalist states (Iraq, Libya, Syria), plus a wide range of Islamist organizations, with financial support from other Muslim countries such as Saudi Arabia, have been fighting the United States and, at times, Britain, France, and other Western states and groups, as well as Israel and Jews generally. Second, it is a quasi war because, apart from the Gulf War of 1990–91, it has been fought with limited means: terrorism on one side and air power, covert action, and economic sanctions on the other. Third, it is a quasi war because while the violence has been continuing, it has also not been continuous. It has involved intermittent actions by one side which provoke responses by the other. . . .

In this quasi war, each side has capitalized on its own strengths and the other side's weaknesses. Militarily it has been largely a war of terrorism versus air power. Dedicated Islamic militants exploit the open societies of the West and plant car bombs at selected targets. Western military professionals exploit the open skies of Islam and drop smart bombs on selected targets. The Islamic participants plot the assassination of prominent Westerners; the United States plots the overthrow of extremist Islamic regimes. . . .

American leaders allege that the Muslims involved in the quasi war are a small minority whose use of violence is rejected by the great majority of moderate Muslims. This may be true, but evidence to support it is lacking. Protests against anti-Western violence have been totally absent in Muslim countries. Muslim governments, even the bunker governments friendly to and dependent on the West, have been strikingly reticent when it comes to condemning terrorist acts against the West. On the other side, European governments and publics have largely supported and rarely criticized actions the United States has taken against its Muslim opponents, in striking contrast to the strenuous opposition they often expressed to American actions against the Soviet Union and communism during the Cold War. In civilizational conflicts, unlike ideological ones, kin stand by their kin.

The underlying problem for the West is not Islamic fundamentalism. It is Islam, a different civilization whose people are convinced of the superiority of their culture and are obsessed with the inferiority of their power. The problem for Islam is not the CIA or the U.S. Department of Defense. It is the West, a different civilization whose people are convinced of the universality of their culture and believe that their superior, if declining, power imposes on them the obligation to extend that culture throughout the world. These are the basic ingredients that fuel conflict between Islam and the West. . . .

Civilizations and Core States: Emerging Alignments

The post–Cold War, multipolar, multicivilizational world lacks an overwhelmingly dominant cleavage such as existed in the Cold War. So long as the Muslim demographic and Asian economic surges continue, however, the conflicts between the West and the challenger civilizations will be more central to global politics than other lines of cleavage. . . . Relations between the United States, on the one hand, and China, Japan, and other Asian countries will be highly conflictual, and a major war could occur if the United States challenges China's rise as the hegemonic power in Asia.

Under these conditions, the Confucian-Islamic connection will continue and perhaps broaden and deepen. Central to this connection has been the cooperation of Muslim and Sinic societies opposing the West on weapons proliferation, human rights, and other issues. At its core have been the close relations among Pakistan, Iran, and China, which crystallized in the early 1990s. . . . The cooperation among the three countries has included regular exchanges among political, military, and bureaucratic officials and joint efforts in a variety of civil and military areas including defense production, in addition to the weapons transfers from China to the other states. . . .

Enthusiasm for a close anti-Western alliance of Confucian and Islamic states, however, has been rather muted on the Chinese side. . . . This position presumably reflected the classical Chinese view that as the Middle Kingdom, the central power, China did not need formal allies, and other countries would find it in their interest to cooperate with China. China's conflicts with the West, on the other hand, mean that it will value partnership with other anti-Western states, of which Islam furnishes the largest and most influential number. In addition, China's increasing needs for oil are likely to impel it to expand its relations with Iran, Iraq, and Saudi Arabia as well as Kazakhstan and Azerbaijan. Such an arms-for-oil axis, one energy expert observed in 1994, "won't have to take orders from London, Paris or Washington anymore" (Friedman 1994,). . . .

Russia's relations with Islam are shaped by the historical legacy of centuries of expansion through war against the Turks, North Caucasus peoples, and Central Asian emirates. . . . It has actively attempted to maintain its political, economic, and military influence in the Central Asian republics, has enlisted them in the Commonwealth of Independent States, and deploys military forces in all of them. Central to Russian concerns are the Caspian Sea oil and gas reserves and the routes by which these resources will reach the West and East Asia. Russia has also been fighting one war in the North Caucasus against the Muslim people of Chechnya and a second war in Tajikistan supporting the government against an insurgency that includes Islamic fundamentalists. These security concerns provide a further incentive for cooperation with China in containing the "Islamic threat" in Central Asia. . . . For the coming decades Russia's relations with Islam will be decisively shaped by its perceptions of the threats posed by the booming Muslim populations along its southern periphery.

During the Cold War, India, the third "swing" core state, was an ally of the Soviet Union and fought one war with China and several with Pakistan. Its relations with the West, particularly the United States, were distant when they were not acrimonious. In the post–Cold War world, India's relations with Pakistan are likely to remain highly conflictual over Kashmir, nuclear weapons, and the overall military balance on the Subcontinent. . . . Chinese power is expanding at the moment; India's power could grow substantially in the early twenty-first century. Conflict seems highly probable. . . .

The relations between civilizations and their core states are complicated, often ambivalent, and they do change. . . . The relatively simple bipolarity of the Cold War is giving way to the much more complex relationships of a multipolar, multicivilizational world (Malik 1993, 75).

11.2

Madeleine Albright

THE MIGHTY AND THE ALMIGHTY (2006)

Although—as I learned late in life—my heritage is Jewish,[2] I was raised a Roman Catholic. As a child, I studied the catechism, prayed regularly to the Virgin Mary, and fantasized about becoming a priest (even a Catholic girl can dream). As I was growing up, my sense of morality was molded by what I learned in church and by the example and instruction of my parents. The message was drilled into me to work hard, do my best at all times, and respect the rights of others. As a sophomore at Wellesley College, I was required to study the Bible as history, learning the saga of ancient Israel in the same way as that of Greece or Rome.[3]

As an immigrant and the daughter of a former Czechoslovak diplomat, I was primarily interested in world affairs. I did not, however, view the great issues of the day through the prism of religion—either my own or that of others. Nor did I ever feel secure enough about the depth of my religious knowledge to think I was in a position to lecture acquaintances about what they should believe. I did not consider spiritual faith a subject to talk about in public. For the generation that came of age when and where I did, this was typical. I am sure there were parts of America where attitudes were different, but the scholar Michael Novak got it right when he asserted in the early 1960s, "As matters now stand, the one word [that could not be used] in serious conversation without upsetting someone is 'God'" (Novak 1965, 17).

The star most of us navigated by in those years was modernization, which many took as a synonym for secularization. The wonders we celebrated were less biblical than technological: the space race, breakthroughs in medicine, the birth of nuclear power, the introduction of color television, and the dawn of the computer age. . . .

In the early 1980s, I became a professor at Georgetown University. My specialty was foreign policy, about which such icons as Hans Morgenthau, George Kennan, and Dean Acheson theorized in almost exclusively secular terms. In their view, individuals and groups could be identified by the nations to which they belonged. Countries had governments. Governments acted to protect their nations' interests. Diplomacy consisted of reconciling different interests, at least to the point where wars did not break out and the world did not blow up. Foreign policy was commonly compared to a game of chess: cerebral, with both sides knowing the rules. This was a contest governed by logic; its players spoke in the manner of lawyers, not preachers. During my adult years, western leaders gained political advantage by deriding "godless communism"; otherwise, I cannot remember any leading American diplomat (even the born-again Christian Jimmy Carter) speaking in depth about the role of religion in shaping the world. Religion was not a respecter of national borders; it was above and beyond reason; it evoked the deepest passions; and historically, it was the cause of much bloodshed. Diplomats in my era were taught not to invite trouble, and no subject seemed more inherently treacherous than religion.

This was the understanding that guided me while I was serving as President Clinton's ambassador to the United Nations and secretary of state. My colleagues felt the same.

When, in 1993, Professor Samuel Huntington of Harvard predicted that the era following the end of the cold war might well witness an interreligious "clash of civilizations" (Huntington 1993, 22–49), we did all we could to distance ourselves from that theory. We had in mind a future in which nations and regions would draw closer as democratic bonds grew stronger, not a world splitting apart along historic fault lines of culture and creed. . . .

Since the terror attacks of 9/11, I have come to realize that it may have been I who was stuck in an earlier time. Like many other foreign policy professionals, I have had to adjust the lens through which I view the world, comprehending something that seemed to be a new reality but that had actually been evident for some time. The 1990s had been a decade of globalization and spectacular technological gains; the information revolution altered our lifestyle, transformed the workplace, and fostered the development of a whole new vocabulary. There was, however, another force at work. Almost everywhere, religious movements are thriving.

In many parts of Central and South America, Protestant evangelicals are contesting the centuries-old dominance of the Catholic Church. In China, authorities saddled with an obsolete ideology of their own are struggling to prevent burgeoning religious and spiritual movements from becoming a political threat. India's identity as a secular society is under challenge by Hindu nationalists. Throughout the former Soviet Union, long-repressed religious institutions have been reinvigorated. In Israel, Orthodox religious parties are seeking more influence over laws and society. Secular Arab nationalism, once thought to embody the future, has been supplanted by a resurgent Islam extending beyond Arab lands to Iran, Pakistan, central and southeast Asia, and parts of Africa. Christianity, too, is making remarkable inroads in Asia and Africa; ten of the world's eleven largest congregations are in South Korea, and the other is in Nigeria. A reawakening of Christian activism is also altering how we think about politics and culture here in the United States. In contrast to Michael Novak's observation four decades ago, people now talk (and argue) about God all the time. Even in Europe, which seems otherwise exempt from the trend toward religious growth, the number of observant Muslims is rising quickly, and a new pope—named for Benedict of Nursia, the continent's patron saint—is determined to re-evangelize its Christian population.

What does one make of this phenomenon? For those who design and implement U.S. foreign policy, what does it mean? How can we best manage events in a world in which there many religions, with belief systems that flatly contradict one another at key points? How do we deal with the threat posed by extremists who, acting in the name of God, try to impose their will on others? We know that the nature of this test extends back to pagan times and is therefore nothing new; what is new is the extent of damage violence can inflict. This is where technology has truly made a difference. A religious war fought with swords, chain mail, catapults, and battering rams is one thing. A war fought with high explosives against civilian targets is quite another. And the prospect of a nuclear bomb detonated by terrorists in purported service to the Almighty is a nightmare that may one day come true.

Leaving government service in 2001, I returned to an earlier love, the university classroom. . . .

Increasingly, in the classes I teach and in discussions with friends and colleagues, I have solicited thoughts about the impact of religion on current events. At first most people are surprised, as if uncertain what to think; then they open up. My request leads not to one set of debates, but to many. It is a Rorschach test, revealing much about the preoccupations and anxieties of those who respond.

My students tend to equate religion with ethics and so frame their responses in moral terms. . . .

My friends who are experts on foreign policy—a somewhat older group—are focused on the threat posed by religious extremists, including the possibility that terrorists will gain access to weapons of mass murder. They are alarmed, as well, about the gap in understanding that has opened between predominately Islamic societies and the West.

Arab leaders to whom I have spoken share this concern. They are upset, too, by the spread of what they consider to be false and damaging generalizations about Islam.

The religious scholars I have consulted are passionate about the need for political leaders to educate themselves in the varieties of faith and to see religion more as a potential means for reconciliation than as a source of conflict.

Political activists, not just Democrats, are agitated about the influence of the religious right on the White House and Congress; this is a subject weighing on the minds of foreign diplomats.

My own reactions are grounded in my various identities, as a daughter of Czechoslovakia, an American who is intensely proud of her adopted country, and a former secretary of state. . . .

. . . All through my years of government service, I maintained a positive outlook. In the Clinton administration, we talked a lot about the twenty-first century and, characteristically, felt sure that America, with others, could find a solution to most problems. I still feel that way, but I worry that we have been making some serious and avoidable mistakes. . . .

Summoning the Better Angels

. . . If God has a plan, it will be carried out. That is heaven's jurisdiction, not ours. If, however, one believes that creation has given us both life and free will, we are left with the question of what to do with those gifts. That is both a practical challenge and a moral one, and it is what this book has been about.

Religion concerns itself with the hopes and fears of all the years; the terms of American presidents are not so expansive. The policies of the United States government have to be based on what we might hope to accomplish in a finite period on Earth, not on postmillennial expectations. At the same time, what we can accomplish on Earth is mixed up with the different understandings people have of God. As I travel around the world, I am often asked, "Why can't we just keep religion out of foreign policy?" My answer is that we can't and shouldn't. Religion is a large part of what motivates people and shapes their views of justice and right behavior. It must be taken into account. Nor can we expect our leaders to make decisions in isolation from their religious beliefs. There is a limit to how much the human mind can compartmentalize. In any case, why should world leaders who are religious act and speak as if they are not? We must live with our beliefs and also with our differences; it does no good to deny them.

This does not mean, however, that we should inflate the importance of those differences. It is human instinct to organize into groups. For most of us, this sorting process is largely passive. The groups to which we belong are part of our inheritance and culture—a consequence of where we were born and how we were raised. My family's heritage was Jewish, but I was raised a Roman Catholic. If, as a child, I had been sent to temple instead of to church, I would have grown to adulthood with a different group identity. I was born overseas. If not for the cold war, my family would have had no cause to emigrate to the United States and I would never have become an American.

Nature allows us to choose neither our parents nor our place of birth, limiting from the outset the groups with which we will ever after identify. True, some of us will weigh competing philosophies and convert from one religion to another out of spiritual enlightenment or intellectual and emotional conviction. Some will find reason to shift allegiance from one country to another. More often, we remain within the same general categories we dropped into at birth or, as in my case, the categories where events beyond our control have placed us. That is not much of an accomplishment.

Logically, then, our differences should not matter so much. People of diverse nations and faiths ought to be able to live in harmony. However, the gap between what ought to be and what actually is has been a recurring source of drama throughout human existence. Decades ago, Reinhold Niebuhr warned us that the brutality of nations and groups cannot be tamed no matter how hard we try. "Social conflict," he wrote, is "an inevitability in human history, probably to its very end." Good and wise people might seek to prevent catastrophe, he conceded, but they would likely be no match for the fears and ambitions that drive groups into confrontation. It is sobering that Niebuhr arrived at this grim judgment before World War II. He was not reacting to the war; he was predicting it.

If Niebuhr is right, the pursuit of peace will always be uphill. And yet, I cannot accept the view that because our characters are flawed there is nothing we can do to improve the human condition. Decision makers can usefully search for ways to minimize the inevitable social conflicts referred to by Niebuhr—not so much with the aspiration of finding Utopia than with the goal of saving us from even greater destruction (Niebuhr 1932). Our inherent shortcomings notwithstanding, we can still hope to create a better future. And we know that the right kind of leadership can do much to prevent wars, rebuild devastated societies, expand freedom, and assist the poor.

I wrote at the start of this book that I wanted to identify ways to bring people together in support of policies that reflect the unifying rather than the divisive aspects of religion. My purpose is not to create a spiritual melting pot in which competing religious claims are reduced to mush; my interest is in solving problems and in responding to a practical political imperative. Technology has made outrages more visible, borders more permeable, weapons more dangerous, and conflicts more costly. In the process of realizing our dreams, scientists have also brought some nightmares closer to reality. The job of our leaders is to foster an international environment in which we can live with as much security, freedom, and justice as possible; this, by its nature, requires communication and cooperation. . . .

Looking ahead, we would be well advised to recall the character of wartime leadership provided by Abraham Lincoln. He did not flinch from fighting in a just cause, but he never claimed a monopoly on virtue. He accepted that God's will would be done without professing to comprehend it. He rejected a suggestion that he pray for God to be on the side of the Union, praying instead for the Union to be on the side of God.

Lincoln led a divided country. We must lead in a divided world. To that end, we should blend realism with idealism, placing morality near the center of our foreign policy even while we debate different understandings of what morality means. We should organize ourselves better to comprehend a globe in which religious devotion is both a powerfully positive force and an intermittently destructive one. We should respond with determination and confidence to the danger posed by Al Qaeda and its ilk. And we should make clear not only what America stands against, but also what we stand for.

Half a century ago, in writing about the cold war, my father argued that, whether we are "American individualists or British laborists, conservatives or progressives, socializing democrats or democratic socialists, white, black or yellow—we can all accept that human dignity and respect for the individual" must be the focus of everything. I believe that, too.

Respect for the rights and well-being of each individual is the place where religious faith and a commitment to political liberty have their closest connection. A philosophy based on this principle has the most potential to bring people from opposing viewpoints together because it excludes no one and yet demands from everyone full consideration of the ideas and needs of others.[4]

Yet the question arises: how can we hope to unite people around a principle—respect for the individual—that is such a uniquely western concept? The answer, of course, is that it is not. Hinduism demands that "no man do to another that which would be repugnant to himself." The Torah instructs us, "Thou shalt love thy neighbor as myself." Zoroaster observed, "What I hold good for myself, I should for all." Confucius said, "What you do not want done to yourself, do not do unto others." Buddha taught us to consider others as ourselves. The Stoics of ancient Greece argued that all men are "equal persons in the great court of liberty." The Christian gospel demands, "Do unto others as you would have done unto you." The Quran warns that a true believer must love for his brother what he loves for himself. Finally, the world's first known legal code had as its announced purpose "to cause justice to prevail and to ensure that the strong do not oppress the weak." This is, we might think, the kind of legal system the world should develop now as a gift to the people of Iraq. In fact, it is the law code of Hammurabi, a gift civilization received four thousand years ago from ancient Babylon, now known as Iraq. . . .

I cannot write a happy ending to this book. We remain in the midst of struggle. As Bill Clinton reminds us, none of us can claim full title to the truth. We may hope, however, for leadership at home and abroad that will inspire us to look for the best in ourselves and in others. Lincoln, again, coined the perfect phrase, appealing in the aftermath of war to "the better angels of our nature"—summoning our capacity to care for one another in ways that cannot fully be explained by self-interest, logic, or science.

This is why the principle matters so much: every individual counts. If we truly accept and act on it, we will have the basis for unity across every border. We will take and hold the high ground against terrorists, dictators, tyrants, and bigots. We will gain from the contributions of all people; and we will defend and enrich liberty rather than merely consume it. In so doing, we may hope to inch our way over time not toward a glistening and exclusive city on a hill, but toward a globe on which might and right are close companions and where dignity and freedom are shared by all.

11.3

Walter Russell Mead

GOD'S COUNTRY?
(SEPTEMBER/OCTOBER 2006)

Evangelicals and Foreign Policy

Religion has always been a major force in U.S. politics, policy, identity, and culture. Religion shapes the nation's character, helps form Americans' ideas about the world, and influences the ways Americans respond to events beyond their borders. Religion explains both Americans' sense of themselves as a chosen people and their belief that they have a duty to spread their values throughout the world. Of course, not all Americans believe such things—and those who do often bitterly disagree over exactly what they mean. But enough believe them that the ideas exercise profound influence over the country's behavior abroad and at home. . . .

Yet the balance of power among the different religious strands shifts over time; in the last generation, this balance has shifted significantly, and with dramatic consequences. The more conservative strains within American Protestantism have gained adherents, and the liberal Protestantism that dominated the country during the middle years of the twentieth century has weakened. This shift has already changed U.S. foreign policy in profound ways. . . .

A Question of Fundamentals

To make sense of how contemporary changes in Protestantism are starting to affect U.S. foreign policy, it helps to understand the role that religion has historically played in the country's public life. The U.S. religious tradition, which grew out of the sixteenth-century Reformations of England and Scotland, has included many divergent ideologies and worldviews over time. Three strains, however, have been most influential: a strict tradition that can be called fundamentalist, a progressive and ethical tradition known as liberal Christianity, and a broader evangelical tradition. . . .

The three contemporary streams of American Protestantism (fundamentalist, liberal, and evangelical) lead to very different ideas about what the country's role in the world should be. In this context, the most important differences have to do with the degree to which each promotes optimism about the possibilities for a stable, peaceful, and enlightened international order and the importance each places on the difference between believers and nonbelievers. In a nutshell, fundamentalists are deeply pessimistic about the prospects for world order and see an unbridgeable divide between believers and nonbelievers. Liberals are optimistic about the prospects for world order and see little difference between Christians and nonbelievers. And evangelicals stand somewhere in between these extremes. . . .

Evangelicals and the Middle Path

Evangelicals, the third of the leading strands in American Protestantism, straddle the divide between fundamentalists and liberals. Their core beliefs share common roots with fundamentalism, but their ideas about the world have been heavily influenced by the optimism endemic to U.S. society. . . .

. . . Like fundamentalists, evangelicals attach a great deal of importance to the doctrinal tenets of Christianity, not just to its ethical teachings. For evangelicals and fundamentalists, liberals' emphasis on ethics translates into a belief that good works and the fulfillment of moral law are the road to God—a betrayal of Christ's message, in their view. Because of original sin, they argue, humanity is utterly incapable of fulfilling any moral law whatever. The fundamental message of Christianity is that human efforts to please God by observing high ethical standards must fail; only Christ's crucifixion and resurrection can redeem man. Admitting one's sinful nature and accepting Christ's sacrifice are what both evangelicals and fundamentalists mean by being "born again. . . ."

Evangelicals also attach great importance to the difference between those who are "saved" and those who are not. Like fundamentalists, they believe that human beings who die without accepting Christ are doomed to everlasting separation from God. . . .

Finally, most (although not all) evangelicals share the fundamentalist approach to the end of the world. Virtually all evangelicals believe that the biblical prophecies will be fulfilled, and a majority agree with fundamentalists on the position known as premillennialism: the belief that Christ's return will precede the establishment of the prophesied thousand-year reign of peace. Ultimately, all human efforts to build a peaceful world will fail. . . .

All Christians, whether fundamentalist, liberal, or evangelical, acknowledge at least formally the responsibility to show love and compassion to everyone, Christian or not. For evangelicals, this demand has extra urgency. Billions of perishing souls can still be saved for Christ, they believe. The example Christians set in their daily lives, the help they give the needy, and the effectiveness of their proclamation of the gospel—these can bring lost souls to Christ and help fulfill the divine plan. Evangelicals constantly reinforce the message of Christian responsibility to the world. Partly as a result, evangelicals are often open to, and even eager for, social action and cooperation with nonbelievers in projects to improve human welfare, even though they continue to believe that those who reject Christ cannot be united with God after death. . . .

Evangelicals are more optimistic than fundamentalists about the prospects for moral progress. The postmillennial minority among them (which holds that Christ will return after a thousand years of world peace, not before) believes that this process can continue until human society reaches a state of holiness: that the religious progress of individuals and societies can culminate in the establishment of a peaceable kingdom through a process of gradual improvement. This is a view of history very compatible with the optimism of liberal Christians, and evangelicals and liberal Christians have in fact joined in many common efforts at both domestic and international moral improvement throughout U.S. history. Although the premillennial majority is less optimistic about the ultimate success of such efforts, American evangelicals are often optimistic about the short-term prospects for human betterment. . . .

The Balance of Power

Recent decades have witnessed momentous changes in the balance of religious power in the United States. The membership of the liberal, historically dominant mainline Protestant churches mostly peaked in the 1960s. Since then, while the number of American Christians has grown, membership in the mainline denominations has sharply dropped. . . . The Pew Research Center reports that 59 percent of American Protestants identified themselves as mainline Protestants in 1988; by 2002–3, that percentage had fallen to 46 percent. In the same period, the percentage of Protestants who identified themselves as evangelical rose from 41 percent to 54 percent.

In 1965, there were 3.6 million Episcopalians in the United States—1.9 percent of the total population. By 2005, there were only 2.3 million Episcopalians—0.8 percent of the population. Membership in the United Methodist Church fell from 11 million in 1965 to 8.2 million in 2005. In the same period, that in the Presbyterian Church (U.S.A.) fell from 3.2 million to 2.4 million, and the United Church of Christ saw its membership decline by almost 50 percent.

The impact of these trends on national politics has not been hard to find. Self-identified evangelicals provided roughly 40 percent of George W. Bush's total vote in 2004. Among white evangelicals, Bush received 68 percent of the national vote in 2000 and 78 percent in 2004. . . . Evangelicals have been playing a major role in congressional and Senate elections as well, and the number of self-identified evangelicals in Congress has increased from around 10 percent of the membership in both houses in 1970 to more than 25 percent in 2004. . . .

Out in the World

The growing influence of evangelicals has affected U.S. foreign policy in several ways; two issues in particular illustrate the resultant changes. On the question of humanitarian and human rights policies, evangelical leadership is altering priorities and methods while increasing overall support for both foreign aid and the defense of human rights. And on the question of Israel, rising evangelical power has deepened U.S. support for the Jewish state, even as the liberal Christian establishment has distanced itself from Jerusalem.

In these cases as in others, evangelical political power today is not leading the United States in a completely new direction. We have seen at least parts of this film before: evangelicals were the dominant force in U.S. culture during much of the nineteenth century and the early years of the twentieth. But the country's change in orientation in recent years has nonetheless been pronounced.

Evangelicals in the Anglo-American world have long supported humanitarian and human rights policies on a global basis. The British antislavery movement, for example, was led by an evangelical, William Wilberforce. Evangelicals were consistent supporters of nineteenth-century national liberation movements—often Christian minorities seeking to break from Ottoman rule. And evangelicals led a number of reform campaigns, often with feminist overtones: against suttee (the immolation of widows) in India, against foot binding in China, in support of female education throughout the developing world, and against human sexual trafficking (the "white slave trade") everywhere. Evangelicals have also long been concerned with issues relating to Africa.

As evangelicals have recently returned to a position of power in U.S. politics, they have supported similar causes and given new energy and support to U.S. humanitarian efforts. Under President Bush, with the strong support of Michael Gerson (an evangelical who was Bush's senior policy adviser and speechwriter), U.S. aid to Africa has risen by 67 percent, including $15 billion in new spending for programs to combat HIV and AIDS. African politicians, such as Nigeria's Olusegun Obasanjo and Uganda's Yoweri Museveni, have stressed their own evangelical credentials to build support in Washington, much as China's Sun Yat-sen and Madame Chiang Kai-shek once did. Thanks to evangelical pressure, efforts to suppress human trafficking and the sexual enslavement of women and children have become a much higher priority in U.S. policy, and the country has led the fight to end Sudan's wars. Rick Warren, pastor of an evangelical megachurch in Southern California and the author of The Purpose Driven Life (the single best-selling volume in the history of U.S. publishing), has mobilized his 22,000 congregants to help combat AIDS worldwide (by hosting a conference on the subject and training volunteers) and to form relationships with churches in Rwanda.

Evangelicals have not, however, simply followed the human rights and humanitarian agendas crafted by liberal and secular leaders. They have made religious freedom—including the freedom to proselytize and to convert—a central focus of their efforts. Thanks largely to evangelical support (although some Catholics and Jews also played a role), Congress passed the International Religious Freedom Act in 1998, establishing an Office of International Religious Freedom in a somewhat skeptical State Department.

Despite these government initiatives, evangelicals, for cultural as well as theological reasons, are often suspicious of state-to-state aid and multilateral institutions. They prefer grass-roots and faith-based organizations. Generally speaking, evangelicals are quick to support efforts to address specific problems, but they are skeptical about grand designs and large-scale development efforts. Evangelicals will often react strongly to particular instances of human suffering or injustice, but they are more interested in problem solving than in institution building. (Liberal Christians often bewail this trait as evidence of the anti-intellectualism of evangelical culture.)

U.S. policy toward Israel is another area where the increased influence of evangelicals has been evident. This relationship has also had a long history. In fact, American Protestant Zionism is significantly older than the modern Jewish version; in the nineteenth century, evangelicals repeatedly petitioned U.S. officials to establish a refuge in the Holy Land for persecuted Jews from Europe and the Ottoman Empire.

U.S. evangelical theology takes a unique view of the role of the Jewish people in the modern world. On the one hand, evangelicals share the widespread Christian view that Christians represent the new and true children of Israel, inheritors of God's promises to the ancient Hebrews. Yet unlike many other Christians, evangelicals also believe that the Jewish people have a continuing role in God's plan. In the seventeenth and eighteenth centuries, close study of biblical prophecies convinced evangelical scholars and believers that the Jews would return to the Holy Land before the triumphant return of Christ. Moreover, while the tumultuous years before Jesus' return are expected to bring many Jews to Christ, many evangelicals believe that until that time, most Jews will continue to reject him. . . .

Evangelicals also find the continued existence of the Jewish people to be a strong argument both for the existence of God and for his power in history. The book of Genesis relates that God told Abraham, "And I will make of thee a great nation, and I will bless thee. . . . And I will bless them that bless thee, and curse him that curseth thee: and in thee all families of the earth be blessed." For evangelicals, the fact that the Jewish people have survived through the millennia and that they have returned to their ancient home is proof that God is real, that the Bible is inspired, and that the Christian religion is true. Many believe that the promise of Genesis still stands and that the God of Abraham will literally bless the United States if the United States blesses Israel. They see in the weakness, defeats, and poverty of the Arab world ample evidence that God curses those who curse Israel.

Criticism of Israel and of the United States for supporting it leaves evangelicals unmoved. If anything, it only strengthens their conviction that the world hates Israel because "fallen man" naturally hates God and his "chosen people." In standing by Israel, evangelicals feel that they are standing by God—something they are ready to do against the whole world. . . .

. . . The extraordinary events of modern Jewish history are held up by evangelicals as proof that God exists and acts in history. Add to this the psychological consequences of nuclear weapons, and many evangelicals begin to feel that they are living in a world like the world of the Bible. That U.S. foreign policy now centers on defending the country against the threat of mass terrorism involving, potentially, weapons of apocalyptic horror wielded by anti-Christian fanatics waging a religious war motivated by hatred of Israel only reinforces the claims of evangelical religion.

Liberal Christians in the United States (like liberal secularists) have also traditionally supported Zionism, but from a different perspective. For liberal Christians, the Jews are a people like any other, and so liberal Christians have supported Zionism in the same way that they have supported the national movements of other oppressed groups. In recent decades, however, liberal Christians have increasingly come to sympathize with the Palestinian national movement on the same basis. In 2004, the Presbyterian Church passed a resolution calling for limited divestment from companies doing business with Israel (the resolution was essentially rescinded in 2006 after a bitter battle). One study found that 37 percent of the statements made by mainline Protestant churches on human rights abuses between 2000 and 2004 focused on Israel. No other country came in for such frequent criticism.

Conspiracy theorists and secular scholars and journalists in the United States and abroad have looked to a Jewish conspiracy or, more euphemistically, to a "Jewish lobby" to explain how U.S. support for Israel can grow while sympathy for Israel wanes among what was once the religious and intellectual establishment. A better answer lies in the dynamics of U.S. religion. Evangelicals have been gaining social and political power, while liberal Christians and secular intellectuals have been losing it. This should not be blamed on the Jews.

The New Great Awakening

The current evangelical moment in the United States has not yet run its course. For secularists and liberals in the United States and abroad, this is a disquieting prospect. Measured optimism, however, would be a better response than horror and panic.

Religion in the United States is too pluralistic for any single current to dominate. The growing presence and influence of non-Christian communities in the country—of Jews, Muslims, Buddhists, Hindus, and, above all, secularists—will continue to limit the ability of any religious group to impose its values across the board.

Liberals, whether religious or not, may want to oppose the evangelical agenda in domestic politics. For the most part, however, these quarrels can cease at the water's edge. As the rising evangelical establishment gains experience in foreign policy, it is likely to prove a valuable—if not always easy—partner for the mostly secular or liberal Christian establishment. Some fears about the evangelical influence in foreign policy are simply overblown. After the attacks of September 11, for example, fears that evangelical Christians would demand a holy war against Islam were widespread. A few prominent religious leaders (generally fundamentalists, not evangelicals) made intemperate remarks; Jerry Falwell, for one, referred to the Prophet Muhammad as "a terrorist." But he was widely rebuked by his colleagues.

U.S. evangelicals generally seek to hold on to their strong personal faith and Protestant Christian identity while engaging with people across confessional lines. Evangelicals have worked with Catholics against abortion and with both religious and secular Jews to support Israel; they could now reach out to Muslims as well. After all, missionary hospitals and schools were the primary contact that most Middle Easterners had with the United States up until the end of World War II; evangelicals managed more than a century of close and generally cooperative relations with Muslims throughout the Arab world. Muslims and evangelicals are both concerned about global poverty and Africa. Both groups oppose the domination of public and international discourse by secular ideas. Both believe that religious figures and values should be treated with respect in the media; neither like the glorification of casual sex in popular entertainment. Both Islam and evangelicalism are democratic religions without a priesthood or hierarchy. Muslims and evangelicals will never agree about everything, and secular people may not like some of the agreements they reach. But fostering Muslim-evangelical dialogue may be one of the best ways to forestall the threat of civilizational warfare. . . .

Similarly, engaging evangelicals in broader foreign policy discussions can lead to surprising and (for some) heartening developments. A group of leading conservative evangelicals recently signed a statement on climate change that stated that the problem is real, that human activity is an important contributing cause, that the costs of inaction will be high and disproportionately affect the poor, and that Christians have a moral duty to help deal with it. Meanwhile, evangelicals who began by opposing Sudanese violence and slave raids against Christians in southern Sudan have gone on to broaden the coalition working to protect Muslims in Darfur.

Evangelicals are likely to focus more on U.S. exceptionalism than liberals would like, and they are likely to care more about the morality of U.S. foreign policy than most realists prefer. But evangelical power is here to stay for the foreseeable future, and those concerned about U.S. foreign policy would do well to reach out. As more evangelical leaders acquire firsthand experience in foreign policy, they are likely to provide something now sadly lacking in the world of U.S. foreign policy: a trusted group of experts, well versed in the nuances and dilemmas of the international situation, who are able to persuade large numbers of Americans to support the complex and counterintuitive policies that are sometimes necessary in this wicked and frustrating—or, dare one say it, fallen—world.

Primary Sources

11.4

St. Thomas Aquinas

THE SUMMA THEOLOGICA. PART II, QUESTION 40
(CIRCA 1274)

We must now consider war, under which head there are four points of inquiry:

1. Whether some kind of war is lawful?
2. Whether it is lawful for clerics to fight?
3. Whether it is lawful for belligerents to lay ambushes?
4. Whether it is lawful to fight on holy days?

Whether It Is Always Sinful to Wage War?

Objection 1: It would seem that it is always sinful to wage war. Because punishment is not inflicted except for sin. Now those who wage war are threatened by Our Lord with punishment, according to Mt. 26:52: "All that take the sword shall perish with the sword." Therefore all wars are unlawful.

Objection 2: Further, whatever is contrary to a Divine precept is a sin. But war is contrary to a Divine precept, for it is written (Mt. 5:39): "But I say to you not to resist evil"; and (Rm. 12:19): "Not revenging yourselves, my dearly beloved, but give place unto wrath." Therefore war is always sinful.

Objection 3: Further, nothing, except sin, is contrary to an act of virtue. But war is contrary to peace. Therefore war is always a sin.

Objection 4: Further, the exercise of a lawful thing is itself lawful, as is evident in scientific exercises. But warlike exercises which take place in tournaments are forbidden by the Church, since those who are slain in these trials are deprived of ecclesiastical burial. Therefore it seems that war is a sin in itself.

On the contrary, Augustine says in a sermon on the son of the centurion [*Ep. ad Marcel. cxxxviii]: "If the Christian Religion forbade war altogether, those who sought salutary advice in the Gospel would rather have been counselled to cast aside their arms, and to give up soldiering altogether. On the contrary, they were told: 'Do violence to no man . . . and be content with your pay' [*Lk. 3:14]. If he commanded them to be content with their pay, he did not forbid soldiering."

I answer that, In order for a war to be just, three things are necessary. First, the authority of the sovereign by whose command the war is to be waged. For it is not the business of a private individual to declare war, because he can seek for redress of his rights from the tribunal of his superior . . . Hence it is said to those who are in authority (Ps. 81:4): "Rescue the poor: and deliver the needy out of the hand of the sinner"; and for this reason Augustine says (Contra Faust. xxii, 75): "The natural order conducive to peace among mortals demands that the power to declare and counsel war should be in the hands of those who hold the supreme authority."

Secondly, a just cause is required, namely that those who are attacked, should be attacked because they deserve it on account of some fault. Wherefore Augustine says (Questions. in Hept., qu. x, super Jos.): "A just war is wont to be described as one that avenges wrongs, when a nation or state has to be punished, for refusing to make amends for the wrongs inflicted by its subjects, or to restore what it has seized unjustly."

Thirdly, it is necessary that the belligerents should have a rightful intention, so that they intend the advancement of good, or the avoidance of evil. Hence Augustine says . . .: "True religion looks upon as peaceful those wars that are waged not for motives of aggrandizement, or cruelty, but with the object of securing peace, of punishing evil-doers, and of uplifting the good." For it may happen that the war is declared by the legitimate authority, and for a just cause, and yet be rendered unlawful through a wicked intention . . .

Reply to Objection 1: As Augustine says (Contra Faust. xxii, 70): "To take the sword is to arm oneself in order to take the life of anyone, without the command or permission of superior or lawful authority." On the other hand, to have recourse to the sword (as a private person) by the authority of the sovereign or judge, or (as a public person) through zeal for justice, and by the authority, so to speak, of God, is not to "take the sword," but to use it as commissioned by another, wherefore it does not deserve punishment. And yet even those who make sinful use of the sword are not always slain with the sword, yet they always perish with their own sword, because, unless they repent, they are punished eternally for their sinful use of the sword.

Reply to Objection 2: Such like precepts, as Augustine observes (De Serm. Dom. in Monte i, 19), should always be borne in readiness of mind, so that we be ready to obey them, and, if necessary, to refrain from resistance or self-defense. Nevertheless it is necessary sometimes for a man to act otherwise for the common good, or for the good of those with whom he is fighting . . .

Reply to Objection 3: Those who wage war justly aim at peace, and so they are not opposed to peace, except to the evil peace, which Our Lord "came not to send upon earth" (Mt. 10:34). Hence Augustine says (Ep. ad Bonif. clxxxix): "We do not seek peace in order to be at war, but we go to war that we may have peace. Be peaceful, therefore, in warring, so that you may vanquish those whom you war against, and bring them to the prosperity of peace."

Reply to Objection 4: Manly exercises in warlike feats of arms are not all forbidden, but those which are inordinate and perilous, and end in slaying or plundering. In olden times warlike exercises presented no such danger, and hence they were called "exercises of arms" or "bloodless wars," as Jerome states in an epistle. . . .

Whether It Is Lawful to Lay Ambushes in War?

Objection 1: It would seem that it is unlawful to lay ambushes in war. For it is written (Dt. 16:20): "Thou shalt follow justly after that which is just." But ambushes, since they are a kind of deception, seem to pertain to injustice. Therefore it is unlawful to lay ambushes even in a just war.

Objection 2: Further, ambushes and deception seem to be opposed to faithfulness even as lies are. But since we are bound to keep faith with all men, it is wrong to lie to anyone, as Augustine states (Contra Mend. xv). Therefore, as one is bound to keep faith with one's enemy, as Augustine states (Ep. ad Bonif. clxxxix), it seems that it is unlawful to lay ambushes for one's enemies.

Objection 3: Further, it is written (Mt. 7:12): "Whatsoever you would that men should do to you, do you also to them": and we ought to observe this in all our dealings with our neighbor. Now our enemy is our neighbor. Therefore, since no man wishes ambushes or deceptions to be prepared for himself, it seems that no one ought to carry on war by laying ambushes.

On the contrary, Augustine says (QQ. in Hept. qu. x super Jos): "Provided the war be just, it is no concern of justice whether it be carried on openly or by ambushes": and he proves this by the authority of the Lord, Who commanded Joshua to lay ambushes for the city of Hai (Joshua 8:2).

I answer that, The object of laying ambushes is in order to deceive the enemy. Now a man may be deceived by another's word or deed in two ways. First, through being told something false, or through the breaking of a promise, and this is always unlawful. No one ought to deceive the enemy in this way, for there are certain "rights of war and covenants, which ought to be observed even among enemies," as Ambrose states (De Officiis i).

Secondly, a man may be deceived by what we say or do, because we do not declare our purpose or meaning to him. Now we are not always bound to do this, since even in the Sacred Doctrine many things have to be concealed, especially from unbelievers, lest they deride it, according to Mt. 7:6: "Give not that which is holy, to dogs." Wherefore much more ought the plan of campaign to be hidden from the enemy. For this reason among other things that a soldier has to learn is the art of concealing his purpose lest it come to the enemy's knowledge, as stated in the Book on Strategy [*Stratagematum i, 1] by Frontinus. Such like concealment is what is meant by an ambush which may be lawfully employed in a just war.

Nor can these ambushes be properly called deceptions, nor are they contrary to justice or to a well-ordered will. For a man would have an inordinate will if he were unwilling that others should hide anything from him.

This suffices for the Replies to the Objections.

11.5

THE SCHLEITHEIM CONFESSION OF FAITH: BROTHERLY UNION OF A NUMBER OF CHILDREN OF GOD CONCERNING SEVEN ARTICLES
(FEBRUARY 24, 1527)

... Dear brothers and sisters, we who have been assembled in the Lord at Schleitheim on the Randen make known, in points and articles, unto all that love God, that as far as we are concerned, we have been united to stand fast in the Lord as obedient children of God, sons and daughters, who have been and shall be separated from the world in all that we do and leave undone, and (the praise and glory be to God alone) uncontradicted by all brothers, completely at peace.[5] Herein we have sensed the unity of the Father and of our common Christ as present with us in their Spirit. For the Lord is a Lord of peace and not of quarreling, as Paul indicates (1 Cor. 14:33). So that you understand at what points this occurred, you should observe and understand [what follows]:

A very great offense has been introduced by some false brothers among us, whereby several have turned away from the faith, thinking to practice and observe the freedom of the Spirit and of Christ. But such have fallen short of the truth and (to their own condemnation) are given over to the lasciviousness and license of the flesh. They have esteemed that faith and love may do and permit everything and that nothing can harm nor condemn them, since they are "believers."

Note well, you members of God in Christ Jesus, that faith in the heavenly Father through Jesus Christ is not thus formed: it produces and brings forth no such things as these false brothers and sisters practice and teach. Guard yourselves and be warned of such people, for they do not serve our Father, but their father, the devil.

But for you it is not so; for they who are Christ's have crucified their flesh with all its lusts and desires (Gal. 5:24). You understand me well, and [know] brothers whom we mean. Separate yourselves from them, for they are perverted. Pray the Lord that they may have knowledge unto repentance, and for us that we may have constance to persevere along the path we have entered upon, unto the glory of God and of Christ His Son. Amen.

The articles we have dealt with, and in which we have been united, are these: baptism, ban, the breaking of bread, separation from abomination, shepherds in the congregation, the sword, the oath. . . .

Article VI. We Have Been United as Follows Concerning the Sword

We have been united as follows concerning the sword. The sword is an ordering of God outside the perfection of Christ. It punishes and kills the wicked and guards and protects the good. In the law the sword is established[6] over the wicked for punishment and for death and the secular rulers are established to wield the same.

But within the perfection of Christ only the ban is used for the admonition and exclusion of the one who has sinned, without the death of the flesh, simply the warning and the command to sin no more.

Now many, who do not understand Christ's will for us, will ask; whether a Christian may or should use the sword against the wicked for the protection and defense of the good, or for the sake of love.

The answer is unanimously revealed: Christ teaches and commands us to learn from Him, for He is meek and lowly of heart and thus we shall find rest for our souls (Mt. 11:29). Now Christ says to the woman who was taken in adultery (Jn. 8:11), not that she should be stoned according to the law of His Father (and yet He says, "What the Father commanded me, that I do") (Jn. 8:22) but with mercy and forgiveness and the warning to sin no more, says: "Go, sin no more." Exactly thus should we also proceed, according to the rule of the ban.

Second, is asked concerning the sword: whether a Christian shall pass sentence in disputes and strife about worldly matters, such as the unbelievers have with one another. The answer: Christ did not wish to decide or pass judgement between brother and brother concerning inheritance, but refused to do so (Lk. 12:13). So should we also do.

Third, is asked concerning the sword: whether the Christian should be a magistrate if he is chosen thereto. This is answered thus: Christ was to be made King, but He fled and did not discern the ordinance of His Father.[7] Thus we should also do as He did and follow after Him, and we shall not walk in darkness. For He Himself says: "Whoever would come after me, let him deny himself and take up his cross and follow me" (Mt. 16:24). He Himself further forbids the violence of the sword when He says: "The princes of this world lord it over them etc., but among you it shall not be so" (Mt. 20:25). Further Paul says, "Whom God has foreknown, the same he has also predestined to be conformed to the image of his Son," etc. (Rom. 8:30). Peter also says: "Christ has suffered (not ruled) and has left us an example, that you should follow after in his steps" (1 Pet. 2:21).

Lastly, one can see in the following points that it does not befit a Christian to be a magistrate: the rule of the government is according to the flesh, that of the Christians according to the spirit. Their houses and dwelling remain in this world, that of the Christians is in heaven. Their citizenship is in this world, that of the Christians is in heaven (Phil. 3:20). The weapons of their battle and warfare are carnal and only against the flesh, but the weapons of Christians are spiritual, against the fortification of the devil. The worldly are armed with steel and iron, but Christians are armed with the armor of God, with truth, righteousness, peace, faith, salvation, and with the Word of God. In sum: as Christ our Head is minded, so also must be minded the members of the body of Christ through Him, so that there be no division in the body, through which it would be destroyed.[8] Since then Christ is as is written of Him, so must His members also be the same, so that His body may remain whole and unified for its own advancement and upbuilding. For any kingdom which is divided within itself will be destroyed (Mt. 12:25).

Article VII: We Have Been United as Follows Concerning the Oath

We have been united as follows concerning the oath. The oath is a confirmation among those who are quarreling or making promises. In the law it is commanded that it should be done only in the name of God, truthfully and not falsely. Christ, who teaches the perfection of the law, forbids His [followers] all swearing, whether true or false; neither by heaven nor by earth, neither by Jerusalem nor by our head; and that for the reason which He goes on to give: "For you cannot make one hair white or black." You see, thereby all swearing is forbidden. We cannot perform what is promised in the swearing, for we are not able to change the smallest part of ourselves (Mt. 5:34–37).

Now there are some who do not believe the simple commandment of God and who say, "But God swore by Himself to Abraham, because He was God (as He promised him that He would do good to him and would be his God if he kept His commandments). Why then should I not swear if I promise something to someone?" The answer: hear what the Scripture says: "God, since he wished to prove overabundantly to the heirs of His promise that His will did not change, inserted an oath so that by two immutable things we might have a stronger consolation (for it is impossible that God should lie)" (Heb. 6:7 ff.). Notice the meaning of the passage: God has the power to do what He forbids you, for everything is possible to Him. God swore an oath to Abraham, Scripture says, in order to prove that His counsel is immutable. That means: no one can withstand and thwart His will; thus He can keep His oath. But we cannot, as Christ said above, hold or perform our oath, therefore we should not swear.

Others say that swearing cannot be forbidden by God in the New Testament when it was commanded in the Old, but that it is forbidden only to swear by heaven, earth, Jerusalem, and our head. Answer: hear the Scripture. He who swears by heaven, swears by God's throne and by Him who sits thereon (Mt. 5:35). Observe: swearing by heaven is forbidden, which is only God's throne; how much more is it forbidden to swear by God Himself. You blind fools, what is greater, the throne or He who sits upon it?

Others say, if it is then wrong to use God for truth, then the apostles Peter and Paul also swore.[9] Answer: Peter and Paul only testify to that which God promised Abraham, whom we long after have received. But when one testifies, one testifies concerning that which is present, whether it be good or evil. Thus Simeon spoke of Christ to Mary and testified: "Behold: this one is ordained for the falling and rising of many in Israel and to be a sign which will be spoken against" (Lk. 2:34).

Christ taught us similarly when He says: Your speech shall be yea, yea; and nay, nay; for what is more than that comes of evil. He says, your speech or your word shall be yes and no, so that no one might understand that He had permitted it. Christ is simply yea and nay, and all those who seek Him simply will understand His Word. Amen.[10]

Dear Brothers and Sisters in the Lord: these are the articles which some brothers previously had understood wrongly and in a way not conformed to the true meaning. Thereby many weak consciences were confused, whereby the name of God has been grossly slandered, for which reason it was needful that we should be brought to agreement in the Lord, which has come to pass. To God be praise and glory!. . .

Watch out for all who do not walk in simplicity of divine truth, which has been stated by us in this letter in our meeting, so that everyone might be governed among us by the rule of the ban, and that henceforth the entry of false brothers and sisters among us might be prevented.

Put away from you that which is evil, and the Lord will be your God, and you will be His sons and daughters (1 Cor. 6:17).

Dear brothers, keep in mind what Paul admonished Titus (Tit. 2:11–14). He says: "The saving grace of God has appeared to all, and disciplines us, that we should deny ungodliness and worldly lusts, and live circumspect righteous and godly lives in this world; awaiting the same hope and the appearing of the glory of the great God and of our Savior Jesus Christ, who gave himself for us, to redeem us from all unrighteousness and to purify unto himself a people of his own, that would be zealous of good works." Think on this, and exercise yourselves therein, and the Lord of peace will be with you.

May the name of God be forever blessed and greatly praised, Amen. May the Lord give you His peace, Amen.

Done at Schleitheim, St. Matthew's Day [February 24], Anno 1527.

11.6

Mennonite Central Committee

A COMMITMENT TO CHRIST'S WAY OF PEACE
(FEBRUARY 1993)

In 1950, delegates from Mennonite and Brethren in Christ church bodies in North America met at Winona Lake, Indiana, to consider their commitment to the biblical way of peace. Their "Declaration of Christian Faith and Commitment" stands as a testimony that has guided our churches in the past 40 years.

Much has changed in our world since 1950, and we as churches have also changed. While the people of God have given a strong witness to peace during this time, the forces of violence have not diminished. We have seen a vast growth in technological means of destruction, with the development of nuclear bombs and missile systems. We have experienced wars in which highly sophisticated weapons distanced many soldiers from seeing the enemy as human beings. While the East-West power struggle which led to a massive build-up in destructive capacity has ended, conflicts between rival groups threaten the hope for peace in many parts of our globe. People everywhere long for an end to war and strife.

As our congregations have reached out to become more diverse, we have grown in our awareness of the effects of sin and the need to be peacemakers. We have learned that violence can be done not only in warfare, but also through economic structures. We have seen the world's fragile ecosystem endangered by careless treatment of the natural environment. We have struggled against the effects of racism. We have come to realize that violence can reach into our churches and into our families.

As our churches have done at various points in history, we find it helpful to once again state clearly our convictions regarding the church's calling to be God's people of peace. We look toward the future with hope because of God's promise to be with us in all situations. We are committed to speaking clearly and courageously as messenger of the good news in a troubled world. Recognizing our own sinfulness, and relying on God's grace and strength, we make the following affirmations and commitments.

Our Convictions

   A. We believe that God created the world and all its inhabitants as good. Despite human sin, God in Christ, through the Holy Spirit continues to offer forgiveness and reconciliation to all. As we personally acknowledge our sinfulness and repent, we are reconciled to God through Christ our Savior, united with the church community, and entrusted with the ministry of reconciliation. Acts 2; II Cor. 5.

   B. We believe that through the life, death and resurrection of Jesus Christ, God has saved us and proclaimed peace to us. This message of peace is central to our witness to God's suffering love which is redeeming the world. Is. 53; Luke 1–2; Matt. 5–7; Eph. 2.

C. We believe that God calls the church to demonstrate by its life the gospel of peace, which it has received through the reconciling work of Jesus Christ, the Prince of Peace. Nurtured by the Holy Spirit, the church gives this witness through expressions of love, peace and justice within its own community and beyond. We believe that God is creating a people—the church—as a sign of God's renewal of the world. I Cor. 12–14; I Peter 2–3; I John.

D. We believe that peace is the will of God, and that peace cannot be separated from the pursuit of justice. God calls us to abandon hatred, strife and violence in all human relations, whether between individuals, within the family, within the church, among nations and races, or between religious factions, and to pursue a just peace for God's whole creation. Is. 2:1–5; Rom. 12–14.

Our Commitments

We have chosen to follow Jesus as our Lord, and to serve him as disciples. As his representatives, we are called to be peacemakers. This call encompasses all of life, requiring certain attitudes, duties and commitments. We recognize that the strength to pursue these goals comes from God, as we together seek God's will in the context of a spiritual community. Asking for God's grace and guidance, we adopt these commitments as a definition of our path and direction.

A. We strive to share with all people the good news that the grace of God in Jesus Christ, experienced in forgiveness and discipleship, changes lives and enables us to be peacemakers. Our love and ministry reach out to all, regardless of race, religion or status, whether friend or foe.

B. We seek to build up the church as a community of love, which welcomes people of every race, class, sex and nation, uniting even those who were enemies. Though the church in its human expressions remains imperfect, it is the body of Christ, heralding the reign of God. Membership in this body which transcends national boundaries unites believers throughout the world in communion and witness.

C. We will contribute to the relief of human need and suffering by giving ourselves and our resources. The needs of our world and the cries of people in many places for justice call us to respond as Jesus did, with compassion. At the same time we recognize our own spiritual and moral poverty and seek to receive the gifts that others, some of whom may be materially poorer than we are, have to share with us.

D. We will live in relationships of love and mutual respect. We seek to model such relationships in our homes, churches and work places, and to refrain from behavior which violates and abuses others physically or emotionally. In the spirit or Christ, we will oppose and seek to correct abusive relationships within our church family.

E. We will pray for and witness to those in authority over our countries. We recognize that governing authorities have an ordering role in society. Some of us may be called to ministries of reconciliation, relief of human need and protection of the environment through service within governmental institutions. As Christians and citizens, we strive to live consistently according to the values of God's reign, and so we offer our witness to the state, reminding those in authority that they are called by God to use their power in ways that are constructive and life-given rather than violent and life-destroying. As Christians we are keenly aware of our primary allegiance to follow the way of God which may at times conflict with the demands of government.

F. We will strive to show by our lives that war is an unacceptable way to solve human conflict. This calls us to refuse to support war, or to participate in military service. When war or war preparations lead to the conscription of ourselves, our money, or our property, we will seek alternative ways to serve humanity and our countries in the spirit of Christ. We support ministries of conciliation which search for peaceful resolution of conflicts. Recognizing the subtle ways in which our loyalties and resources can be conscripted in modern industrial states, we will strive to continually examine our complicity in systems which treat others as enemies.

G. We will resist evil and oppression in the nonviolent spirit of Jesus. Our stand against unjust treatment of people employs the "weapons" demonstrated by Jesus—love, truth, forgiveness and the willingness to suffer rather than inflict suffering. Our witness anticipates God's transformative power in human hearts and institutions. In loving resistance we will stand with people in their struggle against the power of sin, and proclaim the liberation and reconciliation which come with the rule of God.

H. We will work together to discern what God's reign means for our lifestyles and economic systems. As Christians we are called to be compassionate and just in our economic practices, domestically and internationally, and to critique all economic systems according to their impact on the poor. In our nations military expenditures are used to sustain and shape our economic systems. We seek to resist being trapped by the consumerism so prevalent in our societies, and to live modestly as witnesses against greed and militarism.

I. We will work to restore the earth which God has created. God made the earth good, and wills the redemption of the whole creation. The threats to the future of the creation posed by nuclear weapons and environmental degradation are the result of human sinfulness. We seek to live in sustainable ways as inhabitants of the earth, and to respect all of God's creation.

J. We submit ourselves to the study of scripture, the giving and receiving of counsel, and the practice of prayer, as ways to receive the gift of God's peace. Our world is confronted with problems which are beyond the power of unaided human reason and resources to solve. Jesus relied on prayer in his ministry, and continues to intercede for us. In humility we confess that Christ shows us the way and provides strength, guidance and comfort as we walk in the way of peace.

Our Hope

We thank God for the many opportunities we find to learn from diverse peoples around the globe. We yearn to work together in the ministry of peacemaking with all Christians. We are grateful for the faithfulness of all God's people who have sought to follow the way of Jesus Christ, and for our own tradition which has affirmed Christ's way of love and nonresistance, expressed again in these declarations and commitments.

In humility we confess our failures in following this way, and our shortcomings in both demonstrating and proclaiming Christ's love. As we renew our commitment to

Christ's way, we acknowledge our need for God's grace and each other's help in learning and obeying. With the hope that God gives us, we once more commit ourselves to live holy lives worthy of our calling and to discover anew Christ's message of reconciliation and peace for the world today.

11.7

United States Conference of Catholic Bishops

STATEMENT ON IRAQ
(NOVEMBER 13, 2002)

As we Catholic Bishops meet here in Washington, our nation, Iraq and the world face grave choices about war and peace, about pursuing justice and security. These are not only military and political choices, but also moral ones because they involve matters of life and death. Traditional Christian teaching offers ethical principles and moral criteria that should guide these critical choices.

Two months ago, Bishop Wilton Gregory, President of the United States Conference of Catholic Bishops, wrote President George Bush to welcome efforts to focus the world's attention on Iraq's refusal to comply with several United Nations resolutions over the past eleven years, and its pursuit of weapons of mass destruction. This letter, which was authorized by the U.S. Bishops' Administrative Committee, raised serious questions about the moral legitimacy of any preemptive, unilateral use of military force to overthrow the government of Iraq. As a body, we make our own the questions and concerns raised in Bishop Gregory's letter, taking into account developments since then, especially the unanimous action of the U.N. Security Council on November 8th.

We have no illusions about the behavior or intentions of the Iraqi government. The Iraqi leadership must cease its internal repression, end its threats to its neighbors, stop any support for terrorism, abandon its efforts to develop weapons of mass destruction, and destroy all such existing weapons. We welcome the fact that the United States has worked to gain new action by the UN Security Council to ensure that Iraq meets its obligation to disarm. We join others in urging Iraq to comply fully with this latest Security Council resolution. We fervently pray that all involved will act to ensure that this UN action will not simply be a prelude to war but a way to avoid it.

While we cannot predict what will happen in the coming weeks, we wish to reiterate questions of ends and means that may still have to be addressed. We offer not definitive conclusions, but rather our serious concerns and questions in the hope of helping all of us to reach sound moral judgments. People of good will may differ on how to apply just war norms in particular cases, especially when events are moving rapidly and the facts are not altogether clear. Based on the facts that are known to us, we continue to find it difficult to justify the resort to war against Iraq, lacking clear and adequate evidence of an imminent attack of a grave nature. With the Holy See and bishops from the Middle East and around the world, we fear that resort to war, under present circumstances and in light of current public information, would not meet the strict conditions in Catholic teaching for overriding the strong presumption against the use of military force.[11]

Just cause. The *Catechism of the Catholic Church* limits just cause to cases in which "the damage inflicted by the aggressor on the nation or community of nations [is] lasting, grave and certain." (#2309) We are deeply concerned about recent proposals to expand dramatically traditional limits on just cause to include preventive uses of military force to overthrow threatening regimes or to deal with weapons of mass destruction. Consistent with the proscriptions contained in international law, a distinction should be made between efforts to change unacceptable *behavior* of a government and efforts to end that government's *existence.*

Legitimate authority. In our judgment, decisions concerning possible war in Iraq require compliance with U.S. constitutional imperatives, broad consensus within our nation, and some form of international sanction. That is why the action by Congress and the UN Security Council are important. As the Holy See has indicated, if recourse to force were deemed necessary, this should take place within the framework of the United Nations after considering the consequences for Iraqi civilians, and regional and global stability (Archbishop Jean-Louis Tauran, Vatican Secretary for Relations with States, 9/10/02).

Probability of success and proportionality. The use of force must have "serious prospects for success" and "must not produce evils and disorders graver than the evil to be eliminated" (Catechism, #2309). We recognize that not taking military action could have its own negative consequences. We are concerned, however, that war against Iraq could have unpredictable consequences not only for Iraq but for peace and stability elsewhere in the Middle East. The use of force might provoke the very kind of attacks that it is intended to prevent, could impose terrible new burdens on an already long-suffering civilian population, and could lead to wider conflict and in-stability in the region. War against Iraq could also detract from the responsibility to help build a just and stable order in Afghanistan and could undermine broader efforts to stop terrorism.

Norms governing the conduct of war. The justice of a cause does not lessen the moral responsibility to comply with the norms of civilian immunity and proportionality. While we recognize improved capability and serious efforts to avoid directly targeting civilians in war, the use of military force in Iraq could bring incalculable costs for a civilian population that has suffered so much from war, repression, and a debilitating embargo. In assessing whether "collateral damage" is proportionate, the lives of Iraqi men, women and children should be valued as we would the lives of members of our own family and citizens of our own country.

Our assessment of these questions leads us to urge that our nation and the world continue to pursue actively alternatives to war in the Middle East. It is vital that our nation persist in the very frustrating and difficult challenges of maintaining broad international support for constructive, effective and legitimate ways to contain and deter aggressive Iraqi actions and threats. We support effective enforcement of the military embargo and maintenance of political sanctions. We reiterate our call for much more carefully-focused economic sanctions which do not threaten the lives of innocent Iraqi civilians. Addressing Iraq's weapons of mass destruction must be matched by broader and stronger non-proliferation measures. Such efforts, grounded in the principle of mutual restraint, should include, among other things, greater support for programs to safeguard and eliminate weapons of mass destruction in all nations, stricter controls on the export of missiles and weapons technology, improved enforcement of the biological and chemical weapons conventions, and fulfillment of U.S. commitments to pursue good faith negotiations on nuclear disarmament under the Nuclear Non-Proliferation Treaty.

There are no easy answers. Ultimately, our elected leaders are responsible for decisions about national security, but we hope that our moral concerns and questions will be considered seriously by our leaders and all citizens. We invite others, particularly Catholic lay people—who have the principal responsibility to transform the social order in light of the Gospel—to continue to discern how best to live out their vocation to be "witnesses and agents of peace and justice" (Catechism, #2442). As Jesus said, "Blessed are the peacemakers" (Mt. 5).

We pray for all those most likely to be affected by this potential conflict, especially the suffering people of Iraq and the men and women who serve in our armed forces. We support those who risk their lives in the service of our nation. We also support those who seek to exercise their right to conscientious objection and selective conscientious objection, as we have stated in the past.

We pray for President Bush and other world leaders that they will find the will and the ways to step back from the brink of war with Iraq and work for a peace that is just and enduring. We urge them to work with others to fashion an effective global response to Iraq's threats that recognizes legitimate self defense and conforms to traditional moral limits on the use of military force.

Notes

1. For a selection of such reports, see *Economist*, 1 August 1992, pp. 34–35.

2. A full discussion of the discovery of my Jewish heritage, including the shock of learning that three of my grandparents and a number of other family members had died in the Holocaust, is included in my autobiography, *Madam Secretary: A Memoir*, Miramax, New York, 2003, 235–249.

3. Wellesley is a college for women. The school's motto is "Non ministrari sed ministrare": "Not to be ministered unto but to minister." My classmates and I used to joke that it really meant "Not to be ministers, but to be ministers' wives."

4. Respect for the individual is not, as some say, the opposite of respect for the rights of groups. On the contrary, individuals bring their rights to the groups to which they belong. Thus, freedom from discrimination on the basis of race, gender, or religion is *both* an individual and a group right.

5. Beginning with the old parenthesis "(the praise and glory be to God alone)," the closing phrases of this paragraph refer not simply to a common determination to be faithful to the Lord, but much more specifically to the actual Schleitheim experience and the sense of Unity *(Vereinigung)* which the members had come to in the course of the meeting. "Without contradiction of all the brothers" is the formal description and "completely at peace" is the subjective definition of this sense of Holy Spirit guidance. Zwingli considered the very report that "we have come together" to be the proof of the culpable sectarian, conspiratorial character of Anabaptism (*Elenchus, Z,* VI, p. 56).

6. "Law" here is a specific reference to the Old Testament. Significantly the verb here is not

verordnet but merely *geordnet*: conveying less of a sense of permanence or of specific divine institution than "ordained" does. It should be noted that in this entire discussion "sword" refers to the judicial and police powers of the state. There is no reference to war in Art. VI; there had been a brief one in IV.

7. Two interpretations are possible for "did not discern the ordering of His Father." This may mean that Jesus did not respect, as being an obligation for Him, the service in the state in the office of king, even though the existence of the state is a divine ordinance. More likely would be the interpretation that Jesus did not evaluate the action of the people wanting to make Him King as having been brought about (ordered) by His Father.

8. Here the printed version adds Mt. 12:25: "For every kingdom divided against itself will be destroyed."

9. Zwingli's translation fills in the argument here: "If it is bad to swear, or even to use the Lord's name to confirm the truth, then the apostles Peter and Paul sinned: for they swore."

10. This concludes the *Seven Articles*.

11. "Just war teaching has evolved . . . as an effort to prevent war; only if war cannot be rationally avoided, does the teaching then seek to restrict and reduce its horrors. It does this by establishing a set of rigorous conditions which must be met if the decision to go to war is to be morally permissible. Such a decision, especially today, requires extraordinarily strong reasons for overriding the presumption in favor of peace and against war. This is one significant reason why valid just-war teaching makes provision for conscientious dissent." *The Challenge of Peace: God's Promise and Our Response* (1983), #83.

CHAPTER 12

CONCLUSION

This book has displayed and explored many of the dimensions of religion and politics in the United States, from the time of the earliest colonial settlers to the present day. John Winthrop's 1630 declaration of a new "city upon a hill" articulated the hope that this New World would be a place that allowed religion to thrive. To a great extent, America has been and remains a place where religion flourishes. Even proponents of secularization theory admit that the United States is a country where religious participation remains vigorous and where politics is energized—if not always enhanced—by its intersection with religion. This religious vigor, a lasting American feature but a peculiarity among other Western nations, quite possibly may advance rather than inhibit, the U.S. as it makes its way toward the four hundredth anniversary of Winthrop's famous words. It may be that the nation's long experience combining religious vitality with representative democracy uniquely places it as a global bridge between the more secularized Western world and the more religious remainder of the globe.

The readings collected in this volume provide a range of vantage points for the study of religion and politics in the United States. In Chapter 1, John Witte Jr. pointed out that theology, as much or more than Enlightenment liberalism, formed the basis for the emerging American articulations of religious liberty, and ultimately, of a Republic where many religions could exist in the private sphere even as religious people and ideas had a place in the public sphere. The essay and the accompanying primary sources displayed the religious underpinnings of the country as understood by the colonists themselves. The research pieces indicated that the task of untangling the proper relationship between church and state was a precarious one, especially given differing theological views and religious practices. The notion of religious toleration was the basis for much of the thinking about the broader array of liberties eventually granted in the United States.

Chapter 2 highlighted the interesting ironies inherent in the fledgling Republic. While the U.S. was born partially of a zeal for religious freedom from attempts by centralized governments to dictate claims of conscience, state churches, as Daniel Driesbach discussed, were the norm in the new republic even as the national constitution refused preference for a particular faith. While state churches eventually dissolved and the Supreme Court eventually applied the First Amendment religion clauses to state governments, these developments took time. The primary sources included in this chapter deepened our understanding of the early views of church–state relations. Alexis deToqueville's observations of America provided independent confirmation of the centrality of religion to the character and complexity of the United States.

Chapter 3 explored an interesting concept with practical manifestations—civil religion. Civil religion exists alongside other religions, to some extent becoming the unifying national "faith." Functionally, civil religion provides symbols such as the flag, references like "In God We Trust" on coins, and ceremonies such as the placing of the wreath on the Tomb of the Unknown Soldier at Arlington National Ceremony, that engender national purpose, passion, and patriotism. Presidential speeches represent prime opportunities for the proverbial pastors of the polity to articulate the American variant of civil religion.

Chapter 4 demonstrated how evaluations of religion and politics in the United States have evolved over time as scholars have refined their measurement and study of religious beliefs, belonging, and behavior. Corwin Smidt's essay pointed to recent trends that suggest religious beliefs and the depth of religious commitment are eclipsing religious affiliation as key determinants of political behavior. The research pieces indicated that race, culture, and ethnicity are significant variables that help explain religious persons' political activism.

Chapter 5 examined the close relationship between religion and social movements in the United States. The research pieces explored religion's potential to disrupt the status quo at the national level and at the state level. The primary documents showed the myriad ways that social movement leaders referred to religion in their quests for the fulfillment of America's potential on various fronts. From abolition to women's rights to black freedom, religious ideas have been key catalysts for social change.

Chapter 6 detailed the role of religious interest groups in the United States. From Buddhists to Baptists, religious groups play an active role in political debates at all levels and branches of government. Kimberly Conger's essay highlighted the rise of the Christian Right in the United States and its influence in a number of policy domains— most prominently, in moral issues such as abortion and homosexual marriage, but also in areas such as education and welfare. The role of religious interest groups in the courts should not be overlooked; two *amicus curiae* briefs illustrated the importance of religious interest groups in contemporary debates about the role of religion in American society and in the American polity.

Chapter 7 explored the relationship between religion and the presidency. Mark Rozell and Harold Bass noted that regardless of their personal church upbringing or the regularity of their church attendance, all presidents have invoked religious themes and language to garner public support, whether for public approval, electoral advantage, or in the name of national unity. Even though the Constitution bans formal religious tests for the office, the American people seem to impose informal but persistent expectations that presidents appear religious. As the research pieces demonstrated, the faith of many presidents has been vital to their presidencies, and as the primary sources chronicled, religious language has been central to presidential rhetoric throughout American history.

Chapter 8 examined religion and Congress. Almost all members of Congress claim a religious affiliation, and many speak openly about their faith and its influence on their legislative work. Some of the research pieces indicated that religion affects how members vote, and the primary documents allowed members and Senators to talk about their religion in their own words. Religious values often clash when it comes to contentious congressional issues, further complicating the process of finding the compromise necessary to pass legislation.

Chapter 9 considered religion and the Supreme Court, giving particular attention to establishment and free exercise cases. Paul Wahlbeck's integrative essay illustrated that these historic decisions are the result of a combination of the justices' personal policy preferences, adherence to legal precedents and norms, and strategic decision making. The religion cases selected for this chapter are a sharp reminder that the major judicial decisions on critical religious questions defy easy analysis.

Chapter 10 demonstrated the intersection between religion and domestic policy in the United States. Katherine Knutson's essay highlighted the role of religion in policy formation via church resolutions and lobbying on a broad range of issues. The variety of sources in the chapter provided further documentation of the diversity of and contention between different religious perspectives in the public square.

Chapter 11 traced the relationship between religion and foreign policy in the United States. Religious groups and thinkers have debated the proper place of the faithful in war for many centuries. From pacifism to just war to jihad, the proper relationship between religion and foreign policy remains a contested topic. As all of the research pieces indicated, the role of religion in the international realm is escalating, not declining. Thus, the public and policy makers ignore religion in global politics at their peril.

The insights of leading scholars from political science, law, and history all point to the same conclusion: the story of religion and politics in the United States is older than the republic yet continues to unfold. From the Mayflower Compact to Martin Luther King Jr., in institutions and in elections, in policy ideas and in political speeches of elected officials past and present, religion has been a major source of energy and change in American politics and public policy. Religion has been alternatively ignored, misunderstood, and decried by many of those studying American politics. It may be that the experience of the United States as a thoroughly Western and modern nation with a people of robust and varied religious sentiment will help it navigate constructively in an increasingly interconnected global context. In the words of John Winthrop four centuries ago, "the eyes of all people are upon us."

WORKS CITED

Abraham, Nabeel. 2000. Arab Detroit's 'American' mosque. In *Arab Detroit: From margin to mainstream,* eds. Andrew A. Shryock and Nabeel Abraham eds., 279–312. Detroit: Wayne State University.

Abshire, David M. 2003. The wartime faith of Washington, Lincoln, and Roosevelt. Alumni/ae address at the General Theological Seminary, New York.

Adams, Charles Francis, ed. 1854. *John Adams, the works of John Adams, second President of the United States,* vol. IX. Boston: Little, Brown.

Adeney, W.F. 1925. Toleration. In *Encyclopedia of religion and ethics,* vol. 12, ed. James Hastings. New York: Charles Scribner's Sons.

Alinsky, Saul. 1972. *Rules for radicals.* New York: Vintage.

Alley, Robert S. 1972. *So help me God.* Richmond: John Knox.

Altschuler, Albert. 1996. *Rediscovering Blackstone.* 145 U. Pa. L. Rev. 1.

Alvarez, R. Michael, and Lisa Garcia Bedoll. 2003. The foundations of Latino voter partisanship: Evidence from the 2000 election. *Journal of Politics* 65(1): 31–49.

Alwin, Duane, Jacob Felson, Edward Walker, and Paula Tufis. 2006. Measuring religious identities in surveys. *Public Opinion Quarterly* 70: 530–564.

American Muslim Pac endorses George W. Bush for president. 2004. http://www.amaweb.org/election2000/ampcc_endorses.htm

American Muslim Poll: November/December 2001. 2004. http://www.projectmaps.com/PMReport.htm

Aminzade, Ronald A., and Elizabeth J. Perry. 2001. The sacred, religious, and secular in contentious politics: Blurring boundaries. In *Silence and voice in contentious politics,* eds. Ronald A. Aminzade, et. al., 155–178. Cambridge: Cambridge University Press.

Anderson, James. 2006. *Public policymaking,* 6th ed. Boston, MA: Houghton Mifflin.

Angrosino, Michael V. 2002. Civil religion redux. *Anthropological Quarterly* 75(2): 239–267.

Aquinas, Thomas. 1953. Summa Theologica, question 92, article 1. In *The political ideas of St. Aquinas,* ed. D. Bigongiari. New York: Hafner.

Arvizu, John R. and F. Chris Garcia. 1996. Latino voting participation: explaining and differentiating voting turnout. *Hispanic Journal of Behavioral Sciences* 18: 104–127.

Associated Press. 2009. Judge rules against freeze on assets. *The New York Times,* August 19.

Austen-Smith, David. 1993. Information and influence: Lobbying for agenda and votes. *American Journal of Political Science* 37: 799–833.

Bachmeier, Mark D., Elizabeth A. Craft, Elton F. Jackson, and James R. Wood. 1995. Volunteering and charitable giving: Do religious and associational ties promote helping behavior? *Nonprofit and Voluntary Sector Quarterly* 24: 59–78.

Bagby, Ihsan. 2004. A portrait of Detroit mosques: Muslim views on policy, politics and religion. Clinton Township, MI: Institute for Social Policy and Understanding.

Bagby, Ihsan, Raul Perl, and Bryan Froehle. 2001. *The mosque in America a national portrait: a report from the mosque study project.* Washington, DC: Council on American-Islamic Relations.

Banks, Adelle M. 2004. Poll: Americans want a 'deeply religious' person as president. Pew Forum on Religion and Public Life. January 9. http://pewforum.org/news/display.php?newsid=3012.

Barker, Lucius J. 1988. *Our time has come: A delegate's diary of Jesse Jackson's 1984 presidential campaign.* Urbana: University of Illinois Press.

Barna Group. 2008. Presidential race tightens as faith voters rethink their preferences. Barna Group. August 11. http://www.barna.org/barna-update/article/13-culture/28-presidential-race-tightens-as-faith-voters-rethink-their-preference.

Barnes, Fred. 2003. God and man in the oval office. *The Weekly Standard,* March 17, 8.

Barr, James. 1981. *The scope and authority of the Bible.* Philadelphia: Westminster Press.

Bartkowski, John. 1996. Beyond biblical literalism and inerrancy: Conservative Protestants and the hermeneutic interpretation of scripture. *Sociology of Religion* 57(3): 259–272.

Baumgartner, Frank R., and Bryan D. Jones. 1994. *Agendas and instability in American politics.* Chicago: University of Chicago Press.

Bazar, Emily. 2008. Prayer leads to work disputes. *USA Today,* October 16. http://www.usatoday. com/news/nation/2008-10-15-Muslim_N.htm.

Beiner, Ronald. 1993. Machiavelli, Hobbes, and Rousseau on civil religion. *The Review of Politics* 55(4): 617–638.

Bell, D. 1976. *The cultural contradictions of capitalism.* New York: Basic Books.

Bellah, Robert N. 1967. Civil religion in America. In *Beyond belief: Essays on religion in a post-traditionalist world.* Berkeley: University of California Press.

_____. 1974. American civil religion in the 1970s. In *American civil religion,* eds. Russell E. Richey and Donald G. Jones, 255–272. New York: Harper & Row.

_____. 1976. The revolution and the civil religion. In *Religion and the American Revolution,* ed. Jerald C. Brauer. New York: Fortress Press.

_____. 1976. Response to the panel on civil religion. *Sociological Analysis* 37(2): 167–168.

_____. 1980. American Association of Law Schools law and religion panel: Law as our civil religion. *Mercer Law Review,* 31(2): 482–485.

_____. 1986. Habits of the heart: Implications for religion. Lecture, St. Mark's Catholic Church, Isla Vista, California, February 21.

_____. 1987. Conclusion. In *Uncivil religion: Interreligious hostility in America,* eds. Robert N. Bellah and Frederick E. Greenspahn. New York: Crossroad.

_____. 1992. *The broken covenant: American civil religion in time of trial,* 2nd ed. Chicago: University of Chicago Press.

_____. 2000. In God we trust: Civil and uncivil religion in America. Interview. Radio National Encounter, June 25. http://www.abc.net.au/rn/relig/enc/stories/s143139.htm.

Bellah, Robert N., and Frederick E. Greenspahn. 1987. *Uncivil religion: Interreligious hostility in America.* New York: Crossroad.

Bellah, Robert N., and Phillip E. Hammond. 1980. *Varieties of civil religion.* New York: Harper & Row.

Benson, Peter, and Dorothy Williams. 1986. *Religion on Capitol Hill: Myths and Realities.* New York: Oxford University Press.

Berelson, Bernard, Hazel Gaudet, and Paul Lazarsfeld. 1944. *The people's choice.* New York: Columbia University Press.

Berelson, Bernad, Paul F. Lazarsfeld, and William McPhee. 1954. *Voting: A study of opinion formation in a presidential campaign.* Chicago: University of Chicago Press.

Berger, Peter. 1967. *The sacred canopy.* Garden City: Doubleday.

Berlin, Isaiah. 1969. Historical inevitability. In *Four essays on liberty.* New York: Oxford University Press.

Berry, Jeffrey. 1984. *The interest group society.* Boston: Little, Brown.

_____. 2003. A voice for nonprofits. Washington, D.C.: Brookings Institution Press.

Bigongiari, Dino, ed. 1953. *The politics of St. Thomas Aquinas.* New York: Hafner.

Billings, Dwight B. 1990. Religion as opposition: A Gramscian analysis. *American Journal of Sociology* 96(1): 1–31.

Black, Amy E., Douglas L. Koopman, and David K. Ryden. 2004. *Of little faith: The politics of George W. Bush's faith-based initiatives.* Washington, D.C.: Georgetown University Press.

Blackstone, William. 1765. *Commentaries on the laws of England,* facs. ed., 1979. Chicago: University of Chicago Press.

Blumenthal, Sidney. 1994. Christian soldiers. *The New Yorker* 70(18): 66–112.

Blumhofer, Edith L., and Martin E. Marty. Public religion in America today. The Martin Marty Center, University of Chicago Divinity School. http://martycenter.uchicago.edu/research/publicreligion_today.shtml.

Bokenkotter, Thomas. 1998. *Church and revolution: Catholics in the struggle for democracy and social justice.* New York: Doubleday Image.

The book of laws and liberties of Massachusetts. 1975 [1647]. San Marino, CA: Huntington Library Press.

Boorstin, Daniel J. 1958. *The mysterious science of the law.* Chicago: University of Chicago Press.

Boston, Rob. 2004. With a boost from a Jerry Falwell legal group, the conflict over government-sponsored commandments displays has arrived at the Supreme Court. *Church and State* 57(11): 9–12.

Boyer, Peter J. 2008. Party faithful. *The New Yorker,* September 8.

Bozeman, Theodore Dwight. 1986. The Puritans' 'errand into the wilderness' reconsidered. *New England Quarterly* 59: 231–251.

Bradley, Martin B., Normal M. Green, Jr., Dale E. Jones, Mac Lynn, and Lou McNeil. 1992. *Churches and church membership in the United States, 1990.* Atlanta: Glenmary Research Center.

Branch, Taylor. 1988. *Parting the waters: America in the King years, 1954–1963.* New York: Simon and Schuster.

Briggs, Xavier de Souza. 1998. Doing democracy up close: Culture, power, and communication in community building. *Journal of Planning Education and Research* 18: 1–13.

Brown, Steven P. 2002. *Trumping religion: The new Christian Right, the free speech clause, and the courts.* Tuscaloosa, AL: University of Alabama Press.

Buckley, Thomas E. 2007. Thomas Jefferson and the myth of separation. In *Religion and the American presidency,* eds. Mark J. Rozell and Gleaves Whitney, 39–50. New York: Palgrave/MacMillan Press.

Burdette, Amy M., Christopher G. Ellison, and Terrence D. Hill. 2005. Conservative Protestantism and tolerance of homosexuals. *Sociological Inquiry* 75(2): 177–196.

Byrnes, Timothy. 1991. *Catholic bishops in American politics.* Princeton: Princeton University Press.
_____. 1993. The politics of American Catholic hierarchy. *Political Science Quarterly* 108(3): 497–515.

Byrnes, Timothy A., and Mary C. Segers, eds. 1992. *The Catholic Church and the politics of abortion: A view from the states.* Boulder, CO: Westview.

Cain, Bruce E., D. Roderick Kiewiet, and Carole J. Uhlaner. 1991. The acquisition of partisanship by Latinos and Asian Americans. *American Journal of Political Science* 35(2): 390–422.

Calamandrei, Mauro. 1952. Neglected aspects of Roger Williams' thought. *Church History* 21: 239–258.

Calhoun-Brown, A. 1996. African American churches and political mobilization: the psychological impact of organizational resources. *Journal of Politics* 4: 935–953.

Calvo, M.A. and S. J. Rosenstone. 1989. *Hispanic political participation.* San Antonio, TX: Southwest Voter Research Institute.

Campbell, Agnus, Phillip E. Converse, Warren E. Miller, and Donald E. Stokes. 1960. *The American voter.* New York: John Wiley.

Campbell, David E., and Steven J. Yonish. 2003. Religion and volunteering in America. In *Religion and social capital,* ed. Corwin Smidt, 87–106. Waco, TX: Baylor University Press.

Carmines, Edward G., and James A. Stimson. 1989. *Issue evolution: Race and the transformation of American politics.* Princeton: Princeton University Press.

Carnes, Tony. 2008. Talking the walk. *Christianity Today,* October.

Carpenter, Francis B. 1867. *Six months at the White House with Abraham Lincoln.* New York: Herd & Houghton.

Carson, Clayborne. 1981. *In struggle.* Cambridge: Harvard University Press.
_____. ed. 1992. *Papers of Martin Luther King Jr.* Berkeley: University of California Press.

Carter, Jimmy. 1977. "Inaugural Address." Inaugural Address, Washington, D.C., January 20.

Carter, Stephen. 1993. *The culture of disbelief: How American law and politics trivialize religious devotion.* New York: Basic Books.
_____. 2000. *God's name in vain: The wrongs and rights of religion in politics.* New York: Basic Books.

Casanova, José. 1994. *Public religions in the modern world.* Chicago: University of Chicago Press.

Chambers, John W. II. 1998. The agenda continued: Jimmy Carter's post-presidency. In *The Carter presidency: Policy choices in the post–New Deal era,* eds. Gary M. Fink and Hugh Davis Graham. Lawrence: University of Kansas Press.

Chaves, Mark, and James C. Cavendish. 1994. More evidence on U.S. Catholic church attendance. *Journal for the Scientific Study of Religion* 33: 376–381.

Chaves, Mark, and Laura Stephens. 2003. Church attendance in the United States. In *Handbook of the sociology of religion,* ed. Michele Dillon, 85–95. New York: Cambridge University Press.

Chaves, Mark, C. Kirk Hadaway, and Penny Long Marler. 1993. What the polls don't show: A closer look at U.S. church attendance. *American Sociological Review* 58: 741–752.

Cherry, Conrad, ed. 1998. *God's new Israel: Religious interpretations of American destiny, revised and updated ed.* Chapel Hill: University of North Carolina Press.

Chinmayananda, Swami. n.d. *The Holy Geeta.* Mumbai, India: Thomson Press (India) Ltd.

Clinton, William J. 1997. "Second Inaugural Address." Inaugural Address, Washington, D.C., January 20.

Cloud, Matthew W. 2004. "One nation, under God": Tolerable acknowledgment of religion or unconstitutional cold war propaganda cloaked in American civil religion? *Journal of Church and State* 46(2): 311–340.

Cnaan, Ram. A, Amy Kasternakis, and Robert J. Wineburg. 1993. Religious people, religious congregations, and volunteerism in human services: Is there a link? *Nonprofit and Voluntary Sector Quarterly* 22: 33–51.

Cochran, Clarke E., Lawrence C. Mayer, T. R. Carr, and N. Joseph Cayer. 2006. *American public policy: An introduction,* 8th edition. Boston, MA: Wadsworth.

Coffin, Malcolm. 2003. The Latino vote: Shaping America's future. *Political Quarterly* 74: 214–222.

Coleman, John A., S.J. 2003. American Catholicism, Catholic Charities USA, and welfare reform. In *Religion returns to the public square: Faith and policy in America,* eds. Hugh Heclo and Wilfred M. McClay. Washington, D.C.: Woodrow Wilson Center Press.

Colson, Charles W. 1987. The lures and limits of political power. In *Piety and politics: Evangelicals and fundamentalists confront the world,* eds. Richard John Neuhaus and Michael Cromartie. Lanham: University Press of America.

Colson, Charles W., and Nancy Pearcey. 1999. *How now shall we live?* Wheaton: Tyndale House Publishers.

Cone, James H. 1969. *Black theology and black power.* New York: Seabury Press.

_____. 1972. *The spiritual and the blues.* New York: Seabury Press.

_____. 1986 [1970]. *A black theology of liberation.* Reprint, Maryknoll, NY: Orbis.

Conger, Kimberly H. 2009. *The Christian Right in Republican state politics.* New York: Palgrave MacMillan.

Conger, Kimberly H. and Bryan T. McGraw. 2008. Religious conservatives and the requirements of citizenship: Political autonomy. *Perspectives on Politics* 6: 253–266.

Copulsky, Jerome E. 2005. One Nation under Whose God? Judaism, the Pledge of Allegiance, and American civil religion. Lecture, 37th Annual Meeting of the Association of Jewish Studies, Washington, D.C., December 20.

Cotton, John. 1641. *An abstract of the laws of New England, as they are now established.* London: n.p.

_____. 1646. *The controversie concerning liberty of conscience in matters of religion.* London: n.p.

Cranston, Maurice. 1967. Toleration. In *The encyclopedia of philosophy,* vol. 8, ed. Paul Edwards. New York: Macmillan/Free Press.

Cuomo, Mario. 1984. Religious belief and public morality: A Catholic governor's perspective. Paper delivered at the University of Notre Dame, September 13, South Bend, IN.

D'Antonio, William, and Steven A. Tuch. 2004. The religious factor in the United States Congress. Unpublished manuscript.

Dalton, R. 2000. Citizen attitudes and political behavior. *Comparative Political Studies* 33: 912–940.

Davidson, James D., et al. 1997. *The search for common ground: What unites and divides Catholic Americans.* Huntington, IN: Our Sunday Visitor.

Davis, Derek. 1991. *Original intent: Chief Justice Rehnquist and the course of American church/state relations.* Amherst, NY: Prometheus Books.

_____. 2003. Thoughts on the separation of church and state under the administration of President George W. Bush. *Journal of Church & State* 45(2): 229–235.

Davis, Harry R., and Robert C. Good, eds. 1960. *Reinhold Niebuhr on politics.* New York: Scribner's.

Davis, James A. 1992. Changeable weather in a cooling climate atop the liberal plateau: Conversion and replacement in forty-two general social survey items, 1972–1989. *Public Opinion Quarterly* 56: 261–306.

Dawson, Michael C. 1994. *Behind the mule: Race and class in African American politics.* Princeton: Princeton University Press.

Dean, William. 1994. *The religious critic in American culture.* Albany: State University of New York Press.

Deck, Allan Figueroa, and Jay P. Dolan, eds. 1994. *Hispanic Catholic culture: Issues and concerns.* South Bend: University of Notre Dame Press.

Decker, Karl, and Angus McSween. 1892. *Historic Arlington.* Washington, D.C.: Decker and McSween Publishing Co.

de la Garza, Rodolfo O. 2004. Latino politics. *Annual Review of Political Science* 7: 91–123.

de la Garza, Rodolfo O., Jongho Lee, and Daron Shaw. 2000. Examining Latin turnout in 1996: A three-state, validated survey approach. *American Journal of Political Science* 44(2): 332–340.

Delbanco, Andrew. 1989. *The Puritan ordeal.* Cambridge: Harvard University Press.

Demerath, N. J. III, and Rhys H. Williams. 1985. Civil religion in an uncivil society. *Annals of the American Academy of Political and Social Science* 480: 154–166.

den Dulk, Kevin. 2001. Prophets in Caesar's courts: The role of ideas in Catholic and evangelical rights advocacy. PhD diss., University of Wisconsin – Madison.

de Tocqueville, Alexis. 1966. *Democracy in America,* ed. J.P. Mayer and Max Lerner. New York: Easton Press.

Diamond, Sara. 1998. *Not by politics alone: The enduring influence of the Christian Right.* New York: Guilford Publications.

Diaz, William A. 1996. Latino participation in America: associational and political roles. *Hispanic Journal of Behavioral Sciences* 18: 154–74.

Dinan, Stephen. 1997. "Hate crime" probed: Muslim symbol on ellipse painted with swastika. *Washington Times,* December 29.

Dobson, Ed, and Cal Thomas. 1999. *Blinded by might.* Grand Rapids: Zondervan Publishing House.

Dodd, Lawrence C. 1993. Congress and the politics of renewal: Redressing the crisis of legitimation. In *Congress reconsidered,* 5th ed., eds. Lawrence C. Dodd and Bruce I. Oppenheimer. Washington, D.C.: CQ Press.

Dodds, J. 2002. *The mosques of New York City.* New York: Power House Books.

Dowd, Mark. 2004. A Bush that burns: Who does Dubya think he is? Moses? St. John? Or Jesus himself? *New Statesman,* November, 22–23.

Dowd, Maureen. 2004. Casualties of faith. *New York Times,* October 21.

Dreisbach, Daniel. 1996. The Constitution's forgotten religion clause: Reflections on the Article VI religious test ban. *Journal of Church and State* 38: 261–295.

———.1996. In search of a Christian commonwealth. *Baylor Law Review* 48(4): 927–1000.

———. 2002. *Thomas Jefferson and the wall of separation between church and state.* New York: New York University Press.

Eck, Diana. 2001. *A new religious America.* San Francisco: HarperSanFrancisco.

Edelman, Murray. 1985. *The symbolic uses of politics.* Urbana: University of Illinois Press.

Eisenhower, Dwight D. 1957. "Second Inaugural Address." Inaugural Address, Washington, D.C., January 21.

Elizondo, Virgilio, Gaston Espinosa, and Jesse Miranda, eds. 2005. *Latino religions and civic activism in the United States.* New York: Oxford University Press.

Ellis, Richard J. 2005. *To the flag: The unlikely history of the Pledge of Allegiance.* Lawrence: University Press of Kansas.

Ellison, Christopher G., Samuel Echevarria Cruz, and Brad Smith. 2005. Religion and abortion attitudes among U.S. Hispanics: Findings from the 1990 Latino national political survey. *Social Science Quarterly* 86(1): 192–208.

Ellison, Christopher G., and Darren E. Sherkat. 1993. Conservative Protestantism and support for corporal punishment. *American Sociological Review* 58(1): 131–144.

Elshtain, Jean Bethke. 2001. Faith of our fathers and mothers: Religious belief and American democracy. In *Religion in American public life: Living with our deepest differences,* 1st ed., eds. Azizah Y. Al-Hibri, Jean Bethke Elshtain, Charles C. Haynes, and Martin E. Marty. New York: W. W. Norton & Company.

Elster, Jon, ed. 1986. *Rational choice.* New York: New York University Press.

Emerson, Michael O., and Christian Smith. 2000. *Divided by faith: Evangelical religion and the problem of race in America.* Oxford: Oxford University Press.

Epstein, Lee. 1985. *Conservatives in court.* Knoxville: University of Tennessee.

Epstein, Lee, and Jack Knight. 1998. *The choices justices make.* Washington: CQ Press.

Epstein, Steven B. 1996. Rethinking the constitutionality of ceremonial Deism. *Columbia Law Review* 96(8): 2083–2174.

Ewick, Patricia, and Susan S. Silbey. 1998. *The common place of law: Stories from everyday life.* Chicago, IL: University of Chicago Press.

Fairbanks, James David. 1982. Reagan, religion, and the new Right. *Midwest Quarterly* 23(3): 327–345.

Fairchild, Mary. Christian denominations: The history and evolution of Christian denominations and faith groups. About.com. http://christianity.about.com/od/denominations/a/denominations.htm.

Fairclough, Adam. 2000. Being in the field of education and also being a negro . . . seems . . . tragic: Black teachers in the Jim Crow South. *Journal of American History.* 87: 65–91.

Farrand, Max, ed. 1911. The records of the Federal Convention of 1787. 4 vols. New Haven, CT: Yale University Press.

Fatwa Bank: Muslim participation in the political science in the U.S. 2004. http://islamonline.net/fatwa/english/FatwaDisplay.asp?hFatwaID=16542

Feldman, Noah. 2005. *Divided by God: America's church–state problem—and what we should do about it.* New York: Farrar, Straus and Giroux.

Finke, Roger, and Rodney Stark. 1992. *The churching of America, 1776–1990: Winners and losers in our religious economy.* New Brunswick: Rutgers University Press.

Firebaugh, Glenn. 1989. Methods for estimating cohort replacement effects. *Sociological Methodology,* 243–262.

Fischer, Claude, and Michael Hout. 2002. Why Americans have no religious preference. *American Sociological Review* 67: 165–190.

Fish, Stanley. 1980. *Is there a text in this class? The authority of interpretive communities.* Cambridge: Harvard University Press.

Fitzgerald, Frances. 1981. A disciplined, changing army. *New Yorker,* May 18.

Formisano, Ronald. 1983. *The transformation of political culture: Massachusetts parties, 1790s–1840s.* New York: Oxford University Press.

Fraga, Luis Ricardo, and David L. Leal. 2004. Playing the 'Latino card': Race, ethnicity, and national party politics. *Du Bois Review* 1(2): 297–318.

Freeman, Jo. 1973. The origins of the women's liberation movement. *American Journal of Sociology* 78: 792–811.

Freese, Jeremy, and J. Scott Long. 2001. *Regression models for categorical dependent variables using stata.* College Station: Stata Press.

Friedman, Thomas. 1994. OPEC's lonely at the tap, but China's getting thirsty. *New York Times,* May 2.

Froehle, Bryan T., and Mary T. Gautier. 2000. *Catholicism USA: A portrait of the Catholic Church in the United States.* Maryknoll, NY: Orbis.

Frymer, Paul. 1999. *Uneasy alliances: Race and party competition in America.* Princeton: Princeton University Press.

Galanter, Marc. 1974. Why the "haves" come out ahead: Speculations on the limits of legal change. *Law and Society Review* 9: 95–160.

Galeotti, Anna Elisabetta. 1993. Citizenship and equality: The place for toleration. *Political Theory* 21: 585–605.

Gamson, William. 1990. *The strategy of social protest.* Belmont, CA: Wadsworth.

Garcia, John A. 1997. Political participation: resources and involvement among Latinos in the American political system. In *Pursuing Power: Latinos and the Political System,* ed. F. Chris Garcia. Notre Dame, IN: University of Notre Dame Press.

Gardner, Peter. 1992. Propositional attitudes and multicultural education, or believing others are mistaken. In *Toleration: Philosophy and practice,* ed. John Horton and Peter Nicholson. Brookfield, VT: Avebury.

Gaustad, Edwin Scott, and Philip L. Barlow. 2000. *New historical atlas of religion in America.* New York: Oxford University Press.

Geddicks, Frederick Mark. 2004. The Establishment clause gag reflex. *Brigham Young University Law Review* 3: 995–1004.

Geertz, Clifford. 1973. *The interpretation of cultures.* New York: Basic Books.

Gehrig, Gail. 1981. American civil religion debate: A source for theory construction. *Journal of the Social Scientific Study of Religion* 20(1): 51–63.

Genovese, Eugene D. 1974. *Roll, Jordan, roll.* New York: Vintage Books.

George, Robert P. 2000. What can we reasonably hope for? *First Things,* January, 22–24.

George, Tracy E. and Lee Epstein. 1992. On the nature of Supreme Court decision making. *American Political Science Review* 86: 323–337.

George, Marjorie. 2001. And then God created Kansas? The evolution/creationism debate in America's public schools. *University of Pennsylvania Law Review* 149(3): 843–872.

Gilkes, Cheryl Townsend. 1980. The black church as a therapeutic community: suggested areas for research into the black religious experience. *Journal of the Interdenominational Theological Center* 8: 29–44.

Gittell, Ross, and Avis Vidal. 1998. *Community organizing: Building social capital as a development strategy.* Thousand Oaks: Sage.

Glenn, Norval D. 1987. The trend in "no religion" respondents to U.S. national surveys, late 1950s to early 1980s. *Public Opinion Quarterly* 51: 293–314.

Glock, Charles, and Rodney Stark. 1968. *American piety: The nature of religious commitment.* Berkeley: University of California Press.

Goldberg, Michelle. 2005. One nation, divisible. Review of *Divided by God: America's church–state problem—and what we should do about it,* by Noah Feldman. *Salon,* July 23. http://dir.salon.com/story/books/review/2005/07/23/feldman/index.html.

Granovetter, Mark S. 1973. The strength of weak ties. *American Journal of Sociology* 78: 1360–1380.

Grant, Ulysses S. 1869. "First Inaugural Address." Inaugural Address, Washington, D.C., March 4.

Greeley, Andrew. 1972. *The denominational society: A sociological approach to religion in America.* Glenview, IL: Scott, Foresman.

Greeley, Andrew M. 1994. The demography of American Catholics: 1965–1990. In *The Sociology of Andrew Greeley,* ed. Andrew M. Greeley. Atlanta, GA: Scholars Press.

Greeley, Andrew, and Michael Hout. 2006. *The truth about conservative Christians.* Chicago: University of Chicago Press.

Green, John C. 2007. *The faith factor: How religion influences American elections.* Westport: Praeger.

Green, John C., James L. Guth, Lyman A. Kellstedt, and Corwin E. Smidt. 1996. Grasping the essentials: The social embodiment of religion and political behavior. In *Religion and the culture wars*, eds. John C. Green, James L. Guth, Lyman A. Kellstedt, and Corwin E. Smidt, 174–192. Lanham, MD: Rowman & Littlefield.

———. 1997. Is there a culture war? Religion and the 1996 election. Paper presented at the annual meeting of the American Political Science Association, September, in Washington, D.C.

———. 2006. Religious influences in the 2004 presidential election. *Presidential Studies Quarterly* 36: 223–242.

Green, John C., and John S. Jackson. 2007. Faithful divides: Party elites and religion. In *A matter of faith: religion in the 2004 presidential election*, ed. David E. Campbell, 37–62. Washington, D.C.: Brookings Institution Press.

Green, John C., and Lyman A. Kellstedt. 1993. Knowing God's many people: Denominational preference and political behavior. In *Rediscovering the religious factor in American politics*, eds. David C. Leege and Lyman A. Kellstedt, 53–71. Armonk, NY: M.E. Sharpe.

Green, John C., Lyman A. Kellstedt, Corwin E. Smidt, and James L. Guth. 2007. How the faithful voted: Religious communities and the presidential vote. In *A matter of faith: Religion in the 2004 presidential election*, ed. David E. Campbell, 15–26. Washington, D.C.: Brookings Institution Press.

Green, John C., and Geoffrey Layman. 2005. Wars and rumors of wars: The contexts of cultural conflict in American political behavior. *British Journal of Political Science* 36(1): 61–89.

Green, John C., M.J. Rozell, and Clyde Wilcox, eds. 2000. *Prayers in the precincts: The Christian Right in the 1998 elections*. Washington, D.C.: Georgetown University Press.

Green, John C., Mark J. Rozell, and Clyde Wilcox. 2003. *The Christian Right in American politics: Marching to the millennium*. Washington, D.C.: Georgetown University Press.

Gunn, T. Jeremy. 2005. Religious freedom and laïcité: A comparison of the United States and France. *Brigham Young University Law Review* 2: 465–498.

Gusfield, Joseph. 1963. *Symbolic crusade*. Urbana, IL: University of Illinois Press.

Guth, James L., John C. Green, Lyman A. Kellstedt, and Corwin E. Smidt. 2005. Onward Christian soldiers? Religion and the Bush doctrine. *Books and Culture*, July/August.

———. 2006. Religious influences in the 2004 presidential election. *Presidential Studies Quarterly* 36: 223–242.

Guth, James L., John C. Green, Corwin E. Smidt, Lyman A. Kellstedt, and Margaret M. Poloma. 1997. *The bully pulpit: The politics of Protestant clergy*. Lawrence, KS: University Press of Kansas.

Guth, James L., Lyman A. Kellstedt, and Corwin E. Smidt. 2009. The role of religion in American politics: Explanatory theories and associated analytical and measurement issues. In *The Oxford handbook on religion and American politics*, eds. Corwin E. Smidt, Lyman A. Kellstedt, and James L. Guth. New York: Oxford University Press.

Guth, James L., Lyman A. Kellstedt, Corwin E. Smidt, and John C. Green. 2005. Religious mobilization in the 2004 presidential election. Paper presented at the annual meeting of the American Political Science Association, September 1–4, in Washington, D.C.

———. 2006. Religious influences in the 2004 presidential election. *Presidential Studies Quarterly* 36: 2: 223–242.

Hadaway, C. Kirk, Penny Long Marler, and Mark Chaves. 1993. What the polls don't show: A closer look at U.S. church attendance. *American Sociological Review* 58: 741–752.

Haider-Markel, Donald P. 1999. Morality policy and individual-level political behavior. The case of legislative voting on lesbian and gay issues. *Policy Studies Journal* 27(4): 735–749.

Haider-Markel, Donald P., and Kenneth J. Meier. 1996. The politics of gay and lesbian rights: Expanding the scope of conflict. *The Journal of Politics* 58: 332–349.

Hamburger, Philip. 2002. *Separation of church and state*. Cambridge: Harvard University Press.

Hammond, Phillip E. 1992. *Religion and personal autonomy: The third disestablishment in America*. Columbia: University of South Carolina Press.

Hammond, Phillip E., et al. 1994. Forum: American civil religion revisited. *Religion and American Culture* 4(1): 1–23.

Harlan, John M. 1971. Letter to Chief Justice Warren E. Burger, June 22. Harry A. Blackmun papers. Library of Congress, Washington, D.C.

Harris, Fredrick C. 1994. Something within: Religion as a mobilizer of African-American political activism. *Journal of Politics* 56: 42–68.

———. 1999. *Something within: Religion in African-American political activism*. New York: Oxford University Press.

Harrison, William H. 1841. "Inaugural Address." Inaugural Address, Washington, D.C., March 4.

Hart, S. 1992. *What does the Lord require?* New York: Oxford University Press.

Harvey, Paul. 1997. *Redeeming the South: Religious cultures and racial identities.* Chapel Hill: University of North Carolina Press.

Hatcher, Laura. 2005. Economic libertarians, property and institutions: Linking activism, ideas, and identities among property rights advocates. In *The worlds cause lawyers make: Structure and agency in legal practice,* eds. A. Sarat and S. Scheingold. Stanford, CA: Stanford University Press.

Hausknecht, Murray. 1962. *The joiners: A sociological description of voluntary association membership in the United States.* New York: Bedminster Press.

Hausman, Jerry, and Daniel McFadden. 1984. Specification tests for the multinomial logit model. *Econometrics* 52(5): 1219–1240.

Helms, Melissa. 2001. Dalai Lama visit stirs controversy. *Minnesota Public Radio,* May 1. http://news.minnesota.publicradio.org/features/1200105/01_hughes_dalai/.

Henderson, Charles P. Jr. 1975. Civil religion and the American presidency. *Religious Education* 70: 473–485.

Henry, Charles P. 1990. *Culture and African American politics.* Bloomington: Indiana University Press.

Herberg, Will. 1955/1960. *Protestant, Catholic, Jew: An essay in American religious sociology.* Chicago: University of Chicago Press.

Hero, Rodney E. and Anne G. Campbell. 1996. Understanding Latino political participation: exploring the evidence from the Latino national political survey. *Hispanic Journal of Behavioral Sciences* 18: 129–41.

Hertzke, Allen D. 1989. Faith and access: Religious constituencies and the Washington elites. In *Religion and political behavior in the United States,* ed. Ted G. Jelen. New York: Praeger.

———. 2006. *Freeing God's children: The unlikely alliance for global human rights.* Lanham, MD: Rowman & Littlefield.

Heschel, Abraham Joshua. 1996. On prayer. In *Moral grandeur and spiritual audacity,* ed. Susannah Heschel. New York: Noonday.

———. 1972. *God in search of man.* New York: Octagon.

Hobbes, Thomas. 1839 [1651]. *Leviathan.* Vol. 3 of *The English works of Thomas Hobbes,* ed. Sir William Molesworth. London: John Bohn.

Hodgkinson, Virginia A., and Murray S. Weitzman. 1996. *Giving and volunteering in the United States: 1996 edition.* Washington, D.C.: Independent Sector.

Hodgkinson, Virginia A., Murray S. Weitzman, and Arthur D. Kirsch. 1990. From commitment to action: How religious involvement affects giving and volunteering. In *Faith and philanthropy in America,* eds. Robert Wuthnow, Virginia A. Hodgkinson, and associates. San Francisco: Jossey-Bass.

Holl, Jack. 2007. Dwight D. Eisenhower: Civil religion and the Cold War. In *Religion and the American presidency,* eds. Mark J. Rozell and Gleaves Whitney, 119–138. New York: Palgrave/MacMillan Press.

Holmes, Oliver Wendell, Jr. 1991. [1881] *The common law.* New York: Dover.

Horton, John P. 1991. Toleration. In *The Blackwell encyclopedia of political thought.* Ed. David Miller. New York: Oxford University Press.

Horton, John P., ed. 1993. *Liberalism, multiculturalism and toleration.* New York: St. Martin's Press.

Horton, John P., and Susan Mendus, eds. 1985. *Aspects of toleration: Philosophical studies.* London and New York: Methuen.

Horton, John P., and Peter Nicholson, eds. 1992. *Toleration: Philosophy and practice.* Brookfield, VT: Avebury.

Houston, K. 2001. Into the mosque: the GOP should forge friendship with US Muslims. February 13. *Investor's Business Daily News.*

Hout, Michael, and Claude Fischer. 2002. Why Americans have no religious preference. *American Sociological Review* 67: 165–190.

Hritzuk, Natasha and David K. Park. 2000. The question of Latino participation: from an SES to a social structural explanation. *Social Science Quarterly* 81:151–85.

Hunt, John Gabriel, ed. 1995. *Inaugural addresses of the Presidents.* New York: Gramercy Books.

Hunt, Larry L. 1998. The spirit of Hispanic Protestantism in the United States: National survey comparisons of Catholics and non-Catholics. Social Science Quarterly 79: 828–45.

———. 1999. Hispanic Protestantism in the United States: Trends by decade and generation. *Social Forces* 77(4): 1601–1624.

Hunter, James Davison. 1983. *American Evangelicalism: Conservative religion and the quandary of modernity.* New Brunswick: Rutgers University Press.

———. 1991. *Culture wars.* New York: Basic Books.

Huntington, Samuel. 1993. The clash of civilizations. *Foreign Affairs,* 22–49.

_____. 2004. *Who are we? Challenges to American national identity*. New York: Simon & Schuster.

Hurst, James Willard. 1956. *Law and the conditions of freedom in the nineteenth-century United States*. Madison: University of Wisconsin Press.

Hutcheson, Richard G., Jr. 1988. *God in the White House: How religion has changed the modern presidency*. New York: Macmillan.

Hutchings, Vincent L., and Nicholas A. Valentino. 2004. The centrality of race in American politics. *Annual Review of Political Science* 7: 383–408

Ignagni, Joseph A. 1993. U.S. Supreme Court decision-making and the Free Exercise clause. *Review of Politics* 100: 99–113.

_____. 1994. Explaining and predicting Supreme Court decision making: The Burger court's Establishment clause decisions. *Journal of Church and State* 36: 301–327.

_____. 1994. Supreme Court decision making: An individual-level analysis of the Establishment clause cases during the Burger and Rehnquist court years. *American Review of Politics* 15: 21–42.

Intergovernmental Panel on Climate Change. 2001. *Climate change 2001: Synthesis report. Summary for policymakers*. http://www.ipcc.ch/pdf/climate-changes-2001/synthesis-spm/synthesis-spm-en.pdf.

Is abortion a Catholic issue? 1976. *Christianity Today,* January 16.

Ivers, Gregg. 1995. *To build a wall: American Jews and the separation of church and state*. Charlottesville: University of Virginia Press.

_____. 1998. Please God, save this honorable court: The rise of the conservative religious bar. In *The interest group connection,* ed. P. S. Herrnson, R. G. Shaiko, and C. Wilcox. Chatham, NJ: Chatham House.

Jackson, Elton F., Mark D. Bachmeier, James R. Wood, and Elizabeth A. Craft. 1995. Volunteering and charitable giving: Do religious and associational ties promote helping behavior? *Nonprofit and Voluntary Sector Quarterly* 24: 59–78.

Jackson, Jennifer. 1992. Intolerance on the campus. In *Toleration: Philosophy and practice,* ed. John P. Horton and Peter Nicholson. Brookfield, VT: Avebury.

Jackson, Walter A. 1990. *Gunnar Myrdal and America's conscience: Social engineering and racial liberalism, 1938–1987*. Chapel Hill: University of North Carolina Press.

Jacoby, Susan. 2004. *Freethinkers: A history of American secularism*. New York: Henry Holt.

Jamal, A. In press. Mosque participation and gendered differences among Arab American Muslims. *Journal of Middle East Women's Studies*.

Janoski, Thomas, and John Wilson. 1995. The contribution of religion to volunteer work. *Sociology of Religion* 56: 137–152.

Jefferson, Thomas. 1801. "First Inaugural Address." Inaugural Address, Washington, D.C., 4 March.

_____. Letter to Samuel Miller, 23 January 1808. *Writings of Thomas Jefferson,* 11: 428–430.

Jensen, Richard. 1971. *The winning of the Midwest: Social and political conflict, 1888–1896*. Chicago: University of Chicago Press.

Johnson, Edward. 1910 [1658]. *Wonder-working providence of Sion's saviour in New England*. Ed. J. Franklin Jameson. New York: Charles Scribner's Sons.

Johnson, Lyndon Baines. 1965. "Inaugural Address." Inaugural Address, Washington, D.C., January 20.

Johnson, Paul. 2001. A God-fearing White House is safer. *Forbes,* August 20.

Johnson, Timothy R., Paul J. Wahlbeck, and James F. Spriggs, II. 2006. The influence of oral arguments on the U.S. Supreme Court. *American Political Science Review* 100: 99–113.

Jones-Correa, Michael and David Leal. 2001. Political participation: does religion matter? *Political Research Quarterly* 54: 751–70.

Journal of the First Session of the Senate of the United States of America. 1820. Washington, D.C.: Gales and Seaton.

Kao, Grace. Forthcoming. "One nation under God" or taking the Lord's name in vain? Christian reflections on the Pledge of Allegiance. *Journal of the Society of Christian Ethics*.

Kellstedt, Lyman A. Seculars and the American presidency. 2008. In *Religion, race, pluralism and the American presidency,* ed. Gaston Espinosa. Lanham, MD: Rowman & Littlefield.

Kellstedt, Lyman A., and John C. Green. 1993. Knowing God's many people: Denominational preference and political behavior. In *Rediscovering the religious factor in American politics,* eds. David C. Leege and Lyman A. Kellstedt, 53–71. Armonk, NY: M.E. Sharpe.

Kellstedt, Lyman A., John C. Green, James L. Guth, and Corwin E. Smidt. 1996. Grasping the essentials: The social embodiment of religion and political behavior. In *Religion and the culture wars,* eds. John C. Green, James L. Guth, Corwin E. Smidt, and Lyman A. Kellstedt, 174–192. Lanham, MD: Rowman & Littlefield.

Kellstedt, Lyman A., John C. Green, James L. Guth, and Corwin E. Smidt. 1997. Is there a culture war? Religion and the 1996 election. Paper presented at the annual meeting of the American Political Science Association, September, in Washington, D.C.

Kelly, Nathan J., and Jana Morgan Kelly. 2005. Religion and Latino partisanship in the United States. *Political Research Quarterly* 58: 87–95.

Kengor, Paul. 2004. *God and Ronald Reagan: A spiritual life*. New York: Regan Books.

_____. 2007. Ronald Reagan's faith and attack on Soviet communism. In *Religion and the American presidency*, eds. Mark J. Rozell and Gleaves Whitney, 175–190. New York: Palgrave/MacMillan Press.

Kennedy, John F. 1961. "Inaugural Address." Inaugural Address, Washington, D.C., January 20.

_____. 1961. Annual Message to the Congress on the State of the Union. State of the Union Address, Washington, D.C., January 30.

King, Preston. 1976. *Toleration*. London: Allen and Unwin.

King Jr., Martin Luther. 1958. *Stride toward freedom: The Montgomery story*. New York: Harper.

_____. 1992. Autobiography of religious development, Fall 1950. In *The Papers of Martin Luther King Jr.*, ed. Clayborne Carson, 359–79. Berkeley, CA: University of California Press.

_____. 1992. Kings' application to Crozer Theological Seminary, February 1948. In *The Papers of Martin Luther King Jr.*, ed. Clayborne Carson, 142–49. Berkeley, CA: University of California Press.

Kirk, Russell. 1991. *The roots of American order*. Washington, D.C.: Regnery Gateway.

Kissinger, Henry A. 1977. Morality and power. In *Morality and foreign policy: A symposium on President Carter's stance*, ed. Ernest W. LeFever. Lanham, MD: University Press of America.

Kleppner, Paul. 1979. *The third electoral system, 1853–1892: Parties, voters, and political cultures*. Chapel Hill: University of North Carolina Press.

Klineberg, Stephen L. 2005. Houston Area Survey. Computer File. Houston: Rice University, Center on Race, Religion and Urban Life.

Knight, Jack. 1992. *Institutions and social conflict*. New York: Cambridge University Press.

Knight, Jack, and Lee Epstein. 1996. The norm of *Stare decisis. American Journal of Political Science* 40: 1018–1035.

Kobylka, Joseph F. 1989. Leadership on the Supreme Court of the United States: Chief Justice Burger and the Establishment clause. *Western Political Quarterly* 42: 545–568.

Koff, Stephen. 2000. Criticism of Hindu plucked from web. *Plain Dealer*, September 23.

Kohn, Hans. 1961. *The idea of nationalism*. New York: Macmillan.

Kohut, Andrew, John C. Green, Robert C. Toth, and Scott Keeter. 2000. *The diminishing divide: Religion's changing role in American politics*. Washington, D.C.: Brookings Institution Press.

Kosmin, Barry A., and Seymour P. Lachman. 2001. *American religious identification survey: 2001*. New York: Graduate Center of the City University of New York.

Kramnick, Isaac, and R. Laurence Moore. 1996. *The godless Constitution*. New York: W.W. Norton & Co.

Krishnananda, Swami. 1975. *The Brihadaranyaka Upanishad*, Sankaracarya cmt., Swami Madhavananda trans.

Kritzer, Herbert M., and Mark J. Richards. 2003. Jurisprudential regimes and Supreme Court decisionmaking: The *Lemon* regime and Establishment clause cases. *Law & Society Review* 37: 827–840.

Laitin, David D. 1988. Political culture and political preferences. *American Political Science Review* 82: 589–1593.

Lally, Francis J. 1958. Religion and public life. *Commonweal* 69, December 19, 314.

Larson, Edward J. 1985. *Trial and error: The American controversy over creation and evolution*. New York: Oxford University Press.

Laycock, Douglas. 2003. The many meanings of separation: Review of separation of church and state by Philip Hamburger. *University of Chicago Law Review* 70(4): 1667–1701.

Layman, Geoffrey. 2001. *The great divide: Religious and cultural conflict in American party politics*. New York: Columbia University Press.

Lazarsfeld, Paul, Bernard Berelson, and Hazel Gaudet. 1944. *The People's Choice*. New York: Columbia University Press.

Lazerwitz, Bernard. 1962. Membership in voluntary associations and frequency of church attendance. *Journal for the Scientific Study of Religion* 2: 74–84.

Leal, David L. 2007. Latinos and religion. In *A matter of faith: Religion in the 2004 presidential election*, ed. D. E. Campbell. Washington, D.C.: Brookings Institution Press.

Leege, David C., and Michael Welch. 1991. Dual reference groups and political orientations: An examination of evangelically oriented Catholics. *American Journal of Political Science* 35: 28–56.

Leloudis, James L. 1996. *Schooling the new South: Pedagogy, self, and society in North Carolina,*

1880–1920. Chapel Hill: University of North Carolina Press.

Levenick, Christopher, and Michael Novak. 2005. Religion and the founders. *National Review Online*, March 7.

Lewis, John, and Michael D'Orso. 1998. *Walking with the wind: A memoir of the movement*. New York: Simon and Schuster.

Liberty and the weal public reconciled. 1637. London: n.p.

Liebman, Charles S., and Eliezer Don-Yehiya. 1983. *Civil religion in Israel: Traditional Judaism and political culture in the Jewish state*. Berkeley: University of California Press.

Liebman, Robert. 1983. Mobilizing the moral majority. In *The new Christian Right,* eds. Robert Liebman and Robert Wuthnow. New York: Aldine.

Lien, P., C. Collet, J. Wong and K. Ramakrishnan. 2001. Asian Pacific American public opinion and political participation. *PS: Political Science and Politics* 34: 625–630.

Lincoln, Abraham. 1865. "Second Inaugural Address." Inaugural Address, Washington, D.C., March 4.

Lincoln, Bruce. 2002. *Holy terrors: Thinking about religions after September 11*. Chicago: University of Chicago Press.

Lincoln, C. Eric, ed. 1970. *Martin Luther King, Jr.: A profile*. New York: Hill and Wang.

Lincoln, C. Eric. 1989. The black church and black self-determination. Paper presented at the annual meeting of the Association of Black Foundation Executives, April, in Kansas City, MO.

Lincoln, C. Eric, and Lawrence H. Mamiya. 1990. *The black church in the African American experience*. Durham: Duke University Press.

Linder, Robert D. 1996. Universal pastor: President Bill Clinton's civil religion. *Journal of Church and State* 38: 733–749.

Linder, Robert D., and Richard V. Pierard. 1988. *Civil religion and the presidency*. Grand Rapids: Zondervan.

_____. 1991. Ronald Reagan, civil religion and the new Religious Right in America. *Fides et Historia* 23: 66.

Lindner, Arlon. 2001. Rep. Arlon Lindner's comments. *Minnesota Public Radio News*, May 1. http://news.minnesota.publicradio.org/features/ 200105/01_hughes_dalai/lindner.shtml.

Lipset, Seymour Martin. 1963. Religion and American values. In *The first new nation*. New York: Basic Books.

_____. 1991. Comment on Luckmann. In *Social theory for a changing society*, eds. Pierre

Bourdieu and James S. Coleman, 185–188. Boulder: Westview Press.

Lowi, Theodore. 1964. American business, public policy, case studies, and political theory. *World Politics* 16: 677–715.

Luker, Ralph. 1991. *The social gospel in black and white: American racial reform, 1885–1912*. Chapel Hill: University of North Carolina Press.

Lutz, Donald S., ed. 1998. *Colonial origins of the American Constitution: A documentary history*. Indianapolis, IN: Liberty Fund.

Macaluso, Theodore F., and John Wanat. 1979. Voting turnout & religiosity. *Polity* 12: 158–169.

Madison, James. 1787. The same subject continued: The union as a safeguard against domestic faction and insurrection, (Federalist no. 10). *New York Daily Advertiser*. November 22.

_____. 1809. "First Inaugural Address." Inaugural Address, Washington, D.C., March 4.

_____. 1961. The Federalist (no. 51). In *The Federalist papers*, ed. Clinton Rossiter. New York: Mentor.

Malik, J. Mohan. 1993. India copes with the Kremlin's fall. *Orbis* 37:75.

Maltzman, Forrest, James F. Spriggs, II, and Paul J. Wahlbeck. 2000. *Crafting law on the Supreme Court: The collegial game*. New York: Cambridge University Press.

Manza, Jeff, and Clem Brooks. 1999. *Social cleavages and political change*. New York and Oxford: Oxford University Press.

Marsden, George. 1991. *Understanding fundamentalism and evangelicalism*. Grand Rapids, MI: Eerdmans.

Martin, Andrew D., and Kevin M. Quinn. 2002. Dynamic ideal point estimation via Markov chain Monte Carlo for the U.S. Supreme Court, 1953–1999. *Political Analysis* 10: 134–153.

_____. 2007. Assessing preference change on the US Supreme Court. *Journal of Law, Economics, & Organization* 23(2): 365–385.

Marty, Martin. 1974. Two kinds of two kinds of civil religion. In *American civil religion*, eds. Russell Ritchey and Donald Jones. New York: Harper & Row.

_____. 2003. The sin of pride. *Newsweek*, March 10.

Mather, Lynn. 1995. The fired football coach (Or, how trial courts make policy). In *Contemplating courts*, ed. Lee Epstein, 170–202. Washington D.C.: CQ Press.

Mason, John Mitchell. 1880. *The voice of warning to Christians, on the ensuing election of a President of the United States*. New York: G.F. Hopkins.

Mattingly, Terry. 2005. Bush isn't speaking in unknown tongue. *Associated Press.* January 22.

Mays, Benjamin. 1945. Commencement address at Howard University, June 1945. *Journal of Negro Education* 19: 527–534.

Mays, Benjamin and Joseph Nicholson. 1933. *The negro's church.* New York: Institute of Social and Religious Research.

McAdam, Douglas. 1979. Political process and the black Protestant movement 1948–1970. PhD diss., State University of New York at Stony Brook.

McCann, Michael. 1994. Law and social movements. In *The Blackwell companion to law and society,* ed. A. Sarat. Oxford: Blackwell.

McCarthy, John. 1987. Pro-life and pro-choice mobilization: Infrastructure deficits and new technologies. In *Social movements in an organizational society,* eds. Mayer N. Zald and John D. McCarthy, 49–66. New Brunswick, NJ: Transaction.

McClay, Wilfred M. 2003. Two concepts of secularism. In *Religion returns to the public square: Faith and policy in America,* eds. Hugo Heclo and Wilfred M. McClay. Washington, D.C.: Woodrow Wilson Center Press.

McConnell, Michael W., et al. 2006. *Religion and the Constitution,* 2nd ed. New York: Aspen Publishers.

McCormick, Richard L. 1974. Ethno-cultural interpretations of American voting behavior. *Political Science Quarterly* 89: 351–377.

McGreevy, John T. 2003. *Catholicism and American freedom.* New York: W.W. Norton & Company.

McGuire, Kevin T. 1993. *The Supreme Court bar: Legal elites in the Washington community.* Charlottesville: University Press of Virginia.

_____. 1995. Repeat players in the Supreme Court: The role of experienced lawyers in litigation success. *Journal of Politics* 57: 187–196.

McIntosh, Wayne V. 1990. *The appeal of civil law: A political-economic analysis of litigation.* Urbana: University of Illinois Press.

Mead, Sidney. 1963. *The lively experiment.* New York: Harper & Row.

Meernik, James, and Joseph Ignagni. 1997. Judicial review and coordinate construction of the Constitution. *American Journal of Political Science* 41: 447–467.

Meier, Kenneth J. 1994. *The politics of sin: Drugs, alcohol, and public policy.* Armonk, NY: M.E. Sharpe.

Meier, Kenneth J. 1999. Drugs, sex, rock, and roll: A theory of morality politics. *Policy Studies Journal* 27(4): 681–695.

Melton, Gordon J. 2003. *Encyclopedia of American religions.* 7th ed. Detroit: Gale.

Mendelberg, Tali. 2001. *The race card.* Princeton: Princeton University Press.

Mendus, Susan, ed. 1988. *Justifying toleration: Conceptual and historical perspectives.* New York: Cambridge University Press.

Mendus, Susan, and David Edwards, eds. 1987. *On toleration.* Oxford: Clarendon Press.

The Michigan Daily. 1982. November 2.

Miller, Donald E. 1997. *Reinventing American Protestantism.* Berkeley: University of California.

Miller, Perry. 1939. *The New England mind: The seventeenth century.* Boston: Beacon.

Miller, Perry, and Thomas H. Johnson, eds. 1938. *The Puritans.* New York: American Book Company.

Miller, William Lee. 1958. *The Protestant and politics.* Philadelphia: Westminster.

_____. 1980. *Lincoln's second inaugural: A study in political ethics.* Bloomington: Poynter Center.

_____. 2002. *Lincoln's virtues: An ethical biography.* New York: Alfred A. Knopf.

Miller, William Robert. 1968. *Martin Luther King: His life, martyrdom, and meaning for a new world.* New York: Weybright and Talley.

Mirsky, Yehudah. 1986. Civil religion and the Establishment clause. *The Yale Law Journal* 95(6): 1237–1257.

Mitchell, Joshua. 2007. Religion is not a preference. *Journal of Politics* 69: 351–362.

Moen, Matthew C. 1992. *The transformation of the Christian Right.* Tuscaloosa, AL: The University of Alabama Press.

Monroe, James. 1817. "First Inaugural Address." Inaugural Address, Washington, D.C., March 4.

Monsma, Stephen. 2002. Concluding observations. In *Church–state relations in crisis: Debating neutrality,* ed. Stephen Monsma. Lanham, MD: Rowman and Littlefield.

Mooney, Christopher Z. 2001. The public clash of private values. In *The public clash of private values: The politics of morality policy,* ed. Christopher Z. Mooney, 3–18. New York: Chatham House Publishers.

Mooney, Christopher Z., and Mei-Hsien Lee. 1995. Legislative morality in the American states: The case of pre-*Roe* abortion regulation reform. *American Journal of Political Science* 39: 599–627.

Moreno, Sylvia. 2005. Supreme Court on a shoestring. *The Washington Post.* 21 February. A01.

Morgan, Edmund S., ed. 1965. *Puritan political ideas, 1558–1794.* New York: Bobbs-Merrill.

Morris, Aldon D., Shirley J. Hatchett, and Ronald E. Brown. 1989. The Civil Rights movement and black political socialization. *Political Learning in Adulthood*, ed. Roberta S. Sigel. Chicago: University of Chicago Press.

Mueller, Carol McClurg. 1992. Building social movement theory. *Frontiers in Social Movement Theory*, edited by Aldon D. Morris and Carol McClurg Mueller. New Haven: Yale University Press.

Musick, Mark, and John Wilson. 1997. Who cares? Toward an integrated theory of volunteer work. *American Sociological Review* 62: 694–713.

Myrdal, Gunnar. 1962. *An American dilemma: The negro problem and modern democracy*. New York: Harper Torchbooks.

Neuchterlein, James. 2002. Let us pray. *First Things* 122: 8–9.

Neuhaus, Richard John. 1984. *The naked public square*. Grand Rapids: Eerdmans.

Nevins, Allan, ed. 1964. *Lincoln and the Gettysburg Address*. Urbana: University of Illinois Press.

The New York Times. 2009. August 19.

Nice, David C. 1992. The states and the death penalty. *Western Political Quarterly* 45(4): 1037–1048.

Nicholson, Peter. 1985. Toleration as a moral ideal. In *Aspects of toleration: Philosophical studies*, eds. John P. Horton and Susan Mendus. London and New York: Methuen.

Niebuhr, H. Richard. 1937. *Kingdom of God in America*. New York: Harper.

_____. 1956. *Christ and culture*. New York: Harper.

Niebuhr, Reinhold. 1932. *Moral man and immoral society*. New York: Scribner's.

_____. 1935. *Interpretation of Christian ethics*. New York: Harper.

_____. 1952. *The irony of American history*. New York: Scribner's.

Nir, Ori. 2004. AJ-Congress stands alone on pledge issue. *The Jewish Daily Forward*, January 9. http://www.forward.com/articles/ajcongress-stands-alone-on-pledge-issue.

Nixon, Richard. 1969. "First Inaugural Address." Inaugural Address, Washington, D.C., January 20.

Noll, Mark A. 1990. Introduction to *Religion and American Politics*, ed. Mark A. Noll. New York.

_____. 2008. *God and race in American politics: A short history*. Princeton: Princeton University Press.

Noonan, Jr., John T. 1998. *The lustre of our country: The American experience of religious freedom*. Berkeley and Los Angeles, CA: University of California Press.

Novak, Michael. 1965. *Belief and unbelief: a philosophy of self-knowledge*. New York: Mentor-Omega.

_____. 1974. *Choosing our king*. New York: Macmillan.

_____. 2001. *On two wings: Humble faith and common sense at the American founding*. New York: Encounter Books.

Nussbaum, Martha. 2005. Radical evil in liberal democracies. Presentation on Initiative on religion, politics, and peace: The new religious pluralism and democracy at Georgetown University, April 21–22, Washington, D.C. http://berkleycenter.georgetown.edu/8986.html.

Oldmixon, Elizabeth Anne, Beth Rosenson, and Kenneth D. Wald. 2005. Conflict over Israel: The role of religion, race, party and ideology in the U.S. House of Representatives, 1997–2002. *Terrorism and Political Violence* 17: 404–426.

Olson, Mancur. 1965. *The logic of collective action: Public goods and the theory of groups*. Cambridge, MA: Harvard University Press.

Opp, Karl Dieter. 1982. Economics, sociology, and political protest. In *Theoretical models and empirical analyses: Contributions to the explanation of individual actions and collective phenomena*, ed. W. Raub. Utrecht, Netherlands: Explanatory Sociology.

Oswald, Rudy. 1984. The economy and workers' jobs, the living wage, and a voice. In *Catholic social teaching and the U.S. Economy: Working papers for a bishops' pastoral*, eds. John W. Houch and Oliver Williams. Washington, D.C.: University of America.

Patillo-McCoy, Mary. 1998. Church culture as a strategy of action in the black community. *American Sociological Review* 63: 767–784.

Penning, James. 2007. The religion of Bill Clinton. In *Religion and the American presidency*, eds. Mark J. Rozell and Gleaves Whitney, 191–214. New York: Palgrave/MacMillan Press.

Pestana, Carla Gardina. 1991. *Quakers and Baptists in colonial Massachusetts*. Cambridge: Cambridge University Press.

Peterson, Steven A. 1992. Church participation and political participation: The spillover effect. *American Politics Quarterly* 20: 123–139.

Pew Forum on Religion and Public Life. 2002. God bless America: Reflections on civil religion after September 11. Conference, Brookings Institution, Washington, D.C., February 6, in Washington, D.C. http://pewforum.org/events/index.php?eventid=22.

Pfiffner, James P. 2000. Presidential character: Multidimensional or seamless? In *The Clinton scandal and the future of American government*, eds. Mark J. Rozell and Clyde Wilcox, 235–255. Washington: Georgetown University Press.

Phelps, Glenn A. 2001. The President as moral leader: George Washington in contemporary perspective. In *George Washington: Foundation of presidential leadership and character*, eds. Ethan Fishamen, William D. Pederson, and Mark J. Rozell. Westport: Praeger.

Philpot, Tasha S. 2007. *Race, Republicans, and the return to the party of Lincoln*. Ann Arbor: University of Michigan Press.

Pika, Joseph A. 1987–1988. Interest groups in the White House under Roosevelt and Truman. *Political Science Quarterly* 102: 647–668.

The Pluralism Project at Harvard University. Statistics by tradition: Jainism. Harvard University. http://www.pluralism.org/resources/statistics/tradition.php#Jainism.

Poole, Keith T., and Howard Rosenthal. 2007. *Ideology and Congress*. New Brunswick, NJ: Transaction Publishers.

Posner, Richard A. 2001. *Public intellectuals: A study of decline*. Cambridge, MA: Harvard University Press.

Prager, Dennis. 2006. America, not Keith Ellison, decides what book a congressman takes his oath on. Townhall.com, November 28. http://townhall.com/columnists/DennisPrager/2006/11/28/america,_not_keith_ellison,_decides_what_book_a_congressman_takes_his_oath_on.

Prendergast, William B. 1999. *The Catholic voter in American politics: The passing of the Democratic monolith*. Washington D.C.: Georgetown University Press.

Price, David E. 2004. Faith in public office. In *One electorate under God: A dialogue on religion and American politics*, eds. E. J. Dionne Jr., Jean B. Elshtain, and Kayla M. Drogosz. Washington, D.C.: Brookings Institution.

Pritchett, C. Herman. 1948. *The Roosevelt's court: A study in judicial politics and values 1937–1947*. New York: Macmillan.

Pruden, Wesley. 2005. A little God talk from the chief. *Washington Times*, April 23.

Queen, Edward. 2002. Public religion and voluntary associations. In *Religion, politics, and the American experience: Reflections on religion and American public life*, ed. Edith L. Blumhofer, 86–102. Tuscaloosa: University of Alabama Press.

Raboteau, Albert. 1978. *Slave religion: the "invisible institution" in the Antebellum south*. New York: Oxford University Press.

_____. 1995. *A fire in the bones: Reflections on African-American religious history*. Boston: Beacon Press.

Rail, H. F. 1940. *Christianity: An inquiry into its nature and truth*. New York: Scribner.

Raines, Howell. 1977. *My soul is rested*. New York: Putnam.

Reagan, Ronald. 1981. "First Inaugural Address." Inaugural Address, Washington, D.C., January 20.

_____. 1985. "Second Inaugural Address." Inaugural Address, Washington, D.C., January 21.

_____. 1989. "Farewell Address to the Nation." Farewell Address, Washington, D.C., 11 January.

Reeves, Thomas C. 1991. *A question of character: A life of John F. Kennedy*. New York: Free Press.

_____. 1996. *The empty church*. New York: Free Press.

_____. 1997. *A question of character: A life of John F. Kennedy*. New York: Random House.

Reichley, A. James. 1985. *Religion in American public life*. Washington, D.C.: Brookings.

Ribuffo, Leo P. 1989. God and Jimmy Carter. In *Transforming faith: The sacred and secular in modern American history*, eds. M. L. Bradbury and James B. Gilbert. Westport: Greenwood.

Richards, Mark J., and Herbert M. Kritzer. 2002. Jurisprudential regimes in Supreme Court decision making. *American Political Science Review* 96: 305–320.

Richardson, Valerie. 2005. Altered Pledge of Allegiance stuns students. *Washington Times*, April 23.

Rimor, Mordechai, and Gary A. Tobin. 1990. Jewish giving patterns to Jewish and non-Jewish philanthropy. In *Faith and philanthropy in America*, eds. Robert Wuthnow, Virginia A. Hodgkinson, and associates. San Francisco: Jossey-Bass.

Rodriguez, Jeanette. 1994. *Our Lady of Guadalupe: Faith and empowerment among Mexican-American women*. Austin: University of Texas Press.

Rohde, David W., and Harold J. Spaeth. 1976. *Supreme Court decision making*. San Francisco: W.H. Freeman.

Roig-Franzia, Manuel. 2006. New Orleans mayor apologizes for remarks about God's wrath. *The Washington Post*, January 18.

Roosevelt, Franklin D. 1945. Radio address summarizing State of the Union message. January 6. *Presidential Papers of Franklin D. Roosevelt* 13: 517.

Rosenstone, Steven J., and John Mark Hansen. 1993. *Mobilization, participation, and democracy in America*. New York: Longman.

Rouner, Leroy. 1999. What is an American? Civil religion, cultural diversity, and American civilization. *The Key Reporter* 64(3): 1–6.

Rozell, Mark J., and Clyde Wilcox. 1995. *God at the grass roots: The Christian Right in the 1994 elections.* Lanham, MD: Rowman & Littlefield.

Salamon, Lester M. 1995. Explaining nonprofit advocacy: An exploratory analysis. Draft paper prepared for delivery at the Independent Sector Spring Research Forum.

Sarat, Austin, and Stuart Scheingold, eds. 1998. *Cause lawyering.* New York: Oxford.

Schaeffer, Francis A. 1976. *How should we then live?* Old Tappan, NJ: Revell.

_____. 1981. *A Christian manifesto.* Westchester, IL: Crossway Books.

Schaeffer, Francis A., and C. Everett Koop. 1979. *Whatever happened to the human race?* Old Tappan, NJ: Revell.

Scheingold, Stuart, and Austin Sarat. 2004. *Something to believe in: Politics, professionalism, and cause lawyering.* Stanford, CA: Stanford Law and Politics.

Scholzman, Kay L., and John T. Tierney. 1986. *Organized interests in American democracy.* New York: Harper and Row.

Schutz, John A., and Douglass Adair, eds. 1966. *The spur of fame: Dialogues of John Adams and Benjamin Rush, 1805–1813.* San Marino, CA: Huntington Library.

Schwartz, Bernard. 1986. *Swann's way: The school busing case and the Supreme Court.* New York: Oxford University Press.

Segal, Jeffery A. 1984. Predicting Supreme Court decisions probabilistically: The search and seizure cases. *American Political Science Review* 78: 891–900.

Segal, Jeffery A., and Albert Cover. 1989. Ideological values and the votes of U.S. Supreme Court justices. *American Political Science Review* 83: 557–565.

Segal, Jeffrey A., and Harold J. Spaeth. 2002. *The Supreme Court and the attitudinal model revisited.* New York: Cambridge University Press.

Segers, Mary C., and Timothy A. Byrnes, eds. 1995. *Abortion politics in American states.* Armonk, NY: M.E. Sharpe.

Sidey, Hugh. 1984. Taking cues from on high. *Time*, March 19.

Smidt, Corwin E. 2007. Evangelical and mainline Protestants at the turn of the millennium: Taking stock and looking forward. In *From pews to polling places: Faith and politics in the American religious mosaic,* ed. Matthew Wilson, 29–51. Washington, D.C.: Georgetown University Press.

Smidt, Corwin E., Kevin den Dulk, Bryan Froehle, James Penning, Stephen Monsma, and Douglas Koopman. 2010. *The disappearing God gap? Religion and the 2008 presidential election.* New York: Oxford University Press.

Smidt, Corwin E., Kevin den Dulk, James Penning, Stephen Monsma, and Douglas Koopman. 2008. *Pews, prayers and participation: Religion and civic responsibility in America.* Washington D.C.: Georgetown University Press.

Smith, Christian. 1998. *American Evangelicalism: Embattled and thriving.* Chicago: University of Chicago Press.

_____. 2000. *Christian America? What Evangelical Christians really want.* Berkeley: University of California Press.

Smith, Gary Scott. 2005. *Faith and the presidency.* New York: Oxford University Press.

_____. 2007. The faith of George Washington. In *Religion and the American presidency*, eds. Mark J. Rozell and Gleaves Whitney, 9–38. New York: Palgrave/MacMillan Press.

Smith, Gregory. 2006. Attitudes toward immigration: In the pulpit and the pew. *Pew Research Center*, April 26.

Smith, Kenneth L., and Ira G. Zepp. 1986. *Search for the beloved community: The thinking of Martin Luther King, Jr.* Lanham, MD: University Press of America.

Smith, Oran P. 2000. *The rise of Baptist republicanism.* New York: NYU Press.

Smith, Robert C., and Hanes Walton Jr. 2003. *American politics and the African American quest for the universal freedom.* New York: Longman.

Smith, Steven D. 1995/1999. *Foredained failure: The quest for a constitutional principle of religious freedom.* Oxford: Oxford University Press.

Sniderman, Paul M., Richard A. Brody, and Philip E. Tetlock. 1991. *Reasoning and choice: Explorations in political psychology.* Cambridge: Cambridge University Press.

Snow, David, and Robert D. Benford. 1992. Master frames and cycles of protest. In *Frontiers in Social Movement Theory,* ed. Aldon D. Morris and Carol McClurg Mueller. New Haven: Yale University Press.

Snow, David E., Burke Rochford, Jr., Steven K. Worden, and Robert Benford. 1986. Frame realignment processes, Micromobilization, and movement participation. *American Sociological Review* 51: 464–481.

Sorauf, Frank. 1976. *The wall of separation: Constitutional politics of church and state.* Princeton, NJ: Princeton University Press.

Sorens, Jason, Fait Muedini, and William P. Ruger. 2008. U.S. state and local public policies in 2006: A new database. *State Politics and Policy Quarterly* 8(3): 309–326.

Sorensen, Theodore. 1965. *Kennedy*. New York: Harper & Row.

Souza Briggs, Xavier de. 1998. Doing democracy up close: Culture, power, and communication in community building. *Journal of Planning Education and Research* 18: 1–13.

Spaeth, Harold J. 2008. The original United States Supreme Court judicial database, 1953–2007 terms.

Spalding, Elizabeth Edwards. 2007. "We must put on the armor of God": Harry Truman and the Cold War. In *Religion and the American presidency*, eds. Mark J. Rozell and Gleaves Whitney, 95–118. New York: Palgrave/MacMillan Press.

Spiller, Pablo T., and Rafael Gely. 1992. Congressional control or judicial independence: The determinants of U.S. Supreme Court labor-relations decisions, 1949–1988. *Rand Journal of Economics* 23: 463–492.

Spriggs, James E., Forrest Maltzman, and Paul J. Wahlbeck. 1999. Bargaining on the U.S. Supreme Court: Justices' responses to majority opinion drafts. *The Journal of Politics* 61: 485–506.

Stackhouse, Max. 2004. Civil religion, political theology, and public theology: What's the difference? *Political Theology* 5(3): 275–293.

Stark, Rodney, and Charles Glock. 1968. *American piety: The nature of religious commitment.* Berkeley: University of California Press.

Statistical Abstract. 1994. *Statistical abstract of the United States*. Washington, DC: U.S. Census Bureau.

Steensland, Brian. 2002. The hydra and the swords: Social welfare and mainline advocacy, 1964–2000. In *The quiet hand of God: Faith-based activism and the public role of mainline Protestantism,* eds. Robert Wuthnow and John H. Evans. Berkeley: University of California Press.

Stern, Philip, ed. 1940. *The life and writings of Abraham Lincoln*. New York: Modern Library.

Stokes, Anson Phelps. 1950. *Church and state in the United States, vol. I.* New York: Harper.

Strate, John M., Charles J. Parrish, Charles D. Elder, and Coit Ford III. 1989. Life span civic development and voting participation. *American Political Science Review* 83: 443–464.

Stuckey, Mary E. 1991. *The President as interpreter-in-chief*. Chatham, NJ: Chatham House.

Sullivan, Winnifred Fathers. 2002. Neutralizing religion; Or, what is the opposite of "faith-based"? *History of Religions* 41(4): 369–390.

Suskind, Ron. 2004. Without a doubt. *NYT Magazine*, October 17.

Swierenga, Robert. 1990. Ethno-religious political behavior in the mid-nineteenth century: Voting, values, cultures. In *Religion & American politics: From the colonial period to the 1980s*, ed. Mark Noll, 146–171.New York: Oxford University Press.

Taft, William Howard. 1909. "Inaugural Address." Inaugural Address, Washington, D.C., March 4.

Tarrow, Sidney. 1992. Mentalities, political cultures, and collective action frames. *Frontiers in Social Movement Theory*, edited by Aldon D. Morris and Carol McClurg Mueller. New Haven: Yale University Press.

Tatalovich, Raymond, and Byron W. Daynes, eds. 1988. *Social regulatory policy.* Boulder, CO: Westview Press.

Tatalovich, Raymond, and T. Alexander Smith. 2001. Status claims and cultural conflict: The genesis of morality policy. *Policy Currents* 10(4): 2–8.

Tate, C. Neal. 1981. Personal attribute models of voting behavior of U.S. Supreme Court justices. *American Political Science Review* 75: 355–367.

Terry, Sara. 1994. Resurrecting hope. *The Boston Globe Magazine*, July 17.

Thomas, Cal. 2005. Using and abusing God: Part deux. Townhall.com, January 19. http://townhall.com/columnists/CalThomas/2005/01/19/using_and_abusing_god_part_deux.

Thomas, Cal, and Ed Dobson. 1999. *Blinded by might.* Grand Rapids: Zondervan Publishing House.

Thomas, Clive S., and Ronald J. Hrebenar. 1999. Who's got clout. *State Legislatures* 25(4): 30–34.

Thomas, Robert and Friedland, William. n.d. The United Farmworkers Union: From mobilization to mechanization? Ann Arbor, MI: University of Michigan.

Thurman, Howard. 1981. Jesus and the disinherited. Richmond, IN: Friends United Press.

Tilly, Charles. 1978. *From mobilization to revolution.* New York: Mc-Graw Hill.

Timoleon. 1800. A solemn address, to Christians & patriots, upon the approaching election of a President of the United States. In *Answer to a pamphlet, entitled, "serious considerations," &c.*

Tinder, Glenn. 1995. *Tolerance and community.* Columbia, MO: University of Missouri Press.

Tocqueville, Alexis de. 1954. *Democracy in America,* vol. I. New York: Vintage Books.

Tweed, Thomas A., and Stephen Prothero. 1999. *Asian religions in America: A documentary history.* New York: Oxford University Press.

U.S. Bureau of the Census. 1985. Current population reports, Series P-60, no. 149, Monthly income and poverty statues of families in the United States: 1984. Washington, D.C.: U.S. Government Printing Office.

United States Census Bureau. 2003. Population. U.S. Census Bureau. http://www.census.gov/prod/2004pubs/03statab/pop.pdf.

Verba, Sidney, Kay Lehman Schlozman, and Henry E. Brady. 1995. *Voice and equality: Civic voluntarism in American politics.* Cambridge, MA: Harvard University Press.

Verba, Sidney, Kay Lehman Schlozman, Henry Brady, and Norman H. Nie. 1993. Race, ethnicity and political resources: participation in the United States. *British Journal of Political Science* 23: 453–97.

Verter, Bradford. 2002. Furthering the freedom struggle: Racial justice activism in the mainline churches since the Civil Rights Era. In *The quiet hand of God: Faith-based activism and the public role of mainline Protestantism,* eds. Robert Wuthnow and John H. Evans. Berkeley: University of California Press.

Vu, Michelle. 2007. Evangelicals, U.S. gov't promote green churches. *Christian Post,* November 8.

Wahlbeck, Paul J., James F. Spriggs, II, and Forrest Maltzman. 1998. Marshalling the court: Bargaining and accommodation on the United States Supreme Court. *American Journal of Political Science* 42: 294–315.

Wakin, Daniel J. 2004. Rabbis' rules and Indian wigs stir crisis in Orthodox Brooklyn. *The New York Times,* May 14.

Wald, Kenneth D. 1987. *Religion and politics in the United States.* New York: St. Martin's Press.

Wald, Kenneth D., and Allison Calhoun-Brown. 2007. *Religion and politics in the United States.* Lanham, MD: Rowman & Littlefield.

Wald, Kenneth D., Lyman A. Kellstedt, and David C. Leege. 1993. Church involvement and political behavior. In *Rediscovering the religious factor in American politics,* eds. David C. Leege and Lyman A. Kellstedt. Armonk, NY: M. E. Sharpe.

Wald, Kenneth D., and Corwin E. Smidt. 1993. Measurement Strategies in the Study of Religion and Politics. In *Rediscovering the religious factor in American politics,* ed. David C. Leege and Lyman A. Kellstedt, 26–49. Armonk, NY: M.E. Sharpe.

Walker, Wyatt Tee. 1979. *Somebody's calling my name.* Valley Forge: Judson Press.

Walsh, James. 2009. Judge clears way for lawsuit by 6 Imams arrested at Minneapolis airport. *The Minneapolis Star-Tribune,* July 25.

Warner, W. Lloyd. 1962. *American life.* Chicago: University of Chicago Press.

Warren, Mark R. 2001. *Dry bones rattling: Community building to revitalize American democracy.* Princeton: Princeton University Press.

Washington, George. 1789. "First Inaugural Address." Inaugural Address, New York, NY, 30 April.

Washington, James M. 1985. *Frustrated fellowship: the black Baptist quest for social power.* Macon, GA: Mercer University Press.

———. 1986. Jesse Jackson and the symbolic politics of black Christendom. *Annals of American Academy of Political and Social Science.* 480: 89–105.

Washington, James Melvin, ed. 1986. *A testament of hope: The essential writings of Martin Luther King, Jr.* New York: Harper and Row.

Washington, Joseph R. 1964. *Black religion: The negro and Christianity in the United States.* Boston: Beacon Press.

Waskow, Arthur. 1998. "My legs were praying": Theology and politics in Abraham Joshua Heschel. *Conservative Judaism,* Winter–Spring.

Weeks, William. 1992. *John Quincy Adams and the American global empire.* Lexington: University Press of Kentucky.

Weintraub, Jeff, and Krishan Kumar, eds. 1997. *Public and private in thought and practice: Perspectives on a grand dichotomy.* Chicago: University of Chicago Press.

Whale, J. S. 1936. *The Christian answer to the problem of evil.* London: Student Christian Movement Press.

White, Ronald C. 2002. *Lincoln's greatest speech: The second inaugural.* New York: Simon & Schuster.

White, Theodore H. 1961. *The making of the President, 1960.* New York: Atheneum.

Whitehead, John. 1999. *Slaying dragons: The truth behind the man who defended Paula Jones.* Nashville: Thomas Nelson.

Wilcox, Clyde. 1996. *Onward Christian soldiers? The Religious Right in American politics.* Boulder, CO: Westview Press.

Wilcox, Clyde and Joe Wesley. 1998. Dead law: The federal election finance regulations 1974–1996. *PS: Political Science and Politics* 31:14–17.

Williams, Armstrong. 2005. Bush's faith reflects society's beliefs. Townhall.com. February 1.

Williams, Roger. 1963 [1647]. *The bloudy tenent of persecution for cause of conscience, discussed.* Vol. 1 of *The complete writings of Roger Williams,* ed. Samuel L. Caldwell. New York: Russell and Russell.

Wills, Gary. 1990. *Under God: Religion and American politics.* New York: Simon and Schuster.

Wilson, John F. 1989. Religion, government, and power in the new American nation. In *Religion and American politics,* ed. Mark A. Noll, 77–91. New York: Oxford.

Wilson, John, and Thomas Janoski. 1995. The contribution of religion to volunteer work. *Sociology of Religion* 56: 137–152.

Wilson, John, and Marc Musick. 1997. Who cares? Toward an integrated theory of volunteer work. *American Sociological Review* 62: 694–713.

Wilson, Woodrow. 1917. "Second Inaugural Address." Inaugural Address, Washington, D.C., March 5.

———. Quoted in *Equity Inv. V. Paris,* 437 N.Y.S. 2d 1000, 1001(N.Y. Civ. Ct. 1981).

Winthrop, John. 1630. A modell of Christian charity. In *Collections of the Massachusetts historical society, 3rd series,* 7: 31–48. Boston: Massachusetts Historical Society.

———. 1931. *Winthrop Papers,* vol. 2. Boston: Massachusetts Historical Society.

Wood, Richard L. 2002. *Faith in action: Religion, race, and democratic organizing in America.* Chicago: University of Chicago Press.

Woodberry, Robert, and Christian Smith. 1998. Fundamentalism et al.: Conservative Protestants in America. *Annual Review of Sociology* 24: 25–26.

Wuthnow, Robert. 1988. *The restructuring of American religion.* Princeton: Princeton University.

———. 2005. *America and the challenges of religious diversity.* Princeton: Princeton University.

Wuthnow, Robert, and John H. Evans. 2002. Introduction to *The quiet hand of God: Faith-based activism and the public role of mainline Protestantism,* eds. Robert Wuthnow and John H. Evans, 1–24. Berkeley: University of California Press.

Yamane, David. 1998. Religious advocacy in secular society: A neo-secularization perspective. PhD diss., University of Wisconsin-Madison.

Yamane, David, and Elizabeth Oldmixon. 2006. Religion in the legislative arena: Affiliation, salience, advocacy, and public policymaking. *Legislative Studies Quarterly* 31(3): 433–460.

Young, Andrew. 1996. *An easy burden: The civil rights movement and the transformation of America.* New York: Harper Collins.

Young, Robert L. 1992. Religious orientation, race and support for the death penalty. *Journal for the Scientific Study of Religion* 31(1): 76–87.

Zald, Mayer, and John McCarthy. 1987. Religious groups as crucibles of social movements. In *Social Movements in an Organizational Society,* eds. Mayer Zald and John McCarthy. New Brunswick, NJ: Transaction.

CONTRIBUTORS

Harold F. Bass is Dean of the School of Social Sciences and Professor of Political Science at Ouachita Baptist University in Arkadelphia, Arkansas.

Kimberly Conger is Assistant Professor of Political Science at Iowa State University in Ames, Iowa.

Daniel Dreisbach is Professor of Justice, Law, and Society at the School of Public Affairs at American University in Washington, D.C.

Katherine Knutson is Assistant Professor of Political Science at Gustavus Adolphus College in Saint Peter, Minnesota.

Mark Rozell is Professor of Public Policy at George Mason University in Arlington, Virginia.

Corwin E. Smidt is Professor of Political Science and Executive Director of the Paul B. Henry Institute for the Study of Christianity and Politics at Calvin College in Grand Rapids, Michigan.

Paul Wahlbeck is Professor of Political Science at George Washington University in Washington, D.C.

John Witte Jr. is Jonas Robitscher Professor of Law, Alonzo L. McDonald Distinguished Professor, and Director of the Center for the Study of Law and Religion at Emory University School of Law in Atlanta, Georgia.

TEXT CREDITS

Albright, Madeleine: Excerpts from pp. 6–13, 284–292 from THE MIGHTY AND THE ALMIGHTY: REFLECTIONS ON AMERICA, GOD, AND WORLD AFFAIRS by Madeleine Albright. Copyright © 2006 by Madeleine Albright. Reprinted by permission of HarperCollins Publishers.

Bailey, Michael E. and Kristin Lindholm: Excerpts from "Tocqueville and the Rhetoric of Civil Religion in the Presidential Inaugural Addresses" by Michael E. Bailey and Kristin Lindholm, from Christian Scholar's Review, Vol. XXXII No. 3, pp. 259–279. Copyright © 2003 by Christian Scholar's Review. Used by permission.

Bellah, Robert: Excerpts from "Civil Religion in America" by Robert Bellah, published in Daedalus, Journal of the American Academy of Arts and Sciences, Winter 1967, Vol. 96, No. 1, "Religion in America." Reprinted by permission of MIT Press Journals.

Benson, Peter and Dorothy L. Williams: Reprinted with permission from RELIGION ON CAPITOL HILL by Peter L. Benson and Dorothy L. Williams. Copyright © 1982 Search Institute®, Minneapolis, MN; www.search-institute.org. All Rights Reserved.

Buckley, Thomas: "A Mandate for Anti-Catholicism: The Blaine Amendment" by Thomas E. Buckley from America, Vol. 191, Issue 8, September 27, 2004. Reprinted with permission of America Press, Inc. © 2004. All rights reserved.

Chappell, David L.: From A STONE OF HOPE: PROPHETIC RELIGION AND THE DEATH OF JIM CROW by David L. Chappell. Copyright © 2004 by David L. Chappell. Used by permission of the University of North Carolina Press. www.uncpress.unc.edu.

Chaves, Mark: "Political Activities," reprinted by permission of the publisher from CONGREGATIONS IN AMERICA by Mark Chaves, pp. 106–120, Cambridge, Mass.: Harvard University Press, Copyright © 2004 by the Presidents and Fellows of Harvard College.

Christian Coalition of America: Issues page from the 2008 Christian Coalition Presidential Election Voter Guide is reprinted by permission of the Christian Coalition of America.

Cleary, Edward L.: From "Religion at the Statehouse: The California Catholic Conference" by Edward L. Cleary, in Journal of Church and State, Winter 2003, Vol. 45, No. 1, pp. 41–58, by permission of J.M. Dawson Institute of Church-State Studies at Baylor University.

Cornwall Alliance: "An Open Letter to the Signers of 'Climate Change: An Evangelical Call to Action' and Others Concerned About Global Warming" (http://www.CornwallAlliance.org/open-letter/), © 2006 Cornwall Alliance for the Stewardship of Creation (http://www.CornwallAlliance.org). Reproduced by permission. In 2009, the "Open Letter" and accompanying Call to Truth, Prudence, and Protection of the Poor were superseded by An Evangelical Declaration on Global Warming (http://www.CornwallAlliance.org/evangelical-declaration/) and A Renewed Call to Truth, Prudence, and Protection of the Poor: An Evangelical Examination of the Theology, Science, and Economics of Global Warming (http://www.CornwallAlliance.org/ renewed-call-to-truth/).

Danforth, John: "Onward, Moderate Christian Soldiers" by John Danforth, published in The New York Times, June 17, 2005. Copyright © 2005 by The New York Times Co. Reprinted by permission.

den Dulk, Kevin: Adapted from "In Legal Culture, But Not of It" by Kevin den Dulk, from CAUSE LAWYERS AND SOCIAL MOVEMENTS by Austin Sarat and Stuart A. Scheingold. Copyright © 2006 by the Board of Trustees of the Leland Stanford Jr. University. All rights reserved. Used with the permission of Stanford University Press, www.sup.org.

Dunn, Charles W.: Excerpts from "The Theological Dimensions of Presidential Leadership: A Classification Model" from Presidential Studies Quarterly, 14(1), 1984. Copyright © 1984 Center for the Study of the Presidency and Congress. Reproduced with permission of Blackwell Publishing Ltd.